Lander College Library
Lander College
Greenwood, S. C. 29646

A Comparative Study of PARTY ORGANIZATION

edited by

WILLIAM E. WRIGHT

University of Georgia

Charles E. Merrill Publishing Company
A Bell & Howell Company
Columbus, Ohio

MERRILL POLITICAL SCIENCE SERIES

Under the Editorship of

John C. Wahlke
Department of Political Science
State University of New York, Stony Brook

ISBN: 0-675-09875-0

Library of Congress Catalog Card Number: 79-157697

1 2 3 4 5 6 7 8 9 — 79 78 77 76 75 74 73 72 71

Printed in the United States of America

Preface

Any new entry in a field already well-populated with "readers" — as is the field of political parties — should be justified. Like television shows, such readers tend to resemble one another closely; the consumer of readers, like the viewer of television programs, has a large number of offerings, but a limited range of choices.

I have sought to give readers "a choice and not an echo." This volume is a different offering, one that more closely reflects current disciplinary (political science) and interdisciplinary (social science) trends than other readers in this field of study. It also differs either qualitatively or quantitatively in several important respects from alternative offerings. And the overall package makes for considerable difference.

First and foremost, it is a combination text and reader. A serious effort has been made to integrate systematically the seemingly disparate material which has been included. A common problem of readers is their lack of overall coherence; they are more like cafeterias to be enjoyed selectively than carefully coordinated banquets. Some selections fit better than others into any given design or conception. Coherence has been consciously sought in this volume in two ways. Each section is prefaced by an introductory essay that does more than merely summarize the selected studies. Rather, these readings are placed in a theoretical perspective and are related to similar research efforts. References for further reading are listed at the end of each section introduction. Wherever possible, research findings are stated in propositional form. The student is therefore able to use the material to help him find his way about in a larger body of research literature than is usually the case with readers.

Although the material is often pertinent to two or more sections, selections have to be placed in one section of the reader. Integration across sections is brought about partly by cross-references in the section introductory essays. Theoretical integration also has been attempted in another and more significant way. An introductory essay on theoretical party models has been written especially for this volume, and the section essays have been keyed to this overall conceptual framework. Thus a two-stage web of interpretation has been employed which hopefully will enable the user to come to grips systematically with an important area of research. Ultimately, the student is the best judge of how well the attempt to make this volume more than the sum of its parts comes off.

A second distinctive feature of this effort is its genuinely comparative approach to the analysis of political parties. Two-fifths of the selections deal with non-American parties, and all of the introductory essays treat parties in a comparative perspective. The decision to follow this approach was the starting point in plans to make this undertaking. Certainly, one of the clearest trends in political science today is the strong and growing emphasis on comparative, cross-national research. Unfortunately, the study of political parties has lagged behind in this development, in large measure as the result of a theoretical-geographical compartmentalization into American and non-American parties. The party models essay suggests the reasons for this situation and the resulting lack of scholarly communication and hopefully makes a contribution toward overcoming it.

Concern for analytical depth and cumulativeness of research findings necessitates limitations in the comparative perspective taken in this volume. The treatment is restricted to democratic political parties, a choice that is commonly made and which needs no justification. Studies were chosen for inclusion in this volume which employed designs and techniques similar to those of the American studies, rather than being selected primarily on geographic criteria. The research findings pertain only to Anglo-American (American, British, Canadian) and Western European (German, Italian, Norwegian) political parties, although the theoretical perspective has broader implications.

Thirdly, the emphasis in this volume is on empirical theory and research; this fact was a determining criterion for selecting studies for inclusion and only examples of recent research on political parties were chosen. Hopefully, one result will be the stimulation of further research efforts which will extend these studies and fill in the many research gaps, some of which are pointed out in this volume. I have found that undergraduate as well as graduate students can do competent research if properly guided and that they have reacted very positively to actually participating in research efforts instead of merely consuming research findings. Since even a modest experience of this kind of participation greatly aids in the comprehension of research findings, research projects are an excellent teaching device. However, nothing is more frustrating than doing a research project without knowing how to build upon and use previous studies. I hope that this research-oriented volume will provide such a guiding perspective.

Corresponding to the research orientation of this volume is the strong emphasis on theory which provides the essential guidance for research and analysis. The theoretical perspective underlying this volume is both empirical and normative as is true of most theory. The commitment to empirical theory is strong because of the belief in the necessity and efficacy of empirical research. However, this perspective is not blind to the normative components of theory, but is consciously addressed to the value premises which form the often implicit and even unrecognized basis for conceptions of political parties. One of the main purposes which the party models essay serves is to provide sharply contrasting value perspectives by which the performance of political parties may be judged. This perspective is particularly important today in the light of recent criticism of American parties and growing emphasis on participatory democracy.

A fourth distinctive feature of this volume is its exclusive focus on party *organization*, an important aspect of political parties that is usually relegated to one section in readers on American parties. The largely nonorganizational view of American parties, although understandable in the light of their underdeveloped organizational state, is a main deterrent to the comparative analysis of political parties, since concern with party organization has been left largely the domain of non-American (mainly European) scholars. It is an encouraging recent development that American political scientists are now busy remedying this situation, and the studies included in this volume are testimonials to the progress that has been made in this regard.

The focus of this volume is on the lower or grass roots levels of party organization because of the importance assigned these levels in theory, and because most empirical research on party organization has been conducted at these levels. This focus does constitute a limitation, although it is a justifiable one. It is most certainly the case that political parties cover a broad range of phenomena and that there are several other vitally important aspects of party: party organization at higher levels, the governmental party (elected public officials), the party in the electorate, theories of party systems, and, especially, in American parties, candidate-centered and factional organizations. However, these other aspects of party either constitute large and expanding bodies of data (e.g., studies of voting behavior) and are finding specialized treatment, or deserve further research and coherent specialized treatment. The argument is made here that coverage of as many aspects as possible comes at the expense of depth and coherence. The explosion of research efforts and data collection necessitates increasing specialization. Within the above-mentioned limitations, the area covered by this volume is broad indeed, but the breadth does not come at the expense of integration and coherence. By making this volume a combination of a text and reader, flexibility is provided so that it is possible to use this volume alone or along with several of the texts on political parties. It is also hoped that this work will prove useful in courses dealing with political sociology, political behavior, political participation, community politics, and comparative political analysis in which a treatment of the grass roots organization aspects of party can complement the materials normally used. This volume has been designed as not only a coherently specialized, but also a broadly useful work.

Although it is not usually the case that debts of intellectual gratitude are owed in the preparation of a reader, the different character of this undertaking and the thought that went into it makes this gesture both necessary and appropriate. I therefore wish to thank the following individuals for stimulating my own thinking about political parties. Listed in rough chronological order of my intellectual development, they are: Otto Stammer, Wolfgang Hirsch-Weber, and Renate Mayntz, all of the Free University of Berlin; Avery Leiserson, Vanderbilt University; John C. Wahlke, State University of New York at Stony Brook; Samuel J. Eldersveld and Samuel H. Barnes, both of the University of Michigan; Henry Valen, University of Oslo, Norway; and David M. Olson, University of Georgia. I have also learned much from all of the other party researchers whose works appear in this volume. Last, but not least, a special expression of gratitude is due Roger Ratliff, Political Science Editor of Charles E. Merrill Publishing Company, for his ready acceptance of the idea for this kind of treatment of political parties and his quiet patience in awaiting the results.

William E. Wright

Contents

SECTION ONE

Theory

Theory

The study of political parties, as that of all other areas of political science, needs to be guided by theory. Facts have little meaning in and of themselves; theory gives meaning to and enables us to interpret the significance of "facts." However, the study of political parties has been hindered by the lack of the kind of theory that serves to stimulate empirical research. Frank Sorauf (1964) makes a strong indictment of traditional scholarship on American political parties as being generally nontheoretical, nonorganizational, noncomparative, and as failing "to borrow from the concepts, models, and theories of the related social sciences" (p. 177). In Sorauf's view, "An impressive effort of two generations of scholarship on the American parties has failed, above all, to develop a theory of the political party — a theory about its relationship to the political system and other aspects of its environment, or a theory about its structure and function, or its position in a party system" (p. 174). Crotty (1969) criticizes scholarship and research on political parties as lacking "any identifiable accepted focus," theoretical conceptualization, and methodological sophistication. "Theoretical studies of any nature are uncommon in the field" (Crotty, p. 357). Crotty as well as Sorauf stresses "the value of a conceptual focus on party organization" (p. 384).

The terms theory, model, and conceptual framework are used here interchangeably to mean conceptualization of significant variables and their interrelationships. A conceptual framework or theoretical model may be considered an intellectual road map charting the terrain of a set of phenomena (in this case, political parties) being investigated. Before examining party models, three general points need to be considered.

First, we need conceptual schemes since they enable us to organize systematically and thereby gain an overview of the data. Conceptualization inevitably involves simplification — the reduction of a seemingly bewildering array of specifics to broader patterns of relationship. In using a conceptual scheme, significant variables and their interrelationships are specified and degrees of theoretical significance are assigned to selected phenomena; we are led to ask certain kinds of questions that guide our research *and not others.* Thus *any* conceptual scheme operates as a set of lenses through which we view the phenomena being investigated; our investigation is structured by the organizing scheme we choose to employ. In using a scheme we are told what is important, what to look for, and how to evaluate what we find. Thus, two researchers investigating the same phenomena can and often do arrive at conflicting interpretations in terms of different conceptual schemes.

Second, it is important to realize that there is no one theoretical model or conceptual framework that is necessarily *the best* or that most closely corresponds to reality; instead, there are usually competing theories, models, and conceptual schemes and the selection criterion applied is that of research payoff or utility with regard to advancing our understanding of the phenomena under investigation. No one scheme is right and all others wrong.

Thus far it has been argued that conceptualization is essential and necessarily selective. A third point concerns the normative underpinnings or components of theoretical models, some of which are heavily and explicitly normative, i.e., primarily concerned with making prescriptive statements about *what ought to be* — for example, most conceptions of democracy or political philosophers' conceptions of the "ideal state." Less apparent is the fact that even empirical models, which purport to describe *what is,* usually contain potent fundamental normative assumptions or value premises (see Barnes, 1968, p. 107); these are often implicit and may easily be overlooked. Thus, our investigation of political parties "as they are" is usually colored by our conceptions of what they "should be like," how they *should* function. It is therefore necessary to examine competing theoretical models for their explicit and implicit normative assumptions. While social science research is not and cannot be "value free," it is essential to be able to recognize basic value premises and to be alert for the influence these exert in empirical analyses.

Granting these three points, we may turn to an examination of the literature on political parties, which yields a variety of party typologies or models, mostly of the structural variety. The classic example is Michels's (1959) *oligarchic model:* the well-integrated centralized bureaucratic organization (see Introduction to Section Five). In a broader comparative analysis, Duverger (1954) categorized parties in terms of their basic structural element or organizational unit: the *caucus,* an "archaic," nineteenth century organizational form, still characteristic of American parties; the *branch*, for Duverger *the* "modern" form of party organization, the prototype of which is the European Socialist party; and the *cell* (or militia), a centralized, highly disciplined, agitational organizational form which is characteristic of the Communist and Nazi parties (see May, 1969). In a more widely used distinction based on party membership, Duverger contrasted two polar types, the *mass (membership) party* with the *cadre party*. The mass membership party consists of a large number of formally enrolled, active, dues-paying members, well-organized and structurally integrated on the basis of branches (e.g., European socialist parties). The cadre party, of which the major American parties are examples, lacks formal members, has a looser, committee (caucus)-style organization, is decentralized and loosely integrated. Sorauf (1964) and Epstein (1967) make extensive use of these two basic party types in their analysis of political parties.

Eldersveld (1964), holding Michels's hierarchical model inappropriate for the analysis of American parties, formulated a *stratarchy model*, involving limited organizational integration and control and considerable subunit autonomy (see Selection 1.3). Niemi and Jennings (1969) contrast the oligarchic control model, the stratarchy model, and the *decentralization model* which involves local autonomy in terms of intraorganizational communications and is more prevalent in American parties. The central notions involved in the party typology are the distribution of authority and control within the party structure and the extent of organizational integration.

Sigmund Neumann (1956) utilized an essentially functional typology in contrasting the *party of individual representation*, an older conception of "an ephemeral party as a mere electoral committee" which is "characteristic of a society with a restricted political domain and only a limited degree of participation" (p. 404), with a new type, the *party of (social) integration*, the mass membership party which makes more extensive demands of its members. Neumann makes a further distinction between the party of democratic integration, an internally democratic party (e.g., European socialist parties) and the party of total integration, the non-democratic form represented by the Communist and Nazi parties).

The above typologies have been used mainly to analyze European political parties and to differentiate American (cadre) from non-American (mass) parties. Several additional models serve to contrast different organizational types found *within* American parties. The above-mentioned decentralization model may be taken as characteristic of much of American party organization (Sorauf, 1963). Two additional structural party types represent minority patterns, or statistically deviant cases. The first is the "*machine*" *model,* the highly organized, efficient, patronage-based, old-style city machines (Gosnell, 1937; Forthal, 1946; Greenstein, 1963), whose few remaining examples today include Chicago (Snowiss, 1966) and Gary, Indiana (Rossi and Cutright, 1961). A more recent and polar opposite minority pattern is the "*club movement*" *party,* with formal membership criteria and emphasis on member participation, as typified by the California Democratic Council (CDC) and by Democratic political clubs in New York (Wilson, 1962; Carney, 1958; Sorauf, 1964). There are sharp differences between the pragmatic, "get-out-the-vote" orientation and centralized authority of the machine and the policy-orientation and participation of the club party.

A similar typology exists with more of a functional tinge in Wilson's (1962) differentiation of "professional" and "amateur" party organizations, a distinction based on the predominant political style or orientation of the party activists. The political "professional" is power-oriented and interested in winning, rather than being interested in issues; for him, politics is an end-in-itself. In contrast, the "amateur" views political activity as a means to attaining policy ends: "The amateur politician sees the political world more in terms of ideas and principles than in terms of persons" (Wilson, p. 3). The "amateur" is motivated by purposive, and the "pro," by material, incentives (see Introduction to Section Two). Wilson's typology links up with the machine-club party distinction in that the old-style city machine is a classic illustration of the professional organization, whereas the club-movement party is the purest manifestation of the amateur style. There are important organizational consequences of these two political styles involving recruitment characteristics, ideological orientations, and party processes. There are sharp contrasts between the lower-status, patronage or career-oriented, pragmatic, obedient "pro" and the urban-suburban, middle to upper-middle class, volunteer activist who is policy-oriented and who demands a say in party decision-making. A sizable number of recent studies have utilized the contrasting professional and amateur models (see Conway and Feigert, 1968; Hirschfield *et al.*, 1962; Salisbury, 1965-66; Soule and Clarke, 1970; Ippolito, 1969). It should be noted that these are "pure" types and all party organizations (or individual activists) do not fall neatly into one or the other type.

Each of these party typologies and models mentioned is useful for particular purposes; however, each is of limited utility since the typologies tend to be based on a single criterion or dimension. In spite of—or perhaps because of—the overlap between these party typologies, the variety is confusing and it is difficult to select one particular typology as being of broad comparative utility. However, most of the elements involved in the above typologies can be combined into a systematic, multi-factor differentiation of two basic polar-opposite party types which does have broad comparative utility. These may be termed the *Rational-Efficient model* and the *Party Democracy model.* In terms of the above typologies, the Rational-Efficient model incorporates elements of the cadre (caucus) party, the party of individual representation, the stratarchy-decentralization model, and the professional style; the Party Democracy model incorporates the branch-based mass membership party, the party of democratic integration, and the amateur style. In the first essay in this section of the reader, I have attempted systematically to contrast these two party types in terms of common sets of factors pertaining to the role of parties in the political system, party functions, party structure, internal party functions, and evaluative criteria. Briefly summarized, the Rational-Efficient party has exclusively electoral functions and is pragmatically preoccupied with winning elections rather than with defining policy. The Party Democracy type is more policy-oriented, ideological, and concerned with defining policy in an internally democratic manner involving rank-and-file member participation. Electoral success is viewed not as an end in itself but rather as a means to the implementation of policy ends. These models are "pure" types, representing the end points of a continuum along which real world political parties range, approximating to varying degrees one or the other type (see Figure 1 in Selection 1.1).

These two basic party models are used throughout the several section introductions in this reader to integrate the discussion of various aspects of party organization. The viewpoint is taken that the development of theory and research on political parties has been hindered by adherence to one or the other of these two party models, which differ sharply in normative assumptions, identification of significant variables, and evaluations of findings. Different questions of theoretical significance are raised by these two polar models and different aspects of party phenomena are stressed. The result is both a lack of cumulative findings and a lack of communication among advocates of the two competing party models, since these advocates conceive of political parties in such different terms.

A further barrier to communication and the development of comparative party theory and research has been created by reliance on one or the other of these two party models. Use of a particular party model has tended to reflect and reinforce a division that has greatly hindered the comparative analysis of political parties. Almost all of the prominent advocates of the Rational-Efficient model are American social scientists — e.g., Joseph A. Schumpeter (1942), Anthony Downs (1957), Joseph Schlesinger (1965), Leon Epstein (1967) — dealing with American political parties; where they treat non-American parties (as does Epstein), they still tend to rely on the Rational-Efficient model. The strongest advocates of the Party Democracy model tend to be European social scientists such as Robert Michels (1959), Maurice Duverger (1954), Renate Mayntz (1961), and Ulrich Lohmar (1963) dealing primarily with European parties. Schlesinger (1965) hints at these two basic party models in noting the cleavage between continental and Anglo-American conceptions of party concerning "the essential organizational issue of the party's prime beneficiary," which is the electorate (the Anglo-American tradition of the Rational-Efficient model) or the party membership (the continental tradition of the Party Democracy model) (p. 766). As the first selection in this reader notes, in less extreme fashion, reliance of these two basic party models partially accounts for differing views among American political scientists' assessments of American political parties: the Responsible Party School of party reformers (Committee, 1950; James McGregor Burns, 1963) and the club party advocates — have a basic conception of party that is closer to the Party Democracy model than the Rational-Efficient model (with the latter relied on by defenders of the status-quo of American parties).

Our viewpoint is that political parties need not be treated in dichotomous, polarized ("either-or") terms; rather, these two basic party models should be viewed instead as end points of a continuum along which specific political parties range. Since each polar model neglects aspects of party emphasized by the other, what is needed are more comprehensive "hybrid" party models which incorporate significant features of both models so that we have a single conceptual scheme of broadly comparative utility, rather than being forced to choose between these two polar models. While the first two articles in the first section of this reader are intended to clarify these two basic party models (Wright) and to illustrate the Rational-Efficient model (Schlesinger), the pieces by Eldersveld and Barnes illustrate two approaches to the study of political parties that are of such hybrid character and which are of great potential utility for the comparative analysis of political parties.

Schlesinger's basic conception of party has been elaborated in the discussion of the Rational-Efficient model in the first article in this reader. The Schlesinger excerpt (Selection 1.2) elaborates his ideas in more specific terms. This selection, taken from a longer essay (Schlesinger, 1965), lies in the realm of "simple party theory," dealing with "nuclear" party organization; the original essay also develops the notion of the "multinuclear" party and "complex party theory."

It has been noted that Schlesinger's basic conception of party is that of an "office-seeking" organization. It follows, therefore, that the basic unit of party organization is "collective effort devoted to the capture of a single public office." This is the first important concept: the nuclear party organization. The central focus is the public office to be captured. More complex party organizations "emerge out of the relationships among nuclear organizations." The nuclear organization is therefore the building block of party structure. The prospects of electoral success at least in the immediate future is a requirement posed by Schlesinger for a "true nucleus" to exist; otherwise it is considered a "mock nucleus." Schlesinger's second basic concept is that of "contribution" to the party nucleus. He prefers this concept, borrowed from Herbert Simon (1951), to the concept of "membership" on the grounds that the latter term is vague, especially as applied to American parties, and implies a degree of commitment which in practice is highly variable. Schlesinger argues that the concept of "contribution" avoids these difficulties by being more specific and allowing for a wide range of variation. Furthermore, this concept allows us to take into account party-relevant activities by individuals (such as interest group representatives and newspaper publishers) who are not normally recognized as party participants.

The main distinction Schlesinger makes is between "minimal" and "connective" contributions. Minimal contributions—prerequisites for the existence of a party nucleus—consist of candidacy for the nuclear office and votes, which are necessary for capturing the office. To accomplish this objective, several kinds of connective contributions are required. The first and foremost connective contribution is leadership which is necessary to give continuity and direction to party activities and which in the United States is difficult to characterize (in contrast to parliamentary systems). Schlesinger distinguishes between two types of leaders — officeholders or public leaders and party organization or associational leaders. The relationship between these two kinds of party leaders is influenced by patterns of party competition and office turnover factors (formal and informal constraints on tenure). The major task which party leaders face is the selection of a candidate for the office—the recruitment and nomination contribution. The third type of connective contribution is that of issue formulation which is necessary as a rationalization for seeking support of its candidate since power drive is not a sufficient reason. Issues are formulated so as to build a favorable party image in the electorate. Closely related to issue formulation is the contribution of memory, intelligence, and communications. In order to formulate issues, the party needs to gain accurate information about voters' reactions and to disseminate information favorable to the party via the mass media, using public relations techniques. In order to do all of this, the party organization needs and uses the contributions of technical services, typically provided by professional staff men, specialists dedicated to advancing the fortunes of the candidate. The final, but by no means least important, connective contribution which Schlesinger lists is money, essential to the entire operation of the party organization. This selection from Schlesinger's longer essay illustrates his strong adherence to the Rational-Efficient model. Schlesinger places exclusive emphasis on the electoral function: the function of the party organization is to capture elective public office; party activities are functional to the extent to which they contribute to attaining this sole objective. The evaluative criteria applied are rationality and efficiency in pursuit of this single, over-riding objective. In Schlesinger's view, the political party is an electoral machine, nothing more.

Whereas Schlesinger is concerned with developing a theory of party organization, Samuel J. Eldersveld (1964) conducted an extensive study of party organization in the Detroit metropolitan area. There are several points of similarity between Schlesinger and Eldersveld. Both take an organizational view of party (study parties as organizations) and stress the relevance of research on complex organizations for the study of political parties; both view parties as primarily office-seeking organizations, with emphasis on the party's electoral function. But Eldersveld takes a broader, more comprehensive view of party than does Schlesinger. In his study, Eldersveld articulates a theoretical model of party which, while approximating in some respects the Rational-Efficient model, is more comprehensive and of potentially greater utility for the comparative analysis of political parties. Eldersveld views party as "a polity, a miniature political system," with an authority structure, distinctive patterns of power distribution, a representative process, an electoral system, and organizational subprocesses (leadership recruitment, goal definition, conflict resolution, and decision-making).

Eldersveld considers the political party a special type of social organization, distinguished by its primary goal of office-seeking and having relatively distinctive structural features; the classic bureaucratic model, applicable to many other kinds of organizations, is not very relevant for political parties, especially American parties. Eldersveld articulates four theoretical constructs as structural dimensions along which party organizations vary. First, the party is a clientele-oriented structure, an open, expansive, informal, personalized system — seeking to broaden its basis of voter appeal. Second, the party is an alliance of subcoalitions (geographical, demographic-social, ideological, organizational elements). This alliance means inevitable conflict within the party, conflict that must be tolerated. Third, Eldersveld views the party as a stratarchy — meaning relatively autonomous levels of power, rather than a neatly ordered, hierarchical distribution of power. Since power in the party is fragmented, party is a "reciprocal deference structure" and a "rapport system"; higher level party leaders, lacking effective power over subordinates and effective sanctions, must be tolerant of local autonomy, initiative, and inertia. Finally, party is characterized by motivational and career pluralism: individuals participate in party activities out of a variety of motives and constitute a variety of career "classes," rather than a homogeneity of motivations and clearly delineated and institutionalized career lines.

Associated with each of these theoretical constructs is a structural dilemma. First, the party's clientele-orientation makes for problems in harmonizing internal control and perspectives while remaining adaptable. Second, since the party is an alliance of subcoalitions, inevitable tensions between group goals and subcoalitional demands arise. Third, party as stratarchy creates tensions between the need for attaining managerial efficiency on the one hand, while maintaining worker morale on the other. Finally, motivational and career pluralism makes the organizational satisfaction of a diversity of motives and aspirations difficult. Eldersveld is concerned with developing a theoretical model that will adequately characterize the "real world" of political parties. Although less neat and tidy than the Rational-Efficient model, his model incorporates a broader range of variables. Ample evidence of how far American parties depart from the prescriptions of the Rational-Efficient model is apparent throughout Eldersveld's thorough and impressive study.

Probably the most interesting theoretical notion is only partially developed by Eldersveld; he notes the potential contribution of "one important stream of current organizational theory — coalitional theory." Eldersveld makes use of this notion in his construct of party as an alliance of subcoalitions, but does not systematically develop a coalitional model of the political party. This idea is a potentially useful conceptual tool for the comparative analysis of political parties. It would seem to be applicable to a broad range of party phenomena, thus avoiding the limitations of both the Rational-Efficient and Party Democracy models.

The final selection in this section describes a model that could bridge the gap between the Rational-Efficient and the Party Democracy models — a model of broad comparative utility, in terms of which American and European, Western and non-Western, democratic, authoritarian, and totalitarian parties can be compared. Samuel Barnes sketches the outlines of a model of the political party (and, more generally, the political system) based on communications theory. He conceives of the political party as "the communication network that functionally specializes in the aggregation of political communications (that is, communications relating to the authoritative allocation of values) for a polity." Different kinds of parties (democratic, authoritarian, and totalitarian) and kinds of party systems (one-party, two-party, and multi-party) are characterized by different communications networks. Our attention is focused on democratic political systems, whose communications networks, according to Barnes, "are characterized by the existence of multiple autonomous channels connecting subunits at all levels of the system both vertically and horizontally. A channel is autonomous to the extent that its communications are not externally controlled."

The analytical focus of Barnes's research on an Italian Socialist Federation is on party democracy. Such a focus would seem to place him squarely in the tradition of the Party Democracy model, but his critical, less normative, and more empirical orientation enables him to avoid some of the problems entailed in the prescriptions of the Party Democracy model. His analytical focus involves a combination of several theoretical interests: "One of these is the study of party organization. Another is political participation. Still another is leadership. All of these interests converge in the study of party democracy" (1967, p. 15). Concerned specifically as he is with the Italian Socialist Party, he defines party broadly (parties of the left at least) as "more than mere electoral machines," not pursuing electoral success at all costs, centrally concerned with policy formulation, emphasizing member participation in internal party affairs, stressing nonmaterial over material incentives. Barnes is not a spokesman for the Rational-Efficient model: "While some parties pursue electoral success at all costs, it is by no means a universal goal; in many parties it must compete with the goals of ideological purity or the maintenance of internal subcultural integrity. In short, political parties themselves are normative organizations in which goals themselves are a subject of internal debate and possible conflict" (1967, p. 12). Moreover, in Barnes's view, ". . . concern with democracy in organizations is a recurring and perpetual theme in political theory and research, and all substantial work on political parties must come to grips with the conceptual and empirical problems stemming from that concern" (1967, p. 1). (The significant failure of the Rational-Efficient model to usually even raise this question, much less to answer it, has been noted.)

Barnes's brief comparison of the types of political systems, types of parties (especially the working-class mass membership party), and types of party systems in terms of his communications model is stimulating; further conceptualization of this model could lead to significant advances in research on political parties. It should be noted that Barnes's model may be quite comparable with the coalitional model used by Eldersveld. It should be noted that increasingly in recent studies of political parties — e.g., the studies by Eldersveld (1964), Valen and Katz (1964), Barnes (1967), and Seligman (1967) — one finds increasing references to systems theory, organization theory, and communications theory. Anderson (1968) surveyed the literature in organization theory for concepts which may fruitfully be applied to the study of party organization. We have here considerable potential for theoretical convergence which could greatly strengthen and stimulate the development of party theory and comparative research on political parties.

REFERENCES

Anderson, Lee F. "Organizational Theory and the Study of State and Local Parties," in *Approaches to the Study of Party Organization*, edited by William J. Crotty, pp. 375-403. Boston: Allyn and Bacon, 1968.

Barnes, Samuel H. "Party Democracy and the Logic of Collective Action," in *Approaches to the Study of Party Organization*, edited by William J. Crotty, pp. 105-38. Boston: Allyn and Bacon, 1968.

_______. *Party Democracy: Politics in an Italian Socialist Federation*. New Haven: Yale University Press, 1967.

Burns, James McGregor. *The Deadlock of Democracy*. Englewood Cliffs, N. J.: Prentice-Hall, 1963.

Carney, Francis. *The Rise of Democratic Clubs in California*. Eagleton Foundation Case Studies in Practical Politics. New York: Holt, 1958.

Committee on Political Parties of the American Political Science Association. *Toward a More Responsible Two-Party System*. Washington, D.C.: American Political Science Association, 1950.

Conway, M. Margaret, and Feigert, Frank B. "Motivation, Incentive Systems, and the Political Party Organization." *American Political Science Review*, 62 (December, 1968), 1159-173.

Crotty, William J. "The Quest for Scientific Meaning in Analyses of Political Parties," in *A Methodological Primer for Political Scientists*, edited by Robert T. Golembiewski, William A. Welsh and William J. Crotty, pp. 356-88. Chicago: Rand McNally, 1969.

Downs, Anthony. *An Economic Theory of Democracy*. New York: Harper and Brothers, 1957.

Duverger, Maurice. *Political Parties*. New York: John Wiley and Sons, 1954.

Eldersveld, Samuel J. *Political Parties: A Behavioral Analysis*. Chicago: Rand McNally, 1964.

Epstein, Leon D. "The Comparison of Western Political Parties," in *Political Research and Political Theory*, edited by Oliver Garceau, p. 163-89. Cambridge: Harvard University Press, 1968.

_______. *Political Parties in Western Democracies*. New York: Frederick A. Praeger, 1967.

Forthal, Sonya. *Cogwheels of Democracy: A Study of the Precinct Captain*. New York: William-Frederick Press, 1946.

Gosnell, Harold F. *Machine Politics: Chicago Model.* Chicago: The University of Chicago Press, 1937.

Greenstein, Fred I. *The American Party System and the American People.* Englewood Cliffs, N. J.: Prentice-Hall, 1963.

Hirschfield, Robert S., *et al.* "A Profile of Political Activists in Manhattan." *Western Political Quarterly,* 15 (September, 1962), 489-506.

Ippolito, Dennis. "Political Perspectives of Suburban Party Leaders." *Social Science Quarterly,* 49 (March, 1969), 800-15.

Lohmar, Ulrich. *Innerparteiliche Demokratie.* Stuttgart: Fredinand Enke Verlag, 1963.

May, John D. "Democracy, Party 'Evolution,' Duverger." *Comparative Political Studies,* 2 (July, 1969), 216-48.

Mayntz, Renate. "Oligarchic Problems in a German Party District," in *Political Decision-Makers,* edited by Dwaine Marvick, pp. 138-92. New York: The Free Press of Glencoe, 1961.

Michels, Robert. *Political Parties.* New York: Dover Books, 1959 (Original German edition was published in 1911.)

Neumann, Sigmund. "Toward a Comparative Study of Political Parties," in *Modern Political Parties,* edited by Sigmund Neumann, pp. 395-421. Chicago: The University of Chicago Press, 1956.

Niemi, Richard G., and Jennings, M. Kent. "Intraparty Communications and the Selection of Delegates to a National Cenvention." *Western Political Quarterly,* 22 (March, 1969), 29-46.

Rossi, Peter, and Cutright, Phillips. "The Impact of Party Organization in an Industrial Setting," in *Community Political Systems,* edited by Morris Janowitz, pp. 81-116. New York: The Free Press of Glencoe, 1961.

Salisbury, Robert H. "The Urban Party Organization Member." *Public Opinion Quarterly,* 29 (Winter, 1965-66), 550-64.

Schattschneider, E. E. *Party Government.* New York: Rinehart, 1942.

Schlesinger, Joseph A. "Political Party Organization," in *Handbook of Organizations,* edited by James G. March, pp. 764-801. Chicago: Rand McNally, 1965.

Schumpeter, Joseph A. *Capitalism, Socialism and Democracy.* New York: Harper, 1942.

Seligman, Lester E. "Political Parties and the Recruitment of Political Leaders," in *Political Leadership in Industrialized Societies: Stud-*

ies in Comparative Analysis, edited by Lewis J. Edinger, pp. 294-315. New York: John Wiley and Sons, 1967.

Simon, Herbert A. *Administrative Behavior,* New York: Macmillan, 1951.

Snowiss, Leo M. "Congressional Recruitment and Representation." *American Political Science Review,* 60 (September, 1966), 627-39.

Sorauf, Frank J. *Party and Representation: Legislative Politics in Pennsylvania.* New York: Atherton Press, 1963.

———. *Political Parties in the American System.* Boston: Little, Brown, 1964.

Soule, John W., and Clarke, James W. "Amateurs and Professionals: A Study of Delegates to the 1968 Democratic National Convention." *American Political Science Review,* 64 (September, 1970), 888-98.

Valen, Henry, and Katz, Daniel. *Political Parties in Norway: A Community Study.* Oslo: Universitetsforlaget, 1964.

Wilson, James Q. *The Amateur Democrat.* Chicago: The University of Chicago Press, 1962.

Comparative Party Models: Rational-Efficient and Party Democracy

William E. Wright

The objective of this essay is to develop the two basic party models mentioned in the introduction to this section: the Rational-Efficient model and the Party Democracy model. These are two extreme, polar-opposite formulations found in the literature on political parties; they may be considered as endpoints of a continuum along which real-world political parties range. (Figure 1 suggests how several actual political parties might be located along this continuum. The objective of this essay is, however, theory and not a characterization of specific parties.) It is well worth the effort involved in enumerating the sharply differing attributes of these two party models, since scholars of political parties usually operate from one or the other (often implicitly rather than explicitly). Seldom are alternative models identified and systematically contrasted.[1] Futhermore, both models involve potent value premises concerning what political parties should be like which significantly affect the research and analysis that is done.[2] Thus a discussion of

---

[1]The most notable exception to this generalization is the contrast between the professional and amateur organizational models in James Q. Wilson, *The Amateur Democrat* (Chicago: University of Chicago Press, 1962). Also helpful was the comparison of the cadre and mass parties in Frank J. Sorauf, *Political Parties in the American System* (Boston: Little, Brown, 1964), Chapters 3 and 9. See also John D. May, "Democracy, Party 'Evolution,' Duverger," *Comparative Political Studies*, 2 (July, 1969), 216-48.

[2]Schlesinger admits: "How one defines party organization depends as much upon one's value judgments about the function of parties as upon formal definitions." Joseph A. Schlesinger, *Ambition and Politics* (Chicago: Rand McNally, 1966), p. 204.

Figure 1
RATIONAL-EFFICIENT AND PARTY DEMOCRACY CONTINUUM WITH PARTY EXAMPLES

Traditional European Socialist parties	Club movement party (U.S.)	British Conservatives and German Christian Democrats	Democratic & Republican parties	Old-style City Machine (U.S.)
X	X	X	X	X
PARTY DEMOCRACY TYPE				RATIONAL-EFFICIENT TYPE

the attributes of these competing party models in terms of a common set of factors serves several purposes by: (1) systematically comparing and contrasting the two, thus hopefully aiding comparative analysis of political parties;[3] (2) exposing the underlying value premises of each model; (3) linking the attributes of each model together in an integrated whole; and (4) indicating why proponents of each model are so critical of the opposing model.

The Rational-Efficient and Party Democracy models will be systematically contrasted in terms of a common set of factors which are grouped into the following broad classes: (1) the role of parties in the political system or their system functions; (2) the manifest functions of political parties; (3) the salient structural properties of parties; (4) internal party processes; and (5) evaluative criteria. A table giving the specific attributes under each of the above factors will be presented at the beginning of each section. Pertinent quota-

[3]The geographical compartmentalization noted by Schlesinger (although he does not use our terms for the two party models) has been referred to in the Introduction to this section of the reader. See Joseph A. Schlesinger, "Political Party Organization," in *Handbook of Organizations,* ed. James G. March (Chicago: Rand McNally, 1965), pp. 765-66. See also Leon D. Epstein, "The Comparison of Western Political Parties," in *Political Research and Political Theory*, ed. Oliver Garceau (Cambridge: Harvard University Press, 1968), pp. 167-71. The proponents of the Rational-Efficient model tend to be American, and the Party Democracy model, European social scientists — with some exceptions. As can be seen clearly from Wilson's treatment of the amateur Democrats, the club-movement party — the closest American equivalent of the European mass-membership party — is based on the Party Democracy model. The Responsible Party school or party reformers among American political scientists approach the Party Democracy model to varying degrees. On the other hand, Robert T. McKenzie may be considered a proponent of the Rational-Efficient model. See Robert T. McKenzie, *British Political Parties* (London: William Heinemann Ltd., 1955). Nevertheless, the geographical-theoretical cleavage is still a sharp and enduring one, and one which hinders the comparative analysis of political parties.

tions and references illustrating most of the specific characteristics of the two party models have been drawn from the works of prominent proponents of each model. For the Rational Efficient model, these proponents include James Q. Wilson and Leon D. Epstein (in terms of their own orientations), Anthony Downs, and Joseph A. Schlesinger.[4] Advocates of the Party Democracy model include Sigmund Neumann and Maurice Duverger. Illustrations of the Party Democracy Model are drawn from Wilson's analysis of amateur Democrats and Epstein's comments on the mass-membership party.[5] The books by Wilson and Epstein are particularly central to this essay since we have here two Rational-Efficient theorists treating and critically evaluating party phenomena based on the Party Democracy model.

1. System Functions

It is essential to begin with a general consideration of the role assigned parties in the political system and their functions within the system, since it is at this point that a number of value judgments are made — often implicitly — from which specific party attributes derive. Involved here are one's general conception of democracy and the importance of political parties in the political system.[6] Epstein labels the two main conceptions of democratic theory the pluralist and majoritarian views, and he indicates how sharply different conceptions of party (in our terms, the Rational-Efficient and Party Democracy models) derive from each:

> What may be less clear is the relation of the loosely organized, unprogrammatic, and less cohesive American parties to democratic theory. The point is that these very characteristics allow parties to function in accord with a *pluralistic conception of democracy*. The characteristics are deplorable only from the standpoint of a *majoritarian theory*, which is at the heart of the preference, so

[4]Wilson, *The Amateur Democrat;* Leon D. Epstein, *Political Parties in Western Democracies* (New York: Praeger, 1967); Schlesinger, "Political Party Organization"; Schlesinger, *Ambition and Politics*.

[5]Sigmund Neumann, "Toward a Comparative Study of Political Parties," in *Modern Political Parties*, ed. Sigmund Neumann (Chicago: University of Chicago Press, 1956), pp. 395-421; Maurice Duverger, *Political Parties*, trans. Barbara and Robert North (London: Methuen & Co. Ltd., 1954); Wilson, *The Amateur Democrat*; Epstein, *Political Parties in Western Democracies.*

[6]Wilson, for example, raises questions about the desirability and feasibility of intraparty democracy and programmatic parties — a crucial differentiation between the Rational-Efficient and Party Democracy models — and states: "The answers to these questions depend on one's conception of the nature of democracy generally." Wilson, *The Amateur Democrat*, p. 342.

Table 1
POLITICAL SYSTEM ATTRIBUTES

SYSTEM ATTRIBUTES	RATIONAL-EFFICIENT MODEL	PARTY DEMOCRACY MODEL
1. Basic conception of democracy	*Pluralistic* — Party only one type of political actor.	*Majoritarian* — primacy of party.
2. Goal definition function	*Instrumentalist view:* party not a main goal-definer; party defines goals to win elections.	*Purposive view:* party a main goal-definer; party wins elections in order to implement goals.
3. Linkage function	Party only one of a number of linkage mechanisms.	Party is primary linkage institution.
4. Representative function	*Brokerage role* of party. Division of labor: interest groups articulate interests, parties aggregate interests; affirmative view of interest groups.	*Representational role of party:* parties both represent (articulate) and aggregate interests; hostile view of interest groups.
5. Governing function	Less extensive role of party.	Extensive, even dominant role of party.
6. Conflict resolution	Conflict viewed as disruptive; integrative, consensus-building role of party.	Conflict (within limits) viewed as creative; expressive role of party.
7. Political change	*Centrist* view of party as supporting status quo of moderate, consensual change.	*Reformist* role of party as promoting more extensive change.
8. Role of party in democratizing political system	Parties democratized by competition with each other and externally.	Internally democratic parties play primary role in democratizing political system.
9. Party System	Two-party system.	Multi-party system.

often expressed by political scientists, for a large and strong party organization able to mobilize electoral support for programmatic policies to be enacted by a party serving as a governing agency.[7]

The Rational-Efficient model is thus consistent with a pluralistic conception of democracy, in which party is "downgraded" to be only one of a variety of competing political actors including inter-

[7]Epstein, *Political Parties in Western Democracies*, p. 351. (Emphasis added.)

est groups and the like.[8] Epstein for example, is an admitted pluralist[9] and is rather defensive about writing a book on political parties, which he considers important, but not vitally so.[10] Epstein also supplies an excellent statement of the compatibility of the pluralist conception of democracy and what we have termed the Rational-Efficient party model—a characterization of the *brokerage party* which includes a number of the attributes of this model:

> The pluralist's party norm involves more than the avoidance of class consciousness in the older European socialist sense. It also involves a generally non-programmatic character, a leadership capable of responding to diverse electoral considerations, and a transactional or brokerage view of political activity. A party may still be associated with particular policies and interests, presumably in accord with habitual voting patterns of large portions of the electorate, but it preserves, in theory as in practice, a loose and accommodating character. Such a party, while having had patronage-seeking memberships in the past, does not usually have large numbers of program-committed members. The *brokerage party,* by its nature, is unattractive to members of this kind. And it does not have the need of a majoritarian party to legitimize, through mass-membership participation, any program or policies. For electoral purposes, which are of prime importance, a cadre organization suffices.[11]

It is important to note that the leading proponents of the Rational-Efficient party model (Epstein, Wilson, Downs, Schlesinger, and Schumpeter) base their pluralist conceptions of democracy and the brokerage party on an economic analogy. The emphasis is on the competitive struggle in the political market-

---

[8]This point is illustrated by Epstein's view of party activism (member participation): "But parties are *only one kind* of possible political participation, and by no means the most significant, especially in the United States . . . It is hard to say that these other forms of political participation [e.g., voluntary associations and nonpartisan community activity] are less functional in a democratic political system than purely party membership and party activism." Epstein, *Party Politics in Western Democracies*, pp. 357-58. (Emphasis added.)

[9]"On the contrary, it will be plain in much of this book that the pluralist conception of democracy is essential if there is to be a happy acceptance of my main interpretations of party development." Epstein, *Party Politics in Western Democracies*, p. 18.

[10]"What I have sought is a middle ground [between exaltation and condemnation] on which parties can be viewed as important but not overwhelmingly important political agencies." Epstein, *Party Politics in Western Democracies*, p. 8.

[11]Epstein, *Political Parties in Western Democracies*, p. 357. (Emphasis added.)

place, with political leaders viewed as entrepreneurs. Candidates for public office are the commodity, voters are the political consumers,[12] and votes and influence are the medium of exchange. Issue positions and policy stands are part of the packaging, voter surveys are the equivalent of market research, and advertising and public relations techniques perform the same function in both the business and political arenas. Furthermore, politicians appear to hold voters in as low esteem as businessmen do consumers.[13]

Schumpeter denies that political parties are — or need be — ideologically distinctive "for all parties will, of course, at any given time, provide themselves with a stock of principles or planks and these principles or planks may be as characteristic of the party that adopts them and as important for its success as the brands of goods a department store sells are characteristic of it and important for its success. *But the department store cannot be defined in terms of its brands and a party cannot be defined in terms of its principles.*"[14]

Anthony Downs systematically adapts and applies economic theory to political parties;

> Our main thesis is that parties in democratic politics are analogous to entrepreneurs in a profit-seeking economy. So as to attain their private ends, they formulate whatever policies they believe will gain the most votes, just as entrepreneurs produce whatever products they believe will gain the most profits for the same reason.[15]

Crucial to the application of the economic analogy to political behavior is the adoption of the "self-interest axiom" — i.e., winning office or other material gain is for the politician what the profit motive is for the businessman. Downs states: "Thus, whenever we speak of rational behavior, we always mean rational behavior directed primarily towards selfish ends . . . . Therefore we accept the self-interest axiom as the cornerstone of our analysis."[16]

---

[12]"If Chester Barnard and Herbert Simon consider the consumer a member of the firm, so the voters, who stand in the same relationship to the candidates as do the consumers to the firm, may be considered participants in the election." David M. Olson, "The Structure of Electoral Politics," *Journal of Politics,* 29 (May, 1967), 360.

[13]"The ignorance of voters is what makes party government possible." Wilson, *op. cit.,* p. 357. Even more candid expressions of contempt by the campaign technicians — advertising and media specialists — are found in Joe McGinnis, *The Selling of the President 1968* (New York: Trident, 1969).

[14]Joseph A. Schumpeter, *Capitalism, Socialism and Democracy* (New York: Harper, 1942), p. 283. (Emphasis added.)

[15]Downs, *An Economic Theory of Democracy,* p. 295. See especially his first chapter, in which he states: "Thus our model could be described as a study of political rationality from an economic point of view" (p. 14).

[16]Downs, *An Economic Theory of Democracy*, pp. 27-28.

In another classic formulation of the economic analogy, Wilson also applies the self-interest axiom; if anything, he goes further than Downs in differentiating between motivations or incentives for individual action and the social ends that these actions serve:

> This [amateur] approach stands in sharp contrast to the actions of professional politicians who behave as if they believed that politics, like other forms of human activity, only occurs when individuals can realize their private aims and maximize their self-interest. Public policies are the by-product of political self-seeking just as the distribution of goods and services is the by-product of economic self-seeking. In both cases, the incentive for individual action is not the same as the ends served by the system as a whole. The social function of human action is not the reason that action was undertaken.[17]

The value judgments contained in this conception of democracy and the functions of political parties — anti-policy, anti-member participation, and anti-intraparty democracy — are fundamental to a differentiation of the Rational-Efficient and Party Democracy models. The above formulation of the Rational-Efficient model is undoubtedly more "realistic" as far as the actual behavior of most practicing politicians is concerned, but it suffers from a blind spot in the extreme pragmatic view that whatever works is good, that the ends justify the means.[18]

Because of the important implications for a conception of party that follow from the pluralist conception of democracy, especially when based on an economic analogy, this formulation has received considerable stress. The competing conception of democracy upon which the Party Democracy model is based is less clear and explicit. Epstein terms this the majoritarian conception: "The first [model] is the majority rule theory. According to it, more than one-half of a community's electorate may be mobilized to support a policy or set

---

[17]Wilson, *The Amateur Democrat,* p. 20. Wilson cites Schumpeter in support and notes that Downs makes a concession in his "social welfare function." The concern involved in differentiating between individual motives and social (community welfare-public interest) ends is to make politicians seem not too crassly opportunistic, materialistic, and selfish by denying that the one (individual motives) is incompatible with the other (social ends), thus reversing the old adage to read: "Doing good by doing well." Schlesinger also subscribes to the self-interest axiom: "The central assumption of ambition theory is that a politician's behavior is a response to his office goals." Schlesinger, *Ambition and Politics,* p. 6.

[18]Wilson defensively addresses himself to this point: "It is easy to criticize the notion that 'the ends justify the means'; but if the *ends* do not justify the means, it is difficult to imagine what else can." Wilson, *The Amateur Democrat,* p. 348. (Original emphasis.)

of policies, and the majority thus mobilized ought to have the means to enact its policy. The means are to be provided by an organized party."[19] There are several crucial differences between these two conceptions of democracy as far as parties are concerned. First, the primacy of party among competing political actors is advocated in the Party Democracy model: "It is the major function of the party to keep these lines of communication [between leaders and followers] open and clear. *Such a task makes the parties, if not the rulers, at least the controlling agencies of government in a representative democracy*."[20] Other important implications are that parties are expected to be highly organized and cohesive, programmatic (policy-oriented or ideological), to play a crucial governing role, and to encourage member participation and intraparty democracy. These attributes will be discussed below.

One of the most important functions of the political system is what has been variously termed societal goal-definition, or the policy function broadly considered. Mitchell, employing a Parsonian framework, names as the first function of the political system, "the authoritative specification of societal goals."[21] The two party models differ sharply in the role assigned political parties in this important political function. In the Rational-Efficient model, parties are not assigned a vital role; this is due partly to the pluralistic conception of democracy (e.g., competition from other sources), but even more to the instrumentalist view of party, in which policy is viewed as a tactical means to an end. Downs states as the "fundamental hypothesis" of his model: "Parties formulate policies in

---

[19]Epstein, *Political Parties in Western Democracies*, p. 15. Epstein further notes that while "the responsible-party advocacy is not quite the American version of the Duverger model," the party reformers do hold, "in common with the believer in the socialist working-class party, a majoritarian theory of party behavior. There is the same underlying idea that the majority should control government through the agency of a political party representing it" (pp. 355-356).

[20]Neumann, *Modern Political Parties*, p. 397. (Emphasis added.) In his introductory essay to the same volume, Neumann refers to political parties as "the lifeline of modern politics" (p. 1), "critically significant" (p. 1), and "the main agents of public affairs" (p. 4). Schattschneider, a proponent of *some* aspects of the Party Democracy model, states as the thesis of his book: ". . . that the political parties created democracy and that modern democracy is unthinkable save in terms of the parties . . . The parties are not therefore merely appendages of modern government; they are at the center of it and play a determinative and creative role in it." E. E. Schattschneider, *Party Government* (New York: Holt, Rinehart and Winston, 1942), p. 1. Later Schattschneider states: "The parties are *the most important instrumentalities of democratic government*" (p. 59, emphasis added).

[21]William C. Mitchell, *The American Polity: A Social and Cultural Interpretation* (New York: The Free Press of Glencoe, 1962), p. 7.

order to win elections, rather than win elections in order to formulate policies."[22]

Epstein expresses a similar view of party: "*Ideological, principle, program, and policy, if they exist at all, are equally instrumental at every organizational level. There is a strictly business arrangement, rational and efficient, for the narrow purpose at hand* [i.e., winning elections]."[23] This instrumentalist, non-ideological conception of party is also held by Wilson, who states in describing the professional model: "Issues will be avoided except in the most general terms or if the party is confident that a majority supports its position. Should a contrary position on the same issue seem best suited for winning a majority at the next election, the party will try to change or at least mute its position."[24]

From the primacy of party among political actors in the general conception of democracy on which the Party Democracy model is based, it follows that the party is considered the main goal-definer and policy-formulator in the political system. This kind of party, unlike the Rational-Efficient party, is expected to stand for something and seeks power in order to implement goals and policies: "At the root of the belief in programmatic parties is the asumption that parties should be primarily policy-makers . . . [Policies], and the program from which they come, are the party's *raison d'etre*. Elections are won in order to carry them out."[25] Similarly, Wilson stresses this difference between the two party models: "Amateur politicians thus seek to alter fundamentally the way in which the functions of parties are carried out. Instead of serving as neutral agents which mobilize majorities for whatever candidates and programs seem best suited to capturing the public fancy, the parties would become the sources of program and the agents of social change."[26]

---

[22]Downs, *An Economic Theory of Democracy,* p. 28.

[23]Epstein, *Political Parties in Western Democracies,* p. 104. (Emphasis added.) Epstein further notes: "Why should parties assume the kind of coherent policy-making that being programmatic implies? In particular, why should parties so function when, as is thought to be the case for American parties, coherent policy-making might interfere with successful election campaigns by narrowing political appeals? I do not raise the question cynically" (p. 265).

[24]Wilson, *The Amateur Democrat,* pp. 17-18. Similarly, Downs expresses the tactical view of ideology: "Each party realizes that some citizens vote by means of ideologies rather than policies; hence it fashions an ideology which it believes will attract the greatest number of votes." Downs, *An Economic Theory of Democracy,* p. 100. Downs further contends that to view ideology as an end and office, the means, is "irrational" (p. 112).

[25]Epstein, *Political Parties in Western Democracies,* p. 264.

[26]Wilson, *The Amateur Democrat,* pp. 18-19.

The different conceptions of democracy and the status assigned the political party in these two models also accounts for sharply differing judgments as to the role that political parties play as intermediaries linking citizens with government. In the pluralistic conception of democracy which underlies the Rational-Efficient model, the political party is only one among a number of institutions (others being interest groups and the mass media) which compete in performing this linkage function. In the Party Democracy model, on the other hand, the political party is considered the primary linkage between citizens and government, and the primacy thus accorded political parties in large part accounts for the important role assigned parties vis-à-vis other groups in the political system generally. For Sigmund Neumann, party "is the great intermediary which links social forces and ideologies to official governmental institutions and relates them to political action in the larger political community."[27] One of the most important systems functions of party is that of representing "the connecting link between government and public opinion."[28]

Two vital "input" functions of all political systems, as listed by Gabriel Almond, are interest articulation and interest aggregation.[29] In the Rational-Efficient model, again as a result of the pluralist conception of democracy, there is a sharp division of labor between the functions of interest articulation and interest aggregation. Interest groups represent or articulate interests, while political parties, serving as interest brokers, combine or aggregate competing interests and demands into a more manageable number of broader policy alternatives in a kind of electoral calculus. Interest groups offer their electoral support to competing parties in exchange for favorable consideration of policy stands benefitting the group, while parties seek to win the support of competing groups without binding themselves to specific policies. This division of labor between parties and interest groups in the political marketplace found in the Rational-Efficient model entails an affirmative view of interest groups and an appreciation of their performance of this vital func-

---

[27]Neumann, *Modern Political Parties*, p. 396.

[28]Neumann, *Modern Political Parties,* p. 397. Leiserson also stresses the role of party in the linkage function: "The political party, or party system, provides the major connective linkage between people and government, between separate formal agencies and officials of government, and between official and non-official (extra-governmental) holders of power." Avery Leiserson, *Parties and Politics: An Institutional and Behavioral Approach* (New York: Knopf, 1958), p. 35.

[29]See Almond's introductory essay in *The Politics of Developing Areas*, ed. Gabriel A. Almond and James S. Coleman (Princeton: Princeton University Press, 1960), pp. 33-45.

tion; parties and interest groups are friendly colleagues. Epstein, for example, clearly assigns to interest groups the function of interest representation: "It is hard to deny that specialized interest groups provide the most suitable means for policy preferences to be represented in a complex modern society."[30] He also expresses an affirmative view of interest groups and the division of labor between interest groups and political parties — a view based on his electoral, non-ideological conception of party:

> Yet even in the United States some scholars have been reluctant to concede the legitimacy of representation through interest groups. One reason for this reluctance can be traced to the tendency to think of interest groups as rivals that parties must overcome. But there is such a rivalry only if parties are considered as policy-makers. If, instead, they are seen in more exclusively electoral terms, as mobilizers of candidates and not directly for policies, then the function of interest groups in promoting policies is *no more than a sensible division of labor* that frees parties for the task of mobilizing majorities to elect candidates.[31]

Much less of a division of labor between parties and interest groups exists in the Party Democracy model; political parties represent as well as articulate interests.[32] Epstein uses the term *interest group-parties,* defined as "parties combining some of the functions of interest groups and of electoral parties,"[33] found particularly as "single-interest" parties in multiparty systems: "So when political competition is between several parties each based mainly on an interest, the agencies performing the aggregative functions are not differentiated from the interest-articulation agencies. *They tend to*

---

[30]Epstein, *Political Parties in Western Democracies,* p. 279.

[31]Epstein, *Political Parties in Western Democracies,* pp. 280-81. (Emphasis added). He further elaborates this view: "The winning party is the more successful aggregator. Closely enough defined, this aggregative function is compatible with the division of labor between parties and interest groups. . . . Parties responding to their environments by attempting to be very broadly aggregative cannot even *seem* programmatic. Instead they have to be admired, if they are at all, for their pragmatic, compromising spirit" (p. 283). (Original emphasis.)

[32]Valen and Katz discuss the somewhat antithetical and opposed functions of interest representation and compromise-integration (interest aggregation). Whereas American parties emphasize the latter function, Norwegian parties "address themselves seriously to the task of *representing* their major ideological or interest base as well as to the coalition function of including diverse groups under the same party umbrella." Henry Valen and Daniel Katz, *Political Parties in Norway: A Community Study* (Oslo: Universitetsforlaget, 1964), p. 50. (Emphasis added.)

[33]Epstein, *Political Parties in Western Democracies,* pp. 118-19.

be the same."[34] The primacy accorded parties in the political system by the Party Democracy model entails a more hostile view of interest groups, which are considered as representing special interests rather than majority or public interests, as lacking democratic legitimacy since they usually do not operate in a public and democratic manner, and as being manipulative.[35] Neumann hints at the idea that parties outrank interest groups in the Party Democracy model: "It is, indeed, through the network of political parties that the place and responsibilities of pressure groups must be circumscribed if the modern society is not to deteriorate into a neofeudalism of powerful interest groups."[36]

It follows from the general conceptions of democracy and the importance of party, especially with regard to the policy function, that there are sharp differences in the role that political parties are supposed to play in government. In the Rational-Efficient model, the governing role of party is not stressed. Epstein states that emphasis on the governing function of party "is a particular normative view of party functions to which this work does not subscribe;"[37] while "modern parties may also perform governing functions," it is not a necessary party function: "Vote-structuring, however, is their minimum modern function."[38] In the Party Democracy model, modern democratic government is viewed as party government, thus testifying to the extensive, even dominant role that party is expected to play as the main motor of government.[39]

In concluding this discussion of the role of parties in the political system and of the sharply differing implications derived from the two party models, a few other systems factors should be mentioned briefly. Two related processes are social conflict and political change.

---

[34]Epstein, *Political Parties in Western Democracies,* p. 73. (Emphasis added.)

[35]Lohmar makes a further distinction between West German political parties and interest groups: parties are part of the constitutional order whereas interest groups are not. Ulrich Lohmar *Innerparteiliche Demokratie* (Stuttgart: Ferdinand Enke Verlag, 1963), p. 92.

[36]Neumann, *Modern Political Parties,* p. 413. Lohmar warns of dangers of "external control" of political parties by interest groups. Lohmar, *Innerparteiliche Demokratie,* pp. 8-9.

[37]Epstein, *Political Parties in Western Democracies,* p. 315.

[38]Epstein, *Political Parties in Western Democracies,* p. 77. Epstein contends that "the largely nongoverning party may be functional in the American constitutional system. And it may be so in any system founded on the separation of powers," p. 349.

[39]Valen and Katz, for example, note that "Compared with the party systems of many other countries, e.g., the United States, the Norwegian parties play a dominating role in the political process." Valen and Katz, *Political Parties in Norway,* p. 50.

Social conflict may be viewed as the raw material of politics.[40] A main function of the political system shared by other institutions as well is that of conflict resolution, which is related to the goal-definition or policy function. Societal goals are defined and policies formulated in order to reduce conflict. Basic normative judgments concerning conflict have significant implications for the role that political parties are supposed to play with regard to political change.[41] In the Rational-Efficient model, conflict is viewed as disruptive and the integrative role of party in conflict resolution is emphasized; political parties mute conflict by promoting compromise and consensus-building.[42] This view of party determines one's stance with regard to political change: the Rational-Efficient party is oriented toward either preserving the status quo or toward promoting gradual, consensual change.[43] Consensus politics is a familiar term intimately associated with the Rational-Efficient party. Such politics avoids extreme or controversial positions out of a fear of alienating potential supporters. In the Party Democracy model, because social conflict—within limits—is viewed as creative,[44] parties tend to be reformist, advocating more extensive political change,[45]

---

[40]See, for example, Lewis A. Coser, *The Functions of Social Conflict* (Glencoe, Ill.: The Free Press, 1956).

[41]Weiner and LaPalombara identify two types of parties based on different orientations to political change: "In the contemporary scene a distinction is often made between the mobilist party and other kinds of parties. The term 'mobilization' is frequently used to refer to the use of the party as an instrument for affecting attitudinal and behavioral change in a society. The *mobilist party* can be contrasted to the *adaptive party* whose primary concern is its adaptation to the attitudes of the public in its quest for electoral support.... In short, while the goal of the adaptive party is victory, the goal of the mobilist party is social reconstruction." Myron Weiner and Joseph LaPalombara, "The Impact of Political Parties on Political Development," in *Political Parties and Political Development,* ed. Joseph LaPalombara and Myron Weiner (Princeton: Princeton University Press, 1966), pp. 424-25. (Emphasis added.) The Rational-Efficient party is an adaptive party par excellence and the Party Democracy type tends to resemble the mobilist party.

[42]With regard to the conflict management function, Weiner and LaPalombara contend that "it is reasonable to suggest that ideological parties are less able than pragmatic or 'brokerage' parties to handle conflict effectively." LaPalombara and Weiner, "The Impact of Political Parties on Political Development," p. 418.

[43]Epstein expresses the orientation of his book in this regard: "Admittedly, however, the emphasis here, compared with that of party reformers, does reduce the relevance of parties as agents for political change. Indeed, that is the intention." Epstein, *Political Parties in Western Democracies*, p. 9.

[44]For a statement of the view that conflict — within limits — can be creative, see Coser, *The Functions of Social Conflict.*

[45]See the factor of "relationship to the status quo" in Sorauf's table comparing the cadre and mass-membership parties. Sorauf, *Political Parties in the American System*, p. 161.

and serving to express, rather than supress, conflict. The term confrontation politics is more compatible with this party model.

Another systems factor to be noted is the role that is attributed to political parties in democratizing the political system. Several viewpoints are represented, some of which link up with the notion of intraparty democracy which is discussed below. The classic statement of one position is that given by European socialists and based on the Party Democracy model: the party plays the major role in democratizing the political system and needs therefore to practice internal democracy in order to serve as an exemplary model for other institutions. A second view derives from the Rational-Efficient model: political parties make a contribution to democracy in their competitive struggle with opposing parties; they need not be internally democratic to do so. Wilson notes these opposing viewpoints: "The amateurs believe that America's governing institutions are best served if there is democracy within the political parties as well as between them; the adherents of the alternative view argue that while *inter*party democracy is essential, *intra*party democracy is not and, indeed, that the success of the former is reduced by the extent of the latter."[46]

Involved in this brief consideration of the role of parties in effecting political change and in democratizing the political system is the question of whether or not to consider political parties as causal agents, as primarily independent or dependent variables. Epstein accuses European political scientists (e.g., Duverger) and the responsible-party school of American political scientists of holding "a belief in a nearly overwhelming importance of parties in the modern political process,"[47] and counters with his own view: "This more limited way of looking at political parties means that they are not regarded as primarily causal."[48] He considers parties a necessary but not sufficient condition for democracy, as dependent or intervening rather than independent variables.

A final factor which deserves mention relates not to the political system generally but to types of party systems and their compati-

---

[46]Wilson, *The Amateur Democrat*, pp. 343-44. (Original emphasis.) Involved here is the question of whether or not the subunits (e.g., political parties) of a democratic political system must themselves be democratic. Some political scientists, including adherents of the Party Democracy model, give an affirmative answer. Barnes denies that this is necessarily a logical implication: "If the polity is considered the unit of analysis, then democracy within the polity may not be facilitated by democracy within its subunits." Samuel H. Barnes, *Party Democracy: Politics in an Italian Socialist Federation* (New Haven: Yale University Press, 1967), p. 250.

[47]Epstein, *Political Parties in Western Democracies*, p. 7.

[56]Epstein, *Political Parties in Western Democracies*, p. 8.

bility with the two party models. The party system is a particularly important aspect of the political system environment within which political parties operate. Although no neat logical one-to-one correspondence between types of party systems and party models can be drawn, the two-party system is especially congenial to the broadly-based, pragmatic Rational-Efficient party, while the multi-party system allows more leeway to the Party Democracy type. In a multi-party system the ideological party can be electorally successful without being broadly aggregative which is difficult for this type of party. The Party Democracy type tends to be handicapped in a two-party system in which it must get a majority of the votes for attaining a majority usually means appealing to a diversity of social groups in the electorate. The free-wheeling Rational-Efficient party has less difficulty in appealing successfully to diverse interests, since it uses policy stands in a tactical fashion.

Conceptions of democracy and the role of parties in this political system have been discussed in some detail because of the important consequences that basic normative judgments have for more specific party attributes. The outlines of the Rational-Efficient model as the loosely organized, electorally oriented, moderate-pragmatic brokerage party and of the Party Democracy model as highly organized, policy-oriented, ideological, more cohesive, and internally democratic party already have been sketched. These attributes will be discussed below.

2. Party Functions

Sorauf distinguishes between the manifest functions of political parties — the more overt, immediate, and consciously performed tasks — and their latent functions — the more indirect and remote contributions that parties make to the operation of the political system.[49] In the first section of this essay, some of the systems functions of parties have been discussed; here, we turn more explicitly to the party's manifest functions. The two party models differ sharply with regard to their manifest functions and functional characteristics. The Rational-Efficient model is characterized by a narrow range of functions; pre-dominant — even exclusive — emphasis is placed on the party's electoral function. Epstein defines

---

[49]"To put the matter in another way, the party performs certain tasks (the manifest ones) that ensure its own successful functioning, at the same time performing others (the latent ones) that contribute to the functioning of the entire political system." Sorauf, *Political Parties in the American System,* p. 9.

Table 2
PARTY FUNCTIONS

FUNCTIONAL CHARACTERISTICS	RATIONAL-EFFICIENT MODEL	PARTY DEMOCRACY MODEL
1. Manifest functions	Narrow range of functions: almost exclusive emphasis on electoral function; any other functions subordinate.	Broad range of functions: ideological, electoral, and governing; other functions subordinated to ideological function.
2. Activities	Limited and intermittent, geared to election cycle.	Extensive and continuous.
3. Prime beneficiary	Voters (actually elected public officials)	Members
4. Organizational incentives	Material (patronage)	Purposive (especially policy-ideological)
5. Operational style	Pragmatic	Ideological

the political party in terms of this single function: "The single criterion is the functional one: seeking votes for a labelled candidate or candidates."[50] In Epstein's view, although parties may perform other functions, these are to be subordinated to the party's main function: "Organization in one degree or another always exists for this electoral purpose. It may have other purposes as well and still be regarded as that of a party, *provided that the electoral purpose is prominent, if not dominant.*"[51] Other adherents of the Rational-Efficient model present similar views. Wilson, for example, does not even mention the ideological or programmatic function of political parties; in his view, the parties function only to "recruit candidates, mobilize voters, and assimilate power within the formal government."[52] Schlesinger adds to this statement a candid admission of the value judgment involved in this view: "The writer's analysis of party organization accepts the assumption that party organizations in democracies are dominated by their office drives. The decision to view parties narrowly is due to a value preference which derives from the logic of democracy."[53]

[50]Epstein, *Political Parties in Western Democracies,* p. 11.

[51]Epstein, *Political Parties in Western Democracies,* p. 98. (Emphasis added.) Epstein notes the functional difference in the two party models: "The cadre type characterized, from the start, parties with primarily and almost entirely electoral functions. The mass-membership party of the socialists . . . began as movements concerned with other functions. . . ." (p. 99).

[52]Wilson, *The Amateur Democrat,* pp. 16-17.

[53]Schlesinger, "Political Party Organization," p. 767.

In the Rational-Efficient model, the ideological or policy-clarification and goal definition function is rejected, the interest representation function turned over to interest groups, and the party's governing role de-emphasized in order to allow single-minded concentration on the party's basic electoral or vote-mobilization function.[54] If this functional view of the political party is held, one is unable to comprehend and understand parties based on the Party Democracy model which is characterized by a broad range of functions — ideological, electoral, and governing. The electoral function, although important and even crucial, is viewed not as an end-in-itself but as a means to an end. This type of party is expected to stand for something — principles, programs, policies — and it seeks political power via the electoral process in order to implement these. Strictly speaking, the ideological-policy or programmatic function becomes then the dominant function and both winning power (the electoral function) and exercising power (the governing function) are subordinated to it. Neumann lists first among the functions of parties: ". . . the primary task of political parties is to organize the chaotic public will. . . . They are brokers of ideas, constantly clarifying, systematizing, and expounding the party's doctrine."[55] Epstein acknowledges that "basically different conceptions of party functions, it is plain, are involved when policy-making is urged on parties. They are asked to subordinate vote-getting to programmatic considerations. Winning and holding office is a means to another end."[56] We have here a fundamental distinction between the two party models, and one which has a number of significant implications for other party attributes.

These differences in manifest party functions yield two sharply different patterns of party activities. Given the preoccupation with the electoral function by the Rational-Efficient party, it follows log-

---

[54]With regard to the above-metioned division of labor between parties and interest groups, Epstein states that, "in one respect, it affords parties a more limited range of functions." Epstein, *Political Parties in Western Democracies*, p. 218. As far as the policy-making function is concerned, "parties, given their electoral functions, are not especially well qualified to assume the additional functions of policy-making "(p. 269).

[55]Neumann, *Modern Political Parties*, p. 396. Neumann lists the electoral function (termed leader selection by him) last in his list of party functions. So does Kirchheimer in his list of "the functions which European parties exercised during earlier decades (late in the nineteenth and early in the twentieth centuries)." What we have called the ideological function, Kirchheimer terms the "expressive function." Otto Kirchheimer, "The Transformation of the Western European Party Systems," in *Political Parties and Political Development*, ed. Joseph LaPalombara and Myron Weiner (Princeton: Princeton University Press, 1966), p. 189.

[56]Epstein, *Political Parties in Western Democracies*, p. 267.

ically that party activities are limited in scope and intermittant, geared to the election cycle.[57] The typical party organization of this type tends to awaken from a dormant state come campaign time, and to revert to this state during the interim period between elections. The multi-functional Party Democracy type, in contrast, is characterized by extensive, varied, and continuous activities with periodic election campaigns representing a heightened phase of party activity. Campaigning is something else for the party organization to do, in addition to policy discussion and political education activities. Neumann cities as the second function of the political party that of "educating the private citizen to political responsibility."[58] Valen and Katz note the importance of policy discussion and political education activities of Norwegian parties: "All parties place heavy emphasis upon educational activities for members and leaders."[59]

There are two similar ways of classifying types of organizations that are related to the functions of an organization. The first of these is the Blau and Scott organizational typology based on the criterion of *prime beneficiary*,[60] "the criterion of 'who benefits' from an organization's activities."[61] Although Anderson contends that while "typologies such as these are useful in locating party organizations relative to other types, they are of limited value when it comes to analyzing differences among party organizations,"[62] Schlesinger fruitfully applies the Blau-Scott typology in differentiating what we have termed the Rational-Efficient and Party Democracy models:

---

[57]Sorauf characterizes the cadre party by "only periodic activity," and the mass-membership party by "year-around activity." Sorauf, *Political Parties in the American System,* p. 161. For a conceptualization of the "cyclical, recurring character" of party activities, see David M. Olson, "Toward a Typology of County Party Organizations," *The Southwestern Social Science Quarterly,* 48 (March, 1968), especially his discussion of the "electoral-policy cycle" (pp. 563-65).

[58]Neumann, *Modern Political Parties,* p. 397.

[59]Valen and Katz, *Political Parties in Norway*, p. 55. They draw an explicit comparison with American parties: "In comparison with the United States, however, the Norwegian local party organization spends much more time in discussion of the issues and proposals for the party platform. The typical meeting of the local unit of the American party is heavily concentrated upon problems of organization and administration" (p. 64).

[60]Peter M. Blau and W. Richard Scott, *Formal Organizations: A Comparative Approach* (San Francisco: Chandler Publishing Company, 1962).

[61]Lee F. Anderson, "Organizational Theory and the Study of State and Local Parties," in *Approaches to the Study of Party Organization,* ed. William J. Crotty (Boston: Allyn and Bacon, 1968), p. 389.

[62]Anderson, "Organizational Theory in the Study of State and Local Parties," p. 389.

"Cutting through all of these distinctions is the issue of 'Whose party is it?', an issue of great practical and analytical importance. . . . For the party analyst, the answer he gives to this question colors the remainder of his work. If he decides a party belongs to its members, he assumes its need to be responsive to their interests. If he sees the party as an organization aimed at winning elections, he sees it as responsive primarily to the electorate.[63]

Schlesinger notes that "the weight of the continental tradition is clearly on the side of parties as organizations to further the interests of their members, particularly in class or economic terms."[64] The weight of the American tradition, in contrast, is to view the party as responsive to the electorate and thus largely "to ignore the problem of organization."[65] In our view, however, it is logically more consistent with the attributes — especially the "self-interest axiom" — of the Rational-Efficient model to resolve the issue of prime beneficiary in favor of the party's elected public officials rather than the electorate.

The party members are the prime beneficiaries in the Party Democracy model. This type of party has a formal membership which, given the stress on the norm of intraparty democracy, plays an important role in the party. It follows logically that this type of party has a special interest in, and obligation to, its members. It should be noted that the Party Democracy type thus has a problem that the Rational-Efficient party largely — although not entirely — manages to avoid.[66] This problem arises out of tensions produced by a "dual constituency" for elected public officials;[67] conflict arises out of allegiance to members and activists of their party on the one hand, and to the electorate on the other. (There are important consequences for the relationship between the party organization and the governmental party, discussed below.) Although the assumption is made in the Party Democracy model that the politically interested citizen will join and actively participate in the political party closest to his ideological convictions, in practice party membership is usually a small proportion of the electorate, even of party

[63]Schlesinger, "Political Party Organization," p. 765. This is, Schlesinger admits, an issue settled "by value judgments as well as an assessment of the facts" (p. 766).

[64]Schlesinger, "Political Party Organization," pp. 765-66.

[65]Schlesinger, "Political Party Organization," pp. 765-66. See also Epstein, "The Comparison of Western Political Parties," p. 170.

[66]Take, for example, the nomination of a "real Republican" — Barry Goldwater — in 1964. The Republican Party returned to its rational and efficient ways in seeking "a winner" in 1968.

[67]Wilson, *The Amateur Democrat*, p. 296.

supporters (identifiers) in the electorate. Furthermore, party activists represent a distinct minority of the party membership.[68] To the extent that it seriously seeks electoral success, the Party Democracy type must seek in an often difficult task to appeal to sufficiently large numbers of voters without alienating its members — especially the activists.

A second classification is also related to functions performed by organizations. Wilson differentiates two sharply contrasting party types, the "professional" and the "amateur," terms applicable to both individuals and party organizations; these types correspond to the Rational-Efficient and Party Democracy models, respectively. "Professional" and "amateur" refer to distinctive political styles; Wilson's use of these terms is somewhat confusing, since he gives these familiar labels a specialized meaning. He means by "professional" something other than merely whether or not one makes his living from politics; rather, the basic distinction is whether politics is viewed as the end-in-itself of winning, or power, as is the case with the professional, or instead as a means to the end of fulfillment of the public interest, as is the case with the amateur. The goal of the professional is power; the amateur's goal is principle.[69]

The core element of these distinctions is incentive, defined as the means used by the leadership to get individuals to work for an organization and the material or symbolic rewards and satisfactions that motivate these individuals.[70] Elsewhere, Clark and Wilson develop a typology of organizations based on the incentive criterion.[71] They differentiate essentially three types of organizations, based on different kinds of incentives: the utilitarian organization,

---

[68]See Duverger's discussion of membership, supporter, and militancy ratios, whereby these three groups in mass-membership parties may be statistically compared with each other, and with the electorate. Duverger, *Political Parties,* Chapter 3.

[69]Wilson, *The Amateur Democrat,* p. 297. See his first chapter for a discussion of the terms "amateur" and "professional."

[70]Sorauf expresses the notion of incentives used by party organizations in terms of an explicit economic analogy: "If the party is to continue functioning as an organization it must make 'payments' in an acceptable 'political currency' adequate to motivate and allocate the labors of its workers. To continue with analogy to economic organization, each party worker or participant will continue his participation in the party organization only as long as the utility of the incentives to him exceeds the cost to him of the labors the party expects in return." Sorauf, *Political Parties in the American System,* p. 81. Sorauf adds a further note, in similar terms: "Individuals pursue their own aims and goals through work in the political party. The party 'management,' however, seeks to regulate and control the 'payment' of the incentives in order to achieve the goals of the party" (p. 87).

[71]See Peter B. Clark and James Q. Wilson, "Incentive Systems: A Theory of Organization," *Administrative Science Quarterly*, 6 (1961), 129-66.

built on material incentives such as money or patronage; organizations based on solidary incentives, defined by Epstein as including "the intangible values of socializing, congeniality, sense of group membership, conviviality, and general enjoyment";[72] and organizations based on purposive incentives which "also intangible, derive from the stated goals of an association, such as enactment of reform legislation, rather than from the simple act of association itself."[73]

Wilson illustrates these three types by referring to organizational variants within American parties. Typical of the utilitarian-material organization is the strong patronage-based local organization, with a high degree of control and high motivation of the workers; the solidary organization is illustrated by the old-line, decaying regular party club in which the activities are mainly social, and the organization is characterized by low motivation and low degree of control; the best example of the purposive party organization is the amateur, club-movement party typified by the California Democratic Council (CDC), which is based on policy-ideology incentives, and characterized by high motivation, but a low degree of control.[74] Wilson's main contrast, however, is between the professional (patronage) and the amateur (purposive) party organizations. Patronage is the main reward of the professional: "Broadly speaking, patronage refers to any benefit with some material value which a government official can reward at his discretion: a job, a contract, a charter, or a franchise, or even 'inside information' which the recipient can use to his advantage in private dealings."[75] The beauty of material rewards such as patronage, from the standpoint of organizational leaders, is expressed by Sorauf: "As long as it lasted, and for the type of party organization it augmented, patronage was almost the ideal incentive. Its lure was so great . . . that it produced continuous activity. The machine enjoyed complete control over it, the party could deliver the pay-off with almost 100 per cent regularity; and it could in many cases freely revoke it."[76] Wilson expresses a similar view: "Patronage at the disposal of party leaders places those who hold the jobs under an obligation to the leaders. Such an obligation prevents a free expression of opinion and renders intraparty democracy

---

[72]Epstein, *Political Parties in Western Democracies*, p. 101-02.

[73]Epstein, *Political Parties in Western Democracies*, p. 102.

[74]Wilson, *The Amateur Democrat*, pp. 315-16. Sorauf applies a more differentiated typology of incentives to party activists; his incentive categories include: patronage, preferments, political career, economic rewards, personal (social and psychological) rewards, policy and ideology incentives, and organizational loyalty. Sorauf, *Political Parties in the American System*, pp. 82-87.

[75]Wilson, *The Amateur Democrat*, p. 200.

[76]Sorauf, *Political Parties in the American System*, p. 90.

impossible."[77] The "rationality" of this kind of arrangement is cited by Epstein,[78] and Downs clearly draws this implication from the self-interest axiom which is basic to the Rational-Efficient model:

> From the self-interest axiom springs our view of what motivates the political actions of party members. We assume that they act solely in order to attain the income, prestige, and power which comes from being in office. Thus politicans in our model never seek office as a means of carrying out particular policies; their only goal is to reap the rewards of holding office *per se*. They treat policies purely as a means to the attainment of their private ends, which they can reach only by being elected.[79]

Purposive incentives, policy-ideology in particular, rather than material incentives, are basic to the Party Democracy model. Epstein states that "in the absence of large-scale patronage, but not necessarily because of only that absence, many European parties developed membership organizations based largely on nonmaterial incentives."[80] As far as the American representatives of the Party Democracy model are concerned, Wilson observes that "generally speaking, clubs of amateur politicians are examples of purposive organizations,"[81] and, more specifically, that "concern for principles is a crucial incentive for clubs politics."[82] The Party Democracy activist needs a cause to believe in: "A programmatic party, or what is more commonly called an ideological party, is undoubtedly asso-

---

[77] Wilson, *The Amateur Democrat*, p. 210.

[78] "Really the arrangement was quite rational from the standpoint of the party and its workers. Jobs were simply exchanged for party votes." Epstein, *Political Parties in Western Democracies*, p. 109. Epstein also notes that "only the old large-scale American-style distribution of the spoils of office provide the *material* incentive for any large amount of rank-and-file party work" (p. 101, original emphasis). Sorauf states: "No party system has so systematically depended on patronage as the American." Sorauf, *Political Parties in the American System*, p. 82. Greenstein, discussing the old-style urban machine, concluded: "Patronage is the classical lubricant of party organization." Fred I. Greenstein, *The American Party System and the American People* (Englewood Cliffs, N.J.: Prentice-Hall, 1963), p. 42.

[79] Downs, *An Economic Theory of Democracy*, pp. 101-02.

[80] Epstein, *Political Parties in Western Democracies*, p. 111.

[81] Wilson, *The Amateur Democrat*, p. 164.

[82] Wilson, *The Amateur Democrat*, p. 29. Sorauf concurs: "The new club movement builds on personal rewards and policy and ideological incentives." Sorauf, *Political Parties in the American System*, p. 91. Wilson points out that amateur club activists are not only policy-oriented, but very much anti-patronage: "More generally, the amateur believes that political parties ought to be programmatic, internally democratic, and largely or entirely free of a reliance on material incentives such as patronage. . . ." Wilson, *The Amateur Democrat*, p. 340.

ciated with mass-membership organization. The relation is reciprocal . . . The volunteer activist associated with a dues-paying organization needs to have a *cause*. . . . Belief in a cause is the substitute for material interest."[83] Not only principle or policy but participation itself "is a crucial incentive for stimulating amateur — i.e., volunteer — efforts."[84]

The dominant incentives in the two party models are intimately related to party functions: material incentives are geared to electoral success, but are inconsistent with the Party Democracy model's ideological or programmatic function, which translates logically into purposive (especially policy) incentives. From the preceding discussion of system role, party functions, and incentives, it is clear that the two types of parties have basically different operating styles: pragmatic for the power and success-oriented, instrumentalist, patronage-motivated Rational-Efficient party; and ideological for the principled, programmatic, reformist Party Democracy type.[85]

3. Party Structure

The above functional requirements and characteristics have significant implications not only for specific structural attributes, but also for the general importance of organization. In the Party Democracy model, organization is of crucial importance; in the Rational-

---

[83]Epstein, *Political Parties in Western Democracies,* p. 261. (Original emphasis.) Sorauf points out: "Of all the incentives only those of ideology appear to be independent of electoral success." Sorauf, *Political Parties in the American System*, p. 90.

[84]Wilson, *The Amateur Democrat*, p. 182. Sorauf makes the same point — namely that the party organization "may foster solidarity by admitting party workers into the decision-making processes of the party . . . intraparty democracy may perform a useful function for the party as an organization." Sorauf, *Political Parties in the American System,* p. 92. Sorauf does note that the use of ideological incentives by party leaders may reach a "point of diminishing returns" when the costs in voters alienated exceed the efforts "purchased" from party workers (p. 92).

[85]Wilson contrasts the ideological (amateur) and pragmatic (professional) styles: While, "in effect, the amateur asserts that principle, rather than interest, ought to be both the end and motive of political action" (*The Amateur Democrat*, p. 19), in the professional (Rational-Efficient) model, "parties can be regarded as mechanisms for resolving disagreements in ways which reduce to a minimum the number of commitments elective officials must make to policy positions, many of which perforce would be unattainable, unwise, or contradictory" (p. 357). Rather, agreement in this model is produced "by trading issue-free resources" (p. 358). Schlesinger contends that "policy-oriented activists" introduce the "danger of rigidity"; while they must be allowed to participate in party decision-making, "they must be imbued with the primacy of the office goal if the party is to retain its flexibility." Schlesinger, "Political Party Organization," p. 771.

Table 3
STRUCTURAL CHARACTERISTICS

STRUCTURAL CHARACTERISTICS	RATIONAL-EFFICIENT MODEL	PARTY DEMOCRACY MODEL
1. Organizational requirements	Strictly utilitarian view of organization: depends on situational requirements.	Need for extensive, highly integrated structure.
2. Membership	Informal; electoral needs determine organizational size.	Formal membership criteria; many members and strong grass roots organization required for democratic legitimacy.
3. Basic organizational form (structural unit)	Cadre party (committees, cliques of leaders)	Mass membership party (branches or sections)
4. Allocation of authority	Centralization within decentralization (autonomy of sub-units)	Decentralization within centralization (integrated overall structure)
5. Leadership recruitment and career patterns	Open, career pluralism; leaders often recruited from outside party organization or self-recruited.	Institutionalized career patterns; leaders recruited from within.
6. Organizational style	Professional	Amateur

Efficient model, organization is of much less importance. Schlesinger pinpoints the sharp differences in the two party models in this regard. Using Michels as representative of the continental tradition of viewing the membership as the prime beneficiary of the political party, he states: "For Michels, concern with the responsiveness of the party to its membership led to a concern for structure, membership forms, relations among party units, especially those between party members and elected office-holders. His entire analysis flows logically from his original perception of the party as the instrument of its members."[86] In the American tradition of the Rational-Efficient model (e.g., Schumpeter and Downs), on the other hand, "analysts who have assumed that the electorate is the prime beneficiary of party have found the question of structure secondary to that of the party's relation to government. . . . Here there is the tendency to ignore the problem of organization. . . ."[87] In the Ra-

[86]Schlesinger, "Political Party Organization," p. 766.
[87]Schlesinger, "Political Party Organization," p. 766.

tional-Efficient model, as has already been noted, a strictly utilitarian view of organization is taken; organization is functional only to the extent that it facilitates vote mobilization tasks and promotes electoral success. If votes can be mobilized effectively without the benefit of large-scale organization, then so much the better. Epstein clearly subscribes to this view: as a consequence of developments in the mass media (especially television) and other modern campaign techniques, "an organizational apparatus intervening between candidates and voters may be less necessary, or at any rate less efficient, as a vote-getting device. . . . Parties, it may be argued, successfully win votes, perhaps more votes, with fewer organizational members. The new campaign techniques at least facilitate the electoral task."[88] (Just how this perspective leads Epstein to view party members and activists will be shown below.) In the Rational-Efficient model, organizational characteristics are geared to situational requirements: parties may be highly or weakly organized, centralized or de-centralized, strongly or weakly articulated, depending upon the particular situation in the political environment. In contrast, for reasons discussed below, given the nature of its functions and activities, extensive, highly organized and integrated structure is essential to the Party Democracy model.

The structural feature which most visibly differentiates the two party models is the general absence of a formal membership in the Rational-Efficient party and the presence of such in the Party Democracy type. What the Rational-Efficient party has in the way of organization tends to be small and informal; there are usually no formal membership criteria and the size of the organization depends on electoral requirements (i.e., the number of workers needed to get out the vote). The Rational-Efficient organization tends to consist of committees or cliques of leaders.[89] Epstein provides numerous illustrations of these structural characteristics, combined with a critical reaction to the Party Democracy model: "*There is a strictly business arrangement, rational and efficient, for the narrow purpose at hand* [i.e., winning elections]. Organizational membership in any formal sense can be kept fairly small. . . . Size, it must be emphasized, is not an object of an organization of this type. Only enough 'members' are needed for efficient vote-getting. Mass followers are not organized as members. Party work is done by the leaders—little

[88]Epstein, *Political Parties in Western Democracies*, pp. 233, 253.

[89]In his table comparing the cadre and mass-membership parties, Sorauf characterizes the structural unit of the former as "informal cliques and committees." Sorauf, *Political Parties in the American System*, p. 161.

bosses at the neighborhood level and big bosses higher up."[90] Coupled with the anti-organization bias in the Rational-Efficient model is the judgment that formal and extensive membership, characteristic of the Party Democracy model, is largely "dysfunctional," a conclusion that has implications for Rational-Efficient theorists' view on the matter of intraparty democracy (see below). Epstein assesses the value and effect of members in canvassing and contends: "This does not settle the question about the net value of mass-membership organizations. There is still the unresolved question of whether the number of votes the workers obtain are sufficient to justify the considerable professional efforts to organize the workers — which might better be spent on reaching voters directly through the mass media. More particularly, there is the question of whether it would not be more efficient to recruit volunteer workers for each campaign, without the trouble of maintaining membership organizations between campaigns."[91]

On the other hand, Epstein admits that the need for a mass membership is a logical consequence of the functions of the Party Democracy model: "A programmatic party, or what is more commonly called an ideological party, is undoubtedly associated with mass-membership organization. The relation is reciprocal."[92] A prime distinguishing feature of the Party Democracy model is the existence of formal membership criteria for formally enrolled, active, dues-paying members.[93] A strong grass-roots organization is essential not only for the performance of electoral tasks but, more importantly, to provide democratic legitimacy for the party. In this view, a political party must be more than merely an electoral machine; it must have a visible and democratic structure which provides the primary channel of political participation for interested citizens. Since the party stresses the important system function of linking

---

[90]Epstein, *Political Parties in Western Democracies,* p. 104. (Emphasis added.)

[91]Epstein, *Political Parties in Western Democracies,* p. 116.

[92]Epstein, *Political Parties in Western Democracies,* p. 261. He also refers to the American variant of the mass-membership party: "Loosely speaking, the basis is ideological or policy-oriented . . . The mark of the new amateur parties is their regularized dues-paying membership, which sets them apart from the numerous committees created for particular campaigns and candidates" (p. 123).

[93]Duverger states that "The concept of membership is linked with a particular notion of political party that was born at the beginning of the twentieth century along with Socialist parties and that has subsequently been imitated by others. . . . The concept of membership is a result of the evolution which led from the cadre to the mass party." Duverger, *Political Parties,* p. 63; see pp. 71-78 for a description of the formal requirements of membership.

citizens with government, it must be broadly established and responsive at the grass-roots level. This type of party cannot be comprehended except in terms of the role of the membership; as Duverger states, "The members are therefore the very substance of the party, the stuff of its activity. Without members, the party would be like a teacher without pupils."[94]

The basic organizational form of the two party models is the cadre party (the Rational-Efficient model) and the mass-membership party (the Party Democracy model). These terms, which have been widely used in the political parties literature,[95] derive from Duverger, who based his party typology on the basic organizational unit (see Introduction to Section One). The terms cadre party and mass party may be applied to the Rational-Efficient and Party Democracy models respectively; the argument made here is that the latter terms are more useful, in that they are based on multiple criteria that better get at the underlying functional distinctions which give rise to differing structural requirements. The cadre party is a committee style of organization with all leaders and no members while the basic organizational unit of the mass-membership party is the branch or section, composed of the party members who live in the area (usually neighborhood); the party branches are thus roughly equivalent in jurisdiction — although not in structure and function — to the precinct organization of American parties.

The two party models differ in authority structure with regard to both clarity of allocation of power and actual locus of authority. In the Rational-Efficient model, the allocation of authority and control is often unclear and far from obvious, and power tends to be decentralized. Party organization is decentralized to the extent required and consistent with political or governmental structure — which means in the United States highly decentralized. But authority in this model is ideally centralized within organizational subunits, in the interest of organizational rationality and efficiency. The pattern is thus one of centralization within an overall pattern of decentralization. In contrast, in the Party Democracy model, authority is more clearly allocated and visible; organizational integration and effective intra-organizational channels of communication require a more centralized overall structure, but norms of intraparty democracy require decentralization of decision-making authority within

---

[94]Duverger, *Political Parties,* p. 63.

[95]See, for example, Sorauf's differentiation of these two types of parties, including his table of contrasting characteristics. Sorauf, *Political Parties in the American System,* p. 161.

this overall structure. The pattern is thus one of decentralization within centralization.[96] This idea is illustrated by Duverger's statement: "As for the branch, its name implies its integration within a wider community, while the democratic structure of the party, which it aims to bring about, calls for each basic group to play a part proportional to its real importance in the control of the party, and this in turn produces a fairly rigid and fairly strong system of articulation."[97] (In the Party Democracy model, the distribution of authority is vitally related to the notion of intraparty democracy, discussed below).

Another structural characteristic is that of leadership recruitment and career patterns. Differing structural requirements in the two party models entail different leadership selection and career patterns. The leadership selection process in the Rational-Efficient model tends to be more open and fluid, consistent with the emphasis on flexibility in appealing to voter groups and the instrumentalist view of organization in this model. Party leaders, especially candidates for elective public office, are often recruited from outside the party organization—the prime consideration being the voter appeal of the candidate, not organizational service and loyalty; often they are "self-recruited." Eldersveld states that American parties are

---

[96]Sorauf characterizes the cadre party as "tends to be decentralized," and the mass-membership party as "tends to be centralized" in terms of their "internal distribution of power." *Political Parties in the American System,* p. 161. Wilson contrasts the centralized distribution of power in the professional model with the decentralized distribution of power in the amateur model. Wilson, *The Amateur Democrat,* pp. 232-39. Duverger differentiates between centralization-decentralization of authority and degree of *articulation*—i.e., the strength of linkages among organizational units (horizontal and vertical organizational integration). These two dimensions or factors, Duverger cautions, should not be confused: "Strong articulation must not be confused with democratic structure. It is, of course, true that weak articulation is not democratic. . . . But the contrary is not true: a rigid system of articulation may or may not be democratic." Duverger, *Political Parties,* p. 44. Duverger sees a correlation between "the nature of the basic elements which compose the party" and "the strength or weakness of party articulation" (p. 46). The caucus-based party is weakly articulated; the branch-based party, strongly articulated; and the cell or militia-based party, very strongly articulated. Similarly, these three types of party are, respectively, decentralized, centralized, and highly centralized.

[97]Duverger, *Political Parties,* pp. 46-47. Valen and Katz assert: "The membership organization in the Norwegian parties has a clear authority structure. The legislative process in the party is a form of representative democracy. . . . In this process the source of power is at the base of the pyramid. The executive process is also hierarchical but in this case the exercise of authority in implementing party decisions is from the top down." Valen and Katz, *Political Parties in Norway,* p. 84. Wilson contrasts the decentralization of authority in the amateur model with the centralization of authority in the professional model; see Wilson, *The Amateur Democrat,* pp. 232-39.

characterized by career pluralism, rather than highly institutionalized career patterns.[98]

In the Party Democracy model, on the other hand, career patterns are more highly institutionalized and leaders tend to be recruited and promoted from within the organization. Norms of loyalty and service to the organization are important. Leaders must gain and retain the loyalty of the members, as well as appeal to voters as representatives of the party. These patterns are made possible by the more highly organized structure and party control over the nomination of candidates for public office in the Party Democracy model.

It follows clearly from our discussion of these two party models that the organizational style of the Rational-Efficient party is professional, while the amateur style is more in keeping with the Party Democracy type.[99] Just as was the case with the distinctions between the cadre and mass-membership parties, the contrasting professional and amateur styles or models — in Wilson's terminology — are generally equivalent to our Rational-Efficient and Party Democracy types respectively. The same justification for preference for the latter terminology holds.

4. Party Processes

Organizational processes are intimately related to organizational structure. As was the case of structure, organizational processes are of little importance in the Rational-Efficient model; this applies especially to the policy-making process since the party organization is usually — except in the case of city machines — denied any policy role, consistent with its treatment as a service organization by the elected officials as party leaders. As far as the topic of the policy process is concerned, Epstein contends that "the United States

---

[98]See Samuel J. Eldersveld, *Political Parties: A Behavioral Analysis* (Chicago: Rand McNally, 1964), Chapter 7; see also Selection 1.3 in this reader. An exception to this generalization about American parties is the more hierarchical, urban machine form; see Leo M. Snowiss, "Congressional Recruitment and Representation," *American Political Science Review*, 60 (September, 1966), 627-39.

[99]This statement by Wilson referred to American circumstances. The pre-1933 German Social Democratic Party (SPD), a classic prototype of the Party Democracy model, had an extensive and highly developed corps of party "bureaucrats" (salaried party employees). For a discussion of this professionalization of party work and the problems posed for the practice of intraparty democracy, see Michels, *Political Parties*; Duverger, *Political Parties* (New York: John Wiley and Sons, 1954); and Richard N. Hunt, *German Social Democracy 1918-1933* (New Haven: Yale University Press, 1964).

Table 4
PARTY PROCESSES

PROCESS ATTRIBUTES	RATIONAL-EFFICIENT MODEL	PARTY DEMOCRACY MODEL
1. General relevance	Of little importance	Highly important
2. Policy-making process	Largely ignored	Central
3. Intraparty democracy	Little emphasis; member participation tends to be considered dysfunctional.	Strong emphasis on norms of intraparty democracy and encouragement of member participation.
4. Policy role of party organization and governmental party	Autonomy of governmental party; party organization has only service functions.	Inter-dependence in policy-making; norm of strong influence of party organization on governmental party.

provides virtually no illustrative material. . . . More to the point, there has been no nationally organized membership to claim policy-making power."[100] Internal organizational processes generally, and the policy-making process in particular, are of vital importance in the Party Democracy model. Epstein, writing of the European socialist working-class party, the prototype of the Party Democracy model, observes: "Its commitment to organizational policy-making was part of its broader distinctiveness";[101] within this type of party (the programmatic party) there is "a *special* concern with policy-making."[102]

What makes the policy-making process of such great concern in the Party Democracy model is not merely the important policy role claimed by the party in the political system, but the special character of this process, given the commitment to the norm of intra-party democracy. More than even the above-mentioned basic

[100]Epstein, *Political Parties in Western Democracies,* p. 305.

[101]Epstein, *Political Parties in Western Democracies,* p. 314.

[102]Epstein, *Political Parties in Western Democracies,* p. 289. (Original emphasis.) Epstein contends that only the assumption that the party represents a majority of the electorate (e.g., as made by European socialist parties) "can lend democratic credibility to an organized membership's claim to policy-making authority. Otherwise, its credentials seem much less legitimate than those of public office-holders whose policies are tailored to the electorate. The membership must itself be conceived as representing the majority of the population before it can be regarded as any more than another interest group seeking to fashion policy" (p. 314). See Wilson, *The Amateur Democrat,* for an account of the importance of the policy process in amateur Democratic clubs.

functional and structural distinctions, the strong emphasis on intraparty democracy in the Party Democracy model and the absence thereof in the Rational-Efficient model most sharply differentiates these two party models and gives the former its name. Although there are some exceptions,[103] advocacy of programmatic parties is usually coupled with demands for intraparty democracy.

Intraparty democracy is both a simple and a complex term. It includes several elements, one of the most general of which is the responsiveness of the party to its members. This element has several implications, as Wilson notes: "In order to insure that party leaders are responsive to the rank and file, the parties would be internally democratic, with party members choosing party leaders and holding them accountable. Candidates for public office and platforms would be ratified, after some meaningful debate and with real opportunities for choice, by the membership."[104] Members expect to have their voices heard in party policy-making and a commitment to intraparty democracy has several important functional and structural implications: the creation of the requisite structural conditions — especially strong grass-roots organization and extensive two-way channels of communication upwards and downwards in the party structure — and the provision of extensive opportunities for policy discussion and debate within party units. (On these points, see the Introduction to Section Five.) Intraparty democracy exists when the upward flow of ideas and policy views is not completely dominated by the downward flow of views and decisions by party leaders.[105]

It is difficult to exaggerate the centrality of the idea of intraparty democracy in the Party Democracy model. Epstein states: "Intra-

---

[103]Schattschneider, for example, favors more programmatic and cohesive American parties, but does not advocate intraparty democracy: "Democracy is not to be found *in* the parties but *between* the parties." E.E. Schattschneider, *Party Government* (New York: Holt, Rinehart and Winston, 1942), p. 60. (Original emphasis.) It should be noted that Schattschneider erroneously regards partisan voters (party identifiers) as the equivalent of "members." Although clearly not an advocate of ideological parties, Epstein contends: "There is no need, despite some precedents, to posit an improbable degree of intra-party democracy as a necessity for a programmatic party." Epstein, *Political Parties in Western Democracies,* p. 264.

[104]Wilson, *The Amateur Democrat,* p. 341. "Democratizing the party machinery means making the party leaders responsible to party members. . . . The general theme is maximum citizen participation in the party" (pp. 129-30).

[105]Valen and Katz contend that the structure of Norwegian parties is democratic: "Though the dominant pattern of communication does follow vertical lines, it is of crucial importance to realize that the flow is not just one-way." Valen and Katz, *Political Parties in Norway,* p. 95.

party democracy appeared as a nearly essential means for social democrats as it has for the party reformers in the United States. In neither instance has an organized membership in and of itself been the main purpose. Its existence provides a basis for the principled and programmatic policy-making that American reformers, like European socialists, have often wanted."[106] Writing of the amateur Democrats, Wilson emphasizes that "intraparty democracy is not merely a tactically expedient slogan, it is an inherent feature of amateur politics and represents a fundamental break with the professional style. Mass participation and intraparty democracy are crucial to the nature of amateur politics for both theoretical and practical reasons."[107]

For Duverger, the issue is simple. Since democracy is the dominant twentieth century doctrine of legitimacy, "parties must in consequence take the greatest care to provide themselves with leadership that is democratic in appearance. . . . Democratic principles demand that leadership at all levels be elective, that it be frequently renewed, collective in character, weak in authority."[108] According to Duverger, only "where there is coincidence in orientation" between leaders and members, only where the leaders are representative of the members, can a party be called democratic.[109] Mayntz supports Duverger's notion in drawing implications for parties from broad conceptions of democracy: "The ideal model of a functioning democratic system stipulates not only certain outcomes—e.g., selection of *qualified* candidates, statement of *salient* issues — but also certain modes for achieving these outcomes — e.g., not by arbitrary decisions of an oligarchic ruling group, but through democratic processes involving the whole membership."[110] It clearly follows that party functions must be performed in a democratic manner. The importance of norms of intraparty democracy is anchored not only in

---

[106]Epstein, *Political Parties in Western Democracies,* p. 306.

[107]Wilson, *The Amateur Democrat,* p. 181. The stress is not merely on theory but on practice: "In the majority of the reform clubs, intraparty democracy is not only advocated but practiced" (p. 131).

[108]Duverger, *Political Parties,* p. 134. For Duverger, this general notion has further implications for type of party. The mass-membership party is more democratic, and therefore more legitimate, given the general legitimizing norm of democracy: "The branch constitutes the 'legitimate' structure of parties, in the sociological sense of the term: an institution is legitimate when it corresponds to the dominant doctrines of a period, to the most widely held beliefs on the nature and form of power" (p. 26).

[109] Duverger, *Political Parties,* p. 91.

[110]Renate Mayntz, "Oligarchic Problems in a German Party District," in *Political Decision-Makers,* ed. Dwaine Marvick (New York: Free Press of Glencoe, 1961), p. 140. (Original emphasis.)

democratic theory but finds expression in party statutes,[111] and — at least in the case of West Germany — in the constitution.[112]

The opposite side of the coin should be presented — i.e., Rational-Efficient theorists' assessment of member participation and intra-party democracy. It has been pointed out above that these theorists view party membership solely in terms of the performance of electoral, vote-mobilization tasks. Epstein admits the implications of this basic premise:

> This assumes that the principal electoral relevance of a party membership is to provide campaign workers. It leaves aside membership as a source of dues on the ground that there are easier ways of collecting campaign funds (except perhaps for a new working-class party without trade-union support). It also leaves aside membership as a means for programmatic communications between leaders and followers on the ground that this is not a strictly electoral function. *The basic assumption is that the effort to sustain a mass membership is justified primarily by vote-getting considerations.* If other purposes are served, as is likely, they are bound to be of secondary interest to party leaders and candidates who want to win elections.[113]

---

[111]Valen and Katz write of Norwegian parties (especially the Labor Party): "It should be emphasized that the organization of the party not only permits such [policy] discussions at local levels but actually prescribes it." Valen and Katz, *Political Parties in Norway,* p. 90.

[112]Article 21, Section 1, of the Basic Law (*Grundgesetz*) of the Federal Republic of Germany states: "The parties participate in the forming of the political will of the people. They can be freely formed. *Their internal organization must conform to democratic principles.* They must publicly account for the sources of their funds." Aronld J. Zurcher (ed.), *Constitutions and Constitutional Trends Since World War II* (New York: New York University Press, 1955; second ed. revised), p. 294. (Emphasis added.) The Party Law Commission appointed by the Federal Minister of the Interior interpreted this article in the following manner: "Democratic order in the sense of Article 21 of the Basic Law means . . . basing the organization and internal party policy decisions on the expressions of the will of the party members or of the representative bodies which are elected in stages by them. This presupposes a policy-making process which operates 'from the bottom to the top' within the party and stands opposed to authoritarian principles of organization and leadership of the party. The elimination or removal of an active and determinative influence on the part of the party members, a policy-making process controlled 'from above' or 'from outside' the party are contradictory to this goal of the Basic Law." *Rechtliche Ordnung des Parteiwesens: Probleme eines Parteiengesetzes* (Frankfurt: Alfred Metzner Verlag, 1957), p. 157.

[113]Epstein, *Political Parties in Western Democracies*, pp. 113-14. (Emphasis added.) In the same context, Epstein admits: "*This harsh efficiency-minded analysis* neglects the possibility that a few local activists might want lots of members for their own non-electoral purposes" (p. 117). (Emphasis added.)

There is a strong tendency for Rational-Efficient theorists to regard membership participation as dysfunctional: "Most of the members, then, are not functional in an electoral sense. They may even be dysfunctional, since the time spent by local activists in recruiting them might be better used soliciting votes. . . ."[114]

Rational-Efficient theorists are thus critical of the notion of party membership; they are even more critical of the idea of intraparty democracy and of efforts by party members and activists to influence party policy, which they regard as the exclusive domain of elected public officials. Wilson contends that "internal democracy and a commitment to substantive programs would be as irrelevant to the selection of candidates and issues by a party as they would be to the choice of merchandise and sales programs by department stores."[115] He doubts that the main objectives of amateur Democrats — intraparty democracy and programmatic orientation — are "either desirable or feasible" for American parties. He does admit, however, that one's views on this matter depend on "one's conception of the nature of democracy generally."[116] Wilson attacks the notion of intraparty democracy on a broad front; in his view, it gives strategic advantage to the enemy; it leads to outbidding one another in the effort to prove their ideological purity."[117] It also leads the party organization further away from "that crucial middle ground on which all parties must stand if they are to appeal successfully for those crucial votes which are not committed to either extreme."[118] The attending publicity "can deprive such organizations of essential resources,"[119] such as funds if public disclosure is required. Intraparty democracy hinders party discipline. Finally, in the United States, parties which practiced intraparty democracy would not effectively appeal to the lower classes and minority groups, reflecting the view of Wilson and Epstein that this type of American party is not only middle-class in actual composition but

---

[114]*Political Parties in Western Democracies,* p. 116. Epstein discounts the electoral utility of amateur clubs: "The clubs might even get in the way, as suggested earlier, by seeking less 'marketable' policies and candidates" (pp. 125-126).

[115]Wilson, *The Amateur Democrat,* p. 344.

[116]Wilson, *The Amateur Democrat*, p. 342. Wilson goes on to claim: "If the party is to be a competitor for votes, then the requirements of that competition will be, in most cases, the opposite of party democracy. . . . Internal democracy is harmless — and meaningless — when the interparty contest is hopeless" (p. 347). In his discussion of New York amateur Democrats, Wilson contends: "What is surprising is not that intraparty democracy is 'inefficient,' but that it is not a greater problem than it is" (p. 132).

[117]Wilson, *The Amateur Democrat,* p. 347.

[118]Wilson, *The Amateur Democrat*, pp. 347-48.

[119]Wilson, *The Amateur Democrat*, p. 348.

a middle to upper-middle class organizational type of party.[120] Schlesinger further illustrates this hostility to intraparty democracy by noting that American parties use a number of ingenious methods to ward off policy-oriented participants: "There are a number of methods whereby American party organizations have reduced the tensions which come from policy-oriented participants. Techniques of repulsion and insulation are both used."[121]

Questions concerning the role of the party membership in policy-making culminate in a discussion of the relation between the party (membership) organization and the governmental party (elected public officials) and the relative claims to policy influence by each.[122] Epstein contends that the character of this relationship poses a fundamental question:

> In many respects, this controversial point is at the heart of theorizing about the place of a party in a democratic political system. Two conflicting theories of representation are involved. In the older and more traditional one, elected public office-holders, individually and collectively, decide policy. . . . In the second theory, however, the office-holder is considered the agent, although he may be a leader, of an organized following that determines policy. . . . Thus the essence of the second theory of representation is not that it makes for policy agreement among a party's office-holders, but that it makes for this agreement as the result of decisions of an organized party membership.[123]

---

[120]Wilson, *The Amateur Democrat*, p. 253; see also Epstein, *Political Parties in Western Democracies*, pp. 122-26. Wilson takes the view of democracy expressed by Schumpeter (and other Rational-Efficient theorists) — a conception based on "the choice of leaders rather than policies." The political process is viewed from the perspective of elected public officials, who should be freer "from the vetoes of uninformed opinion"; opposed is "a system which will have enlarged powers for imposing vetoes on the judgment of elected officials" — officials who "will find a programmatic party a burdensome constraint." Wilson, *The Amateur Democrat*, p. 346.

[121]These include telling the would-be participants that "parties and government deal with matters of little importance," spreading the "notion that politics is unsavory," and isolating them in their own organizations, in order to "keep people with policy motives from invading the parties." Schlesinger, "Political Party Organization," p. 772. Elsewhere, Schlesinger warns of the inflexibility which he sees associated with ideology: "How can a party, responsible for government, retain the flexibility necessary to respond effectively to complex international and domestic problems if it is controlled by men with strong ideological convictions?" Schlesinger, *Ambition and Politics*, p. 208.

[122]"So there are at least two possible foci of policy-making in a party with a mass membership attracted by the party program: the public office-holders, actual or potential, and the organized membership." Epstein, *Political Parties in Western Democracies*, p. 290.

[123]Epstein, *Political Parties in Western Democracies*, p. 292.

Duverger discusses three stages in the evolution of this relationship between the party organization and the governmental party, along with related variations in basic organizational units and control structure. The first pattern is that of policy dominance by the governmental party, as represented by the Rational-Efficient model of a decentralized cadre party; in this model, the party organization, which serves in a service capacity to elected public officials and which is subordinate to them, makes no claim for a role in party policy-making. This pattern is based on the first-mentioned theory of representation noted by Epstein. The second pattern is that represented by the Party Democracy model: it is based on the second theory of representation noted by Epstein. The second pattern exhibits a state of rivalry and tension between the membership organization and the governmental party.[124] In the Party Democracy model, there are separate and potentially conflicting bases of power,[125] and the membership does stake a claim to influence in policy-making:

> If the membership is not always accorded an actual policy-making role, it is nevertheless certain that it is a potential claimant to the role. It could hardly be otherwise with a group whose organized existence owes so much to a programmatic commitment. The problem of how policy is made in a programmatic party revolves around the part to be played by the organized membership.[126]

The membership organization, in theory if not always in practice, is accorded a strong influence on "their" elected representatives in public office. Valen and Katz, in discussing Norwegian parties, assert that "in other words the formal structure enables party members to have a very effective voice in determining the line which leaders of the governmental party will take, but whether members

---

[124]"There exists a state of tension, if not of equilibrium, between the internal leaders and the parliamentary representatives." Duverger, *Political Parties,* p. 190. The third pattern, that of party organization dominance in policy making, is represented by the cell-based, highly centralized party typified by the Communist parties.

[125]"Yet the point remains that the public office-holders and the organized membership have inherently separate bases for claiming policy-making authority, and these separate bases can conflict." Epstein, *Political Parties in Western Democracies,* p. 290.

[126]Epstein, *Political Parties in Western Democracies,* p. 290. Epstein admits that party members and activists, "it must be stressed, have certain democratic credentials for challenging the claims of the party's public office-holders. These credentials do not exist in a cadre or skeletal party, where there is no substantial membership to provide the numerical basis for a democratic claim. . . . It is such a basis that a dues-paying mass membership clearly provides" (pp. 290-91).

take advantage of their opportunities is up to them."[127] (The relationship between the party organization and the governmental party is discussed more fully in the Introduction to Section Five.)

5. Evaluative Criteria

The effectiveness of these two types of parties is judged in terms of different sets of criteria; the sole test of the effectiveness of the Rational-Efficient party is effective vote mobilization and electoral success. It is not how you play the game that counts, but whether you win or lose that is all-important. Although electoral success is important in the Party Democracy model in order to give party leaders power to accomplish established policy objectives, the main criteria are the effectiveness of policy clarification and intraparty democracy.

Table 5
EVALUATIVE CRITERIA

Evaluative Criteria	Rational-Efficient Model	Party Democracy Model
1. Party effectiveness (criteria)	Sole criterion is electoral success.	Effectiveness of policy clarification and intraparty democracy.
2. View of opposite model	PD model viewed as inefficient in vote mobilization and inflexible.	RE model viewed as an opportunistic, manipulative electoral machine lacking in democratic legitimacy

Included in each model is a sharply hostile view of its opposite number, evidence of which can be seen throughout this essay. In terms of the Rational-Efficient model, the Party Democracy type is viewed as inflexible and unadaptable, often extremist, and inefficient in vote mobilization. Its greatest sins are its principled or

[127]Valen and Katz, *Political Parties in Norway,* pp. 89-90. "In Norway, however, party decisions are definitely the result of a mutual process of influence between the two subsystems": the governmental party and the membership organization (p. 88). Which has greater influence on policy? "The formal structure of the party gives the decisive weight to the membership organization" (p. 89). This is particularly true of the parties of the Left: "The Communist and Labor Parties explicitly state that the party organization shall decide the party policies, and that the elected representatives have to follow these decisions. Similar provisions are not included in the statutes of the other parties. They have, however, established cooperation between party caucuses and membership organizations" (p. 66).

programmatic orientation, generally, and its allowing the membership to have a voice in policy-formulation, in particular. From the standpoint of the Party Democracy model, the Rational-Efficient party is considered to be too opportunistic, manipulative, merely an "electoral machine," and as lacking in "democratic legitimacy" — i.e., as lacking a large membership to participate in and thereby legitimize decisions, and as lacking internally democratic procedures.

No summary of the attributes of the two party models is really needed here. Each party model has its own frame of reference and internal logic. Each model rests firmly upon fundamental value premises; each model has potent built-in biases, including a rejection of the opposing model. This fact goes a long way toward explaining the biases of Duverger, who operates from the Party Democracy model, against American parties; and reverse biases of Epstein, who operates from the Rational-Efficient model, in favor of American parties and against the mass-membership party; and the criticisms of Wilson as a Rational-Efficient advocate of the amateur Democratic club parties, the closest American equivalent of the Party Democracy model. It is hoped that this attempt to portray systematically the attributes of these two party models has adequately illuminated the basic reasons for the lack of communication among scholars which has greatly hindered the comparative analysis of political parties.

The Nucleus of Party Organization

Joseph A. Schlesinger

The basic unit of party organization is the collective effort devoted to the capture of a single public office. Such an organization is here called a *nucleus*. That a nucleus out of the relationships among nuclear organization has been borne out by such an intensive study of city politics as the Cutright and Rossi work (1958b, p. 269). They, too, concluded that local "party organization" often means *candidate* organization.

A nucleus may be a very simple array of activities involving only a candidate and a few supporters, or it may be the multiple activities involved in an assault on the presidency. Complex party organizations emerge out of the relationships among nuclear organizations. At this point, however, the discussion is concerned with the principal organizational questions posed by a nucleus. Note that a nucleus is not the same thing as a precinct, or the smallest unit into which the electorate is divided. The precinct is frequently described as the smallest party unit, and it is, in the formal structure of parties. Where a precinct controls a desirable office, a nucleus will certainly form. But the need to record votes or to fill out the formal party structure does not assure party organization in the precinct.

Reprinted from *Handbook of Organizations*, ed. James G. March (Chicago: Rand McNally and Company, 1965), pp. 775-86, by permission of the publisher. See Schlesinger's extensive bibliography for references, pp. 797-801.

For a true nucleus to exist, there must be the expectation that at some time, if not in the immediate future, organizational activity will lead to the capture of the nuclear office. Thus, it is possible for a candidate to run for an office without the development of a true party nucleus if the candidate and his supporters have no expectations that the office can ever be won. This is frequently the case for the minority party in one-party areas of the United States, for Republican candidates in southern states, and Democratic candidates in a state such as Vermont in the not too distant past. In these instances, candidates may contribute to other nuclear organizations, most commonly the presidential organization of their parties. But their activities will be aimed not at the offices for which they are the ostensible candidates, but at such offices as postmasterships and judgeships which are in the control of the presidential nucleus.

The maximum number of party nuclei and their location depend on the structure of the state and its means of selecting officers. As noted, in the United States there is an extraordinary number of independently elected public officials, ranging from the President down to ward alderman, and each of these may develop an independent organization. Where the selection of two officers is related, however, as is the case of the President and vice-president, or the governor and lieutenant governor in New York, only a single nucleus will form. It is true that candidates for vice-president may develop their own independent organizations, but these have as their goal influence within the presidential nucleus and depend entirely for their success upon that influence.

Contributions to the Party Nucleus

In further describing the nucleus, the writer follows Simon's suggestion (1951, p. 112) and uses the concept of "contribution" rather than the concept of "membership" commonly used with respect to parties. The concept of membership connotes a degree of commitment which is misleading in political parties. It leads to a fruitless discussion of where to draw the line at membership. In the United States, the legal control of formal party structure produces a variety of tests of membership which have little utility (Berdahl, 1942), while in popular parlance party membership is an extraordinarily loose concept, some 75 percent of the electorate choosing to call themselves either Republicans or Democrats (Campbell et al., 1960, p. 125). Furthermore, self-identification is highly variable. The cross-cultural study of Converse and Dupeux (1962), for example, demonstrates that the French voter is far less willing than the American to identify himself with a political party.

Type of Identification An important characteristic of contributions to the nucleus is that many are not openly identifiable as organizational activity. It is easy enough to recognize those persons who take part in clearly labeled party activities, those who run for office on a party ticket, who attend conventions, or who register openly as members. But the newspaper publisher, the interest-group leader, financial backers, and open primary voters can and do take part in organizational decisions without being broadly recognized as participants in the party.

Looseness of identification permits the party to be flexible in seeking contributions. It need depend on overt contributions for little. Precinct workers can be drawn from union offices; candidates for the highest offices can be apolitical luminaries, men such as Willkie and Eisenhower, whose party identification becomes clear only after they have become active candidates for the presidential nomination.

For the contributor, the more circumspect his identification with the party, the more flexible his relations with the organization, leaving him ultimately the opportunity of withdrawal and transfer to the opposite party. Thus, the realignment in American politics wrought by the New Deal came among the least prominent of both parties. The ordinary party voter, the financial contributor, the newspaper publisher were least hampered by organizational ties in switching party allegiance. Even minor party officials, as a study of Pittsburgh precinct workers has shown (Keefe & Seyler, 1960, p. 519), were able to make the change.

On the other hand, the most conspicuous contributor to the party nucleus, the office-holder himself, is most restricted, causing him to counteract the influence of circumspect identification for organizational instability. Thus, during the New Deal, dissident Republicans such as George Norris and Fiorello La Guardia made their accommodations within their party of origin, and the disgruntled Democratic leader of the twenties, Alfred E. Smith, found solace in a nonparty association, the Liberty League (A. M. Schlesinger, 1960, p. 519). There have been few instances of major officeholders moving successfully from one party to the other. The transfer of Senator Wayne Morse from the Republican to the Democratic Party is the only recent example. Again, the officeholder is the centripetal force for party organization.

Primary and Secondary Contributions Another relevant characterization of nuclear activity is the distinction between continuous and transitory or *primary* and *secondary* contributions. A primary contribution involves direct contact and therefore occurs in a fixed location. Primary contributions go beyond the two-month election campaign held every two to four years. They are the activities traditionally associated with flourishing local party organizations— favors, courtship of ethnic groups, and the agreements among political activists. Primary contributions are made most easily within the nucleus itself. Where the social cohesion of the nucleus is weak, however, parties seek primary contributions among special groups, the work group, the business association, the religious and ethnic organization, whose activities can reach outside the single nucleus.

In contrast, secondary contributions are characterized by their cross-nuclear and transitory nature. They can be made quickly; more important, they are readily transferable. Money, as distinct from the collection of money, is a secondary contribution. Once in hand, it can be used anywhere. Campaign oratory, publicity, party stands, and even leadership can be secondary contributions.

It should be made clear that the distinction between primary and secondary contributions is not between the important and the unimportant. Although secondary contributions are more fluid and transitory, they may have more influence on the party's decisions on nominees and policy stands. The distinction will become most relevant when the discussion deals with the problem of the multinuclear organization, since it defines what one organization can contribute to another.

Minimal and Connective Contributions For the immediate purpose of discussion the most useful distinction between types of nuclear activity is that between the minimal and the connective contribution. As defined here, a nucleus must have both a candidate and the expectation that the candidate will win office or that his activity will eventually lead to the winning of enough votes to capture office. Candidacy and votes, then, are minimal contributions without which there would be no nucleus.[1]

[1]Voting behavior is an aspect of political activity which has been subjected to extensive research. A thorough review of the literature up to that time is Lipset et al. (1954). Lane (1959) brings together not only literature on voting but other aspects of political participation as well. Critical essays on various voting studies are in Burdick and Brodbeck (1959). The principal works of the "sociological" school emanating from Columbia University are Lazarsfeld, Berelson, and Gaudet (1944) and Berelson, Lazarsfeld, and McPhee (1954). The "social-psychological" school associated with the University of Michigan is represented by Campbell et al. (1954; 1960).

No additional contributions need be made to join the voter and the candidate. Those which are made are here called connective contributions. Connective contributions differ from the minimal contributions also in that their impact is not self-evident and is indeed most difficult to assess. The principal types of connective contributions are discussed under the following headings: (a) leadership, (b) recruitment and nomination, (c) issue formulation (d) memory, intelligence, and communications, (e) technical services, and (f) money.

Leadership. In party organization, leadership is a connective contribution of first importance. The fluctuating, ephemeral, and largely voluntary character of most contributions to party activity makes it most useful for someone to move people to participate, to make agreements with other leaders, and to bring together the materials of party combat. In this sense, a party leader is more akin to the business enterpreneur than to the manager, and his risks and potential gains are commensurate.

Yet in parties more than in any other type of formal organization, the official lines of authority are suspect, and there is always implicit the question, Who is the "real" leader or, in the terms of this chapter, Who really makes the contribution of leadership? This is true in great part because a political party is a leader-producing organization, and the ambitious men attracted to parties find it advantageous at least to seem to be playing a major role. If the "real" party leader is often difficult to locate, it is because many competitors for leadership have a stake in keeping it so. They are aided by the fact that positive as distinct from negative tests of power are not easily made (Dahl, 1958).

The contribution of leadership is also difficult to assign because there are two broad categories of party leaders, which in fact may or may not merge. There are the *public* leaders, or men who also represent the party as its candidates for public office; there are the *associational* leaders, or men whose office is limited to the party organization. Often there is no sharp distinction in personnel between the two categories; men move from one to the other or hold both public and party office concurrently. In addition, leaders of nonparty organizations, such as corporations, farm groups, and labor unions, may at times also perform leadership functions in parties, particularly when they perceive an identity of interests.

The difficulties for analysis presented by these overlapping categories pertain especially to the American system. In American parties there is no formal hierarchy of authority or delineation of functions. The committees, chairmen, and conventions which range from the locality to the nation have no consistent authoritative relation with each other or with the parties' officeholders and nominees. At the same time, the actual conditions for officeholding in the United States, numerous public offices with a high rate of turnover, favor the distinction in leadership. This situation contrasts with that of the parliamentary system, where the availability to the party of "safe" public offices or seats almost always assures the merger of both categories of leaders. Thus, whatever the original source of the party leader's strength, organization work or officeholding, party and public leadership easily combine and provide the necessary continuity in an organization where most activity is transitory.

The criterion of tenure in office, easily satisfied by the party leader in the parliamentary system, provides a test for leadership in the American party organization. It permits correcting the model which favors the officeholder as the contributor of leadership to the nucleus by taking into account factors in the political situation which encourage the independent associational leader.

Observation leads to the conclusion that the relative tenure of the two types of officials varies with the type of nucleus and that the officeholder is by no means disfavored. While there is no systematic study of this problem, it is evident that at the national level party chairmen do not necessarily hold office longer than public leaders. Within the state office nucleus, there is considerable variation among states, but certainly a number duplicate the national picture. The example of the independent associational leader who outlasts a series of public officials comes largely from local politics. Yet even here, the ability of such public officials as Mayor Wagner of New York to outlast their associational leaders must be weighed against the staying power exhibited by Carmine De Sapio's predecessors.

On the other hand, the conditions for officeholding can affect the tenure of the public official, causing variation within types of nuclei and allowing the party official to make the principal contribution of leadership. Three such conditions may be singled out: the level of party competition, the legal and customary stipulations for officeholding, the place of office in the political career system.

A major reason for turnover in public office is party competition. Although competition is a variable of several dimensions, the most important for the present analysis is the rate of party turnover in office: here a party change means a personnel change. The more competitive a constituency, then, the more fleeting the tenure of public leaders and the more likely that power will flow to independent associational leaders who are not subject to defeat by the other party. Competition enhances the value of continuity in the nuclear organization. The party's ambitious office-seekers find their expectations raised, while the need for cooperative effort in defeating the opposing party is magnified. This drive for unity is reflected in the reduction of overt conflict in primary elections where party competition is greatest (Key, 1949; Key, 1956). It is difficult to conclude whether such unity is due to associational leadership or agreements among the office-seekers. Probably it is due to both. Still, the value of organizational continuity in competitive nuclei does make it more likely that the independent associational leader will make the principal contribution of leadership.

A similar effect may be accomplished by the legal and customary stipulations for officeholding. Thus, for some offices, notably the Presidency and certain governorships, there are constitutional limitations on re-election (Kallenbach, 1952). These requirements, however, reflect on adverse attitude toward longevity in these offices which operates without legal sanction. Governors generally have brief tenures, and the traditional two-term limitation on Presidents was broken only by Franklin Roosevelt. In contrast, long tenure for congressmen and senators is acceptable to voters and party workers.

Finally, the position of a particular office in the political career system can limit office tenure and reduce the role of the officeholder. Offices with little prestige, power, or pay, such as those in many state legislatures, have high turnover rates (Hyneman, 1938). Offices which may have no inherent power but which are good steppingstones, such as lieutenant governor, will also have high turnover. Where the officeholder's stay is automatically brief, the advantage will go to the associational leader.

Taking into account both the concept of nuclear organization and the conditions critical to tenure in public office, four possible solutions to the problem of assigning the connective contribution of leadership may be suggested (Fig. 1):

1. A high level of party competition combined with legal or traditional limitations on public office balances the influence of public and associational leader, while subjecting both to the most rigorous tests. At the same time, the nucleus finds its need for leadership most critical. Thus, the office of President and governorships in competitive states tend to produce well-defined associational leadership which does not, however, appear to dominate. Observation leads to the conclusion that Presidents and governors of competitive states

Figure 1.

RELATION BETWEEN CAUSES OF PERSONNEL TURNOVER IN PUBLIC OFFICE AND ORGANIZATIONAL LEADERSHIP

Level of Interparty Competition	Noncompetitive Factors in Turnover (Formal or traditional restraints on tenure): High	Noncompetitive Factors in Turnover (Formal or traditional restraints on tenure): Low
High	1 Continuity in nuclear party. Association leader prominent but not necessarily dominant. (e.g., presidency, governorships in competitive states)	3 Continuity, tendency towards domination by public leaders, especially incumbents in office. (e.g., competitive congressional seats)
Low	4 Discontinuous organization, dominated by sporadic public leaders. (e.g., state offices in one-party states) or Continuous organization dominated by associational leaders. (e.g., urban "machines")	2 Continuous organization dominated by public leaders. (e.g., safe congressional seats)

hold their own against party chairmen, who, in fact, are often the choice of the public leader. For if a high level of party competition can make organization more valuable and assure the existence of associational leadership, it also enhances the value of the public leader who can win elections. Furthermore, if discontinuity in control of office weakens the public leader, it also deprives the associational leader of the influence which comes from unbroken control of government. At the same time, the very difficulties posed for both types of leader by the political situation puts a high premium on leadership for the nucleus.

2. A low level of office turnover made possible by the formal and customary stipulations for officeholding, such as those allowing indefinite re-election to congress, swings the balance of influence in favor of the public leader. If there is also a low level of party competition, the leadership of the dominant party is almost certainly assured the officeholder, as is clear in the majority of one-party congressional districts. Longevity in office strengthens the officeholder, while nominal competition stifles the impulse for continuous organization and the need for independent associational leadership. Even when the incumbent leaves office and a struggle for succession takes place among various groups, organizational conflict quickly subsides.

3. Where there is competition for offices without legal and customary restrictions, the public leader still tends to remain domi-

nant, surviving even electoral defeat. For example, Ackerman found (1957) that in one out of eight contested congressional elections, the candidates were the same as in the previous election. In the political situation such as that posed by competitive congressional contests, former officeholders and even former candidates can retain their strength.

4. In contrast, high office turnover due to legal and customary stipulations combined with a low level of party competition favors the associational leader. The older urban "machine" thrived in such conditions, aided also by the division of public authority among a host of officials. Brief tenure and limited power for the public local official favored party organization and the independent associational leader who could provide the necessary continuity and coordination in government. When public and associational leadership merge, tenure in the mayor's office appears to increase.

The fourth political situation, however, may also produce the fluid, factional leadership characteristic of many one-party states in the South. In these states, despite a lack of party turnover, frequent changes in office-holders are assured by restraints on re-election. For example, in Alabama, to which Key (1949) assigned the most transient leadership, the governor and all other statewide elective officers are constitutionally unable to succeed themselves. Perhaps ineffective state government is more tolerable than ineffective local government, and no continuous party organization need emerge within the state nucleus, even when the political situation is the same. Thus, given the complexities of the American political scene, leadership as a connective contribution must vary both with the type of nucleus and the political situation determining nuclear organization.

Recruitment and nomination. The major task facing the leaders of the nuclear organization is to choose its candidate for office. Who contributes to this task and how is it accomplished? There are two aspects to the process. One is the recruitment — and discouragement — of candidates for the nomination. The second is the choice of the nominee from among the active seekers. The latter aspect is more overt and is normally surrounded by rules of procedure which serve to make the nomination authoritative. But the recruitment process is equally critical in defining the choices which can be made within the party.

Although there are few empirical studies of the recruitment process, those which exist place the burden of the task with the aspirants themselves. There is little evidence from which to conjure the picture of an organization actively seeking candidates. Thus, for state legislative office, Seligman (1961) found that in competitive districts or in the dominant party of noncompetitive districts there was little if any direction in the choice of candidates. Only in the minority party of noncompetitive districts was there evidence of conscription. Interviews with state legislators and candidates for that office indicated further that the largest number saw themselves as "self-starters," relatively few as having been recruited by the political party (Rosenzweig, 1957; Seligman, 1959; Wahlke et al., 1962). Although most had placed themselves in a milieu in which they could make contacts with party workers or other political groups, only in competitive New Jersey did most of the legislators see the party as the sponsor of their careers (Eulau et al., 1961, pp. 226-229). In the less competitive states, fewer than one in four attributed their careers to the party.

The process of self-recruitment becomes even clearer within the nuclear organization surrounding higher offices. The individuals who hold stepping-stone positions often make themselves available. When, for example, lieutenant governors, attorneys general, or legislative leaders seek the governorship, one need not infer that they have been recruited by a party organization. Nor is there necessarily any party recruitment when a congressman or a governor seeks a senatorial nomination. When a party has no hope of winning an election, it may have to search for candidates. But when the nomination is of value, the nuclear organization normally responds to choices presented by men coming from the various paths of progression. Few organizations show any signs of long-range planning or grooming of candidates for promotion through offices. Once various candidates have made themselves known, however, party officials may discourage some to the advantage of others. Or, as Cutright and Rossi (1958a) pointed out in their discussion of the selection of candidates for minor offices, party leaders may wait until the individual candidates have demonstrated their strength and then pass the "word" in support of the apparent victor.

As with leadership, the aspirants who contribute to recruitment vary with the nuclear office. In the United States there is no clearly marked *cursus honorum* or set stages of office advancement. Nor are there any offices, including the very highest, which have not gone to men from outside the ranks of officeholders or active party workers. But there is a commensurate relation between social, economic, and political status (Matthews, 1954). Two groups of individuals can expect to assault a particular office. There are the officeholders who are within promotional range, such as congressmen and governors in relation to the United States Senate or governors and senators in relation to the presidency. There are the nonofficeholders whose extra-political claims, economic success, military fame, or some special condition of notoriety, make them acceptable. Although recruitment is distinctly not bureaucratic, it as far from being unstructured (J. A. Schlesinger, 1957).

The contribution of nomination which follows recruitment is equally complex and often obscure. In the United States, reforms such as the convention and the direct primary have clarified some aspects.[2] But there remains decisive activity which takes place in private. Much of the organizational activity in a nomination consists of discouraging other men's ambitions and, if the organization is to succeed at the polls, tying their ambitions to those of the candidate. Therefore, the nomination ideally combines a maximum of discouragement of all but one of the ambitious with a minimum of public disgrace for the others.

The discouragement process takes place within a set of rules according to which one man gains the designation "nominee" of the party. In a stabilized party system, capture of the label is important, and the state frequently acts to assure that only candidates selected according to the rules can pose in the general election under that label. This does not prevent office-seekers, however, from organizing their own campaigns to capture the label. As with recruitment, nomination is less a case of an organization's selecting candidates according to qualifications than it is of providing the framework within which they contest for the nomination.

Rival aspirants, then, must largely discourage their own competitors. The resources available to them are: (a) Outright threat of sanctions, economic, social, or political. The candidate whose supporters in the constituency have control of such sanctions is in a strong position to discourage others. (b) Withholding of resources necessary for effective contesting of the nomination. This is particularly successful when the contest requires substantial financing, as it does for state office or the presidency. (c) Offers of alternative outlets for ambition, either for positions within the jurisdiction of the office being sought, or for aid in seeking some office outside the nuclear office goal. (4) Situational, the obviously superior strength

[2]On early American nominating systems, Dallinger (1897) is the best source. For the presidential nominating conventions, David, Goldman, and Bain (1960) provides the most thorough history and analysis. On the direct primary, Merriam and Overacker (1928) provides an early account. In addition to Key (1956), Turner (1953) and Standing and Robinson (1958) have analyzed the operation of the direct primary in the states in relation to their competitive structures.

of one candidate to that of all other candidates. Such is normally the case when an incumbent officeholder who has not aroused great opposition seeks renomination. All resources are not equally available to each candidate. It can be said, however, that the situational factor is critical, and that the other resources for discouragement tend to follow. Because office ambition is central to party organization, a candidate who is demonstrably a front runner will most easily amass the other resources to reinforce his position. The appearance of victory creates the "bandwagon effect" or fear of the consequences of not being with the winner.

Whatever the contribution of nomination, whether it be the discouragement of ambitions or their open defeat, it is disfunctional if it leaves the nominee too weak to win at the general election. Thus, although not all of the actors may be so motivated, all of the candidates who do hold office ambitions will be under a common restraint at least not to oppose and preferably to support the nominee. The most effective control the party has is the defeated candidate's own hope for preferment. It is peculiar to party organization that at one and the same time it encourages men to open conflict and then forces them to curb animosity to achieve a subsequent goal. Much of the two-facedness of political activity as it appears to external observers comes from this inherent characteristic of nuclear organization. That burying the hatchet is not easy is evident from the frequency with which it is not done, or if done, is done grudgingly. Still, the constant process of personal advancement through organized conflict either repels or weeds out personalities incapable of sustaining the tension. In his earlier work, Lasswell (1948) emphasized the dominance of power drives in the personality of political leaders. More recently, he has come to note that such persons do not rise to the top in democracies (Lasswell, 1954; Lane, 1959, pp. 124-128). The pure power seeker, as distinct from the man with office ambitions who sees office as instrumental to other goals, can probably find more satisfactory outlets in areas other than politics. An important aspect of the contribution of nomination is that self-interest must control itself and create cooperation out of what might be the most divisive and corroding of ambitions, the drive for political power.

As opposed to the discouragement process, the actual choice of a candidate takes in the broadest range of contributors. American parties in varying degrees have been required by law to widen the range and permit any voter to take part in direct primary elections. The principal reason for this was that the two-party mold, unevenly distributed among the states, made intraparty democracy the only effective way of giving the voters in one-party states any choice at all (Key, 1956, pp. 85-97). During the Progressive era, this peculiar invention was strengthened by the antiparty ideology and spread to states where there was two-party competition. It stands today as the means of nominating candidates for most public offices in the United States.

A broad range of contributors in such a vital function as nominations raises for party organization serious questions of both competence and goals. Even if one assumes that all primary voters accept the goal of electoral victory and vote in terms of their perception of which candidate is most likely to win in the general election, it is reasonable to conclude that their individual judgments will be less competent than those of experienced politicians. On the other hand, their collective judgment may, if it is reasonably representative of the party's likely voters, be better than that of a professional. Survey research has not yet been extended to the primary voter, but there is evidence from aggregate election data that primary voters come disproportionately from those areas in which the party is strong and may not serve as a cross-section of the electorate (Key, 1956, pp. 145-165). Yet when the primary has resulted in irrational decisions by the party, corrective techniques have developed. In California, where the cross-filing system damaged the Democratic Party (Carney, 1958), and in Wisconsin, where the Progressive conflict threatened conservative control of the Republican Party, pre-primary or extra-legal party organization emerged (Sorauf, 1954).

Issue formulation. Once the nuclear organization chooses its candidate, it must seek support for reasons other than its power drives. Although it is known that the voters' response to parties involves much more than a choice between policy stances, there is a good deal of issue content to electoral decisions, and to succeed a party must devise a program or platform. The position of the party as seen by both its leaders and voters is only partially covered by the formal "platform." Therefore, one must ask who contributes the issues. To a great extent, the process of leader selection decides the policies for which the party will stand. But beyond the party leader there are individuals, intellectuals, specialists in public affairs, scholars, and journalists on whom the party can call for contributions in devising policy. This discussion is not concerned with the motivations of these men, for even an issue specialist can be attracted to a party by material or solidary incentives. What is of relevance at this point is the contribution he makes.

The intellectuals' function is severely limited by the way in which competitive governing parties are forced to devise policy. A party in control of government must make choices, but its range of alternatives is usually narrow. The party is restricted by time, internal differences, the administrative apparatus of government, and other relevant elements of the political system, including foreign relations. A drastic reformulation of public policy, therefore, requires either massive continuous support or the elimination of the competitive rules. Otherwise, the party in government finds its position defined largely by the way it responds to issues which arise during its tenure. Thus, the formulators of the party's position must consist largely of its elected leaders as well as of the administrative corps. Although the party out of power presumably has greater freedom in defining its stand, it also must respond to the issues as they arise and to the government and allow public officials the major role.

A second limitation on the intellectual or issue specialist as the contributor of issues is the manner in which the electorate, at least that of the United States, responds to the parties. Only a minute fraction of the voters sees the parties in anything resembling ideological terms (Campbell et al., 1960, pp. 216-265). More important, a substantial part of the response to the difference between the parties derives, not from the voters' perception of the parties' policy stances, but rather from the voters' feeling that a party is a good or bad instrument of government in such general areas of policy as economic prosperity or peace. Students of American voting in attempting to ascertain the impact of issues on the vote have had to recognize the impossibility of placing on any simple left-right continuum such critical issues in American history as prohibition or corruption. Thus, Berelson, Lazarsfeld, and McPhee (1954, pp. 184-198) distinguished between "position" and "style" issues. Stokes (1963) has refined the distinction further and speaks of "position-issues," e.g., levels of taxation, issues on which the electorate can be expected to divide, and "valence-issues," e.g., prosperity or peace, issues on which there is little disagreement about what is desirable. "Valence-issues" are relevant because they help determine the voters' favorable or unfavorable perception of the parties. Such reactions, however, derive not from the parties' active decisions on the issues but from the association of the parties in government with periods of peace, prosperity, or corruption.

Because the electorate responds to the parties in terms of their governmental record, the intellectual's role is reduced to that of apologist. Party leaders need most ideas which can get across to the voters the virtues of their position. Thus, rather than originating policy, the intellectual is most often confined to stating existing issues in the role of speech-writer, official biographer, or as a specialist in public relations.

Memory, intelligence, and communications. Along with issue formulation, memory, intelligence, and communications are important connective contributions within the nuclear organization. Given the individualistic, transitory, and uncertain character of much organizational activity, information which can reduce this state is naturally a valuable commodity. Yet most often contributions of information merely reflect the dominant characteristics of the nucleus. Thus, information tends to be gathered and stored by individuals within the organization for their own advantage, and information is frequently disseminated by groups outside the party for purposes which may even be hostile.

Within the nucleus, the seemingly innocuous contribution of memory and recording is very often a private enterprise, indicating the value of every organizational sign for the ambitious. Nuclear organizations have notoriously poor arrangements for gathering and keeping data even about such obvious and vital questions as who has given money or worked for the party. Mere systematic data on the duties of party staff workers may be treated as the private property of the party chairman (Bone, 1958, p. x). In a situation where much is fleeting, any record of organization becomes a precious raw material not to be passed casually from hand to hand.

The intelligence as opposed to the memory contribution is also greatly dependent upon private initiative. Nor has the recent appearance of the professional pollster or the high-speed computer as contributors appreciably altered this state. Information about voters' reactions to personalities and issues is vital to individual aspirants within the party in making career choices and strategies. Traditionally, they have counted on the face-to-face canvassing of the precinct worker or other party faithfuls whose ardor and efficiency have varied considerably. Recent technological advances in the sample survey, along with the social deterioration of the neighborhood, have tended to outmode the personal canvasser and replace him with the more reliable professional poller and even the computer (Pool & Abelson, 1961). But it is not yet apparent that this has resulted in a complete, permanent, and objective source of intelligence for the nucleus. Pollers work for one or the other party and service different individuals within them.

As for the dissemination of information, this contribution is very often made by groups which have no identification with the nucleus and may even be hostile. Thus, the most ubiquitous poll-takers and disseminators of their results are newspapers. The press also gathers and disseminates other information, such as polls of convention delegates and the announcements of individual candidacies. The resources of the press may well be superior to any that the nucleus has for distributing such information. These external groups, therefore, have a powerful means of influencing the nucleus, for they provide some of its most important channels of communication.

The precise impact of the independent channel of communication is not clear. The media of communication are under some restraint to present information they have gathered truthfully. This is particularly true when the accuracy of the information can be tested. Thus, newspaper polls are more successful the more accurately they predict the electoral outcome. On the other hand, where tests of accuracy are less refined, as, for example, in the reporting of factional conflicts, partisan preferences may well affect the flow of information. One consequence is clear, therefore: much of the parties' organization is devoted to influencing what does get into the news media. Among the first permanent staff hired by parties and prominent in any nuclear organization are the press agent, the public relations man, or the press representative (Ebel, 1960).

Another result of the independent channel of communication is that it raises party etiquette to the level of international diplomacy. When a man plans to seek a nomination, it is advisable that he at least inform other party leaders before the announcement, even if he knows they will be opposed. To make them dependent upon the press for information is to infer their demotion from leadership rank. The surest sign that an individual is unimportant within the nucleus is his failure to be consulted or even told what is going to happen. With an external source always capable of exposing ignorance, the giving and withholding of information inside the nucleus become a political tactic and an indication of status and importance.

Technical services. The nuclear organization can use many technical contributions. Periodic contact with the electorate, quite apart from testing their sentiment, is useful in keeping track of the party's supporters. Every campaign creates a surge of possible tasks for which volunteers must be recruited. Each party affair, rally, or coffee hour involves bringing together as many people as possible to give the appearance that the party enjoys popular support. On election day itself, there are many things which an organization can do to make sure that the committed voter gets to the polls and has his vote tallied.

Characteristically, in American parties, technical contributions are made by small permanent staffs which blossom during the campaign. Such professional staff men exhibit no tendency to develop a sense of direction independent of party leaders. They gain influence in their relations with associational or public leaders of the party, not as a separate bureaucracy (Ebel, 1960). But it is important to recognize also that there is much more professional substance to some nuclear party organizations than appears to be the case from examination of the purely formal extra-governmental party. American civil-service traditions have not prevented public officials from using at least the close members of their staff for continuous electoral purposes. Most major officeholders enjoy at public expense the services of people to write and distribute their newsletters in their constituencies, to arrange their schedules, to do field work among leaders and voters. Such services relieve incumbent officeholders of the need to obtain aid through their own resources. Because incumbents have at their disposal a paid staff, they gain enormous advantages in establishing their leadership.

Money. Since useful services are by no means all voluntary, money is a prime contribution within the nuclear organization. Money represents "instant" organization by helping to satisfy the periodic need to expand activities rapidly. The active nucleus, therefore, puts much effort into gathering money.

Money may come in small amounts from many people. In addition to providing funds, the small contribution also serves to reinforce popular identification with the party. The small contribution may also be used to clarify party membership when it is regularized in the form of dues. This procedure is common in European parties but is not unknown in major American state organizations, as in Wisconsin (Epstein, 1958, p. 81) and Michigan (Sawyer, 1960, p. 213). Since the effort required to gather money in small amounts probably limits its financial value, the small contribution should be considered as part of a general leadership strategy aimed at producing broad participation in the nucleus (Hennessey, 1960).

The greatest proportion of money collected by American parties comes in large contributions, Heard's study (1960, p. 28) reveals that about 10 per cent of the contributions to the Republican National Committee in the presidential elections of 1948, 1952, and 1956 were less than $100, while around 70 per cent were in amounts of over $500. The Democratic Party was only slightly more dependent on small contributions, with about 20 per cent under $100. Although state and local nuclear organizations depended more upon small contributions, the greatest share for both parties came in amounts of over $100 (p. 51).

The devices used to gather money reflect the place of the nucleus in the economic and social system. Individuals with a direct stake in the organization's victory, such as candidates and public employees dependent upon them, can be expected to contribute, as can businessmen such as contractors or others needing licenses from the state. To these traditional techniques of gathering income, nuclear organizations have added methods devised by charitable groups, the fund-raising dinner, the expensive advertising brochure, and various businessmen's committees, each with a quota. The Republican Party, with its closer ties to the business community, has been able to use these devices more effectively than the Democrats. On the other hand, the Democratic Party, with its close ties to the union movement, has been able to utilize the effective fund-raising capacities of the unions.

The impact of financial contributions, both on the competitive chances of the parties and also upon the internal distribution of power in the organization, has been of wide concern. The amounts which individuals can give to parties as well as the amounts which parties can spend in any given campaign are regulated by both federal and state laws. Although these controls are ineffective, they do reflect a distrust of the influence of large contributors upon political organizations. . . .

A Theory of the Political Party

Samuel J. Eldersveld

The political party is a social group, a system of meaningful and patterned activity within the larger society. It consists of a set of individuals populating specific roles and behaving as member-actors of a boundaried and identifiable social unit. Goals are perceived by these actors, tasks are assigned for and by them, and communication channels are maintained. The party is thus one social organism. But the party is also a polity, a miniature political system. It has an authority structure, although the manner in which authority is graded and legitimated may differ considerably from other social groups. The party has distinctive patterns of power distribution. It has a representative process, an electoral system, and subprocess for recruiting leaders, defining goals, and resolving internal system conflicts. Above all, the party is a decision-making system, although, again, how "authoritative" the decision-making process is remains a subject of inquiry. The political party, thus, conforms to the common characteristics of social groups. Herbert Simon, for example, has defined a group as a system of "interdependent activity, encompassing at least several primary groups and usually characterized . . . by a high degree of rational direction of behavior towards

---

Reprinted from *Political Parties: A Behavioral Analysis* (Chicago: Rand McNally and Company, 1964), pp. 1-13, by permission of the publisher.

ends that are objects of common acknowledgement and expectation."[1] The party, as studied here, is such a group. It fulfills, at least minimally, these requirements, although we seek through empirical analysis to determine the degree to which "interdependent activity," "rationality," and "common acknowledgement" in fact exist.

In the study of the party as a social group, we are intially concerned with the empirical discovery of structural properties, those characteristic modes of activity which may distinguish the party as a social collectivity. To this end, it is necessary to develop and test empirical theory about the perspectives and behavior of individuals holding positions at all major levels of the hierarchy, their vertical and horizontal relationships with others in the group, and the meaning of this behavior for the subunits (or "primary groups") as well as for the total organization. Structure is people acting in relationship to others, not merely *some* actions and particular relationships, or *some* actors, for then only a segment of the structure will be revealed. The party is more than its executive elite, or campaign workers, or precinct activists, analyzed in isolation. It is a meaningful organizational system of interpersonal relationships. Concentration on those "in power," or the "inner circle," or the "activist cadre," while helpful and suggestive, cannot by itself lead to comprehension of the structure as a whole. Too much party research in America has had to settle for partial images of political reality.

In attempting to delineate the properties of the party, we assume that our knowledge of its tasks and roles in the larger political system will be enhanced. Parties came into existence to perform certain critical functions for the system, and derived their basic form in the process of implementing these functions. If one is interested in understanding the tasks presumably fulfilled by parties, it is necessary to analyze the party as a functioning structural subsystem. This is not to say that all party groups perform the same functions and possess identical structural properties. Social and political environmental conditions vary from one culture to the next. The same is true of "functional priorities." Parties are merely a particular structural response, therefore, to the needs of a social and political system in a particular milieu.

The student of party organization is interested in many of the theoretical propositions and problems which occupy the attention

---

[1] "Comments on the Theory of Organizations," *American Political Science Review,* XLVI, No. 4 (Dec., 1952), 1130.

of students of other large-scale social groups. He may be concerned with problems of rule enforcement, morale, task performance, productivity, regulatory mechanisms, and reward systems. But he must also be alert to the probability that the party, as a political-power motivated and instrumental group, is a specific subclass of social organizations, with particular types of substructures and specialized activity patterns. Above all, he must be alert to the probability that party structures have specific group properties, which are basic to understanding the party as a structural organism, and as a functional unit in the socio-political system.

Although other approaches to the study of party structure are feasible, the analysis presented here begins with a specification of the primary structural properties of the party. It then proceeds to the utilization of these theoretical images, after the presentation of empirical evidence attesting to their validity or invalidity, in three ways. First, we are interested in determining the impact of these structural conditions on the ideology, role perception, and motivation of party leaders at different levels of the hierarchy. Second, we are concerned with the patterns of internal organizational relationships as they reflect these structural properties — in what respects is the communication system defective, in what areas does managerial control break down, and to what extent is decisional involvement achieved? Third, we feel that such knowledge of the party as a structure of leadership perspectives and as a structure of interpersonal hierarchical relationships will lead to a better understanding of the quality of the party group as a functional unit. Our major foci are, therefore, the *congruence* of leadership perspectives, the *coherence* of hierarchical relationships, and the *competence* of the group in the fulfillment of social and political functions.

Political party structures have certain common tendencies differentiating them from other groups such as families, churches, labor unions, business firms, lodges. This is a proposition not easily defended. In the long run it can be demonstrated only by the development of probable differentiae and the testing of these through empirical research. In taking the position that there are common structural tendencies, we do not mean to imply that party structures do not vary. They do, both in the same society and in different societies. But, despite such variations which are primarily the product of particular adaptations to special environmental conditions, parties exhibit structural similarities in certain basic respects. We view the party as a specialized system of action in democratic societies, with a special meaning and purpose in the political and social order. It is distinguishable by its primary goal (to occupy at least some of the governmental leadership posts), by its competitive-electoral relationships with similar groups, and by its special pattern of public-support and adaptation strategies. As will be suggested below, certain key structural styles emerge in parties and are inherent in the party type of social organization. Perhaps it can be said that parties are unique structurally because they are groups oriented to the achievement of special goals and functions under unique environmental conditions in the society. Whether these structural properties are maximally conducive to goal and function realization is a major object of our investigation.

In attempting to spell out the relevant structural dimensions of parties as tentative theoretical positions for subsequent analysis, it must be recognized that parties do not possess many of the conventional attributes of the bureaucratic system. In particular, the bureaucratic prerequisites of impermeability, depersonalized human relationships, strict devotion to regulations and rule enforcement, precise allocation of obligations, duties, and roles, discipline, and sanctions, even low circulation of personnel, are found wanting in most party structures. We sense that the Republican and Democratic parties are structurally different from General Motors, the Catholic church, the AFL-CIO, or the Farm Bureau; how they differ is the task of empirical theory and research. We suggest the following four theoretical constructs in a genuinely exploratory sense, conscious that they are indeed "dimensions," with great variation among individual party structures along each dimension, and that they are a mere beginning for theory. Parties may combine these properties differently, emphasizing some more than others. In our opinion, however, it is likely that elements of each of these constructs are not only relevant to all party structures but are also critical for comprehending their essential nature as functioning social and political organisms.

The party must first be understood as a clientele-oriented structure. In contrast to the bureaucratic model, the party is almost by definition an open, informal, personalized system. Roberto Michels wrote long ago of the "omnibus tendency" of parties. He saw party as an "organization ever greedy for new members," adding, "the party no longer seeks to fight its opponents, but simply to outbid them." The result, claimed Michels, was that the party would "sacrifice its political virginity, by entering into promiscuous relationships with the most heterogeneous political elements. . . ."[2] Al-

[2]See Alfred de Grazia, *Roberto Michels' First Lectures in Political Sociology* (Minneapolis: University of Minnesota Press, 1949), p. 145, and Robert Michels, *Political Parties* (Glencoe, Ill.: Free Press, 1949), pp. 374-76.

though Michels was writing particularly about socialist parties a half-century ago, his observations are insightful and have been repeated by many scholars of party politics. The party is always "potential-clientele" conscious. It is open at its base to new recruits for party work as well as to nonactivist supporters. It is often open at the higher levels also, indeed, sometimes at the elite apex, if such a strategy will profit the party's power aspirations. Thus it is permeable and adaptive, even in societies with multiparty systems in which the probability of seducing the small number of "floating voters" is minimal. Singularly reliant on votes as the arithmetic of power, the party reflects structurally an inherent tendency toward joint advantage. The party is a mutually exploitative relationship — it is joined by those who would use it; it mobilizes for the sake of power those who would join it. This porous nature of the party — at its base, sides, and apex — has tremendous consequences for individual perspectives and organizational relationships. Where adaptation is maximal, internal managerial control is difficult, factional pluralism multiplied, operational efficiency likely to be impaired, and goal orientations and ideological consensus highly noncongruent; where adaptation is minimal, such consequences for internal control and perspectives will doubtless be less severe. This is the first theoretical dilemma the party must face.

The second empirical image follows from the first. The party is a structural system seeking to translate or "convert" (or be converted by) social and economic interests into political power directly. It consists of a set of socio-economic interests groping for political recognition, articulation, and control. As such the party can be conceptualized as an alliance of substructures or subcoalitions. Many writers have implicitly recognized this character of the party organization. Charles Merriam made the point well 40 years ago:

> Of great significance in the composition of any political party are the numerous types of social groupings. These are fundamental in any scientific study of the political party, and too great emphasis cannot be laid upon them. . . . The practical politician is never guilty of the omission of the study of social groupings, but the students of politics have sometimes proceeded as if parties were working in a social vacuum.[3]

The subcoalitions within the party may be identified variously — in terms of geographical boundaries, on the basis of organizational status, as demographic or social categories, or on the basis of ideo-

[3]*The American Party System* (New York: Macmillan, 1922), p. 3.

logical division. In addition, there may be organizational entities almost completely self-reliant, such as the legislative wing of the party (or the congressman with his own "machine"), women and youth auxiliaries, a political club "movement," and affiliated business, labor, or farm suborganizations.

The party, in this image, exists as an intermediary group representing and exploiting multiple interests for the achievement of direct control over the power apparatus of the society. The party becomes inevitably, then, a conflict system. Conflict among the competing interests in the structure can be managed, channeled, avoided — in fact, the structure many times seems constituted to maximize conflict avoidance. But above all, and this is the unique structural characteristic of the party in this regard, conflict within the party must be tolerated. As a power-aspiring group, "greedy" for new followers, the party does not settle conflict; it defers the resolution of conflict. The party is thus no genuine mediator; it seeks to stabilize subcoalitional relationships and interactions so that these multiple interests will remain committed to the organization, after partial acquiescence to their demands, without permitting intergroup rivalries to collide with the party's grand design for power. Tension between the group goal and subcoalitional demands is, therefore, the second basic structural dilemma of the party.

This theoretical position is similar to, and borrows from, one important stream of current organizational theory — coalitional theory.[4] In adapting this theory to the party structure, each subcoalitional participant can be considered as possessing its own set of demands and goals (or "preference orderings"). The party organization as a single enterprise "bargains" with these subgroups, enters into a coalition agreement with them "for the purposes of the (political) game," and thus develops a "joint preference ordering" of organizational objectives. This, presumably, is the result of "side payments" to the subcoalitions, a subtle calculus of reciprocal strengths, needs, and contributions to the total party structure. Once the "bargain" has been consummated the party is able to move ahead, goal-setting is finalized, and the group can operate as a single "entrepreneur." Variations on this basic model have been advanced, and strong reservations have been suggested. In its applicability to the political party these reservations should certainly be underlined. Yet it is a valuable theoretical formulation with which to work, though the process for determining coalitional objectives, the final-

[4]See, for example, Richard M. Cyert and James G. March, "A Behavioral Theory of Organizational Objectives," in Mason Haire, ed., *Modern Organization Theory* (New York: Wiley, 1959), pp. 76-89.

ity of the agreement, as well as the resultant implication that organizational unity will be attained, are obscure elements in the model. The chief value of the model is that it begins to operationalize insights about the structural properties of parties which have remained vague and unresearchable for many years. If clarified and systematically utilized, it is a construct which will prove useful in explaining internal organizational relationships as well as leadership perspectives. The nature of decision-making, communicative contacts, consensus, role perceptions, and goal orientations will probably be more strikingly different in a moderately pluralized party structure than in a rigidly pluralized structure of three or four distinct subcoalitions tenaciously clinging to conflicting "preference orderings" and with whom "side payments" are not easily arranged. In the latter context, to say that the party functions with a single entrepreneurial goal may be superficial, as the coalition theorists would be the first to admit. In sum, if the view of the party in coalitional terms is not employed mechanically, and is linked to the view of the party process as joining with, and instrumental for, the social process, it may represent a theoretical image of considerable explanatory power.

A third theoretical position concerning the party's structural properties emerges with the question, What type of hierarchy or structure of power is a party? That the party is a hierarchy is generally not disputed, since certainly a coarchal pattern of perfectly equal power distribution does not exist. Whether the party structure is an "oligarchy," however, has been the subject of speculation since Michels' famous theory of the "iron law of oligarchy." Some insist that a minority inevitably assumes leadership and control of parties, with all the expected oligarchic phenomena which Michels predicted. Others note that even in the most carefully structured American party "machines," a reciprocal pattern of influence and responsibility obtains between the "boss" and his precinct captains.[5] We do not wish to grapple with all the alleged features of oligarchy within the party. Rather, we take issue with the necessity of one crucial assumption in that "iron law," the assumption that control of the party structure is inexorably concentrated in the hands of a single leadership corps, the top, elite, managerial nucleus of the structure. In contrast to this theory we suggest the following alternative image of the pattern of control within the party.

The possibility clearly exists that a special type of hierarchy obtains in parties — one which, to borrow Harold Lasswell and

[5]See, for example, Edward C. Banfield, *Political Influence* (New York: Free Press, 1961), pp. 235-62.

Abraham Kaplan's phrase, we will call *stratarchy*.[6] The general characteristics of stratarchy are the proliferation of the ruling group and the diffusion of power prerogatives and power exercise. Rather than centralized "unity of command," or a general dilution of power throughout the structure, "strata commands" exist which operate with a varying, but considerable degree of, independence. Such allocation of command and control to specified "layer," or "echelon," authorities is a pragmatic necessity. The very heterogeneity of membership, and the subcoalitional system, make centralized control not only difficult but unwise. In the process of adaptation, then, the party develops its own hierarchical pattern of stratified devolution of responsibility for the settlement of conflicts, rather than jeopardize the viability of the total organization by carrying such conflicts to the top command levels of the party. Further, the party must cope with widely varying local milieus of opinion, tradition, and social structure, and this encourages the recognition and acceptance of local leadership, local strategy, local power. In addition, the desperate need in all parties for votes, which are scarcely mobilized at the apex of the hierarchy, results in at least some, if not pronounced, deference to the local structural strata where votes are won or lost. Thus, a kind of "balkanization" of power relations occurs, with variations in the extent of autonomy in middle and lower hierarchical strata from one habitat to the next. While admittedly party systems in different countries will vary in degree of stratarchy, exploratory research suggests the real probability that there is a stratarchical element in all such systems, despite the custom of referring to them in such simple terms as "centralized," monolithic, or unitary.

The political party is thus to be visualized as a "reciprocal deference structure." Contrary to the bureaucratic and authoritarian models of social organization, the party is not a precisely ordered system of authority and influence from the top down, though as a "paper" structure it may give this appearance. The organization does not function through the issuance of directives from the top which are obeyed without question. Rather, there is tolerance of autonomy, local initiative, local inertia. The factors contributing to this property of the party are several: sparsity of activists, voluntary nature of recruitment for party work, limited rewards available to activists and irregularity of their loyalty. But, primarily, this "downward deference" stems from the absence of effective sanctions, the strong drive for votes, the instinctively adaptive tactics of

[6]*Power and Society* (New Haven: Yale University Press, 1950), pp. 219-20.

success-minded party leaders, and the need for lower-echelon support. More than any other social organization, the critical action locus of the party structure is at its base. And since there is high potential for inefficiency, indifference, and displacement of group (leadership) goals with personal goals among activists at the base, leaders defer. In fact, the basis for the authority of the leadership of party organizations is one of the most puzzling to understand. It does not seem to be a function of expertise, or of role, or of normative expectations. Rather, the party structure appears to be characterized as a "rapport system."[7] Rapport is basic to status. Rapport between the top elite, middle-level cadre, and local activists rests on mutual perspectives concerning the strategy of electoral success, or mutual tolerance of ineptness (and inaction) in the face of sure defeat. The relationship between the executive elite and the "hard-core" activists in the party structure is above all, therefore, one of accommodation — of "centralist" (leadership) drive and strategy for power to "localist" interests, demands, and support. In this structural context the party faces another crucial dilemma — the need for managerial efficiency while maintaining worker morale.

Closely related is a fourth major image which emphasizes the special type of elite careerism patterns found in the party. Here, again, we take issue with an important component in the theory of oligarchy, the picture of the party as possessing a single elite cadre, "one directive social group," well-organized, self-conscious, self-perpetuating, congruent, conspiring. In its place we suggest and empirically examine the possibility of another image of the party elite. We see the party elite as consisting of pluralized sets of separable "career classes" or "career categories," with considerable differentiation in congruence, communicative interchange, and self-consciousness. Furthermore, we hypothesize differently the character of "circulation" of the party elite, as well as the basis for the structural stability of the party in the face of such circulation. There is indeed a high turnover in party leadership at all levels of the hierarchy, just as individual mobility for the determined careerist can occur at unbelievable rates. But this is not a *pro forma* turnover, as the oligarchic theorists would contend, a circulation resulting from the "amalgamation" by the old elite of "new elite" elements which are considered "safe." This is not primarily a process of absorption. It is often a process of genuine renovation, adap-

---

[7]For one discussion of this problem, see Robert V. Presthus, "Authority in Organizations," in Sidney Mailick and Edward H. Van Ness, eds., *Concepts and Issues in Administrative Behavior* (Englewood Cliffs, N.J.: Prentice-Hall, 1962), pp. 122-36.

tation, and reconstitution of the sub-coalitional balance of power within the party structure. Or it is often genuine evidence of the loss of power.

The party leader's basis of authority leans heavily on rapport, and yet is essentially quixotic, dependent as it is on an ever changing balance sheet of votes won and lost, as well as on the competitive struggle for power among the organizational subgroups with which he must contend. In addition, although party leadership cadres may indeed have some *esprit de corps*, this is quite different from that of a bureaucratic cadre. In the latter case, *esprit de corps* rests heavily on a vocational security, professional associations, expectations of permanency, and a desire to protect the group from its environment. The party, however, is an open structure; tenure is unstable; personal relationships are uncertain. Thus power vanishes easily within a political party, but the saving grace is the existence of career groups of individuals who are not essentially aspiring to power. For many of these the party means "status," not "power," and the continuity of their commitment to party tasks contributes to stability in the face of constant flux and potential disequilibrium. The party structure, thus, has a peculiar career system, which, despite insecurity of tenure and high circulation, does result in durability, due primarily to the continuous renewal of those separable career categories so indispensable to the fulfillment of party goals. But the dilemma of the party is clear, for it must accomplish the simultaneous fulfillment of "mobility" and "status" demands and satisfactions in an organization which is heterogeneous in membership, eclectic in ideology, and voluntaristic in motivational orientation.

These four images of the basic properties of the party structure are obviously not mutually exclusive. The argument here is that if the party as a social organization is distinctive from other organizational types, and we postulate that it is, then these tentative constructs may help identify its special character. It is not to be implied that all parties are equally characterized by these theoretical images. They are merely "dimensions," and party structures differ in the degree to which they approximate these properties. The coalitional character of certain party structures may be most relevant in certain locales; in others "reciprocal deference" and stratarchy may be more basic; and certainly parties vary in adaptiveness and clientele-consciousness. The suggestion is that an internal logic about the nature of party structure in a democratic system does exist, which theoretically differentiates it from other social structures. Two common elements in democratic societies contribute to the existence of party groups with these inherently unique structural styles: political power rests on votes; and groups compete for power. Where these components of the democratic system are strong, party groups will manifest their stylistic attributes maximally; where the components are weak, party attributes are also weak.

The specification of these structural properties should not lead to an analysis of the party in an intellectual vacuum, or to complete normative pessimism. In our opinion there are three major clusters of factors responsible for the party structure as it is. One such cluster consists of environmental pressures, both the socio-economic conditions with which the party must contend in a particular area, and the political history and climate of the area. The competitive conditions of political life interact with the social complexion of the area to impress on the party structure certain properties which are in a sense structural responses to environmental demands. Secondly, there is the "internal dynamic" cluster of variables, including the personal orientations and styles of political activism within the power process in a given area. This is the "political subculture" of the area — the normative and operational codes adhered to in the power process, communicated widely to participants in this process, and continually re-enforced by the system itself. The party and its leadership is but one segment of this subculture. Finally, the developmental or chronological component in the analysis of party structure, the factor of time, must be considered. Parties gradually evolve characteristic modes or properties which tend to become accepted and tolerated in a given area and culture. But change can and does occur, and it is possible that at critical points in time party structures do develop reorientations. Thus, although we are rather committed to accepting the basic theory outlined above, as having generalizable validity for modern-day parties in democratic societies, we accept the possibility that these, or their degree of manifestation at this point in time, are not fixed and unalterable. Human institutions do change. Social groups are dynamic. We are not locked into a structural system which is forever imprisoned by identical and constant social pressure . . . .

Democracy and the Organization of Political Parties: Some Speculations

Samuel H. Barnes

Communications Models of the Polity

A communications model of a democratic system can best be identified by contrasting it with models of other types of political systems. Existing political systems can be divided into three types according to how their communications networks channel conflicting demands. As all polities are "mixed," these three types should be considered as analytic constructs. Actual political systems (and other units) can be described in terms of the particular patterning of the mix of these models found within them. The authoritarian and the totalitarian will be discussed first.

In the authoritarian model only one or a greatly restricted number of communications channels are permitted to influence governmental policy. A system is authoritarian to the extent that subunits remain unmobilized and are barred from influencing the authoritative allocation of values of the system. There is no logical incompatibility between authoritarianism and constitutionalism (in the sense of effectively limited government). Indeed, some authoritarian systems have also been constitutional systems, for example,

Reprinted from *Party Democracy: Politics in an Italian Socialist Federation Organization* (New Haven: Yale University Press, 1967), pp. 238-55, by permission of the publisher.

eighteenth-century England, perhaps contemporary Spain and Portugal, and some Latin American dictatorships. Nor, as the examples mentioned above would indicate, is authoritarianism incompatible with pluralism if by pluralism is meant the existence of autonomous communications networks. The networks exist — in churches, universities, business, ethnic communities, and various associations — but most simply have no political influence. Throughout most of its history India was an example of a society that was pluralist in this sense and yet authoritarian politically. When only a limited segment of the population is mobilized, the political system as a whole is generally authoritarian even though intraelite relations may be quite democratic.

A totalitarian system is similar in that only communications issuing from a single channel have authority. But the totalitarian system goes further — it seeks to control all the communications channels of a society. Those channels it cannot control it destroys; and if channels do not exist to bind all the subunits together, it creates them. It is total in its control of communications, so that every subunit is "plugged in" the network in some way through an officially sanctioned channel.

An authoritarian system seems to function best where political competence, which is essential to the operation of communications channels, is not widely distributed. The importance of education has been demonstrated. The combination of authoritarianism and a wide diffusion of political competence leads to rising frustration, anomic means of communicating demands (demonstrations, strikes, assassinations, and so on), and, in turn, repression. Although mankind has lived under authoritarian systems throughout most of history, this form without adaptation is unlikely to survive the entry of the masses into politics. The logic of mass mobilization leads either to democracy or to totalitarianism.

The totalitarian system manipulates consent or at least acquiescence through control of communications channels. Contemporary systems differ from the totalitarian polar ideal in several ways. The first concerns the depth of the penetration of the communications networks into the subunits. In the U.S.S.R., for example, subunits such as the family seem to be achieving greater autonomy; other subunits also seem to be increasingly independent. Significantly, these tendencies have emerged first in areas less overtly political, as in the family, arts, and religion; and the autonomy tolerated is not permitted to threaten the political system. A second variable is the degree to which communications channels are in fact effectively controlled. In National Socialist Germany, for example, and even more so in Fascist Ialy, many networks, such as the state bureaucracy, the army, the Catholic Church, and some economic channels, were only superficially controlled. Insofar as this was the case, Germany and Italy veered toward the authoritarian pole, though the Fuhrer and the Duce and their respective parties certainly had totalitarian intentions.

The communications networks of democratic political systems are characterized by the existence of multiple autonomous channels connecting subunits at all levels of the system both vertically and horizontally. A channel is autonomous to the extent that its communications are not externally controlled.[1] These channels permit and facilitate the building of coalitions binding together levels in order to aggregate the demands of subunits, filter them, and translate them into policy alternatives. The existence of multiple channels renders difficult the blocking of communication, for the "outs" are generally receptive to potential coalition partners. And autonomy prevents the channels from being manipulated for the benefit of the "ins."

It should be emphasized that communication is two-way in all types of political systems. Feedback exists in all of them; the differences lie in the role played by feedback.[2] The content of communications is constantly being affected by feedback. This is why repeated communications in a system with open and free channels at best leads to adjustment of demands, to compromise. At the very least, communications and feedback increase rationality, for information reduces uncertainty and hence the extent of miscalculation and unintended consequences. In Deutsch's terms, it results in learning. It also, in Deutsch's terms, requires "good will," the willingness to learn, to adapt; and it is in this respect that some belief systems may be more conducive to democracy than others, because some emphasize "will" as opposed to "learning."[3]

Parties and Communications Networks

Multiple autonomous communications channels are the strategic factor in democracy. In a formal sense these channels need not be political parties. However, due to the division of labor that characterizes complex societies it is difficult for a contemporary polity to

[1]This is similar to Dahl's conception of autonomy in *A Preface to Democratic Theory*, p. 78.

[2]See the discussions of feedback in Karl Deutsch, *The Nerves of Government* (New York, Free Press, 1963).

[3]Ibid.

function without political party or parties. The political party is the communications network that functionally specializes in the aggregation of political communications (that is, communications relating to the authoritative allocation of values) for a polity. It is the political communications channel par excellence, and in democracies parties generally sustain multiple autonomous channels.

Different party systems are associated with different communications patterns. Where existing political elites have aggregated demands from new units entering the political communications network, two-party systems have emerged in which both parties are in principle open to demands from almost all subunits. The degree to which parties even in two-party systems are receptive to communications from all subunits is an empirical question. Certainly parties are not equally responsive to communications from all subunits even in two-party systems, and the tendency toward restrictiveness is more pronounced in multi-party systems.

There is probably no single historical explanation for the emergence of multi-party systems. They are associated with discontinuities that inhibit communication across critical boundaries of the polity, such as religious divisions, class antagonisms, regional boundaries, and ideological differences. Their common feature is the inability of channels to aggregate communications from across the critical boundaries. The unwillingness of those who dominated existing channels to heed demands of the new subunits entering into political consciousness, at least until too late, has resulted in the establishment of new parties to serve as channels.

In totalitarian politics the party is a principal channel for political communications. It is an instrument of mobilization in a system in which all subunits must be "plugged in" a communications network. The party infiltrates all structures but maintains its identity. In authoritarian systems, on the other hand, the primary goal of elites is to set limits on behavior rather than to mobilize the population, and governmental bureaucracies, police, and army are generally adequate for these purposes. Hence the party tends to lose its position as the dominant communications channel; it mingles with other networks within the machinery of state; thereby becoming only one of several competing channels. Compare, for example, the Communist Party of the Soviet Union with the Italian Fascist Party in its later years or some of the single-party regimes of the developing nations.

This conception of the party as a communications channel connecting politically relevant subunits places cadre, mass, totalitarian, and democratic parties within the same analytical framework. All of these parties serve as communications channels, but within political systems that structure communications networks differently. For example, in the past parties of notables have been able to incorporate all politically relevant units; but they have lost ground to mass parties in countries where the electorate has expanded greatly, for mass parties are unequaled for maintaining wide communications networks.

Two-party systems probably incorporate more people into influential communications networks than multi-party systems. The coalition-building process in two-party systems makes it difficult for either party to ignore completely communications from any weighty unit. The "outs" in particular exploit the grievances of disaffected units. The multi-party system, on the other hand, generally restricts the spread of communications received by any single party. A governmental coalition often can ignore communications from units outside the coalition, as has been the case with the extreme left in France and Italy and the conservative parties of several countries. But even when conservative parties are denied formal participation, the superior communications facilities available to the upper classes often assure them alternative means of access while the inadequate communications resources of the lower classes render formal channels indispensable. Hence multi-party systems often deprive some units of de facto influence, though comparable units may have more formal representation than in two-party systems.

Multi-party systems complicate choice. Two-party systems reduce policy alternatives, and the dynamics of coalition building tend to ensure, even require, a majority preference for one policy. A party that cannot succeed at this over time flounders. Most policy is made by politicians as skilled in weighing intensity and influence — the weight to be attached to communications received — as mere votes. The debate over policy serves to clarify and polarize alternatives, at least among those concerned with the issue, so that one policy has a majority. But when there are more than two choices a curious inconsistency can result. Assuming that choices are transitive, it is quite possible that regardless of which policy is adopted, a majority would have preferred another one. This "paradox of voting," sometimes referred to as the "Arrow Problem," deserves more attention than it has received from students of parties.[4]

[4]See Kenneth Arrow, *Social Choice and Individual Values* (New York, Wiley, 1951); William A. Riker, "The Paradox of Voting and Congressional Rules for Voting on Amendments," *American Political Science Review*, 52 (1958), 349-66; Anthony Downs, *An Economic Theory of Democracy* (New York, Harper, 1957); Duncan Black, "The Decisions of a Committee Using a Special Majority," *Econometrica, 16* (1948), 262-70; and Dahl, *A Preface to Democratic Theory*.

Some ramifications of these characteristics of a multi-party system deserve mention. If inputs are relatively similar, if there is a high degree of consensus, especially on the "rules of the game," then a multi-party system based largely on differences in inputs in the socioeconomic sphere may function quite well as in the Scandinavian countries. Also, where party communications channels cut the polity vertically, as in some religious parties, few units will be completely denied consideration. But horizontal blocks in communications channels, as in class-based party systems, serve to fragment rather than to integrate the communications networks and important units may be blocked from communicating with the authoritative networks. Parties in two-party systems possess wider communications networks.

The Organization of Working-Class Parties

The significance of the level and unit of analysis for the study of political parties can now be indicated more clearly. Units can be either polities or subdivisions of polities. A democratic polity can contain democratic, authoritarian, and even totalitarian subunits within it as long as they serve to provide the multiple autonomous communications channels that are essential to democracy. Business organizations, for example, are usually authoritarian in their communications patterns. The Catholic Church, with its multiple channels serving specific groups in the church, veers in the totalitarian direction. Even in democratic politics the Communist Party seeks a total control over the channels dealing with the member or supporter — party, union, press, recreation, and so on. However, the experiences of both these associations demonstrate that without control over the official networks it is impossible to sustain a communications monopoly even over limited segments of a population. Compare the Communist parties of Britain and the U.S.S.R., for example, or the Catholic Church in contemporary Spain and France.

Even in a democracy some groups are more likely to have their demands effectively communicated by authoritarian or even totalitarian networks than by democratic ones. The reasons for this are important to an understanding of working-class parties and thus merit a brief analysis.

Class differences in communications patterns reflect the unequal distribution of political competence. Although research is limited, there is strong evidence that socioeconomic status correlates highly with education, knowledge, and sense of political efficacy. The ability to communicate political information is indisputedly related both to a sense of efficacy and to some minimal skill in articulating and transmitting demands. People find it difficult to articulate their feelings, much less to feed them in a refined form into a communications network; on the other hand, they can respond to the formulations of others, and hence are available for political mobilization.

Most elites possess a well-developed group life, wide personal contacts, superior communications resources, and an elevated sense of political efficacy. Elites thus have communications advantages that partially offset their numerical inferiority. Despite considerable functional specialization, members of the socioeconomic elite in most polities customarily have access to important political communication networks.

This is not true of people of lower socioeconomic strata. Throughout most of history they have been objects, not subjects, of politics. Their entry on the political stage is the drama of our times. The diffusion of democratic ideals has sanctioned their participation, but ideals have often been implanted in poorly prepared soil. Political competence may be lacking. Crude demands may exceed the material capacity of the polity: the revolution of rising expectations may give way to one of rising frustrations.

A crucial problem is leadership. How can lower strata secure capable leadership? Several universal patterns exist. One is clientelism, which relates individuals to a communications network by means of personal ties with one of its members. This is a widespread arrangement, found in feudal and industrial societies alike. Clientelism results in vertical communications channels that leave elites unchallenged; it nullifies the major weapon of the lower socioeconomic strata — their numbers. Political competition is restricted to the elite and may be irrelevant to the needs of their clients. Troublesome clients can be bought off, co-opted, or in some systems physically eliminated. Clientelism seldom results in effective communication of demands from those of low political competence; the sophisticated customarily receive preferential treatment. In general, horizontal channels are necessary for extensive and sustained efforts on behalf of lower strata.

Another pattern is the mass movement. Spontaneous mass movements are not unknown in political history. Lower socioeconomic strata have periodically communicated their demands through demonstrations, peaceful and otherwise, and even heroic manifestations of discipline and courage. Popular leaders have emerged from the masses, sometimes exhibiting considerable skill. More often, however, spontaneous mass movements burn themselves out in futile violence and rage, for leaders lack the requisite skills to direct these energies into meaningful sustained activity. Many peasant uprisings and proletarian movements share this failing, and the major distinction between prepolitical and political movements, to use Hobsbawm's categories, may well lie in the lack of communications viability of the former.[5]

Lower socioeconomic strata thus are faced with trying problems in acquiring adequate leadership, for individuals with the requisite political competence often have alternative career outlets. In the more class-conscious societies of Western Europe, trade union and Socialist leaders have often been quite able, as the talented European worker, at least in the past, found few outlets for his ambition outside of working-class organizations. Deficient in political competence and alternative communications networks, lower socioeconomic strata have had to rely heavily on specifically political organizations, especially parties and trade unions (which are almost everywhere more political than they are in the United States).

Leadership emerges easily among higher strata, but lower strata must *construct associations*, often bureaucratic organizations, to support stable, competent, and trustworthy leadership. As members of lower strata are particularly susceptible to demagoguery and other maladies of the mass society, bureaucratic organization is probably more important for them than for those of higher strata.[6]

The lower strata have sometimes been aided by pre-existing organizations. The Catholic Church has fostered an entire working-class subculture in several countries, and the role of Nonconformist Churches in the early years of the British Labor party is well known. In these instances, the maintenance of communications between social strata has been facilitated. In other European countries the churches acted too late, and communication broke down. Significantly, continental churches were more successful with workers and regions that lagged behind in industrialization, as in Flanders and the French Rhineland.

The emerging proletariat suffered repeated defeats until it painfully learned to convert numbers into influence through organization. Severed from existing networks, it seemingly had to displace the authoritative channels and create new ones. Marxism as an

---

[5]Eric Hobsbawm, *Printing Rebels: Studies in Archaic Forms of Social Movement in the 19th and 20th Centuries* (Manchester, Manchester University Press, 1959).

[6]Max Weber noted this relationship between democracy and bureaucracy in political parties, but he wrongly attributed it to the desire for equality rather than the necessity to support a leadership ("Bureaucracy," in H. H. Gerth and C. Wright Mills, *From Max Weber* [New York, Oxford, 1958], pp. 211, 225).

ideology justifies this outlook, and many of its basic tenets have taken deep roots within continental lower strata. Communism supplied two things these strata desperately needed: first, an explanation of the environment that could prevent the futile actions resulting from crude passionate demands (hence "scientific" socialism); and, second, an organizational structure to support political action.

Communism converted the Marxian analytical method into dogma proclaimed by Moscow and the party into an organizational weapon to achieve the goals posited by dogma.[7] As organizational theory suggests, the more strictly defined are the goals of an organization, the less significant is free communication within it. With basic policies not subject to wide debate, European Communist parties could act with a single-mindedness seldom matched by their democratic Socialist rivals. This often seemed a virtue. For the Communist method of organization, whether in a multi-party system or a Communist single-party system, permits and even requires widespread mobilization regardless of political competence and classic notions of participatory democracy. Although it tends to eliminate goal conflict and the structural independence of constituent units that are so important to democracy, communism replaces them with strength, unity, and a sense of meaningful if largely vicarious participation on the level of the larger units. As this study has shown, substantial portions of those low on political competence perceive this as adequate from the democratic point of view. As levels of participation and education rise, this type of mobilization may be increasingly viewed as unsatisfactory by the individuals involved, as may be the case at present in some countries, including Italy. But the party itself can take steps to overcome many of the negative aspects of this type of mobilization by permitting freer internal debate and a more important role for the rank and file. If this process of internal "democratization" is carried out skillfully, a long time can elapse before the party loses the strengths of its former system and before the rank and file play a genuinely determining role within the party. Perhaps the Communist method is ultimately unsuited to units with widespread political competence. But once established it may decay slowly over a long period of time. Thus its long-range viability may be questionable, given the educational and other trends existing throughout the world today. However,

[7]In the words of Lenin: "The proletariat has no other weapon in the fight for power except organization." Quoted in Philip Selznick, *The Organizational Weapon* (New York, Free Press, 1960), p. 8.

the Communist system of organization is in jeopardy in only a few countries; in many others, the Communist system for mobilizing the politically incompetent is well-adapted to the human resources with which politicians must work.

The Italian Communist Party may thus be perceived by its supporters as being both effective and democratic. It is uncertain that the effectiveness of the PCI will be maintained once open internal debate is permitted, as seems to be beginning at least in Italy. Perhaps the rising level of political competence among lower strata will lead to a rejection of this form of party organization. It is of course also possible that the party will accommodate its structure to the changed socioeconomic environment. Regardless, in the historical period under discussion the PCI provided one model for resolving the problems of political competence and working-class politics: the model of the democratic Socialist Party is another.

Party Democracy

If the Communist system is well adapted to the characteristics of people of low political competence, there still remains the problem of maximizing the democratic potential of organizations. This means finding ways to maintain multiple autonomous channels of communication. Political competence, goal conflict, and structural bases all seem to be very important in their maintenance.

The first requisite for the existence of these channels is competent people to man them. Varying with the unit, an ample number of people with a sufficient level of political competence is required. This obvious fact merits more systematic attention than it has received. Unless those seeking a hearing form a significant portion of the total unit or possess some adequate substitute for numbers, they are unlikely, for logical reasons, to succeed. But not only must there be sufficient numbers; there must also be sufficient competence to communicate. As units and problems become more complex the level of competence required for meaningful communication rises. Competence is a relative thing, of course, but it is seldom distributed equally within units and between units, with dire consequences for democracy. Some units — parties, trade unions, and other organizations of the poor, for example — are often extremely deficient in competence. Sometimes skills are barely adequate to man the official channels. In this case, the unit literally may not be able to afford a second autonomous channel. This is probably the most important single impediment to democracy within working-class organizations. It also often applies to polities as well, as is evident from the experiences of many developing countries.

Other units, especially parties of notables, voluntary associations dominated by middle-class members, and rich Western democracies, may have a superabundance of political competence as operationalized in this study. These possess numerous informal communications networks and channels. As mentioned previously, it seems that as a general rule the lower the average level of competence within a unit the more important are the formal channels as a means of communicating with the larger unit. Industrialists and middle-class people in a democracy have many channels available to them for communicating demands. The poor, whether European industrial workers or American immigrants, often find the political party itself or its associated structures to be the sole or principal channel open to them. Classical liberalism and socialism thus both reflect some pragmatically important properties of communications networks, in that both implicitly recognize the class bias inherent in the liberal conception of the role of the state.

If the polity is considered the unit of analysis, then democracy within the polity under certain circumstances may not be facilitated by democracy within its subunits. For there are substantial groupings of people who presently lack the political competence to participate democratically. If they are to gain a hearing it will likely be through nondemocratic structures. To insist upon classical notions of democracy as participation might enhance the spread of democracy within the subunits of a polity but it is also certain to reduce the quantitative level of democracy, that is, the portion of the total population plugged into meaningful communications networks. Until the political incompetence of large portions of the population is reduced, democratic mobilization on the polity-wide level is incompatible with an insistence on democratic structures for all of the subunits of the polity. Such is the dilemma of contemporary democracy. It is a paradox the dimensions of which can in principle be expressed quantitatively. Under some circumstances, democratic participation is incompatible with total mobilization.

The level and unit of analysis problem enters again here also, for democracy is meaningless unless some choice between goals is available to the individual. But does this choice have to exist within every unit and subunit to which an individual belongs?[8] Undoubt-

---

[8]For the argument that it does, or at least that democracy is facilitated if it does, see Eckstein, *A Theory of Stable Democracy*.

edly, if the individual has no choice as to the unit to which he belongs, then this unit must be organized democratically if he is to participate democratically in the polity. This is one of the chief criticisms that can be made of American trade unions — that they are seldom truly voluntary associations. It is a point on which the situation of American and Italian workers differ greatly. But if an individual can choose among several organizations, then democracy in the polity would not seem to require that each of its subunits be democratically organized. In other words, the Communist Party of the Soviet Union does not contribute to democracy in the polity as it has been operationalized, but the Italian Communist Party may very well do so despite its system of organization. Indeed, it may mobilize segments of Italian society that would not be mobilized in any other fashion.

When the lower classes are a largely undifferentiated mass, as Marx conceived them and as often seems to be the case in developing societies, then having a single party represent them may not be as unreasonable as classic democrats are wont to argue. But development brings increasing differentiation and complexity along with a growing divergence, if not conflict, of interest within the lower classes. There is genuine goal conflict that a single party can resolve only with difficulty, and not at all if the legitimacy of goal conflict is denied. In this case, several parties representing the lower classes may facilitate the democratic mobilization of people of low political competence better than one democratic party, for this situation may give them a more realistic choice than would emerge from their formal participation in a seemingly democratic decision-making process. In this sense the Italian lower classes have more alternatives available to them in both the party and trade-union spheres than do Americans of comparable political competence. Whether they are more effectively and democratically mobilized is another question.

Goal conflict within units thus seems to be essential for the existence of multiple autonomous communications channels within the unit. Without such conflict, it is difficult to organize the potential for internal opposition that exists within most organizations.

A final factor that greatly facilitates the existence of democracy within a unit is that of structural bases for opposition. Political pluralists have realized that democracy is greatly facilitated by the existence within a polity of structures independent of one another and of the state. Certainly the ability to maintain a separate structure is necessary to democracy within a unit. Thorough-going pluralism is perhaps not a necessary condition, but it is undoubtedly conducive to democracy. There are functional equivalents for traditional pluralism. People of great political competence and some minimum resources of time and money can create separate structures even in the absence of pre-existing structural discontinuities. And in the absence of political competence and goal conflict pluralism will not lead to democracy, a point evident in the absence of a relationship between pluralism and democracy in many polities.

But democracy is a matter of tendencies, and a given level of structural pluralism can compensate for a given deficiency in political competence or in goal conflict. If separate structures exist they can be utilized in politics even in the absence of the competence necessary for the establishment of specifically political structures. And if separate structures exist they tend to persist even if there is a minimum of significant goal conflict between them, as is often the case with political parties. All things being equal, therefore, in any particular unit internal democracy is facilitated by the existence of structural discontinuities that give it a pluralistic character. Any structural arrangement that reduces the capacity of unit elites to coerce secondary leaders and rank and file encourages the survival of internal opposition and hence democracy.

The autonomy of constituent units is one such arrangement. This is the insight of federalism, but the same dynamics work within other units, for if the subunits are independent then elites must bargain and convince, as they cannot command.

The same results may be achieved by the existence of related but independent structures based upon function or clientele. In the PSI the trade unions — associated with the party but not completely under its control — achieved the same results. And in many labor movements Communist or Socialist parties, or at least individuals loyal to Communist and Socialist principles, have provided the structural bases for internal opposition. This is an example of the democratic requirements of political competence, goal conflict, and structural bases being met by the same source. It is also an example of the advantages the Communist system of front organizations has over less professional forms of opposition, as the party structure implements competence, provides guidance on goals, and ensures a structural basis for opposition. It is a formidable organizational weapon, and even more imposing among people of low political competence. Its very success usually leads to the destruction of internal democracy, because the party claims for itself — and is usually technically able to implement its claim — a monopoly of competence, goal setting, and control of structure.

Making unions and other organizations "nonpolitical" is thus one way of frustrating democracy, as political differences, especially when they reflect party differences, are one way of sustaining an internal opposition. An emphasis on limited goals and functions, on consensus, and on expertise among leaders has the same effect. The implications for democracy of a politics of material abundance, consensus, and technocracy are rather discouraging.

Democracy in the Polity

Although little firm evidence is available, one can speculate that the nature of the structural bases of opposition has a great deal to do with the quality of a polity's politics.[9] Some structural types of opposition have a built-in limitation as a means of mobilizing discontent. Regional, ethnic, linguistic, and religious structures may sometimes serve to develop competence and provide a structural basis for opposition without formulating alternative goals of a nature encouraging national integration. Often, for example, conflict over particular policies is replaced by conflict over the rules of the game. Rather than integrating opposition it may fragment it further. The result is often not democracy but warfare. Where these divisions do not coincide, or where there is a great deal of fragmentation, however, these types of differences may facilitate democracy. Encouraging the development of these nonpolitical structures as a basis for democracy is thus a dangerous game: it may facilitate opposition but make a thoroughgoing democratic mobilization more difficult to achieve.

There is much to be said for opposition structures based on political differences. From the viewpoint of democratic mobilization the encouragement of political differences, as, for example, economic and welfare policy and the like, is probably more desirable than other forms of division. For though religious, ideological, ethnic, linguistic, and regional differences all involve political differences, they also involve differences that are not political, or at least for which there is no simple political solution. In this case they are better left out of the political communications system, for they tend to overload what is already a heavily burdened network. Again, the advantages of political channels over nonpolitical ones are evident.

---

[9]For a thorough discussion of this topic see Dahl, ed., *Political Oppositions in Western Democracies.*

He who makes use of a pre-existing nonpolitical network for political purposes brings into politics much that could better be left out.

On the other hand, the growing agreement on political matters in Western countries may mean that opposition will have to come from other areas of life. The very success of technocracy in achieving material well-being — which seems to be what interests masses if not elites — threatens to eliminate narrowly political opposition, converting it into a "how-to-do-it" or "I-can-do-it-better" debate. Perhaps the revitalization of democracy requires a more radical critique of goals than is likely to emerge from existing political structures. How such a critique will be made compatible with the realities of organizational dynamics is difficult to say.

The most important unknown in this respect is the impact of increased education. The upgrading of entire populations through education should greatly increase the portion of the population that is participant, politically competent, and ideologically sophisticated — in short, the part that can create and sustain democratic structures. On the other hand, the extent to which these qualities have the impact ascribed to them only in this present era and Western culture is unknown. There are indications that participation was much higher, at least in the United States, in earlier times when the population ranked lower than today on most indices conventionally associated with participation.[10] Education may not lead to an increase in the quality of participation; under some circumstances it may even increase the potential for manipulation. Certainly its impact is the great unknown in the future of democracy.

The theorist of democracy thus can suggest certain methods for increasing the democratic potential of organizations, including political parties. He can at least better understand what limits internal democracy in some types of organizations and why this is not always undesirable. He can understand why organizations that are themselves not democratic internally can contribute to democracy on the level of the polity. But situations change, and democrats can only win battles in a war that never ends. The nature of democracy in the epoch ahead may differ from that presented here. Michel's cruel game continues.

---

[10]See Walter Dean Burnham, "The Changing Shape of the American Political Universe." *American Political Science Review*, 59 (1965), 7-28.

SECTION TWO

Recruitment

Recruitment

Political recruitment is the process by which political roles are filled; in Gabriel Almond's conceptual scheme (Almond and Coleman, 1960), recruitment is one of the important functions of all political systems. Moreover, as Lester Seligman (1967) notes, it is a function in which "political parties play a special and sometimes exclusive function" (p. 315) as "sponsors and gatekeepers to leadership recruitment" (p. 299). The role of political parties in the recruitment process covers a wide range of roles and offices (members, activists, party officials, elected public officials) and variables (environmental, organizational, and individual).

More research on political parties falls under the broad heading of recruitment than any other, with attention focused on both the characteristics of the individuals selected and the means by which they are recruited. The two basic party models differ sharply: recruitment in the Rational-Efficient model is more open in both regards than is the case of the Party Democracy model. A more open and flexible recruitment process is compatible with the Rational-Efficient model because party leaders, concerned with maximizing chances for electoral success, recruit from a diversity of groups to whom the party wishes to appeal. (See the use made of the notion of deviant subgroups by Eldersveld, 1964.) There are less institutionalized political career patterns and more self-recruitment in this model. In the Party Democracy model, on the other hand, the appeal is to a more homogeneous clientele in terms of social-demographic and/or ideological characteristics and political career patterns are more highly institutionalized. There tend to be clear career lines in the Party Democracy model through which party leaders and candidates for public office rise within the organizational structure.

Generally speaking, there are two recruitment models with different analytical foci. The first, the Political Participation model, raises the question of who the leaders (activists, public officials) are and how they differ in terms of social, demographic, attitudinal, and personality characteristics from voters generally. The theoretical interest in this line of research is elite-mass differences in political behavior since the findings of such studies add cumulatively to the growing body of knowledge about types and correlates of political participation generally (see Lane, 1959; Milbrath, 1965). A good bit of the research on political parties has been based implicitly or explicitly on the Political Participation model. In such studies, party activists are treated as a sample of political activists and interest tends to be focused on individual attributes; the organizational implications of the findings are often not clear.

Although the recruitment process should be broadly construed to encompass a wide range of variables, including social background characteristics, patterns of political socialization, modes of entry into political and party activity, motivations and incentives for political activity, politically relevant attitudes, and political career patterns and aspirations, most studies deal only with selected aspects. After surveying the political recruitment literature, Herbert Jacob (1962) concluded that although "we have excellent descriptions of isolated fragments . . . too little of this research has concerned itself with the whole of the recruitment process" (p. 703). "The time is ripe," Jacob contends, "for a more comprehensive, integrated, and theoretical approach" (p. 708). Toward this end, he has formulated a recruitment model that adds personality, community, and political structure variables to the usual social background variables.

Bowman and Boynton (Selection 2.1) have developed a recruitment model more directly tied to the Political Participation model. Their recruitment model involves four broad classes of variables: (1) social background (social status — occupation and education); (2) political socialization (parental political activity, sources of political activity); (3) personality factors (e.g., motivations for political activity); and (4) political attitudes (e.g., sense of political efficacy, sense of subjective political competence). Approaching political recruitment from the standpoint of these two efforts, we can view the recruitment process as involving individuals who tend to come from advantaged social backgrounds and have personality characteristics which predispose them toward political activity. These predispositions tend to be reinforced by earlier and/or later socialization experiences which generate activity-sustaining political orientations and attitudes. The opportunities for political activity are structured by community and political structure factors which at least partially determine which kinds of individuals become active politically. However, relatively few of even those individuals possessing "favorable" social-demographic and attitudinal characteristics actively participate in politics. According to Lester Milbrath (1965), something else is needed to push individuals across the "threshold" from spectator to gladiatorial political roles. More research attention needs to be given to various kinds of activity-triggering factors.

The type of recruitment model thus far considered focuses largely on individual characteristics and is theoretically anchored in political participation research, especially in the identification of elite-mass differences. The inclusion of environmental and organizational variables adds new dimensions of theoretical significance. The second kind of recruitment model is the Process Model, in terms of which recruitment is viewed as an organizational or institutional process. Of central interest here are the organizational modes of recruitment and the consequences for the organization of different recruitment patterns and the kinds of individuals selected.

An example of this kind of recruitment model is found in the recent work of Lester Seligman (1967). Seligman, taking an organizational view of party, sees it as a crucial factor in the recruitment process, and conceptualizes political leadership recruitment as "the product of the interaction between the internal organization dynamics and diverse party environments as mediated by the structure of political opportunity and political risk. Recruitment is a facet of the exchange between the party organization with the polity and the society" (p. 295). In other words, Seligman views the party as an organization which must be understood in terms of how it interacts with, affects, and is affected by environmental influences. His conceptual scheme may also be termed an organizational-environmental (systems) model. The dependent variable to be explained in this scheme is leadership selection; independent variables are environmental factors (e.g., electoral system, party competition). Intervening variables are political opportunity factors (formal and informal barriers and conditions, resources, skills, motivations of aspirants) and political risk factors — "the extent of the losses in status, income, and influence when a person loses political office" (p. 299). These intervening variables are viewed as "filters" which screen leadership aspirants — factors which are to varying degrees defined or influenced by the party system. Party is also influential in a more dynamic fashion. Internal organizational dynamics involve goal-setting, decision-making, and environmental adaptation — all vitally related to leadership selection outcome. Seligman's model considers such matters as the organizational loci of recruitment decision (centralization-decentralization with the parties, the role of interest groups); party organizational selection mechanisms (self-recruitment, sponsorship, conscription, co-optation); and recruitment outcomes and organizational consequences. The research potential of such a recruitment model for the comparative analysis of political parties is exciting, especially since this approach is consistent with new directions in conceptualization (notably systems theory and organization theory) which are increasingly being applied to the study of political parties. Certainly more attention needs to be devoted to conceptualizing political recruitment broadly in process terms, and to conceptually linking individual and organizational variables.

In considering substantive research findings, it is impossible concisely to do more than state some general propositions derived from a rather extensive line of research. This list of propositions is intended to be illustrative rather than exhaustive. The studies selected for inclusion in this section of the reader can be better understood within the context of such a general survey of research findings.

The first three propositions illustrate the role of social background factors — notably socio-economic status — in politicial recruitment.

1. *Political leaders and activists tend to be of higher socio-economic status than party members, identifiers, and voters generally.* It is a well-established proposition of cross-national validity that socio-economic status correlates positively with political participation generally (Lane, 1959; Milbrath, 1965) and party activity specifically. Generally, political activists from the grass-roots level up tend to be drawn from the relatively higher socio-economic status groups (Bowman and Boynton, 1966a; Eldersveld, 1964; Frost, 1961; Hartenstein and Liepelt, 1962; Hirschfield,*et al.*, 1962; Kornberg, Smith and Bromley, 1969; Patterson, 1963; Valen and Katz, 1964). However, in areas with strong patronage systems, many party activists are drawn from relatively lower-status backgrounds (Rossi and Cutright, 1961; Salisbury, 1965-66).

2. *Furthermore, the higher the leadership level, the higher the socio-economic status of office incumbents; SES tends to increase with the level of party or public office.* Increasing status within the party ranks from identifiers, to members, activists, and officials and at all levels of government office — local, state and national — tends to be associated with increasingly higher socio-economic status of individuals holding these positions. This, too, is a finding of cross-national applicability (Eldersveld, 1964; Hartenstein and Liepelt, 1962; Mayntz, 1961; Pomper, 1965; Valen, 1966).

3. *Leaders, activists, and members of parties of the Right tend to have higher socio-economic status than their counterparts in*

parties of the Left. The fact that the Republican party draws its electoral support and leaders disproportionately from higher-status groups compared with the Democratic party is a well-documented finding of studies of American voting behavior (Campbell *et al.*, 1960; Lane, 1959). These party-related status differences also tend to be found in studies of the recruitment of party activists and officials (Bowman and Boynton, 1966b; Eldersveld, 1964; Marvick and Nixon, 1961; Pomper, 1965). However, exceptions to this general pattern have been found: two studies of party activists in Manhattan (Hirschfield *et al.*, 1962) and Nassau County, New York (Ippolito, 1969) found no significant status differences between Republican and Democratic party officials. At least two studies found Democratic county chairmen to be of higher socio-economic status than their Republican counterparts; in both states —Oklahoma (Patterson, 1963) and North Carolina (Crotty, 1967) — the Democratic Party had been dominant for a long time, had acquired the status of the "establishment" party and was thus able to draw upon higher status groups in the community. Socio-economic status tends to be even more strongly related to party affiliation in other countries where members, activists, and leaders of parties of the Left (Labor, Social Democratic, Communist) tend to draw more heavily from lower-status groups, while parties of the Right (Conservative, Liberal, Christian Democratic) find their support more concentrated among higher-status groups (Epstein, 1967; Hartenstein and Liepelt, 1962; Lipset, 1960; Milbrath, 1965; Valen and Katz, 1964; Valen, 1966).

Although most studies consider occupational status to be the most significant of this class of recruitment variables, some studies have stressed other related variables. In his study of members of an Italian Socialist federation, Samuel H. Barnes (1966, 1967) attaches great importance to level of education as a key variable. He believes education provides skills and competence that have important implications as far as recruitment is concerned, especially in an organization in which the general level of education is quite low. Other studies identify occupational mobility as a key determinant of one's ability to rise within the party. In these studies, party officials are characterized not only by higher socio-economic status but also — and importantly — by upward social mobility (Bowman and Boynton, 1966b; Crotty, 1967; Eldersveld, 1964; Valen and Katz, 1964). Still another view emphasizes occupational role as the most important dimension. The nature rather than the status of the job is considered crucial; this view involves the idea that certain occupations (notably "brokerage" occupations such as law) impart skills that are useful in politics and that individuals in these occupations are more likely to engage in political activity (Jacob, 1962; Bowman and Boynton, 1966b).

A second class of recruitment variables concerns the political rather than the social background of political leaders and activists — i.e., political socialization. The role of the parental family and other socialization and recruitment agents, the timing and circumstances of the development of interest in politics and the entrance into political activity are questions raised in this context. Prewitt (1965) reviews classes of variables (social stratification, skill requirements, personality, and socialization) held to be related to political leadership recruitment patterns; he stresses political socialization variables in formulating his hypothesis of "overexposure" to political stimuli emphasizing the socialization role of the family. In the research that has been done on political socialization, a relatively new area of political research, two related propositions stress the often important role of the parental family.

4. *Leaders and activists tend to a greater degree than voters generally to have been raised in "politicized families" — i.e., to have grown up in homes where at least one parent was politically interested and active.* Research on political socialization generally and on party activists in particular tends to support the general proposition that the parental family has considerable influence in stimulating an initial interest in politics and entry into political activity (Barnes, 1967; Converse and Dupieux, 1962; Eldersveld, 1964; Key, 1961; Kornberg, Smith, and Bromley, 1969; Marvick and Nixon, 1961; Prewitt, 1965; Valen and Katz, 1964). In his study of Democratic club members in St. Louis, Salisbury (1965-66) notes the importance of the parental family in stimulating political interest more than activity, especially for those party activists whose political behavior was habitual rather than purposive. In his study of Italian socialists, Barnes (1967) arrives at a similar conclusion: that conventional or traditional socialists (from working-class, socialist family backgrounds) participated less actively in party affairs than members from middle-class, non-leftist backgrounds. Both studies find significant differences between those activists who joined the party as a matter of habit or family tradition and those who joined for more conscious and purposive reasons.

5. *A related aspect of the socialization role of the parental family is the transmission of partisan loyalties to their offspring; leaders and activists tend to a greater extent than voters generally to follow the parental party.* The general literature on political socialization has documented the tendency of voters to follow in their parents'

footsteps as far as partisan ties are concerned (Dawson and Prewitt, 1969; Hyman, 1959; Key, 1961; Lane, 1959, Langton, 1969). This tendency may be even stronger for political leaders and activists (Valen and Katz, 1964).

6. *Leaders and activists tend to develop an interest in politics and acquire partisan loyalties at an earlier age than voters generally.* That is, not only are political activists distinguished from the mass electorate by their greater interest and involvement in politics, but this interest tends to develop earlier in life for the activists. This finding attests to the often strong influence of early socialization experiences that stimulates attitudes and orientations favorable to political interest and activity (Kornberg, Smith and Bromley, 1969; Marvick and Nixon, 1961; Salisbury, 1965-66; Valen and Katz, 1964; Wahlke *et al.*, 1962). While the above propositions emphasize the influential socialization role of the family and the early development of political interest, it should be noted that political socialization is an ongoing process and that later, more directly political experiences and other socializing agents such as the school or peer groups often have considerable — even greater — impact (Almond and Verba, 1963; Hess and Torney, 1967; Jennings and Niemi, 1968; Wahlke *et al.*, 1962).

Political attitudes comprise the third class of recruitment variables. Several propositions which relate to ideology and motivations are treated in more detail in the third section of this reader and are thus only briefly noted here.

7. *Leaders and activists tend to have a greater sense of political efficacy and subjective political competence than do voters generally.* Political efficacy and subjective political competence are widely identified as strongly related to political participation generally (Almond and Verba, 1963; Lane, 1959; Milbrath, 1965). These variables have sometimes been included in research on political parties, although too little has been done in this regard (Bowman and Boynton, 1966b; Barnes, 1967). There is a reciprocal relationship between these political attitudes and political participation. A person who does not feel efficacious and competent is less likely to engage in political activity. On the other hand, actual participation may generate these political attitudes which tend to be a product of education and/or strong early socialization experiences (Barnes, 1966; Barnes, 1967).

8. *Leaders and activists tend to be more ideologically sensitive and consistent than are voters generally.* A growing body of research on elite-mass differences in political behavior has documented the low level of conceptualization and sophistication of mass publics;

ideology is more salient for the politically active stratum of the electorate and political leaders and activists are relatively more consistent ideologically in their policy views (Campbell *et al.*, 1960; Converse, 1965; McClosky, 1964). Several studies of party activists furnish support for these findings (Barnes, 1966; Barnes, 1967; Eldersveld, 1964; McClosky *et al.*, 1960).

Individuals become active in politics for a variety of reasons and there are often significant organizational consequences of the kinds of individuals who become politically active and the reasons they become active (these two factors are often related.) It will be recalled that motivational diversity and career pluralism are considered key variables by Eldersveld (Selection 1.3).

The concepts of incentive and motivation are attracting increasing attention as theoretical constructs crucial to the study of political leadership and organizations. Clark and Wilson (1961) construct a theory of organization based on types of incentives (material, solidary, and purposive); Payne (1968) applies the concept of incentive (status *versus* program) to an explanation of patterns of political conflict in Columbia; Schlesinger (1966) posits ambition as the prime motivation of elected public officials in the United States; Wilson (1962), in his study of club movement Democrats, uses the concept of incentive to differentiate two basic and sharply contrasting political styles: "professional" (material incentives) *versus* "amateur" (policy incentives). We have noted earlier that material or patronage incentives are emphasized in the Rational-Efficient model while ideological or policy incentives are emphasized in the Party Democracy model.

Greenstein (1963) and Sorauf (1964) note a relative shift from material to policy incentives in American parties as a result of decreasing patronage resources and the environmental changes of increasing urbanization and education. An increasing number of studies of American party activists have stressed the important role that policy and other purposive incentives apparently play in the recruitment of party activists (Bowman, Ippolito, and Donaldson, 1969; Conway and Feigert, 1968; Hirschfield *et al.*, 1962; Ippolito, 1969; Marvick and Nixon, 1961; Marvick, 1968). The next proposition is:

9. *Leaders and activists tend to be motivated more by ideological or policy incentives than by material incentives.* An exception is in areas where there are still ample reservoirs of patronage at the disposal of party leaders and "machine" style organizations (Rossi and Cutright, 1961; Snowiss, 1966). Valen and Katz (1964) com-

pare motivational patterns of Norwegian and American (Detroit) party activists and find that within a context of broad similarities the former tend to be more political and ideological and less individualistic than the Americans. Eldersveld (1964) stresses the complexity of motivational patterns and changes in motivational direction from impersonal to personal satisfactions over periods of time. Conway and Feigert (1968) also investigate incentive change — from initial to sustaining motivations — and find a relative shift from purposive to solidary and material incentives in the careers of Democratic and Republican activists in two counties in Maryland and Illinois.

Another tentative proposition regarding the role of motivation in recruitment that has been advanced is:

10. *It is probably not the method of recruitment (self-generating versus recruitment by others) but the initial motivation for participation which is most indicative of those who will rise to higher positions within the party and governmental structure.* Reasons for initially becoming active in politics may be influential in determining initial recruitment patterns and influencing subsequent political career patterns and office aspirations (Barnes, 1967; Eldersveld, 1964; Hirschfield *et al.*, 1962; Marvick and Nixon, 1961).

We still know very little about the motivations of political activists and need to give more attention to the conceptual and methodological problems involved in the use of incentive and motivation as a crucial recruitment and career variable as well as to the organizational consequences of motivational patterns.

The propositions thus far advanced have emphasized characteristics of political activists; they tap a growing body of research which is extending the kind of knowledge we already have of voters to cover political activists as well. A second, and equally, if not more important, aspect of recruitment involves the selection of candidates for elective public office; in fact, most people tend to think of "recruitment" in the latter connotation. In this area we not only have fewer empirical studies, but also fewer propositions of broad scope, given the wide variation cross-nationally and within the United States of formal and effective opportunities and candidate selection procedures. As far as American parties are concerned, the degree of party competition is the variable most often mentioned among the determinants of candidate recruitment patterns and characteristics of the candidates selected. There are basically two different situations: low competition, where one party is dominant; and high competition, or closely competitive situations. Several studies have generated propositions regarding candidate recruitment in these two types of situations.

11. *In low-competition situations, the minority party tends to more actively recruit candidates, while leaders of the majority party can often rely on their dominant position in the community to produce an ample supply of available candidates; they need not recruit actively and may play an inactive or neutral role.*

12. *In situations marked by a high degree of party competition, leaders of both parties are likely to actively recruit candidates.* Evidence supporting this pair of propositions may be found in Seligman (1961), Patterson (1963), and Crotty (1968). We should however be most cautious, especially as far as American parties are concerned, in simply linking party competition and candidate selection. Certainly the degree of involvement of party organizational leaders in pre-primary candidate selection varies greatly and is a factor neither entirely nor consistently determined by the competitive status of the parties. No general proposition concerning the role of party organizational leaders in pre-primary candidate selection procedures can be advanced. Bowman and Boynton (1966a) note that "little systematic evidence is available about the extent to which parties are involved in the pre-primary selection of candidates and much of it is contradictory" (p. 135). Pennsylvania local parties have been found to play an active role in candidate selection (Sorauf, 1963) while little organizational activity on the part of Wisconsin local party leaders was found by Epstein (1958). The activities of Oklahoma county officials varied according to party competition (Patterson, 1963); sporadic patterns of activity by North Carolina and Massachusetts ward and precinct officials were found by Bowman and Boynton (1966a) and the same was found in an Oregon study by Seligman (1961). Snowiss (1966) found that Congressional candidate recruitment patterns in the Chicago metropolitan area varied sharply by both party and type of Congressional districts (inner city, outer city, and suburban). The Seligman and Snowiss studies are good illustrations of the interacting role that differing environmental conditions and organizational characteristics play in candidate recruitment; however, since both kinds of factors vary so widely in the United States, much more research of this kind is needed in order to find patterns and, hopefully, to be able to state broader propositions.

Outside the United States, the candidate selection process is markedly different and little studied; generally, in the absence of the direct primary system for nomination of candidates for elected public office, the party organization controls the candidate selection process. In Britain, in spite of the formal powers of the central party organization to recommend and even veto candidates, local constituency parties are largely autonomous in this regard. However, British local parties are composed of national partisans who adopt parliamentary candidates in accordance with national rather than local criteria; consequently, local control does not limit the cohesiveness of the parliamentary parties (Epstein, 1967; Ranney, 1965; Ranney, 1968).

The term "recruitment" covers a broad research terrain. It is an area in which there has been a great deal of effort, but we need much more research on selected aspects of the recruitment process as well as more theory and conceptualization to show us how the pieces fit together and what aspects have been under-researched.

REFERENCES

Almond, Gabriel A., and Coleman, James S., eds. *The Politics of Developing Areas.* Princeton: Princeton University Press, 1960. (Introductory Essay).

Almond, Gabriel A., and Verba, Sidney. *The Civic Culture.* Princeton: Princeton University Press, 1963.

Barnes, Samuel H. "Participation, Education, and Political Competence." *American Political Science Review,* 60 (June, 1966), 348-53.

________. *Party Democracy: Politics in an Italian Socialist Federation.* New Haven: Yale University Press, 1967.

Bealey, Frank J.; Blondel, J.; and McCann, W.P. *Constituency Politics: A Study of Newcastle-under-Lyme.* New York: The Free Press, 1965.

Berry, David. *The Sociology of Grass Roots Politics: A Study of Party Membership.* London: Macmillan, 1970.

Bowman, Lewis, and Boynton, G.R. "Activities and Role Definitions of Grassroots Party Officials." *Journal of Politics,* 28 (February, 1966), 121-43.

________. "Recruitment Patterns Among Local Party Officials: A Model and Some Preliminary Findings." *American Political Science Review,* 60 (September, 1966), 667-76.

Bowman, Lewis; Ippolito, Dennis; and Donaldson, William. "Incentives for the Maintenance of Grassroots Political Activism." *Midwest Journal of Political Science,* 13 (February, 1969), 126-39.

Browning, Rufus P. "Hypotheses about Political Recruitment: A Partially Data-Based Simulation," in *Simulation in the Study of Politics,* edited by William D. Coplin, pp. 303-25. Chicago: Markham, 1968.

———. "The Interaction of Personality and Political System in Decisions to Run for Office: Some Data and a Simulation Technique." *Journal of Social Issues,* 24 (July, 1968), 93-109.

Campbell, Angus; Converse, Philip E.; Miller, Warren E.; and Stokes, Donald E. *The American Voter.* New York: John Wiley and Sons, 1960.

Clark, Peter B., and Wilson, James Q. "Incentives Systems: A Theory of Organization." *Administrative Science Quarterly,* 6 (1961), 129-66.

Converse, Philip E. "The Nature of Belief Systems of Mass Publics," in *Ideology and Discontent,* edited by David Apter, pp. 206-61. New York: Free Press, 1965.

Converse, Philip E., and Dupieux, George. "Politicization of the Electorate in France and the United States." *Public Opinion Quarterly* 26 (1962), 1-24.

Conway, M. Margaret, and Feigert, Frank B. "Motivation, Incentive Systems and the Political Party Organization." *American Political Science Review,* 62 (December, 1968), 1159-173.

Crotty, William J. "The Party Organization and Its Activities," in *Approaches to the Study of Party Organization,* edited by William J. Crotty, pp. 247-306. Boston: Allyn and Bacon, 1968.

———. "The Social Attributes of Party Organizational Activists in a Transitional Political System." *Western Political Quarterly,* 20 (September, 1967), 800-15.

Dawson, Richard E., and Prewitt, Kenneth. *Political Socialization.* Boston: Little, Brown, 1969.

Eldersveld, Samuel J. *Political Parties: A Behavioral Analysis.* Chicago: Rand McNally, 1964.

Epstein, Leon D. *Political Parties in Western Democracies.* New York: Frederick A. Praeger, 1967.

———. *Politics in Wisconsin. Madison*: The University of Wisconsin Press, 1958.

Fiellin, Alan. "Recruitment and Legislative Role Conceptions: A Conceptual Scheme and a Case Study." *Western Political Quarterly,* 20 (June, 1967), 271-87.

Flinn, Thomas A., and Wirt, Frederick M. "Local Party Leaders: Groups of Like-Minded Men." *Midwest Journal of Political Science,* 9 (February, 1965), 77-98.

Frost, Richard T. "Stability and Change in Local Party Politics." *Public Opinion Quarterly,* 25 (Summer, 1961), 221-35.

Greenstein, Fred I. *The American Party System and the American People.* Englewood Cliffs, N.J.: Prentice-Hall, 1963.

Hartenstein, Wolfgang, and Liepelt, Klaus. "Party Members and Party Voters in W. Germany." *Acta Sociologica,* 6, 1-2 (1962), 43-52.

Hess, Robert D., and Torney, Judith V. *The Development of Political Attitudes in Children.* Chicago: Aldine, 1967.

Hirschfield, Robert S., *et al.* "A Profile of Political Activists in Manhattan." *Western Political Quarterly,* 15 (September, 1962), 489-506.

Holt, Robert T., and Turner, John E. *Political Parties in Action: The Battle of Barons Court.* New York: Free Press, 1959.

Hyman, Herbert. *Political Socialization.* New York: Free Press, 1959.

Ippolito, Dennis. "Political Perspectives of Suburban Party Leaders." *Social Science Quarterly,* (March, 1969), 800-15.

Jacob, Herbert. "Initial Recruitment of Elected Officials in the U.S. — A Model." *Journal of Politics,* 24 (November, 1962), 703-16.

Janosik, Edward G. *Constituency Labour Parties in Britain.* New York: Frederick A. Praeger, 1968.

Jennings, M. Kent, and Niemi, Richard G. "The Transmission of Political Values from Parent to Child." *American Political Science Review,* 62 (December, 1968), 169-84.

Key, V.O., Jr. *Public Opinion and American Democracy.* New York: Alfred A. Knopf, 1961.

Kornberg, Allan; Smith, Joel; and Bromley, David. "Some Differences in the Political Socialization Patterns of Canadian Party Officials: A Preliminary Report." *Canadian Journal of Political Science,* 2 (March, 1969), 64-88.

Lane, Robert E. *Political Life.* Glencoe, Ill.: Free Press, 1959.

Langton, Kenneth P. *Political Socialization.* New York: Oxford University Press, 1969.

Lipset, S.M. *Political Man.* Garden City, N.Y.: Doubleday, 1960.

Marvick, Dwaine. "The Middlemen of Politics," in *Approaches to the Study of Party Organization,* edited by William J. Crotty, pp. 341-74. Boston: Allyn and Bacon, 1968.

Marvick, Dwaine, and Nixon, Charles. "Recruitment Contrasts in Rival Campaign Groups," in *Political Decision-Makers,* edited by Dwaine Marvick, pp. 193-216. New York: The Free Press of Glencoe, 1961.

Mayntz, Renate. "Oligarchic Problems in a German Party District," in *Political Decision-Makers,* edited by Dwaine Marvick, pp. 138-92. New York: The Free Press of Glencoe, 1961.

McClosky, Herbert, *et al.* "Issue Conflict and Consensus Among Party Leaders and Followers." *American Political Science Review,* 54 (June, 1960), 406-27.

McClosky, Herbert. "Consensus and Ideology in American Politics." *American Political Science Review,* 58 (June, 1964), 361-79.

Milbrath, Lester W. *Political Participation.* Chicago: Rand McNally, 1965.

Patterson, Samuel C. "Characteristics of Party Leaders." *Western Political Quarterly,* 16 (June, 1963), 332-52.

Patterson, Samuel C., and Boynton, G.R. "Legislative Recruitment in a Civic Culture." *Social Science Quarterly,* 50 (September, 1969), 243-63.

Payne, James L. *Patterns of Conflict in Columbia.* New Haven: Yale University Press, 1968.

Pomper, Gerald. "New Jersey County Chairman." *Western Political Quarterly,* 18 (March, 1965), 186-97.

Prewitt, Kenneth. "Political Socialization and Leadership Selection." *The Annals,* 361 (September, 1965), 96-111.

Ranney, Austin. "Candidate Selection and Party Cohesion in Britain and the United States," in *Approaches to the Study of Party Organization,* edited by William J. Crotty, pp. 139-58. Boston: Allyn and Bacon, 1968.

———. *Pathways to Parliament.* Madison: The University of Wisconsin Press, 1965.

Rossi, Peter, and Cutright, Phillips. "The Impact of Party Organization in an Industrial Setting," in *Community Political Systems,* edited by Morris Janowitz, pp. 81-116. New York: The Free Press of Glencoe, 1961.

Salisbury, Robert H. "The Urban Party Organization Member." *Public Opinion Quarterly*, 29 (Winter, 1965-66), 550-64.

Schlesinger, Joseph A. *Ambition and Politics: Political Careers in the United States.* Chicago: Rand McNally, 1966.

Schwartz, David C. "Toward a Theory of Political Recruitment." *Western Political Quarterly*, 20 (September, 1969), 552-71.

Seligman, Lester E. "Political Parties and the Recruitment of Political Leaders," in *Political Leadership in Industrialized Societies: Studies in Comparative Analysis,* edited by Lewis J. Edinger, pp. 294-315. New York: John Wiley and Sons, 1967.

_______. "Political Recruitment and Party Structure: A Case Study." *American Political Science Review,* 55 (March, 1961), 77-86.

Snowiss, Leo M. "Congressional Recruitment and Representation." *American Political Science Review,* 60 (September, 1966), 627-39.

Sorauf, Frank J. *Party and Representation: Legislative Politics in Pennsylvania.* New York: Atherton Press, 1963.

_______. *Political Parties in the American System.* Boston: Little Brown, 1964.

Valen, Henry. "The Recruitment of Parliamentary Nominees in Norway," in *Scandinavian Political Studies,* vol. 1, pp. 121-66. New York: Columbia University Press, 1966.

Valen, Henry, and Katz, Daniel. *Political Parties in Norway: A Community Study*. Oslo: Universitetsforlaget, 1964.

Wahlke, John C., *et al. The Legislative System.* New York: John Wiley and Sons, 1962.

Wilson, James Q. *The Amateur Democrat.* Chicago: The University of Chicago Press, 1962.

Recruitment Patterns Among Local Party Officials: A Model and Some Preliminary Findings in Selected Locales

Lewis Bowman
G. R. Boynton

Introduction

An ongoing political system requires a continuing process of recruitment in order to maintain the small but active cadre of citizens who assume the primary responsibility for the operation of the system. These political activists are involved in recruiting the official leadership, campaigning for their election and sometimes serve as governors of the system themselves. In American politics, the recruitment of political activists is effected through processes which political scientists have only recently begun to investigate in depth. Most of the studies of recruitment to positions of political activism have investigated the social backgrounds and the patterns of recruitment of public officials.[1] Not as much attention has been directed toward the personnel who operate the local political party organizations, and

[1]See, for example, Lester Seligman, "Recruitment in Politics," *PROD* (1958), 14-17; and "Political Recruitment and Party Structure: A Case Study," REVIEW, 55 (1961), 77-86; John Wahlke, *et al., The Legislative System* (New York: John Wiley and Sons, 1962); Frank J. Sorauf, *Party and Representation* (New York: Atherton Press, 1963); Donald R. Matthews, *The Social Background of Political Decision-Makers* (New York: Random House, 1954), and *U. S. Senators and Their World* (Chapel Hill: The University of North Carolina Press, 1960); Herbert Jacob, "Initial Recruitment of Elected Officials in the U. S. — A Model," *Journal of Politics*, 24 (1962), 703-16.

Reprinted from the *American Political Science Review*, LX (September, 1966), 667-76, by permission of the American Political Science Association and the authors.

the processes of their recruitment.[2] Our data add to the literature about political party activists at the lower echelons of the party organizations by reporting the findings of research conducted among local party officials in selected locales in North Carolina and Massachusetts. These local party officials constitute the lowest level of party officialdom in their respective party organizations. We have investigated the process of their recruitment to their party positions, and have used the data to test a model of political recruitment. Several questions guiding our research included: What are the social correlates of recruitment to local party positions? What are the patterns and channels of recruitment? What triggers political party activism — is there an identifiable "threshold" or "political opportunity structure" which serves as an indicator of political party activism? Are recruitment patterns and channels related to role definitions? We have also examined the relationship between the recruitment pattern of the party worker and his orientation to his job as party worker.

Methodology and Settings

We interviewed local party officials in three Massachusetts communities and in two North Carolina communities during the fall of 1963. These communities are not representative of Massachusetts or North Carolina communities, and no such implication is intended.

---

[2]Several recent research efforts have added to our knowledge of local party activists. See: Samuel J. Eldersveld, *Political Parties: A Behavioral Analysis* (Chicago: Rand McNally and Co., 1964); R. S. Hirschfield, B. E. Swanson, and B. D. Blank, "A Profile of Political Activists in Manhattan," *Western Political Quarterly,* 15 (1962), 489-506; Peter H. Rossi and Phillips Cutright, "The Impact of Party Organization in an Industrial Setting," in Morris Janowitz (ed.), *Community Political Systems* (Glencoe, Illinois: The Free Press of Glencoe, 1961), pp. 81-116; Phillips Cutright and Peter H. Rossi, "Grass Roots Politicians and the Vote," *American Sociological Review,* 23 (1958), 171-79; Samuel C. Patterson, "Characteristics of Party Leaders," *Western Political Quarterly,* 16 (June, 1963), pp. 332-52; Phillip Althoff and Samuel C. Patterson, "Political Activism in a Rural County," *Midwest Journal of Political Science,* 10 (February, 1966), 39-51.

The following research also provides helpful insights about party officials and/or leaders at other organizational levels or through different research approaches than that reported in our study. For more about the activities of county party chairmen, see: Leon D. Epstein, *Politics in Wisconsin* (Madison: University of Wisconsin Press, 1958), especially, pp. 77-97; Eugene C. Lee, *The Politics of Nonpartisanship* (Berkeley: University of California Press, 1960), pp. 97-119. For information about volunteer party workers, see: Dwaine Marvick and Charles R. Nixon, "Recruitment Contracts in Rival Campaign Groups," in Dwaine Marvick (ed.), *Political Decision-Makers: Recruitment and Performance* (New York: The Free Press of Glencoe, 1961), pp. 138-92.

Rather, we selected the communities as research sites for reasons of convenience (proximity), because the party organizations were fairly active, and because they offered some partisan balance. Both of the party systems in the two North Carolina communities can be characterized historically as modified one-party, although the Republicans recently made sizeable inroads on the traditional Democratic strength in one. In the two-party politics of Massachusetts, one of the community's party systems is strongly Democratic, one is strongly Republican and the third is two-party.

We designated the ranking official of each party's precinct organization in the North Carolina communities, and the two ranking officials in each party's ward organization in the Massachusetts communities as our universe.[3] In this universe, a structured interview of one-half to one hour in length was administered to a total of 138 local party officials. The response rate was 80.2 per cent.[4]

A Recruitment Model

In a democratic system the recruitment of the highly active political elite may be viewed as a part of the more general investigation of all forms of political participation.[5] Political participation in the Amer-

---

[3]The organizational arrangement is such in the Massachusetts communities that two officials in each ward had to be designated in order to inflate the universe to practical size. This means that for the purposes of this study "local party official" has been defined as the Republican and Democratic precinct chairmen in the North Carolina communities and as the two highest ranking Republican and Democratic ward officials in the Massachusetts communities. In some cases these are not exactly comparable because of the wide variations in the legal arrangements of the party systems of the states: nevertheless, these are the grass roots party officials in both systems and are comparable in that important respect. They represent roughly comparable functional and organizational levels.

[4]Apparently, a low response rate, while never desirable, must be faced as a usual problem when interviewing "grass roots politicians." See the problems encountered by Hirschfield and his associates, *op. cit.*, p. 490, and by Eldersveld, pp. 103-04.

[5]Two strands of the literature of political science are relevant to the theoretical model used for this study. The studies of the recruitment of party and public officials provide hypotheses for investigation. For citations to this literature generally, see: *supra*, p. 1, note 1. We found Herbert Jacob's review of this literature particularly helpful. The recent work of Samuel Eldersveld, *op. cit.*, also furnishes important theoretical insights and empirical comparisons.

The literature on the more general questions of political participation also offers suggestive hypotheses. See especially: Angus Campbell, *et al.*, *The American Voter* (New York: John Wiley and Sons, 1960), Chapters 2 and 5; Robert Lane, *Political Life* (Glencoe, Illinois: The Free Press of Glencoe, 1959); and Lester W. Milbrath, *Political Participation* (Chicago: Rand McNally and Co., 1965).

ican system may range from little more than exposure to political communication to the active extreme of holding either party or public office. This broad continuum may be divided into four levels of political participation.[6] Some members of society never participate in politics. This is the portion of the population often designated individually as "apathetics." They do not expose themselves to political communication and they do not vote. Only slightly more active are those who may talk about politics, and who may read about politics or may be exposed to political events through television and the radio. This portion of the public may vote (particularly in elections of high interest) usually on a party basis because of habit.[7] Those constituting a more active group expose themselves to political communication, vote in almost all elections, and participate in campaign activities in behalf of the candidates they support. A fourth, and the most active group, perform most or all of the previously mentioned activities as well as holding an official position in either the party organization or in the government itself. This is a a very small group constituting no more than about one per cent of the total population.

Past research on political participation and the recruitment of party and public officials suggests a number of factors which help explain why certain members of the polity participate actively and others less actively or not at all. The first broad group of factors has to do with the individual's background. Those who are active in politics come from backgrounds of higher social status.[8] Also, a large proportion of the politically active have occupations of high social status. As one would expect, a high level of education is congruent with the high occupational achievement of most political activists.

A second background factor is the level of political activity in the home environment in which political activists grow up. For example, a study of legislators in four states found that a large number of the legislators came from homes in which one or both parents had been politically active.[9]

A third background factor is the personality development of political activists. Many political scientists have been persuaded that certain personality characteristics lead to a high level of political

---

[6]See Milbrath, *ibid.*, pp. 5-38, for a general discussion of the problems in conceptualizing political participation.

[7]These are roughly equivalent to the "peripheral voters" described by Angus Campbell. See "Surge and Decline: A Study of Electoral Change," *Public Opinion Quarterly*, 24 (1960), 397-418.

[8]The high occupational status of the fathers of public officials has been amply documented by Donald R. Matthews. See his two books, *op. cit.*

[9]See Wahlke, *et al., op. cit.*, p. 83.

activity.[10] There has been little evidence that would justify the wholesale generalizations from these hypotheses and tentative findings to all political office holders. However, in his study of political party leaders, Eldersveld suggests that:

> a consciousness of power as the goal of the party is intimately related to the individual's own psychological makeup, his own ambitions, interests, and drives in political organizationl life.[11]

The background of political activists produces two types of intervening factors which further help explain why this group is highly involved in politics. One intervening factor is the competence to operate easily in a political environment. Jacob has pointed out in detail the role certain occupations play in providing training in skills which are useful in politics.[12] They are also likely to place the individual in contact with the political environment, thus facilitating the development of political activity. Education also provides training which is valuable to the politician. The ability to conceptualize political issues and verbalize these conceptions is importantly related to educational achievement. The development of skills essential to political activity will also be facilitated if the child sees these skills practiced by members of his home environment. Thus, the political activity of parents contributes to the development of political competence in their children.

The background of political activists also produces attitudes which are important in explaining the involvement of this group in politics. Political efficacy (the feeling that one's actions can have an impact on the government) has been shown to be related to level of political activity. A recent study of this feeling of individual competence (called "subjective competence" by the authors) in five nations showed that subjective competence was related to the level of political activity of the individual.[13] Also, they found that the

---

[10]For a summary of this work, see Milbrath, *op. cit.*, pp. 72-80. In the main, the various scales relating to trait psychology, rather than psycholanalytical techniques, have been utilized in an effort to operationalize investigation of this factor.

[11]*Op. cit.*, p. 243.

[12]*Op. cit.*, p. 710. He says: "Occupation is the crucial social variable in our model. But counter to the assumptions of elite theories, political officials in the U.S. emerge from all levels of the social structure. Occupational role rather than status alone is the important factor. Certain occupations frequently place their practitioners into a bargaining role where they deal with outsiders (non-subordinates) and try to reach a mutually satisfying agreement. The lawyer is the classic example. . . ."

[13]See Gabriel Almond and Sidney Verba, *The Civic Culture* (Princeton: The Princeton University Press, 1963), Ch. 7.

development of the feeling of subjective competence was directly related to educational and occupational achievement.

The duty to participate in politics is a second attitude which helps explain why some people are active and others are not. Almond and Verba found that a sense of obligation to participate in community life is more widespread in the United States than in any of the other four countries.[14] The more strongly one feels obliged to participate in politics the more likely he is to participate.[15] The belief that it is a part of the duty of a citizen to participate in the politics of his country is an important element of the democratic creed, and those from higher social background, who have had more education, are more likely to subscribe to the creed than are other members of the society.[16]

The strength of partisan commitment has been shown to be an important variable in explaining political participation.[17] Partisanship seems to be completely unrelated to social status. People of high social status do not seem to be either more or less committed to their political party than do people of low social status.[18] However, party identification is passed from parents to children in a quite striking fashion. It seems reasonable to assume that the same thing would be true of the strength of partisan commitment.

A fourth attitudinal variable which is importantly related to political participation is interest in politics. The more interested an individual is in politics the more likely he is to participate. Interest in politics has been shown to be related to both strength of partisanship and to the social background of the individual.[19]

Past studies of political leadership have clearly shown background characteristics on which political leaders differ from the population as a whole. These background characteristics produce the competence to operate easily in the work of politics as well as a set of attitudes which dispose the individual to take an active part in the political world. However, this is not enough to explain why some people are interested and active enough to become political officials and others are not. There are far more people who have all of these characteristics than there are people who actually hold political office. This larger group forms a pool from which political

---

[14]*Ibid.*, p. 169.

[15]Campbell, *et al., op. cit.*, p. 106.

[16]See V. O. Key, Jr., *Public Opinion and American Democracy* (New York: Alfred A. Knopf, 1961), Ch. 13.

[17]Campbell, *et al., op. cit.*, p. 97.

[18]George Robert Boynton, *Southern Republican Voting in the 1960 Election* (unpublished Ph.D. thesis, University of North Carolina, 1963), p. 21.

[19]Campbell, *et al., op. cit.*, p. 103.

leadership is drawn.[20] Milbrath points out the apparent necessity of some extra push in moving an individual from one level of political participation to a higher one.

> There seems to be a kind of threshold that must be crossed before a person changes role; this is especially characteristic of transition from spectator to gladiator. A person needs an extra strong push from the environment (e.g., earnest solicitation from a friend) or needs to feel very strongly about an issue as a candidate before he will cross the threshold and become a political combatant. Once the threshold is crossed and the new team member integrated in his role, he usually participates in a wide repertoire of political acts.[21]

The final push from being interested in politics to holding office is the major concern of this paper. What is the nature of this final push for local party officials? By examining this question for local party officials we hope to provide further evidence of the existence of such a threshold and begin to systematically examine the nature of the stimuli which propel individuals across this threshold.

Not all of the suggested model can be tested in this study. The social and political background of the local party officials can be examined as well as their present occupation. Political competence is very difficult to test but a minimal level of political competence can be assumed, given the fact that the individuals interviewed hold official positions in the party organizations. The attitudes mentioned cannot be examined, but based on the generalizations which have been established in the literature on political participation it is a fairly safe assumption that the party officials would score high on each of the attitudinal scales. It is possible to examine the factors which initiated the party officials' interest in politics, and to investigate the factors involved in their recruitment to office.

Recruitment Patterns: Fitting Data to the Model

The Backgrounds of Local Party Officials. As expected, more Republicans than Democrats come from families of white collar workers (see Table 1). The fathers of 53% of the Massachusetts Republicans and 43% of the North Carolina Republicans had white collar jobs. Only slightly fewer (37%) of the North Carolina Demo-

---

[20]Jacob, *op. cit.*, p. 711.
[21]Milbrath, *op. cit.*, pp. 20-21.

crats came from white collar backgrounds, while the Massachusetts Democrats have the highest percentage coming from blue collar backgrounds.

The social status of the local party officials is significantly higher than their fathers'.[22] Eighty-seven percent of the Massachusetts Republicans and 83% of the North Carolina Republicans have white collar occupations. The North Carolina Democrats are again only slightly lower (79% white collar) than the Republicans, and only 50% of the Massachusetts Democrats have white collar jobs. In contrast Eldersveld reports that 69% of the Republican precinct leaders hold white collar occupations as opposed to only 43% of the Democrats in Wayne County, Michigan.[23]

Education, a second measure of social status, further illustrates the relatively high social status of the local party officials (see Table 2). One-fourth of the officials only have a high school education or less, but 40% have at least a college education and one-fifth have gone beyond the college degree in their education.[24]

Occupational role may be as important as social status in developing political competence and in recruitment. One important source of political activists is the profession of law. The lawyer must learn how to bargain, inspire confidence, and his occupation requires a high degree of the skills which, according to conventional wisdom, are important in a political career. Of the local party officials, 11% (thirteen) are lawyers. However, eight of the thirteen lawyers are North Carolina Democrats, while only three are Massachusetts Republicans, two are Massachusetts Democrats, and there are no lawyers among the North Carolina Republicans. There are, of course, occupations other than the law which may provide training

---

[22]The slightly larger difference in the North Carolina communities probably reflects the relatively greater opportunity for increased wihte collar employment for the current generation there as compared to the Masschusetts communities.

[23]Eldersveld found less occupational status differential between precinct leaders and their fathers than we have found. See *op. cit.*, p. 52, Table 3.1.

[24]We found a higher portion of local party officials to have at least a college level education than Eldersveld found to be the case in Wayne County, Michigan (see *ibid.*). One plausible explanation is that political parties recruit among "safe groups" more in the five community locales of our study than in the metropolitan area af Detroit. See Eldersveld's discussion of the emphasis on groups who have "deviant potential" rather than emphasizing recruitment among "traditional safe groups" (*op. cit.*, p. 71).

This interpretation is supported by the findings of Marvick and Nixon. (See *op. cit.*, p. 203, Table 6.) They found approximately one third of the party campaign workers to be college graduates but they did not find the party officials making efforts to accumulate helpers among the "deviant potentials" in the fashion Eldersveld describes.

TABLE 1
OCCUPATIONAL STATUS OF THE LOCAL PARTY OFFICIALS AND OF THEIR FATHERS

	PERCENT HOLDING WHITE COLLAR OCCUPATIONS*			
	N.C. REPS.	N.C. DEMS.	MASS. REPS.	MASS. DEMS.
Party officials	83%	79%	87%	50%
Fathers of the party officials	43%	37%	53%	27%
Percentage point difference	40	42	34	23
N =	(34)	(41)	(40)	(23)

*Includes the following occupational categories: professional and technical; managers, officials, and proprietors; clerical and sales.

in skills relevant to a political avocation. Jacob has provided a tentative listing of occupations which required a "brokerage" role.[25] He included such occupations as general practitioners, lawyers, newspapermen, auto dealers, fuel dealers, independent merchants, insurance salesmen, local union officials, undertakers, and others. Using the list Jacob developed, we can estimate the "brokerage" training provided in terms of these occupations (Table 3). Fifty-nine percent of the North Carolina Democrats and 50% of the Massachusetts Republicans work in jobs which provide training in political skills. The Massachusetts Democrats are third, with 39% involved in "brokerage occupations," and the North Carolina Republicans are last. The overall difference in the status ranking and the "brokerage occupations" ranking, and particularly the difference for the North Carolina Republicans, illustrates the independence of status and brokerage role training. Eighty-three percent of the

TABLE 2
EDUCATION OF LOCAL PARTY OFFICIALS

	N.C. REPS.	N.C. DEMS.	MASS. REPS.	MASS. DEMS.	TOTAL
College or more	44%	46%	38%	26%	40%
Some education beyond high school	47	27	33	35	35%
High school or less	9	27	28	39	25%
N =	(34)	(41)	(40)	(23)	(138)

[25] *Op. cit.*, pp. 709-710.

TABLE 3
Local Party Officials Holding Brokerage Occupations

	N.C. Reps.	N.C. Dems.	Mass. Reps.	Mass. Dem.	Total
Involved in brokerage occupations	21%	59%	50%	39%	44%
N =	(34)	(41)	(40)	(23)	(138)

North Carolina Republicans have white collar jobs, which ranks them second in terms of social status, but only 24% are involved in jobs with brokerage roles, ranking them last. The North Carolina Republicans have drawn on accountants, engineers, and other professionals who have high social status, but who have little opportunity to exercise "political" skills in their profession.

Past studies have shown that political leaders tend to come from highly politicized family backgrounds. The local party officials were asked about the political activity of their family. Controlling for state locale, the Democrats were considerably more likely to have grown up in a family having one or more members politically active. The North Carolina Democrats have the largest number of officials coming from politically active families. The North Carolina Republicans and the Massachusetts Democrats fall in the middle (about 40% coming from politically active families), and the group with the fewest coming from politically active backgrounds are the Massachusetts Republicans.

The background factors, which have been suggested as important components of a model of political recruitment, exist among a relatively large portion of these party officials. Many are of high social status, are highly educated, and come from highly politicized backgrounds. A considerable portion of the party officials hold occupational positions assumed to be conducive to the development of skills needed for success in politics. Tangential questions are suggested by these findings: Do differential social status, education, or politicization backgrounds make any difference in the role definitions which they hold of their party position? Do those engaged in "brokerage occupations" define their roles differently from those holding "nonbrokerage occupations"?[26]

[26]Of course, other questions could be asked. For example: How are these variations associated with efficacy at party tasks? How are these variations associated with policy orientations?, *etc.* However, our data are not adequate to speak to these questions. We are convinced that further investigations into these and similar questions are desirable.

In terms of the oft-used "white-collar" and "blue-collar" dichotomy, occupational status for the party officials is unrelated to their definition of their roles.[27] The important dimension of occupational status seems to be mobility (see Table 5). The upwardly-mobile are clearly more campaign-oriented than the others. Although the number of cases are too small for safe generalization, the fact that almost half of those who are downwardly-mobile are primarily oriented

TABLE 4
POLITICAL ACTIVITY OF FAMILY OF LOCAL PARTY OFFICIALS

	N.C. Reps.	N.C. Dems.	Mass. Reps.	Mass. Dems.
One or more members of the family were politically active	38%	49%	28%	39%
N =	(34)	(41)	(40)	(23)

TABLE 5
THE RELATION OF THE LOCAL PARTY OFFICIALS' OCCUPATIONAL MOBILITY TO THEIR ROLE DEFINITIONS

Role Definition	Upwardly-mobile[a]	Others	Total
	%	%	%
Campaign	72	46	59
Organization	24	33	28
Other[b]	4	21	13
N =	(71)	(67)	(138)

[a] Includes each local party official whose occupation is at least one status-level above that of his father.
[b] Includes ideological, nomination, or other primary role orientation.

toward party organizational activities seems particularly suggestive in comparison with the strong campaign orientation of the upwardly-mobile aggregate. This indicates that the upwardly-mobile local party officials are concerned with winning elections, and presumably moving ahead, rather than with clinging to the party organization and its activities at such a low level in the party hierarchy. Even stronger support for this interpretation is found when one

[27] The four basic role definitions are: campaign-related; party organizational; ideological; and nominations. These were assigned on the basis of the local party officials' answers to this question: "How would you describe the job of being (current party office) — what are the most important things you do?"

examines the role definitions of those local party officials whose occupational status is two levels or more above their fathers'. These are even more campaign-oriented with less than one-fifth being oriented toward party organizational activities.[28]

The other background factors are not significantly related to the role definitions of the local party officials. The level of education and the level of political activity by members of the local party officials' families show only slight differences when associated with role definition.[29] Most surprising, however, is the fact that practically no variation in role definition occurs when one compares those engaged in "brokerage occupations" with those party officials engaged in "non-brokerage occupations."[30]

Initial Political Involvement. The local party officials were asked how they first got interested in doing something more in politics than just voting.[31] A number of reasons were given for their initial involvement in a highly active role in politics. The most frequently mentioned general reason (by 26% of the respondents) was that they were *asked* to take a more active part. Of these, almost one-half

---

For a longer discussion of the derivation and of the application of these role definitions, see "Activities and Role Definitions of Grass Roots Party Officials," by Lewis Bowman and G. R. Boynton, *The Journal of Politics,* 28 (February, 1966), 121-43.

[28]This suggests that the idea of "marginality" has not been adequately explored as an explanatory factor in analyzing recruitment to political leadership. See the work of James C. Davies, *Human Nature in Politics* (New York: John Wiley and Sons, 1963), especially pp. 85-94, 287-88, 345-48, for an interesting discussion of extreme examples of marginality as a factor in leadership recruitment.

[29]It should be reported that our data generally support the contention that the dominant party attracts the "best people" (in socio-economic terms). The variations are not very large, however. For support for this hypothesis, see Patterson, *op. cit.,* p. 337ff.

[30]In view of the recent work of Heinz Eulau and John D. Sprague, this is less surprising than one might have thought earlier. They found no significant differences between lawyers (the prime brokerage occupation) and non-lawyers in politics: see their book, *Lawyers in Politics* (Indianapolis: The Bobbs-Merrill Co., 1964). They pointed out, *"Preoccupation with real or alleged dysfunctional consequences* of the lawyer's ubiquity in politics has had the effect of orienting research toward analysis of differences rather than of similarities in the behavior of the politician who is a lawyer and the politician who is not" *ibid.,* p. 123.

[31]One must be careful in interperting this kind of data because it requires the respondent to recall circumstances of earlier periods in his life. Nevertheless, this is almost the only way to collect this important data in a systematic fashion. But it must be kept in mind that these are the "recollections" of the local party officials rather than their feelings at the time they were first interested in active political participation (See the warning about the use of this kind of data in Jacob, *op. city.*, p. 713.).

said that they were asked by their friends or relatives to take a more active role.

The second general reason most often mentioned was a concern with policy matters. Almost one-fourth of the respondents said that they were dissatisfied with present conditions, they wanted to see better government, or mentioned specific policies that had been of particular interest to them.

Direct party or campaign involvement was the third general reason most frequently mentioned (by 16% of the respondents) as leading to active participation. The party officials mentioned both attachment to political parties and interest in particular campaigns as the kind of political involvement which led to such participation.

"Interest in politics" is closely akin to poiltical involvement as a reason for becoming active. Almost 10% of the local party officials found the excitement of campaigns and the related thrill of "politicking" to be a key factor in increasing their level of activity. Their high level of interest led quite naturally to their taking an active part in politics.

Two other specific reasons for initial involvement were given. Six percent of the respondents said they got involved because political activity would help their business. Five percent said their initial involvement was the result of their admiration of a political figure. Other scattered responses constituted 13% of the answers.

When analyzed by party groups in differing locales, several recruitment variations develop (see Table 6). The most striking variation is by those who give business as a reason for initial activist

TABLE 6

REASONS FOR INITIAL POLITICAL INVOLVEMENT BEYOND VOTING

	N.C. Rep.	N.C. Dem.	Mass. Rep.	Mass. Dem.
Was Asked	22%	20%	31%	30%
Concern with policy	30	23	24	20
Party and/or campaign involvement	27	14	10	15
Like politics	11	14	4	10
Business reasons	0	18	12	0
Admire political figure	0	2	8	15
Other	10	9	21	10
	100%	100%	100%	100%
N =	(34)	(41)	(40)	(23)

involvement in politics. Eight of the nine local party officials who gave this as a reason were North Carolina Democrats. More of the Massachusetts officials reported being asked to take an active role in politics and seven of the eight officials who report admiration for a political figure as a primary reason for involvement are from Massachusetts. The North Carolina Republicans indicate a greater concern with policy matters, and a disproportionate number of them say that prior political involvement prompted them to become active.

Whether the initial political involvement was self-generated or from influences outside the party official seems to have no association with their role definitions. This finding is in line with recent work which has cast some doubt on the earlier assumptions scholars held about the direct relationship between initial political involvement and political careers. For example, Kenneth Prewitt[32] has reported that discontinuity existed between initial political interest and policy decisions by city councilmen in the San Francisco Bay area. Even though Prewitt was concerned with "early" or "late" starting whereas our concern here is with "self-generated" political interest as opposed to initial interest by "outside influences," it seems to follow that the happenings at the point of recruitment to office may be of greater significance in policy and role definitions than earlier career events.

Variations do occur in sources of initial political involvement according to party and locale. As shown in Table 7, the local party officials in the two North Carolina communities indicate a disproportionate share of outside influence was involved in getting them to participate politically beyond the mere act of voting.

Recruitment to Party Office. After asking how they first got involved in politics, the party officials were asked about the circumstances of their first election to party office. Why did they first decide to run? Sixty percent of the local party officials report that they were recruited by the political party for their present position. (This happened to a larger portion of the Massachusetts party officials than in the North Carolina party officials.) Of all the party officials, 11% report that other groups such as unions, business organizations, and others asked them to seek the position. This is true of a larger percentage of the North Carolina Democrats than of the other three aggregates. Only 29% of the party officials say that they

---

[32]See his paper, "Career Patterns of Local Elected Officials," delivered at the American Political Science Association meeting in Chicago, 1964.

were self-recruited to office. North Carolina Republicans have the largest percentage who say that they were self-recruited for the good of the party. The party organization is developing there and a higher percentage say that they have joined the organization in order to bolster it.

TABLE 7
SOURCES OF INITIAL POLITICAL INTEREST

SOURCE OF INTEREST	N.C. REPS.	N.C. DEMS.	MASS. REPS.	MASS. DEMS.	TOTAL
Outside influence	62%	54%	42%	44%	51%
Self-generated	29	34	40	30	34
Other	9	12	18	26	15
	100%	100%	100%	100%	100%
N =	(34)	(41)	(40)	(23)	(138)

TABLE 8
THE RECRUITMENT OF LOCAL PARTY OFFICIALS

	N.C. REPS.	N.C. DEMS.	MASS. REPS.	MASS. DEMS.	TOTAL
Asked by the party	59%	51%	69%	67%	60%
Self-recruited	35	26	27	33	29
For personal gain	(4)	(3)	(12)	(13)	(6)
For the good of the party	(31)	(23)	(15)	(20)	(23)
Asked by other groups	6	23	4	0	11
	100%	100%	100%	100%	100%
N =	(34)	(41)	(40)	(23)	(138)

TABLE 9
RECRUITMENT PATTERNS TO LOCAL PARTY OFFICE

SOURCE OF RECRUITMENT	N.C. REPS.	N.C. DEMS.	MASS. REPS.	MASS. DEMS.	TOTAL
Outside influence	62%	70%	45%	44%	57%
Self-generating forces	32	25	18	17	23
Other*	6	5	37	39	20
	100%	100%	100%	100%	100%
N =	(34)	(41)	(40)	(23)	(138)

*Includes "accidental involvement," other vague or uncodeable responses, and single answers.

Eldersveld[33] has subsumed the sources of political recruitment for party work at the precinct level under three main categories: "outside influences," "self-generating forces," and "accidental involvement." Although the comparisons are not exact (due to coding and other variations), the distribution of the recruitment patterns to party office which he found in Wayne County, Michigan, and those we found for the total sample from the five North Carolina and Massachusetts study sites are in the same directions (see Table 9). For example, in Wayne County, Michigan, 56% of the precinct leaders were rescruited by outside influences (such as friends, political clubs, etc.). We found 57% giving this as their channel of recruitment. However, we found significant variations between the recruitment channels of the North Carolina aggregates and the Massachusetts aggregates. Many of the Massachusetts party officials maintained that they had come by the party office through default of others to run, or because they were "as good as others holding the posts," *etc.* In Eldersveld's terminology this is "accidental involvement," and when one finds relatively large numbers following this recruitment pattern, the relative unimportance of organizational effects, as compared to individual influences, is probably being underscored.

It seems quite clear, also, that the majority party accumulates a disproportionate share of those local party officials coming into the job through impetus of outside influences (see Table 10). This may be because of more efficient organization on the part of the majority party, or it may be due to its more extensive membership.

Those local party officials who come to party work because of outside influences are more likely to define their primary role in

TABLE 10
THE RELATION OF RECRUITMENT PATTERNS TO THE MAJORITY-MINORITY PARTY DIFFERENTIATION

RECRUITMENT PATTERN	MAJORITY PARTY	MINORITY PARTY
Outside influence	63%	49%
Self-starting	23	24
Other	14	27
	100%	100%
N =	(73)	(65)

[33]*Op. cit.*, p. 127, Table 6.2 (Our categories include comparable items as outlined by Eldersveld in this table.)

terms of campaign activities (Table 11). This indicates, perhaps, that the majority party accumulates a disproportionate share of the party officials for campaign purposes.

TABLE 11
THE RELATION OF THE LOCAL PARTY OFFICIALS' RECRUITMENT PATTERN TO THEIR ROLE DEFINITIONS

ROLE DEFINITIONS	RECRUITMENT PATTERNS			
	OUTSIDE INFLUENCE	SELF-GENERATING	OTHER	TOTAL
Campaign	67%	56%	43%	59%
Organizational	26	32	32	28
Other	7	12	25	13
	100%	100%	100%	100%
N =	(78)	(32)	(28)	(138)

Discussion

In order to develop a conceptual scheme for understanding the recruitment of local party officials, we thought of general political participation as being divided into four levels: no participation; only passive participation; quite active participation, but short of being elected to or assuming party or public office; and holding party or public offices. Although our concern was with local party officials — persons categorized in the last, and most active, of the participatory levels — we assumed that part of the explanation of political activism could be found in those factors which are associated with the various levels of political participation among the general population. The model which we developed, and the data which we related to it, sought in a tentative and exploratory way to get at very basic questions: why do politically active people assume positions in local party organizations? What finally triggers such active political involvement?

Certainly several background factors are likely to predispose individuals toward becoming political activists. The social status of the individual and the political "training" which his occupation affords are likely to facilitate, or diminish, skills in interpersonal relationships as well as produce a set of attitudes, more or less, conducive to political activism. Our data (and comparable data) indicate that even local party officials are drawn from higher social backgrounds and more active political backgrounds than are the averages for these two factors in the individual communities of each leader aggregate. But many people possessing the same social and political backgrounds have not become political activists. Without using a control group, which would have been helpful, we have investigated this phenomenon by asking the party officials in five communities about their perceptions of the recruitment factors relating to their rise to official party positions. They were able to recall a number of factors, ranging from admiration for a current political figure to extreme ideological concern about public policy. Almost three-fourths, however, thought the triggering mechanism had involved situations in which some politically active group or individual asked them to seek or to fill a local party position. Thus, the major stimulus to party office holding was external. Many persons in each of the five communities undoubtedly possessed quite similar social and political correlates but did not assume or compete for party posts because external stimuli did not give them a final push across the threshold.

This finding supports that plausible hypothesis, which is oft-asserted in leadership literature: if adequate educational levels and occupational skills are represented among the population of a community, then the proportion of potential political activists actually involved in political activities at a given time depends on the openness of the leadership recruitment system of that particular community. Our data support this hypothesis, illustrating that the nature of a community's politics is an intervening factor between the social and political background variables and actual activist participation. In one of the communities we studied (Greensboro, North Carolina) the Republicans had no long history of adequate party organization. In their recent drive for more active party leaders, the Greensboro Republicans made a point of recruiting "bright young articulate" business types, who wanted to get ahead fast. Except for the nature of party politics in the community at that moment, it seems unlikely that such a specific drive for upward-mobiles would have occurred. Except for this situation, they probably would have gravitated to the majority party, or have invested their energies in other than politcal forms of activism. This in turn illustrates the differential intervention of the community factor, and the interplay between it and individual social background variables.

The important social background factor may not be that preponderance of occupations involving brokerage skills — as has often been assumed to occur under all circumstances of leadership recruitment. Rather than occupations per se being the important social background factor, occupational marginality may be the critical factor. These persons are marginal in the sense that they have moved at least two rungs up the occupational ladder above their fathers' occupations. They are looking for fast avenues to success— in politics as much as in business. Hence, we found that they tended to be self-starting as well as more campaign-oriented. This may have been both because they were interested in winning, and because of the selective process of recruitment used by the minority party in securing their services. It is likely that other comparative studies in differing political cultures will show that upwardly-mobiles are attracted into politics in disproportionate numbers in areas where, and when politics is unusually competitive and salient. This should be true in very competitive two-party situations or where a long-standing minority party is actually challenging an entrenched but embattled majority party. Relatedly, in communities where relatively "closed" recruitment systems dominate the political landscape — whether because of one-partyism or excessively dominant factional control within each party in a two-party situation — persons embodying the social and political correlates associated with the highest level of political activism will not be encouraged to seek party or public offices because wider cooptation of potentially activist elites will be considered unnecessary.

Some Differences in the Political Socialization Patterns of Canadian and American Party Officials: A Preliminary Report*

Allan Kornberg
Joel Smith
David Bromley

This paper reports on selected aspects of an extensive comparative study of a major segment of an elite group of political actors in two metropolitan areas of the United States and Canada respectively—party officials and influentials, hereafter generally referred to as party "activists." Of particular interest have been the political socialization, the recruitment, the party careers of such activists, the patterns of relationships among these, and the factors that may help explain such patterns. The investigation has been pursued in a comparative framework consistent with two of the canons of the comparative method laid down by Emile Durkheim[1] (i.e., the comparison of subcultural differences within a particular society, and the comparison of societies generally alike but differing in certain aspects).

*This is a revised version of a paper presented at the annual meeting of the Canadian Political Science Association at Calgary, June 5-7, 1968. The research is supported by a grant from the National Science Foundation, GS-1134. We are indebted to Mr. Larry Suter, Department of Sociology and Anthropology, Duke University, for his assistance in preparing some of these data for analysis.

[1]Emile Durkheim, *Les règles de la méthode sociologique* (Paris, 1895), p. 139.

Reprinted from the *Canadian Journal of Political Science*, II (March, 1969), 64-88, by permission of the Canadian Science Association and the authors.

At this point, the research and related reports are, frankly, atheoretical, though, we hope, exploratory analyses such as this will lead to the formulation of testable theory. Until such analyses are possible, however, such reports are not without their relevance for certain matters of theoretical concern. For example, the paucity of systematic and quantitative comparative research generally, and the lack of such data on Canadian and American party activists in particular, justifies the study. Moreover, we shall be considering issues which fall within, and contribute to, what David Easton[2] in a recent article termed "system-persistence" theory. Parenthetically, since party officials generally have had ascribed to them the function of recruiting and electing the individuals[3] who help to attain and at times even to specify the goals of the larger society, this research may also bear on what Easton distinguishes as "allocative theory."[4] Thus, although this paper is a frankly empirical report of the early political socialization of 1257 party activists in Vancouver, Winnipeg, Seattle, and Minneapolis, it is theory-relevant although not theory-testing.

We shall first compare the social characteristics of Canadian and American party activists. Because Canadian society has been characterized as a mosaic,[5] and American society as a melting pot,[6] we would expect that the Canadian party activists would be a more heterogeneous group, symbolically representing the several social groups in their society, while the Americans would be more homogeneous. The reasoning that underlies this expectation is that in the melting pot those who rise to positions of importance will tend also to represent symbolically the anticipated ultimate synthesis of the

---

[2]"The Theoretical Relevance of Political Socialization," *Canadian Journal of Political Science*, I (June, 1968), 125-46. See also his *A Systems Analysis of Political Life* (New York, 1965) and *A Framework for Political Analysis* (Englewood Cliffs, 1965).

[3]For example, see Lewis Bowman and G. R. Boynton, "Recruitment Patterns among Local Party Officials: A Model and Some Preliminary Findings in Selected Locales," *American Political Science Review,* LX (1966), 667-76; and Frank Sorauf, *Party Politics in America* (Boston, 1968), 1-25.

[4]Because Easton's work is connected with the earlier work of Talcott Parsons in at least an evolutionary sense, similar references to the theoretical relevance of these materials could be made in Parsonian terms. Of course, the work of both builds on that of others and so this could become an exercise in endless references. The point is that the data do bear on matters of repeated and historical theoretical relevance.

[5]John Porter, *The Vertical Mosaic: An Analysis of Social Class and Power in Canada* (Toronto, 1965).

[6]The term derives from the title of Israel Zangwill's popular drama. Recently new attention has been stimulated by the study of Nathan Glazer and Daniel P. Moynihan, *Beyond the Melting Pot* (Cambridge, Mass., 1963).

on-going assimilative process, whereas in the mosaic those who become important will be the leaders of each of the markedly different and independent interest groups involved in the shifting coalitions in which power is aggregated and applied.

It would be unrealistic to expect such macro-characterizations to apply and give guidance in mechanical fashion. It has been argued, for example, that the process of the melting pot stops at a point subsequent to minimum accommodation and produces something like a frozen mosaic. John Porter, in considering Canada, argues that the mosaic is not a flat pattern comprised of equally powerful segments but has a vertical dimension that reflects differential power. Without torturing the implications of these observations, it could be shown that, from these points of view, the expectations regarding differences in heterogeneity and homogeneity between the two countries would be just the reverse of those stated above.

Still a third way of approaching this matter is to start with the premise that both societies are enough alike, and that the holding of high party position is a sufficiently exclusive and prestige-giving attainment, for differences between the two groups with respect to heterogeneity to become minimal — that is, both groups would tend to reflect the higher social strata of their populations. Major differences might occur only where there are structural differences that lead to differences in what is exclusive and bestows prestige (e.g., in Canada levels of both education and income tend to be lower than in the United States). Hence, while we have started with one hypothesis about societal differences that develops from what is perhaps the most prevalent view about the differences in the structures of the two societies, it is hard to hold it with much confidence. Our comparisons should clarify which of these three competing perspectives are most appropriate. Finally, it should be noted in this regard that our concern with societal differences does not obviate the fact that that there may also be differences between the officialdoms of the separate parties in both countries.[7]

After examining the social characteristics of our populations we shall consider selected aspects of political socialization (including the patterns of development of party identifications, first political awareness, and patterns of changing political interest) and the ap-

[7]See Joel Smith, Allan Kornberg, and David Bromley, "Patterns of Early Political Socialization and Adult Party Affiliation," *Canadian Review of Sociology and Anthropology*, V (Aug., 1968), 123-55; and Joel Smith and Allan Kornberg, "Awareness, Identification, and Interest as Aspects of the Political Socialization of Party Elites" (mimeographed).

proximate ages which define them. Howard Scarrow[8] has suggested that the relative political instability of Canadian party politics, particularly the sharp fluctuations in voter support for the several parties, can be explained in part by the fact that Canadians, in comparison to Americans, identify neither as frequently nor as faithfully with their parties. If his belief can be extrapolated to this select group of party officials, it seems reasonable to expect that Canadian party activists will identify with a party at a later age, and that their identification with a single party will be less constant than will the party identities of their American counterparts.

A third subject of concern will be the relative and differential contributions of various socializing agents to key developments in the process. Previous research suggests that these are still matters open to question. For example, Herbert Hyman,[9] while recognizing the importance of other agents, ascribed a preeminent position to the family. However, subsequent empirical investigations by Hess and Torney[10] and by Jennings and Niemi[11] have raised serious questions concerning the family's importance as a socializing agent. In so far as political actors are concerned, a comparative study of the development of political interest among Canadian MPs and American Congressmen[12] indicates that Canadians tend most frequently to cite the family, and American legislators the school, as the agent associated with the development of political interest. Since the majority of Canadian MPs tend to be active in local party organizations prior to becoming incumbents of parliamentary positions and, in fact, frequently use their positions in such organizations as vehicles for entry into the House of Commons,[13] we also might expect, at the risk of committing the ecological fallacy, the Canadian party activists more often than the Americans to cite the family as the agent that generated their interest in politics and public affairs. Finally, we shall try to assess the effects of the political characteristics of parents on both the early political socialization of the re-

---

[8]Howard A. Scarrow, "Distinguishing between Political Parties — The Case of Canada," *Midwest Journal of Political Science*, IX (1965), 61-76.

[9]Herbert H. Hyman, *Political Socialization* (Glencoe, 1961), 69-91.

[10]Robert D. Hess and Judith V. Torney, *The Development of Political Attitudes in Children* (Chicago, 1967).

[11]M. Kent Jennings and Richard G. Niemi, "The Transmission of Political Values from Parent to Child," *American Political Science Review*, LXII (1968), 169-84.

[12]Allan Kornberg and Norman C. Thomas, "The Political Socialization of National Legislative Elites in the United States and Canada," *Journal of Politics*, XXVII (1965), 761-75.

[13]See Allan Kornberg, *Canadian Legislative Behavior: A Study of the 25th Parliament* (New York, 1967).

spondents and their adult party careers, for studies of both party officials and mass publics have shown, respectively, that having parents who are active politically[14] and knowing which party they prefer[15] can have an important effect on one's adult political behaviour.

Before describing the measures that were employed, we should like to comment on the population being studied. The reasons for the selection of the four research sites are described in detail elsewhere, as is the rationale for trying to include a total population rather than a sample of holders of positions in the organizations above a certain level of scope and authority.[16] Very briefly, the Canadian sites were selected on the assumption that they contained viable New Democratic and Social Credit party organizations. The selection of the two American sites then was circumscribed by three requirements: demographic characteristics that approximated those of the Canadian cities; the presence of viable Republican party organizations after the Goldwater debacle of 1964; and the ability to establish productive contacts with local party leaders. Happily, the cities of Minneapolis and Seattle satisfied these requirements.

Rather than sample the several strata of the party organizations in each city, an effort was made to identify and to interview (*a*) all holders of offices in the formal party organizations from the level of Ward Leader in the United States and above the level of Poll Captain in Canada; and (*b*) all other party members deemed either by local party "knowledgeables" or by consensus of respondents holding formal party office as playing roles of at least equal importance.[17] Thus, except for those who were consistently unavailable or refused to be interviewed (both groups together being approximately 20 per cent of the total listed), the study population includes an elite of the "real" holders of power in the formal and informal party organizations. It also contains a substantial number of individuals who carry out the policy decisions made by the party leaders and who perform the routine but necessary maintenance tasks of any organization. However, it could be argued that even with the inclu-

---

[14]Dwaine Marvick and Charles Nixon, "Recruitment Contrasts in Rival Campaign Groups," in Dwaine Marvick, ed., *Political Decision-Makers: Recruitment and Performance* (Glencoe, 1961), 193-217.

[15]Philip E. Converse and George Dupieux, "Politicization of the Electorate in France and the United States," *Public Opinion Quarterly*, XXVI (1962), 1-24.

[16]Allan Kornberg and Joel Smith, "The Development of a Party Identification in a Political Elite" (mimeographed).

[17]A somewhat similar attempt to define a population of party activists in both the formal and informal organizations was made by Marvick and Nixon during their study of Los Angeles. See Marvick and Nixon, "Recruitment Contrasts."

sion of the latter group the interviewed group can be termed an elite simply because they are part of that select 2-4 per cent of the population in most Western societies whose involvement in political parties goes beyond mere membership or identification.[18] At any rate, to the extent that there are party organizations in these cities whose members engage in activities which have been described as necessary albeit not sufficient for maintaining democratic polities,[19] we are confident that the present study focuses on the people who give life to these organizations.

Methods and measures

The concept of political socialization as it is employed in political science research entails something far broader than simply becoming aware of significant others in one's environment. It is usually conceptualized as the process by which the individual acquires political values, attitudes, interests, and knowledge of the political community, the regime, its institutions, and incumbent leaders.[20] As such it is too broad to indicate relevant topics for study. These must be settled by questions in hand. For us, in addition to the effect of politicized parents, the problem leads to a concern with four other aspects of political socialization: the development and any subsequent changes in a psychological identification with a party[21]; the

---

[18]Lester Milbrath, *Political Participation* (Chicago, 1965), 21-2.

[19]Leon D. Epstein, *Political Parties in Western Democracies* (New York, 1967).

[20]Excellent surveys of the more recent literature on political socialization are currently available in Fred I. Greenstein, *Children and Politics* (New Haven, 1965); and Hess and Torney, *Development of Political Attitudes in Children.* Also see the bibliographical essay by Richard E. Dawson, "Political Socialization," in James A. Robinson, ed., *Political Science Annual, 1966* (New York, 1966); and the bibliography of published, unpublished, and research in progress, by Jack Dennis, "Recent Research on Political Socialization" (University of Wisconsin, mimeographed).

[21]The concept of a psychological identification with a party was first discussed in detail by George Belknap and Angus Campbell, "Political Party Identification and Attitudes toward Foreign Policy," *Public Opinion Quarterly*, XV (1951), 601-23. It was subsequently developed by Angus Campbell, Gerald Gurin, and Warren E. Miller, *The Voter Decides* (Evanston, 1954), 88-111; Angus Campbell and Homer C. Cooper, *Group Differences in Attitudes and Votes* (Ann Arbor, 1956), 38-61; and Angus Campbell, Philip E. Converse, Warren E. Miller, and Donald E. Stokes, *The American Voter* (New York, 1960), 120-67. For a review of some of the other literature, see Lewis Froman and James Skipper, "An Approach to the Learning of Party Identification," *Public Opinion Quarterly*, XXVII (1963), 473-85.

development of political awareness;[22] the development and change in the level of political interest;[23] and the agents[24] that help generate political interest and party identification. Identification is used here in the sense of "appropriation and commitment to a particular identity or series of identities,"[25] where the identification is the *content* of the role and status.[26] This use is in the symbolic interactionist rather than the Freudian sense and is reflected in various scholarly writings.[27]

Although political interest and political awareness are sometimes treated as though they develop simultaneously,[28] we do not accept this view. Rather, awareness is simply conceived as the state of knowing of the existence of something and may differ from the interest, which denotes a "caring about." The latter differs, in turn, from identification, which, as has already been indicated, is the sense of being at one with and is obviously a special psychological state. The world of sports provides a good setting in which it is conventional to distinguish the referents of these terms. Thus, one can be aware of sports without devoting any attention to them (awareness); one can follow what is going on by reading sports reports or attending sporting events (interest); but one may or may not be an avid "fan" of a team or individual (identification).

---

[22]In so far as awareness is concerned, the inference to be drawn from the studies of the political socialization of children such as those by Greenstein, and Hess and Torney, is that political awareness occurs relatively early in a child's life and varies with factors such as age, intelligence, and sex. The only present concern is with the age at which awareness of politics occurs.

[23]There has been considerably less research on political interest than on party identification. The principal finding to date is that an interest in politics can develop at any stage of the life cycle. See studies such as Heinz Eulau, "Recollections," in John C. Wahlke, *et al.*, *The Legislative System* (New York, 1962), 77-95; and Kornberg and Thomas, "Political Socialization of National Legislative Elites."

[24]In addition to the family and school, other important socializing agents that have been cited in the literature are peer groups (Karlsson); work experiences (Almond and Verba); cataclysmic events (Wright); and social conditions (Kornberg and Thomas).

[25]Nelson Foote, "Identification as the Basis for a Theory of Motivation," *American Sociological Review*, XVI (1951), 17.

[26]*Ibid.*, 16.

[27]See, for example, Helen M. Lynd, *On Shame and the Search for Identity* (New York, 1961); and Gregory P. Stone, "Appearance and the Self," in Arnold M. Rose, ed., *Human Behavior and Social Processes* (Boston, 1962), 86-118.

[28]See Kenneth Prewitt, Heinz Eulau, and Betty Zisk, "Political Socialization and Political Roles," *Public Opinion Quarterly*, XXX (Winter, 1966-67), 569-82.

In view of these distinctions, political awareness was ascertained by asking respondents: "Would you go back as far as you can remember to tell us two things. What is the first aspect of politics or public affairs that you were aware of? How old were you at the time?" With regard to identification, the approach was: "Suppose I were a poller who had been coming to see you each year from the time you were four, asking which political party you then identified with — that is, the party you were sympathetic and loyal to. Let's take this card and, if we start at when you were four, would you tell me where to draw this line to record your preference each year?" To delineate the agents associated with the development of a first and any later identifications, the respondents were asked: "Which of the two things on this card were important factors in the development/the change of your sympathies from the.................................. party to the............................party at age....................?"

Two questions were formulated (*a*) to ascertain the presence of an interest in politics and any noticeable changes in that interest during the period, and (*b*) to detect factors that may have been responsible for such changes. These questions were asked for as many periods between the beginning of high school and the start of the career in party work as were applicable in each person's case. For those persons who were not in school for all or some part of the period, equivalent ages of 14-18, 18-22, 22-26, and 26 and over were substituted. An interest typology then was derived from these response sets. For simplicity's sake, only the basic form of the question on interest is cited here: "During (your high school years) how would you describe the level of your interest in politics?" A card was presented which contained the following six options for choice:[29]

[29]Whenever any one of the last four alternatives was selected, a second card detailing various potential agents of change was presented and the respondents were asked whether any were important factors in the change. From an analysis of responses to the sets of "interest-change" questions for the appropriate age periods, we develop a typology of various courses of developing interest among current party functionaries. In anticipation of the difficulties that would be introduced into our analysis by low frequencies of occurrence, we based our typology on five circumstances that might obtain in each of four time periods. The typing started with the observation that some respondents entered the first period as workers, or early on in that period became workers. At the other extreme a considerable number answered all questions and even after age 26 had not become workers. The third group was somewhere in between. If the start of an active career is interpreted as the peak of a developing interest, then one aspect of the developing course of interest is how far through the adolescent-early adult period the respondent has passed without having started a career as a worker. With respect to the beginning of a career as a worker, then, three categories were recognized. Essentially, those who began as workers no later than the high school period were considered (1) early

"I had no interest in politics; I had an interest in politics, but it did not change appreciably; I had an interest in politics, and it increased considerably; I had an interest in politics, and it increased somewhat; I had an interest in politics, and it decreased somewhat; I had an interest in politics, and it decreased considerably."

We have had to rely on the respondents' recollections of all these events. The recognized hazards involved in this procedure probably are most succinctly outlined in a recent paper by Richard G. Niemi.[30] We were cognizant of these hazards during the construction of the survey instrument and, accordingly, included a number of probes to check the accuracy of the events and the time periods recalled by the respondents. Moreover, several models of systematic error and bias in recall also have been applied to the data as checks, and, fortunately, none of them fit. However, it is always *possible* that the data have been affected by recall error or bias in a manner

---

workers; those who began during either college or professional/graduate school periods were considered intermediate workers; and those whose careers started at a later period were considered late workers.

Two distinct types of intermediate workers with regard to interest were separated. In examining the responses for preceding periods of people whose careers began during these intermediate periods, it was apparent that some had had an interest for at least two of the preceding periods whereas others either did not report an interest at all before beginning work or reported one in only the preceding period. On this basis, we separated (2) intermediate workers with short-term interests from (3) intermediate workers with longer-term interests in politics.

By far the largest block of late workers also showed a restricted number of interest patterns. Like the intermediate workers they either reported active interests throughout the period or did not do so until they reached a somewhat more advanced period of age or schooling. Essentially, we found it feasible to distinguish those who reported an interest during every one of the four periods from those who reported no interest either for at least the first period, or for subsequent periods if they had reported an interest in the first period. Further examination of the reports of interest revealed that many of the interest patterns showed constant increases whereas others were characterized by one or more periods of unchanging interest at the end of the time periods covered by the questions. Therefore, taking both these matters into account, we also chose to distinguish four types of late workers: (4) those with a continuous rising interest; (5) those with a continuous stable interest; (6) those with a late but rising interest; and (7) those with a late but stable interest.

Reports of declines in interest have not been mentioned in setting up these types because there were very few of them. Whenever such reports occurred, they were set aside for later consideration. After inspecting them, it was decided that they could not be fitted to some of the other types as minor variants, but, rather, should be treated as a separate type of (8) extreme fluctuators. (See Figure 1 for summary of these types.) There is an additional category in Canada, respondents who reported no interest or virtually no interest in politics until, presumably, the eve of their entry into party work.

[30]Richard G. Niemi, "Collecting Information about the Family: A Problem in Survey Methodology" (mimeographed).

that still is not apparent. Having registered this caveat, we must still suggest that recall is the only realistic means currently available for studying the political socialization experiences of a fairly exclusive adult sub-population. Because there is no way of predicting which children eventually will become party activists, to study the process longitudinally by following a group of children through to the adult stage of life (in addition to taking up the better part of our own professional lifetime) would require support from an agency with the resources of Croesus and the patience of Job. Such research support, readers will agree, is difficult to find.

Socio-economic characteristics

An examination of the social origins and, particularly the current life status of this group of party activists reveals that neither the Canadians nor the Americans are "just plain folks." Rather, a substantial proportion, by their own admission, were raised in households which, by the standards of the time, could be described as "somewhat better than average" and/or "very well off." As a group, they were solidly upper middle class in their origins; fully 49 per cent of the Americans and 43 per cent of the Canadians had fathers who were either professionals or managers and proprietors of businesses. Conversely, only 12 per cent of the fathers of the American respondents and 13 per cent of the Canadians' fathers were semi-skilled, unskilled, and service workers. On the average, they had gone to school for considerably longer periods of time than other citizens in the communities of which they are a part.[31] A disproportionate number, in comparison to the general population of their communities, were professionals and proprietors or managers of business establishments. Perhaps the most striking indicator of the favoured positions they enjoyed *vis à vis* their fellow citizens is shown in Table 1 which compares family incomes taking into account the occupations of heads of households in each community.[32]

---

[31]Data not shown here are available upon request.

[32]Wherever possible these incomes as reported are the medians. Because we currently lack the comparable Canadian data, we have shown median incomes for party officials and average incomes for provincial populations. The average incomes, particularly for upper income categories, tend to be larger than are the median incomes for these categories. Thus, in this respect the comparisons we are making actually favour the cross-sectional populations. Fortunately, our American data permit us to make direct comparisons of median incomes for party officials and for the county rather than for the state as a whole.

TABLE 1
A Comparison of the Median Incomes of Party Activists and Average Incomes of Cross-Sections of Population in the Several Occupations

	Occupation of Head of Household					
	Professional	Managerial	Clerical	Sales	Skilled	Non-skilled
Vancouver						
Party officials' median family income	$13,028	$11,830	$7,043	$9,671	$8,000	$6,650
British Columbia average family earnings	$ 6,882	$ 7,421	$5,003	$5,542	$5,006	$4,629
Percent by which median exceeds provincial average	89.4%	59.4%	40.8%	74.5%	59.8%	43.7%
N	114	119	21	40	26	32
Winnipeg						
Party officials' median family income	$14,065	$11,930	$6,459	$10,625	$8,126	$6,622
Manitoba average family earnings	$ 6,617	$ 7,297	$4,778	$ 5,408	$4,515	$4,421
Percent by which median exceeds provincial average	112.6%	63.5%	35.2%	96.5%	80.0%	49.8%
N	97	83	18	13	25	16
Minneapolis						
Party officials' median family income	$17,028	$16,768	$7,028	$13,500	$10,714	
Hennepin County average family earnings	$ 8,542	$ 9,482	$6,484	$ 7,966	$ 7,278	
Percent by which median exceeds county average	99.3%	76.8%	8.4%	69.5%	47.2%	*
N	123	104	114	31	17	
Seattle						
Party officials' median family income	$16,328	$15,356	$10,000	$15,937	$10,000	
King County average family earnings	$ 9,021	$ 9,374	$ 6,552	$ 8,025	$ 7,314	
Percent by which median exceeds county average	81.0%	63.8%	52.6%	98.6%	36.7%	*
N	117	103	18	26	23	

SOURCES: *Census of Canada, 1961*, "Households and Families," Vol. III, Part 1, Bulletin 2, 1-9, Table 81. US Bureau of the Census, *Census of Population, 1960*, "Detailed Characteristics," PC(1)D(Minnesota and Washington), Table 145; US Summary, Table 230; and US Bureau of the Census, *Current Population Reports*, Series P-60, Table 4.

*Too few non-skilled heads of households to calculate.

Even if the community incomes are adjusted for the general increase in incomes that has occurred since 1960, it seems clear that the annual incomes of Canadian party officials in the various occupational categories, other than clerical and less-than-skilled, exceed the incomes of occupational counterparts in their respective provinces; and the incomes of Minneapolis party activists in all but the clerical group and of the Seattle officials in all but the lowest status group are higher than the comparable community averages.

With regard to the three homogeneity-hetereogeneity theses described above, inspection of the data in Table 2 indicates that they really do not support either of the first two expectations. That is, one group is not clearly more homogeneous or hetereogeneous than the other. The only thing that can be said with some assurance is that both groups of activists tend to overrepresent the higher social strata of their populations. Despite the permeability of the lower levels of party organizations in the United States and Canada (individuals move in and out of the lower levels of organizations so easily that officials are usually unable to identify most of them), it appears that the holding of high party office remains so sufficiently special that it tends to be denied to people of relatively low status. As was indicated, the study population, in theory, includes the incumbents of all such positions in the four cities. Thus, the differences between the two groups with respect to relative hetereogeneity tend to be minimal.

The substantial current differences which can be observed in the educational attainments and family incomes of the Canadian and American party activists reflect general societal differences in living standards rather than differential selectivity in recruitment. Their essentially similar socio-economic origins tend to support a point made in a recent macro-analysis of the United States and Canada by Nathan Keyfitz.[33] The more favourable economic position of Americans, in great part, is a function of the longer education Americans enjoy.[34] And, although over the years the length of formal education has been increasing in both countries, the American increase has been substantially larger. In fact, as Keyfitz points out,[35] the differences between the two countries are presently such that

---

[33]Nathan Keyfitz, "Human Resources," in Richard Leach, ed., *Contemporary Canada* (Durham, NC, 1968), pp. 10-31.

[34]J. J. Servan-Schreiber also points to the superiority of the American educational system as the most crucial difference between Americans and Europeans — a difference upon which American economic hegemony ultimately rests. See J. J. Servan-Schreiber, *The American Challenge* (New York, 1968).

[35]Keyfitz, "Human Resources," pp. 26-29.

young Canadians in the sixties actually are at a greater disadvantage than were their countrymen of a generation ago.

TABLE 2
PERSONAL AND SOCIO-ECONOMIC CHARACTERISTICS OF CANADIAN AND AMERICAN PARTY ACTIVISTS (PERCENTAGES)

VARIABLE	CANADIANS	AMERICANS
Sex:		
Males	81.1	66.6
Females	18.9	33.4
Region:		
Protestant	62.1	69.9
Catholic	14.3	19.7
Jewish	4.5	4.2
None	19.0	6.3
Age:		
29 years and under	8.2	8.6
30-34 years	10.7	14.9
35-44 years	33.2	36.3
45-54 years	24.5	22.0
55 and over	22.9	18.0
Relative class of family of origin:		
Below average to destitute	21.5	24.4
Average	44.4	37.7
Better than average to very well off	34.4	37.9
Respondent's father's occupation:		
Professional	14.2	19.0
Proprietors, managers, officials	28.9	30.1
Clerical and sales	10.2	11.1
Farmers	15.8	12.8
Skilled craftsmen	18.6	13.6
Semi-skilled, unskilled, and services	12.3	12.8
Respondent's education:		
High school and less	62.1	26.7
College 1-3 years	14.3	18.9
College graduate	4.5	25.4
Post-baccalaureate (graduate and/or professional school)	19.1	29.0
Occupation of head of household:		
Professional	33.8	38.1
Proprietors, managers, officials	31.3	34.3
Clerical and sales	14.7	13.6
Skilled to service workers	8.1	9.4
Less than skilled, and not in labour force	12.0	4.6
Annual family income:		
Under $10,000	48.2	22.4
$10,000 to $12,499	17.4	17.3
$12,500 to $17,499	15.5	25.7
$17,500 to $24,999	10.6	22.3
$25,000 and over	8.3	12.3
N	625	627

Identification, awareness, and interest as aspects of political socialization

While the data thus far considered suggest that the major party activists in both countries emerge from the same higher social strata, to the extent that societal differences permit, it does not necessarily follow that they tread the same paths to their current positions of eminence. For information on this matter we look to their reports of their personal political developments with respect to political awareness, interest, and identification.

Angus Campbell and his colleagues have shown that for most Americans a psychological identification with the party develops early in life, and that, once it occurs, an identification with either of the two major parties tends to be held with remarkable constancy. Until recently, comparable Canadian data were unavailable. Consequently, Howard Scarrow was speculating when he suggested that the relative instability of Canadian party politics could be explained in part by the failure of Canadians to identify as frequently or as faithfully with their parties as do Americans. Happily, the work of John Meisel has begun to fill this void. The 1965 study of the Canadian electorate done by Meisel and his associates indicates that approximately 77 per cent of a national population sample identified with one of the four major parties.[36] In 1964, 75 per cent of Americans were Democratic or Republican identifiers.[37] Contrary to Scarrow's expectations, then, approximately the same proportions of Canadians[38] as Americans are identified with a party. However, as

---

[36]The question Meisel employed was: "Generally speaking, do you usually think of yourself as Conservative, Liberal, Social Credit, Creditiste, NDP, Union Nationale, or what?" The survey to which we refer was initiated by Meisel and carried out by him and P. E. Converse, M. Pinard, P. Regenstreif, and M. A. Schwartz. The results have not yet been published and we are grateful to Meisel and his associates for making the data available.

[37]The question employed by Campbell and his associates of the Survey Research Center to delineate adult party identifications is the now-familiar, "Generally speaking, do you usually think of yourself as a Republican, a Democrat, an Independent, or what? (If Republican or Democrat) Would you call yourself a strong (R) (D) or a not very strong (R) (D)? (If Independent) Do you think of yourself as closer to the Republican or Democratic Party?"

[38]Fully 63 per cent of Meisel's sample identified with the two major Canadian parties; 10.1 per cent were NDP identifiers; 5.6 per cent were Social Credit-Creditiste identifiers; approximately 1 per cent identified with the Union Nationale and "other" parties; 17 per cent said no party; and the remaining 3 per cent "did not know." When the 20 per cent who did not identify were asked: "Well, do you generally think of yourself as a little closer to one of the parties than the other? (If 'yes') Which party?" only 10.6 per cent said 'no.' This group approximates the 9-10 per cent of Americans who, when probed, say they are "Independents," and do not "lean" toward either the Democrats or Republicans.

Scarrow *had predicted*, Canadians are less constant in their identifications. Thus, although approximately 76 per cent of a 1964 American sample[39] had never changed their partisan identification, only 49 per cent of those interviewed in the 1965 study by Meisel and his colleagues had never changed. Further, among the Canadians, only 58 per cent now identify with a single party at *both* the national and provincial levels, and they constitute only 46 per cent of those with a partisan identification.

The tendency to identify with more than one party can be observed among the Canadian party activists. Their average age of first identification also was higher than the American — 14.8 years versus 11.6 years. As might be expected, unlike the general public, all the officials currently accept a party label. Both groups of activists also are similar in that there was approximately a ten-year period, on the average, between an initial identification and any subsequent switches. Since individuals who changed identifications one or more times probably needed to start identifying at an earlier age in order to squeeze a checkered identification history into a relatively short career, we find that the propensity to change tends to be inversely related to the mean ages of first identifications among both groups — the more changes, the lower the age of identification (see Table 3).

Such movement, of course, rarely results in any basic realignment of party strength in general, although it certainly may strongly affect the outcome of particular electoral contests. The taking on of a new identity is not an asymmetrical process. Agents of particular personal relevance (e.g., marriage, taking a new job) that lead an individual to change in one direction may move another the opposite way, so that at any time, even though the proportion of people changing identifications may become quite large, any net changes in prevailing attitudes are likely to be insignificant. In contrast, cataclysmic social events which may also serve as agents, such as depressions or wars, can be experienced simultaneously by whole nations. Such events, if they are of sufficient duration, may have important political consequences; they can move large groups, even whole classes of people, from one party to another without offsetting movements in other directions. Although politics may rank fairly low in a hierarchy of interests, even for party activists, specifically political events such as elections[40] (if the feelings they arouse

---

[39]These percentages are calculated from the totals contained in the code book for the 1964 national election study conducted by the Survey Research Center of the University of Michigan and made available through the Inter-University Consortium for Political Research.

[40]V. O. Key, "A Theory of Critical Elections," *Journal of Politics,* XVII (1955), 3-18.

TABLE 3
MEAN AGES OF FIRST IDENTIFICATIONS AND SUBSEQUENT CHANGES OF CANADIAN AND AMERICAN PARTY OFFICIALS

NUMBER OF IDENTIFICATIONS	PER-CENTAGE	MEAN AGE FIRST IDENT.	MEAN AGE FIRST CHANGE	MEAN AGE SECOND CHANGE	MEAN AGE THIRD CHANGE	MEAN AGE FOURTH CHANGE	MEAN AGE FIFTH CHANGE
Canadian party officials ($N=614$)							
1 identification only	60%	15.5 years					
1 change	24	14.3	25.0				
2 changes	11	13.7	21.9	26.8			
3 changes	5	9.9	17.9	23.0	27.4		
4 changes	*	14.5	20.0	21.5	23.0	27.5	
5 changes	*	9.0	16.5	21.0	25.0	27.5	33.5
American party officials ($N=626$)							
1 identification only	68%	11.8 years					
1 change	16	11.8	23.5				
2 changes	12	9.7	20.0	24.7			
3 changes	2	11.3	16.3	22.1	26.9		
4 changes	1	9.7	17.0	18.3	23.0	24.3	
5 changes	*	6.0	8.0	9.0	11.0	19.0	20.0

*Less than 1 per cent.

are sufficiently widespread and intense) also can produce significant changes in the balance of partisan forces. That the elections following the Civil War generated a "normal" Republican majority that endured until 1932 is accepted by most students of American voting behaviour. The "Grand Coalition" put together by Roosevelt that year resulted in a Democratic majority that may even survive the Great Society and the predatory incursions of Eugene McCarthy on the Left and George Wallace on the Right. Thus, despite the rarity of really fundamental partisan realignments, critical elections such as those of 1896 and 1912, figures such as Presidents Eisenhower and Kennedy, and critical events such as the Korean and Vietnamese wars periodically have detached fairly large segments of the electorate from partisan moorings that have their origins in the families and a specific social milieus.

Similar events and conditions can be pointed to in Canada. For example, critical elections such as those of 1911, 1935, 1958, and 1968, events such as the Manitoba schools controversy and the conscription crises, and charismatic figures such as Diefenbaker and Trudeau have probably induced substantial numbers of Canadians to change their party identities; and catastrophies such as the Second World War and the Great Depression have helped align the electorate in a Liberal plurality which, while atrophied, continues to endure. These generalizations are fairly well supported by the data delineating the agents recalled by respondents as being intimately associated with the development of and subsequent changes in their identifications with parties (see Table 4).

For example, they indicate that the initial partisan identifications of a majority of both groups of activists had their origins in the nuclear and extended family, here termed "kin." Somewhat surprisingly, since Kornberg and Thomas reported in their paper on Canadian parliamentary and American Congressional leaders that the responses of the former more often than the latter revealed a conscious attempt on the part of families to indoctrinate partisan affiliations and attitudes, we found that fewer (54 per cent) Canadian than American (69 per cent) party officials cited "kin" as the agent involved in their first partisan identification. Nor can this difference be attributed simply to the fact that the Canadians, on the average, first identify with a party at a later age when influences outside the family are more likely to become operative, since it persists even when the differential effect of age, which is negatively related to the citing of kin, is controlled. However, the fact that Canadian party officials tend to cite family less frequently than the Canadian parliamentary leaders referred to above may simply reflect the overlapping populations involved; although a majority of Canadian members of Parliament at some time have held an office in their party organizations, not all party officials become members of Parliament. In addition to "kin," four other general categories of socializing agents were named; peer groups (school friends and schoolmates, non-school friends, neighbours, and acquaintances); experiences and activities (with teachers and teaching materials, with religious functionaries and religious activities, with recreational, fraternal, and work groups, and with work experiences); public figures (such as presidents, prime ministers, members of Parliament and Congress, cabinet officials, military leaders, and bureaucratic officials); and public events(such as the Second World War, the Depression, public meetings, and political campaigns). Of these, the latter two categories were most frequently and consistently mentioned. School-related agents were most important during high school and undergraduate days, although the Canadians were less inclined to cite these as factors involved in identity changes. Indicative of the broad importance of the various peer groups as socializing agents[41] was the fairly consistent tendency to cite them as

[41]Peer groups are also fairly important socializing agents in Sweden. See Georg Karlsson, "Political Attitudes among Male Swedish Youth," *Acta Sociologica,* fasc. III (1958), 236.

TABLE 4

AGENTS ASSOCIATED WITH THE DEVELOPMENT AND CHANGES IN PARTISAN IDENTIFICATIONS CITED BY CANADIAN AND AMERICAN PARTY OFFICIALS (PERCENTAGES)

	Kin	Friends and Neigh-bours	School Friends	School Materials	School Teachers	Work	Religion	Recre-ation	Public Figures	Public Events	Other
First identification											
Can. (N=614)	54	26	7	5	9	6	6	4	33	25	10
Amer. (N=622*)	69	27	11	5	10	5	3	3	28	26	5
First change											
Can. (N=241)	17	23	9	4	7	10	5	4	38	34	28
Amer. (N=211)	19	22	11	10	16	15	3	5	44	37	22
Second change											
Can. (N=96)	9	28	4	4	4	18	3	3	41	32	30
Amer. (N=101)	13	17	9	4	18	16	1	4	44	38	24
Third change											
Can. (N=29)	10	31	3	7	3	21	3	7	55	45	41
Amer. (N=23)	17	17	9	13	17	22	—	4	48	26	30
Fourth change											
Can. (N=4)	—	—	—	—	—	—	—	—	25	75	25
Amer. (N=5)	20	—	—	20	—	—	20	20	40	80	60

*Numbers are less than the total because of missing informatiion.

TABLE 5

Agents Associated with Changes in Political Interest Cited by Canadian and American Party Officials (Percentages)

Time periods	Kin	Friends and neigh-bours	School friends	School materials	School teachers	Work	Religion	Recre-ation	Public figures	Public events
High School Equivalent										
Can. ($N=257$)	35	13	19	14	25	8	6	9	29	44
Amer. ($N=218$)	16	5	10	13	18	2	3	4	19	27
College Equivalent										
Can. ($N=288$)	16	13	19	12	9	21	4	12	40	42
Amer. ($N=268$)	9	7	15	13	13	12	3	6	22	30
Grad./Prof. Equivalent										
Can. ($N=241$)	15	16	10	6	8	26	4	6	40	39
Amer. ($N=247$)	9	10	7	6	5	15	2	4	22	26
26 years and over										
Can. ($N=269$)	15	21	2	2	3	27	5	8	47	46
Amer. ($N=274$)	18	28	1	5	3	34	6	10	50	55

factors involved in both the development and change in partisan identity and interest levels. (See Tables 4 and 5).

Although there were a few fairly substantial cross-national differences in terms of the various agents cited, the similarities were more impressive. Among both groups of officials, social events and conditions are more important socializing agents, seemingly, than personal experiences. This finding is consonant with that of Campbell and his colleagues who, in studying the 1956 American electorate, were struck by the fact that only a small proportion of the individuals who had identified with a different party than their current one explained the change in terms of personal experiences such as a new job, a change of residence, or meeting new friends.[42] Further, for both Canadians and Americans, the principal importance of the family appears to be in transmitting a partisan identification. This finding again is consistent with more recently reported research on the political socialization of public school children and of high school students and their parents. The influence of parents is a subject to which we will return. Not unexpectedly perhaps, but yet important to demonstrate, the kinds of agents cited by both groups of party activists do vary with the life cycle. That is, as the individual ages and becomes exposed to, and aware of, the world outside of his family and school, the frequency with which he cites family and school-oriented agents declines while his public events, public figures, and work-related experiences are increasingly mentioned. Of particular interest is the fact that religious figures and experiences are rarely cited as socializing agents. Whether this finding would be replicated in a less secular social environment such as in Quebec or Louisiana is worth exploring.

The manner in which political interest develops and then rises and falls also is relatively similar for both American and Canadian activists. As is indicated in Figure 1 and Table 6, a majority of both the Canadian and American party activists were interested in politics long before they became active in a political party. For most of these, the level of their interest either remained stable or rose gradually over the years. The interest of a small number (type 8) periodically surged and declined rather sharply, and although these individuals constitute only a very small proportion of the officials in each country, their interest patterns are important to delineate because they and the Canadian type 9 — individuals with virtually no interest — probably are characteristic of a majority of the population of both countries. Despite the fact that we lack really com-

[42]See Campbell, *et al.*, *The American Voter*, p. 50.

parable data, the weight of empirical evidence[43] suggests that in both countries the activities of politicians go virtually unnoticed. Short of scandal, only occasionally does a public figure impinge on the consciousness of the average citizen or a public policy become sufficiently salient for him so that it is of concern for even a brief interval. We may infer then, that one factor that sets party activists apart from their general populations is a sustained and relatively intense interest in public affairs.

Going a step further, one can speculate that a sustained and intense interest may well be a common (although obviously neither a necessary nor sufficient) condition for becoming politically active. In fact, if one can conceptualize the awareness-interest-identification triad as a socialization process through which all activists necessarily pass, one could assume that this is both a reasonable and the actual sequence in which these events are experienced. In part, the data contradict this belief. In a cohort of emerging party officials developing politically through time, the hierarchy seems to be a sequence of realizing that something exists (political awareness), associating oneself with a particular party or, in the case of independents, with a particular position (partisan identification), and subsequently developing more than a passing curiosity about the political world (political interest). This in itself is worthy of note. One might ordinarily expect identification with referent objects to

---

[43]For example, Campbell, *et al.* found that only 27 per cent of a 1956 sample of the American electorate were in the "highly involved" position of a political involvement index. The index is based on responses to questions concerning the respondent's interest in following the 1956 presidential campaign and concern about its outcome. Four years later, 26 per cent said they cared "very much" which party won the presidential election, and 19 per cent said they followed politics "very closely" between campaigns. During the 1964 campaign, 38 per cent said they were "very much interested" in the campaign and another 30 per cent claimed they followed what was going on in government "all the time." These figures compare very closely to the data gathered by John Meisel in his 1965 national electoral study. Only 26 per cent of the Canadian sample said they cared "a good deal" about what was going on in politics. Nor is the situation different in other Western countries. Almond and Verba found about the same level of political apathy in Great Britain, more in West Germany, and especially apathetic populations in Italy and Mexico.

Thus, although Lester Milbrath was describing only the American public, his characterization is probably highly appropriate for Canada and most other Western democracies as well. According to Milbrath, "About one-third of the American adult population can be characterized as politically apathetic or passive; in most cases, they are unaware, literally, of the political part of the world around them. Another 60 per cent play largely spectator roles in the political process; they watch, they cheer, they vote, but they do not battle. In the purest sense of the word, probably only 1 or 2 per cent could be called gladiators." See *Political Participation*, p. 21.

FIGURE 1

TYPES OF PATTERNS OF REPORTS OF DEVELOPING POLITICAL INTEREST

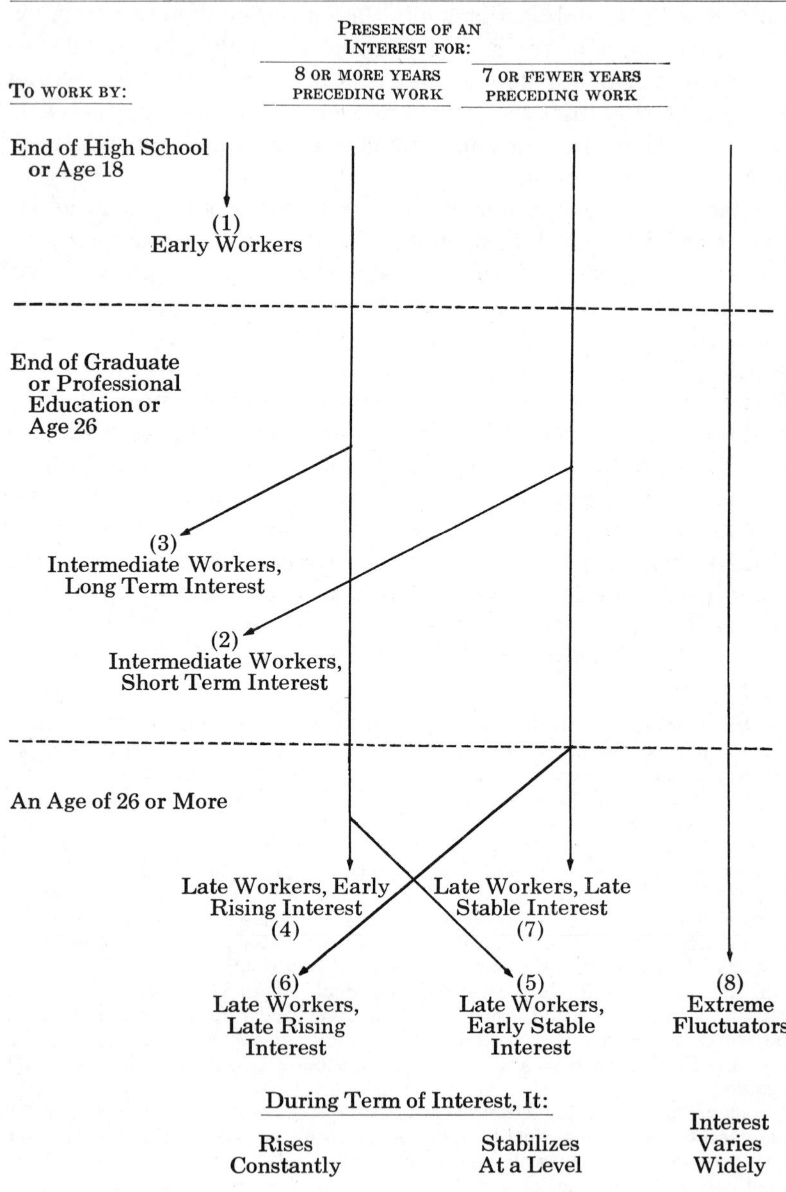

occur for objects in areas of interest *only after these areas of interest have been developed.* The findings suggest that, at least as regards the area of politics and the two groups of party activists, this is not the case. Frequently, objects (i.e., parties) are invested with affective sentiments (i.e., partisan identifications are formed) without the prior existence of interest in the domain of objects. This is

TABLE 6
TYPES OF ADOLESCENT-EARLY ADULT POLITICAL INTEREST PATTERNS REPORTED BY PARTY ACTIVISTS IN CANADA AND THE UNITED STATES

	CANADA		UNITED STATES	
TYPES OF PATTERNS	*N*	%	*N*	%
1. Early workers	80	13%	54	9%
2. Intermediate workers, short-term interest	39	6	33	5
3. Intermediate workers, long-term interest	136	22	124	20
4. Late workers, early rising interest	134	21	183	30
5. Late workers, early stable interest	45	7	48	8
6. Late workers, late rising interest	110	18	92	15
7. Late workers, late stable interest	28	4	48	8
8. Extreme fluctuators	40	6	34	5
9. No interest	13	2	—	—
Total	625	100%	616*	100%

*Missing cases due to incomplete data.

TABLE 7
PROPORTIONS OF CANADIAN AND AMERICAN PARTY ACTIVISTS WITH POLITICAL AWARENESS, POLITICAL IDENTITIES, AND POLITICAL INTERESTS BY AGE 18 ACCORDING TO AGE OF BEGINNING PARTY WORK

	PERCENTAGE WHO BY 18 ARE:		
AGE OF STARTING TO WORK FOR A PARTY	AWARE	IDENTIFIED	INTERESTED
Canadians			
18 years or less	100	96	100
19-25 years	92	75	79
26 years or more	92	74	63
Americans			
18 years or less	98	93	98
19-25 years	95	84	81
26 years or more	98	77	67

reflected in Table 7 which shows that, for both groups, the later the period of going to work for a party, the more does the development of interest lag in comparison with awareness and identification. A relatively high level of interest, then, appears to be the last rather than the second threshold necessary for party work.

The table hides the additional fact that a substantial number of American party activists and a smaller proportion of Canadians also identified with a party before they actually become politically aware. Virtually similar proportions report awareness and identification occurring in the same year (see Table 8). Previous research has indicated that a psychological identification with a party first develops as an affective attachment to a symbol rather than as a consequence of a rational evaluative calculus.[44] That is, for a large percentage of the American public, what becomes a life-long attachment is assumed at a time when political information is almost totally lacking. To the extent that this identification subsequently serves them as a surrogate ideology,[45] it seems to introduce an element of irrationality to the political process.

TABLE 8

Age of First Identification by First Awareness for Canadian and American Party Activists (Percentages)

	Canadian party activists	American party activists
Identification before awareness	12	23
Identification and awareness in same year	39	42
Identification after awareness	49	34

Any such irrationality as may be suggested by the fact that identifications can precede awareness and/or interest might be thought to be more prevalent in the United States than in Canada because

[44]Herbert Hyman noted that party affiliation develops without much cognitive content. See *Political Socialization*, 46. And Greenstein writes, "Party identifications probably develop without much explicit teaching on the part of parents, more or less in the form of a gradual awareness by the child of something which is part of him." See *Children in Politics*, p. 73.

[45]A partisan identification seemingly functions as a kind of conceptual net that permits individuals to organize and evaluate whatever incoming political information they receive. See Donald E. Stokes, "Party Loyalty and the Likelihood of Deviating Elections," *Journal of Politics*, XXIV (1963), 689-702.

Americans report an average age of first identification earlier enough to imply that their reports are more likely to recall experiences which are affective and devoid of political substance. However, other aspects of the data suggesting irrationality in the process contradict any such conclusion concerning differences between the two countries. For one thing, the pattern of identifications forming prior interest is equally prevalent in both. For another, the rate of identification-switches (if switches may be taken to indicate a certain degree of emptiness and frivolity in the earlier attachment) for Canadians is like that of Americans. They simply occur later. If anything, since ages reported for most of these events in Canada are higher, the data seem to bear more on differences in the extent to which politics suffuse the entire social environments in the two countries than on differences between them in the degree of rationality in the socialization processes. The later ages at which all of the events considered here are reported by Canadians, then, are perhaps simply repeated indicators of a less politicized social environment.

Parental influences

The assumption (anchored in the Freudian theory of personality) that childhood experiences in the family strongly affect the formation of attitudes and behavior patterns of adults has long been held by social psychologists, sociologists, and, more recently, political scientists who have studied the process of political socialization as it occurs among children.[46] Some political scientists while conceding that the family generally transmits a partisan identification to the child, have argued that much of the child's political information and many of his values and attitudes toward the political world and its

[46]See, for example, the review of early literature by Irvin L. Child, "Socialization," in Gardner Lindzey, ed., *Handbook of Social Psychology*, II (Cambridge, Mass., 1959), pp. 655-92. See, also, Frederick Elkin, *The Child and Society: The Process of Socialization* (New York, 1960); H. H. Remmers, "Early Socialization of Attitudes," in Eugene Burdick and Arthur Brodbeck, eds., *American Voting Behavior* (Glencoe, 1959), pp. 55-67; Robert E. Lane, "Fathers and Sons: Foundations of Political Behavior," *American Sociological Review*, XXIV (1959), 502-11; Herbert McCloskey and Harold E. Dahlgren, "Primary Group Influence on Party Loyalty," *American Political Science Review*, LVIII (1959), 361-82; Greenstein, *Children in Politics*; Hess and Torney, *Development of Political Attitudes in Children*; James E. Davies, "The Family's Role in Political Socialization," and Frank Pinner, "Parental Overprotection and Political Distrust," both in *Annals of the American Academy of Political and Social Science* (1965), pp. 10-19 and 58-70.

actors are produced in and by the public school. Hess and Torney,[47] in particular, have pointed to the American public school as the most important instrument, at least potentially, of political socialization. Their findings and others by Karlsson,[48] Abramson,[49] and Jennings and Niemi[50] support, although at times obliquely, the contention by Almond and Verba that although "family experiences do play a role in the formation of political attitudes . . . the gap between the family and the polity may be so wide that other social experiences, especially in social situations closer in time and structure to the political system, may play a larger role."[51] The data on the agents associated with changes in partisan identification and political interest levels presented previously also tend to support this assumption — to the extent that agents such as public figures and public events are mentioned more frequently by party activists than the family. Here, however, we are concerned with assessing the impact that politicized parents have on both initial political awareness and identification, events that occur relatively early in the lives of most respondents, and political party work, an adult activity for most.

Marvick and Nixon were struck by the extent of parental political activity reported by Los Angeles party officials and, especially, by the fact that a disproportionate number of party influentials tended to have had politically active parents. According to them, in "both parties, campaign-workers with politically active parents were much more likely to be in the ranks of the powerful than were workers whose parents were not active. The inference, of course, is that for volunteer politics the politicized family may be a crucial training ground for future campaign workers."[52] They concluded that the concept of the politicized family needs to be more fully developed. Abrams and Little[53] also were impressed with how politically involved were the parents of the young British party activists whom they studied. Research by Converse and Dupeux[54] suggests another

---

[47]Hess and Torney, *Development of Political Attitudes in Children*, pp. 212-25.

[48]Karlsson, "Political Attitudes among Male Swedish Youth."

[49]Paul Abramson, "The Differential Political Socialization of English Secondary School Students," *Sociology of Education*, XL (1967), 246-69.

[50]Jennings and Niemi, "The Transmission of Political Values."

[51]Gabriel A. Almond and Sidney Verba, *The Civic Culture* (Princeton, 1963), p. 373.

[52]Marvick and Nixon, "Recruitment Contrasts," 209.

[53]Philip Abrams and Alan Little, "The Young Activists in British Politics," *British Journal of Sociology*, XVI (1965), 315-32.

[54]Converse and Dupieux, "Politivization of the Electorate in France and the United States," 9-15.

aspect of politics in the family that requires study: they found that knowing which political party one's father prefers can have important consequences for adult political behaviour.

In thinking about how the concept of the politicized family can be developed as Marvick and Nixon suggest, there appears to be a conceptual difference with regard to the development of the child's political being in the two aspects of the parental role model revealed by the separate matters of parental party support and parental political activity. Activity is public and, hence, visible. It may be assumed by the parent to carry its own message to the offspring. But, regardless of whether it does, it is directed first to the outside world and, perhaps, only incidentally to the child. Parental party preference, in contrast, if it is known about, must have been communicated. Hence, when adults are able to report parents' party preference they also are reporting some active effort on the part of the parent that must have fallen within the child's sphere of perception and cognition. In this special sense, unlike work (the import of which may only be incidentally conveyed to the child), a parent's party preference is directly conveyed to the child. As such, it actually may provide more of an object lesson than would involvement in the "gutwork" of politics and, conversely, not knowing the preferences of both parents might be thought to be a real detriment to early political socialization and political party activity. We were able to isolate this group of individuals, and will report on them below. The more frequently employed measure of homogeneity was obtained by dividing the respondents between those who reported that both parents supported the same party, regardless of what that party was, and those who said that their parents supported different parties, or else, said their parents were not interested in politics, or were not alive (when they first became politically aware), or did not know which party their parents preferred. With respect to party activism, we have classified any respondent who reported that one or both parents either held a party office, engaged in campaign work, talked informally in favour of a party," or, engaged in other overtly partisan activities, as "politically active." They are distinguished from respondents who said their parents never did these things or did not know whether their parents engaged in such activities.

Analysis indicates that a smaller proportion of Canadian than American party activists reported that their parents supported the same party — 51 per cent versus 68 per cent. Similarly, 47 per cent of the Americans but only 35 per cent of the Canadians had one or more parents who can be characterized as politically active. In terms of these two gross measures, then, the Canadian party officials appear to have been raised in less politicized families than were the Americans. In fact, if either the respondent's failure to know his parents' partisan preference or the fact that they had none also can be taken as indicators of less politicized family environments, than the Canadian party leaders clearly emerged from the less politicized environments. Fourteen per cent of them but only 5 per cent of the Americans report that to their knowledge neither parent had a party preference. Another 17 per cent of the Canadians could not report a preference for one parent, in contrast to 9 per cent of the Americans. In all, 31 per cent of the Canadians are totally or partially unaware of paternal political preferences whereas only 15 per cent of the Americans are in this condition.[55] The joint effect of these differences is that Canadians more frequently report "apolitical" family origins — in the sense that the parents were neither active nor supported the same parties (43 per cent versus 23 per cent) whereas the Americans more frequently report the inverse conditions (38 per cent versus 28 per cent).

The data in Table 9 which show that Canadians (a) report becoming politically aware and identify with a party later than do the Americans; (b) take longer to go to work after finishing their formal schooling; and (c) have shorter continuous party careers in their current parties than their American counterparts, reflect both the joint affect of homogeneity and activity as well as the differential cross-national frequencies with respect to these two dimensions of politicalization. These data do support a previous suggestion that the road along which Canadian party officials pass in their journey from becoming aware of the political world to becoming active in the party is relatively the same as that taken by the Americans. The essential difference is that the Canadians seem to postpone making the trip.

Although the data also indicate that being raised in a politicized environment generally affected the Americans more than the Canadians, they do not show the separate effect of homogeneity and activity when each variable's effect on the other is controlled. In Table 10, therefore, we examined the role of parental agreement on party preference and parental political activity *separately under each condition of the other variable*. Here the first column of each set of three shows the difference in mean number of years that is attributable to the presence of the facilitative factor *irrespective of*

[55]Converse and Dupieux found that 86 per cent of a cross-sectional sample of the American electorate knew at least their father's party preference, but only 26 per cent of a French sample were similarly informed. See *ibid.*, p. 12.

TABLE 9

Average Ages of Moving to a Career as a Party Official as Related to Parental Agreement on Party Preference and Political Activity

	Parent(s) active		Parents' party preference		Parent(s) active		Parent(s) inactive		
	Yes	No	Same	Different	Support same party	Support different party	Support same party	Support different party	Total
Age of first awareness									
US	9.2	11.5	9.3	12.7	9.0	10.0	9.8	13.7	10.4
Canada	10.0	11.9	10.4	12.0	10.1	9.5	10.9	12.4	11.2
Age of first identification									
US	9.8	13.1	10.1	14.6	9.3	11.1	11.9	15.7	11.6
Canada	12.6	15.9	13.4	16.2	12.5	13.1	14.4	16.7	14.8
Number of years between completion of schooling and party work									
US	9.1	11.0	8.9	12.7	8.5	11.6	9.4	13.3	10.1
Canada	11.9	13.5	12.4	13.5	12.2	10.5	12.6	14.0	12.9
Age of first party work									
US	29.5	32.1	30.0	32.6	29.1	31.0	31.1	33.3	30.9
Canada	28.7	31.6	30.0	31.1	28.9	27.9	31.4	31.6	30.6
Age of going to work for present party									
US	30.1	32.1	30.2	33.0	29.5	32.5	31.1	33.3	31.2
Canada	29.6	32.5	30.7	32.4	26.6	29.5	32.1	32.8	31.5
Years of continuous work with present party									
US	11.5	10.3	10.1	11.7	11.1	12.9	9.5	11.3	10.8
Canada	8.9	7.4	8.5	7.3	9.4	6.7	7.4	7.4	7.9
*N** (US)	294	332	425	201	238	56	187	145	626
*N** (Canada)	217	408	316	309	177	40	139	269	625

*Totals vary slightly in some cases due to missing data.

TABLE 10

Relative Importance of Partisan Homogeneity and Party Activity of Parties

Measure	Differences in mean number of years related to:						Polar types
		Parental agreement			Parental activity		Parents active
	Main effect	Parent(s) active	Parent(s) inactive	Main effect	Parents agree	Parents disagree	Agree vs. neither
Age of first awareness							
US	3.4[c]	1.0[a]	3.9[b]	2.3[c]	.8[b]	3.7[b]	4.7[b]
Canada	1.6	—.6	1.5[b]	1.9[c]	.8[a]	2.9[b]	2.3[b]
Age of first identification							
US	4.5[c]	1.8[b]	3.8[b]	3.3[c]	2.6[b]	4.6[b]	6.4[b]
Canada	2.8[a]	.6	2.3[b]	3.3[c]	1.9[b]	3.6[b]	4.2[b]
Number of years between completion of schooling and party work							
US	3.8[c]	3.1[a]	3.8[b]	1.9	.9	1.6	4.7[b]
Canada	1.1	—1.7	1.4	1.6	.4	3.5[a]	1.8
Age of first party work							
US	2.6[a]	1.9	2.2[a]	2.5[a]	1.9[a]	2.3	4.2[b]
Canada	1.1	—1.0	.2	2.9[b]	2.5[a]	3.7[a]	2.7[b]
Age of going to work for present party							
US	2.8[b]	3.0[a]	2.2[a]	2.0	1.6[a]	.8	3.8[b]
Canada	1.7	—.1	.7	2.9[a]	2.4[a]	3.3[a]	3.2[b]
Years of continuous work with present party							
US	—1.3[a]	—1.8	—1.8[a]	1.2[a]	1.6[a]	1.3	—.2
Canada	1.2	2.7	.0	1.5	2.0[a]	—.7	2.0[a]

[a] .05 level [b] .01 level [c] .001 level

the condition of the other factor. The second and third columns report the same difference *when the influence of the other factor is controlled*. The tests of main effects are from two-way analysis of variance while the test for each variable within conditions of the other are one-tailed directional *t* tests. Finally, the last column assesses the difference between the polar facilitating and inhibitory conditions. The minus sign indicates when the difference is not in the predicted direction.

In Table 10 it may be seen that parental agreement on party preferences serves as a stimulant to activity more in the United States than in Canada, no matter the level of the activity. Although, in general, under the condition of parental agreement on preference, political activity is a comparable stimulant to the child's political development in both countries, *in Canada alone* do we find that when parents disagree on party preference, the disagreement serves as a stimulus to getting into party work more quickly after completing school, and beginning party work at an earlier age. One possible explanation for this finding is suggested by dissonance theory. Cognitive dissonance is a psychological tension having motivational characteristics. The theory, as developed by Leon Festinger,[56] concerns itself with the conditions that arouse dissonance for the individual and the ways in which it can be reduced. One way in which the Canadians in this group could reduce the dissonance generated by the special condition of having parents who actively work for different parties would be for them to become active relatively early in a party different from those preferred by the parents. The data indicate that, for 11 of the 40 individuals involved (28 per cent), this is now the case.

Although this explanation may be theoretically attractive, a more likely cause may be the greater impact of federalism in Canada. Certainly the data provided by Meisel and his associates suggest that it is not uncommon for Canadians to vary their party identification with governmental level — to identify with one party at the national level and with another party provincially. If in Canada, in the special case in which parents are politically active as well as being differently identified, the parents' interests were differentiated as regards the national, provincial, and local levels, then disagreement in identification rather than creating stress for the child may actually have betokened the seriousness and importance of politics. If so, it would have facilitated early socialization. With regard to the later possibility, Table 9 has already revealed that among Cana-

[56]Leon Festinger, *The Theory of Cognitive Dissonance* (Stanford, 1957).

dians this group reports earliest ages of political awareness, working for any party, and working for a party after leaving school. In the United States where (until recently) the incidence of split identification of levels of interest probably has been relatively small, this group is not the earliest on any of the measures.

Finally, we had suggested that knowing either of one's parents' party preference might facilitate political socialization and the beginning of a party career even more than would having politically active parents. Conversely, not knowing either of their preferences might be especially inhibiting. Examination of the data for Canadians and a much smaller group of Americans who do not know either parent's preference indicates that only the age at which they first identify with a party is appreciably affected by the lack of information regarding parents' preferences. Contrary to this expectation, then, the mean ages at which political awareness takes place and party work begins are not markedly different for them than for their colleagues.

Summary and discussion

This paper has reported on certain aspects of the political socialization of approximately 1250 officials in the formal and informal party organizations in four metropolitan areas in Canada and the United States. An examination of their social backgrounds and current life status has suggested that neither group is clearly more socially homogeneous or heterogeneous. Given that both groups so clearly over-represent the upper socio-economic strata of their respective populations, it appears that sufficiently high prestige is attached to the holding of high party office to attract people of relatively high status. Despite this similarity, there were cross-national differences with respect to the ages when American and Canadian party officials became politically aware and when a partisan attachment was first formed. In both instances, the event occurred at a later age among the Canadians. The latter also tended to change their partisan identities somewhat more frequently than did their American party counterparts. Other aspects of their pre-party socialization experiences were fairly similar. Thus, the initial partisan identities of a majority of both groups of officials had their origins in the family. And, for both Canadians and Americans, social events and conditions seemingly were more important agents of change in partisanship and levels of political interest than were personal experiences. The agents they named tended to vary with relative age — moving from personal involvement in family and school to common aspects of their social environment. A majority of both groups were interested in politics long before they actually became active in a party. With regard to the sequence in which the socializing events occur, we found that frequently parties are invested with an affective attachment without the prior existence of interest in the general domain of politics. Further, about a quarter of the Americans and a smaller group of Canadians actually appropriated a party label to themselves before they were even aware of the political world. Finally, the average ages at which both awareness and identification took place varied significantly with the political environment in the respondents' families; those who recalled that their parents supported the same party and were relatively active politically reported becoming aware and identified earlier, on the average, than those who did not. Generally, the Americans were raised by more politicized parents and were more strongly affected by the experience than were the Canadians.

Periodically during the course of this discussion, we have extrapolated from our data to the general population and from the findings of studies of more or less representative cross-sections of children and adults to the present study of party activists. Thus, we have suggested that Canadians seem to go through the same general process of political socialization as do Americans, but that for the former the events take place somewhat later in life. Rather than claim that Canadians are more rational politically than are Americans because they tend to postpone events such as identifying with a party to an age when, presumably, they have more political information, we have suggested instead that this may be but one indicator of a generally less politicized Canadian social environment. The occurrence of politically socializing experiences at later ages also may indicate a greater element of partisan discontinuity in Canada, an opinion that, in part, is supported by our finding that a fairly substantial proportion of the Canadian officials were unaware of their parents' party preferences, or else said their parents were not interested in parties sufficiently to have had an overt preference. It is also supported by the fact that over half of the Canadians (51 per cent) are currently working in parties which neither parent supported, whereas only 30 per cent of the Americans are so engaged. Inversely, whereas the parties of 54 per cent of the Americans were those of both parents, this was the case for only 37 per cent of the Canadians. Such partisan discontinuity may facilitate the relatively high (in comparison to the American) rate of switching Meisel, *et al.* report among Canadian electors. At the mass level, their data suggest that partisan discontinuity seems to extend to identifying with different parties at different levels of government. Parenthetically, it may be noted that by recognizing the possibility that the electorate in a federal system can identify simultaneously with more than one party, and by trying systematically to measure the extent of this "split-identity" phenomenon, Meisel and his colleagues have added a new dimension to the concept of party identification, one that certainly will be investigated in future empirical studies of both the United States and Canada.

Extrapolating from cross-sectional to specific populations and *vice versa* is dangerous, and we have tried to point to some of the hazards involved. Thus, we have suggested that, although only a very small proportion of the party officials were relatively uninterested in politics, or else were only spasmodically interested before becoming activists, this pattern is probably the dominant one in both societies. Similarly, experiences with teachers and curriculum at the high school level may have been important for the political development of the officials of both countries, but they need not have been and, at least one report[57] indicates, *are not* equally relevant for the less politically implicated. Again, although both groups of officials continuously tend to cite social events and conditions that have affected their interest in politics and identity with parties, we are not suggesting that public events and political figures are particularly important agents of political socialization in general publics, because it is likely that only a small proportion of the latter are even peripherally attentive to the political element of their environment.

It would also be unwise to assume that a more generalized condition of intergenerational partisan discontinuity in Canada (in part reflected by the tendency to multiple-party identifications, particularly among cross-sections of population) can be attributed to the multi-party system. A more likely explanation, in addition to the less politicized social environment that we have suggested exists in Canada, is that regardless of their socio-economic status a majority of the Canadians do not perceive insurmountable ideological differ-

---

[57]A recent article focusing on the relationship between the number of civics courses taken in American public and private high schools and the political knowledge, interest, efficacy, etc., of 1669 high school seniors indicates that such courses are rather poor predictors of variation in students' attitudes and behaviour. The authors conclude that "our findings do not support the thinking of those who look to the civics curriculum in American high schools as even a minor source of political socialization." See Kenneth P. Langton and M. Kent Jennings, "Political Socialization and the High School Civics Curriculum in the United States," *American Political Science Review*, LXII (1968), 865.

ences among the four parties.[58] Again, however, this is a speculative inference based on an "eyeball" inspection of our own data and on cross-sectional data made available by Meisel and his associates. Future analysis of data we are currently gathering on a specially matched non-party group as well as a random sample of population in Winnipeg and Vancouver, and our ability to obtain comparable data from similar groups in the two American research sites, should enable us to delineate more completely and with greater certainty whatever unique aspects are involved in the political socialization of party activists. Through continued systematic study interested scholars can increment existing data and begin to formulate the general political theory of political socialization that David Easton has called for. Until the various theoretical lacunae are filled, however, reports such as this must remain, in part, speculative and descriptive.

---

[58]For example, in response to the question, "Which of our federal parties do you feel are most alike?" Meisel, *et al.* found that more than half the electorate (54.8 per cent) thought the Liberals and Conservatives were the same, and an additional 6.7 per cent thought the Liberals and the NDP were similar. This constitutes rather striking empirical support for Gad Horowitz who argues that the electoral success of the Liberals and, relatedly, their refusal to appear as a class party forces both right (Conservative) and left (NDP) to mitigate their class appeals and themselves to become centre parties. See Gad Horowitz, "Conservatism, Liberalism and Socialism in Canada: An Interpretation," *Canadian Journal of Economics and Political Science*, XXXII (1966), 143-71. John Porter's position that there are few if any basic differences between Liberals and Conservatives is best articulated in *The Vertical Mosaic*, pp. 373-79.

With regard to public images of American parties, the authors of *The American Voter* recognize that such images are far from being sharply different, but note that the public tends to link the Democratic party with a positive attitude toward social welfare issues such as governmental underwriting of medical costs, aid to education, guaranteed employment, etc. Since 1964, there is little doubt that the national Democratic party also has been seen as one favouring desegregation and protection of Negro rights in areas such as jobs and housing. *The American Voter*, pp. 202-203.

The Character of Party Leadership

Henry Valen
Daniel Katz

All organizations face the problem of leadership recruitment and leadership succession. Political parties as voluntary organizations have added problems in attracting able leaders to the system and holding them in it. In this chapter we will present evidence on three major aspects of the leadership problem: (1) the types of political and social background from which leaders are recruited, (2) their organizational experience, and (3) the motivational and value orientations of leaders. These problems will be analyzed by looking for differences among parties. Further, with regard to the first problem the responses of leaders and followers within the individual party will be compared.

The Leadership Sample

In all, 149 political leaders were interviewed in the Stavanger study. The group represents a complete coverage, rather than a sample, of the following limited universe: (1) the chairmen and the secretaries

---

Reprinted from *Political Parties in Norway: A Community Study* (Oslo, Norway: Universitetsforlaget, 1964) by permission of the publisher and Henry Valen.

of the five party organizations at the province level, (2) the chairmen and secretaries at the commune level, (3) the chairmen and secretaries of the party's youth organization at the province and commune levels, (4) the chairmen of the party's organization for women at the province and commune levels and secretaries at the province level, and (5) the chairmen of the local ward organization (or their functional equivalents where no officially designated ward leader existed). (Relative proportions from the different levels are given in Table 1.) In other words, with the exception of the secretaries of the commune organization for women, our sample constituted the official party leadership for the membership organization in the area under investigation.[1]

TABLE 1
DISTRIBUTION OF LEADERS ACCORDING TO LEVEL IN THE PARTY STRUCTURE

	PARTY OF LEADERS:				
LEVEL:	LABOR	LIBERAL	CHRISTIAN	AGRARIAN	CONS.
	%	%	%	%	%
Province	14	23	19	16	17
Commune	53	50	31	37	46
Ward	33	27	50	47	37
TOTAL	100%	100%	100%	100%	100%
N	43	26	26	19	35

We found that some of our leaders held more than one position. For example, a province chairman might also be a commune chairman. In such instances, the leader was assigned to his highest position in any comparison of levels.

In evaluating the data it is necessary to keep in mind three limitations:

(1) The sample is drawn exclusively from the membership organizations. Political leaders holding public office were included

[1]Another exception was made in the case of the Labor Party to include representation of the affiliated trade unions at the local level. It will be recalled that at the communal level the trade unions are part of the membership organization. Chairmen of affiliated local unions have membership in the communal assembly of the Labor Party and have the same political roles as do the women and youth organizations. From the 22 local union chairmen in the Labor Party five were selected at random to supplement the sample of Labor Party leadership.

in the sample only if they also held a position in the party organization as listed above. Our sample is thus not necessarily representative of the governmental party.

(2) The national level of the membership organizations has not been represented. Our sample, therefore, consists of leaders from the lower and middle echelons of the organizations.

(3) Finally, the sample is drawn from one specific community. Therefore, we are not justified in drawing conclusions concerning the behavior of lower and middle rank political leaders across the nation. It is probable, however, that in several respects party structure in one sizeable community will reflect the nature of party structure in other communities. We shall assume that our findings concerning party differences are suggestive of general tendencies in the Norwegian political system.

In the following section we shall describe the demographic and background factors of our sample of political leaders, as well as the political involvement of their parents.

Demographic Background

In all, some 14 percent of the leaders are women, and the variation in the sex proportions among the parties is insignificant. This proportion of women in our sample is not low compared with their distribution in the governmental organization. Thus at the 1957 election only 17 percent of the candidates were women; and because women tended to get an unfavorable position on the slates, they constituted less than 7 percent of the elected representatives.[2]

Table 2 shows that young people are not very numerous in the local leadership. Less than 13 percent of our leaders are under 31 years of age, whereas 23 per cent are more than 50 years old. Compared with the age distribution of the governmental party, however, our local leaders are rather young. Thus of the candidates nominated in 1957 (for the whole nation) only 5 percent were under 31 years old, whereas 42 percent were over 50.

It is not surprising that all local leaders in the lowest age bracket belong to the Conservative Party, the Liberal Party and the Labor

---

[2]On sex differences in the recruitment of political leaders see Stein Rokkan and Henry Valen, 'The Mobilization of the Periphery,' in *Acta Sociologica*, 6(1-2), 1962, 111-58.

TABLE 2
AGE DISTRIBUTION OF LEADERS

	PARTY OF LEADERS:				
AGE:	LABOR	LIBERAL	CHRISTIAN	AGRARIAN	CONS.
	%	%	%	%	%
30 years or less	9	12	—	—	34
31-50	72	46	77	74	49
Over 50	14	42	23	26	17
No answer	5	—	—	—	—
TOTAL	100%	100%	100%	100%	100%
N	43	26	26	19	35
Average age	42	46	45.5	42.5	37.5

Party, since these parties have the most active youth organizations in the Stavanger area. When we compare the average age we find that the Conservatives have the youngest leaders, the Liberals and the Christians have the oldest, whereas the Laborites and Agrarians fall in between.

Occupational Background

Consistent with the patterns of the voters, our local leaders show corresponding differences in occupational distribution. Half of the Labor leaders are workers, whereas the other half are distributed in white collar occupations. Liberal and Conservative leaders are almost exclusively drawn from white collar occupations. Agrarian leaders are with one exception, farmers, whereas the Christian People's Party has drawn leaders from all occupational groups. With respect to clerical employment there is an interesting difference among the parties. All white collar Conservative leaders are in private employment, whereas white collar leaders in Labor, the Liberal Party and the Christian People's Party are about equally distributed between private and public employment. Again this finding corresponds with a tendency among the voters for white collar workers in private employment to be attracted to the Conservative Party. But the tendency is less clear for voters than for leaders. And this greater occupational differentiation of party leaders is a general tendency (Table 3). The only exception is the Labor Party, where the proportion of workers is higher for voters than for leaders.

TABLE 3

OCCUPATION OF LEADERS (OCCUPATION OF HEAD OF HOUSEHOLD)

	PARTY OF LEADERS:				
OCCUPATION:	LABOR	LIBERAL	CHRISTIAN	AGRARIAN	CONS.
	%	%	%	%	%
Workers	51	4	19	5	6
White collar, public	16	31	19	—	—
White collar, private	14	38	19	—	43
Journalists, secretaries, in party organizations	10	4	5	—	8
Independents in business	7	19	19	—	34
Farmers	—	4	19	95	3
No information	2	—	—	—	6
TOTAL	100%	100%	100%	100%	100%
N	43	26	26	19	35

In order to explore this difference further we may compare different levels in the party structure with regard to socio-economic background. For the voters we will differentiate between strong party identifiers and ordinary voters (i.e., weak identifiers and independent voters).

Table 4 shows that the parties tend to move toward distinctiveness the higher we move up in the system. In the Liberal Party and the Christian People's Party the proportions of white collar workers are highest for the local leaders and lowest for the voters. Similarly, in the Agrarian Party the proportion of farmers increases as we move from voters to leaders. In the Conservative Party the proportion of white collar workers and self-employed whether in business, agriculture, or other occupations, increases with increasing level, although in this case the changes from one step to another are not quite as regular. It is interesting to note that in all the non-Socialist parties the proportions of blue collar workers are highest among the voters and lowest among the leaders. The general finding then is that for the non-Socialist parties the higher we move in the party system the more we find that the lower occupational groups are marginal to these parties. The group norm for the more prestigeful occupational groups supports an appropriate party identification. With this identification goes greater party activity and resulting positions of leadership.

Comparative analysis indicates that this tendency is prevalent in both the United States and Norway, and possibly may be a general phenomenon.[3] Table 4 also shows that the parties are most likely to draw their leadership from the most important base groups. The Labor Party, however, constitutes an exception in this respect. Strong party identifiers do not differ from ordinary voters with regard to occupational background. When we move from identifiers to leaders we find a substantial drop in the proportion of blue collar workers who comprise the leadership group in the party. Our leadership sample was a compromise at the communal level in that it gave full representation to locals based upon individual membership in the Labor Party, whereas collectively affiliated trade unions were under-represented (only five out of 22 such unions were included). It is possible, therefore, that our Labor Party leadership group would have been made up of more blue collar workers if all 22 of the union chairmen had been included. Nevertheless, a comparison of the Labor leadership sample with the membership organization, excluding people who have membership through being in a collectively associated union, shows essentially the same relationship with respect to occupational composition as would a sample of all members, including collectively associated unions. The data indicate that the membership of the Labor Party has the same occupational composition whether we speak of its individual members or its total membership including union locals.

The fact that the Labor Party draws more heavily for leadership upon the white collar group than its composition would suggest may be due to the higher education, greater skills and knowledge, and social prestige of people in the higher occupational categories. This, however, is not the whole story. Many of the white collar leaders in the Labor Party are socially mobile people whose parents belong to the working class. Some of them may even have begun their careers as manual workers themselves. Hence, it may be that Labor Party members accept white collar workers in leadership positions not so much because they are just white collar workers, but because they are perceived as people like themselves who nevertheless enjoy superior status. In other words, there may be a tendency toward upward identification provided that there is a basis for a common linkage between the identifier and his model. Thus the person identifying can take on the superior qualities of the model. It is also true that

---

[3]See Stein Rokkan and Angus Campbell, "Citizen Participation in Political Life, Norway and the United States of America," in *International Social Science Journal*, 12 (1960), and Angus Campbell and Henry Valen "Party Identification in Norway and the United States," in *Public Opinion Quarterly*, 25 (1961).

the upwardly mobile workers may obtain leadership in part because the same qualities of drive, intelligence, and energy which enable them to move up the occupational ladder make it possible for them to move up the political ladder.

Table 5 deals with the relationship between political participation and another component of socio-economic status, namely, amount of income. Again as we move upward in the income brackets the more likely people are to identify strongly with some party, and the more likely they are to become party leaders. This tendency is consistent for all parties. The trend is to be expected for the non-Socialist parties but it is of interest that in the Labor Party, too, the higher the income the more likely we are to find strong identification with the party. This is true in spite of the fact that the occupational composition of strong Labor Party identifiers and ordinary party supporters is the same. Obviously, the Labor Party does not derive its strength from the lowest income categories.

The income differences among the parties reflect a continuum with the Labor Party being at the lowest end of the income distribution and the Conservative Party at the top end. The Liberals follow the Conservatives and the Christian People's Party and the Agrarian Party are the closest to the Labor Party.

Educational Background

Educational differences between parties and across levels within a party by and large follow the same pattern as we have found for occupational background (Table 6). In all parties the level of education is substantially higher for leaders than for voters and identifiers. Moreover, there is a tendency for strong identifiers to have more education than ordinary voters. There is, however, no difference between identifiers and voters in the Labor Party — a finding consistent with the pattern of occupational background. Another noticeable exception is the Christian People's Party where the proportion of people with only elementary school is in fact highest for identifiers.

Since education is to some extent an index of socio-economic status, and since people with high status tend to be most numerous on the higher levels in the system, leaders obviously have higher education than identifiers and ordinary voters.

The consistency between educational and occupational level is not only apparent in comparing different echelons within the indi-

TABLE 4

Occupation of Local Leaders, Strong Identifiers, and Voters, by Party

Occupation:	Labor Ldrs.	Labor Iden.	Labor Vtrs.	Liberal Ldrs.	Liberal Iden.	Liberal Vtrs.	Christian Ldrs.	Christian Iden.	Christian Vtrs.	Agrarian Ldrs.	Agrarian Iden.	Agrarian Vtrs.	Conservative Ldrs.	Conservative Iden.	Conservative Vtrs.
	%	%	%	%	%	%	%	%	%	%	%	%	%	%	%
Workers	52	83	79	4	25	34	19	36	50	5	3	24	6	8	27
White collar	41	13	13	73	54	39	43	29	21	—	6	8	55	64	36
Independents in agriculture	—	1	3	4	13	7	19	16	22	95	91	67	3	4	6
Independents, others	7	3	5	19	8	20	19	19	7	—	—	1	36	24	31
TOTAL	100%	100%	100%	100%	100%	100%	100%	100%	100%	100%	100%	100%	100%	100%	100%
N*	42	116	246	26	24	143	26	31	58	19	32	63	33	25	86

*A few respondents whose occupation was not ascertained are not included in the Table.

TABLE 5

Income of Local Leaders, Strong Identifiers, and Voters, by Party

Income:	Labor Ldrs.	Labor Iden.	Labor Vtrs.	Liberal Ldrs.	Liberal Iden.	Liberal Vtrs.	Christian Ldrs.	Christian Iden.	Christian Vtrs.	Agrarian Ldrs.	Agrarian Iden.	Agrarian Vtrs.	Conservative Ldrs.	Conservative Iden.	Conservative Vtrs.
	%	%	%	%	%	%	%	%	%	%	%	%	%	%	%
12,000 kroner or less	39	58	66	11	32	50	29	53	67	19	47	45	21	17	41
13,000-20,000	56	37	31	55	52	34	63	27	21	50	33	43	35	44	39
More than 20,000	5	5	3	34	16	16	8	20	12	31	20	12	44	39	20
TOTAL	100%	100%	100%	100%	100%	100%	100%	100%	100%	100%	100%	100%	100%	100%	100%
N*	41	117	241	26	25	135	24	30	57	16	30	58	34	23	76

*A few respondents whose income was not ascertained are not included.

TABLE 6

Education of Local Leaders, Strong Identifiers, and Voters, by Party

Education:	Labor Ldrs.	Labor Iden.	Labor Vtrs.	Liberal Ldrs.	Liberal Iden.	Liberal Vtrs.	Christian Ldrs.	Christian Iden.	Christian Vtrs.	Agrarian Ldrs.	Agrarian Iden.	Agrarian Vtrs.	Conservative Ldrs.	Conservative Iden.	Conservative Vtrs.
	%	%	%	%	%	%	%	%	%	%	%	%	%	%	%
Elementary school only	50	78	78	24	32	47	39	68	59	27	59	59	6	30	41
Continuation school or equivalent	24	13	15	8	24	27	22	26	36	63	38	29	3	15	17
High school	7	7	6	20	24	21	9	—	3	5	3	9	27	44	33
Gymnasium or more	19	2	1	48	20	5	30	6	2	5	—	3	64	11	9
TOTAL	100%	100%	100%	100%	100%	100%	100%	100%	100%	100%	100%	100%	100%	100%	100%
N*	42	117	248	25	25	146	23	31	59	19	32	63	33	27	86

* A few respondents whose education was not ascertained are not included.

TABLE 7

Class Identification of Local Leaders, Strong Identifiers, and Voters, by Party

Q.: If you were to place yourself in one of these groups, would you then say that you were in the upper class, middle class, working class?

Class identification:	Labor Ldrs.	Labor Iden.	Labor Vtrs.	Liberal Ldrs.	Liberal Iden.	Liberal Vtrs.	Christian Ldrs.	Christian Iden.	Christian Vtrs.	Agrarian Ldrs.	Agrarian Iden.	Agrarian Vtrs.	Conservative Ldrs.	Conservative Iden.	Conservative Vtrs.
	%	%	%	%	%	%	%	%	%	%	%	%	%	%	%
Middle class*	7	20	17	58	74	60	73	61	56	68	74	62	63	86	80
Working class	74	79	80	—	22	36	12	36	40	—	21	27	3	7	18
Other classes or refuses to take a stand	19	1	3	42	4	4	15	3	4	32	5	11	34	7	2
TOTAL	100%	100%	100%	100%	100%	100%	100%	100%	100%	100%	100%	100%	100%	100%	100%
N**	43	123	243	26	27	140	26	36	45	19	34	66	35	27	79

* Only three of the leaders and nine of the voters classified themselves as 'upper class.'
** A few respondents whose class identification was not ascertained are not included in the Table.

vidual parties, but the same pattern is also clear in a comparison among parties. The Labor Party, which has the largest proportion of working class support, also has on the average the lowest level of education. Next come the Christian People's Party and the Agrarian Party, then the Liberal Party, with the Conservative Party showing the highest educational level.

Psychological Class Membership

Social class can be measured by objective indices of occupation, income and education, and by psychological identification. Both voters and leaders were asked to indicate which class they belonged to. From Table 7 we may draw two conclusions:

(1) Leaders are less inclined than voters to classify themselves according to categories of social classes. This is due partly to the fact that leaders seem to hold a more differentiated perception of society. They are not willing to accept the working, middle, and upper class designations because they consider them inadequate. On the other hand, several leaders indicated that there were no 'social' differences among people any longer, but they tended to see differences according to level of education and type of work, e.g. between rural and urban occupations. In particular, Agrarians had difficulty in placing themselves in either the 'middle' class or the 'working' class. Moreover, a number of leaders rejected the concept of social class for ideological reasons. They see the concept of 'social classes' as a source of hatred and conflict in society. The class concept seems to be contradictory to the notion of a 'people's party,' because such a party claims that it represents almost all groups in society; to recognize the existence of social classes might imply that the party had to take a stand on conflicts originating from such differences. The Liberal party and the Conservative party, which are both influenced by liberal ideas, have traditionally opposed the notion of social classes. Hence, substantial proportions of the leaders of these parties refused to take a stand on the question of class identification. It is interesting, however, that quite a few Labor leaders responded the same way. Until World War II the Labor party declared itself to be a Marxian party, and it is in the postwar period that the party has changed its label from being a 'class' party to a 'people's' party. The change in ideology seems to have had an impact on the Labor leaders' perception of society. The voters, however, are more ready to accept the class concept and to classify themselves accordingly.

(2) If we omit those who refuse to take a stand, then the higher we move in the party structure the more we approach distinctiveness with respect to class identification. In the non-Socialist parties strong identifiers are more inclined than voters to say that they belong to the middle class, and the tendency to identify with the middle class is even stronger for the non-Socialist leaders (only four out of 106 non-Socialist leaders indicated that they belong to 'working' class). This finding is consistent with the distribution of occupation and income within these parties. The pattern of class identification is less consistent with occupational distribution in the Labor party. It is not surprising that four out of five voters as well as identifiers say they belong to the working class. This ratio corresponds almost exactly to the proportion of blue collar workers in the two categories. But although Labor leaders are drawn equally from white collar and blue collar occupations, only 7 percent say that they belong to the middle class. There are two reasons for this apparent lag between socio-economic status and class identification. (1) The Labor leaders in white-collar occupations are still closer to the working class objectively because of their family background. Their fathers were workers and some of them started their careers as blue collar workers. Our data indicate that only 40 percent of the white collar Labor leaders have any high school or gymnasium training as compared to 78 percent of the white collar leaders in other parties. (2) Ideologically the Labor Party is still the party of the workers. If leaders were too conspicuous in their middle class identification, this would create psychological distance between themselves and their followers.

Political Socialization and Party Leadership

The socialization process through which the growing individual becomes a member of his society has long occupied the attention of social scientists, but that aspect of the process concerned with political induction into the role of citizen has seen little direct study. H. Hyman in assembling the research data available on political socialization found only scanty evidence on the problem and this evidence consisted mostly of the reports of voters on the political affiliation of their parents (Hyman, 1959). Our findings extend this subarea of investigation by differentiating and comparing the political background of party leaders and ordinary voters.

One important dimension of political background is the *party* allegiance of parents. To what extent do the leaders work for the same party to which their parents belonged when they were growing up? Do the leaders differ in this respect from ordinary voters? Our respondents were asked about party preference of both father and mother. Since the reported voting patterns are almost identical for both parents we will present only the Tables for the father's vote.

Leaders tend to inherit their political beliefs from their parents (Table 8). In all parties the proportion of respondents whose father voted for the respondent's own party is much higher for the leader than for the average voter.

TABLE 8
PARTY PREFERENCE OF FATHER FOR LEADERS AND VOTERS

Q.: Which party did your father belong to (when you were growing up)?

PARTY PREFERENCE OF FATHER:	LEADERS					VOTERS				
	LAB.	LIB.	CHR.	AGR.	CONS.	LAB.	LIB.	CHR.	AGR.	CONS.
	%	%	%	%	%	%	%	%	%	%
Communist	—	—	—	—	—	1	—	—	—	1
Labor	77	8	—	—	—	47	13	7	5	13
Liberal	7	73	27	—	14	23	53	51	28	34
Christian	—	—	4	—	—	1	2	—	—	—
Agrarian	2	4	11	63	3	5	10	17	48	5
Conservative	2	—	19	16	52	7	11	13	11	38
Others	—	—	4	—	—	—	—	—	—	—
Changed party*	5	11	23	21	11	—	—	—	—	—
Don't know	5	—	8	—	14	14	11	11	8	9
No answer	2	4	4	—	6	2	—	1	—	—
TOTAL	100%	100%	100%	100%	100%	100%	100%	100%	100%	100%
N**	43	26	26	19	35	365	171	90	95	113

*Less than 1 percent of the voters report that their father changed party.
**For voters the percentage basis is the total reporting the vote preference for given party.

For both leaders and voters, however, there are some striking differences among the parties with respect to these proportions. Almost no one reports that his father voted for the Christian People's party — obviously because this party was established less than one generation ago, and it did not run slates at elections in the province of Rogaland until 1945. Similarly, the Agrarian party is relatively new (established in 1921), and therefore the proportion of Agrarian leaders who report that their parents changed party is at least double that of the three older parties. In these older parties the proportion of leaders whose father belonged to the same party is substantially lower for Conservative than for Liberals and Laborites. The tendency is similar for voters.

The Conservative party gains increasing support from upwardly mobile people, middle class people whose parents were workers, and apparently also from people who have moved socially from the lower middle class to the higher middle class. It is the movement from lower middle class status that apparently accounts for the substantial proportion of Conservative leaders with a family background in other parties, since not a single one of our Conservative leaders reported that his father had been a Labor party supporter. The Liberals also attract socially mobile people to some extent. The Liberal party is the only party which has recruited leaders whose family background was Labor. The Labor party in turn has recruited a few leaders from Liberal homes (8 percent) but is otherwise virtually restricted to its own parental background for leadership. The Agrarian party has its major recruitment of leaders from families in which the parents voted Agrarian (63 percent) with a minority from parents of Conservative background. Although the Christian People's party had its origin in a factional split from the Liberal party, its leaders also are drawn from families supporting the Conservative party (19 percent).

In comparison with leaders the ordinary voters show much more deviation from the political faith of their fathers. Moreover, the deviations are wider in terms of the political spectrum. Thus some 13 percent of the Conservative voters came from Labor party family background. And 7 percent of the Labor vote comes from sons and daughters of Conservative voters. The greatest gain for the Labor party is from the Liberal party, some 23 percent of Liberal sons and daughters — reflecting a similar but less pronounced tendency found among the leaders. Of the older parties the Conservative party is the one in which the members are least likely to be recruited from similarly minded parents. The sons and daughters of Liberal fathers are almost as large an element in the Conservative party as are the children of Conservative parents. The changing character of the Conservative party in generations is in part due to the attraction it holds for the upwardly mobile people in Norwegian society but it is also due in part to the losses it sustains as members of the younger generation shift to the other parties. But whereas the Conservative losses are more than made up by its gains, the

Liberal party, without counting the defections to the Christian People's party, loses considerably more than it has gained across generations.

Though some people of Labor family background move into the Conservative party they do not assume positions of leadership in that party. On the other hand, the movement from Liberal family background into the Conservative party is accompanied by some change in Conservative party leadership. And there is a much heavier reliance in the Agrarian party upon those from Conservative backgrounds for leadership than their numbers justify.

The tendency to come from one specific background party is much stronger for leaders than for voters. Moreover, when change has occurred, the new party tends to be a close neighbor in the party spectrum more often for leaders than for voters. Thus, politically mobile Liberal leaders have a tendency to come from either Labor or Agrarian background, mobile Agrarian leaders come exclusively from Conservative families, and Conservative leaders come from Liberal or Agrarian families. It is also of interest that all leaders of the Christian People's party have grown up in families with non-Socialist preferences. Labor leadership is recruited from the extreme right in the negligible proportion of 2 percent and the Conservative leadership has no recruits from the Labor party.

Political socialization in the family is thus even more significant for political leaders than for voters in general. Though a heavy plurality of people follow the political allegiance of their fathers the influence of family background is even more important for political leadership in that a clear majority of all leaders reflect the partisan identification of their parents. The exact mechanisms at work here are not clear and three possibilities need further exploration. *(1)* The leaders may come from homes in which the political indoctrination was more intense. *(2)* The attainment of leadership in a party may be easier for the person whose family background prepares him for that party. He will be more readily accepted because of this background and the resulting values and position he holds. *(3)* The commitment to a leadership role in contrast to the voter role means more ideological involvement of the individual. It is easier for a person to desert his parental family by voting differently than by public participation as a leader in an opposition party. And it represents less of a wrench to his own values to support another party than to accept its policies and ideology as a leader is expected to. And similar reasoning would explain why the leaders who have departed from family tradition tend to move to the closest neighbor in the party spectrum. Such a change would not necessitate a complete break with their earlier philosophy. For voters, however, the weaker ideological involvement can result in movement from one extreme of the political spectrum to the other.

Familial Influence in the Recruitment of Leaders

The importance of the immediate family in political socialization is shown by the fact that a sizeable proportion of the local leaders (43 percent) grow up in politically active families (Table 9). The nationwide survey of voters found in contrast that only 11 percent had

TABLE 9
POLITICAL ACTIVITY OF PARENTS
PUBLIC OFFICE HELD BY FATHER

Q.: Can you remember whether your parents participated actively in political work while you were growing up?

	LEADERS				
	LABOR	LIBERAL	CHRISTIAN	AGRARIAN	CONS.
	%	%	%	%	%
Yes, they were active	44	54	38	48	34
No	49	42	62	47	60
No answer	7	4	—	5	6
TOTAL	100%	100%	100%	100%	100%
N	43	26	26	19	35

Q.: Can you remember whether your father (and mother) ever held public office?

	LEADERS				
	LABOR	LIBERAL	CHRISTIAN	AGRARIAN	CONS.
	%	%	%	%	%
Yes, held office	28	73	38	63	37
No	68	27	58	37	60
Don't know, can't remember	2	—	—	—	—
No answer	2	—	4	—	3
TOTAL	100%	100%	100%	100%	100%
N	43	26	26	19	35

parents very active politically and 16 percent had parents somewhat active politically. Liberal leaders are more likely than other party leaders to report that their parents were active and Conservatives and Christian People's party leaders the least likely. Party differerences on the whole, however, are not great if we consider the size of the sample.

On the question of whether the parents held public office, a similar proportion (44 percent) of the leaders answered in the affirmative (Table 9). But on this question there are great variations among the parties. Again the Liberals are ahead of other leaders, in that almost three out of four reported that parents held public office. They are closely followed by the Agrarians, whereas the corresponding proportions in the other parties are much lower. The data indicate that in the Liberal and the Agrarian Party the proportion of parents who actually did hold office exceeded the proportion who are reported active. The major reason is that a number of the leaders come from communities where local parties did not exist when the respondent grew up, and that therefore local office holders were recruited through nonpartisan slates. This discrepancy can easily be demonstrated when political activity of parents is related to office-holding.

TABLE 10
POLITICAL ACTIVITY OF PARENTS RELATED TO OFFICE-HOLDING

DID FATHER HOLD PUBLIC OFFICE?	WERE PARENTS ACTIVE?		
	YES	NO	DON'T KNOW, NO ANSWER
	%	%	
Yes	77	19	
No	20	78	
Don't know, no answer	3	3	
N	65	78	6*

*Too few cases for computation of percentages.

Of those who reported that parents were active, four out of five said their father held public office, whereas only one out of five of the non-active parents held public office. Altogether 54 percent of the leaders indicated that their parents were either active or held public office, or both.

Leaders differ from ordinary voters in family background in two respects: (1) they are more likely to come from homes in which the parents were politically active and (2) they are more likely to adhere to the partisan faith of their fathers. It would seem plausible that the former factor, of greater political activity in the home, accounts for the greater political stability of the leader in that he comes from a family where the political influences in a given partisan direction were stronger. When, however, we compare the active and politically inactive homes the differences in the anticipated direction, though present, are not great (Table 11). Ten percent more of the people with parents, politically active, follow the father's political faith than of the people with parents politically inactive. And the holding of public office by parents bears no relation at all to adherence to the father's political faith. Apparently the political activity of the parents is not the critical variable in producing generational stability of partisan identification though it does contribute to generational stability of political leadership in general. Children whose parents were political leaders tend to become leaders themselves but not inevitably of the same political party as their parents. Having a parent in party politics or in public office does create a favorable model for the youngster for a political role in general more than it does for a role in a particular party. . . .

TABLE 11
PARTY PREFERENCE OF PARENTS RELATED TO POLITICAL ACTIVITY

	PARENTS ACTIVE		PARENTS HELD PUBLIC OFFICE	
	YES	NO	YES	NO
	%	%	%	%
Parents belonged to respondent's party	72	62	65	68
Parents belonged to different party	28	38	35	32
TOTAL	100%	100%	100%	100%
N*	54	69	60	63

*Leaders from the Christian People's Party excluded from the Table.

Congressional Recruitment and Representation*

Leo M. Snowiss

This is a study of the relationship between local political organization, candidate recruitment, and representation in the United States House of Representatives. It seeks to ascertain the effects which different systems of recruitment have upon the kinds of men who enter public life and the public policies they espouse. A case study of metropolitan Chicago is used to demonstrate the utility of this kind of analysis. The objective is to distinguish distinct systems of recruitment in the Chicago area, describe the factors associated with each and note the consequences of each for representation in Congress.

---

* This is a revised version of a paper delivered at the annual meeting of the American Political Science Association, Washington, D.C., September, 1965. The original version was written while the author was a Fellow at The Brookings Institution. Additional assistance was provided by the Institute of Government and Public Affairs at the University of California, Los Angeles. The author gratefully acknowledges the helpful comments made by Gerald Bender, Martin Edelman, James Guyot, Duncan MacRae, Jr., John Manley, Stephen V. Stephens, and Raymond E. Wolfinger.

Reprinted from the *American Political Science Review,* LX (September, 1966), 627-39, by permission of the American Political Association and the author.

Recruitment and Organization

Political recruitment is the process by which public officials attain office. The study of recruitment and the study of representation are complementary. Knowledge of representative institutions gives direction to analyses of recruitment; in turn, knowledge of factors affecting recruitment may explain much about the behavior of legislative bodies.

The Necessity of Organization. Congressional recruitment is essentially a problem of organization. Congressional districts, with populations generally in excess of 400,000, are typified by social diversity and the dispersion of politically relevant power. The concentration of sufficient power for the nomination and election of candidates for Congress is a difficult problem. Congressional districts are rarely "natural" political units, neatly corresponding to local governmental lines or to concentrations of particular population groups and interests. Local politicians generally do try to establish relatively homogeneous districts in which there are favorable concentrations of politically relevant power. But demographic homogeneity and concentration of power are not optimally achieved even in the most favorable circumstances, such as those found in the relatively compact districts of central Chicago. While the population of a central city district may be relatively homogeneous in terms of some relevant variables (e.g., income and home ownership), its population may show signs of diversity and conflict with regard to others (e.g., race and ethnicity); it may contain potentially conflicting units of state and local governmental power (e.g., wards and state assembly districts); and it will very likely have numerous politically interested and potentially conflicting organizations (e.g., party factions, unions, ethnic and service clubs).[1]

Systems of Recruitment. The organization of effective power for recruitment is not unstructured or haphazard. To the extent that distinct processes of concentrating power can be isolated, patterns of recruitment and their consequences for representation can be classified and analyzed. A *system* of recruitment is a complex of variables affecting the organization of constituency power in a way which pro-

[1]Even Adolph Sabath (d. 1952), dean of the House and Chairman of its Rules Committee, was not immune to political attack by various party factions. On several occasions high-ranking national leaders, acting through Mayors Kelly and Kennelley, had to intervene to save his seat from ward committeemen anxious to displace him in the name of their own ethnic communities. Even within the well disciplined Democratic party, only strong leadership could maintain unity.

duces identifiable types of legislators. A system of recruitment is essentially a system of organization.

I have utilized five major variables in analyzing the organization of power for recruitment in the Chicago area:

(1) Social Bases of Organization. Social structures set the parameters for political systems. This is certainly manifest in the well-documented correlations between key socio-economic variables and both party identification and electoral support.[2] However, insofar as the systematic organization of power for recruitment is concerned, it is the primary electorates which are crucial. They provide the most active party workers, the most dependable electoral support, and the major sources of intraparty factionalism and competition. This distinction is important because primary electorates do not simply mirror the social structure of general electorates. On the contrary, primary turnouts tend to distort and exaggerate the social bases of partisan support which are manifest in general elections.[3]

(2) Organizational Resources. If primary electorates provide the social bases for organization support, the availability and suitability of particular resources affect the actual exploitation of those bases. Distinct systems of recruitment tend to be associated with the extent to which types of material or non-material incentives (patronage or issues, respectively) are applied to particular kinds of primary electorates.[4]

(3) Organizational Structure. The utilization of particular kinds and quantities of resources largely determines the character of organizational authority and the capacity of organizations to resist external influence. The use of material incentives tends to be associated with party organizations which are relatively hierarchic (evincing centralized leadership, discipline and unity) and impermeable (resisting external influences upon their decision-making processes), while reliance on non-material incentives tends toward dispersed authority and permeable decision-making structures.

---

[2]For a summary of the relevant literature see, Nelson W. Polsby and Aaron B. Wildavsky, *Presidential Elections* (New York: Charles Scribner's Sons, 1964), chs. i and iii.

[3]A general discussion of the effects of the primary on the party system is found in V. O. Key, Jr., *American State Politics: An Introduction* (New York: Alfred A. Knopf, 1956), chs. iv-vi. The social bases of party organization in Los Angeles are analyzed in Dwaine Marvick and Charles R. Nixon, "Recruitment Contrasts in Rival Campaign Groups," in Dwaine Marvick (ed.), *Political Decision-Makers* (Glencoe: The Free Press, 1961), ch. v.

[4]The effects of material and non-material resources upon organizations are treated in Peter B. Clark and James Q. Wilson, "Incentive Systems: A Theory of Organizations," *Administrative Science Quarterly,* 6 (September, 1961), 129-66.

(4) Organizational Ethos. The dominant resources and prevailing structures tend to promote characteristic organizational values. Materially-oriented party organizations with elaborate structures of authority tend to promote certain skills (such as bargaining and compromise) among their personnel, while issue-oriented party organizations are more inclined to emphasize ideological commitment.[5]

(5) Organizational Control. If congressional recruitment is essentially a process of organizing power, it is imperative to ascertain the extent to which particular organizations can control their electoral environments in both primary and general elections. In the Chicago area, the regular party organizations control recruitment with varying degrees of success, depending on their internal structure, the extent of electoral competition, and the character of organized non-party counter-elites in the primary electorates. Party organizations which are faction-ridden and/or confronted with well-organized and readily available non-party opposition in primaries, tend to lose control over recruitment at the nominating stage. In districts where general elections tend to be highly competitive (irrespective of the primary situation), the regular party organizations may not actually lose control over recruitment, but deliberately tend to recruit from sources outside the party organizations. Insofar as the regular party organizations tend toward internal recruitment, organizational ethos has a decisive impact on the character of the men who run for Congress. Where external recruitment prevails, party organizational ethos is less important and the character of non-party elites takes on greater significance.

Metropolitan Chicago: Three Types of Districts

The fundamental character of post-war representation in Congress from the Chicago area was established by the Apportionment Act of 1947, the first congressional redistricting in Illinois since 1901. The new apportionment delineated three systems of political recruitment among the districts allotted to Cook County. These have been five safely Democratic *inner city* "machine" districts, five (four after the apportionment of 1961) *outer city* swing districts, and three Republican-oriented *suburban* districts. The three areas are relatively distinct in regard to their socio-economic characteristics and divisions of partisan sentiment. These differences are summarized in Tables 1 and 2, below.

[5] *Ibid.,* James Q. Wilson, *The Amateur Democrat* (Chicago: University of Chicago Press, 1962); James Q. Wilson, "The Economy of Patronage," *The Journal of Political Economy*, 69 (August, 1961), 360-80.

I. The Inner City Districts. The apportionment of 1947 created five congressional districts in the center of Chicago (the 1st, 5th, 6th, 7th, and 8th). They cut a wide swath through the city, from Lake Michigan in the east, out along the slum wards adjoining the Chicago River and Sanitary Canal, and westward into mixed residential and industrial areas. This area is the least affluent in Cook County and has always been heavily populated by ethnic and racial minorities.

TABLE 1

INDICES OF SOCIO-ECONOMIC STATUS, BY TYPE OF DISTRICT, 1960[a]

	PERCENTAGES		
	INNER CITY	OUTER CITY	SUBURBAN
Family Income Under $5,000	37	26	16
Family Income Over $10,000	14	26	33
Minority Groups (Negroes plus foreign stock)	65	55	36
High School Graduates	25	42	50
Home Ownership, single family	14	26	62
Home Ownership, total	29	36	72
White Collar	32	49	53

[a] Compiled from. U.S. Bureau of the Census, *U.S. Census of Population and Housing: 1960 Census Tracts*, Final Report PHC (1)-26. (Washington, D.C., U.S. Government Printing Office, 1962.) The districts are for the apportionment of 1947. The reapportionment of 1961 did not alter these figures significantly.

Inner City Democratic Organization. The inner city districts are the domain of the Democratic party organization. The basic character of the organization throughout Cook County has been molded here, where its most extensive electoral support lies. This organization is a classic political "machine," a kind of party organization which relies primarily upon material incentives for its ward and precinct workers and supplies local services for its voter constituents. Non-material rewards, for workers or voters, generally are not needed or used.[6] With large stocks of patronage available from city, county, and state offices, and with relatively centralized control over

[6] The early formation and contemporary operation of the Democratic organization in Chicago have been described and analyzed so often elsewhere that the analysis here need not go beyond a few summary remarks. For detailed treatments see: Edward C. Banfield, *Political Influence* (Glencoe: The Free Press, [1961]; Edward C. Banfield and James Q. Wilson, *City Politics* (Cambridge; Harvard University Press, 1963), ch ix; Harold F. Gosnell, *Machine Politics, Chicago Model* (Chicago: The University of Chicago Press, 1937); Martin Meyerson and Edward C. Banfield, *Politics, Planning and the Public Interest* (Glencoe: The Free Press, 1955), chs. iii and xi; James Q. Wilson, *Negro Politics* (Glencoe: The Free Press), ch. iii.

the distribution of those stocks, the organization is both massive and disciplined. This is especially true in the inner city wards of Chicago, where the low socio-economic status of the people is conducive to a materially-oriented organization.

Six attributes of the Democratic organization have decisively affected inner city congressional recruitment:

(1) Although party structure is formally based upon ward level organization, party leaders have been able to centralize the distribution of patronage and maintain a relatively hierarchic structure of authority throughout the city and county.

(2) The centralization of patronage has enabled party leaders to ensure unity among ward and township organizations. Committeemen cannot oppose the organization slate of candidates with impunity in either primary or general elections.

(3) Unity and hierarchy have made organization decision-making relatively impervious to the influences of rival non-party groups, associations, and elites in the primary electorate. Although the preferences of external groups (e.g., unions and ethnic associations) are considered, the slating of candidates for Congress is controlled entirely by the party leaders.

(4) The predominance of material incentives and the need to maintain the unity of a rather complex organization have contributed to an ethos which tends to inhibit the use of issues for obtaining either personnel or public support. The organization is able to maintain unity through intricate bargaining over the allocation of patronage. Issues, on the other hand, are deemed irrelevant at best and dangerously divisive at worst. Under such conditions, skills at bargaining, negotiation, and compromise are fostered and rewarded.

(5) The availability of important local offices as the major sources of patronage and of prestigious career objectives has produced a strong local orientation in the organization and among its personnel. The office of congressman is not highly regarded because it has no patronage worth mentioning and no apparent influence upon local politics. High city, county, or state-wide offices, with relatively broader jurisdictions, considerable administrative responsibilities, and greater visibility, are more eagerly sought than seats in Congress.

(6) Since the inner city organization is in large part an alliance of numerous ward-based ethnic, racial and religious groups, such affiliations have become important criteria for determining the distribution of patronage and elective office — in effect, the allocation of power within the organization.

TABLE 2
Metropolitan Chicago Congressional Voting Trends: Averages by Type of District[a]

	Per Cent Democratic								
District Type	1948	1950	1952	1954	1956	1958	1960	1962	1964
Inner City	71	65	66	74	63	76	74	71	77
Outer City	51	46	47	56	51	62	58	55	62
Suburban	42	35	36	40	35	42	40	35	41

[a] Sources: *The Congressional Quarterly Almanac* (Washington, D.C., 1957), XIII, 180-81; *ibid.*, 1961, XVII,1039-1040; *The Congressional Quarterly Weekly Report*, April 5, 1963, Part 1, p. 482, and March 26, 1965, Part 1, p. 477.

Inner City Recruitment. The recruitment of congressmen from the inner city districts has been an internal affair of the Democratic party organization during the last thirty years. Massive, hierarchic, unified, impervious to external pressure, and without serious Republican opposition, the Democratic organization has been able to exercise absolute control over the nomination and election of inner city congressmen. Long-standing membership in the organization has been the single most important criterion of selection. The congressmen have been chosen by party regulars from among party regulars.[7] They have risen through the party apparatus following career lines shaped by the distribution of power and the existence of established traditions. The party tends to funnel certain racial, ethnic, and religious groups to specific organizational and public positions. A given office may be reserved for Irishmen, or particular ward organizations may by tradition be awarded specified offices or patronage jobs. And offices are traded as patronage in bargains among different factions within the party. In this manner, prospective careers are determined and paths to Congress established.

Internal recruitment has had certain pronounced effects upon the character of inner city representation in Congress:

(1) Reflecting the material ethos of the organization, inner city congressmen have been well-schooled in and appreciate the value of quiet bargaining, negotiation, and compromise — virtues amply

[7] The fifteen men who have represented the inner city between 1932 and 1964 have owed much to the local organization. Seven of the congressmen had been slated by the organization and elected to legislative positions (in the State Assembly or the City Council) before going to Congress and two others had been elected to local executive offices. Four of the others had held high patronage positions in Chicago. Six of the fifteen were ward committeemen.

rewarded in the House. But few are skilled orators or advocates. Such abilities are not often needed in the House, but when they are, the inner city congressmen are handicapped.

(2) The local, non-ideological orientation of the organization generally has not been conducive to the recruitment of men who know much about questions of national policy. The nature of organization business has given few the time or incentive to prepare themselves for an office of national stature.

(3) Democrats who have risen through the disciplined and unified local party organization are well aware of the virtues of party unity. Local experience has taught them that in unity there is power. Chicago Democratic congressmen, particularly those from the inner city, value party cohesion as a positive good in need of little or no justification.

(4) Inner city Democrats abjure personality politics. Since recruitment is entirely controlled by the organization, there is little incentive for individuals to cultivate personal publicity or personal followings among the electorate. Inner city congressmen tend to resent individuals who consciously attempt to attract personal publicity. There is even some inclination to regard those who frequently make policy pronouncements as somewhat opportunistic and sensationalistic. Politics tends to be viewed as a cooperative, organizational enterprise.

(5) Inner city Democrats tend to be relatively old when they go to Congress. The elaborate structure of the organization usually entails a lengthy tenure and ascent through the hierarchy of organization-controlled offices. Since 1932, all but two of the fifteen inner city congressmen have been at least forty-five years old when first elected. Ten were over fifty, and one was seventy-eight. Although its utility to the organization is low, the office is not without its glamor and has tended to become a reward for long and loyal service.[8]

II. The Suburban Districts. The three suburban districts (the 4th, 10th, and 13th) have been the most safely Republican in metropoli-

[8]For comparative data, see Tables 3 and 4, below. Even the youngest man ever elected to Congress from an inner city district, Dan Rostenkowski, had considerable experience within the organization. His father was a Democratic committeeman. Mr. Rostenkowski grew up in the organization, served two terms in the State General Assembly, was elected Treasurer of the Cook County Young Democrats, and was elected to Congress in 1958 at the age of thirty. He became a party committeeman when his father was appointed to a federal job in 1961.

tan Chicago.[9] Three features of suburban society have decisively affected suburban organization for recruitment. First, as Table 1 indicates, these are the most affluent districts in the area. There are, however, numerous suburbs with large working class populations, concentrations of heavy industry, and pockets of poverty — a fact of decisive importance for Democratic township organization. Secondly, with thirty townships and over 100 municipalities, the dispersion of power and population is especially great.[10] Thirdly, there is a widely shared political ethic which is antagonistic to, if not incompatible with, organization politics. This ethic is manifest in the non-partisan local governments of most suburban municipalities, which deny to the parties potentially large stocks of patronage.[11]

Suburban Republican Organization. Just as the Democratic organization in metropolitan Chicago takes its characteristic form in central Chicago, the archetype of the Republican organization is found in the suburbs, where its voting support is most secure. Republican party organization and recruitment here have been shaped by the inadequacy and ineffectiveness of patronage in the suburban political milieu. Because the districts are so large, with dispersed populations living in individual homes, effective precinct work requires very large corps of party workers. The patronage needed is much greater than the supplies available from suburban sources. Moreover, the relatively high socio-economic status of the people and the ethic antagonistic to the use of patronage severely limit the utility of that which is available. The Republican township organizations encounter these conditions and beliefs more than the suburban Democratic party organizations and in exaggerated form. The Republicans must appeal to those more affluent country towns and townships where the suburban ethic is strongest and the middle and upper classes largest. This is true for the general and especially for the primary electorate.

---

[9]Only four Democratic candidates received as much as 45 per cent of the vote in individual suburban districts between 1948 and 1964. No Republican candidate for Congress has received a comparable percentage of the inner city vote during this period.

[10]District densities vary from 1,556 (4th C.D.) to 5,164 (10th C.D.) persons per square mile. In the city of Chicago, densities range from 9,880 (2nd C.D.) to 30,600 (9th C.D.). Source: U. S., Bureau of the Census, *Congressional District Data Book (Districts of the 88th Congress)* — A Statistical Abstract Supplement (Washington, D.C.: U. S. Government Printing Office, 1963), pp. 128 and 135.

[11]For an extensive treatment of the use of patronage in suburban Cook County, see David McCoy, "Patronage in Suburbia" (Unpublished Ph.D. dissertation, Department of Political Science, University of Chicago, 1963).

Republican township leaders have had to make extensive use of issue-oriented volunteer workers as the fundamental basis of party organization in the suburbs. The result in each of the three districts has been an organization which is non-materially oriented, undermanned, undisciplined if not disunited, decentralized, and easily penetrated by external elites from the primary electorate. The fact that the Republican committeemen have little useable patronage is of decisive importance. Without it they lack the resources to attract sufficient campaign workers and have no effective sanctions with which to discipline their organizations. In primary elections, township committeemen cannot rely on their volunteer precinct captains to work for the entire organization slate. Congressional district caucuses cannot even rely upon individual committeemen to adhere to caucus-endorsed candidates for Congress. Even when the organization is united, it cannot assure a safe primary vote, because non-patronage volunteers do not work their precincts all year and cannot build personal ties with their constituents.

The character of the major Republican counter-elites in the primary electorate has also affected the structure of the party organization. Generally speaking, although the party depends upon the good will and support of the business community in general elections, businessmen have had a rather disruptive influence on the party structure in primary elections. The party simply does not know when a prosperous businessman will decide to embark upon a political career or support a non-organization Republican for some office. If the Republican primaries were controlled by strong party organizations this would not be possible. On the other hand, the presence of prosperous businessmen who finance their own or help to finance someone else's campaign is an independent factor which damages already precarious organization control of the Republican primaries. Public spirited businessmen have upset regular Republican organization expectations on all levels of government in Illinois — from the ward or township to the governorship. In primary elections for public offices, it is not uncommon for a segment of the regular party to ally itself with some businessman and oppose other elements in the regular party who have endorsed some other candidates.

Suburban Republican Recruitment. In sharp contrast to the inner city Democratic pattern, suburban Republican recruitment generally has not been from within the party organization.[12] The non-

[12]Since the creation of the three suburban districts in 1947, only one of the seven Republicans elected had previously held a party organization position of any consequence. Given the uncertainty of the primaries, few committeemen have sought the nomination.

hierarchic, highly permeable structure of Republican organization has compelled Republican candidates for Congress to rely upon personal initiative and personal resources. The system tends to foster extreme sensitivity to the character of the primary electorate, which candidates must scrupulously cultivate.

External recruitment has had the following concrete effects upon the character of suburban congressmen and representation:

(1) These Republican congressmen have tended to be issue-oriented conservatives. They have had to cultivate primary electorates which are generally among the most prosperous and traditionally conservative in the entire county. From these primary electorates they have had to enlist large numbers of volunteer workers[13] (to supplement or combat the weak regular party organizations, as the case may be), solicit financial contributions, and obtain whatever support they can from prestigious businessmen. The primary constituency has set certain broad limits to the process of recruitment, while the influence of the business community and issue-oriented volunteers, drawn from among the more activist Republican elements in the primary electorate, have further influenced the process.

(2) Insofar as the Republicans elected to Congress have been issue-oriented and ideologically inclined, they have tended to put less emphasis on skills of bargaining or negotiation and more on oratory and public advocacy. The contrast with the inner city Democrats is particularly great.[14]

(3) In the absence of adequate organizational control, suburban Republican congressmen must engage in personality politics. They have either begun their congressional careers with relatively well-known names (two of the seven were school district superintendents) or have made every honorable effort to publicize their names and cultivate personal followings.

(4) Suburban Republican congressmen seem to place considerably less value on party cohesion for its own sake than do inner city Democrats. The Republican recruitment process is hardly conducive to traditions of unity and even less to any capacity to enforce it.[15]

---

[13]In some cases personal organizations have been exceptionally large. This has been particularly true of the 13th C. D., where the last two representatives could rely on well over 1,000 volunteers in primary or general elections.

[14]Speeches and insertions in the *Congressional Record* are a helpful (albeit inadequate) index to the differences between the two groups in this regard. On the whole, suburban Republicans have shown a greater propensity for oratory and on a wider range of issues than have the inner city Democrats.

[15]During the post-war period under study, Illinois Republican congressmen have not caucused with anything approaching the regularity of the Demo-

(5) Suburban candidates of both parties tend to be the youngest in Cook County. The seven suburban Republican congressmen who have served since 1949, the products of the most open, unstructured and uncertain system of recruitment in metropolitan Chicago, have averaged about forty-seven years of age when first elected to Congress.[16]

Suburban Democratic Organization. Democratic recruitment is very different from its Republican counterpart in the suburbs. Because the Democratic organization in Cook County is relatively centralized, it has access to stocks of patronage in a variety of offices outside of the suburbs and can distribute them in townships where they are scarce. Many township committeemen themselves have patronage jobs controlled by the central committee. In each of the three suburban districts, Democratic party organization is characterized by the patronage-service concept with hierarchic, unified leadership not easily permeated by external elites. The Democratic party has been able to build township organizations of this type because its primary electorate is largely composed of lower status groups who are amenable to the non-issue service appeals associated with patronage-oriented organizations. While it is true that the size of this electorate is sharply restricted in relation to the general electorate in most townships, it has been adequate to give the organization firm control over primary elections.

This control is facilitated by the structure of the potential counter-elites in that electorate — the labor unions. Labor cannot wheel into Democratic primary politics the way businessmen can enter Republican primaries. While businessmen can act as individual entrepeneurs, unions must act as collective entities — they are bureaucracies whose political decisions must be bureaucratic, not individual. The labor movement and the Democratic party in Cook County are both relatively centralized. Union leaders must think of the long-term effects and ramifications of opposition to a cen-

---

cratic delegation, which has consciously sought to maintain high cohesion on roll call votes. Unity among Illinois Republicans is much less deliberately cultivated.

[16]The nine outer city Republicans who have served in Congress during this same period have averaged fifty-three years of age when first elected. No Republicans have been elected from inner city districts since 1934. Although Republican candidates are nominated in all five inner city districts, the action is perfunctory because the election is viewed almost invariably as an impossible cause by party officials and nominees alike. Moreover, since the Republicans are patronage-poor, the nomination cannot even be used as a qualification for obtaining some other office. The analysis of recruitment is not an especially fruitful enterpise under these circumstances.

tralized and powerful Democratic political organization. They must also consider how best to allocate the limited political resources of their organizations. These officials are not individualistic entrepeneurs free to spend their own fortunes. Consequently the suburban Democratic primaries are highly structured — the party organizations are strong and disciplined and the only source of countervailing power is weaker and disinclined to risk adventuresome political fliers.

Suburban Democratic Recruitment. In each of the three suburban townships the Democratic organization is strong enough to control its own internal affairs, including the recruitment of candidates for public office. This strength, however, is built upon a severely restricted primary electorate. In general elections, where the public at large must be solicited, patronage-based Democratic organizations are much less effective. Not only are they too small for the task; they are the wrong kind of organization for the suburban milieu. The very factors which give the Democratic organization control over primary elections hurt their effectiveness in general elections. Then, when Democratic candidates must broaden their appeal to the wider general electorate, the ideals of the suburban ethic or "political culture" come into conflict with the image projected by the Democratic township organizations. The use of patronage, closed primaries, and central committee influence in the township political organizations are not viewed with favor in the middle class suburbia which decides the outcome of the general elections.

Although Democratic recruitment is internally controlled, Republican predominance in the general electorate has decisively affected the recruitment of Democratic candidates. Because there is no presumption of victory in the general elections (the Democrats have won only one suburban election since 1948), old line organization stalwarts have not valued the nomination. On the contrary, it has been sought by ambitious young men, mostly lawyers, seeking to establish themselves politically or professionally. The committeemen, in turn, tend to use the power of endorsement as a kind of incentive to induce aspirants to join their township organizations and serve for some time prior to receiving the nomination. Twenty-six organization-backed candidates were nominated in the three suburban districts between 1948 and 1964; seventeen, or about two-thirds were attorneys, compared to one-third of the inner city congressmen during the same period. These divergent patterns are an indication of the relative professionalization of career expectations in the inner city organization, where the probability of recruiting candidates from an independent profession is less likely than in the suburbs.

The disadvantageous competitive situation in general elections has affected internal recruitment in other important aspects. The average age of the suburban nominees has been forty-four years, some six years younger than the average for the inner city congressmen when first elected. (Of the seventeen suburban lawyers, eight were under forty when nominated.) The fact that suburban nominees have not had to rise through the Democratic party hierarchy largely accounts for their relative youth. Moreover, the candidates tend to be issue-oriented and are, like their Republican opponents, compelled to indulge in personality politics.[17]

III. The Outer City Districts. Nowhere in metropolitan Chicago is the influence of organization upon recruitment more evident than in the outer city districts (the 2nd, 3rd, 9th, 11th, and former 12th). The heterogeneous and intermediate socio-economic status of the people in these districts has provided ample social bases for the organizations of the two parties in their characteristic forms. The extremes of poverty and affluence are more evenly divided in this area than in either of the other two sets of districts. (See Table 1.) Neither party is compelled to build its outer city organization on severely attenuated primary electorates. Nor has either party had to face almost certain defeat in general elections throughout the entire period under study, as has been the case in the suburbs and inner city. At the same time, there have been gradual changes in the demographic and political environments within which the organizations must function. While the organizational structures have remained relatively stable in form, the districts have evolved from marginally Republican to marginally (and in some cases safely) Democratic.[18] (See Table 2.) Analysis of these districts over time

---

[17]Since, with a single exception, these candidates were not elected, it was not possible to ascertain their orientation toward party unity and the utilization of particular skills in concrete legislative situations. Issue-orientation and personality politics were evident in their campaigns and in interviews. Not infrequently, these propensities among suburban Democratic candidates created strains between them and the non-issue-oriented organizations which nominated them.

[18]Population trends since the apportionment of 1947 have contributed greatly to the increasing outer city Democratic pluralities shown in Table 2. The principal sources of the trend have been the expansion of the Negro ghetto, especially into a few wards in the 2nd and 3rd congressional districts, and the outmigration of Jews from the west side into some wards in the 2nd, 9th, and old 12th congressional districts.

reveals the variable influences of party organization and constituency upon candidate recruitment.

Outer City Republican Organization and Recruitment. Like Republican organizations throughout Cook County, those in the outer city are poorly disciplined, understaffed, and readily permeated by external elites because they have little patronage and must rely heavily on volunteer workers. Again the most important consequence of party organizational weakness is the enhanced influence of the primary electorate in the recruitment process. As in the suburbs, the system has tended to produce conservative candidates who have been issue-oriented, inclined (if not actually compelled) to cultivate personal followings and personal volunteer organizations, and disinclined to treat party unity as a cardinal virtue.

The influence of the Republican primary electorate has been more evident in the outer city districts than in the suburbs, where the dispersion of the electorate has tended to diffuse the influence of particular townships, municipalities, and population groups. On the other hand, a Republican legislature created the outer city districts with specific traditionally Republican areas of support at the heart of each. These communities are pockets of prosperity which serve as sources of money, volunteer personnel, and candidates in congressional elections. The founding of the districts in 1947 actually helped to structure power and recruitment in the primary constituency. As long as these communities have remained intact, they have dominated a recruitment process which has culminated in the nomination of outspokenly conservative candidates for Congress. This has been especially evident in the 3rd and 11th Districts. In each case, the candidates have come from a single ward dominated by long-established communities. In the case of the 3rd C.D., that community is formally organized into an association which has exercised considerable influence over the weak, disunited Republican party organization in the key Republican ward. In the 2nd C.D. two wards generally dominated, while in the 9th C.D. it was the Lake Shore Gold Coast area in general.

But changes in outer city social structure and party competition during the last decade have promoted deviations in the old patterns of recruitment in a number of districts:

(1) When population changes have altered the balance of party competition and the composition of Republican primary electorates, significant changes in candidate recruitment have occurred. This has been most evident in the Lake Shore districts, which have had a

large immigration of Jews. By the late 1950's these districts (especially the 2nd and old 12th) were beginning to slate avowedly liberal candidates for Congress. Where the effective primary electorate changed, so too did the available and influential elites, the personnel of the ward organizations, and eventually the kind of candidates recruited.[19]

(2) Where population changes have altered party competition but have not affected the structure of the Republican primary electorate, recruitment patterns have tended to remain relatively stable. Republican party leaders have known for some time that population trends were fundamentally altering the balance of partisan support in the outer city. But in districts with stable primary electorates, the party has not nominated candidates who could appeal to the new general electorates. This has been true particularly in the 3rd and 11th districts, where the balance of partisan sentiment has been least unfavorable to the Republicans and the primary electorates have been the most stable.

(3) As the outer city districts have become increasingly Democratic, Republican candidates have tended to become younger. The average age of outer city Republican nominees from 1950 through 1956 was fifty-two years; since 1958 the average has dropped to about forty-six years.

Outer City Democratic Organization and Recruitment. The Democratic organizations in the outer city wards are patronage and service-oriented, disciplined, hierarchic, and relatively impervious to external influences upon recruitment. Although the socio-economic conditions of the outer city are not ideal for this form of organization, considerable patronage has been invested there and organizations thoroughly capable of controlling primary elections and of appreciably influencing general elections have been created. Two factors have contributed to the success of outer city Democratic organizations. First, population changes have made some outlying wards very much like wards found in central Chicago. Secondly, the large electoral base which the Democrats have in the poor areas of "mixed" wards gives them power to exert considerable influence in the more affluent areas of those wards — by distributing the prestigious patronage and emoluments to which a ruling party

---

[19]The permeability of the Republican party organization has admitted a number of liberal Republican committeemen, many of them Jewish. This is particularly true in the northern Lake Shore wards, where the largest numbers of Jewish people have moved in the last decade. With only one exception, the highly structured Democratic organizations in these same wards have remained in the hands of Irish Catholics.

has access and by recruiting volunteers with practical interests in joining the ruling party of the wards and city. Republican committeemen complain that some of their best captains are enticed into the enemy camp.

Although the Democratic organizations are strong enough to control the outer city primary electorate, the marginality of the general electorate has compelled candidates to seek organized support beyond that which the party can supply. Notwithstanding this dependence on outside groups, particularly labor, recruitment has not been affected. Labor's hierarchic organizational ties to the Democratic party in the city as a whole are such that bolting the ticket (in primaries or general elections) in these districts could not be done without risking too much elsewhere in the city.

Nevertheless, electoral marginality has had a decisive impact on outer city Democratic recruitment. Although the process is internal, marginality has tended to divert the recruitment process away from old-line politicians of the type sent to Congress from the inner city districts. Most Democratic candidates and congressmen from the outer city have not held important party positions. In these districts, the kind of candidate slated for Congress has depended upon the party committeemen's assessments of the electoral situation at a given time. When the prospects for victory have seemed remote, the candidates chosen have been outsiders with tenuous links to the organization, or loyal men being rewarded with the candidacy or being groomed for more important (i.e., local) offices.[20]

Information is available on nineteen of the twenty-one Democrats who have been nominated in the outer city area since 1932 (the 2nd, 3rd, and 9th Districts) and 1947 (when the 11th and 12th Districts were created). The average age of the nineteen candidates when first slated is 47 years. Table 3 compares the averages of the three district categories in this regard. The fact that the outer city average falls between the other averages is a useful indicator of the overall differences between the three district categories. Where the party organization is highly structured and entrenched and where electoral security is most certain, candidates tend to be recruited internally from among organization men who have served the party for many years. Where the opposite conditions prevail, younger men with tenuous ties to the organization are recruited. The political

---

[20]In the 3rd C. D., for example, the seat was marginal during the 1940's and early 1950's, moving with national trends. But a large influx of Negroes gradually changed the partisan balance and, in 1958, an organization committeeman, William Murphy, decided the time was ripe to send himself to Congress and did so.

significance of these age differentials must be emphasized. It is the men who come from the marginal and unsafe districts who tend to be young enough to acquire seniority and with it power and leadership potential in Congress. But it is precisely these men who have the least chance of electoral survival.

TABLE 3
AGE OF DEMOCRATIC CANDIDATES WHEN FIRST NOMINATED 1932-1964

DISTRICT TYPE	AVERAGE AGE	PER CENT UNDER 40	TOTAL CASES[a]
Inner City	50	13	15
Outer City	47	37	19
Suburban	44	44	26

[a] Two outer city districts (11th and 12th) and two Suburban districts (4th and 10th) were created in 1947, so information dates from 1948.

The age differential is by no means the most important consequence of the different recruitment patterns in the inner and outer city districts. Like the suburban candidates, outer city Democrats have not been systematically socialized into norms which have become second nature for typical inner city congressmen. The differences are obvious and important for understanding the operation of the Chicago Democratic delegation in Congress. It is the outer city congressmen who have been the most inclined to seek personal publicity, least committed to the intrinsic value of party unity, most articulate, and most issue-oriented.

Chicago Democrats in Congress

For the past decade, Democrats have dominated the Chicago delegation in the House. Although Democratic candidates have failed to carry a suburban district since the election of 1948, they have won every congressional election in the inner city since 1934 and in the outer city since 1958. The impact which different systems of recruitment have upon representation can be evaluated by examining the means utilized by the Democratic delegation in exploiting the principal sources of influence in the House: the seniority and committee systems, bloc voting, and the skills and knowledge of individual members.

The Seniority and Committee Systems. When they were first elected to Congress, the average age of the twenty-one Democrats who have represented Chicago since 1949 has been fifty years (median fifty-three). The eleven from the inner city averaged fifty-two, while those from the outlying districts averaged forty-eight. Only five (twenty-four per cent) were under forty when first elected — four of them having come from unsafe outer city districts which were marginally Republicans when they were first elected.[21] During this same period, House Democrats who have served as committee chairmen have averaged forty-one years of age (median forty) when first elected to Congress. The Chicago delegation has been under a considerable handicap in achieving senior committee rank.[22]

Bloc Voting. Leadership of the delegation has perforce accrued to the safe inner city members with close ties to the local party organization. Without adequate important committee or subcommittee chairmanships during most of the post-war period, delegation leaders have had to be concerned with the cultivation of personal friendships among congressional leaders, a willingness to go along with the requests of others, and the promotion of delegation cohesion as a bargaining instrument. Long experienced in the practical political arts, the inner city members have been well trained for such tasks. Under their leadership, the delegation has maintained extraordinary unity on roll call votes. Since 1949, delegation leaders could rely on nine or ten sure votes, which, taken with those of a few downstate Democrats, have composed a sizeable bloc on close roll calls. These votes were readily expendable when other congressmen or delegations became indebted to the Chicago group.

The principal source of delegation unity has been the common organization background of most of the members, especially those from the inner city. They have been well aware of the utility of unity. To the organization stalwarts this is a self-evident truth which needs little explanation and no justification.

The principal source of disunity and deviant roll call voting during the period studied almost invariably came from those outer city congressmen who had the most tenuous ties to the organization when they were first elected. Some of these members were also prone to seek personal publicity to a degree that disturbed delega-

[21]Two of the four (James Murray [3rd C. D.] and Chester Chesney [11th C. D.]) were defeated after one term. A third, Sidney R. Yates (9th C. D.), retired temporarily in 1962 and ran unsuccessfully for the United States Senate.

[22]The problem has been especially noticeable since the death of Mr. Sabath in 1952. Generally speaking, by the time Chicago Democrats have begun to accumulate seniority and committee rank, they have been too old to enjoy the fruits of power for any length of time, if at all.

tion leaders.[23] Insofar as the leaders sought to maintain group solidarity, they tried to minimize these sources of tension emanating from outer city recruitment.

Skills and Knowledge. The recruitment process in Chicago generally has not supplied the Democratic delegation with men who have been knowledgeable about and capable of significantly contributing to the formulation of important national policies. The most articulate, interested, and best informed have almost invariably come from the outer city. But insofar as the delegation has acted in concert, the values of the inner city representatives have prevailed. Their practical, instrumental outlook and their preoccupations with tangible, highly specific goals have helped them to acquire much of value for the city. When necessary, credits could be collected on roll call votes in the House and even in the Senate. Pursuing limited, specific, tangible goals, they have been able to exercise considerable influence over the disposition of federal public works. In view of the recruitment patterns of the congressmen, it is not surprising that the federal projects and financing which the delegation has sought for Chicago typify the service ethos characteristic of the local political organization. Rivers and harbors, highways and housing have been their forte. Lobbyists have complained that no one on the delegation adequately understands the complexities of new fields, particularly those relating to electronics. Moreover, inner city congressmen rarely have initiated legislation of signal importance to the city. They generally have looked to local government and private business for requests — the highly specific kind best handled under the circumstances in the House. The justifications for these ideas and particularly the arguments for them on the floor of the House (when that was necessary) were generally left to the outer city congressmen.

Opportunities for Future Research

The general effects of recruitment upon the functioning of the House must await systematic, extensive study of that body. The development of appropriate categories relative to the functioning

[23]These habits are at least in part necessitated by the close electoral situation in these districts and the consequent need to rely on personal followings, the press, and non-party organizations for supplementary electoral help. But the marginality of the districts is also part of the original recruitment process which tends to funnel non-organization types to Congress in the first place.

of the House is clearly a prerequisite to the most useful application of recruitment analysis. Even without this knowledge, however, the variety of organizational forms in the cities throughout the nation provides an unusually large source of data for the study of political recruitment. A cursory examination of the major cities, using a very simple classification of organizational forms, is indicative of the research possibilities. Differences in the structures of the political systems within metropolitan Chicago suggest great differences between (and within some) other big cities and metropolitan areas.[24] Do these constituency differences have any systematic effects upon urban recruitment and representation in the House?

Chicago is the model of a strong, centrally-directed, patronage-oriented political organization. Labor, although relatively well organized for political action, is relegated to a decidedly secondary position in the recruitment process. The situation in Los Angeles is very different. There, as in California generally, local parties lack effective precinct level organization, cannot control the nominating process, and have no patronage.[25] In the absence of effective local party organization, the recruitment of Democrats in Los Angeles is decisively affected by the endorsements of important groups — particularly the press, labor, and the California Democratic Council, a liberal, issue-oriented, volunteer organ of the Democratic club movement.[26] In marked contrast to Chicago, local party leaders in California are primarily concerned not with local affairs, but with issues of state and national interest.[27] The general effect has been the recruitment of ideological liberals to serve in Congress. Detroit presents a third kind of political structure in which a labor union under ideologically liberal leadership has effectively dominated a

---

[24]For more detailed comparisons of big cities, see the following: Charles E. Gilbert, "National Political Alignments and the Politics of Big Cities," *Political Science Quarterly,* 79 (March, 1964), 25-51; J. David Greenstone, "Labor Politics in Three Cities: Political Action in Detroit, Chicago, and Los Angeles," (Unpublished Ph.D. dissertation, Department of Political Science, University of Chicago, 1963); James Q. Wilson, "Politics and Reform in American Cities," in Ivan Hinderaker (ed.), *American Government Annual* (New York: Holt, Rinehart, and Winston, Inc., 1962); Wilson, *The Amateur Democrat;* Edward C. Banfield and James Q. Wilson, *City Politics* (Cambridge, Mass.: Harvard University Press, 1963); "City Bosses and Political Machines," *Annals of the American Academy of Political and Social Science* (May, 1964), entire issue. The most detailed studies are found in the series edited by Edward C. Banfield, "City Politics Reports" (Cambridge: Joint Center for Urban Studies of the Massachusetts Institute of Technology and Harvard University, 1959-63).

[25]Wilson, *Amateur Democrat,* p. 101.

[26]*Ibid.,* pp. 110-11, 118-20, 248.

[27]*Ibid.,* pp. 125, 149, 162.

weak and disunited regular Democratic party. As in Los Angeles, a local non-partisan tradition and scarcity of patronage have crippled the Democratic party organization. But in Detroit, unlike Los Angeles, a strong, politically conscious union exists. The UAW, via its control of the local COPE organization, frequently in alliance with activist liberal or ethnic groups, has stepped into the organizational void.[28] But nowhere in Detroit has COPE been able to exercise the degree of control over recruitment which the Democratic party organization has everywhere in Chicago. The incompleteness of organizational control by either party or labor is manifest in the importance of personality in determining the outcomes of primary elections in most Wayne County congressional districts.[29]

Other major cities more or less approximate these three types. Those with a strong, centralized, patronage-oriented Democratic party organization which can control political recruitment, as in Chicago, include Gary, Pittsburgh and Philadelphia.[30] Other machines are weak and highly factionalized, such as those in Cleveland, Jersey City, Kansas City, and St. Louis.[31] In Boston, the Democratic organization is weak and local patronage is scarce, but state legislators do have considerable patronage and can influence the local factions.[32] There are also machines which are not city-wide. Such organizations have been strong in Baltimore and in Kings (Brooklyn) and Bronx Counties in New York City. In other areas of the city patronage resources have been inadequate to sustain professional party organizations strong enough to dominate the political system.[33] Finally, there are cities which resemble Los Angeles or Detroit in being genuinely nonpartisan locally, with little or no patronage, and no party machines in the classic sense of the term.

---

[28]Greenstone, *op. cit.*, ch. ii; *The Annals of the American Academy of Political and Social Science* (May, 1964), pp. 47-48; Banfield and Wilson, *City Politics,* pp. 286ff.

[29]See Greenstone's discussion of the nominations of Charles Diggs, Jr. (Thirteenth), Harold Ryan (Fourteenth), John Dingell, Jr. (Fifteenth), John Lesinski, Jr. (Sixteenth), and Martha Griffiths (Seventeenth).

[30]For a detailed account of the Democratic organization in Philadelphia, see Robert L. Freedman, *A Report on Politics in Philadelphia* (Cambridge: Joint Center for Urban Studies of the Massachusetts Institute of Technology and Harvard University, 1963). See also James Reichley, *The Art of Government: Reform and Organization Politics in Philadelphia* (New York: The Fund for the Republic, 1959).

[31]Wilson, *American Government Annual* (1962), p. 38.

[32]*Ibid.,* p. 40; Banfield and Wilson, *City Politics,* pp. 116, 136, 152, 161, and 230.

[33]This is particularly true of Queens and, lately, of Manhattan, where Tammany Hall has steadily lost control. The Bronx organization has also deteriorated.

The major cities of this type include Milwaukee, Minneapolis, St. Paul, and San Francisco. Labor is especially well organized and militant in San Francisco. In Minneapolis and St. Paul, labor has joined a coalition of Democratic party leaders and liberal intellectuals in the Democratic-Farmer-Labor party, which emerged as a dominant political force in 1948.[34] As we noted previously in regard to Los Angeles, the political systems in all of these cities, in marked contrast to the machine organization cities (whether centralized, factional, or partial), tend to encourage the recruitment of Democratic congressmen who are issue-oriented ideological liberals.

The simple classification of machine and non-machine recruitment can be shown to have general, systematic effects in the House. We see the distinction between the ideological, issue-oriented liberal Democrats, who founded the Democratic Study Group, and the non-ideological, machine liberals, who took much less interest and provided almost no leadership for the DSG during its formative years.[35] We see the distinction, too, in the different recruitment ages of northern metropolitan Democrats (Table 4). Irrespective of district marginality, non-machine Democrats tend to enter Congress with a career-potential advantage of two to three terms. The nonmachine congressmen, however, have tended to represent districts whose electoral marginality gives the least promise of long careers in the House.

It has been pointed out that the increasing number of safe Democratic seats in the urban North and the decrease of such seats in the South portends significant changes in the distribution of power in the Democratic party in the House.[36] What kind of men will represent these urban districts? What interests and skills will they bring

---

[34]Banfield and Wilson, *City Politics*, pp. 285-89.

[35]Mark Ferber lists 27 M.C.'s whom he calls the "inner core" of leaders in the DSG when it was organized formally during the 86th Congress. Only three were from big cities having political machines in the traditional sense of the term, while seven were from non-machine urban districts, which had a total of only 27 Democratic representatives at that time. There were nearly twice that number of machine congressmen. For the list of DSG leaders and members during the 86th Congress, see Mark F. Feber, "The Democratic Study Group: A Study of Intra-Party Organization in the House of Representatives" (Unpublished Ph.D. dissertation, Department of Political Science, University of California, Los Angeles, 1964). A DSG official has estimated that in the 88th Congress only one-third of the machine Democrats in the House actually belonged to the DSG and that many who did were there at the request of the leadership.

[36]Raymond E. Wolfinger and Joan Heifetz, "Safe Seats, Seniority, and Power in Congress," this REVIEW, 59 (June, 1965), 337-49. See also, Charles O. Jones, "Interparty Competition for Congressional Seats," *Western Political Quarterly*, 17 (September, 1964), 461-76.

TABLE 4

NORTHERN METROPOLITAN DEMOCRATS: AGE AT FIRST ELECTION 1953-1961, BY TYPE OF DISTRICT

	DISTRICT TYPES[a]					
	SAFE		UNSAFE		ALL	
AGE	MACHINE (39)	NON-MACHINE (12)	MACHINE (28)	NON-MACHINE (28)	MACHINE (67)	NON-MACHINE (40)
Average	45.2	40.9	45.7	40.5	45.4	40.7
Median	44.0	40.0	44.0	40.0	44.0	40.0
Under 40	23%	50%	32%	46%	27%	48%

[a] Cox index of inter-party competition. Edward F. Cox, "Congressional District Party Strength and the 1960 Election," *Journal of Politics,* 24 (May, 1962), 277-302. "Unsafe" includes three of Cox's categories: "generally" Democratic, "marginal" and "generally" Republican. Metropolitan districts are defined in *Congressional Quarterly Almanac,* 12 (1956), 788-791.

Machine and non-machine categories are based on the characteristics of political organization analyzed in the discussion above. The major machine-dominated areas include: Baltimore, Boston, The Bronx, Brooklyn, Buffalo, Cleveland, Gary, Jersey City, Kansas City, Manhattan, Newark, Philadelphia, Pittsburgh, and St. Louis. A number of anti-machine congressmen have been elected in machine cities. Such men have the support of independent political organizations and are classified as non-machine in the Table. They include: Bolling (Mo.), Donovan (N.Y.), Powell (N.Y.), Roosevelt (N.Y.), and Ryan (N.Y.).

to the House? The decline in strength of a number of party machines and recent increases in the number of safe Democratic seats in non-machine areas may ultimately have a significant impact upon the character of the Democratic representation and leadership from the urban North.

Future analyses of recruitment need not be confined to the simple categories used for illustrative purposes here. Even the machine, nonmachine distinction can be reclassified into numerous types according to the extent of centralization, sources of resources, local goal-orientations and organizational age.

SECTION THREE

Ideology

Ideology

The concept of ideology, one of the most frequently used terms of political analysis, is closely linked to political parties as a prime conveyor of competing sets of political beliefs. It has been noted that the Rational-Efficient and Party Democracy models differ fundamentally in evaluation of the role that ideology plays in political parties. Ideology is viewed in the Rational-Efficient model as a tactical means to the end of electoral victory; party leaders are concerned with adopting policy stands that are designed to win elections, rather than with winning elections in order to implement a particular set of policies (Downs, 1957; Schlesinger, 1965; Epstein, 1967). The elevation of ideology into an end-in-itself is viewed in this model as irrational and dysfunctional. Proponents of the Rational-Efficient model tend to favor such material incentives as patronage and career advancement over ideological incentives or motivations for political activity; they believe that a commitment to ideological principles endangers the successful operation of the pragmatic, bargaining, brokerage style party in that either specific voter groups or the mass of voters of the moderate center are likely to be alienated by such party appeals.

Ideology is a more vital and integral component in the Party Democracy model; here, the party is assigned a preeminent role in societal goal-definition and governmental policy-making. From the viewpoint of this model, a political party is supposed to stand for something, and it seeks power in order to implement basic policy views; it is expected to be something more than merely an electoral machine. It follows then that party leaders and activists tend to be motivated by ideological or policy incentives, rather than by material concerns. One engages in political activity in order to give expression to his own political views, not in hope of some material gain.

Opposing general propositions concerning ideology are derived from these two party models. From the standpoint of the Rational-Efficient model, American parties are viewed as being basically non-ideological and undifferentiated, Tweedledum and Tweedledee, as wine bottles holding essentially the same contents, although bearing different labels. (For statements of and critical reactions to this common view of American parties see Flinn and Wirt, Selection 3.1; and Marvick and Nixon, 1961.) A set of propositions related to ideology follows from the Party Democracy model: first, political parties are expected to be ideologically distinctive; second, party leaders and activists are ideologically oriented; and third, party activists or "militants" are held to be ideological purists who put principle ahead of winning and who are more extreme ideologically than party leaders and voters (Duverger, 1954; Butler, 1960; Epstein, 1967; May, 1969; McKitterick, 1960).

Recent empirical research has cast doubt about the above propositions derived from both party models. American parties appear to be more ideological and European parties less ideological than the Rational-Efficient and Party Democracy models suggest. It makes more sense to reject such simple dichotomies stated as polar opposites of *either* ideology *or* pragmatism and to think instead of a continuum involving a broad area between these two extremes in which ideology is operative in political parties (Wright, Selection 3.5). Before examining individual studies of the ideological perspectives of party activists, it is first necessary to indicate how the concept of ideology has been conceptualized and measured. A large part of the problem with the concept of ideology is that it has been vaguely and broadly used. Overviews of the variety of usages of this term are presented by Minar (1961) and Lane (1965). Among attempts to gain a clearer and more precise grasp of the concept of ideology, the efforts of Converse (1965) and Barnes (1966a) are notable. Converse considers the term ideology so "thoroughly muddied by diverse uses" that he uses instead the term "belief system," which he defines as "a configuration of ideas and attiudes in which the elements are bound together by some form of constraint or functional interdependence" (p. 207). The notion of constraint is central. Converse extends the line of research begun in *The American Voter* (Campbell, *et al.*, 1960) on voters' levels of conceptualization to voters' recognition and understanding of the terms liberalism and conservatism. His main thesis is that ideological sensitivity and sophistication is mostly a property of political elites, which in a broad sense mean the politically interested and active stratum of the electorate, and that it declines rapidly within mass publics the lower one goes in the scale of political involvement and participation (pp. 219-27).

This approach to ideology as "a belief system which is internally consistent *and* logically held," with elites viewed as the "hosts of ideology" is extended by Samuel Barnes (1966a). Following Converse, Barnes views ideology as an analytical framework; he admits the intellectual bias and argues that ideology should be distinguished from "ideology by repetition" or traditionalism and "ideology by proxy" which means merely "repeating the party line" without necessarily understanding it. Barnes makes an important contribution in presenting the case that ideology should be viewed in an *organizational* context; he stresses the important role of political organizations — especially political parties — in mediating between the elite and the mass electorate. Converse and Barnes, in viewing ideology as a constrained and intergrated political belief system which is possessed mainly by the political elite and is transmitted to the politically less sophisticated mass electorate, have made a promising start toward salvaging this classic concept of political analysis.

Ideology is a complex concept; herein lies a great deal of the difficulty. The term is broadly applied, but usually only selected aspects of relevant phenomena are studied. Ideology should be conceptualized as involving several rather than a single dimension: "Ideology is not an undifferentiated concept; it has many interpretations and dimensions" (Barnes, 1967, p. 158). Three main dimensions of ideology are analyzed by Barnes (1967) and Converse (1965). The first dimension, that of *saliency* or sensitivity and intensity; this gets at the question *how ideological*; it indicates the extent to which ideological perspectives are applied as a frame of reference to the interpretation of political phenomena. The second dimension is degree of constraint or consistency and interdependence among an individual's political beliefs. A third, and more familiar, dimension is that of content or direction; this refers to the substance of the political ideas, to what the ideology is about. Involved here are the familiar left-right and liberal-conservative continua. The additional dimensions of the range or scope and the complexity of the belief system are related to constraint and are implied in the traditional usage of the concept of ideology, although they are less frequently studied empirically. Political ideologies may provide cues over a narrow or broad range of political issues; they may be simple or complex. In this regard, Communism is a broad, systematic, and complex ideology when compared with liberal democracy as a belief system. Congruence or consensus is a dimension of ideology which refers not to an individual's political beliefs, but rather to the degree of homogeneity-diversity of perspectives within and between groups — e.g., among leaders or between leaders and followers (see McClosky *et al.*, 1960).

A belief overview of approaches that have been taken to the operationalization of the concept of ideology is found in Wright (Selection 3.5). The most commonly used approach in survey research involves ascertaining the respondent's positions (agree-disagree, favor-oppose) in controversial policy areas such as social and economic policy, civil rights, and foreign policy which involve liberal-conservative differences. A less widely used though related approach seeks agreement-disagreement with liberal and/or conservative philosophic principles, rather than with current issues (McCloskey, 1958). Both approaches are designed to measure the content and congruence dimensions and scaling techniques are often applied. The approach most often taken with regard to the saliency dimension involves ascertaining the respondents' perceptions of salient political issues and/or differences between the political parties and candidates; their responses to open-ended questions are coded for references to ideology and evidence of ideological perspectives (Campbell, *et al*, 1960; Eldersveld, 1964; Barnes, 1967). The simplest, although more subjective, approach is simply to ask the respondents to classify themselves along a liberal-conservative continuum ranging from strong liberal to strong conservative and to ask the underlying reasons in terms of principles or issues for their self-classification. Given the lack of ideological sensitivity of mass publics, this approach is more feasible with elite samples.

A number of studies of American parties have raised the questions of how ideological are party leaders and activists (the saliency dimension), how cohesive are the Democratic and Republican parties ideologically (the congruence dimension), and to what extent do Democrats and Republicans differ ideologically in liberal-conservative terms (the content dimension). Three general findings have emerged from this line of research: first, ideology is more salient for political activists than for voters generally; second, there are significant ideological differences between Democratic and Republican party leaders and activists: Democrats tend to be more liberal and the Republicans, more conservative; third, party activists appear often to be motivated more by ideology and policy than by material incentives. Finally, ideology appears to be a party-related phenomenon; in most of the studies examined, party is more strongly associated with ideological differences than other variables — such as socio-economic status or religion — examined. Given the use of differing approaches, it is helpful to look at individual studies as their findings bear on the above propositions. The dimensions of ideology investigated and the measures used should be noted.

Herbert McClosky and associates (1960) studied the ideological perspectives of Democratic and Republican leaders (1956 national convention delegates and alternates) and followers (partisan voters from national cross-section surveys). Their instrument was the respondents' policy views on a set of 24 national issues and their findings pertain to the three dimensions of saliency, content, and congruence. They found, first, ideology to be more salient for party leaders than followers (see also McClosky, 1964). Second, they found the two parties to be relatively distinctive ideologically; the Democrats (leaders and followers) tended to be more liberal and the Republicans, more conservative. Third, party leaders differed more sharply than did followers. The two groups of party leaders differed significantly on 23 of the 24 issues; the followers, on only 7 of 24. Fourth, they found Republican supporters to be closer in their policy views to the Democratic leaders than they were to leaders of their own party. The inference from this study that the Republican party leadership is ideologically out-of-tune and more conservative than either the electorate as a whole or even Republican voters was echoed in the 1964 Republican campaign and again in the 1968 pre-convention polls.

Flinn and Wirt (Selection 3.1) replicated McClosky's study on samples of Ohio Democratic and Republican county party officials. They used McClosky's original set of 24 national issues, and found essential similarity of ideological perspectives of both groups of Ohio leaders with their national counterparts, although the Ohio Democrats were slightly more liberal and the Ohio Republicans slightly more conservative than the corresponding samples of national convention delegates. Flinn and Wirt note that this suggests an "informal linkage" between levels of American parties that "contrasts with many facts demonstrating the federal and local character of American parties." Flinn and Wirt went beyond the McClosky study in adding separate sets of items concerning state issues and civil liberties questions. They found reduced party differences on state issues and even slighter differences on civil liberties questions; furthermore, for both groups of party officials there was only a moderate positive correlation (.52) between positions on social and economic national issues and on similar state issues and virtually no relationship between positions on civil liberties matters and *either* national or state issues, thus suggesting that "those are different dimensions of opinion." Very little in the way of correlates of ideology was found apart from party. Flinn and Wirt concluded: "It appears that the contrasting attitudes and attitude structures which divide Republicans from Democrats relate to party itself and not to some other factor lurking behind and operating through party." Flinn and Wirt argue that the ideological function is important in any visible democratic political system, including the American, and are critical of what we have called the Rational-Efficient model: "A model of American party politics presuming free maneuver of leaders exclusively concerned with electoral victory is dubious."

In his systematic study of political parties in the Detroit metropolitan area, Samuel J. Eldersveld (1964, Chapter 8) analyzed the intensity or saliency, congruence, and direction or content of ideological perspectives of party officials at the congressional district and precinct levels. He used issue positions as a measure of content and congruence and perceptions of party differences as a measure of saliency. Eldersveld found, first, that the two party leadership groups differed significantly in ideological perspectives in the expected direction (Democrats more liberal, Republicans more conservative), although neither party was a monolithic ideological structure. Second, the inter-party ideological differences were greatest for the top district leaders, who were more ideologically sensitive and homogeneous than the precinct leaders. Third, Eldersveld found greater ideological diversity in the Democratic leadership ranks; the Republican leaders were ideologically more homogeneous and more conservative. Fourth, as far as leader-follower congruence is concerned, Eldersveld furnished only partial support for McClosky's findings. There were sharper ideological differences between the two groups of party leaders than was the case for the followers (party identifiers, from a cross-section sample). But, *contra* McClosky, there was even closer correspondance of leader-follower policy views in the Wayne County Republican party than among the Democrats; the policy views of the independent voters, however, were closer to those of the Democratic precinct leaders.

Eldersveld also examined a number of correlates of ideology. Particularly interesting are two of his findings: first, contrary to much impressionistic evidence, ideological conflict between the two parties was greatest in the politically competitive, marginal congressional districts; second, he found striking ideological differences among district organizations within each party. He concluded: "A prominent and consistent finding, with explanatory power, is that ideology is a phenomenon related to party organization" (p. 218).

In a study of Nassau County (New York) executive committeemen, Ippolito (1969) collected data on the dimensions of ideological saliency, content, and congruence by means of questions concerning issue positions, perceived issue-differences between the parties, and motivations for entering and continuing party activity. Ippolito found sharp liberal-conservative differences between Democratic and Republican party officials. He found further that ideology was quite salient for both groups of party officials and that it played a strong role — especially among Democrats — as an incentive for political activity and in their perceptions of party goals. In examining correlates of ideology, Ippolito found party to be most strongly related to ideological differences.

Hirschfield and associates (Selection 3.2) studied Democratic, Republican, and Liberal county committeemen in Manhattan and found sharp ideological differences (content), with the Republicans being the most conservative group and the Liberals the most liberal, with the Democrats falling between but closer to the Liberals. They used issue positions, identification with prominent national political leaders, attitudes towards minority groups and political change, and reasons given by the party officials for their having become interested in politics as measures of ideology. Hirschfield and associates also contended that ideological incentives played a stronger role than material incentives as motivations for political activity and concluded that political allegiance and affiliation of these urban political activists was determined more by ideological convictions than by socio-economic status or demographic characteristics.

A study of Democratic and Republican campaign workers in Los Angeles (Marvick and Nixon, 1961) included a treatment of ideology, touching on the dimensions of saliency, content, and congruence. Marvick and Nixon used as measures of ideology questions concerning motivations for joining the party, perceived differences between the parties, and issue positions. They concluded that ideology was a significant motivational factor for these political activists: "When active workers were asked why they belonged to their parties and what differences they saw between parties, they consistently answered in rudimentary ideological terms" (p. 211). Marvick and Nixon noted also: "There is some evidence that ideological convictions were important in activating people, especially when they felt a sense of ideological *disharmony* with their daily associates" (p. 212, original emphasis). In addition, they found sharp party differences in ideological perspectives (content) and, due partly to greater socio-economic diversity, more ideological tension within the Democratic party ranks. They concluded generally that their findings did not support the view of American parties as "basically non-ideological in character."

A few studies have tested propositions derived from the Party Democracy model, especially the hypothesis, associated with Duverger (1954) and Butler (1960), which states that party activists are more extreme ideologically than party leaders and voters. One such study, which in a very limited fashion tested this propostion on American parties, is included in this section. Costantini (Selection 3.3) sent a mail questionnaire to the members of the California delegation to the 1960 Democratic national convention. Delegate selection procedures enabled Costantini to differentiate three levels of party leaders and activists: the top leaders (elected public officials); middle level leaders (delegates selected in district caucuses); and lower level leaders or activists (rejected caucus nominees, to whom questionnaires were also sent). The two latter groups were composed heavily of members of the California Democratic Council (CDC), "the unofficial, mass-membership arm of the state's Democratic party." (See Carney, 1958; Wilson, 1962). Costantini's measures of ideology consisted of the respondents' self-classification on a five-point liberal-conservative scale, their preferences as to the party's presidential nominee, and positions on a set of issues. Costantini's findings support the Duverger-Butler hypothesis: "The superstructure of the party's leadership tends to be more 'moderate' and 'centrist' than the substructure," whom he found to be more radical and liberal than the top leaders. Costantini suggests that his findings are not inconsistent with McClosky's; while top party leaders may be more ideological than party voters, they may also be more moderate than the lower-level party leadership (activists), thus being ideological intermediates within the party. It should be noted that Costantini's findings differ from Eldersveld's (1964), who found top party leaders to be more ideological sensitive and extreme than lower-level precinct leaders. However, Eldersveld's top party leaders were party officials, rather than elected public officials. In any case, a contribution of both studies lies in the analysis of ideological differences among party leadership strata. Too often, leaders are considered a single, undifferentiated stratum, and more research is needed on intra-leadership differences.

Richard Rose (Selection 3.4) also tested the Duverger-Butler hypothesis attributing ideological extremism to party activists. Unlike the foregoing studies, which utilized data on individuals, Rose analyzed resolutions submitted by constituency parties to the annual conferences of the British Conservative and Labour parties over a five year period (1955-60). Rose used as indices the proportion of resolutions which he classified as "ideological" or policy-oriented statements and "extremist" positions which deviated from current party policy. His main conclusion was that "ideological extremism . . . is extremely limited in both parties." Only 54 per cent of the resolutions were classified as "ideological" (Labour slightly more than Conservative), and only 18 per cent of the Labour (and 11 per cent of the Conservative) constituency parties were classified as "ideologically extreme," based on the submitted resolutions. Further analysis revealed that ideology was not related to party competition and Rose concluded that contituency parties were not "firmly anchored in ideological position." His findings thus fail to support either the Duverger-Butler hypothesis or characterizations of British party activists as ideological extremists. However, an important limitation of this approach should be noted; namely, the assumption that such resolutions accurately reflect the ideological convictions of party activists, a dubious assumption as Janosik (1968, p. 177) notes.

In his study of Italian Socialist Party (PSI) members, Barnes (1966, 1967) developed measures of three dimensions of ideology: saliency, constraint, and content. Adapting the measure of ideological sensitivity used in *The American Voter* (Campbell, *et al.*, 1960) and by Converse (1965), Barnes's findings strikingly parallel the American data. Only 14 per cent of the PSI members qualified as ideologues (1967, p. 163). This finding is at variance with the Party Democracy model and is surprising given the status of the Italian Socialist Party as perhaps the last surviving Western example of the classic Marxist socialist party. Education was found to be the variable most strongly related to ideological saliency: "Ideological sensitivity is almost a monopoly of the educated members" (1967, p. 353). Barnes also found a rather low level of constraint due to ideology, although it was somewhat greater for the educated members. As far as content was concerned, a majority of the PSI members were leftists, although there was considerable diversity and factionalism; the party was not a monolithic ideological structure. Only a minority of the members were classified as ideological extremists; Barnes's findings thus lend little support to the Duverger-Butler hypothesis concerning the ideological zeal of party activists.

A different approach to measuring the saliency of ideology is in the last selection in this section; here, I (Wright, Selection 3.5) develop the notion of an ideology-pragmatism continuum along which party activists can be located. A set of items concerning perceptions of party constituted an acceptable Guttman scale with which to compare local officials of the German Social Democratic (SPD) and Christian Democratic (CDU) parties. Consistent with the findings of several of the above-mentioned American studies, party was the variable most strongly related to ideology; since this was the case, party was controlled in the search for other correlates of ideology. The most interesting broad finding was the emergence of different party-related patterns of ideological correlates: generally working-class correlates of ideology for SPD officials and middle-class correlates of ideology for CDU officials.

The variety of approaches to ideology in these studies testifies to still unresolved conceptual and methodological problems. Nevertheless, a promising beginning has been made, and already the findings of such studies lead us to question some of the standard generalizations made about the role of ideology in political parties.

REFERENCES

Barnes, Samuel H. "Ideology and the Organization of Conflict." *Journal of Politics,* 28 (August, 1966), 513-30.

———. "Participation, Education, and Political Competence." *American Political Science Review,* 60 (June, 1966), 348-53.

———. *Party Democracy: Politics in an Italian Socialist Federation,* Chapters 10 and 11. New Haven: Yale University Press, 1967.

Bealey, Frank J., Blondel, J., and McCann, W.P. *Constituency Politics: A Study of Newcastle-under-Lyme,* Chapter 14. New York: The Free Press, 1965.

Berry, David. *The Sociology of Grass Roots Politics: A Study of Party Membership.* London: Macmillan, 1970.

Brown, Steven R. "Consistency and the Persistence of Ideology: Some Experimental Results." *Public Opinion Quarterly,* 34 (Spring, 1970), 40-68.

Butler, David. "The Paradox of Party Difference." *American Behavioral Scientist,* 4 (November, 1960), 3-5.

Campbell, Angus, *et al. The American Voter.* New York: John Wiley and Sons, 1960.

Carney, Francis. *The Rise of Democratic Clubs in California.* Eagleton Foundation Case Studies in Practical Politics. New York: Holt, 1958.

Costantini, Edmond. "Intraparty Attitude Conflict: Democratic Party Leadership in California." *Western Political Quarterly,* 16 (December, 1963), 956-72.

Converse, Philip E. "The Nature of Belief Systems of Mass Publics," in *Ideology and Discontent,* edited by David Apter, pp. 206-61. New York: Free Press, 1965.

Downs, Anthony. *An Economic Theory of Democracy*, New York: Harper, 1957.

Eldersveld, Samuel J. *Political Parties: A Behavioral Analysis*, Chapters 8 and 19. Chicago: Rand McNally, 1964.

Epstein, Leon D. *Political Parties in Western Democracies*, Chapters 10 and 11. New York: Frederick A. Praeger, 1967.

Fishel, Jeff. "Party, Ideology, and the Congressional Challenger." *American Political Science Review*, 63 (December, 1969), 1213-232.

Flinn, Thomas A., and Wirt, Frederick M. "Local Party Leaders: Groups of Like-Minded Men." *Midwest Journal of Political Science*, 9 (February, 1965), 77-98.

Hirschfield, Robert S., *et al.* "A Profile of Political Activists in Manhattan." *Western Political Quarterly*, 15 (1962), 489-506.

Ippolito, Dennis S. "Political Perspectives of Suburban Party Leaders." *Social Science Quarterly*, 49 (March, 1969), 800-15.

Janosik, Edward G. *Constituency Labour Parties in Britain*. New York: Frederick A. Praeger, 1968.

Lane, Robert E. *Political Ideology*. New York: The Free Press of Glencoe, 1962.

Luttbeg, Norman R. "The Structure of Beliefs among Leaders and the Public." *Public Opinion Quarterly*, 32 (Fall, 1968), 398-409.

Marvick, Dwaine, and Nixon, Charles. "Recruitment Contrasts in Rival Campaign Groups," in *Political Decision-Makers*, edited by Dwaine Marvick, pp. 193-216. New York: The Free Press of Glencoe, 1961.

McClosky, Herbert. "Conservatism and Personality." *American Political Science Review*, 52 (March, 1958), pp. 27-45.

________. "Consensus and Ideology in American Politics." *American Political Science Review*, 58 (June, 1964), 361-79.

McClosky, Herbert; Hoffman, Paul J.; and O'Hara, Rosemary. "Issue Conflict and Consensus Among Party Leaders and Followers." *American Political Science Review*, 54 (June, 1960), 406-27.

McKitterick, T.E.M. "The Membership of the Party." *The Political Quarterly*, 31 (July-September, 1960), 312-23.

Minar, David W. "Ideology and Political Behavior." *Midwest Journal of Political Science*, 5 (1961), 317-31.

Rose, Richard. "The Political Ideas of English Party Activists." *American Political Science Review*, 56 (June, 1962), 360-71.

Sartori, Giovanni. "Politics, Ideology, and Belief Systems." *American Political Science Review*, 63 (June, 1969), 398-411.

Schlesinger, Joseph A. "Political Party Organization," in *Handbook of Organizations*, edited by James G. March, pp. 764-801. Chicago: Rand McNally, 1965.

Wilson, James Q. *The Amateur Democrat*. Chicago: The University of Chicago Press, 1962.

Wright, William E. "Ideological-Pragmatic Orientations Among West Berlin Local Party Officials." *Midwest Journal of Political Science*, 11 (August, 1967), 381-402.

Local Party Leaders: Groups of Like-Minded Men

Thomas A. Flinn
Frederick M. Wirt

In the conclusion to his recent survey of opinion data V. O. Key, Jr. remarked,

> "... as we have sought to explain particular distributions, movements, and qualities of mass opinion, we have had to go beyond the survey data and make assumptions and estimates about the role and behavior of that thin stratum of persons referred to variously as the political elite, the political activists, the leadership echelons, or the influentials. In the normal operation of surveys designed to obtain tests of mass sentiment, so few persons from this activist stratum fall into the sample, that they cannot well be differentiated, even in a status description, from those persons less involved politically. The data tell us almost nothing about the dynamic relations between the upper layer of activists and mass opinion. The missing piece of our puzzle is this elite element of the opinion system."[1]

There are, of course, some data that bear on the attitudes of the leadership stratum. Organizational leaders' attitudes toward civil

---

[1]*Public Opinion and American Democracy* (New York: Knopf, 1961), p. 537.

Reprinted from the *Midwest Journal of Political Science,* IX, No. 1 (February, 1965), 77-98, by permission of Wayne State University Press.

rights have been studied by Stouffer. Representative role concepts have been examined by Eulau, *et al.* with reference to state legislators and by Miller with reference to congressmen while a survey of business attitudes of senators was made by Hacker and a survey of policy attitudes of presidential convention delegates by McClosky, *et al.*[2] Still the essential correctness of Key's assessment is beyond dispute, and it is the aim of this study to provide some additional information concerning the opinion of political activists, specifically county party leaders in Ohio.[3]

In particular, we wish to describe these party leaders in terms of attitudinal characteristics on public policy issues. This section of our study is in part a replication of McClosky's using, however, a different population. For some this will be mere replication, but we trust that others will agree with us that it is important to see if we know what we think we know and to see whether what is true in one situation is true also in another. An additional objective of our inquiry is to test for the presence of attitude structures. Finally, we will make a serious effort to explain attitudinal differences between and within the parties.

Method

The data were collected by use of a mail questionnaire. In preparation for its mailing, a list was made containing the names of all the chairmen and secretaries of the county central and executive committees of the Ohio Republican and Democratic parties who were elected in 1958 or in 1960. Duplications were eliminated as were the names of officers who had co-operated with an earlier version of the

---

[2]Samuel A. Stouffer, *Communism, Conformity, and Civil Liberties* (New York: Doubleday, 1955). Eulau, *et al.*, "The Role of the Representative: Some Empirical Observations on the Theory of Edmund Burke," *American Political Science Review*, (Sept., 1959), pp. 742-56. Warren Miller, "Majority Rule and the Representative System," paper delivered at the 1962 APSA meeting. Andrew Hacker, "The Elected and the Anointed: Two American Elites," *American Political Science Review* (Sept., 1961), pp. 539-49. Herbert McClosky, *et al.*, "Issue Conflict and Consensus Among Party Leaders and Followers," *American Political Science Review* (June, 1960), pp. 406-27.

[3]The studies on which the publication is based were made under a grant from The Maurice and Laura Falk Foundation of Pittsburgh through the Eagleton Institute of Politics, Rutgers, The State University. However, the Foundation is not the author, publisher, or proprietor of this publication and is not to be understood as endorsing, by virtue of its grant, any of the statements made or views expressed herein. Gratefully appreciated and necessary assistance has come also from the Ohio Center for Education in Politics and from a Ford Fund grant to Oberlin College for the study of public affairs.

study. A list of 565 remained, 298 Republicans and 267 Democrats. Several waves of questionnaires were sent to them early in 1962. Replies were received from 135 (45%) of the Republicans and from 127 (48%) of the Democrats. Respondents appeared to be representative of the original list of party officers (see the *Appendix* p. 000 on the "Sample").

The questionnaire consisted of three parts, the first dealing with political career, the second with socio-economic characteristics, and the third with opinion on policy issues. The last part, which contained 35 items, provides the larger part of the data to be analyzed here. The first 24 items were the national issue items McClosky used in his study of leader-follower relations.[4] The next 4 items dealt with civil liberties and the last 7 with state government issues. The first 24 items in this series of 35 will be referred to as the national issues schedule, the next 4 as the civil liberties schedule, and the last 7 as the state issues schedule.

In the questionnaire these items were simply listed, national issues first, civil liberties second, and state government issues last. Instructions preceding the list asked respondents to indicate whether they thought government support for an issue should increase, decrease, or remain the same. The three alternative responses were then stated in the space below each listed issue. Incidentally, our instructions were identical with those used by McClosky.

For the purpose of analysis we employed two measures: (1) an "Individual Support Ratio," and (2) a "Party Support Ratio." As will appear, each permits somewhat different analyses. Every respondent received three "Individual Support Ratios" corresponding to the three schedules, and "Party Support Ratios" were computed for each item in the questionnaire. The first measure (ISR) indicates where a respondent stood over a range of topically related issues while the second measure (PSR) shows where all members of each party stood on an issue or set of issues.

As a first step in the computation of Individual Support Ratios we selected 10 items from the national issues schedule.[5] One reason for the move was to reduce the required number of computations. Another was to limit analysis to items with high salience. Determination of salience is, of course, difficult; and doubt may arise concerning the selections that were made. What we did was to choose

---

[4]McClosky, *et al., op. cit.*

[5]The items selected were those which appear in Table 2 with the following numbers: 1,2,3,6,9,10,12,13,14,24. It may be of interest to note we have subsequently discovered that these items when applied to a population of state legislators constitute a Guttman scale.

items which we thought were issues familiar to political activists over a long period of time. Another reason for limiting this analysis to 10 items was to segregate domestic policy from foreign policy on the chance that these are different dimensions of opinion for members of our sample. All of our selected items deal with domestic matters.

The actual procedure used in scoring respondents on each schedule was as follows: every reply favoring increased governmental activity was given a value of 100; every reply favoring decreased governmental activity was given a value of 0; every reply favoring neither an increase nor a decrease was given a value of 50; failures to reply[6] were also given a value of 50. The total value of the responses in each schedule was divided by the number of items in the schedule which yielded an Individual Support Ratio for the schedule. Computation of Party Support Ratios required as a first step the grouping of all Democratic and of all Republican responses to each item in the questionnaire. For each party group replies were then scored in accordance with the procedure described above.[7]

Differences between and within the Parties

Our first effort was to determine the extent to which the policy views of Ohio Republican and Democratic leaders differ. The next

TABLE 1

PERCENTAGE DISTRIBUTION OF INDIVIDUAL SUPPORT RATIOS BY PARTY AND BY ISSUE SCHEDULE

Individual Support Ratio	National D	National R	State D	State R	Civil Liberty D	Civil Liberty R
100-80	21%	0%	14%	2%	49%	62%
79-60	48	7	40	17	26	21
59-40	23	44	36	35	9	13
39-20	6	35	7	30	10	2
19-0	1	14	3	15	5	2
	99%	100%	100%	99%	99%	100%
Mean	64	37	62	42	74	81

[6]Nearly all respondents completed every item in the opinion section of the questionnaire.

[7]The procedure was devised by McClosky with the exception that a scale of 100 is used here while he used a scale ranging from .00 to 1.00. In a subsequent comparison of the Ohio findings with McClosky's, his scores are converted to the scale of 100.

and closely related task was to measure differences within each party.

On national and state issues the inter-party differences are striking. On national issues, very few Republicans appear in the highest and very few Democrats in the lowest quintile; two-thirds of the Democrats have scores of 60 or more and half of the Republicans have scores under 40. On state issues, very few Republicans appear in the highest and very few Democrats in the lowest quintile; more than half of the Democrats have scores of 60 or more and almost half of the Republicans have scores under 40. The Democratic mean ISR on national and state issues is 64 and 62 respectively compared to 37 and 42 for the Republicans. Democrats are obviously much more in favor of governmental activity than Republicans, whether that government be in Washington or Columbus. It should be added, however, that there is an area of overlap in regard to both national and state issues; that is, there are Republicans and Democrats at the center in terms of ISR scores who agree with each other despite differences in party membership.

With reference to civil liberties, members of both parties urge stronger governmental action to restrain films, teachers, and Communists, with one-half of the Democrats and three-fifths of the Republicans placing in the highest ISR quintile. At the other end of the scale, there are more Democrats than Republicans with ISRs under 40, and the Democratic mean is slightly lower than the Republican. In general, the leaders of neither party appear as libertarians although the Democratic position seems to be a little less strongly anti-libertarian than is the Republican.

Another inference which may be drawn from the table above is that a high level of intra-party agreement exists with some exceptions and qualifications. This is an inference which we cannot "prove" statistically, but we can show how we reasoned from the quantitative data to the qualitative judgment. Note that on national issues about 70% of the Democrats are in the range from 40 to 80. In other words, the large majority of the party favors the status quo or offers moderate support for increased governmental activity, which appears to us to be a narrow range of opinion. The same thing may be said of the Republicans in regard to national issues with the differences that the range of opinion in the large majority of the party is from the status quo to moderate preference for less governmental activity. On state issues the range and character of opinion in each party is much the same as on national issues with the exception that the Republicans in particular show a slightly greater range of opinion. In the area of civil liberties the Republicans are united, but the Democrats show signs of intra-party conflict. Thus we agree with McClosky's conclusion that examination "of the opinions of Democratic and Republican leaders (on national issues) shows them to be distinct communities of co-believers. . . ."[8] We would add that this statement applies only slightly less well to state issues but substantially less well to questions involving civil liberties.

Party stands on specific issues are shown by the table below.

TABLE 2

Democratic and Republican Party Support Ratios, Issues Listed in Order of Greatest to Least Disagreement by Schedule

Issue	Subject	Dem.	Rep.	D-R
	National Issues			
1	Federal Aid to Education	76	31	45
2	Business Regulation	48	13	35
3	Social Security Benefits	86	53	33
4	Slum Clearance & Public Housing	87	59	28
5	Public Ownership of Resources	70	42	28
6	Utility Regulation	77	50	27
7	Foreign Aid	37	10	27
8	Reliance on the UN	67	40	27
9	Minimum Wages	76	49	27
10	Corporate Income Tax	54	28	26
11	Tariffs	31	54	−23
12	Farm Price Supports	38	18	20
13	Tax on Business	43	23	20
14	Tax on Large Incomes	59	39	20
15	US Participation in Military Alliances	65	47	18
16	Enforcement of Integration	65	47	18
17	Public Control of Atomic Energy	72	56	16
18	Defense Spending	54	41	13
19	Tax on Middle Incomes	36	25	11
20	Trade Union Regulation	74	66	8
21	Immigration	33	27	6
22	Restrictions on Credit	60	54	6
23	Tax on Small Incomes	13	16	−3
24	Enforcement of Anti-Trust	64	63	1
	State Issues			
25	Level of State Services	69	39	30
26	State Taxes	58	32	26
27	Unemployment Compensation	56	31	25
28	Mental Health Program	94	75	19
29	Establish State Corp. Income Tax	42	24	18
30	State Aid to Education	79	63	16
31	Establish State Individual Income Tax	37	25	12
	Civil Liberties Issues			
32	Loyalty Oaths for Teachers	66	80	−14
33	Investigations of Communism	71	85	−14
34	Enforcement of Laws Against Communism	87	96	−9
35	Motion Picture Censorship	69	68	1

[8]McClosky, *op. cit.*, p. 426.

The data may be more easily grasped if issues are collected in subject matter categories, and for this purpose we use the categories employed by McClosky with the addition of state and civil liberties categories. The stand of each party in each issue category is designated as the mean of all PSRs in the group. Thus we find that Democratic and Republican positions in various issue categories are as follows:

TABLE 2a

DEMOCRATIC AND REPUBLICAN PARTY SUPPORT RATIOS BY CATEGORIES OF POLICY ISSUES

	DEM.	REP.	D-R
Equalitarianism and Human Welfare (items 1, 3, 4, 9, 16, and 21)	70	44	26
Foreign Policy (items 7, 8, 15, and 18)	56	34	22
Public Ownership (items 5 and 17)	71	49	22
Taxes (items 10, 13, 14, 19 and 23)	41	26	15
Governmental Regulation of the Economy (items 2, 6, 11, 12, 20, 22, and 24)	56	45	11
State Issues (items 25, 26, 27, 28, 29, 30, and 31)	62	41	21
Civil Liberties (items 32, 33, 34, and 35)	73	82	−9

Mean differences are fairly large in all categories with the exception of the categories labeled "Governmental Regulation of the Economy" and "Civil Liberties"; but even in the first of these two categories there are some items on which party differences are substantial, i.e., business regulation (35 points difference), utility regulation (27 points difference), and farm price supports (20 points difference).

Additional use may be made of the data on Table 2 by making the rearrangement shown in the table below.

TABLE 3

DISTRIBUTION OF PARTY SUPPORT RATIOS ON 35 POLICY ISSUES

REP. PSR	DEM. PSR				
	0-25	26-45	46-55	56-75	76-100
0-25	1	6	1	—	—
26-45	—	1	2	6	1
46-55	—	1	—	3	3
56-75	—	—	—	4	3
76-100	—	—	—	2	1

* Boxed categories are those which contain issues on which Democratic and Republican PSRs fall in the same range.

An illustration may make reading of the table easier. The item which appears in the top row and in the center column is the item, "Regulation of Business" (item 2). The Democrats had a PSR of 48 and the Republicans a PSR of 13.

Proceeding now to inferences, note that only 7 of the 35 issues fall into the boxed categories. The measure is rough, but one can only conclude that the parties disagree much more than they agree. Note also that 23 Democratic Party Support Ratios fall to the right of the vertical lines and that only 10 Republican Party Support ratios fall below the horizontal lines indicating that the Democrats are much more than the Republicans in favor of governmental activity. These conclusions coincide, of course, with those made earlier on the basis of analysis of Individual Support Ratios.

So far, heavy emphasis has been laid upon inter-party disagreements, but further analysis of the data in Table 2 reveals an unexpected area of agreement between the parties. The item on the national issues schedule which Ohio Democrats support most strongly is slum clearance and public housing, and their second favorite is social security benefits. Ohio Republicans also give these issues strong support relative to the support they give other issues. More systematic investigation of the order of preferences expressed by Democratic and by Republican leaders shows that there is on the national issues schedule a rank order of correlation of plus .64. On the state issues schedule there is an even higher rank order correlation: plus .80.[9] It is obvious that Democratic and Republican respondents agree fairly well on priorities although the Democrats are more in favor of government action than are the Republicans.

Attitude Structure

It is occasionally asserted that the good conservative not only opposes governmental regulation of economic relations but also the governmental interference with individual non-property rights or that the true liberal favors government action to deal with economic and social problems but opposes governmental interference with freedom of speech and assembly. Stripped of their normative content, such statements are actually hypotheses concerning attitude structures; that is, they assert that attitudes on one subject predict attitudes on another due to some common underlying dimension of opinion.

[9]The coefficients are Spearman rank order correlation coefficients.

One way to test for the presence of attitude structures is to correlate scores on one attitude test with scores on another attitude test, and that was done in this study. What we did, for instance, was to take the individual scores of all Democratic respondents on the 10 selected national issues and to correlate these with the scores of the same respondents on state issues and then on civil liberties issues. Results are reported below.

TABLE 4

PRODUCT MOMENT COEFFICIENTS EXPRESSING CORRELATIONS BETWEEN INDIVIDUAL SUPPORT RATIOS ON THREE SCHEDULES BY PARTY AFFILIATION

	Democrats			Republicans		
	Natl.	State	Civ. Lib.	Natl.	State	Civ. Lib.
Civil Liberties	−.073	−.099	—	+.077	+.025	—
National Issues	—	+.525	−.073	—	+.519	+.077
State Issues	+.525	—	−.099	+.519	—	+.025

It appears that ISR scores on national issues relate positively to ISR scores on state government issues and that the relationship is virtually the same for Democrats as for Republicans, .525 and .519 respectively. A party official who views national government action favorably is also favorable to state government action; the same consistency holds if one desires that government restrain its action. Party leaders in Ohio evidently do not endorse the argument that federal activities should be restrained in order to create greater opportunities for state government action. It must be added, however, that national issue positions predict state issue positions imperfectly since there is considerable unexplained variance.

Further inspection of Table 4 shows that there is no relation between responses to national issues and responses to civil liberties issues no matter which party group is viewed. The same is true with regard to the relation of state issues to civil liberties issues. Evidently our respondents put the liberties questions in one compartment different from and unrelated to national and state policy questions.

We conclude that the data support the view that pro-government action views on national policy tends to predict somewhat similar views on state policy. However, the data contradict the notion that pro-government action views related to the handling of social and economic matters correlates positively and closely with civil libertarianism. These are different dimensions of opinion. It also appears that on these points opinion structure in the two major parties is essentially similar.

Sources of Opinion

So far analysis has indicated that each set of Ohio party leaders tends to be a group of "co-believers" whose outlook differs substantially from that of the opposite set of party leaders and that there are underlying ideologies. One explanation may be that Democrats, for example, agree among themselves and disagree with Republicans because of a common socio-economic background which is different from that of the Republicans; and our data permit us to test this hypothesis in several operational forms.

It is possible that inter-party disagreement arises because Republican leaders have high incomes and Democratic leaders relatively low incomes. The facts are, however, contrary to the hypothesis. There are in each party considerable differences in the income of leaders, but the distribution of income within the respective parties is surprisingly parallel.

TABLE 5

Percentage Distribution of Ohio Party Leaders by Income and by Party

	Under $5000	$5-7500	$7500-$10,000	$10-15,000	Over $15,000	
Dems. (N=120) *	15%	31%	27%	17%	10%	100%
Reps. (N=125) *	21%	30%	23%	16%	10%	100%

* The number of responses reported in the table is less than the total number of respondents because a few members of each party did not reply to the income question.

Similar analyses can be made substituting other factors for income. In the table below that is done by introduction of the variables: age, education, and occupation.

It may be seen easily that there are age, educational, and occupational differences in each party and that the distribution does not vary with party with one exception: the number of housewives and the number of hourly paid workers is somewhat greater in the Democratic group than in the Republican group which includes on the other hand relatively more farmers; however, these occupational differences are not great. It seems fair to say that the similarities are more striking than the differences. Thus it appears that the leadership levels of the Ohio Democratic and Republican parties do not differ substantially with respect to income, age, education, and occupation.

They do, however, differ with respect to religion. Twenty-seven per cent of the Democratic respondents who gave their religious affiliation (N=124) were Roman Catholics, 72% were Protestants,

TABLE 6

PERCENTAGE DISTRIBUTION OF OHIO PARTY LEADERS BY AGE, EDUCATION, OCCUPATION AND BY PARTY

	Age				
	26-35	36-45	46-55	56-65	65 +
Dems. (N=126) *	6%	26%	35%	22%	10%
Reps. (N=130) *	4%	25%	34%	18%	18%

	Education					
	Completed 8 Grades	Completed 9-11 Grades	Completed 12 Grades	Attended College	College Degree	Advanced Degree
Dems. (N=123) *	5%	6%	35%	21%	13%	20%
Reps. (N=128) *	2%	5%	35%	21%	16%	20%

	Occupation								
	Housewife	Lawyer	Other Prof.	Business, Self-Employed	Business, Salaried	Clerical	Hourly Pd. Manual	Farmer	Other
Dems. (N=124) *	10%	18%	3%	26%	6%	4%	11%	6%	15%
Reps. (N=126) *	5%	19%	4%	27%	5%	3%	6%	20%	11%

* The number of resopnses reported in the table is less than the total number of respondents since a few members of each party did not reply to one or more of the relevant items.

and 1 Democrat stated that he had no religious affiliation. In contrast to the Democrats, only 8% of the Republicans who gave their religious affiliation (N=130) were Roman Catholics and 92% were Protestants. One Republican stated that he belonged to no religious group. It is conceivable that part of the difference between Democratic and Republican policy preferences may be due to differences in religious background. Inspection of Table 7 below suggests no strong relationship between religious affiliation and opinion within the respective parties. The chi-square test confirms what inspection suggests: it produces no value significant at the .10 level. It is interesting to note in particular that religious affiliation does not relate significantly to leadership opinion on civil liberties, a finding which is contrary to Stouffer's finding that Roman Catholics living in the north are slightly less sympathetic to civil liberties claims

TABLE 7

DISTRIBUTION OF INDIVIDUAL SUPPORT RATIOS AROUND THE PARTY MEAN BY RELIGION AFFILIATION

	NATL. ISR		STATE ISR		CIV. LIB. ISR	
	MEAN OR ABOVE	BELOW MEAN	MEAN OR ABOVE	BELOW MEAN	MEAN OR ABOVE	BELOW MEAN
Dems.						
RC	17	17	18	16	23	11
P	48	41	49	40	54	35
Reps.						
RC	4	6	7	3	8	2
P	61	58	63	56	70	49

than are Protestants in the same region;[10] however, not too much should be made of this point since the number of Roman Catholics in our sample of party leaders is small. The principal point to be made here is that religious affiliation does not relate significantly to intra-party difference of opinion and hence cannot explain differences between Republicans and Democrats.

Therefore, our general conclusion is that leaders of the two parties do not differ in attitudes toward public policy issues because of differences in background. It appears that the contrasting attitudes and attitude structures which divide Republicans from Democrats relate to party itself and not to some other factor lurking behind or operating through party.[11]

---

[10]Stouffer, *op. cit.*, p. 144.

[11]Note that we do not attempt to say whether the development of attitudes and ideology precede or follow identification with the party and entrance to its leadership level. One study, at least, suggests that the development of similar attitudes in a party member follows rather than precedes party "membership." Belknap and Campbell, "Political Party Identification and Attitudes Toward Foreign Policy," *Public Opinion Quarterly* (Winter, 1951-52), pp. 601-23.

Not only are there differences between the parties but also within each and some effort should be made to explain their presence. It has already been stated that they do not relate to religious affiliation; but it is possible, of course, that these differences do relate to some other socio-economic or demographic factors. Evidence is provided by the table below.

TABLE 8

PRODUCT MOMENT CORRELATIONS OF SELECTED VARIABLES WITH ISRS BY PARTY

	NAT'L. ISR		STATE ISR		CIV. LIB. ISR	
	REP.	DEM.	REP.	DEM.	REP.	DEM.
Age	.03	.04	—.09	—.09	—.01	.28
Ed.	—.19	—.13	.06	.00	—.30	—.44
Inc.	—.18	—.18	—.03	—.06	—.30	—.23
% U	—.05	.11	.07	.01	—.01	—.18
% M&M	—.08	.00	.04	—.07	.00	.00
% RF	.09	.01	—.14	.06	—.02	.10
Ct. Hse.	—.05	.05	.01	.11	—.13	.04
% Dem.	.09	.07	.15	.08	.23	.01

Legend:

Age—age with values assigned from lowest to highest age category.
Ed.—education with values assigned from lowest to highest grade completed.
Inc.—income with values assigned from lowest to highest income category.
% U—per cent of county population classified urban in 1950.
% M&M—per cent of county population employed in mining and manufacturing in 1950.
% RF—per cent of county population classified rural farm in 1950.
Ct. Hse.—county court houses classified as Democratic, Mixed, and Republican according to the number of victories won by each party in 1956 and 1958 elections excepting the office of coroner; values assigned from least to most Republican.
% Dem.—county median Democratic vote for president, 1940-1956 (5 elections).

The independent variables in Table 8 are of three kinds: (1) personal, i.e., age, education, and income; (2) ecological, i.e., per cent urban, per cent mining and manufacturing, and per cent rural farm; and (3) electoral, i.e., party control of court house offices and median percentage of the presidential vote, 1940-1956. In general, no variable has a consistently close relation to attitudes on policy issues, and in no *instance* does any single variable explain more than 20 per cent of the variation in Individual Support Ratios within either party.

In the areas of state and national issues there is no relationship as strong as .2, which is very weak, of course. In regard to civil liberties, it can be noted that there are some stronger relationships. They indicate that low ISRs (i.e., the more libertarian outlook) are associated with high income, high education, and youth which is a finding consistent with Stouffer's finding that higher occupational status, higher educational achievement, and youth are positively related to tolerance[12] assuming a rough eqivalence of occupational status and income. It appears also that age has a negative relation to civil liberties in the Democratic Party. The most interesting feature of this analysis is that certain personal variables operate to influence opinion most strongly in the area of civil liberties where party ideology does not run. Its absence evidently frees and permits the operation of factors associated particularly with education and income.

Another explanation for differences of opinion within the parties in addition to those explored above is that these differences relate to the personal associations of leaders, with those who associate most with persons of the same party taking policy positions most consistent with the dominant tendency in their party. To test this hypothesis leaders of each party were divided into classes according to the politics of their friends, and mean class ISRs were computed. (Some respondents were not included in this analysis since they had failed to answer one or more questions concerning the politics of their friends.) Analysis of variance was deemed an appropriate and flexible method for determining the relation of these personal associations to attitudes.[13] Results are reported in a series of equations which are forms of the equation

$$S = b_1A_1 + b_2A_2 + b_3A_3 \ldots$$

where S is the *actual* line of regression, b the class mean, and A_1, A_2, etc, the classes. The object is, of course, to discover how much of the variance can be accounted for by classification in terms of the specified variable; and this is expressed by R-values which if squared state the per cent of total variance which is explained.

The Republicans were divided into 6 classes with the aim being to create the largest possible number of classes without establishing classes with excessively few members. In the case of Republicans, however, it was impossible to avoid the creation of one very large class since the pattern dominant in the party was association with friends of the same party. The same thing was less true of the Democrats. Analysis of Individual Support Ratios on national issues yields the following:

$$S = 34A_1 + 38A_2 + 32A_3 + 51A_4 + 51A_5 + 38A_6$$
$$R = .402$$

---

[12] *Ibid.*, p. 139 and pp. 89-93.

[13] See A. M. Mood, *Introduction to the Theory of Statistics* (New York: McGraw-Hill, 1950), pp. 318-26.

where A_1 is a class whose members associate most with Republicans and A_2 is a class whose members associate next most frequently with Republicans, etc. The finding is in accord with the hypothesis. Combination of classes 1, 2, and 3 (Ns=70, 12, and 7 respectively) and of classes 4, 5, and 6 (Ns=7, 5, and 7) straightens the line of regression with this result:

$$S=34A_{1\text{-}2\text{-}3}+47A_{4\text{-}5\text{-}6}$$
$$R=.357$$

In words, Republicans who associate less with members of their own party give most support to government action, a position characteristic of Democrats; however, it should be added quickly that only a relatively small part of intraparty variance is accounted for in this way.

Analysis of Individual Support Ratios on state issues yields the following outcome:

$$S=39A_1+48A_2+44A_3+45A_4+55A_5+45A_6$$
$$R=.229$$

Reduction to 2 classes (A_1 and $A_{2\text{-}6}$) which seems reasonable, given the shape of the line of regression, yields this result:

$$S=39A_1+47A_{2\text{-}3\text{-}4\text{-}5\text{-}6}$$
$$R=.199$$

The outcome is in accord with the hypothesis, but the relation between the variables is very weak.

Similar consideration of individual responses to civil liberties issues produces the following result:

$$S=80A_1+79A_2+88A_3+93A_4+80A_5+87A_6$$
$$R=.193$$

Reduction to 2 classes seems to be in order. Analysis produces the following:

$$S=80A_{1\text{-}2}+87A_{3\text{-}4\text{-}5\text{-}6}$$
$$R=.158$$

Thus, it appears that Republicans who associate less with members of their own party support the party position more than others, a finding which is contrary to the hypothesis; however, it would be a mistake to rest much on this finding since the relation between the variables is almost negligible.

The Democrats were divided into 4 classes with the aim again being to create the largest number of classes without establishing excessively small ones. The number of members in each class is as follows: $A_1=41$, $A_2=28$, $A_3=24$, and $A_4=10$. Analysis of Individual Support Ratios on national issues yields the following:

$$S=72A_1+67A_2+55A_3+55A_4$$
$$R=.473$$

where A_1 is a class whose members associate most with Democrats, A_2 is a class whose members associate next most frequently with Democrats, etc. It can be seen that Democrats whose friendships are less with other Democrats give less support to national issues, a finding which supports the hypothesis.

Analysis of Individual Support Ratios on state issues yields this result:

$$S=67A_1+66A_2+60A_3+58A_4$$
$$R=.194$$

The line of regression is in accord with the hypothesis, but very little is explained by classification.

Similar consideration of individual responses to civil liberties issues produces the following result:

$$S=77A_1+75A_2+69A_3+54A_4$$
$$R=.260$$

It appears that Democrats who associate more than others with non-Democrats are more favorable to civil liberties. Evidently this group of Democrats helps to give the Democratic leadership group the appearance of being slightly more libertarian than the Republican; however, it must be quickly added that the relation between the politics of friends and attitudes on civil liberties is weak even though the line of regression is consistent with the hypothesis.

To summarize this section, we can say that Republican and Democratic leaders who associate more with members of their own party have attitudes more consistent with the tendency of their party on national issues than do other leaders. The same statement may be made with reference to state issues, but the relation is substantially weaker. The relation between the politics of friends and attitudes on civil liberties issues varies in direction with party and is strong in neither case, but this is not surprising. It has been noted that civil liberties is a dimension of opinion apart from national and state issues and that party positions on civil liberties are neither distinctive nor well-established. Consequently, it is reasonable to expect that the partisan preference of friends will have little to do with opinion on liberties issues.

State and National Leaders

So far our analysis has been confied to the attitudes of county party leaders in Ohio. It is possible to add another dimension by comparing their attitudes with the attitudes of national party leaders[14] as reported by McClosky. In an item by item comparison of responses to national issues Ohio Republicans show higher support ratios (PSRs) than do national Republicans on 9 items, lower support ratios on 12 items, and the same support ratio on 3 items. The median difference is 5 points. We may conclude that Ohio Republican leaders are slightly less in favor of governmental action than were national Republican leaders; however, it is the essential similarity of outlook which must be emphasized. Furthermore, issues receiving relatively strong support from one group also receive relatively strong support from the other. The order of preference shown by these 2 groups correlates with a coefficient of plus .928.[15]

Ohio Democratic leaders show higher support ratios (PSRs) than do national Democratic leaders on 17 national issues, lower support ratios on 5 national issues, and the same support ratio on 2 other national issues. The median difference is 5 points. Thus Ohio Democrats emerge as being somewhat more sympathetic to governmental action than were Democratic national leaders, but once again it is the essential similarity between the state and national groups which must be emphasized. Furthermore, issues popular with one group are popular with the other; and issues opposed by one are likely to be opposed by the other. The order of preference shown by the 2 Democratic groups correlates with a coefficient of plus .867.[16]

It is a fair inference to say that the opinions of county party leaders in Ohio are not unique. They resemble closely the opinions of national party leaders even though Ohio Democratic leaders are

---

[14]McClosky defined national leaders as delegates to the 1956 national conventions.

[15]The coefficient is a Spearman rank order correlation coefficient.

[16]*Idem.*

slightly more "liberal" than national Democratic leaders and Ohio Republican leaders, slightly more "conservative" than their opposite numbers. There is, therefore, an informal linkage between important leaders in basic units of party organization on the one hand and on the other leaders who may be identified as belonging to the national party. This is a finding which contrasts with the many facts demonstrating the federal and local character of American parties.

Summary

1. Ohio Democratic and Republican leaders differ sharply on issues involving national and state government policies with Democrats favoring relatively more governmental action than Republicans. The difference is slightly greater on national than on state issues.

2. The national issues which show the greatest inter-party conflict are such familiar items as slum clearance and public housing, federal aid to education, and social security benefits.

3. Democrats and Republicans agree on priorities or on their order of preferences concerning national and state issues despite generally different attitudes towards government action.

4. In the area of civil liberties both leadership groups strongly favor government action which has the effect of restraining the liberties involved; Democrats are, however, slightly less anti-libertarian than Republicans.

5. Each group of party leaders tends to be internally united although there are differences of opinion within each party on national, state, and civil liberties issues. Internal unity is greatest on national issues, slightly less on state issues, and least on civil liberties issues where the Democrats can hardly be said to be united at all.

6. The attitude of individual leaders to national issues relates positively to their attitudes toward state issues. Leaders favoring federal action tend also to favor state action. There are what may be called government action and government inaction ideologies.

7. Attitudes toward civil liberties cannot be predicted, however, by attitudes toward either state or national issues. Civil liberties is a separate dimension of opinion.

8. Inter-party differences of opinion cannot be attributed to differences in the backgrounds of Democratic and Republican leaders since these differences are either non-existent or unrelated to opinion.

9. Differences of opinion within the respective parties concerning national and state issues do not relate to differences in personal background, county demography, and county politics unless some very weak relations are counted as exceptions.

10. Intra-party differences of opinion concerning civil liberties are, however, related to income, education, and age. Higher income, extended education, and youth relate positively to libertarian positions. The absence of government action ideologies in this area evidently permits operation of these factors.

11. Leaders whose friends mostly belong to their own party show on national issues attitudes more consistent with the dominant tendency of their party. The same statement may be made concerning the relation of personal associations to state issues, but the relationship is weak.

12. The partisan preferences of friends relate to opinion on civil liberties in a way which is contradictory and inconclusive, but this is reasonable since stands on these issues have little relation to party affiliation.

13. Ohio Democratic and Republican leaders have attitudes on national issues which closely resemble the attitudes of the national leaders of their respective parties. There is in this way an informal linking of local and national parties.

14. In general, there is a consistent point of view on national and state issues within each party which is shared by most of their members and which contrasts with that of the opposing party. Neither inter-party nor intra-party differences on national and state issues can be attributed to differences in personal characteristics or in background. Inter-party differences are based on attitudes which we think are corollaries of party membership and leadership, and intra-party differences are to some extent consequences of the politics of friends.

In other words, party leaders are not issue neutrals. Furthermore, their attitudes on national and state issues are not functions of social status. Rather, these attitudes may well be correlates of party itself (or of some variable which we neither locate nor suggest) and of associations which re-enforce or wear away loyalties to party stands. These statements are more true when applied to national issues than to state issues which are tied a little less closely to party. At bottom, there is in each party a distinctive issue orientation which apparently cannot be reduced to non-political variables.

Different conclusions are in order when civil liberties are considered. Both groups of Ohio party leaders are generally anti-libertarian. However, intra-party differences exist; and they relate to variables which have been found in other studies to affect attitudes on civil liberties issues. Most important for this study is the fact that views on civil liberties are not to any significant extent a part of the well-developed issue orientations which distinguish Republican leaders from Democratic leaders.

Comment. Political parties have been described in terms of the face they show the electorate. One type is the party which emphasizes policy and which seeks to clarify and perhaps to magnify differences between groups in the electorate in order to gain the cherished goal which is, of course, public office. Another type is the party which de-emphasizes policy and which seeks to blur and minimize group conflict in order to gain majority support; and this kind of party is in some circles referred to with approval as an agent of consensus, a not too well defined condition which is presumably healthy. This concept supposes relatively free manipulation of issues for electoral advantage. A closely related concept of party is that of party as the "honest broker." It maintains that party goes between competing groups, offers compromises without prejudice, and through its own electoral success or failure reflects in policy the strength of the contending groups. Another view of party, often advanced only for the purpose of presenting an error with which to contrast the truth, is that of party as a group of like-minded men banded together in order to win the offices required for the effective expression of their common convictions (the Burkean view).

Our finding is that local party leaders in Ohio tend to be groups of like-minded men whose agreement is not easily reducible to something other than membership and leadership in party itself. This lends support to the Burkean view of party, although we would not for a moment claim it is a completely adequate view since party is, after all, a complex phenomenon that varies from time to time and place to place. Conversely, our finding suggests that contrasting views of party ought not to be swallowed whole.

The fact that our party leaders are not issue neutrals suggests that they may not be able to freely manipulate issues for the sake of electoral triumph as the agency of consensus model of party activity supposes. They may well take risks for what they themselves prefer and their preferences may prejudice what appear to be purely "practical" decisions about the use of issues. Along the same line, it is to be doubted whether parties are honest brokers; and adding an impression which is outside those suggested by our data, we doubt that many major interest groups suppose that the parties are honest brokers. We would suggest instead that, at least, the party organizations we have considered are composed of leaders who have definite policy preferences which will influence their perception of electoral necessities and their tactical decisions. A model of American party politics presuming free maneuver by leaders exclusively concerned with electoral victory is dubious. One last important implication of our findings is that party may well have the function of providing a method for the expression of ideology in political life, a function groups organized around one or a few issues cannot perform easily; and we would add that in our opinion this function may be needed in a viable democratic system.

Appendix: The Respondents as a Sample. Our respondents constituted an accidental or self-selected sample, but we are convinced that they are representative and that the sample is not seriously biased. Our reasons are as follows: (A) The whole population is homogeneous in that all members have more than usual interest and involvement in politics or, at least, than can be safely assumed. (B) Respondents were compared with non-respondents in regard to place of residence and it was found that the two groups were generally similar with reference to county demography and politics. For example, respondents were neither more nor less urban than non-respondents. (C) Attitude scores of early respondents were compared with those of later respondents. The theory was that if non-residents differed from respondents in attitude the later respondents would differ from earlier in the same way but to lesser degree. There was, however, no significant difference between early and late Democratic respondents in attitude toward any set of issues. Nor did early and late Republican respondents differ in attitude toward state and civil liberty issues; they did differ on national issues with late respondents being more in favor of government action ($X^2 = 8.8$, df = 1). However, the relation was weak (phi coefficient = .259); so we once again concluded respondents and non-respondents were probably similar. (D) A small random sample was collected (some of it as much as a year or more after the first sample) for the purpose of comparing its characteristics with those of the larger self-selected sample. Insofar as possible the two samples were compared item by item through the use of chi-square tests. We found that there was a probability of .7 or higher that differences in regard to age, place of residence, and politics of friends were due to chance. The probabilities for education were .3 and .4 respectively for the Democrats and Republicans. On the 19 national issues where it was possible to compare Democrats in the random sample and Democrats in the self-selected sample it was found that there was a probability of .9 or higher that differences on 7 items were due to chance.

The probability was .7 or .8 or another 7 items, and .5 on 3 other items. On only 2 items were probabilities as low as .3. They were the items dealing with military alliances and with integration. It is possible that the former was a fairly meaningless issue and that opinion on the latter had changed. Neither of these items was used in computing Individual Support Ratios. Comparison of Republicans in the 2 samples on national issues produces the same general pattern; that is, there is a very strong probability that nearly all differences are due to chance. There are 2 exceptions. One is the item dealing with restrictions on credit, but we are confident this issue was virtually without meaning in 1962-1963. The other exception is responses to several tax items. Members of the random and later sample were significantly less in favor of tax cutting than were members of the self-selected and earlier sample. This difference may easily be attributed to changes of opinion since the clearly articulated Republican Party position in 1963 was opposition to tax cuts. Thirteen chi-square tests were run on state issues, 6 comparing the 2 groups of Republicans and 7 the 2 groups of Democrats. On 4 issues the probabilities were .9 or higher, on 3 issues .8, on 4 issues .5, and on only 2 issues lower than .5. It was not possible to run chi-square tests on Republican responses to civil liberties items, but inspection of the frequencies shows little difference between the samples. Chi-square tests were run on Democratic responses to 3 civil liberties items, and produced in each case a probability of .3. Random and later respondents were somewhat more libertarian on these issues. Differences might be due to bias, changes of opinion, or to instability of opinion. In view of the fact that the 2 samples resemble each other closely over a long range of national and state issues we are inclined to rule out bias. Evidence in this study suggests that opinion on civil liberties may not be very well organized and that instability may be the explanation. In general, we feel that our self-selected sample has the characteristics of our random sample.

A Profile of Political Activists in Manhattan

Robert S. Hirschfield
Bert E. Swanson
Blanche D. Blank

Introduction

Although urban areas dominate the American political scene today, our firsthand knowledge of big-city politics and politicians is surprisingly limited. Most of the literature in this field deals descriptively with "bosses" and "machines." Few empirical studies have been concerned with the less sensational aspects of urban political organization or personnel, and almost none have investigated the attributes and attitudes of those big-city political activists who are representative of their parties' general membership.

The subjects of the present study are the elected committeemen of Manhattan's three parties — Democratic, Republican, and Liberal. They were considered the group most representative of their parties' organizations with regard to demographic background, policy attitudes, and political activity. The result is a profile of the urban political activist. In many instances this profile confirms widely held impressions; in others, it raises doubts regarding accepted political stereotypes. The data revealed significant differences as well as striking similarities among the party representatives. On

---

Reprinted from the *Western Political Quarterly,* XV (September, 1962), 489-506, by permission of the University of Utah,

the basis of these findings a number of propositions concerning the nature of American politics will be advanced.

The research project on which this study is based was conducted from October, 1959 to June, 1960.[1] A 20 per cent random sample (787) was taken from an official list of 3,749 committeemen and women provided by the New York County Board of Elections. Interviews based on an 86-item questionnaire were completed with 409 committeemen (51.9 per cent of the sample or 10.9 per cent of the total universe). Among the respondents, 233 were Democrats (65.9 per cent of the Democratic sample), 124 were Republicans (36.5 per cent of the Republican sample) and 52 were Liberals (55.7 per cent of the Liberal sample).[2]

The legal duties of the county committeeman are few.[3] His real work is his informal, year-round effort in behalf of the party. According to his particular skill and inclination, he may engage in canvassing, registering, getting out the voters, proselytizing, fund-raising or providing services for constituents. He may occasionally make patronage recommendations, help choose candidates for office, and assist in formulating party policy. Ordinarily he has little or no influence in these last areas of party activity, but he is nonetheless an important link between (a) the voter and the party and (b) the party members and their leaders.

NOTE: The writers wish to express their thanks to Citizenship Clearing House for financial aid and the assistance of D. D'Amico, P. Landan, E. Main, and D. Rosenfield.

[1]Blanche Blank, Robert Hirschfield, and Bert Swanson, "An Experiment in Political Education," *Journal of Higher Education*, 31 (November, 1960), 428-34.

[2]The study was conducted with the endorsement of the county chairmen of all three parties. The investigators were hampered by a number of complex factors peculiar to urban living. Access to the apartment-dweller was limited because of the difficulty of getting past doormen and the fact that many participants had unlisted telephones. The list of committeemen kept by the Board of Elections (the only central list available) was sometimes inaccurate. Often it contained names of individuals who had been appointed by party leaders but had little interest or participated minimally in party affairs and therefore refused to be interviewed. An extra effort was made (three to six contacts) to gain cooperation from those who either were difficult to locate or refused to be interviewed. The reasons offered were (a) lack of interest; (b) too busy; (c) wrong address; (d) out of town; (e) no telephone; (f) illness; (g) "lack of knowledge"; and (h) death. This experience points up the need to explore further the methodological problem of sample survey research in the large urban centers where the life of anonymity is highly valued.

[3]For comparative purposes, the county committeemen of our study conform to precinct captains described in earlier studies in other cities.

The Manhattan Environment

Manhattan, although not essentially different from other great urban centers, has certain special aspects which must be taken into account. Most important, perhaps, is the racial and religious composition of its population. Over 20 per cent of the island's people are Negro and an almost equal percentage are Puerto Rican, constituting the most densely populated communities of these two groups in America. Manhattan contains twice the number of Negroes and three times as many Puerto Ricans as any of the neighboring four counties which comprise Greater New York City. The population also includes disproportionately large numbers of Catholics and Jews. Although Manhattan is the most Protestant of the boroughs, Jews constitute approximately 17 per cent of the population and Catholics, 24 per cent. It has been estimated that if persons unaffiliated with any church were distributed according to religious background or identification, the results for New York County would be: Protestant, 36.5 per cent; Roman Catholic, 43.6 per cent; Jewish, 17.7 per cent.[4] In addition, the number of foreign-born persons is higher in New York than in other urban areas, 20 per cent of its people having come to the United States as immigrants. Manhattan is the focus of national and international activity in a variety of fields, the mecca of itinerant diplomats and politicians, the most cosmopolitan of American cities — all of which heighten the political consciousness of its citizens.

An unusual feature of the Manhattan environment, one of great political significance, is the fact that the dominant Democratic party is divided into two competing groups — "regulars" (members of the long-established party organization clubs or Tammany Hall) and "reformers" (members of new dissident clubs affiliated with the Committee for Democratic Voters). Though the other boroughs also have reform groups, Manhattan is the stronghold of the movement and the arena of the current regular-reform struggle.

Manhattan is not, in short, the "typical American community," and any political study must consider that fact. However, with regard to urbanization, political structure and processes Manhattan (as well as the Greater New York area) is comparable to urban communities throughout the nation. The present findings, therefore, may well be applicable beyond the confines of Manhattan.

---

[4]Ralph A. Straetz and Frank J. Munger, *New York Politics* (New York: New York University Press, 1960), pp. 36 and 37.

Propositions

Seven tentative propositions, representing the conclusions reached in this study, will serve as a frame of reference for the present discussion.

1. *Socio-economic status (class) is not the dominant determinant in the composition of urban political organization.*

Paul Lazarsfeld has stated that "social characteristics determine political references."[5] Herbert McClosky agrees that "a voter's political attachments are strongly affected by both his or his family's 'life style' (occupation, income, education and religion)."[6] Avery Leiserson adds, "There are any number of indices of group affiliation in the sense of interpersonal association and contact, as well as subjective identification and class consciousness, that are correlated with political attitude."[7] The data presented here modify these theories. In contrast to all these statements, few substantial socio-economic differences were found among the parties' representations.

2. *The major determinants of political affiliation are ideological; there are significant ideological differences among the political parties.*

Both party leaders and the rank-and-file, says Alfred De Grazia, lack "firm and homogeneous political convictions." When a party is at peak efficiency, "it is not very concerned with issues and the flights of fancy that sometimes overtake amateurs."[8] Wallace Sayre and Herbert Kaufman[9] also consider that political parties (except perhaps the Liberal party) show less interest in issues than in power. Murray Levin reports that "Boston politics continues to revolve around personal obligations and strong personal loyalties."[10] This seems a generally accepted view, but the present findings do not support it. New York committeemen divide along party lines, and the key to that division is essentially ideological. Ideas regarding people, politics and policies offer the best clue to party affiliation.

---

[5]Paul Lazarsfeld, Bernard Berelson, and Hazel Gaudet, *The People's Choice*, 2d ed (New York: Columbia University Press, 1948), p. 27.

[6]Herbert McClosky and Harold Dahlgren, "Primary Group Influence on Party Loyalty," *American Political Science Review*, 53 (September, 1959), 775.

[7]Avery Leiserson, *Parties and Politics* (New York: Knopf, 1958), p. 153.

[8]Alfred De Grazia, *The American Way of Government* (New York: Wiley, 1957), p. 214.

[9]Wallace S. Sayre and Herbert Kaufman, *Governing New York City* (New York: Russel Sage Foundation, 1960), pp. 67-70, 452-58.

[10]Murray E. Levin, *The Alienated Voter* (New York: Holt, Rinehart and Winston, 1960), p. 7.

3. *The political activist views his party organization primarily as an instrument for effectuating policies rather than as a source of personal gain.*

The classic descriptions of urban politics emphasize the boss-dominated "machine," concerned almost exclusively with getting out the vote, getting in the brother-in-law and maintaining itself in power. The present study indicates a significant change among political activists regarding their view of the party's function and their own rewards. The committeeman's principal objectives are neither political power per se nor personal aggrandizement.

These three are the most significant propositions which were developed. All three modify prevailing generalizations about American politics. The four propositions which follow either support the mainstream of current political studies or deal with concepts largely ignored in those studies.

4. *All urban political parties draw their personnel largely from the "middle class."*

5. *The party in power occupies the "middle of the road" in urban politics; the other parties deviate from center in inverse proportion to their chances of winning office.*

6. *The dominant party's personnel are much more "professional" in their political attitudes and activities than the members of the minority parties.*

7. *Religious affiliation and depth of family roots in America are major factors in determining the member's degree of "liberalism" or "conservatism."*

These are the most noteworthy conclusions drawn from the study of Manhattan committeemen. The material which follows will describe and analyze the results of that study in detail, with the data arranged according to demographic background, policy attitudes and political activity. In each section the differences among the three parties will be discussed and the relationships between the present results and those of other empirical studies will be noted.

Social Background of Manhattan Committeemen as Compared with Earlier Studies

Since no previous studies of Manhattan or New York City committeemen are available, it is difficult to make statistical comparisons to indicate how the 1960 party representatives differ demographically from their earlier counterparts. However, the pioneer studies of Chicago precinct workers by Gosnell between 1928 and 1936, of the same group by Sonya Forthal in 1946, of upstate New York committeemen by Mosher in 1932, of Philadelphia politicians by Kurtzman in 1935, and of Seattle "grass roots" leaders by Bone in 1952 are all relevant and will be referred to in our discussion of the Manhattan committeemen.[11]

William Mosher pictured the upstate New York politicians in 1932 as a group of lower-class "hacks" feeding at the public trough and concluded that the "most fruitful of reforms in government is to see to it that really representative and broad-gauged citizens are drafted for positions of committeemen."[12] His plea for more respectable and more representative party activists has been answered by the Manhattan committeemen of 1960, for if anything characterizes them it is middle-class (or even upper middle-class) solidity and respectability. Moreover, there is no significant distinction among the parties, the portrait of each party's committeemen being only a variation of the same middle-class prototype.

The "new look" among party activists is most apparent in the data regarding education, for the old-time poorly educated "hack" finds little company in the 1960 Manhattan organizations. Only 7.3 per cent of the committeemen have had no more than a grammar school and only a quarter no more than a high school education, while fully two-thirds have gone to college or beyond. Among Chicago politicians of the past the comparable percentages for 1928 and 1936, respectively, were: grammar school or less, 58 and 40; high school, 26 and 40; college or beyond, 16 and 20. Even as recently as 1952 only 53 per cent of the Seattle Republican committeemen had a college education or more. The 1960 Manhattan committeeman is not only better educated than his predecessors but also better educated than most of his constituents.

The data on occupation and income also bear out the middle- to upper middle-class character of the 1960 Manhattan political activist. One-fourth are professional people today, as compared to one-tenth in Chicago and upstate New York in the mid-thirties and one-seventh in Seattle in 1952. Even more outstanding, since public employment has so often been regarded as a reward of political activity, is the fact that only 5 per cent of the 1960 Manhattan com-

---

[11]Harold F. Gosnell, *Machine Politics: Chicago Model* (Chicago: University of Chicago Press, 1937); Sonya Forthal, *Cogwheels of Democracy* (New York: William-Frederick Press, 1946); William Mosher, "Party Government Control at the Grass Roots," *National Municipal Review*, Vol. 24 (1935); David H. Kurtzman, *Methods of Controlling Votes in Philadelphia* (Philadelphia: privately printed, 1935); Hugh Bone, *Grass Roots Party Leadership* (Seattle: University of Washington Press, 1952).

[12]Mosher, *op. cit.*, p. 15.

mitteemen are on the public payroll, while in 1928 almost 60 per cent of the Chicago precinct workers were government employees. Finally, the vast majority of committee members have incomes greater than the national average, with well over half reporting more than $10,000 a year.

Another striking difference between the 1960 committeemen and the traditional stereotype is revealed by the data on religious affiliation. Over half of Chicago's precinct captains in 1928 were Catholic; eight years later Catholics still held 42 per cent of these positions. But if Catholics were once considered the backbone of the Manhattan political "machine," today they have been displaced by both Jews and Protestants. Only a quarter of the 1960 committee positions are filled by Catholics; Protestants hold one-quarter and, most significantly, Jews occupy two-fifths. Even taking into account Manhattan's sizable Jewish population, this is a most interesting development, bearing out Roy Peel's observation in 1935 that Jews were becoming increasingly active in the major parties and were slowly gaining "positions of vantage within the regular organization."[13] One explanation for this high rate of Jewish political participation may be the relative freedom which Jews feel when they are not a small minority; another may be the Jew's desire to guarantee his oft-threatened personal security by assuring his political influence; still another explanation may be found in the professional background of Jews, since many are lawyers and lawyers have a natural affinity for politics. Whatever the reasons, the Jew has become an important cog in the Manhattan party wheel.

Data regarding the committeemen's origin (paternal) also reveal a strong deviation from the stereotype. The number born outside the United States is quite low — only 8 per cent (in Chicago in 1936 the figure was 18 per cent). This is particularly noteworthy since New York has always been the nation's greatest immigration center. The decline may well be explained by the fact that immigration has slowed to a trickle during the past thirty-five years. In any event, among the major party committeemen today, more than half have had roots in America for two generations or longer. Equally interesting is the relatively small proportion of Irish committeemen (only 9 per cent), since the Irishman is so familiar in the traditional literature of urban politics.[14] Today the two major parties' representatives are distributed fairly evenly among all the substantial

---

[13]Roy Peel, *The Political Clubs of New York City* (New York: Putnam, 1935), p. 253.

[14]Harold Zinc, *City Bosses in the United States* (Durham: Duke University Press, 1930), p. 3.

European-origin groups to be found in New York's variegated population. Puerto Ricans, the glaring exception, are virtually unrepresented; Negroes, despite their numbers and long residence in the community, hold only 11 per cent of the committee seats.

A few final points of special interest were revealed by the study. One is the fact that almost one-quarter of the committee posts are held by persons under thirty-five years of age, demonstrating both that interest in political activity has become more prevalent among younger people and that old-time party workers no longer dominate their organizations as they did even a generation ago. In Chicago, for example, those over thirty constituted 88 per cent of the party personnel studied in 1928 and 85 per cent in 1936. It is also notable that one-third of the committeemen were born outside the New York City area, since deep roots in a community are often considered a political necessity. Finally, since precinct-level political activity has traditionally been depicted as a rough and decidedly masculine business, it is particularly interesting to find that over 44 per cent of the Manhattan committee*men* are women, indicating a change in the nature of the job, as well as the increasingly important political role being assumed by American women. This change was first noticed by Gosnell in his Chicago studies, where the percentage of female precinct workers doubled (from 5 to 11 per cent) between 1928 and 1936. The 1960 Manhattan figures reflect still more marked growth in female political activity during the past thirty years. Since over one-third of the committee members are single, one may speculate that many unmarried women, and bachelors as well, are attracted to politics for social reasons.

The 1960 Manhattan committeeman resembles neither the fictional stereotype nor the actual machine cog of earlier political studies. He is younger, better educated, higher paid, more "American." He may be a Jew. "He" is not unlikely to be a woman. Finally, the big-city machines reflect their middle-class constituencies. This characteristic defies party label, for the next section demonstrates that there is little demographic difference among the committeemen of Manhattan's three parties.

Demographic Characteristics of the Members of the Three Major Parties

In socio-economic terms the Democrats, Manhattan's dominant party, occupy a middle position. In almost every demographic cate-

TABLE 1

Demographic Characteristics of New York County Committeemen: 1960

Characteristic	Democrat Number	Democrat Per Cent	Republican Number	Republican Per Cent	Liberal Number	Liberal Per Cent
Education						
Grade school	13	6	9	7	6	11
High school	46	20	37	28	9	17
Trade school	7	3	2	2	12	23
Some college	30	13	16	13	12	23
Completed college	37	16	28	23	4	8
Graduate work	90	38	29	23	21	30
No answer	10	4	2	2	1	2
Occupation						
Professional	33	14	16	13	12	23
Business executive	12	5	12	10	5	9
Small businessman	55	24	29	24	12	23
Salesman	26	11	8	7	6	11
Skilled worker	46	20	16	13	11	21
Unskilled worker	29	12	18	15	2	4
Public servant	8	3	6	5	1	2
Clerical	4	2	10	8	0	0
No answer	19	8	7	6	4	8
National Origin of Father						
Italian	14	6	13	11	1	2
Irish	25	11	13	11	3	6
German	16	7	15	12	8	15
Russian	34	15	9	7	18	34
Polish	20	9	7	6	7	13
English	20	9	13	11	3	6
Puerto Rican	6	3	1	1	0	0
Other	83	36	47	38	13	25
No answer	15	6	5	4	0	0
Immigrant Status						
New immigrant	22	9	8	7	14	26
First generation	86	37	34	28	26	49
Second generation	44	19	21	18	5	9
Third generation	23	10	12	10	3	6
Fourth generation	37	16	36	29	2	4
No answer	22	9	12	10	3	6
Religion						
Protestant	56	24	38	31	7	13
Catholic	52	22	36	29	5	9
Jewish	104	44	35	28	34	64
Other	11	5	9	7	3	6
No answer	11	5	5	4	4	8
Age						
Under 35	62	28	21	18	4	8
35-54	105	47	61	52	19	38
Over 55	58	26	35	30	27	54

gory studied they will be found between the Republicans and the Liberals (a phenomenon which will be noted again with regard to policy attitudes). This might be expected, since Democratic control of New York County politics is pervasive (it is often said that the city has a one-party system). It is surprising, however, to note that in background the Democratic committeemen resemble their Republican counterparts more than they do the Liberals, a fact of even greater interest if one remembers that Democratic-Liberal election alliances are a regular occurrence in New York City. The cement of these alliances, it would seem, is not simple demographic or socio-economic similarity.

The Liberals are demographically the most distinctive of the three committee groups, a fact which is interesting to note, since their organization — with its roots in the labor movement — is often regarded as a pressure group rather than a party. Indeed, the representatives of the Liberal party fail to conform to most of the generalizations established by prior studies of political activists. Despite their policy orientation, they are the best educated and the most affluent of the three groups. They number proportionately more professional people, more oldsters and more males than either of the other two. The Liberal party has the greatest proportion of Jews and those of immigrant status.

A comparison of the three groups, therefore, reveals primarily that the Democrats occupy the broad center of social background characteristics and that the Liberal or "third" party is the least conforming in character.

All three committee groups have a high educational level, with over two-thirds having gone beyond high school. Since a higher level of education generally is regarded as characteristic of the Republican party,[15] it is interesting to note that among those who have had some college education the parties differ only slightly (Republicans, 69 per cent; Democrats, 67; Liberals, 72). Only one out of seven Republicans holds a graduate degree, while one out of four Democrats and Liberals has completed a graduate degree. Finally, the type of graduate work pursued by committeemen is worthy of comment, for 19 per cent of the Liberals were trained in the liberal arts, as were 11 per cent of the Democrats, but only 5 per cent of the Republicans. This corresponds with Rossiter's view that "one important qualifying footnote should be appended to the generalization that the further Americans go with their education, the more likely they are to be Republicans. This may be true of persons who

[15] Angus Campbell, Gerald Gurin, and Warren E. Miller, *The Voter Decides*, rev. ed (Evanston: Row, Peterson, 1954), p. 152.

have had postgraduate education for professions like law, medicine and engineering; it is certainly not true of persons with higher degrees in the sciences, humanities and social sciences."[16]

Occupational status assumes a pattern similar to that of education. Over one-third of the Liberals are professional people, while only one-fourth of the Democrats and one-seventh of the Republicans fall in this category. Likewise, with regard to income of $10,000 a year and over, members of all three parties are alike. With regard to age, of those forty-five years and over, there are more Liberals (54 per cent) than Republicans (30 percent) or Democrats (26 per cent).

The failure of Liberals to conform to accepted socio-economic theories of politics seems to reflect the most distinctive single fact about this group, namely that so large a percentage is Jewish — 64 per cent, as compared with 44 per cent for Democrats and 28 for Republicans. Education and professionalism are highly prized and encouraged in Jewish families, and the Liberals' Jewish background may well account for their high percentage in these areas. In any event, Rossiter's comment that in their voting habits Jews tend to "ignore consideration of status and income"[17] seems true also with regard to active participation in party affairs.

In at least one respect the Republican committeemen reflect the expected pattern — they are the most Protestant of the three groups (31 per cent, as against the Democrats' 24 and the Liberals' 13 per cent). But more interesting, in view of the fact that the big-city political activist is so often pictured as a Catholic Democrat, is the fact that more Republican committeemen (29 per cent) than either Democratic (22 per cent) or Liberal (less than 10 per cent) are Catholics. This supports Caldwell's observation that "it seems probable that the political influence of the Roman Catholic Church has in recent decades become more evenly divided between the major parties, perhaps as a result of a shift of allegiance among conservative Catholics from the Democratic to the Republican Party."[18]

In racial terms, all three groups are overwhelmingly (80-90 per cent) white. Similarly, all three draw their members almost exclusively from European national-origin groups; only the Democrats have a noticeable (3 per cent) Puerto Rican contingent. Readers whose image of the Manhattan Democratic politician is colored by

---

[16]Rossiter, *op. cit.*, p. 102.

[17]*Ibid.*, p. 98.

[18]Lynton K. Caldwell, *The Government and Administration of New York* (New York: Crowell, 1954), p. 40.

the succession of Irish bosses — Tweed, Croker, Murphy, Plunkitt — may be surprised to learn that only 11 per cent of the 1960 Democratic committeemen are Irish, the same percentage as Republicans. While Roy Peel's prediction that "the future of New York, at least the immediate future, belongs to the sons of Italy"[19] may have proved true of the top leadership of Tammany Hall, it is not borne out at the committee level. Not only is the percentage of Italian-origin committeemen small in all parties, but the majority of these are Republicans (percentages: Republicans, 11; Democrats, 6; Liberals, 2). Only the Liberals may be said to have a dominant national-origin group — Russo-Polish (47 per cent) — again a fact which is probably attributable to the large number of Jews in the Liberal party.

The image of the Republican party as the haven of long-time Americans in an ethnically-polyglot urban community is substantiated by the present findings.[20] Almost 30 per cent of the Republicans have American roots extending back four generations or more, while only 16 per cent of the Democrats and less than 4 per cent of the Liberals can make a like claim. Among the Liberals half are first-generation and one-fourth are new immigrants. The Democrats and Republicans may claim to be more deeply-rooted in New York City, since 61 and 57 per cent respectively were born in the metropolis, as compared to the Liberals' 49 per cent.

Finally, since politics has long been viewed as a masculine domain, and since women generally are considered a conservative political influence, it is significant that the Republican committee is almost evenly divided between the sexes; 66 per cent of the Liberals are men, and the Democrats have 44 per cent female committeemen.

The data on socio-economic background indicate, then, that in Manhattan the committee personnel of the dominant Democratic party rank closer to their Republican counterparts than to their political allies in the Liberal party. Neither Republicans nor Democrats show the demographic characteristics usually attributed to them. This is true also of the Liberal committeemen, who also present more of a single image than either of the major parties. The reasons for this last are probably the strongly Jewish character of the Liberal party and the fact that it is as much a pressure group as a third party.

---

[19]Peel, *op. cit.*, p. 252.

[20]Campbell, *et al.*, *op. cit.*, p. 78.

Ideology and Attitudes of Manhattan Committeemen

Party differentiation among the Manhattan committeemen becomes sharper and more meaningful in light of their basic views of people, politics, and policies. Party labels, often blurred demographically, become more distinct when related to the committeemen's attitudes regarding established institutions and ideas, social change, governmental power, minority group attitudes and similar matters which reveal basic political orientation. In terms of these ideological considerations the Liberal is well-named; the Republican becomes more noticeably conservative (although in Manhattan he is probably more liberal than in the nation as a whole); and the Democrat — while remaining in the center — diverges more sharply from the Republican than he did demographically and moves more positively in the direction of the Liberal. We conclude, therefore, that ideological considerations mainly determine political allegiance and affiliation.

An initial clue, although admittedly highly impressionistic, to the ideological differences among the three committee groups lies in the types of political personalities with whom they identify. When given a list of well-known political figures and asked to rank each on an approval scale ranging from "strongly approve" to "strongly disapprove," the committeemen provided the following results. (See Table 2.)

TABLE 2

ATTITUDE OF NEW YORK COUNTY COMMITTEEMEN*
TOWARD LEADING NATIONAL POLITICIANS: 1960
(*in percentages*)

	Agree Strongly			Agree			Undecided			Disagree			Disagree Strongly		
Political Figure	D	R	L	D	R	L	D	R	L	D	R	L	D	R	L
Eisenhower	14	79	6	26	19	23	8	1	8	28	2	25	24	—	39
Stevenson	60	12	76	22	26	14	5	9	4	6	19	4	5	35	2
Nixon	9	63	8	17	27	9	5	4	2	22	3	20	47	3	61
Kennedy	31	23	29	44	34	44	12	18	14	12	17	12	1	9	2
Rockefeller	13	65	29	32	24	31	15	3	12	18	5	20	23	3	8
Johnson	9	19	4	31	25	26	31	30	24	15	14	18	15	11	28
Humphrey	29	4	40	36	30	35	32	41	21	3	12	—	—	14	4

*Number of Respondents: D (Democrats) — 221; R (Republicans) — 119; L (Liberals) — 51.

Senator Hubert Humphrey, generally regarded as an unequivocal "liberal," was strongly approved by only 4 per cent of the Republicans but by 29 per cent of the Democrats and 40 per cent of the Liberals. Adlai Stevenson, identified with moderate liberalism and appealing to intellectuals, found strong approval among Democrats (60 per cent) and even more among Liberals (76 per cent), but met with strong disapproval among Republicans (35 per cent). On the other hand, President Eisenhower, popularly considered a moderate conservative, received strong Republican approval (79 per cent), while 24 per cent of the Democrats and 39 per cent of the Liberals strongly disapproved. Finally, Vice President Nixon, who was regarded — at least during the pre-campaign period — as a conservative, won strong approval from 63 per cent of the Republicans, but from only 9 per cent of the Democrats and 8 per cent of the Liberals.

Perhaps a more significant measure of party differentiation is found in the responses to a series of questions dealing with attitudes toward Negroes and Puerto Ricans. When asked, with regard to intelligence, responsibility, morality, and ambition, whether they considered the members of these groups to be *by nature* "the same as" or "inferior to" other citizens, the Republicans consistently rated both minorities lower than did the Democrats or Liberals. Considering all four attributes together, half the Republicans regarded Puerto Ricans as "inferior" to others, while one-fourth of the Democrats and Liberals held this opinion. Similarly, while one-third of the Republicans considered Negroes naturally inferior, only one-fifth of the Democrats and Liberals concurred. Attitude toward minority groups, therefore, demonstrates an important index of differentiation among the parties.

The attitudes of committeemen toward religion also reveal political differences. Again there are significant differences between the two major parties, although these differences nearly disappear when compared with the strikingly "irreligious" attitude of the Liberals. Almost 60 per cent of the Republicans regard religion as "very important" in their lives, an attitude expressed by only 40 per cent of the Democrats. Twice as many Democrats "never attend church" as Republicans (18 per cent Democrats, 9 per cent Republicans). The Liberals, however, are much the least concerned about religion. Over 40 per cent never attend church and a solid majority (79 per cent) do not regard religion as very important.

Further indications of the division among the parties are their attitudes toward social, political, and economic change. Here, as before, the Liberals live up to their name, but the Democrats, although generally moderate, differ noticeably from the Republicans with regard to governmental power and policies. When offering their reasons for entering politics, 43 per cent of the Liberals, 29 per cent of the Democrats, and only 20 per cent of the Republicans claimed "a desire to bring about change in the community." When asked about alteration of party rules — an important issue among New York City Democrats — Republicans were much more strongly opposed to any change; 60 per cent resisted change, as compared to 40 per cent of the Democrats. A miniscule 4 per cent of the Liberals thought there should be no change.

With regard to the role of the national government in effecting changes in society, the "liberal-conservative" split[21] is apparent. The respondents were given a series of questions dealing with major policy issues and asked to register their views of government's proper role in each issue. In every instance the Republicans took more "conservative" positions (i.e., against governmental intervention to effectuate the policy) than either the Democrats or Liberals. For example, Table 3 shows that only 36 per cent of the Republicans feel strongly that the government should "help people get doctors and hospital care at low cost," while 68 per cent of the Democrats and 83 per cent of the Liberals strongly support such a view. The issue of government support for school construction drew strong approval from Liberals and Democrats, less from Republicans. Similarly, Liberals and Democrats strongly favored government activity in securing fair employment and housing practices for Negroes. Table 4 shows distinct and comparable patterns on the issues of full employment, public ownership versus private enterprise in electric power and housing, and limiting the political power of large corporations. The three groups showed more agreement about the government's role in achieving integrated education, although even here there were significant differences.

All these results indicate that the committeemen of the two major parties — as well as of the third party — *are* distinguishable, but that the differentiation is related more to their ideas and attitudes than to their socio-economic backgrounds. Although the study shows demographic similarity among the party groups, with the Democrats leaning toward their Republican opponents, when the tests involve ideology and attitudes, the Democrats move away from the Republicans toward their Liberal political allies. It may well be true that "a large majority of the American people believe that the parties do not represent sharp alternatives,"[22] but if party commit-

---

[21]The liberalism-conservatism index was designed by members of the University of Michigan Survey Research Center as part of a national voting study.

[22]De Grazia, *op. cit.*, p. 210. Also, cf. *New York Times,* July 26, 1959, report of a University of Michigan study of Wayne County voters conducted by Samuel Eldersveld and Daniel Katz. Among the conclusions: "More than half the adult population could see no difference between Republicans and Democrats. Among precinct leaders more than one-third saw no difference."

TABLE 3

REASONS OF NEW YORK COUNTY COMMITTEEMEN FOR INTEREST IN POLITICS

REASONS	DEMOCRAT		REPUBLICAN		LIBERAL	
	NUMBER	PER CENT	NUMBER	PER CENT	NUMBER	PER CENT
Desire to change community	67	29	25	10	23	43
Friends	27	12	14	11	3	6
Personality	21	9	11	9	7	13
Enjoy dealing with people	21	9	14	11	6	11
Family or relatives in politics	15	6	26	16	2	4
Make job and business contacts	10	4	6	5	2	4
Desire for prestige	7	3	0	0	1	2
Acquaintances on job	3	1	3	2	1	2
Influence of teacher	3	1	1	1	2	4
Other	22	10	15	12	4	6
No answer	38	16	14	11	2	4

teemen do reflect their constituents and their organizations, then at least in Manhattan the matter of political affiliation (on the part of either the activist or the voter) is not simply a choice between Tweedledum and Tweedledee or, in this instance, Tweedledoo.

Political Activities of Manhattan Committeemen

The final section of this study analyzes the ways in which the three groups of committeemen differ as they conceive of and play the game of politics. Leiserson states: "Although we might be better able to understand the politician if we knew his *real* motivation, to inject a generalized motive to him as a member of a class is often an extremely unreliable index to the politician's behavior in particular situations."[23] The data drawn from the present study, however, conclude that the members of the dominant Democratic party are more serious, more active, and more "profesional" in their approach to political life than those of the minority parties, and that the Liberal, though the most ideologically oriented, is the least involved in practical politics.

Today the differences among the three political parties in Manhattan, however, are not as significant as those separating the entire group of committeemen from their counterparts in the 1930's. Gos-

[23] Leiserson, *op. cit.*, p. 14.

TABLE 4

POLITICAL POLICY ATTITUDES OF THE NEW YORK COUNTY COMMITTEEMEN:* 1960

(*in percentages*)

Policy Statement	Strongly Agree			Agree			Disagree			Strongly Disagree		
	D	R	L	D	R	L	D	R	L	D	R	L
1. The government ought to see to it that everyone who wants to work can find a job.	43	36	52	31	26	37	13	10	9	13	28	2
2. The government ought to help people get low-cost doctors and hospital care.	68	36	83	16	28	11	8	11	6	9	25	0
3. If Negroes are not getting fair treatment in jobs and housing, the government should see to it that they do.	65	43	85	18	22	9	8	16	2	9	19	4
4. The government ought to see to it that big U.S. corporations don't have much say about how the government is run.	51	32	53	25	27	27	9	20	15	14	21	4
5. If cities and towns around the country need help to build more schools, the government ought to give more money.	58	36	64	22	20	27	10	20	2	10	24	7
6. The government should leave things like electric power and housing for private business concerns to build.	22	35	14	19	28	12	21	18	21	38	18	52
7. The government should stay out of the question of whether white and colored children go to the same school.	14	20	7	6	8	4	12	12	5	67	61	83

*Number Responding: D (Democrats)—216; R (Republicans)—118; L (Liberals)—46.

nell and Forthal found that the promise of concrete economic rewards was the Chicago precinct worker's most frequent reason for entering politics in the 1930's. Samuel Koenig commented that the New York City party organization of the same period was kept in line by the committeemen's loyalty to the county leader, a loyalty based "not only on respect and admiration, but also on patronage . . . not only jobs for himself . . . but jobs for his constituents."[24] Not only is the 1960 representative better educated, more affluent, and more firmly entrenched in the middle class, but he is also more likely to enter politics because of his ideas concerning government and society than for personal economic gain. These data agree with Bone's conclusion in 1952 that economic gain and patronage benefits "do not appear particularly significant among the western Washington party officials. Party organizations in Seattle must, for the most part, find other inducements for attracting men and women to precinct leadership."[25] In short, as the character of the party representatives has changed, so, too, have their motives for entering politics.

A large majority of the committeemen interviewed (over 60 per cent) deny ever receiving any personal benefits from political activity. It is interesting to note, however, that when the respondents were asked whether they believed political activity to be instrumental in securing such benefits (appointments, clients, contracts), over 50 per cent replied affirmatively. This may mean that today's party worker still accepts the older stereotyping but considers himself an exception to the rule. It is more likely that while self-interest remains an important consideration in entering politics, most activists consciously or unconsciously subordinate it to a concept of "public interest." In any event, the committeemen's responses indicate that changes in their backgrounds have been accompanied by related changes in their motivation toward political activity.

Despite similar motivation, however, each group of committeemen projects a different image of its own political character, function, and purpose. The Liberal in Manhattan appears primarily as an intellectual who considers his party the ideological forerunner of social progress. Wedded to ideas and ideals, and proud of his independence, he is neither "in" nor "of" politics in the professional sense. He rejects its organizational aspects. He remains steadfast within the Liberal party, however, because it is the most likely of

---

[24]Samuel Koenig, *Oral History Collection* (New York: Columbia University, n.d.), p. 233.

[25]Bone, *op. cit.*, p. 25.

the three to espouse the causes to which he is intellectually committed. The Democrat, though ideologically close to the Liberal, is much more the political "pro." He is concerned with ideas and policies, but he is in politics to win. His associations and activities, his mode and degree of participation in party work, are the most political and professional of the three groups. Except for ideological differences, the Republican resembles the Democrat; were he in power his behavior would probably be quite similar. Interestingly enough, however, the Republican more often considers himself a strong party adherent (80 per cent) than either the Democrat (76) or the Liberal (70). Similarly, the Republicans are more loyal in their party allegiance, with 71 per cent never having even thought of themselves as "other than Republicans," as compared to the Democrats' 65 and the Liberals' 42 per cent.

The Democrats' more profesional approach to politics appears in their responses regarding the "best way of affecting local governmental policy." While the largest number of Liberals would "vote in elections" (33 per cent) and the largest number of Republicans (24 per cent) would "circulate a petition," the first choice of the Democrats (27 per cent) was to "go to your local political party officials." As with other questions of this nature, one reason for the Democratic approach probably lies in the fact that they are the "in" party. They also are better attuned than the other groups to the use of those more subtle and manipulative techniques which are hallmarks of the political professional.

A better index of professionalism is the type and intensity of participation in party activities. The Democrat's view of himself as a provider of services for his party's constituents — as a buffer between the citizen and an increasingly complex government — is part of his more professional pattern. A third of the Democrats visit their clubhouses to "handle constituent problems." Again, as members of the dominant party, they are better able to function in this way, but it is significant, nonetheless, that only a quarter of the Republicans and less than 15 per cent of the Liberals deal with constituents' problems. In fact, 62 per cent of the Liberals never visit the clubs at all. Morever, while a third of both Democrats and Republicans go to their clubhouses to "meet friends" or "be seen," only 19 per cent of the Liberals who frequent their clubs do so for these reasons.

Most of the New York committeemen prefer "policy making" to more public or more tedious (or less impressive) political activities. Here again the Liberals are most distinctive, almost 80 per cent choosing policy formulation as opposed to about 65 per cent in each of the other groups. As for "running a campaign," 45 per cent of the Democrats and 43 per cent of the Republicans choose this more "practical" activity, as compared to only 28 per cent of the Liberals. The height of political activity — "being a candidate for office" — attracts 19 per cent of the Democrats and 17 per cent of the Republicans, but only 11 per cent of the Liberals.

Other activities reveal the Democrats' deeper commitment to and greater professionalism in politics. Some two-thirds have been involved actively in an issue of local concern during the past few years, as compared to half of both Republicans and Liberals. Some 85 per cent of the Democrats have attended public meetings concerned with such issues, compared to 76 per cent for the Republicans and 81 per cent for the Liberals. Only a third of the Democrats report "no activity" on local issues, while half of the Republicans and two-fifths of the Liberals were inactive. While 17 per cent of the Republicans and 21 per cent of the Liberals engaged in "no political activity" during nonpresidential election years (when the amateur's interest often flags), this applied to only 10 per cent of the Democrats.

Democrats, to a greater extent than Republicans and Liberals, limit their social contacts to those holding similar political views and party affiliation. McClosky points out that "stable voters have the highest proportion of peers who share their preferences."[26] Over 72 per cent of the Manhattan Democrats limit their close friendships to other Democrats. Only 42 per cent of the Republicans and 53 per cent of the Liberals are so insular. Moreover, while over half the Democrats belong to organizations whose membership is predominantly Democratic, only a third of the Republicans and a fourth of the Liberals say that their organizations are mainly Republican or mainly Liberal in composition. Whether dominated by their own kind or not, however, the Democrats exceed the other groups in the average number of extra-party organizations to which they belong. Only 3 per cent belong to no social, civic, or religious organizations, while 11 per cent of the Republicans eschew "joining."

Both Democrats and Liberals "talk politics" with friends more frequently than do Republicans (68 and 70, as compared with 59 per cent). But more striking is the fact that while only 4 per cent of the Democrats "never talk politics" with civic leaders, 24 per cent of the Republicans and 32 per cent of the Liberals hold no discus-

[26]McClosky and Dahlgren, *op. cit.*, p. 771.

sions at a higher level of power. The Democrats' greater willingness to discuss community affairs and their greater contacts among community leaders are further reflected in the fact that more people consult *them* with regard to local government and political party problems.

The Manhattan Democratic committeeman — partly because of his political orientation and partly because of his membership in the dominant party — is more active, more purposeful, more practical and more professional in politics than either his Republican or Liberal counterparts. The Republican does not differ basically in his political methods but he is limited by his minority-party status. The Liberal, by reason of his ideological commitment, issue orientation, and intellectual emphasis, is the least professional of the party representatives. The "new look" in political life is as evident in party activities as it is in both demography and ideology.

Conclusion

The Manhattan Democratic committeemen belong to the dominant party in New York City politics; they occupy the broad center on virtually every dimension developed in this study. With regard to demographic background, policy attitudes, and political activity, the Democrat ranks consistently between the Republican and the Liberal. He is closer to the former in his socio-economic position and party activity and closer to the latter in his basic political philosophy and his attitudes toward governmental power and public policies. The Democratic committeeman is more "liberal" than the Republican and more professional than the Liberal.

The Republican, while resembling the Democrats in background and mode of operation, differs primarily in policy orientation. He is noticeably more "conservative" than the Liberal. This may be traced partly to the fact that the Republicans are, as a group, furthest from immigrant status and most representative of the nation's Protestant majority.

The Liberals, more a pressure group than a party, refute most of the established axioms of political behavior. They are, in fact, the most "liberal" of the three groups. Although the most firmly committed to policies which they approve, they also are the least involved in practical political activity. The principal factor responsible for this Liberal paradox — and the third party's most distinctive feature — is its large number of Jews. Intellectually oriented and socially conscious, liberal from both conviction and necessity, their attachment to their party's principles supersedes considerations of economic status.

The data gathered on all three parties leads to two general conclusions regarding the nature of urban politics in the United States. First, ideological orientation — more than socio-economic status — is apt to determine the urban activists' political affiliation. The parties' memberships are characterized far less by income, education, and occupation than by varying attitudes toward social and political change, governmental power and policies, minority groups, and established institutions and ideas. Second, there is a "new look" among today's political activists. They are "respectable," solid middle-class citizens. The party "hack" of fiction, films, and the traditional literature is hard to find among the young, well-educated, affluent, and socially-acceptable committeemen — and women — of the nineteen-sixties. Concomitantly, both the nature of political motivation and the character of political activity have changed. The contemporary politician considers his party organization an instrument for effectuating policy rather than a haven of personal security. He tends to be more interested in social reform than in catering to individual constituents.

What do these general conclusions mean for the future of American politics? On the one hand they point to increasing interest in politics among intelligent and informed citizens, on the other to a sharper conflict between the two major parties on ideological grounds and structural weakening of the party organizations. If the results of this study of urban political activists reflect definite trends, American politics — at least in the great population centers like New York City — promises to be characterized in the future by parties which are more broadly based, by politicians who are more policy-oriented and by a political system which is more dynamic than in the past.

Intraparty Attitude Conflict: Democratic Party Leadership in California

Edmond Costantini

Attitude conflict is a phenomenon occurring within as well as between political parties. And if party members are differentiated in terms of their political dispositions, so too are they differentiated in terms of the status they have within their party. The relationship between these two forms of differentiation — between membership stratification and attitude conflict — is the central concern of this study. It is a relationship which has recently been the subject of some interest to students of political behavior.

David Butler, for example, has suggested that a principal dilemma of party leaders is that they are caught between the disparate demands of their followership: "Their most loyal and devoted followers tend to have more extreme views than they have themselves, and

NOTE: I would like to express my appreciation to the Falk Foundation, to Professor Eugene C. Lee and the Institute of Governmental Studies, University of California at Berkeley, and to James Earle Sandmire for their generous assistance in this study and in the larger study of California party leadership of which it is a part.

Reprinted from the *Western Political Quarterly,* XVI (December, 1963), 956-72, by permission of the University of Utah.

to be still farther removed from the mass of those who actually provide the vote." The leaders therefore have "to conciliate those who support them with money or with voluntary work, without alienating that large body of moderate voters whose attitudes make them most likely to swing to the other party and thus to decide the next election."[1]

Professor Butler's definition of "party leader" is limited to the elected government official, and the elaboration of his hypothesis is limited to diagrammatic representations which, he concludes, "are no more than pedagogic devices." And yet his suggestion seems to bear significantly on another recent study, more comprehensive and more empirical in nature, conducted by Herbert McClosky, Paul J. Hoffmann, and Rosemary O'Hara. They have demonstrated that "whereas the leaders of the two [American] parties diverge strongly, their followers differ only moderately in their attitudes toward issues," one conclusion among several drawn from the results of questionnaire studies of delegates to the 1956 national party conventions and of a nationwide sample of adult voters.[2]

The Butler hypothesis is not incompatible with the findings of McClosky and his colleagues. It does suggest, however, that the relationship between party status and attitudes may be significantly more complex than the leadership-followership dichotomy would indicate.

The research reported here seeks to put a slightly revised version of Butler's hypothesis to a limited empirical test: it seeks to compare the political perspectives of differentiated groups of party leaders which, taken together, are somewhat more inclusive than Butler's elected government officials. The hypothesis is simply that the substructure of party leadership deviates in attitudes more radically from the actual political center than does the superstructure; that the top party leaders are, indeed, faced with the dilemma not only of a voting public holding more centrist, or moderate, views — amply demonstrated by McClosky and his colleagues — but also of a more extremist group of party militants standing below them in the hierarchy of party leadership.[3]

[1]David Butler, "The Paradox of Party Difference," *American Behavioral Scientist,* 4 (November 1960), 3-5.

[2]"Issue Conflict and Consensus among Party Leaders and Followers," *American Political Science Review,* 54 (June 1960), 406-27.

[3]The fact that Butler considers the party militant to be a part of the party followership rather than leadership arises from his more limited definition of party leadership and poses a terminological difficulty which does not seem to affect materially the efficacy of the conclusions herein drawn. Indeed, what will be identified as one of the groups composing the substructure of party leadership — the "caucus nominees" — is quite similar to what Butler calls the "party militant" group.

Focus

The data used to test this hypothesis are focused on the California delegation to the 1960 Democratic national convention.[4] As would be true of any other delegation, such a focus allows us to compare different levels of party leadership by differentiating delegates from alternates.[5] But there are characteristics of this particular delegation which are advantageous for the purposes of this paper while not being of such universal incidence. Of prime significance in this respect is the exceptional degree to which the delegation constituted a generous cross-section of the state's Democratic leadership. Replete with party notables of all sorts, it was characterized by a representativeness which is not always found among convention delegations.

The fact that there was no contest between rival party factions in the June, 1960 presidential primary, that there was only one authentic party slate presented to the Democratic voters, meant that no group of party leaders was excluded from the delegation through defeat at the polls.[6] But the primary served more to confirm than to cause the cross-sectional nature of the California contingent to the Democratic convention. A delegation selection committee had met four months earlier, in February, and had drawn up the slate of delegates pledged to the "favorite son," Governor Edmond G. Brown, which was subsequently presented to the Democratic pri-

---

[4]The story of this delegation is lucidly told by John H. Bunzel and Eugene C. Lee, *The California Democratic Delegation of 1960,* Inter-University Case Study No. 67 (University, Alabama: University of Alabama Press, 1962). See also Eugene C. Lee, "Organization and Administration of a Large Delegation: California Democrats," in Paul Tillett (ed.), *The National Conventions* (Dobbs Ferry, New York: Oceana Publications, 1962).

[5]The term "delegation" will be used throughout these pages to include both delegates and alternates.

[6]A delegation slate pledged to George McLain, old-age pension promoter, managed to attract some 646,387 votes in the Democratic presidential primary — almost half the number of votes given to the slate pledged to Governor Brown. However, by no stretch of the imagination can the McLain slate be considered to have been a repository of state Democratic leadership.

The 1960 situation stands in marked contrast to those of 1952 and 1956. In 1952 a delegation slate largely composed of political unknowns and pledged to Senator Estes Kefauver carried the presidential primary after the last-minute withdrawal of President Truman from the race had left the "regular" slate without its candidate. In 1956 California Democrats were treated to a primary contest between two real contenders for the presidential nomination — Kefauver and Adlai Stevenson. Each was represented by a reasonably strong delegation slate; neither had a monopoly of state party leadership supporting him.

In both 1952 and 1956, then, primary contests meant that the delegations sent by California to the Democratic national conventions were something less than cross-sections of state party leadership. Despite the McLain phenomenon, this was not true in 1960.

mary voters. There was no domination of that committee by a particular party group or faction.[7] Nor was there a commitment to any bona fide candidate to give his supporters inordinate preferential treatment, or to exclude his opponents from consideration in the selection of the delegation members.[8] Indeed, the selection committee—with all deliberateness—attempted to design a delegation slate on which every leadership element within the party was represented and from which no party group was seriously omitted. Success in this attempt, it was felt, would effectively discourage any challenge in the primary by a rival slate pledged to a bona fide presidential aspirant. A costly fratricidal contest would thus be averted, while, at the same time, a delegation which in effect was uncom-

---

[7]The ten-member selection committee included: the chairman and vice-chairman of the Democratic State Central Committee, the chairman of the Women's Division of the Democratic State Central Committee, the Democratic national committeeman and committeewoman from California, the president of the California Democratic Council, the dean of the California Democratic delegation to the U.S. Congress, a second congressman designated by U.S. Senator Clair Engle, the speaker of the state Assembly, and the president pro tempore of the state Senate.

Additionally, a twenty-nine-member Advisory Committee was appointed to assist the selection committee in its duties. This included representatives of each of the following groups: Democrats holding elective office in the state and national governments; officers of the official party machinery, i.e., of state and county central committees; and officers of the unofficial "citizen" wings of the party, principally of the California Democratic Council. While the Advisory Committee never met, some of its members did submit lists of names for the consideration of the delegation selection committee.

[8]Paul David has recently written that in pre-primary negotiations in California Senator John F. Kennedy successfully "pressed for the inclusion of a substantial number of his own supporters in the Brown delegation." See "The Presidential Nomination," in Paul David (ed.), *The Presidential Election and Transition, 1960-1961* (Washington: Brookings, 1961), p. 9. There is little evidence, however, that there was any pressure from the Kennedy organization which significantly affected the delegation selection committee in its deliberations, or, indeed, that the committee was even concerned with the presidential preference of those people whom it was considering for a place on the delegation. In fact, late February, when the delegation members were chosen, was somewhat early for presidential preferences to be developed among party leaders. The Kennedy objective of the moment was achieved nonetheless, a consequence of the decision to construct a delegation broadly representative of party leadership throughout the state: a fair sample of California Democrats was bound to include "a substantial number" of Kennedy supporters.

The charge sometimes heard among California Democrats that the selection committee was biased against Stevenson and toward Kennedy seems particularly questionable in view of the fact that, in the final analysis, only three of its members voted for Kennedy at the national convention, while six of the remaining seven voted for Stevenson.

mitted would presumably maximize California's influence at the Democratic national convention.[9]

In sum, a thoroughgoing and conscious attempt was made to construct a delegation which was as representative of all leadership elements within the party as possible.[10] And there is every reason to believe that the conclusion of McClosky and his colleagues that national convention delegates represent "as faithful a cross-section of . . . party leadership as could be had without an extraordinary expenditure of money and labor"[11] is especially appropriate to California Democrats, 1960.

The decision to make the delegation a repository of as many party leaders in the state as possible was an opportune one for the purposes of this study; and it involved two fortunate ancillary consequences. Coupled with the amplitude of the delegation's membership — there were 162 delegates and 80 alternate posts to fill — it meant that official status at the national convention was to be extended to 74 Democratic congressmen and state legislators and to

---

[9]In 1960 the California *Election Code* required not only that each delegation slate entered in the presidential primary be committed to a particular candidate, but that that slate have the endorsement of its candidate before presentation to the primary voters. Thus, a commitment to Governor Brown as a "favorite son" was the nearest possible thing to an "uncommitted delegation." Thus, too, Senator Kennedy, or any other candidate, would have had to approve explicitly any attempt to challenge the Governor and his "strong" delegation in the primary.

[10]This cross-sectional nature of the California delegation was achieved at a high price. As Eugene Lee and William Buchanan conclude: "Forestalling a primary contest by selecting a delegation on which every faction was represented made it impossible for the delegation to act in a unified and coherent fashion." "The 1960 Election in California," *Western Political Quarterly,* 14 (March 1961), 312. Thus, by convention-time the unity achieved at the primary had been completely dissipated. So, too, had been the hopes that the state might play a decisive role at Los Angeles.

The California vote at the Democratic convention for the various presidential aspirants serves as the most obvious demonstration of the delegation's divisiveness: 67 of the delegates voted for Kennedy, 63 for Stevenson, 16 for Symington, 15 for Johnson, and one for Governor Brown. In only four other instances did delegations fail to give a particular candidate a majority of their respective votes; and the combined vote of these delegations—those of Hawaii, Idaho, Nevada, and South Dakota — was only a little over half that of California. Indeed, no delegation had so wide a discrepancy between potential and performance, between sanguine hopes for political influence and the disappointing reality of political effeteness.

But the practitioner's bane is the analyst's boon, and it is this very conflict within the delegation — born of the cross-sectional nature of its membership — which makes it particularly interesting for the student of party leadership.

[11]*Op. cit.*, p. 405.

8 elected officials of the state executive branch.[12] This extraordinary representation of elected officeholders serves further to commend the California delegation to the 1960 Democratic national convention as the focal point for a study of attitude conflict between differentiated groups of party leaders.

The second fortunate consequence of the desire to create a broadly representative delegation was the adoption of the caucus nominee system. Caucuses of local party leaders were called by the delegation selection committee in each of the state's thirty congressional districts to nominate candidates for positions on the delegation.[13] These caucuses were instructed not to include elected state or national government officials among their nominees, because the delegation selection committee was to consider them separately. Indeed, the approximately 300 men and women nominated by the caucuses were by and large voluntary contributors of time and energy to party endeavors whose personal political ambitions were limited in nature. Their partisan activities tended to be focused more on their localities and less on Sacramento, California in general, or Washington than those of the other Democratic leaders considered in this paper. Again more than these other leadership groups, the caucus nominees tended to play active roles in the California Democratic Council, the unofficial, mass-membership arm of the state's Democratic party.[14] Francis Carney describes the motives of men and

---

[12]Thus, over 80 per cent of those Democrats holding such office were on the delegation. The selection committee did not follow a policy of deliberately excluding any Democratic officeholder for personal or political reasons. The fact that 17 of them were not on the delegation is attributable to other considerations, principally their own decision not to serve and the fact that the state Senate is apportioned in such a way that there were more legislators in some rural congressional districts than were permitted on the delegation.

[13]The following were invited to attend these caucuses: (1) all members of the Democratic State Central Committee from within the congressional district; (2) all members of Democratic County Central Committees from within the district; (3) all Democrats holding elective office as mayor, city councilman or county supervisor within the district; (4) all Assembly District, Congressional District, and County Council officers from within the district; (5) one delegate for every twenty members of each club within the district chartered by the Democratic County Central Committee or the California Federation of Young Democrats, or authorized to participate in the 1960 convention of the California Democratic Council.

[14]Of the 141 caucus nominees responding to questionnaires sent in connection with this study, 110 (77 per cent) claimed to be active members of the California Democratic Council, with 50 of these saying that they were officeholders in the organization. Eight of the remaining 31 failed to respond to this particular question, 3 denied membership, and 20 claimed that they were not very active members.

In contrast, only 39 (48 per cent) of the 81 respondents who were on the delegation but who were not caucus nominees claimed to be active in the C.D.C., and only five of these said they held official status in the organization. Fourteen of the remaining 42 failed to respond to this particular question, 10 denied membership, and 18 claimed that they were not very active members.

women such as these when he discusses those who attend annual C.D.C. conventions: "The overwhelming majority of them have no personal or financial interest in politics, no ambitions to be served, no enemies whose jugulars must be pierced."[15] But however limited the focus of political activity and the motives of the caucus nominees, they can nevertheless be considered party leaders. The recognition extended by their fellow partisans at the local nominating caucuses serves as testimony to that fact. And for some — 86 of the approximately 300 — recognition was further extended by the top party leadership in the state when they were selected as members of the delegation.[16]

Thus, the California delegation to the 1960 Democratic national convention is a particularly appropriate focus for a study of attitude conflict between differentiated groups of party leaders. (1) Unlike many other delegations, it was, by conscious design and a series of circumstances, the repository of top leaders from all elements within the party. (2) It was unusual in that it included among its members a large number of elected government officials, the traditional object of analysis for students of party leadership. (3) It was unusual in that a finite group of "grass roots" party leaders was specifically considered and in substantial part deliberately rejected for membership on the delegation.

Substantial as its advantages are, however, our focus is clearly a limited one. And the distinctive characteristics of California politics — the heritage of nonpartisanship and a weak party discipline, the tradition of progressivism and of the political maverick, the strength and nature of the Democratic club movement, the power limitations of the governorship, the extraordinarily high esteem with which Adlai Stevenson is held, etc. — were all reflected in the story of the California delegation to the 1960 Democratic national convention. Certainly this study should be seen in terms of the context of California politics. And certainly its findings are, at best, suggestive rather than validating, heuristic rather than conclusive.

Procedures

Questionnaires designed for self-administration were sent to all delegation members, with 99 of the 162 delegates (61 per cent) and 59 of the 80 alternates (74 per cent) responding. Additionally, questionnaires were sent to 115 of the 203 congressional district

---

[15]Francis Carney, *The Rise of Democratic Clubs in California,* Eagleton Foundation Case Studies in Practical Politics (New York: Holt, 1958), p. 12.

[16]Each caucus could nominate up to 10 names, of which the delegation selection committee was pledged to select at least two for delegate or alternate status.

caucus nominees who had been denied a place on the delegation by the selection committee (hereafter referred to as "rejected caucus nominees"). Some 67 (58 per cent) of these were returned. Virtually all of the transactions — remission and receipt of the questionnaires — occurred during the two months immediately preceding the national convention at Los Angeles in July, 1960.

The questions with which this discusion will be concerned relate to the political attitudes of the respondent. (1) He was asked to evaluate his own position within the party on a five-point liberal-conservative scale. (2) He was asked to register a preference for the Democratic presidential nomination. Six candidates were listed for his consideration, and although he was permitted to write in another choice the respondent was specifically requested to exclude Governor Brown, the favorite son candidate whom each member of the delegation was formally pledged to support. (3) He was asked, finally, to express his attitudes toward each of nine national issues by indicating whether he was "very much," "somewhat," "very little," or "not at all" favorably disposed toward the proposed policy.

To analyze the latter data a technique very similar to the "ratio of support score" used by McClosky and his colleagues has been adopted, the principal difference being a consequence of the fact that McClosky used a three-point scale — "increase," "remain as is," and "decrease" — as opposed to the four-point scale herein employed. Table 4 does more than merely present the percentage of each leadership group favoring each proposed policy "very much," "somewhat," etc. For ease of analysis it also presents a single statistic for each policy proposal — a "ratio of support" — which simultaneously takes account of all four percentages of policy acceptance or rejection among the members of the party group being considered. The "ratio of support" was arrived at by assigning a weight of 1.000 to each "very much" response, 0.667 to each "somewhat" response, 0.333 to each "very little" response, and 0.000 to each "not at all" response. Thus, it may vary from zero to unity, with support for a proposed policy increasing as the score approaches unity.

It should be noted that in all of the groupings used for this analysis our Democratic respondents registered larger support ratios on each issue than did a sample of delegates and alternates from California to the 1960 Republican national convention.[17] Thus, the

[17]Unfortunately, the Republican respondents cannot be grouped in a manner corresponding to that in which the Democrats have been grouped (see pp. 962-63). There were few (less than 20) elected government officials on the Republican delegation; and there were no congressional district caucuses

higher the support ratios for the Democratic groups here being considered the greater their "radicalism" or their deviation from the mean score of the two rival delegations. In view of the nature of our two parties, of the policies being proposed, and of the relationship between the policy questions and the other attitude questions under consideration, we shall also speak of a higher ratio of support score as indicating a more "liberal" orientation. The terminology is not as important as the direction and magnitude of attitude differences between different respondent groupings.

A technique similar to the ratio of support score is used to evaluate the response of the question regarding liberal-conservative self-evaluation. By assigning a weight of 1.00 to each "very liberal" response, 0.75 to each "somewhat liberal" response, 0.50 to each "middle of the road" response, 0.25 to each "somewhat conservative" response, and 0.00 to each "very conservative" response a single statistic is derived which, for simplicity's sake, shall be termed a "liberalism ratio."

To evaluate the question relating to candidate preference the political facts of the pre-convention presidential sweepstakes among California Democrats are assessed in the following manner: Bowles, Humphrey, and Stevenson tended to be the candidates of "liberals"; Johnson, Kennedy, and Symington tended to be the candidates of "conservatives." The relationship between the candidate preference and liberal-conservative self-evaluation of our Democratic respondents is shown in Table 1, and it would seem to support this contention. Between 30 and 40 per cent of those who preferred either Bowles, Humphrey, or Stevenson considered themselves to be very liberal. On the other hand, 20 per cent of those enamored of Symington, and 7 per cent of the Kennedy supporters, claimed to be very liberal. Not one Johnson supporter so evaluated himself. Applying the liberalism ratio technique, we find that Bowles, Humphrey, and Stevenson supporters achieved liberalism ratios of 0.790, 0.808, and 0.810 respectively, as contrasted to the 0.475, 0.650, and 0.700 for the supporters of Johnson, Kennedy, and Symington, respectively.

---

called to nominate possible delegation members. Indeed, even differentiating delegates from alternates seems unjustified because of the small size of the delegation and the consequent small number of respondents in each category. For these reasons, and for others, an analysis of data arising from questionnaires sent to the members of the Republican delegation will not be presented in this paper. Footnote 20, however, presents the ratio of support scores for the Republican respondents in the aggregate. Suffice it to say at this point that their issue posture is substantially different from that of the Democrats. In fact, there was no issue on which the mean Republican score was even two-thirds the magnitude of the mean Democratic score.

Findings

For each of the three sets of questions (candidate preference, liberal-conservative self-evaluation, issue orientation), the respondents are grouped in three ways. First, differences between delegates, alternates, and rejected caucus nominees are distinguished. Second, elected state and national government officials on the delegation are compared with the remainder of the delegation and with the rejected caucus nominees. Third, those members of the delegation

TABLE 1

RELATIONSHIP BETWEEN CANDIDATE PREFERENCE AND LIBERAL-CONSERVATIVE SELF-EVALUATION: ALL RESPONDENTS (DELEGATION MEMBERS AND REJECTED CAUCUS NOMINEES)

(in percentages)

	CANDIDATE PREFERENCE					
SELF-EVALUATION	BOWLES (N:18)	HUMPHREY (N:13)	STEVENSON (N:97)	JOHNSON (N:10)	KENNEDY (N:32)	SYMINGTON (N:24)
Very liberal (N:58)	39	31	41	—	6	21
Somewhat liberal (N: 94)	44	61	43	20	59	46
Middle-of-the-road (N: 35)	11	8	12	50	25	25
Somewhat conservative (N: 13)	6	—	3	30	9	8
Very conservative (N:0)	—	—	—	—	—	—
Liberalism Ratio	0.790	0.808	0.810	0.475	0.650	0.700

TABLE 2

LIBERAL-CONSERVATIVE SELF-EVALUATION OF VARIOUS LEADERSHIP GROUPS

(in percentages)

SELF-EVALUATION	DELEGATES (N:94)	ALTERNATES (N:55)	ELECTED GOVERNMENT OFFICIALS (N:42)	OTHER DELEGATION MEMBERS (N:107)	NON-CAUCUS NOMINEES ON DELEGATION (N:77)	CAUCUS NOMINEES ON DELEGATION (N:77)	REJECTED CAUCUS NOMINEES (N:66)
Very liberal	23	27	17	28	21	30	36
Somewhat liberal	48	44	40	49	42	51	50
Middle-of-the-road	22	22	36	17	30	14	9
Somewhat conservative	6	7	7	6	8	6	5
Very conservative	—	—	—	—	—	—	—
Total	99	100	100	100	101	100	100
Liberalism Ratio	0.715	0.728	0.668	0.748	0.695	0.768	0.792

who were not caucus nominees are compared with those that were and, again, with the rejected caucus nominees. Given the nature of the total sample under consideration, these three groupings would seem to be the most appropriate for an analysis of the attitudes of differentiated levels of party leadership. The distinctions may be diagrammatically represented as follows:

High-level leadership	Delegates	Elected government officials (state and national) on delegation	Non-caucus nominees on delegation
Middle-level leadership	Alternates	Members of delegation who were not elected government officials	Caucus nominees on delegation
Low-level leadership	Rejected caucus nominees		

The results of the questionnaire analysis clearly sustain our basic hypothesis. In each case, the group which tends to include the superstructure of party leadership in California (delegates, government officials, non-caucus nominees on the delegation) is less "radical" or "liberal" than the groups beneath it in the party edifice. The group which most nearly represents the substructure of party leadership (rejected caucus nominees) is consistently more "radical" or "liberal" than the groups above it in the party edifice.

1. In differentiating delegates, alternates and rejected caucus nominees in terms of their own assessment of their place on the political spectrum, we find that 23 per cent of the delegates, 27 per cent of the alternates, and 36 per cent of the rejected caucus nominees consider themselves "very liberal" (see Table 2).[18] The delegates register a liberalism ratio of 0.715, the alternates, 0.728, and the rejected caucus nominees, 0.792.

A similar relationship prevails for these three groups on the question of candidate preference. The delegates divided in half in their support of the three liberal versus the three conservative candidates (see Table 3). In contrast, two-thirds of the alternates preferred the three liberal candidates. And of the group farthest removed from top party leadership — the rejected caucus nominees — more than four-fifths preferred the three liberal candidates. In respect to four of the six candidates, the progression conforms to the hypothesized pattern. That is, the higher the place of the group in the party hierarchy the more the conservative candidate is preferred

[18]No answer responses are excluded from consideration in all of this paper's tabulations.

and the less the liberal candidate is preferred. In one of the other two cases the alternates evince a greater preference for a liberal candidate (Bowles) than do the rejected caucus nominees, and in the other case the alternates evince a lesser preference for a liberal candidate (Humphrey) than do the delegates.

With reference to issue orientation, again our basic hypothesis is supported: the lower the respondent's status in the leadership hierarchy the more "radical" or "liberal" he tends to be (see Table 4). That is, he tends to accentuate the differences between the top leadership of the two parties and to have a programmatic posture which would generally be considered more liberal. For seven of the nine issues presented in our questionnaire, the highest ratio of support score is achieved by the rejected caucus nominees, and in five of these the alternates register the next highest ratio of support score. The mean support ratios for the nine issues clearly conform to the hypothesized pattern: delegates have a mean score of 0.714, alternates, 0.726, and rejected caucus nominees, 0.798.

2. In comparing incumbent elected state and national government officials with the rest of our respondents on the delegation, we find that this top leadership group stands in the same relationship — although the hypothesized differences are even more exaggerated — to the groups lower in the party hierarchy as did the delegates in relation to alternates and rejected caucus nominees.[19] The officials consider themselves less liberal than the other members of the delegation; and the latter, in turn, feel they are less liberal than the rejected caucus nominees (see Table II). Thus 17 per cent of the officials evaluate themselves as very liberal, as opposed to 28 per cent of the other delegation members, and, as indicated, 36 per cent of the rejected caucus nominees. The liberalism ratio for the government officials is 0.668, while the others on the delegation achieved 0.748 and the rejected caucus nominees 0.792.

On candidate preference and on issue orientation our hypothesis is again sustained. Less than one-half of the elected government officials prefer the three liberal candidates, as contrasted with three-fifths of the other delegation members, and, as indicated, more than four-fifths of the rejected caucus nominees (see Table III). For five of the six condidates, the higher the place in the party hierarchy the

[19]Thirty-two respondents were elected state or national government officials with delegate status at Los Angeles; fourteen were alternates. Forty-one of the forty-six officials were state legislators or congressmen, and three of the remaining five neglected to indicate whether they were in the state executive or legislative branch. As indicated, none of the rejected caucus nominees were state or national government officials.

TABLE 3

CANDIDATE PREFERENCE OF VARIOUS LEADERSHIP GROUPS
(in percentages)

	DELEGATES (N:84)	ALTERNATES (N:55)	ELECTED GOVERNMENT OFFICIALS (N:39)	OTHER DELEGATION MEMBERS (N:100)	NON-CAUCUS NOMINEES ON DELEGATION (N:71)	CAUCUS NOMINEES ON DELEGATION (N:65)	REJECTED CAUCUS NOMINEES (N:64)
Bowles	5	15	5	10	6	12	11
Humphrey	5	2	—	5	3	5	14
Stevenson	40	51	44	45	38	51	58
Three Candidate Total	50	68	49	60	47	68	83
Johnson	8	5	13	5	10	5	2
Kennedy	23	15	18	20	20	18	12
Symington	19	13	20	15	24	9	2
Three Candidate Total	50	33	51	40	54	32	16

more the conservative candidate is preferred and the less the liberal candidate is preferred. In the other case the non-government officials on the delegation indicate a preference for a conservative candidate (Kennedy) which surpasses that of the government officials.

At the same time, on six of the nine issues the hypothesized differences prevail, with the support ratios progressing in magnitude from government officials on the delegation, to others on the delegation, to rejected caucus nominees (see Table 4). Indeed, the mean support ratios for the nine issues conform to this progression as follows: 0.649 for the government officials, 0.747 for the other delegation members, and, again, 0.798 for the rejected caucus nominees. On no issue do the government officials register a higher support ratio than the rejected caucus nominees.

3. The same general relationships hold true in our final rearrangement of Democratic leadership groups in California. Those members of the delegation who were selected from lists submitted by congressional district caucuses tend to be more "radical" or "liberal" than those who were appointed directly by the delegation selection committee, i.e., than the group which is largely composed of heavy financial contributors, interest group representatives, high party functionaries, and government officials. At the same time, the caucus nominees on the delegation are less "radical" or "liberal" than the rejected caucus nominees, i.e., than those who were nominated by the same congressional district caucuses but who were re-

TABLE 4

Issue Orientation of Various Leadership Groups

(in percentages)

	Delegates	Alternates	Elected Government Officials	Other Delegation Members	Non-Caucus Nominees on Delegation	Caucus Nominees on Delegation	Rejected Caucus Nominees
For recognition of Communist China	(N:85)	(N:50)	(N:39)	(N:96)	(N:74)	(N:69)	(N:58)
Not at all	39	34	54	30	46	25	17
Very little	18	24	15	22	16	25	19
Somewhat	34	26	23	34	29	34	40
Very much	9	16	8	14	9	16	24
Support Ratio	0.377	0.413	0.283	0.440	0.337	0.470	0.570
For abolition of the House Committee on Un-American Activities	(N:87)	(N:51)	(N:39)	(N:99)	(N:67)	(N:69)	(N:65)
Not at all	15	20	23	14	19	13	11
Very little	15	14	20	12	19	9	3
Somewhat	25	16	36	16	29	15	20
Very much	45	51	20	58	33	63	66
Support Ratio	0.667	0.663	0.507	0.727	0.587	0.760	0.803
For nationalization of selected basic industries	(N:84)	(N:48)	(N:41)	(N:91)	(N:67)	(N:63)	(N:62)
Not at all	63	58	66	59	61	60	37
Very little	26	21	22	25	24	25	27
Somewhat	5	13	2	10	7	8	18
Very much	6	8	10	5	7	6	18
Support Ratio	0.180	0.237	0.187	0.200	0.197	0.197	0.390
For increasing the federal minimum wage from $1.00 to $1.25	(N:89)	(N:52)	(N:43)	(N:98)	(N:71)	(N:67)	(N:67)
Not at all	2	2	5	1	3	1	1
Very little	9	2	7	6	7	4	1
Somewhat	13	25	19	17	21	15	10
Very much	75	71	70	76	69	79	87
Support Ratio	0.867	0.883	0.850	0.893	0.853	0.903	0.940

For medical aid to the aged tied to the Social Security program	(N:93)	(N:53)	(N:43)	(N:103)	(N:74)	(N:69)	(N:66)
Not at all	4	2	5	3	4	3	—
Very little	1	2	2	1	3	—	2
Somewhat	22	21	21	21	23	19	17
Very much	73	75	72	75	70	78	82
Support ratio	0.880	0.897	0.867	0.893	0.863	0.907	0.940
For power projects entirely developed with federal funds over those developed through federal private partnership	(N:91)	(N:53)	(N:43)	(N:101)	(N:72)	(N:69)	(N:66)
Not at all	7	6	9	5	8	4	3
Very little	10	9	9	10	11	9	6
Somewhat	22	21	30	18	26	17	24
Very much	62	64	51	67	54	70	67
Support Ratio	0.800	0.810	0.740	0.823	0.750	0.843	0.850
For greater economic aid to under-developed countries	(N:92)	(N:51)	(N:44)	(N:99)	(N:73)	(N:68)	(N:65)
Not at all	3	2	7	1	5	—	3
Very little	7	2	11	2	10	—	5
Somewhat	28	22	39	20	32	21	22
Very much	62	75	43	77	53	79	71
Support Ratio	0.830	0.903	0.727	0.910	0.777	0.930	0.873
For federal aid to school construction	(N:93)	(N:53)	(N:44)	(N:102)	(N.74)	(N:69)	(N:67)
Not at all	1	6	4	2	4	1	1
Very little	2	4	9	—	5	—	3
Somewhat	12	13	14	12	14	12	12
Very much	85	77	73	86	77	87	84
Support Ratio	0.937	0.870	0.853	0.940	0.880	0.950	0.930
For a federal Fair Employment Practices Commission	(N:90)	(N:52)	(N:41)	(N:101)	(N:71)	(N:68)	(N:66)
Not at all	4	2	7	2	6	1	2
Very little	3	8	2	6	6	4	5
Somewhat	12	21	24	12	21	10	20
Very much	80	69	66	80	68	84	74
Support Ratio	0.890	0.857	0.827	0.900	0.840	0.920	0.890
Mean Support Ratio for Nine Issues	0.714	0.726	0.649	0.747	0.676	0.764	0.798

jected by the selection committee. It will be recalled that more than 35 per cent of those in the latter group evaluate themselves as very liberal. In contrast, approximately 20 per cent of the non-caucus nominees on the delegation and 30 per cent of the caucus nominees on the delegation make such a claim (see Table 2). As for comparative liberalism ratios, the non-caucus nominees on the delegation compile a mean ratio of 0.695, the caucus nominees on the delegation, 0.768, and the rejected caucus nominees, 0.792.

Similarly, somewhat less than half the non-caucus nominees on the delegation prefer one of the three liberal candidates, whereas over two-thirds of the selected caucus nominees and over four-fifths of the rejected caucus nominees are so inclined (see Table 3). In the case of only one candidate does the pattern of support fail to conform to the hypothesized pattern: Bowles is preferred by a greater proportion of caucus nominees on the delegation than of rejected caucus nominees.

On six of the nine issues the hypothesized progression prevails (see Table 4). And again, on no issue do the rejected caucus nominees achieve a lower ratio of support score than the top leadership group — the non-caucus nominees on the delegation. It will be recalled that for the former group the mean support score is 0.798. For the latter group it is 0.676. As before, our middle-level leadership group — in this case, the caucus nominees on the delegation — falls between the other two leadership groups under consideration, its mean support ratio being 0.764.

4. Table 5 presents a partial recapitulation of the data developed on the issue orientation of the various groups under consideration. It compares low-level leadership with high-level leadership in terms of the ratio of support scores achieved on each issue. The issues are ranked in order of the magnitude of the differences between each pair of groups. The rejected caucus nominees are treated as the lowest level of party leadership in each of the three sets of comparisons. The highest levels are alternately the members of the delegation who had delegate status, the elected government officials on the delegation, and the members of the delegation who had not previously been nominated by congressional district caucuses. Inasmuch as there are nine issues and three groupings, there are twenty-seven comparisons made. Three features of the comparisons summarized in Table 5 might be noted.

In the first place, in twenty-five of the twenty-seven comparisons the basic hypothesis of this paper is sustained, i.e., the low-level leadership group has a higher ratio of support score than each of the high-level leadership groups with which it is compared. Additionally, taking the differences in average support scores between the groups, we find that the hypothesized relationship applies in all three instances.

In the second place, three issues clearly stand out in terms of the magnitude of differences in support scores between high-level and low-level leadership groups. On these issues — the recognition of Communist China, the nationalization of selected basic industries, and the abolition of the House Committee on Un-American Activities — intraparty conflict is greatest, and the willingness of the rejected caucus nominees to support the proposed policies, while less than in the case of the other issues, is markedly higher than that of the delegates, government officials, and non-caucus nominees on the delegation. What can be said about the nature of these issues? (1) Unlike the others, they do not stand in any clear relationship to the established position of the Democratic party. The proponent of recognition, of abolition, or of nationalization is not acting on the basis of any authoritative pronouncement by the national party. And the opponent is not acting in violation of party norms or expectations. (2) Unlike the others, these three issues are of such a nature as to make any public approval of the proposed policies an act of political courage. Such approval would probably be unpopular in the general community and might even inspire public ridicule. (3) These three policy proposals are precisely those to which a sample of the California delegation to the Republican national convention is most markedly opposed.[20] On none of the other proposals do the Republican respondents so nearly approach a posture of total rejection.

In sum, of the nine issues presented to the Democrats considered in this study, those dealing with Communist China, the House Committee on Un-American Activities, and nationalization of basic

---

[20]The Republican ratio of support scores follow:

1. Recognition of Communist China (N:54) 0.047
2. Abolition of the House Committee on Un-American Activities (N:53) 0.033
3. Nationalization of selected basic industries (N:53) 0.020
4. Increasing the federal minimum wage to $1.25 (N:50) 0.353
5. Medical aid to the aged tied to the Social Security Program (N:51) 0.280
6. Federal development of power projects (N:52) 0.170
7. Greater economic aid to underdeveloped countries (N:50) 0.527
8. Federal aid to school construction (N:52) 0.493
9. Federal Fair Employment Practices Commission (N:50) 0.427

Mean support ratio 0.261

TABLE 5

Issue Orientation — Rank Order of Differences in Support Scores for Low-Level versus High-Level Leadership Groups

Rejected caucus nominees versus delegates	
1. Nationalization of selected basic industries	0.210
2. Recognition of Communist China	0.193
3. Abolition of House Committee on Un-American Activities	0.136
4. Increasing federal minimum wage to $1.25	0.073
5. Medical aid to the aged tied to social security program	0.060
6. Federal development of power projects	0.050
7. Greater economic aid to underdeveloped countries	0.043
8. Federal Fair Employment Practices Commission	0.000
9. Federal aid to school construction	−0.007
Difference in Mean Support Ratios	0.084
Rejected caucus nominees versus elected government officials	
1. Abolition of House Committee on Un-American Activities	0.296
2. Recognition of Communist China	0.287
3. Nationalization of selected basic industries	0.203
4. Greater economic aid to underdeveloped countries	0.146
5. Federal development of power projects	0.110
6. Increasing minimum wage to $1.25	0.090
7. Federal aid to school construction	0.077
8. Medical aid to the aged tied to social security program	0.073
9. Federal Fair Employment Practices Commission	0.063
Difference in Mean Support Ratios	0.149
Rejected caucus nominees versus non-caucus nominees on delegation	
1. Recognition of Communist China	0.233
2. Abolition of House Committee on Un-American Activities	0.216
3. Nationalization of selected basic industries	0.193
4. Federal development of power projects	0.100
5. Greater economic aid to underdeveloped countries	0.096
6. Increasing federal minimum wage to $1.25	0.087
7. Medical aid to the aged tied to social security program	0.077
8. Federal Fair Employment Practices Commission	0.050
9. Federal aid to school construction	0.050
Difference in Mean Support Ratios	0.122

industries seem to involve the most critical tests of political radicalism—most critical in the sense that support of the suggested policies would be derived independent of the guidance of official party pronouncement, would be in least conformance with community norms, and would be most at odds with the virtually unanimous opposition of the Republican party. It is on these very three issues that the lowest level leadership group—the rejected caucus nominees—differs most markedly from the high-level leadership.

The third feature which might be noted from the comparisons summarized in Table 5 is that the elected government officials are the least "radical" top leadership group. In fact, Table 4 indicates that of the seven leadership groupings considered, the elected government officials achieve the lowest support ratio on seven of the nine issues, and in each of the other two instances their support ratio is slightly higher than that of only one other group. Similarly, on the self-evaluation question, the officials score the lowest liberalism ratio and have the smallest percentage of "very liberal" respondents. The officials also least prefer two of the liberal presidential candidates, Bowles and Humphrey. To the extent that the government officials stand as the most conservative leadership group under consideration, this study serves to support the specific hypothesis proffered by David Butler.

Summary and Conclusions

The research described in this paper was principally designed to apply a limited empirical test to a hypothesis regarding the relationship between two rather obvious facts of American political life: political party leadership is, in the first place, stratified, and, in the second place, heterogeneous in attitudes. Questionnaires were sent to approximately 350 Democratic leaders from California, selected for study because they were either delegates and alternates to their party's 1960 national convention or had been specifically considered but then rejected for delegation membership. The resulting sample of approximately 225 was grouped according to status within the party leadership hierarchy. The groups, in turn, were compared in terms of their responses to questions regarding certain political attitudes, i.e., questions regarding selected policy proposals, presidential preference, and liberal-conservative self-evaluation. All of these comparisons supported the original hypothesis: the superstructure of party leadership tends to be more "moderate" and "centrist" than the substructure.

Is this finding applicable to other parties in other places at other times? A substantial body of literature has been developed concerning very much the same phenomenon within British political parties. Further inquiry into the extent of its incidence in this country would seem to be in order, for such an inquiry would have considerable bearing on questions to which students of American politics have long been addressing themselves.

One of these questions concerns the extent to which the leaders of the two parties have tended to ignore the cleavages in attitude and programmatic demands within the electorate and between their respective followers. For some, the Tweedledum and Tweedledee character of party leadership has had salutary effects. To Clinton Rossiter, for example, the essence of American political history is that "the parties have been the peacemakers of the American community, the unwitting but forceful suppressors of the 'civil war potential' we carry always in the bowels of our diverse nation."[21] To Pendleton Herring, "the accomplishment of party government [in the United States] lies in its demonstrated ability for reducing warring interests and conflicting classes to cooperative terms."[22] Similarly, John Fischer, in defending the American party system, has concluded: "The purpose of European parties is, of course, to divide men of different ideologies into coherent and disciplined organizations. The historic role of the American party, on the other hand, is not to divide but to unite."[23]

For others, the mitigation of ideological divisions within the electorate by party leaders is cause for concern and reason for reform. More than fifty years have elapsed since James Bryce critically characterized American political parties as two empty bottles differing only in their labels and suggested that "a time for a reconstruction of parties is approaching."[24] Since then many observers have repeated Bryce's characterization in one form or another, and have sought to encourage and hasten the ever-approaching "time for a reconstruction." Stephen K. Bailey, for example, has recently advocated a program of political readjustment which would allow the parties "to appeal to the natural ideological divisions within the population and within us as individuals."[25]

Certainly many of the salient features of American politics seem to have been conducive to the rise and perpetuation of programmatically similar party leaders. And yet, put to an empirical test, the notion that these leaders tend to mitigate ideological divisions

[21]Clinton Rossiter, *Parties and Politics in America* (Ithaca: Cornell University Press, 1960), p. 59.

[22]Pendleton Herring, *The Politics of Democracy* (New York: Holt, Rinehart and Winston, 1940), p. 132.

[23]John Fischer, "Unwritten Rules of American Politics," *Harper's*, 197 (November, 1948), 32.

[24]James Bryce, *The American Commonwealth* (rev. ed.; New York: Macmillan, 1910), II, 29. The characterization and prediction both first appeared in the 1910 edition, although their spirit was evident in earlier editions.

[25]Stephen K. Bailey, *The Condition of our National Political Parties* (The Fund for the Republic, 1959), p. 4. It must be noted, however, that Bailey insists that the needed "political reform does not include making the parties any more ideological than they are now." The problem is not one of ideological effeteness but rather "that neither party has a sufficiently unified structure to enable it to dramatize its program around its ideology; neither has the power, even if it had the right structure, to carry out the program; neither has sufficiently clear and unambiguous lines of political accountability running to the voters."

within the electorate seems unfounded: Professor McClosky and his colleagues have demonstrated that the party leader is less "moderate" or "centrist" than the party follower, that the ideological differences that exist between the rank-and-file supporters of the two parties are, in fact, magnified by their leaders. The McClosky study concludes the description of its findings by stating: "Little support was found for the belief that deep cleavages exist among the electorate but are ignored by the leaders. One might, indeed, more accurately assert the contrary, to wit: that the natural cleavages between the leaders are largely ignored by the voters."[26] It would seem, then, that American party leaders tend to divide rather than to unite.

To the extent that the findings of this study have bearing beyond the California Democracy of 1960, they indicate that the leader-follower dichotomy adopted by McClosky may conceal significant aspects of the complex pattern of clash and counterpoint within a political party. These findings suggest an explanation of the magnification of inter-follower cleavage by the top party leaders which would stand in addition to those appearing in McClosky's catalogue of causative factors: the top leaders may be drawn to less centrist positions by the radicalism of lower-level leaders. Or, to put it somewhat differently, the radicalism of lower-level leaders may serve as a counterforce to the "natural" tendency of top leaders to gravitate toward the political center as a consequence of their public responsibilities and of the overriding objective of electoral success.

While the top party leader may be less moderate than his followers — as McClosky's evidence indicates — the present findings suggest that he may still be an ideological intermediate within his party. That is, he may be faced not only with a more moderate followership but with a more radical lower-level leadership. As V. O. Key, Jr., has concluded, "the top party leadership must try to restrain the extremists within the party ranks. . . . Lower-level leaders may flourish by the fanning of extremist and particularist emotions, but the top echelon must seek to hold together divergent and often conflicting elements."[27] In sum, it is possible that the top party leaders of the two parties at once magnify the ideological differences between their respective followers and blunt the differences between their respective lower-level leaders. If top party leaders divide, as Herbert McClosky so well demonstrates, they may also unify, as John Fischer believes.

---

[26]Herbert McClosky, *et al., op. cit.*, p. 426.

[27]V. O. Key, Jr., *Politics, Parties and Pressure Groups*, 4th ed (New York: Crowell, 1958), p. 241.

The Political Ideas of English Party Activists*

Richard Rose

If a democracy is to function successfully, the great mass of the population need instruments for communicating their views to political leaders. The chief channels for communication are parties and pressure groups. English politics provides much scope for study of these conduits, because both parties and pressure groups are highly organized and well-articulated. Although the part played by party activists in policy formulation is only one small aspect of this network, the study of that part throws considerable light upon the interplay of parties and pressure groups, and challenges as well some prevailing notions about the policy demands of party activists.

Party activists in Britain have only comparatively recently been regarded as potentially capable of participating in discussions of public policy. Both the Conservatives and Liberals originated as small coteries of parliamentary notables who controlled, or were

---

*This is a revised version of a paper read at the International UNESCO Seminar on Political Participation, held at the Christian Michelsen Institute, Bergen, Norway in June, 1961.

The author is indebted to Mrs. T. Collins and her associates in the computer section of the University of Manchester for considerable assistance in tabulating the data discussed herein.

Reprinted from the *American Political Science Review,* LVII (June, 1962), 360-71, by permission of the American Political Science Association and the author.

independent of rank-and-file party workers. Writing in 1908, A. Lawrence Lowell characterized the two party organizations as shams — the Liberals, with their formal devices for rank-and-file policy-making as an opaque sham, and the Conservatives as transparent shams.[1] He noted that in 1903 Conservative Party members were so deferential that when the Cabinet was split on tariff reform the annual membership conference "shrank from saying what it thought." Both Conservative and Liberal parties have maintained this aloofness from activists in matters of policy discussion up to the present day. The official report on Conservative Party reorganization prepared after the 1945 *debacle* noted that the size of the annual party conference made it "a demonstration of strength and enthusiasm" and made impossible "the more intimate circumstances necessary to thoughtful debate."[2] Since the farcical intervention of activists in policy-making at the 1958 Liberal Assembly, Jo Grimond has successfully emphasized the need to keep Liberal policy-making in the hands of a small circle.

The Labour Party, in theory and to some extent in practice, has always stood for participation by rank-and-file party members in policy-making. A current party pamphlet states: "The right to a voice in determining policy is important to any member. . . . The individual member has a chance to use the machinery of the party to secure support for ideas on every aspect of party policy."[3] In recent years a harassed Labour leadership has begun to stress Robert T. McKenzie's thesis that it is unconstitutional for party members to make policy to which MPs are bound, because MPs must be responsible to those who elect them and not to that allegedly unrepresentative faction who constitute active party members. The Labour leadership is reverting to the Burkean position maintained by many Conservatives that an MP owes his constituency party supporters nothing more than his informed and independent judgement.[4] Except for Ralph Miliband, who has argued that the influence of the active Labour minority should not be reduced because

[1]A. L. Lowell, *The Government of England* (London, 1921 edition) vol. I, pp. 578, 584. See also M. Ostrogorski, *Democracy and the Organization of Political Parties* (London, 1902), vol. I, p. 161 ff; J. L. Garvin, *The Life of Joseph Chamberlain* (London, 1932), vol. I, ch. 14; W. S. Churchill, *Lord Randolph Churchill* (London, 1906), esp. chs. 6-8.

[2]*Final Report of the Committee on Party Organization* (National Union, London, 1949), p. 27.

[3]S. Barker, *How the Labour Party Works* (London, 1955), p. 6.

[4]See R. T. McKenzie, *British Political Parties* (London, 1955), esp. chs. 1, 10; *Report of the Fifty-Ninth Annual Conference of the Labour Party* (London, 1960), p. 159 ff; and Morgan Phillips's *Memorandum on the Constitution of the Labour Party* (London, 1960).

of the apathy of the majority,[5] there is a consensus among students of British politics that party activists cannot and should not make party policy, or even influence it greatly.

It does not follow, however, that the views of party activists are of no interest. There are several reasons for analyzing them. First, activists may be mobilized to support a faction within the elite when there occurs what Michels treated as "The Struggle Among the Leadership Themselves."[6] Sometimes, a section of the counter-elite and of the activists appear to work together and respond to a common stimulus. Second, activists are a major channel of communication between MPs and party leaders and the electorate at large. Third, they are presumed to be the last stronghold of ideologues within the party system. Last but hardly least, there has never been any systematic study of the policy views of activists in Britain, although there has been no lack of generalizing on this subject.

Many students of political parties, most notably Duverger, have claimed that the views of activists differ significantly from those of most party voters; hence, the description of an activist as a militant.[7] (American experience would suggest that many active party workers are far from being ideologically militant, but this has not until recently been thought relevant to European politics.) Such leading writers on British politics as Bagehot, Lowell and McKenzie have also argued this with reference to Britain.[8] Leon Epstein has explained the alleged extremist views of these activists as follows:

> The voluntary and amateur nature of these associations ensures that they attract zealots in the party cause, and particularly so at the local leadership level, where there are many routine political chores which only the devoted are likely to perform. Principles, not professional careers, are what matter here.[9]

---

[5] "Party Democracy and Parliamentary Government," *Political Studies*, vol. 6 (1958), pp. 170-74. Wilfrid Fienburgh, then research secretary of the Labour Party, implicitly took this position in "Put Policy on the Agenda," *Fabian Journal*, no. 6 (1952), pp. 25-27.

[6] *Political Parties* (Dover edition, New York, 1959), p. 164 ff. McKenzie ignores this phenomenon.

[7] *Political Parties* (London, 1954), p. 101 ff. *Cf.* A. Leiserson, *Parties and Politics* (New York, 1958), pp. 191, 274.

[8] Bagehot, quoted in N. Nicolson, *People and Parliament* (London, 1958), p. 166; A. L. Lowell, *Public Opinion and Popular Government* (New York, 1914), p. 92; R. T. McKenzie, *op. cit.*, pp. 196-97, p. 506. See also T. E. M. McKitterick, "The Membership of the [Labour] Party," *Political Quarterly*, vol. 31 (1960), p. 316 ff.

[9] "British MPs and their Local Parties: The Suez Case," this Review, vol. 54 (1960), p. 385. Epstein wrongly suggests that rank-and-file extremism strengthens the position of party leaders. This is because he generalizes from the extremist position of the leadership on Suez; the instance is, however, exceptional.

Nigel Nicolson, the victim while a Conservative MP of a constituency association which disowned him because of his centrist views, has argued that the extremist outlook of activists threatens to endanger parliamentary government, because Parliament is losing power to Cabinet and Cabinet is dominated by party. Nicolson claims that parliamentary leaders rightly see problems in terms of "the intrusive grey," whereas activists see things in black and white terms. Political activity only intensifies their militant beliefs. Hence, in the constituencies, warfare between the parties is "a grim reality."[10]

To use the terminology of Martin Lipset in *Political Man*, the influence of activists in party policy-making is said to give heavy emphasis to ideological cleavage without a compensating statement of consensus, whereas both the theory and practice of British government value consensus much more than cleavage. It is theoretically possible that constituency parties may act as a safety valve through which extremist pressures escape, but this argument has not been advanced. It is the crux of Nicolson's case that the steam being generated by extreme-minded activists threatens to scald the engine drivers of democracy and endanger all the passengers.

I

Party activists have the same formal method of influencing policy in both parties — sending resolution to the annual party conferences.[11] This is not sufficient proof of policy concern, but it is almost certainly a necessary condition which activists must meet if they wish their views to be considered by the national party leadership. The other major channel — lobbying one's MP — is informal and indirect. Furthermore, half the constituenices have an MP from the opposition party. There are no inhibitions surrounding conference resolutions. If anything, there is an expectation that resolutions will be used by extremists to voice complaints to and about leaders.

The circumstances in which policy resolutions are drafted, debated and approved differ widely from constituency to constituency. Resolutions are likely to originate in committee meetings of local parties; alternatively, suggestions or amendments may be made at party meetings, where attendance will invariably be only a small fraction of a constituency party's membership, and an extremely

---

[10] *Op cit.*, p. 169. His fear is not new. *Cf.* Ostrogorski, *op. cit.*, vol. I, p. 493 ff.

[11] See S. Barker, *op. cit.*, p. 7 ff; *Party Organization* (Conservative & Unionist Central Office, London, 1961), p. 23 ff; R. T. McKenzie, *op. cit.*, pp. 231-58, 532-46.

small fraction of the party vote in the constituency.[12] Thus, the method and setting facilitate domination by a small group determined to foster a particular set of ideas. The extent to which policy is discussed in local parties appears to vary considerably.[13] Motives for tabling resolutions may be mixed and several. Expressions of opinion may spontaneously originate within the local caucus from concern with an immediate event in the news. MPs or candidates may stimulate resolutions favouring views they wish to advance. Sometimes resolutions are presented in efforts to gain publicity, either for the local party or for the person who may be chosen to move it in an auditorium crowded with delegates.

The resolutions analyzed herein are those submitted to Conservative and Labour annual party conferences from 1955 to 1960 inclusive. No list of resolutions was published for the cancelled 1959 Conservative conference. The omission of one year's total from the sample is offset by the fact that there is no limit on the number of resolutions which a Conservative constituency may forward. In the Labour Party, a constituency normally may send only one resolution, and occasionally an amendment. Because of alterations to constituency boundaries prior to the 1955 election, the analysis could not be accurately carried further back in time.

Each resolution has been assigned to one of four categories — Right, Left, Partisan or Nonpartisan. Resolutions in the first three categories contain a distinctive element of partisan ideology; those in the last tend to reflect pressure group concerns or general cultural values not integrally a part of party ideology. The definitions follow, with examples taken from conference programs.

Partisan: Enunciation of an agreed party policy which is opposed to that of the other party and which has an ideological basis.

Conservative example: "That this Conference congratulates the Government on its economic policy, which has resulted in full employment, stable prices and the highest standard of living in our history, but urges the removal of the many impediments still hindering the spread of ownership throughout the community." (No. 177, 1960)

---

[12]*Cf.* reports of low participation by trade unionists in discussions of union policy, in B. C. Roberts, *Trade Union Government and Administration in Great Britain* (London, 1956), p. 95 ff; M. Harrison, *Trade Unions and the Labour Party Since 1945* (London, 1960), ch. 3.

[13]*Cf.* D. V. Donnison and D. E. G. Plowman, "The Functions of Local Labour Parties," *Political Studies*, vol. 2 (1954), p. 156 ff; A. H. Birch, *Small Town Politics* (Oxford, 1959), p. 44 ff.

Other favored Conservative themes include: requests for maximum economy in public expenditure, denunciation of further nationalization, protection of property rights in land compulsorily acquired by the state, support for the Commonwealth, and approval of the tripartite division of secondary education.

> Labour example: "This Conference believes that a substantial measure of public ownership is essential for the nation's well-being. It therefore instructs the NEC to prepare for presentation to the 1961 Annual Conference a practical programme of public ownership for the next Labour Government, based on the needs of the economy, workers and consumers' interests." (No. 203, 1960)

Labour resolutions in this category often deal with: world disarmament through the United Nations, support for colonial freedom and attacks upon the Conservative colonial policy, attacks upon advertising, the need for economic planning and controls, demands for an end to profiteering in land prices, and support for a comprehensive secondary education system.

> *Nonpartisan:* Enunciation of a policy which is not the subject of controversy along party lines, either because it reflects the views of pressure groups working within both parties or because it is generally regarded as desirable within the culture. A nonpartisan resolution is not necessarily nonpolitical.
>
> Conservative example: "That this Conference is of the opinion that in view of the statement made at the time of the General Election that old age pensioners were to share in the prosperity of the country, an increase in their pensions should now be made." (No. 126, 1960)

Other popular themes for nonparty resolutions at Conservative conferences include: assistance for particular industries or for agriculture, calls for more teachers and smaller class sizes, demands for more roads and safer roads, tax relief for homeowners, changes to strengthen local government in its work, changes in electoral law to simplify the job of party workers, and improvements in party organization.[14]

---

[14]Resolutions dealing with the mechanics of party organizatiion have been scored nonpartisan because they show bureaucratic rather than ideological concerns. Interestingly, a number of resolutions ostensibly dealing with party principles are also nonideological. They simply stress the need for unity on principle, or promoting principles, without any indication of which particular principles (if any) should be emphasized.

Labour example: "This Conference urges the Government to grant an immediate increase for old age pensioners." (No. 344, 1960)

Among a welter of Labour themes that were basically nonideological were: assistance for shipbuilding, coal, other industries and for agriculture, calls for more teachers and smaller class sizes, requests for more hospitals and removal of alleged anomalies in welfare services, changes to strengthen local government in its work, more roads and safer roads, better railway services, and relief of the housing shortage and need for slum clearance.

Right-wing Conservative: A policy statement which calls for widening the gap between the two parties through adoption of a reactionary variant of party policy.

Example: "That in the opinion of this Conference the monopoly of omnibus transport in large cities and towns should be abolished and that responsible operators be allowed to compete, thereby giving the public a better service." (No. 48, 1960)

Right-wing Conservatives concentrate upon: pleas for weakening taxes which tend to redistribute income, requests for laws to curb trade unions and strikers, demands for a return to flogging and heavy reliance upon capital punishment to fight crime, the absolute reduction of government spending and services, the denationalization of various industries, and reducing benefits available through welfare services.

Left-wing Labour: A statement calling for a radical transformation of the domestic mixed economy welfare state, or of the existing system of international relations, in order to make the breakthrough to a Socialist society. Such statements are usually out of harmony with the declared policy of the leadership.

Example: "This Conference instructs the National Executive Committee to appoint a subcommittee to investigate and report to the 1961 Annual Conference the most practical way in which all the means of production, distribution and exchange can be brought under public ownership, ensuring that the workers and consumers alike can participate in the management of each industry." (No. 206, 1960)

Under this heading come resolutions: asking for unilateral nuclear disarmament, demanding large-scale extension of nationalization and/or workers' control, reaffirming Socialist principles in terms of root-and-branch rejection of a capitalist-influenced society, and those calling for compulsory closure of the public boarding schools.

> *Left-wing Conservative/Right-wing Labour*: Statements of policy which deviate so markedly from conference policy that they tend to be in harmony with the policies of the opposing party.
>
> Conservative example: "That this Conference requests the Minister of Housing and Local Government to examine the position of the tenants of furnished accommodation with a view to introducing legislation to guarantee an adequate standard of furnishings and fittings, and a reasonable security of tenure." (No. 331, 1960)
>
> Labour example: "This Conference moves that the Labour Party, being a social and democratic movement, seeks to determine by means of a social-political survey, such questions as the image of the party in the minds of the electorate, their social habits and background, and their wishes concerning the fundamental issues of the day, with the aim of studying the results of such an inquiry and deciding to what extent they should influence future party policy." (No. 424, 1960)

The number of these resolutions is so few that one cannot generalize much. In the Conservative Party, left-wing resolutions seemed to come either from constituency parties in working-class areas, which voiced Labour-inclined views on social services and economic policy, or from constituencies where progressive Conservatives had some sympathies with Labour's overseas policy. Labour deviation seemed largely motivated by a desire to repudiate traditional Socialist ideology, with an occasional repudiation resulting in virtual alignment with Conservative positions.

Any system of categorizing data is open to criticism. The headings here employed have been designed to group together views which signify, either explicitly or by their nuance, association with one or another faction within the two parties. This is the standard used by many speakers on resolutions at party conferences, who discuss them in terms of left/right tendencies, and the same standard is characteristically employed in descriptions of conference debates by journalists.

II

The analysis immediately reveals that the description of local parties as a force constantly pressing extremist views upon national party leaders is false. The total proportion of ideological (i.e., left-wing, right-wing and partisan) resolutions is 54 per cent; those which are nonideological constitute 46 per cent of the total (Table 1A). In other words, constituency parties are nearly as apt to be voicing views derived from general cultural values or from interest group links as they are to voice those clearly associated with a partisan ideology.

When the scores are analyzed according to parties, one finds that the Conservatives are more inclined to press non-partisan resolutions on their leaders than are Labour constituencies. But the differences are not great and Labour parties do not show strong partisanship; 42 per cent of their resolutions are nonpartisan, compared with 50 per cent of Conservative ones (Table 1B, 1C). The variation in the number and orientation of resolutions from year to year appears to reflect the temper of the times. A party's adversity would seem to stimulate extremist views.

An analysis of the number of resolutions submitted by individual constituency parties reveals the existence of wide variations in con-

TABLE 1A

TOTAL SCORES FOR ALL CONSTITUENCY RESOLUTIONS

TYPE	No.	%
Extremist (Rt, Con; Left, Lab)	1398	30
Partisan (Con and Lab)	1013	22
Misplaced partisanship (Left, Con; Rt, Lab)	97	2
Nonpartisan (Con and Lab)	2090	46
Totals	4598	100

TABLE 1B

TOTAL SCORES OF CONSERVATIVE CONSTITUENCY RESOLUTIONS*

YEAR	RIGHT	PARTISAN	LEFT	NON-PARTISAN	TOTAL
1955	50	52	17	173	292
1956	137	109	10	137	393
1957	130	60	6	216	412
1958	90	141	12	204	447
1959	(No resolutions published)				
1960	98	41	17	259	415
Totals No.	505	403	62	989	1959
Per Cent	26	21	3	50	100

*This table, like 1A and 5A, includes resolutions filed by Welsh constituency parties and minor federated bodies, as well as those from English parties. Welsh resolutions are omitted from all other calculations because the party system there is not quite the same as in England; minor parties are twice as strong. The federated bodies are omitted because they are not comparable to Labour ones. Omittted groups have similar scores to those fully analyzed. Scotland and Northern Ireland are not included in any Conservative tabulations, because these parties are separate and have their own conferences.

cern with policy. Approximately one-third of Conservative constituency parties did not present a single resolution in the five-year period studied; only 26 per cent forwarded an average of one resolution or more a year (Table 2A). This disinterest in pressing policy views cannot be attributed to poor party organization, because virtually all English Conservative constituencies are sufficiently well organized to have a full-time party agent. It may well be related to the deferential relationship which exists, socially as well as politically, between party leaders and members. Balfour is reported to have said that he would as soon take orders from his valet as from a Conservative Party annual conference.[15] Perhaps some party members would equally regard it as wrong to depart from the obligations of their station in life.

In the Labour Party, concern with matters of policy is more widely diffused, as one might expect from a party which has always boasted of its ideological basis. The gap between individual constituency parties is not so great, because of the limit of one resolution and one amendment for each party at each conference (Table 2B). Although the Labour Party has more constituencies which will sometimes file a resolution, there is little difference in terms of heavy activity, insofar as different regulations permit of comparison. Among Conservative constituencies, 74 per cent file resolutions less than once a year on average; in the Labour Party, the proportion is 79 per cent.

Concern with questions of policy is not the same as partisanship. In order to isolate those constituencies which reflected particularly

TABLE 1C

TOTAL SCORES OF LABOUR CONSTITUENCY RESOLUTIONS*

YEAR	LEFT	PARTISAN	RIGHT	NON-PARTISAN	TOTAL
1955	123	98	5	198	434
1956	109	119	5	169	402
1957	127	140	4	172	443
1958	173	89	6	160	428
1959	152	73	3	186	414
1960	209	91	12	216	528
Totals No.	893	610	35	1101	2639
Per Cent	34	23	1	42	100

*This table, like 1A and 5B, includes resolutions from Welsh and Scottish constituency parties, and from trade unions and other affiliated bodies. There is no significant variation in scores as between those groups fully analyzed and those omitted elsewhere.

[15]Quoted in McKenzie, *op. cit.*, p. 82. See also Earl Balfour, *Chapters of Autobiography* (London, 1930), p. 158 ff.

strong partisanship, the groups were divided into four categories, according to the extent to which they varied from the average party score. In the Conservative table, partisan views are those scored right or partisan; in the Labour table, those scored left or partisan. From this we find (Tables 3A, 3B) that the proportion of constituency parties which regularly press partisan views is less than one-quarter in each party. There is a skewed distribution among the Conservatives, for 59 per cent of the constituencies show less than

TABLE 2A

Frequency Distribution of Resolutions Filed by Conservative Constituency Parties

Number of Resolutions	No. of Parties*	% of all Parties	Cumulative Percentage†
0	165	32	32
1	90	18	50
2	49	10	60
3	42	8	68
4	29	6	74
5	23	5	79
6	22	4	83
7	14	3	86
8	15	3	89
9	12	2	91
10	7	1	92
11-20	33	6	98
21-30	4	0.8	98.8
31-40	3	0.6	99.4
46	1	0.2	99.6

* Bolton West and Huddersfield West are omitted from this and subsequent calculations because they do not nominate parliamentary candidates, standing aside in favour of the Liberals.

† Percentages do not add up to 100 because of rounding off.

TABLE 2B

Frequency Distribution of Resolutions Filed by Labour Constituency Parties

Number of Resolutions	No. of Parties	% of all Parties	Cumulative Percentage*
0	28	6	6
1	48	9	15
2	62	12	27
3	72	14	41
4	94	18	59
5	102	20	79
6	96	19	98
7	7	1.4	99.4
8	2	0.4	99.8

* Percentages do not add up to 100 because of rounding off.

average partisanship. Absence of partisanship does not, of course, mean absence of ideological commitments; it is evidence that parties so labeled are little interested in advocating ideological views. There is more interest in proclaiming partisan views in the Labour parties.

TABLE 3A

PARTISANSHIP IN CONSERVATIVE CONSTITUENCY PARTIES*

CATEGORY	No.	PER CENT
No partisan resolutions	164	35
Low (1-34%) partisanship	113	24
Average (35-64%) partisanship	120	26
High (65% or more) partisanship	71	15

* Constituencies which submitted only one resolution in the period, and that one partisan, have been omitted, because this was regarded as insufficient evidence for categorization.

TABLE 3B

PARTISANSHIP IN LABOUR CONSTITUENCY PARTIES*

CATEGORY	No.	PER CENT
No partisan resolutions	88	18
Low (12.5-40%) partisanship	83	17
Average (41-75%) partisanship†	208	42
High (above 75%) partisanship	113	23

* Constituencies presenting only one resolution, and that partisan, have been omitted from this table.

† This category is not as large as it appears, for only seven parties could have scored between 41-49.9%.

The incidence of ideological partisanship is certainly no cause for concern; few could criticize party activists for pressing party policy upon their leaders, when the leaders accept the ideas, as well as

TABLE 4A

EXTREMISM IN CONSERVATIVE PARTIES*

CATEGORY	No.	PER CENT
No extremist resolutions	314	66
Low (1-16.5%) extremism	20	4
Average (16.6-37.4%) extremism	92	19
High extremism (37.5% or more)	52†	11

* Those constituencies submitting one extremist resolution and filing only one or two in the period are omitted.

† Consists of 24 parties submitting up to 5 resolutions each in the period and 28 parties submitting more than 5 resolutions each in the period.

many voters. Ideological extremism is a far greater force for social cleavage, but it is extremely limited in both parties. (Tables 4A, 4B) Even though the definition of high extremism in the Conservative Party does not require a constituency to express extremist views as much as half the time, only 11 per cent qualify for that appellation — and only 6 per cent are both extremist and quite active in pressing views. Although more Labour constituencies are extremist than Conservative, they form only 18 per cent of the total. The median Labour constituency will only forward one extremist resolution in a six-year period, and the median Conservative one will not even forward a single extremist resolution in a five-year period.

The foregoing tables indicate that party workers on opposite sides of the political fence are not so partisan as electoral contests suggest, and not so extremist as some theorists suggest. A breakdown of resolutions by subject matter and by policy orientation provides a list of areas of common agreement within both parties (Tables 5A, 5B). A notable feature of Conservative resolutions is concentration upon domestic issues, notwithstanding the importance of international affairs to the government and to the electorate. Only 3 per cent of resolutions concerned foreign policy and defence questions, compared to 29 per cent in the Labour Party. The latter devotes less attention to politically important domestic questions. The virtual absence in both parties of expressions on highly explosive racial, religious and constitutional questions should not be overlooked.

Analysis by topics suggests that the partisanship and extremism of party activists is not so strong in several fields as the pull of interest group or general cultural standards.[16] In four areas of public concern — education, welfare services, transport, and pensions — partisan standards are applied less than half the time by activists

TABLE 4B

EXTREMISM IN LABOUR PARTIES*

CATEGORY	No.	PER CENT
No extremist resolutions	191	38
Low extremism (20% or less)	47	9
Average (25-50%) extremism	172	35
High (above 50%) extremism	87	18

* Those constituencies submitting only one resolution, and that extremist, have not been categorized.

[16] *Cf.* S. H. Beer, "Pressure Groups and Parties in Britain," this Review, vol. 50 (1956), pp. 1-23.

in both parties. When facing these questions they may ask for 'more schools' or 'higher pensions'; this is a cry of beneficiaries and benefactors, not of ideologues. This non-party emphasis is the more striking because there are clear ideological differences between the parties on education, welfare and transport. For instance, although the method of organizing secondary education is a point of sharp difference between the parties and affects the whole electorate, 64 per cent of Labour resolutions and 56 per cent of Conservative ones steer clear of all partisan controversy on education. The proportion of ideological resolutions rises in areas of economic policy, where interest group and ideological standards are likely to be the same for most activists; partisan ideology is thus intensified. For instance, all of the 19 Labour resolutions on industrial relations were partisan, and only 12 per cent of the 133 Conservative resolutions on this topic were non-partisan.

Some activists appear more concerned with the mechanics of party organization than with party policy. This shows in Conservative resolutions on party structure and on election law, and in organizational resolutions in the Labour Party, and resolutions asking for party unity — without any sign of preference concerning the program upon which unity should be based.

III

Examination of conference resolutions has shown that constituency parties differ considerably in their political attitudes. The question is then raised: Do they differ in relation to other measurable social or political factors? Unfortunately, the data available for cross tabulation is strictly limited,[17] but sufficient exists to test several important hypotheses.

One hypothesis concerns the relationship between party strength and attitudes of activists. It has been argued[18] that in areas where the strength of both parties is nearly equal, policies will tend to converge. In safe seats, extremist policies may be more readily found. The most important index of party strength is the margin by which a constituency is won or lost at the general election. A safe seat may conveniently be defined as one in which the winner had a majority of more than 10 per cent; a marginal seat as one in which the majority is less than that; and a hopeless seat one as in which

[17]For instance, census data cannot be related to parliamentary constituencies because of boundary differences.

[18]*E.q.*, Sir Ivor Jennings, *The Queen's Government* (Harmondsworth, 1960), pp. 60-61.

a candidate lost by more than 10 per cent[19] Nearly 85 per cent of English seats were either safe, marginal or hopeless at both the

TABLE 5A

TOPICS FOR CONSERVATIVE RESOLUTIONS

Topic	Right	Partisan	Left	Non-Partisan	Total
Economic affairs	121	142	28	64	355
Housing	22	35	4	107	168
Industrial relations	73	37	7	16	133
Party organization	5	8	3	112	128
Education	33	18	2	72	125
Pensions	6	2	—	104	112
Taxes	56	17	—	29	102
Compulsory purchase	16	79	—	4	99
Crime	63	13	4	11	91
Transportation	5	1	—	82	88
Election law	—	—	—	85	85
Commonwealth & colonies	31	14	4	7	56
Local government	—	—	—	51	51
Welfare services	21	—	—	29	50
Agriculture	5	—	—	42	47
Foreign policy	6	16	5	5	32
Defence	1	18	2	7	28
Immigration	21	—	—	—	21
Party principles	9	2	—	6	17
Miscellaneous	11	1	3	156	171

TABLE 5A

TOPICS FOR LABOUR RESOLUTIONS

Topic	Left	Partisan	Right	Non-Partisan	Total
Foreign policy, defence	594	145	14	20	773
Economic affairs	117	141	10	188	456
Housing and land	10	85	—	80	175
Party organization	14	4	1	130	148
Pensions	2	1	—	143	146
Welfare services	7	31	—	94	132
Education	17	19	—	64	100
Commonwealth & colonies	8	82	3	1	94
Local government	7	43	—	44	94
Socialist principles	57	15	2	5	79
Transportation	4	3	—	56	63
Party unity	18	2	1	31	52
Industrial relations	6	13	—	—	19
Miscellaneous	32	26	4	245	306

[19]On electoral swing and margins of victory, see D. E. Butler, *The British General Election of 1955* (London, 1955), p. 202 ff; D. E. Butler and Richard Rose, *The British General Election of 1959* (London, 1960), p. 236.

1955 and 1959 elections. In what follows only these three major groups are discussed, because the numbers in the others are so small as to be of negligible significance. Safe Labour seats may be assumed to be heavily working-class; safe Conservative seats are likely to be disproportionately middle-class, though manual workers may still form a numerical majority in the constituency. It is probable that these differences in turn are reflected in the composition of party activists in different areas, although there is no conclusive evidence on this point.

The analysis shows no relation between partisanship in policy outlook and safety of seat in Conservative constituencies, and only a limited relationship in the Labour Party. (Tables 6A, 6B) In both parties there is a clear but strictly limited relationship between ideological extremism and electoral support. In the Conservative Party, safe seats display on average 9.1 per cent more extremist resolutions than hopeless seats. In the Labour Party, hopeless seats adopt 9.2 per cent more extremist resolutions than safe seats. A further check was made to test this finding because of its importance. Constituency parties were divided according to degrees of partisanship and extremism, as in Tables 3A-B, 4A-B, to see whether each group had a fair cross-section of parties with strong, medium and weak electoral support. This was the case.

TABLE 6A

PARTISANSHIP, EXTREMISM AND ELECTORAL SUPPORT FOR CONSERVATIVE CONSTITUENCY PARTIES

CATEGORY	NO. OF SEATS	TOTAL RESO-LUTIONS	% PARTISAN	% EXTREME
Safe	213	788	48.4	29.3
Marginal	123	512	49.8	25.0
Hopeless	110	193	49.7	20.2

TABLE 6B

PARTISANSHIP, EXTREMISM AND ELECTORAL SUPPORT FOR LABOUR CONSTITUENCY PARTIES

CATEGORY	NO. OF SEATS	TOTAL RESO-LUTIONS	% PARTISAN	% EXTREME
Safe	110	383	50.6	28.2
Marginal	123	462	55.2	32.7
Hopeless	217	829	60.0	37.4

In both parties the variation between these two factors was of the order of one resolution in ten. But it takes a Conservative constituency party on average about 14 years to submit ten resolutions, and a Labour party about 12 years. The major conclusion must be that policy views are randomly distributed among constituency parties without regard to their electoral strength, for the statistical differences are of negligible political significance. One may note but hardly stress that parties in the most markedly middle-class areas are slightly more extremist on both sides than in working-class areas.

The author began his investigation with the hypothesis that the smaller a constituency party's membership, the higher the incidence of extremism. This was based upon the assumption that the number of extremist party supporters is very small, and that they could more easily dominate a small party. This hypothesis could only be tested for the Labour Party. There are 140 English parties which affiliate to headquarters on the minimum membership of 800; the extremism score for this group averaged 36 per cent. For the 61 parties with above average memberships ranging from 2,000 to 3,000, the extremism score averaged 34 per cent; for the 35 parties reporting membership above 3,000, the figure was 30 per cent. Similarly, parties with high extremism scores average 22 party members for every 1,000 electors, compared to a figure of 26 for those with average scores, and 25 for those with no extremist resolutions. The differences are hardly of a size to lend much support to the hypothesis.

Constituency parties may also seek to influence policy by pressing MPs or prospective candidates to act as spokesmen for the local party caucus. Candidates are selected by small groups representing less than 1 per cent of the electorate, and these nominations cannot be effectively challenged. In a normal election, nomination is tantamount to election in at least three-quarters of the constituencies; nomination is virtually tantamount to election for life in upwards of half the constituencies. Most students of British politics have commented upon the failure of constituency parties to exercise their considerable potential powers over candidates in such a way as to produce MPs with views like their own.[20] This generalization needs testing by reference to extremism scores because these writers have usually assumed that constituency selection committees are dominated by extremists. The wide range of opinion within both parliamentary parties might reflect an absence of policy concern in the selection process — or it might reflect a tendency for constituency

[20]See especially John Biffen, "The Constituency Leaders," *Crossbow*, vol. 4, no. 13 (1960), p. 30.

parties to adopt candidates with views compatible with their own.

The emergence of unilateral nuclear disarmament as a major factional issue within the Labour Party provides one test for the coincidence between extremism in candidates and in parties. We find that there is some relationship between extremism in a constituency party and a candidate who is extreme on this issue. Parties showing high extremism constitute 18 per cent of all local parties, but 29 per cent of those nominating unilateralist candidates. Unilateralist candidates are least likely to be found where extremism is low or non-existent (Table 7). Like many statistical findings, this one is only important if it is an indication of a trend. Further checks showed no tendency for unilateralist candidates to be nominated particularly for hopeless seats, nor were they especially favoured in the adoption of new candidates. Counterbalancing this absence of association was the tendency of constituencies with trade union sponsored candidates to score below average on extremism. Of 102 constituencies categorized, only 5 per cent were extremist, and 55 per cent had submitted no extremist resolutions in the period.

A similarly meaningful issue was not available for testing Conservative MPs. A rundown of the 16 Conservative MPs who took extremist positions on the Suez affair showed that two-thirds of their constituency parties scored below average on extremism. A check was made on Conservative parties which had Privy Councillors as MPs; it was assumed that the responsibility of these MPs, and their closer identification with generally moderate government policies, would damp down party extremism. In fact, the distribution of extremism scores among the 46 parties categorized was virtually identical with the distribution for all Conservative constituency parties. The most significant relationship found had on the face of it no connection with policy. It was that safe Conservative seats choose 84 per cent of their candidates from those with expen-

TABLE 7

EXTREMISM AND THE NOMINATION OF UNILATERALIST CANDIDATES BY CONSTITUENCY LABOUR PARTIES

CATEGORY*	NO. CANDIDATES	NO. UNILATERALIST	PER CENT UNILATERALIST
No extremism	191	14	7
Low extremism	47	5	11
Average extremism	172	31	18
High extremism	87	20	23
Totals	497	70	14

* Constituency parties submitting only one resolution, and that one extremist, have not been categorized.

sive public school educations, and only 31 per cent of the time take men with local connections. In hopeless seats, only 44 per cent have been at public schools, and 60 per cent of candidates have local connections. Marginal seats fall between these two groups. (No such pattern exists in the Labour Party.) One might speculate that the return of members of a national social-political elite by safe constituencies tends to increase the independence of MPs from constituency parties, for such persons are more likely to be independently minded, or influenced by a national peer group, than to submit to pressure from lower status activists.

IV

The fundamental conclusion which arises from this study is that attitudes on questions of policy are randomly distributed among constituency parties and, it may be tentatively assumed, among party activists as well. One cause of the diversity would appear to be the plurality of motives leading individuals to become active in party politics, together with the plurality of functions which local parties may perform.[21] The following list of motives is not exhaustive, nor is any particular one meant to exclude the operation of others within the same individual.

Motives for volunteer political work

A. Overtly political

- — Desire to advance party program
- — Desire to modify party program to bring it more into line with one's own ideological beliefs
- — Desire to modify party program to bring it more into line with the program of one's interest group
- — Local government concerns
- — Sense of civic duty
- — *Ex officio* involvement — e.g., as trade union official.

B. Non-political

- — Occupational careerism
- — Status seeking
- — Gratification of desire for power
- — Pleasure from group activities
- — Pleasure from a 'sporting' contest
- — Friendship with active party workers.

---

[21] A. Leiserson, *op. cit.*, is notable for the allowance he makes for diversity. See also Robert E. Lane, *Political Life* (Glencoe, 1959), for much evidence on motives for political participation.

The functions which constituency parties fulfill are also numerous. Some have a bearing on national party policy, but others do not:

Functions of English constituency parties

— Propagate national party policy
— Advise upon national party policy
— Organize and conduct election contests
— Nominate parliamentary candidates
— Manage local government affairs
— Act as pressure group for local interests
— Provide social facilities for the community
— Finance and maintain local party office.

An immediate consequence of this diversity is the flexibility which it gives to party leaders. At annual party conferences leaders are not faced with a mass of extreme-minded activists, demanding the adoption of socially divisive policies as the price of continuing to do menial work.[22] Opposition comes from only a fraction of the rank-and-file. Another portion is likely to support the leadership and a significant group may have no clear views, or even interest, in questions of party policy. In such circumstances support of the rank-and-file assembly may be gained simply by giving a clear policy lead. Lacking firm anchorage in an ideological position, constituency parties may be willing to trust their leaders wherever they lead. The pressure from above, the effect as it were of the gardener's lawn-mower upon grass roots activists, is considerable. The classic illustration occurred when the Conservative government was able to keep the party virtually united behind it when it unexpectedly attacked Egypt, and again when it abruptly accepted a cease-fire there in 1956. This flexibility is less in the Labour Party; a small contributing factor is the greater attachment which activists have to ideological standards.

Robert T. McKenzie has suggested that representative democracy presupposes a near identity in views between persons at different levels in parties, and half-suggested that democratic parties should have views tending towards identity.[23] Hence, his polemics against the participation of alleged extreme-minded activists in

---

[22]Some British politicians still regard local party organizations with the respect they received in the days of open voting and bribery. The Nuffield studies find no evidence to support this. See most recently D. E. Butler and R. Rose, *The British General Election of 1959* (London, 1960), pp. 143, 232 ff.

[23]See especially "Parties, Pressure Groups and the British Political Process," *Political Quarterly*, vol. 29. no. 1 (1958), p. 12 ff; and "The 'Political Activists' and Some Problems of 'Inner Party' Democracy in Britain" (mimeo, International Political Science Association, Paris, 1961), p. 5 ff.

party policy-making. But on the basis of their resolutions, constituency parties do not seem to be pulling the parties apart. While recognizing the simplifications involved, one might consider party differences as being ranked on a scale from 0 to 100, with 0 being extreme right-wing and 100 being left-wing extremism. Simple consensus based upon an identity of views within and between parties would occur if all opinion rested at 50; more realistically, consensus would result if the center of gravity of opinion[24] within both parties was at 50. But a situation of balanced disagreement would operate if one of the parties centered at 60 and the other at 40, assuming a normal distribution frequency. An imbalance would result only if one party tended towards the center while the other balanced near an extreme. Balance, of course, is not a good in itself. Theoretically, a balance would occur if one party rested at 90 and another at 10. Furthermore, balance could produce stagnation when a radical shift in one direction was required by objective social circumstances. If we distribute resolutions along such an axis, we see that much of the weight of constituency views is closer to the center than to the extremes. The leftward bias is largely the result of the greater frequency of Labour resolutions. When a correction is made for differences in expressing views as between the parties, the point of balance turns out to be three per cent to the left of center.

There has been no systematic investigation of political attitudes in an effort to find out what differences, if any, exist between voters, activists, MPs, and leaders in parties. There is evidence to indicate that the spread of opinion is wide at all levels of both parties. For instance, a 1959 national survey found that 45 per cent of Conservative sympathizers accepted the *status quo* in the nationalized industries, and 40 per cent wished to denationalize one or more industries. In addition, 42 per cent of Labour sympathizers were opposed to further nationalization, whereas 36 per cent supported it.[25] In 1960, when 34 per cent of constituency party resolutions were extremist, 33 per cent of Labour MPs voted against Hugh

---

[24]*Cf.* D. E. Butler "The Paradox of Party Difference" *American Behavioral Scientist,* IV: 3 (1960), pp. 3-5, where the concept of centers of party gravity is developed.

[25]See D. E. Butler and R. Rose, *op. cit.,* p. 244, and also p. 71. The opinion surveys regularly reported in the monthly *Gallup Political Index* (London) by the British Institute of Public Opinion, and by Mark Abrams, in M. Abrams and R. Rose, *Must Labour Lose?* (Harmondsworth, 1960) also bear out the point that party sympathizers are divided into partisans, extremists, deviants and indifferents on almost all issues. Cf. also S. E. Finer, H. Berrington and D. Bartholomew, *Backbench Opinion in the House of Commons 1955-59* (London, 1961).

TABLE 8

DISTRIBUTION OF THE POLICY VIEWS OF ACTIVISTS*

SCALE:	0 RT. CON.	25 PARTI- SAN CON.	50 NON- PARTI- SAN	75 PARTI- SAN LAB.	100 LEFT LAB.
No. of resolutions	505	438	2090	672	893
Per Cent of resolutions	11	10	45	15	19

* Resolutions showing misplaced partisanship are assigned to the partisanship category for the other party.

Gaitskell in a contested election for the parliamentary party leadership. During the past decade the resignations of such leading Cabinet ministers as Aneurin Bevan, Lord Salisbury and Peter Thorneycroft have provided public evidence of the frequent suspicions of sharp divisions within a theoretically united Cabinet. Thus, it appears that the dilemma which David Butler has posed for party leaders — "their most loyal and devoted followers tend to have more extreme views than they have themselves, and to be still farther removed from the mass of those who actually provide the vote"[26] — does not really exist. Differences in policy exist within parties, and conflict is sometimes great, but this is not conflict between a monolithic bloc of activists and a monolithic leadership. Rather, it would seem that factional disputes divide parties vertically, joining some Privy Councilors, MPs, lobbyists, activists and voters into a faction which is in conflict with another which also contains members drawn from all ranks of the party.

[26] D. E. Butler, *op. cit.*, p. 5.

Ideological-Pragmatic Orientations of West Berlin Local Party Officials*

William E. Wright

Ideology is one of the most frequently used concepts of political analysis; it is also one of the more slippery terms. Debate rages over its "proper" definition and whether the concept is to be defined "broadly" or "narrowly"; how ideology may be differentiated from what it is *not* (our vocabulary has been enriched by such terms as "belief systems," "ideology by proxy," "near ideology," and "surrogates for ideology"); its distribution within a given population and whether ideology is declining or increasing in saliency (the "end of iedology" debate); the extent to which researchers improperly ascribe ideological sensitivity to the people whose behavior they are studying; and how the concept of ideology may best be measured empirically.[1] We are concerned here with the last-mentioned of the above considerations — the operationalization and empirical measurement of the concept "ideology." It is hoped, however, that the

* The present research was supported by a Social Science Research Council Research Training Fellowship.

[1]For a review of the various usages of the concept of ideology, see David Minar, "Ideology and Political Behavior," *Midwest Journal of Political Science*, vol. 5 (November, 1961), pp. 317-31. See also Robert E. Lane, *Political Ideology* (New York: The Free Press, 1962), Chapter 1. For an excellent discussion of some of the problems of conceptualization and empirical measurement of ideology, see Samuel H. Barnes, "Ideology and the Organization of Conflict: On the Relationship Between Political Thought and Behavior," *Journal of Politics*, vol. 28 (August, 1966), pp. 513-30, especially his argument for studying ideology in an organizational context—i.e., the impact of political organization on the ideological orientations of elites and members (pp. 521-24).

Reprinted from the *Midwest Journal of Political Science*, XI, no. 3 (August, 1967), 381-402, by permission of Wayne State University Press.

efforts reported below will make a small contribution to the conceptual clarification of the term.

Several approaches to the empirical measurement of ideology have been taken by social scientists. The most widely used approach is one based on the familiar "liberal-conservative continuum," "one judgmental dimension or 'yardstick' that has been highly servicable for simplifying and organizing events in most Western politics for the past century. . . ."[2] In survey research the respondents are ranked along a liberal-conservative continuum and classified as "liberals" or "conservatives" on the basis of agree-disagree responses to items; the construction of a cumulative scale is often attempted.[3] Although these items usually refer to (American) political issues, in some cases the items consist of statements of liberal and/or conservative principles.[4] The basic notion involved is that of an underlying liberal-conservative continuum along which respondents can be located. A key question posed by the use of this approach is whether it is useful to think in terms of a single liberal-conservative continuum, or whether we should think in terms of several liberal-conservative continua, representing different policy areas.[5]

A second approach attempts to measure the "saliency" of ideology — i.e., classifies respondents as more or less ideological, usually on the basis of their responses to open-ended questions concerning policy issues and/or perceptions of political parties, candidates, groups, and the like.[6] Such an attempt to measure saliency of ideol-

---

[2]Philip E. Converse, "The Nature of Belief Systems in Mass Publics," in *Ideology and Discontent*, ed. David Apter (New York: The Free Press of Glencoe, 1964), p. 214.

[3]See, for example, Angus Campbell, *et al.*, *The American Voter* (New York: John Wiley & Sons, 1960), pp. 194-209; John C. Wahlke, *et al.*, *The Legislative System* (New York: John Wiley & Sons, 1962), pp. 372-75, and p. 475.

[4]See Herbert McClosky, "Conservatism and Personality," *American Political Science Review*, vol. 52 (March, 1958), pp. 27-45.

[5]Lipset distinguishes between liberalism-conservatism in the two areas of economic policy and civil rights. See S. M. Lipset, *Political Man* (London: Mercury Books, 1963), pp. 101-05 and pp. 298-301. Campbell and associates provide separate liberalism-conservatism scales in two policy areas: domestic (social welfare) and foreign (internationalism). Campbell, *et al.*, *op. cit.*, pp. 194-209.

[6]See Seymour Martin Lipset, Martin A. Trow, and James S. Coleman, *Union Democracy* (Garden City, N.J.: Anchor Books, 1962), pp. 101-14, for a measure of ideological sensitivity, based on union members' perceptions of parties, candidates, and union politics in terms of policy or issues. See also Samuel J. Eldersveld, *Political Parties: A Behavioral Analysis* (Chicago: Rand McNally & Co., 1964), pp. 196-98, for a measure of saliency of ideology, based on local party officials' perceptions of (issue) differences between the parties.

ogy may or may not be accompanied by an effort to determine the "content" or "direction" of the ideology (e.g., liberal or conservative). Thus Angus Campbell and associates constructed two liberal-conservative (issue) scales and also provided a measure of saliency of ideology in their investigation of the "levels of conceptualization" which respondents in a national sample of the adult U. S. population applied to politics (perceptions of parties and presidential candidates).[7] One of the co-authors of this study, Converse, carried the analysis one step further in relating levels of conceptualization to the respondents' "recognition of ideological dimensions of judgment" (i.e., to their recognition and understanding of the terms "liberalism" and "conservatism").[8] An important consideration that emerges from this line of investigation pertains to elite-mass differences: political articulates, influentials, activists, and leaders are more ideological (i.e., ideology is more salient for them) than respondents in a cross-section sample; ideological sensitivity declines rapidly as one goes lower in the scale of political involvement and participation.[9]

A third approach to an understanding of the concept of ideology is taken in this article; it is one that is often used in discourse but which has not been subjected to empirical investigation. This approach involves the notion of an "ideological-pragmatic" continuum. This judgmental yardstick or dimension is as common to political analysis as the above-mentioned "left-right" or "liberal-conservative" continuum: political parties, other groups, candidates, citizens, political cultures, and political systems are frequently compared and ranked along the ideological-pragmatic dimension. For LaPalombara and Weiner, "The second dimension along which we classify competitive [party] systems is the ideological-pragmatic. These characteristics refer to the parties themselves, and we believe it is of vital importance to be able to judge parties in terms of where they fall along this continuum."[10] In this same volume, Giovanni Sartori, in analyzing European political parties, defines "ideology [as] the opposite of pragmatism; that is, it implies a doctrinaire and

---

[7]Campbell, *et al., op. cit.*, Chapter 10. In addition to their measure of ideological sensitivity, Lipset, Trow, and Coleman also constructed a Liberal-Conservative Index. (*Op. cit.*, Appendix I, pp. 487-89). See also Eldersveld, *op. cit.*, Chapter 8, for an analysis of the direction (liberal-conservative), and saliency of ideology for Detroit party leaders.

[8]Converse, *op. cit.*, pp. 219-27.

[9]*Ibid.*, p. 213; see also Herbert McClosky, "Consensus and Ideology in American Politics," *American Political Science Review*, vol. 58 (June, 1964), pp. 372-73; Barnes, *op. cit.*, pp. 516-17.

[10]Joseph LaPalombara and Myron Weiner, "The Origin and Development of Political Parties," in LaPalombara and Weiner (eds.), *Political Parties and Political Development* (Princeton: Princeton University Press, 1966), p. 36.

somewhat unrealistic way of framing political issues."[11] Sidney Verba contrasts ideology and pragmatism as major polar political styles and states:

> It is likely that this distinction between ideological and pragmatic politics involves several different dimensions. One can distinguish between open and closed belief systems; between explicit and implicit belief systems; and between belief systems that stress expressive behavior and those that stress instrumental behavior.[12]

Verba notes that the pragmatic political style emphasizes "open, implicit, and instrumental political beliefs," thus facilitating "compromise and bargaining."[13]

The data reported below explore the ideological-pragmatic dimension in the form of a cumulative scale tested on a sample of German local party officials. The approach used in the present article combines features of the first two approaches to the measurement of ideology mentioned above, but differs from both. It is similar to the first approach in that respondents are ranked along a continuum on the basis of agree-disagree responses to a set of attitudinal statements and a cumulative scale was constructed; however, the continuum involved here is that of "ideology-pragmatism" rather than "liberalism-conservatism." It is similar to the second approach in that it also measures the "saliency" of ideology on the basis of respondents' perceptions of party (and what they would like their party to be); however, in the present case equal emphasis is given to exploring the other end of the continuum (i.e., pragmatism). The construction of the ideology-pragmatism scale will be spelled out below.

I. Study and Instrument

The present data are from a broader study of social characteristics, socialization and recruitment patterns, and role perceptions of local party leaders of the German Social Democratic Party (SPD) and the Christian Democratic Union (CDU) in all twelve boroughs in West Berlin.[14] The interviews, averaging one hour in length, were

---

[11]Giovanni Sartori, "European Political Parties: The Case of Polarized Pluralism," in LaPalombara and Weiner, *op. cit.*, p. 158.

[12]Sidney Verba, "Comparative Political Culture," in *Political Culture and Political Development*, ed. Lucian W. Pye and Sidney Verba (Princeton: Princeton University Press, 1965), p. 545.

[13]*Ibid.*, p. 548.

[14]For a detailed report on the research, see William E. Wright, "Local Leadership in Two West Berlin Political Parties" (unpublished Ph.D. dissertation, Vanderbilt University, 1966).

conducted in 1962-63 with incumbents of three key local party offices: the highest elected party officials on the two lowest levels of German party organization, the district chairmen (with the district organizations corresponding to the West Berlin borough jurisdictions) and the branch chairmen (the party branches being organized on an electoral district or neighborhood basis). The third party office selected was that of district secretary (SPD only) — the only full-time, salaried party official on the two lower levels of German party organization. Two hundred thirteen (83 per cent) of all 256 incumbents of these party offices were successfully interviewed; the great majority of the party officials were branch chairmen, the closest equivalent to the American precinct leader.

The Berlin setting of the study may be relevant to an interpretation of the findings regarding saliency of ideology in two regards: the fact that the CDU has been in a minority role in Berlin elections since its founding in 1945 (minority status may be conducive to stronger ideological orientations); secondly, the fact that the Berlin SPD, under the leadership of Willy Brandt, has strongly supported the "modernization" of the party and the adoption of the Godesberg Program in 1959 — a change in the party's program, goals, tactics, and image — directed at making the party less doctrinaire, less ideological, and more flexible and pragmatic.[15] It may be that Berlin SPD leaders are more "pragmatic," and Berlin CDU officials, more "ideological" than their colleagues in the Federal Republic; in any case, one cannot generalize the Berlin findings to other areas of West Germany.

The main instrument of the study, as far as the present article is concerned, is an ideology-pragmatism scale. The party leaders were asked to agree or disagree (on a four-point scale) with a series of items stating that their party should be more (or less) "principled" or "pragmatic," that the party should seek as broad an appeal as possible to voters (segments of the electorate), and that adaptability of party goals and "compromise" was or was not desirable. The following four items formed an acceptable Guttman scale:[16]

1. My party should always stand fast to its goals and principles, even if this should lead to a loss of votes.

---

[15]See Douglas A. Chalmers, *The Social Democratic Party of Germany: From Working-Class Movement to Modern Political Party* (New Haven: Yale University Press, 1964) and Arnold J. Heidenheimer, *The Governments of Germany* (New York: Thomas Y. Crowell Co., 2nd ed., 1966), Chapter 3.

[16]The Coefficient of Reproducability (C.R.) of the four-item scale was .938 and the C.R.s of the individual items were .930, .933, .934, and .945. Scale error was randomly distributed. Of the 213 party leaders interviewed, 205 (or 96 per cent) completed the scale items.

2. My party should attempt to win the votes of as many voter groups as possible and to represent their interests in the state.
3. Politics is more a matter of getting the best possible out of a given situation than of stubbornly sticking to principles.
4. My party needs a *Weltanschauung* basis for its goals and policies.

Responses pertaining to the unwillingness to compromise party principles in the political arena, adherence to party goals regardless of electoral consequences, emphasis on a more limited basis of party support, and the need for a *Weltanschauung* foundation of the party were considered ideological responses; emphasis on adaptability, compromise, broad appeal of the party, and the rejection of a necessarily *Weltanschauung*-based party were considered pragmatic responses. The party officials were divided into four groups on the basis of their scale scores; these groups were labeled "very pragmatic," "fairly pragmatic," "fairly ideological," and "very ideological."[17]

Although we have no test of the degree of internal consistency of the party ideologies, since the scale items did not tap the content of salient ideologies, and although we have little to go on in the way of the relationship between ideology-pragmatism and behavior (apart from some data on political career patterns and role perceptions), other data from the study yield some insight into the content of the salient ideologies, and an examination of a number of correlates of ideology-pragmatism furnish a fair degree of confidence in the measure. Not only does the ideology-pragmatism scale appear to be a potentially useful measure of the saliency of ideology, but the present data add to our substantive understanding of German politics, especially with regard to the role that religion plays in the ideological orientations of CDU officials and the extent to which the deideologization of the SPD has filtered down to lower levels in the party hierarchy.

II. Distribution of Scale Types

The distribution of ideological-pragmatic scales types within the two parties is presented in Table 1. Two findings emerge from these

---

[17]The scale items were scored on the basis of pragmatic responses; thus the higher the score, the more pragmatic; the lower the score, the more ideological. Scale scores ranged from 0 to 15. The two lowest scale scores (0 and 1) comprised the "very ideological" category; the "fairly ideological" grouping was defined by scale scores 2-4; the "fairly pragmatic," by scores 5-9; and the "very pragmatic" category, by the remaining scores (10-15).

data. First, a majority of the officials in both parties are ideologues rather than pragmatists. Second, and more striking, is the finding that considerably more CDU leaders than SPD officials are found in the two ideological types (CDU: 73 per cent; SPD: 51 per cent); the party differences are statistically significant ($p<.02$). The party differences are even greater in the "very pragmatic" category (24 per cent SPD in contrast to only 9 per cent CDU). There were no significant differences within each party by office. These findings run counter to the traditional image of the SPD as an ideological workers' party and the CDU as a pragmatic (even "Americanized") electoral party.[18] It may be that these data reflect the minority status of the CDU in West Berlin; in any case, they would seem to indicate that the de-emphasis on ideology in the SPD has been communicated to the lower party echelons.

The scale items pertain to pragmatic *versus* ideological approaches to politics; they say nothing about the content of the party ideologies. Some insight into the latter can, however, be gained from the party officials' responses to other questions from the study dealing with political socialization and party recruitment. These were open-ended questions which permitted the officials to make ideological responses, but which did not call for such statements ("How did you become interested in politics?" "How did you come to join the SPD or CDU?"). Ideological responses to the open-ended political socialization and party recruitment questions thus do *not* provide an accurate measure of the extent to which the Berlin party officials are ideologically oriented; these data do, however, provide some insight into the content of the party ideologies.

---

[18]On German party "images," see Ulrich Lohmar, *Innerparteiliche Demokratie* (Stuttgart: Ferdinand Enke Verlag, 1963), Chapter 1; Arnold J. Heidenheimer, *Adenauer and the CDU* (The Hague: Martinus Nijhoff, 1960); U. W. Kitzinger, *German Electoral Politics: A Study of the 1957 Campaign* (Oxford: Oxford University Press, 1960). Kitzinger notes the "time lag" involved in the SPD's attempt to change its image: "In view of the party's own insistence on its traditions the less well-informed public was hardly to be blamed if it regarded the SPD as being still largely an ideological party that derived its inspiration from Marx and hankered after the nationalization of all means of production, distribution and exchange." (p. 127). Later surveys indicate that the SPD has had difficulty persuading the West German electorate that it has "changed." Almost two-thirds of a national sample in October, 1960 felt that the two major parties had not drawn closer together, and in April, 1961 only one-quarter believed that the SPD has freed itself from its past and was on the way to becoming a genuine people's party; an additional one-quarter perceived the "new spirit" in the SPD but were sceptical as to how much things had changed; the remainder thought that the change in the party's image could not be trusted, that this was only a tactic to fool the electorate. See K. D. Eberlin, "Die Wahlentscheidung vom 17. September 1961: Ihre Ursachen and Wirkung," *Zeitschrift fuer Politik*, vol. 9 (1962), 244.

TABLE 1

IDEOLOGICAL-PRAGMATIC ORIENTATIONS OF SPD AND CDU OFFICIALS

SCALE TYPE	SPD	CDU
Very Ideological	24%	37%
Fairly Ideological	27%	36%
Fairly Pragmatic	25%	18%
Very Pragmatic	24%	9%
Total	100%	100%
	(N=131)	(N=74)

$X^2=10.21$, $df=3$, $p < .02$

References of the following kinds were coded as "ideological references" in the political socialization and party recruitment context. First, considered as indicators of an ideological orientation were references to politically relevant belief systems (e.g., "socialism," "Marxism," "Catholicism," "religious principles"). Second, "anti-positions" such as the expression of anti-Communist, anti-socialist, anti-clerical, and anti-bourgeois attitudes were noted, although these might be considered as weaker indicators of ideology in some cases (i.e., they might represent a single isolated attitude rather than constitute an element of a more extensive belief system). Third, expressions of socio-economic ("we workers," "the working class," "class consciousness") or religious ("we Christians," "as a Catholic") group identification were regarded as ideological indicators.[19] The following quotes from the recorded interviews illustrate these categories.

I. *General Belief Systems:*

SPD: "Since I am a convinced socialist — and Marxist — I saw the SPD as the best chance for the realization of my political views."

CDU: "I joined the party in spite of my SPD relatives because of my Catholic *Weltanschauung* . . . . I wanted to join a Christian party or none at all."

[19]Converse states that although group interest "perceptions run to the more tangible core of what has traditionally been viewed as ideological conflict," respondents who replied in these terms were not classified as ideologues in his study (or in *The American Voter)* because they constituted a mass public whose general level of conceptualization about politics was very low. (Converse, *op. cit.*, p. 216.) We are dealing with a relatively sophisticated political elite and will regard group interest perceptions as indications of an ideological orientation.

II. *Anti-Positions:*

SPD: "My views are such that I cannot stand the clerical and religious element in politics. Religion has to be kept out of politics."

CDU: "Through my conscious anti-Communist orientation."

III. *Group Identification:*

SPD: "As a worker, the SPD is the only party for me."

CDU: "Especially the idea of uniting all religious faiths in one party impressed me and decided me for the CDU."

The extent to which the local officials of the two parties referred to these types of ideological indicators in the socialization and party recruitment context may be seen in Table 2. Considerably more CDU officials than SPD leaders volunteered ideological references; the party differences are statistically significant ($p<.01$). This finding is consistent with the party differences on the ideology-pragmatism scale. Furthermore, as Table 3 demonstrates, there is a positive relationship (Gamma=.17)[20] between volunteered references to ideology in the socialization-party recruitment context and scores on the ideology-pragmatism scale. However, it should be repeated that the socialization-recruitment data are not necessarily accurate estimates of the saliency of ideology for the two groups of party officials. Thus, more SPD officials than CDU leaders referred simply to family tradition in the socialization-recruitment context,

TABLE 2

REFERENCES OF IDEOLOGY IN THE SOCIALIZATION-PARTY RECRUITMENT CONTEXT

TYPE OF IDEOLOGICAL REFERENCE	SPD	CDU
General belief system	10%	27%
Anti-positions	19%	18%
Group identification	8%	21%
No reference to ideology	63%	39%
Total	100% (N=136)	105%* (N=77)

* This column totals more than 100 per cent because a few CDU officials referred to more than one type of ideological category.

[20] Gamma is a measure of association proposed by Leo A. Goodman and William H. Kruskal, "Measures of Association for Cross-Classifications, I," *Journal of the American Statistical Association*, vol. 49 (December, 1954), pp. 740-64. Gamma equals Yule's Q in the case of a fourfold table and may be thought of as a generalization of Yule's Q for tables larger than 2 × 2.

which might have concealed references to ideology. These reservations notwithstanding, the consistency of the findings regarding saliency of ideology in two separate contexts of the study appears noteworthy. As far as the types of ideological references made in the socialization and party recruitment context are concerned, the same proportion (about one-fifth) of leaders of the two parties

TABLE 3
VOLUNTEERED IDEOLOGICAL REFERENCES TO SOCIALIZATION AND RECRUITMENT QUESTIONS AND IDEOLOGICAL-PRAGMATISM SCALE TYPES, WITH PARTY CONTROLLED

Ideology-Pragmatism Scale Type	Socialization-Recruitment Content			
	SPD		CDU	
	Ideological Reference	No Ideological Reference	Ideological Reference	No Ideological Reference
Ideological	52%	48%	72%	68%
Pragmatic	44	49	26	26
No answer	4	3	2	6
	100% (N=50)	100% (N=86)	100% (N=46)	100% (N=31)

referred to "anti-positions," whereas almost three times as many CDU as SPD officials mentioned belief systems and group identification.

There were clear-cut differences in the context of the ideological references by the two groups of party leaders. Almost all of the SPD officials who responded in ideological terms expressed beliefs in socialist principles, anti-bourgeois and/or anti-clerical attitudes, or a sense of working-class identification. The only exceptions were one SPD official who referred to "liberalism" as a belief system and two who held strongly pacifistic attitudes. The CDU officials, on the other hand, stated their ideological orientation (if at all) almost entirely in terms of religious beliefs (e.g., the sense of Christian responsibility to participate in politics only within the framework of a Christian or specifically Catholic *Weltanschauung*) or they expressed anti-Communist or anti-socialist attitudes or expressed a sense of religious group identification as governing their choice of a party.[21] These findings indicate the strong role that religion played

[21]In their discussion of German party images, Almond and Verba note that "The striking difference between the German pattern, on the one hand, and the British and American, on the other, is the large percentage of Germans — almost identical for Christian Democrats and Socialists — who describe the supporters of the Christian Democratic party as 'religious people.'" Almond and Verba, *op. cit.*, p. 127.

in the recruitment of CDU officials as well as its role in the party ideology. Although Berlin CDU officials appear to be more ideological than SPD leaders, it seems safe to conclude that the socialist ideology is more consistent internally and directly relevant politically than the CDU ideology, which Otto Kirchheimer characterized thusly: "In the CDU, ideology was from the outset only a general background atmosphere, both all-embracing and conveniently vague enough to allow recruiting among Catholic and Protestant denominations."[22] We are not able to say anything more definite about the content of the party ideologies on the basis of the present data, but only about the extent to which Berlin local party officials think of their party in ideological (i.e., programmatic or "principled") terms. In this regard, the two parties are presently in different situations: the SPD is consciously becoming less ideological and more pragmatic, whereas there are indications that at least some CDU leaders desire to move their party in the opposite direction, and are seeking to have the party formulate a party program of principles and goals.[23] Although the Berlin CDU leaders' ideological statements strongly stress religious principles, we should not assume that this is the only source of the party's ideology.

III. Correlates of Ideology-Pragmatism

A number of independent variables hypothesized to be related to ideology-pragmatism were examined. These independent variables include age, socio-economic status, religion, and the socio-economic composition of the population of the party districts, as well as political career status and role perceptions of the party officials.[24] The rationale for these hypothesized relationships will be spelled out below. Since there were significant party differences in ideology-pragmatism, party was controlled in all cross-classifications. This meant, however, that the four ideology-pragmatism categories had to be collapsed into broader "ideological" and "pragmatic" types, because of the small number of cases involved when party is controlled.

---

[22]Kirchheimer, *op. cit.*, p. 187.

[23]For a discussion of what appears to be a counter-trend in the two parties, see Ulrich Lohmar, *Innerparteiliche Demokratie* (Stuttgart: Ferdinand Enke Verlag, 1963), pp. 14-18. The minority status of the CDU in West Berlin may have increased the saliency of ideology for these leaders.

[24]It may be noted that sex was not included among the independent variables that might be related to ideology-pragmatism. Almost all (96 per cent) of the party leaders interviewed were men.

Age. Age is one variable that might be related to ideology. Since German parties are becoming less ideological, we would hypothesize that the younger leaders of both parties would tend to be less ideological and more pragmatic than the older leaders. This should apply especially to the SPD, since this party is in the process of moving from its traditionally ideological stance to a more pragmatic position; we would expect the younger SPD leaders to be stronger proponents of this transition and, therefore, less ideological than their older colleagues. As Table 4 shows, age does correlate positively with ideology (gamma = .19) for the SPD leadership group — the saliency of ideology increases with age. However, this relationship is not strong. For the CDU leadership group, there is no relationship between age and ideology: the youngest leaders (40 and under) are as ideological as the oldest age group (55 years and over); the CDU leaders in the middle age group (41 to 55) are slightly less ideological. The SPD data support the hypothesis concerning the relationship of age to ideology; the CDU data do not. The CDU pattern might mean that religion is highly salient for the oldest CDU leaders, whereas the youngest CDU leaders are more concerned about the fact that the CDU has "neglected" to state its principles and formulate a party program and feel that such an attempt is needed, especially if the CDU is to become more of a "membership" party and less exclusively an "electoral" party. The younger leaders may also be more concerned than older leaders about the CDU's minority status in Berlin and may feel that their party has not sufficiently differentiated itself from the SPD, the dominant partner in a SPD-CDU coalition which governed West Berlin for most of the postwar period (until the CDU left the coalition in 1963).

Religion. Religion is another variable which might be related to ideology. This hypothesized relationship raises two questions. First,

TABLE 4

AGE AND IDEOLOGY-PRAGMATISM, WITH PARTY CONTROLLED

Ideology-Pragmatism	SPD			CDU		
	40 and under	41-55	Over 55	40 and under	41-55	Over 55
Ideological	46%	49%	63%	80%	65%	80%
Pragmatic	54%	51%	37%	20%	35%	20%
Total	100% (N=48)	100% (N=55)	100% (N=27)	100% (N=20)	100% (N=34)	100% (N=20)
	gamma = .19			gamma = 0		

TABLE 5

RELIGION AND IDEOLOGY-PRAGMATISM, WITH PARTY CONTROLLED

IDEOLOGY-PRAGMATISM	SPD			CDU		
	CATHOLIC	PROTESTANT/OTHER	NONE	CATHOLIC	PROTESTANT/OTHER	NONE
Ideological	25%	52%	52%	74%	72%	0
Pragmatic	75%	48%	48%	26%	28%	0
Total	100% (N=4)	100% (N=58)	100% (N=69)	100% (N=35)	100% (N=28)	0 0

are Catholic CDU leaders more ideological than their Protestant colleagues — i.e., is the CDU ideology a specifically Catholic one? Second, since agnosticism and anti-clericalism are traditional elements of the socialist ideology, are SPD nonbelievers more ideological than their party colleagues who are church-members? Both questions are answered negatively. There is almost no relationship between religion and ideology for either group of party leaders: Catholic CDU leaders are only slightly more ideological than Protestants, and Protestant SPD leaders are no less ideological than their colleagues without church affiliations. (Table 5). Since only four of the SPD officials are Catholics, no reliable conclusions can be drawn for this subgroup.

Socio-economic Status. Socio-economic status is another variable (or set of variables) that is frequently related to ideology. Since a major objective of the current de-emphasis on ideology in the SPD is to increase the party's appeal to middle-class voters, we hypothesize that the younger, middle-class, better-educated SPD leaders would tend to be less ideological, while the older, working-class, less-educated SPD leaders would tend to retain the traditional image of the SPD as an ideological, primarily working-class party. That is, SES variables should correlate negatively with ideology for SPD leaders. On the other hand, since the CDU is more of a middle-class party than the SPD (in terms of the composition of the party leadership, party membership, and electorate),[25] it might be expected that ideology would correlate positively with socio-economic status for the CDU leadership group — i.e., that higher SES CDU leaders would tend to be more ideological than CDU leaders of lower socio-economic status.

[25]For a comparison of the demographic profiles of party voters and members of the SPD and CDU, see Wolfgang Hartenstein and Klaus Liepelt, "Party Members and Party Voters in W. Germany," *Acta Sociologica*, vol. 6, nos. 1-2 (1962), pp. 43-52.

Several indicators of socio-economic status were used in the present study: family background, education, and a composite measure that includes occupation, education, and income. Since the job descriptions of the party leaders were sometimes incomplete, and since a majority of the leaders in both parties were civil servants or government employees (SPD: 56 per cent; CDU: 53 per cent), a composite measure based on occupation, income, and education was constructed, and the party leaders were grouped into three categories: high socio-economic status (university education, white-collar occupation, and a net monthly income of over 1500 DM); medium SES (at least some secondary education, white-collar occupation, and net monthly income between 800 and 1500 DM); and lower SES (elementary or trade/vocational school education, manual or low status white-collar occupation, income of less than 800 DM per month), As Table 6 demonstrates, there is a relationship between socio-economic status and ideology, and in the predicted direction for the two party leadership groups: negtaive for SPD leaders (gamma = −.24) and positive for the CDU leadership group (gamma = .33). That is, middle-class SPD leaders are less

TABLE 6

SOCIO-ECONOMIC STATUS AND IDEOLOGY-PRAGMATISM, WITH PARTY CONTROLLED

IDEOLOGY-PRAGMATISM	SPD			CDU		
	LOW SES	MEDIUM SES	HIGH SES	LOW SES	MEDIUM SES	HIGH SES
Ideological	67%	48%	45%	77%	60%	87%
Pragmatic	33%	52%	55%	23%	40%	13%
Total	100% (N=30)	100% (N=61)	100% (N=40)	100% (N=13)	100% (N=30)	100% (N=31)
	gamma = −.24			gamma = .33		

ideological than their party colleagues of lower socio-economic status, whereas the reverse is true of CDU leaders; medium SES CDU leaders are, however, the least ideological CDU subgroup. However, the relationship between socio-economic status and ideology was not strong. When we focus specifically on education and compare the party leaders with at least some university education with those of less education, we find a stronger relationship to ideology, again in the predicted direction: gamma = −.56 for the SPD and .58 for the CDU. (Table 7). Whereas only 28 per cent of the highly-educated SPD leaders are ideologues, this is the case of 87 per cent of the CDU leaders with the highest level of education.

TABLE 7

EDUCATION AND IDEOLOGY-PRAGMATISM, WITH PARTY CONTROLLED

IDEOLOGY-PRAGMATISM	SPD		CDU	
	LOW AND MEDIUM EDUCATION	AT LEAST SOME UNIVERSITY	LOW AND MEDIUM EDUCATION	AT LEAST SOME UNIVERSITY
Ideological	58%	28%	64%	87%
Pragmatic	42%	72%	36%	13%
Total	100% (N=98)	100% (N=32)	100% (N=44)	100% (N=30)
	gamma = −.56		gamma = .58	

Another socio-economic status variable, father's occupational status, was also examined for its relationship to ideology-pragmatism. For the SPD leadership group, we again find a negative relationship between SES and ideology, of about the same magnitude (gamma = −.21) as our summary SES measure. For the CDU leadership group, father's occupational status correlates positively with ideology-pragmatism; this time the magnitude of the relationship between SES and ideology is even stronger (gamma = .58) than was the case with the summary SES measure. (Table 8). Again, we have working-class correlates of ideology in the SPD and middle-class correlates in the CDU.

TABLE 8

FATHER'S OCCUPATIONAL STATUS AND IDEOLOGY-PRAGMATISM, WITH PARTY CONTROLLED

IDEOLOGY-PRAGMATISM	SPD		CDU	
	MANUAL	NONMANUAL	MANUAL	NONMANUAL
Ideological	54%	43%	52%	84%
Pragmatic	46%	57%	48%	16%
Total	100% (N=67)	100% (N=58)	100% (N=21)	100% (N=51)
	gamma = −.21		gamma = .58	

Borough Type. Is there a relationship between the environment of the party organization and ideological-pragmatic orientations of the party leaders? The 12 West Berlin boroughs were classified by socio-economic status (of the borough population) and party competition; unfortunately, census data were not available for the smallest (branch) party units. The percentage of manual workers in the borough population labor force was taken as a simple index of borough SES: the three boroughs with more than 54 per cent workers in the labor force were classified "working-class"; the three boroughs with less than forty per cent workers were considered "middle-class"; and the remaining six boroughs with between 40 per cent and 54 per cent workers were labeled "mixed."[26]

Our classification of the boroughs according to party competition reflects the dominant status of the SPD in West Berlin *Land* and borough elections. Whereas the SPD has won an absolute majority of the votes cast in all six Berlin elections since 1945 in three (of the 12) boroughs, and an absolute majority in more than one-half of the elections in three other boroughs, the CDU has not received an absolute majority in any borough in any single election. The CDU has won a plurality of the votes cast in three boroughs in two elections (1954 and 1958) and the Free Democratic Party (FDP) has also received its largest vote in these three boroughs, in which the SPD has been weakest.[27] These three boroughs are the only ones which can be considered "politically competitive." The three boroughs in which the SPD has been strongest were classified "safe SPD," and the remaining six boroughs were characterized as "tending to SPD."

There is an almost perfect relationship ($r = .98$) between borough socio-economic status (percentage workers) and party vote (per cent SPD in the 1963 Berlin election). Thus the "safe SPD" boroughs are the three working-class districts; the "tending to SPD" boroughs are the six mixed (SES) districts; and the competitive boroughs are the three middle-class districts. As Table 9 shows, borough socio-economic status and party competitiveness (since these two factors are highly correlated, we cannot say whether we are measuring one of the other or both) are related to ideological-pragmatic orientations of the party leaders, but in opposite directions for the two parties. As far as the SPD is concerned, the more middle-class and politically competitive the district, the less ideological are the SPD leaders (gamma $= -.23$). For the CDU, the reverse is true: the more middle-class and competitive the district, the more ideological are the CDU leaders (gamma $= .23$). Although these relationships are not strong, their directions are consistent with previous findings regarding socio-economic status and ideology.

Political Career Status and Role Perceptions. Two final independent variables were examined for their relationship to ideology-pragmatism — political career status and role perceptions. It was hypothe-

[26]The percentages of workers in the borough labor force (as of June 6, 1961) were taken from Statistisches Landesamt Berlin, *Statistisches Jahrbuch Berlin, 1964* (Berlin: Kulturbuch-Verlag, 1964), pp. 62-63.

[27]Berlin election statistics were taken from *ibid.*, p. 159.

TABLE 9

Borough SES and Party Competitiveness and Ideology-Pragmatism, with Party Controlled

Ideology-Pragmatism	Borough SES and Party Competitiveness					
	SPD			CDU		
	Working-Class, Safe SPD	Mixed, tends to SPD	Middle-Class, competitive	Working-Class, Safe SPD	Mixed, tends to SPD	Middle-Class, competitive
Ideological	62%	48%	43%	69%	70%	83%
Pragmatic	38%	52%	57%	31%	30%	17%
Total	100% (N=39)	100% (N=64)	100% (N=28)	100% (N=16)	100% (N=40)	100% (N=18)
	gamma = −.23			gamma = .23		

sized that the party leaders of higher career status and those who emphasized vote mobilization tasks in their role perceptions would tend to be more pragmatic and less ideological than leaders of lower career status and those who were primarily concerned with internal party tasks. The rationale states that the former leaders would, because of their political experience and emphasis on the party's external relations with the public, meet competing interests and different views of local groups, leaders of other parties, and voters, and therefore tend to be more flexible, adaptive, and pragmatic than the latter. It was thus hypothesized that political career status and emphasis on vote mozilization tasks would correlate negatively with ideology.

The measure of political career status consisted of two components: the extent of upward mobility in the party hierarchy and level of aspiration.[28] The highest elective public office achieved was taken as the best single indicator of upward mobility: those party leaders who had held public offices higher than that of borough assemblyman were considered highly mobile; those who had served only as borough assemblyman were considered moderately mobile; and those who had never held elective public office were classified as nonmobile (or of low mobility). High aspiration means that the leaders aspire to both higher party and public office; moderate aspiration, that they sought public office only; and low aspiration, that they sought party office only, or did not aspire to any higher office. On the basis of these two criteria, three levels of political career status were distinguished: high (high mobility and moderate

[28]Eldersveld's career typology was adapted to the present data. See Eldersveld, *op. cit.*, pp. 139-45.

to high aspiration), medium (moderate mobility and moderate to high aspiration), and low (low mobility and low aspiration).

As Table 10 shows, higher status CDU leaders are less ideological, but the relationship is not very strong (gamma = −.27). Higher status SPD leaders, on the other hand, are more ideological than those of lower status (gamma = .14); it is the middle-status SPD leaders (the "potential careerists") who are the least ideological. The relationship of age to ideology probably accounts for the SPD differences: the middle status SPD leaders are younger than the other two career groups. In any case, our hypothesis is not supported at all by the SPD data and is not strongly supported by the CDU findings.

TABLE 10

POLITICAL CAREER STATUS AND IDEOLOGY-PRAGMATISM, WITH PARTY CONTROLLED

IDEOLOGY-PRAGMATISM	POLITICAL CAREER STATUS					
	SPD			CDU		
	LOW	MEDIUM	HIGH	LOW	MEDIUM	HIGH
Ideological	51%	43%	68%	82%	71%	67%
Pragmatic	49%	57%	32%	18%	29%	33%
Total	100% (N=47)	100% (N=56)	100% (N=28)	100% (N=27)	100% (N=17)	100% (N=30)
	gamma = .14			gamma = −.27		

Emphasis on vote mobilization tasks,[29] as predicted, correlates negatively with ideology as far as the SPD group is concerned (gamma = −.21), but positively for the CDU leadership group (gamma = .24) (Table 11). That is, the SPD leaders who stress their relations with the public are less ideological than their colleagues; the reverse is true of the CDU leaders. Perhaps the minority status of the CDU in West Berlin partly explains these party differences. There was no consistent relationship between borough type and role perceptions; however, the highest proportion of the "vote mobilizers" was found in the competitive, middle-class bor-

[29]Vote mobilization tasks, as the term is used in the present study include any tasks designed to increase the party's influence with the public. A broader classification than strictly campaign-related tasks, these include propaganda efforts, group contacts, and the like. These data come from open-ended role perception questions asking party officials to describe their jobs. Those party officials who listed vote mobilization tasks as their most important are considered "high" on the present "vote mobilization" measure and the other leaders, "low" on this measure.

TABLE 11

ROLE PERCEPTION (EMPHASIS ON VOTE MOBILIZATION TASKS) AND IDEOLOGY-PRAGMATISM, WITH PARTY CONTROLLED

IDEOLOGY-PRAGMATISM	EMPHASIS ON VOTE MOBILIZATION TASKS			
	SPD		CDU	
	LOW	HIGH	LOW	HIGH
Ideological	53%	43%	71%	80%
Pragmatic	47%	57%	29%	20%
Total	100% (N=103)	100% (N=28)	100% (N=59)	100% (N=15)
	gamma = −.21		gamma = .24	

oughs, where SPD leaders tended to be at least ideological and CDU leaders, most ideological.

IV. Summary and Conclusions

In an attempt to operationalize and empirically measure one important dimension of ideology, an ideology-pragmatism scale was tested on a sample of officials of the German Social Democratic Party and Christian Democratic Union in West Berlin. Four items pertaining to perceptions of the party in terms of adaptability, compromise, a broad basis of party appeal, and the necessity for a *Weltanschauung* foundation of the party formed an acceptable cumulative scale in the Guttman sense. The ideology-pragmatism scale discriminated sharply between the two groups of party leaders: CDU leaders were more ideological than SPD officials. Although no statement concerning the content or substance of the party ideologies could be made on the basis of the scale items, data from another aspect of the study (political socialization and party recruitment) indicated that, consistent with the images of the two parties, SPD officials who responded in ideological terms referred to socialist principles or working-class identification, whereas CDU leaders referred to religious beliefs or religious group identification.

A number of independent variables were examined for their relationship to ideology-pragmatism; almost all of these were related to ideology-pragmatism in opposite directions for the two groups of party leaders. The correlates of ideology for SPD leaders were those expected of a political party currently undergoing a transition from an ideological workers' party into a "modern," pragmatic, "people's party": the younger leaders of higher socio-economic status, generally, and higher educational level, in particular; those from middle-class family backgrounds; and the officials who served in middle-class, politically competitive districts were less ideological and more pragmatic. The older SPD officials of working-class origins, of lower socio-economic status, and from working-class districts that are SPD strongholds were more ideological. Not only do the less ideological SPD officials tend to have the characteristics of those segments of the population to whom the party hopes to appeal, but the relatively low saliency of ideology for SPD officials on the local level indicate the extent to which the party's attempt to change its image has filtered down to the base of the party hierarchy. The possibility that some SPD officials are more ideological than they care to admit could not be examined on the basis of the present data. Also, strong support for the SPD's Godesberg Program came from the Berlin party leadership under Willy Brandt and most (but not all) of the local party organizations; this might mean that de-emphasis on ideology is perhaps stronger on the lower levels of party organization in West Berlin than in other parts of the Federal Republic.

Whereas we found working-class correlates of ideology for the SPD leadership group, we found middle-class correlates of ideology for the CDU group. The party officials of middle-class origins, of higher socio-economic status generally (and especially higher educational level), and who served in middle-class districts were the most ideological subgroup of CDU officials. These findings suggest greater relevance of socio-economic group identification than was found in the ideological references of CDU officials in the socialization and party recruitment contexts, where almost all of the ideological references of CDU officials pertained to religious principles and religious-group identification (plus the expression of anti-socialist and anti-Communist attitudes). These data document the important role that religion played in the recruitment of CDU officials and the party ideology; it may be, however, that socio-economic principles and group identifications are "concealed" by references to religious principles and religious group identification. The possibility that the saliency of ideology for CDU officials was related to the minority status of the party in West Berlin was noted.

We conclude that the ideology-pragmatism scale is a potentially useful measure of an important dimension of ideology, one that deserves further testing. Additional items should be formulated to further probe this dimension and more attention should be given to the content of the party ideologies — i.e., this should be directly related to the scale items. We noted that the scale items said nothing about the proximity of ideology to the world of politics, and that the less immediate political relevancy of the CDU ideology should be taken into account in interpretating the finding that Berlin CDU officials were more ideological than SPD leaders. It was also noted that we could say nothing about the internal consistency of the idea-elements of the leaders' belief systems, and very litle about the extent to which the leaders' ideological orientations "constrained" their political behavior. On the latter point our data are inconclusive: we examined two variables, political career patterns and role perceptions (in terms of vote mobilization tasks). Higher status CDU officials were indeed less ideological; the reverse was true of the SPD leaders. On the other hand, the SPD leaders who were most concerned with vote mobilization tasks were less ideological; the reverse was true of the CDU officials.

Ideology is not a simple concept. The ideology-pragmatism scale appears to be of potential utility in furthering our understanding of this important conceptual focus of political analysis. It is hoped that the present effort will help to spur additional empirical research in this area.

SECTION FOUR

Activities and Roles

Activities and Roles

In the two previous sections, the stress was placed largely on who party officials are — i.e., on their social-demographic and attitudinal characteristics. In this section, the focus is shifted to what it is that party officials do — i.e., what kinds of activities they engage in and how they view their roles in the party organization. This is an important area of research since implications for the structure and functioning of party organization may be drawn from such data which are more directly linked to organizational characteristics.

As was noted earlier, the two basic party models differ sharply in the view taken of party functions from which types of party activities and role definitions are derived. Different patterns of party activities stem from different functions. Since the electoral function is considered paramount in the Rational-Efficient model — often to the exclusion of other functions — this model entails a conception of party activities and roles drawn almost exclusively in power-oriented vote-mobilization terms. Party officials, especially those at the precinct level, tend to be viewed in this model as being single-mindedly concerned with vote mobilization tasks (see Eldersveld, Selection 4.2; Leiserson, 1958, pp. 188, 192). The Party Democracy model, on the other hand, is multi-functional. This type of party acquires other and even more important activities than the electoral function; it has, in addition, policy-ideological, governing, and even social integration functions (Neumann, 1956). There is in this type of party a highly developed organizational life apart from election campaigning; in contrast to the cyclical character in the Rational-Efficient party, activities are varied and continuous. Given the strong emphasis on the ideological function in the Party Democracy model, important activities of the party organization involve the political education of the membership which is designed to enable them to participate in policy discussion and opinion-formation within the party.

These attributes of the two party models are significant since assumptions we make about what political parties do that is important and what their functions are and should be often structure empirical research. Such is the case, for example, when party officials are interviewed and asked about their performance of certain selected activities; the researcher has made basic assumptions about the importance of specific party tasks and has structured his questions accordingly.

Two different, although complementary, approaches have been taken in research on this aspect of party. The first approach is task performance: questions are asked about the performance of selected party activities, often in the form of a check-list of specified activities. The second approach is the role approach, which gets at the party officials' own conception of their job. The latter approach usually takes the form of an open-ended job description question (e.g., "How would you describe your job as county chairman — what are the important things you have to do?"). Party officials' references to types of activities and, especially, their designation of their most important task are the basis of the analysis which results in the construction of a role typology. Although these two approaches are complementary, the first does not necessarily lead to the latter. Task performance will be considered first since it is the basis for the role approach and since some studies do not go beyond an analysis of activities. Subsequent discussion will build upon this basis and hopefully will demonstrate the analytic utility of going beyond the performance of specified activities to an investigation of party roles. In both respects, the discussion will center on local party leaders since most of the empirical research has been made at this level of party organization. This emphasis is not meant to deny the importance of higher levels of party organization, or the need for more research of this kind at all levels of the party.

Tasks and Activities

Before looking at empirical findings, it is first necessary to get an idea of the kinds of party activities and the ways these activities are categorized in the literature. Although there is no standard classification of party activities and leadership tasks, apart from the fact that task classifications are geared primarily to the electoral function and have been applied mainly to American parties, there is considerable similarity in such classifications. Katz and Eldersveld (1961) formulated a seemingly broad classification of local party leadership tasks: "(1) the leader as the organizer of his own precinct workers, *the internal function;* (2) the leader as the communication center between the party organization above him and his precinct organization, *the representative function;* (3) the leader as the influential contact with the outside community, *the external function;* (4) the leader as the administrator of standard organizational practices, *the administrative function . . .*" (p. 4, original emphasis). In the listing of *specific* tasks under each of the above functions, however, it is clear that most of these relate directly or indirectly to the party's electoral function. In his analysis of task performance of precinct leaders, Eldersveld (1964, Chapter 13) used the following task classification: organizational work; campaign activities; inter-election activity consisting of political education, voter contact, worker training, and service activities and "environmental adaptation" — i.e., working with the influential groups and segments of the local electorate. Valen and Katz (Selection 4.4) employed the Katz and Eldersveld task typology in their study of Norwegian local party organization. They hold the same expectations of the ideal local party leader as does Eldersveld: "Each of these functions is essential for an effective local party organization. ... In other words, the effective local party leader must relate well to three different groups of people, his own workers, his superiors in the party structure and the voters in the community. . . . In the political party, the local leader is in a key position in that in spite of his lowly status he must assume all four of these roles."

Bowman and Boynton (Selection 4.3) differentiate four main task areas: campaign activities, organizational work, ideological activities which includes policy clarification, and participation in candidate selection or nomination. One additional category that tends to be subsumed under one of the above headings but may be examined separately is that of service activities which involve aiding "constituents" with advice, patronage jobs, funds, intercession with government authorities, or other benefits. The activities of local party officials will be discussed under the following headings: campaign activities, organizational tasks, representative tasks, service activities, candidate selection activities, and ideological tasks.

Campaign Activities. Vote mobilization and related organizational activities constitute the bulk of tasks performed by American local party officials. Bowman and Boynton found that "the bulk of the activities are concentrated in the campaign and in the organizational categories." Ippolito (1969) found that between two-thirds and three-quarters of Nassau County (New York) local party officials referred to one or the other of these types of activities in their job descriptions. Of the two, campaign activities comprise the task area most stressed in research and most emphasized by party officials.

There are several "check-lists" of standard campaign activities. Bowman and Boynton used a list of "six standard campaign techniques: personally talking to voters, door-to-door canvassing, transporting voters to the polls, collecting money, distributing campaign literature, and organizing telephone campaigns." Eldersveld (Selection 4.2) had a similar list of eight campaign activities which also included voter registration and media techniques. Of these eight he considered three to be the most important: voter registration drives, personalized canvassing (house-to-house and/or telephone), and election day round-up of votes. Crotty (1968, p. 303) formulated a Campaign Activities Scale, using six selected activities from a list of 14 campaign techniques, six of which concerned the mass media and advertising. Frost (1961) worked with a list of 33 specific campaign techniques. Apart from differentiating pre-campaign activities (e.g., voter registration) from the campaign proper and election-day activities (e.g., Crotty used a separate Election Day Activities Scale), most of the differences in these check-lists arise from treating types of campaign activities in a generic sense or in a more detailed fashion.

Which campaign activities are most often performed? On the basis of available data, the safest generalization that can be made is that the more traditional and routine activities (e.g., personal contact with voters, rallies, distributing campaign literature) are more often performed than the more systematic and modern techniques, such as systematic compilation of voter records, systematic canvassing, and the use of the mass media — all activities which require either a higher level of skill and/or coordinated organizational (as opposed to individual) effort. For American data supporting this proposition, see Bowman and Boynton, 1966; Eldersveld, 1964, Chapter 13; Frost, 1961.

Two studies of non-American parties support these findings. Valen and Katz (Selection 4.4) found that Norwegian local party leaders tended to restrict their campaign activities to traditional routine techniques — distributing campaign literature and holding public meetings and open membership meetings. They found also that canvassing, a standard American campaign technique, "is used relatively little. Apparently the leaders believe that voters dislike it as an invasion of their privacy and the leaders themselves regard it as improper." Data on German Social Democratic and Christian Democratic local party leaders (Wright, 1970) reinforce the Norwegian findings — namely, the performance of limited and routine campaign tasks such as the distribution of campaign literature and holding of rallies, and the almost total absence of systematic personal canvassing (as distinct from just "talking to voters").

Organizational Work. The task area emphasized second only to campaign activities is the organizational category. The category of organizational maintenance tasks, as used in American studies, includes the following specific activities. First, the factor of personnel — recruiting and organizing campaign workers and staffing precinct positions—is more problematic for American parties with their cyclical activity and generally high turnover of campaign workers than it is for the mass membership party, with its built-in reservoir of workers. Other organizational maintenance activities include the coordination of subunit activities, liaison with other party units, and record-keeping — especially records on the precinct's voters. Organizational maintenance tasks in the Rational-Efficient party are related to campaign activities. In the Party Democracy model, they are related mainly to membership activities, as can be seen by Mayntz's (1961) use of the term "organizational maintenance tasks" to refer to "admission and registration of members, dues collection, distribution of funds, reporting, sending invitations to meetings, and so forth" (p. 165).

Organizational tasks in American parties tend to be regarded as a necessary means to the end of electoral victory. Bowman and Boynton, in their study of Massachusetts and North Carolina local party officials, concluded: "Thus, while the organizational activities are perceived as necessary, they are viewed as necessary for the performance of the major task of campaigning." Exceptions to this generalization are found in two very different kinds of situations. The first is where a party organization must first be created in order to combat an entrenched majority party (e.g., the situation of the Republican party in the South today) or where the organization must be strengthened to be competitive with the previously dominant majority party, as Ippolito (1956) found to be the case with Nassau County (New York) Democrats. The reverse situation is found where there is an organizational style of politics and where one party is dominant and therefore need not be overly concerned with campaigning (e.g., as was the case with the Republican party in Pennsylvania); in this case, winning elections serves to maintain organizational success.

Two types of organizational maintenance activities deserve to be singled out for special attention. These are "service" activities and representative tasks.

Service Activities. Service activities may be viewed as maintaining both organizational viability and voter support. This function involves the provision of the kinds of assistance (jobs, favors, aid, and advice) which were the hallmark of the old-style city machine (see Greenstein, 1963; Merton, 1957; and Sorauf, 1964). This type of party activity still receives considerable attention today, especially in urban areas with a tradition of strong patronage-based party organization. Even though Detroit does not fit into this category, Eldersveld (1964, Chapter 13) labeled about three-fifths of the Democratic and two-fifths of the Republican precinct leaders "welfare promoters," although "they did not see this as their major task" (p. 352). Hirschfield, Swanson, and Blank (Selection 3.2) characterized Manhattan Democratic committeemen thusly: "The Democrat's view of himself as a provider of services for his party's constituents — as a buffer between the citizen and an increasingly complex government is part of his more professional pattern. A third of the Democrats visit their clubhouse to 'handle constituent problems.' " Frost (1961) found a generally high level of performance of service tasks to be a traditional component of New Jersey local party officials' jobs: "The leaders report that they are engaged in numerous broker tasks involving people and government. They provide entree. They are expediters. The party is the great humanizer" (p. 234). Cutright (1964) also found a high rate of performance of service activities in Partisan City, but not in Nonpartisan County In another report on party organization in Partisan City, Rossi and Cutright (1961) emphasized the role that patronage and service activities play, especially in the Democratic party and in Negro precincts. Negro Democratic precinct committeemen averaged 18 requests a month for aid from their constituents (p. 93).

In research on Berlin local party organization, Wright (1970) found that party members expected party officials to aid them with their problems, and a large number of branch chairmen stated that they were sought out and that they did provide information and advice and did intercede with local government agencies on behalf of their constituents. The Berlin party officials appeared to view such service activities as a necessary organizational maintenance task; it was not an important element in their job descriptions.

Representative Tasks. Eldersveld (1964, Chapter 14) and Valen and Katz (1964, Chapter 4) employ the term representative tasks to refer to communications activity within the party structure. This is a task area that has received little research, but one that deserves attention because of its theoretical importance. The communications process — who communicates with whom, when, how, and about what — is an important aspect of any kind of organization. Eldersveld contends that this may be especially true of political parties: "Because of the critical interdependence of goal strategy and tactical implementation in a party, one might, indeed, theorize that the nature of 'information flow' in a party structure may be more important than in other large-scale organizations" (pp. 334-35). One of the sharpest contrasts between the two basic party models concerns the nature and extent of intraparty communications. The Rational-Efficient party tends to be characterized by little, intermittent, and often inefficient communication, dealing mainly with electoral strategy. The Party Democracy type is characterized by extensive, continuous intraparty communication about policy, by means of well-developed and institutionalized communications channels.

Although Barnes (1967) used a communications model in his study of Italian Socialist party activists, and Niemi and Jennings (1969) examined an aspect of intraparty communications among Michigan Republicans, Eldersveld (1964, Chapter 14) has made the most extensive analysis of communications among leaders at several levels in the party structure. Eldersveld's findings may be briefly summarized, since they furnish excellent illustration of attributes of the Rational-Efficient model. First, he found no "pyramidal" communications relationships integrating the party organizational levels in Wayne County; rather, levels or strata in the party structure were often skipped or ignored. Second, he found a variety of communications styles with different degrees and kinds of inter-leader contacts. Third, as far as the content of intraparty communications was concerned, Eldersveld found this to be "heavily vote-oriented." He concluded:

> These data attest consistently and dramatically to the great preoccupation of party leaders with the tactical and organizational problems of "getting out the vote." At all levels of the hierarchy, discussions of party goal perspectives seem to be minimized. The party did not appear to be a team of activists seeking consensus on broad goals or specific issues" (p. 372).

Finally, with regard to the last-mentioned point, Eldersveld found that even where local party leaders were exposed to policy discussion, the party units were so electorally oriented "that whatever broader issues were discussed, at any level, made very little impact" (p. 373).

Beyond campaign and organizational tasks, there is a great fall-off in the performance of other kinds of activities, as reflected in the job descriptions of American party officials. The two main task areas that fall into the "neglected" or "low mention" category are candidate selection tasks and ideological activities such as policy discussion and political education. Since these types of activities tend to be gotten at by way of open-ended job description questions rather than specific questions, the empirical findings should be interpreted with some caution. The fact that a given type of activity is not singled out by party officials as most important does not mean that it is considered unimportant or that it is not performed (Ippolito, 1969). Nevertheless, the fact that very few American party officials stress candidate selection and ideological tasks in their job descriptions is an interesting datum.

Candidate Selection (Nominating) Activities. It was pointed out in the Introduction to Section Two that candidate recruitment is an important party function and that there is considerable variation, especially within American parties, in the role that the party organization plays in this regard. In the present context of a discussion of tasks and role, it should be noted that very few local party officials identify candidate selection activities as their most important task (Bowman and Boynton, Selection 4.3; Ippolito, 1969). This does not mean that local party officials are uninvolved in candidate selection. But, to be sure, candidates for public office in the United States are often self-recruited or recruited by groups and individuals other than party leaders. And, within the parties, there may be more activity of this kind at higher party levels. However, when local party officials are asked specific questions, it appears that they are more involved in candidate selection than their job descriptions indicate. Sorauf (1963) found local party leaders in Pennsylvania to be very active in candidate selection, and Patterson (Selection 4.1) found a moderately high level of candidate recruitment activity by Oklahoma county chairmen, especially in the minority Republican party. Ippolito (1969) found that while only a very few local party officials listed candidate recruitment as their most important activity, at least one-third of Nassau county party leaders included such activities among their important tasks. Bowman and Boynton (Selection 4.3) noted that local party officials may be individually active in candidate recruitment, even where the party organization is not officially active. When asked a specific question, 71 per cent of the local party leaders interviewed stated that they had been contacted by prospective candidates, mostly for local office; however, this was not a frequent occurence. There was a lower rate of reported candidate contacts which had been initiated by the party officials.

Candidate recruitment activities thus pose an interesting case for further investigation; local party officials perform these tasks with some frequency but do not stress them in their job descriptions. It may be that party leaders are, consistent with the Rational-Efficient model, geared primarily to electing candidates, not to selecting them, i.e., in performing a service role for public officials.

Ideological Activities. Even less study has been made of ideological tasks such as policy discussion, formulation, and political education in American parties. This research gap is due in large measure to the generally accurate assumption that party officials play no significant role in this regard. (Recall that this question is considered to be largely irrelevant in the Rational-Efficient model.) Since this matter will receive further attention in the subsequent discussion of role definitions, only two examples of the neglect of this kind of activity in American parties will be cited here. It was noted in the discussion of representative tasks above that Eldersveld found that party goals and policies represented a very small part of intraparty communications. Bowman and Boynton asked local party officials if they communicated policy preferences to public officials. (Note that this question is phrased in terms of the Rational-Efficient model — namely, the assumption that policy-making is the exclusive domain of elected public officials.) Bowman and Boynton concluded that although the party officials were more active in this regard than even the most active group in the electorate, they "did not think of communication of policy beliefs as one of their more important activities."

Task Performance. The discussion of party activities can best be summarized by comments on the level of task performance. Most measures of task performance deal with campaign activities. The level of performance of campaign activities by local party officials is generally rather low in terms of the empirical measures used and certainly low by "ideal" standards. Crotty (1968) found that only one-quarter of North Carolina county chairmen scored "high" on his Campaign Activities Scale (p. 304). Eldersveld (1964, Chapter 13) found the same proportion of Wayne County precinct leaders performing all three critical campaign tasks. Bowman and Boynton constructed an Index of Campaign Efficiency similar to that used by Eldersveld with similar results: only about one-quarter of Massachusetts and North Carolina ward and precinct officials performed all four campaign tasks. In a comparative study of *primary* election activity in Partisan City and Nonpartisan County, Cutright (1964) found an expected higher level of performance in Partisan City. But even here only slightly more than one-third of the party officials scored "high" on his campaign task performance measure.

There are fewer explicit measures of level of performance of organizational tasks, but a correspondingly low level of performance is usually indicated (Crotty, 1968; Eldersveld, 1964, Chapter 13; Bowman and Boynton, 1966). A better overall picture emerges from examination of the few performance measures that take into account a variety of task areas. The general picture that emerges is one of a limited conception by local party officials of their role, and a level of task performance that falls far short of what is expected of them both by political scientists and, to some extent, by higher-level party officials. As a general proposition, the more task areas that are added to the performance measure, the lower the overall performance level. Eldersveld (1964, Chapter 13) combined campaign and organizational tasks and found that "only 7 per cent of the Democratic and 3 per cent of the Republican precincts met these criteria of [high] task performance" (p. 350). Even when these criteria were relaxed somewhat, only about one-fifth of the precinct leaders "could be considered as operating near the peak of potential performance" (p. 350). When inter-election activity was added to the task performance measure, Eldersveld found that only one-fifth of the Democratic and only 4 per cent of the Wayne County Republican precinct leaders were "active during campaigns *and* between elections" (p. 353, original emphasis).

Valen and Katz (Selection 4.4) concluded that slightly more than one-third (38 per cent) of Norwegian local party leaders "had a truly comprehensive notion of their role and 26 per cent had a very limited notion." In research on Berlin SPD and CDU officials, Wright (1970) found that slightly more than one-fifth of the branch chairmen viewed their roles broadly as entailing organizational, ideological, and campaign tasks; the same percentage viewed their roles narrowly, citing only one of these three task areas.

The following discussion of role definitions builds on the discussion of task perception and performance and adds a more analytical component and more depth to the analysis.

Role Definitions

The term "role" has occasionally been used in the above discussion. This is a widely used concept in social and political analysis, but one which has a number of meanings and therefore needs to be elaborated briefly. Biddle and Thomas (1966) made a survey of the ways that the role concept has been defined and concluded: "Perhaps the most common definition is that role is the set of prescriptions defining what the behavior of a position incumbent should be" (p. 29). We make everyday use of this notion in speaking of the role of parents, students, teachers, policemen, and political officials. The component elements of role definitions will be described below. Eulau (1963) stresses the analytic utility of this concept: "Political behavior, then, is always conduct in the performance of a political role. . . . Whatever its uses in everyday language or scientific research, role seems to commend itself as a basic unit of social and political analysis" (p. 40). Increasing use of the role concept is being made in political research, especially in the area of legislative behavior (see Wahlke, *et al.*, 1962; Barber, 1965; Kornberg, 1967). It is a concept that lends itself to the comparative analysis of political institutions, as seen in Kornberg's study of legislative behavior in the Canadian House of Commons.

The concept of role has several advantages over the approach in terms of tasks and activities. First, role is a more inclusive concept, in that it is not restricted to task performance, but includes such elements as expectations of relevant others, norms, sanctions, and "style." Second, the role concept is more sensitive to the position incumbent's own view of his job. Third, and perhaps most important, the concept of role links the individual to the institution or organization being studied. Organizations or institutions may be thought of as networks of interwoven roles.

Several of the studies cited in the above discussion of party activities make explicit use of the role concept (e.g., Bowman and Boynton, Eldersveld, Ippolito, Mayntz, Patterson, and Wright). In spite of the limited amount of data available, several propositions about party roles may be tentatively advanced for the purpose of illustrating the potential utility of this approach in the comparative analysis of political parties. These propositions concern the clarity with which party roles are defined and the scope and content of these role definitions.

1. Party leadership roles tend not to be explicitly and comprehensively defined, either formally or informally. Three main elements make up role definitions: first, the formal (or "official") definition, found, for example, in party and election statutes; second, expectations of relevant others (e.g., higher-level party officials, elected public officials, party members); and third, the individual position incumbent's own conception of his job—his "private" or discretionary role definition. One seldom finds in the party statutes

a clear and comprehensive statement of the duties and responsibilities of party officials. If one wished to find out just what a county chairman or a precinct leader, for example, does, the party statutes are of little help and may even be misleading. Party statutes tend to be most explicit with regard to organizational maintenance tasks, since these are the easiest to define (Mayntz, 1961, p. 165).

The expectations that relevant others hold of the incumbents of a given role are an important element in role definitions, particularly in situations where roles are not clearly and comprehensively defined in a formal sense. As was the case of the formal element in role definitions, expectations tend to be geared to organizational maintenance requirements. In her study of a CDU district party organization, Mayntz (1961) concluded that the "formal as well as widely shared informal expectations concentrated heavily on maintenance activities, and neglected such functions as citizen involvement and lower-level policy-making participation" (p. 175).

2. Even where reasonably clear expectations are held by relevant others, these are often contradictory and tend to be poorly communicated. In his study of role definitions of Wayne County precinct leaders, Eldersveld (Selection 4.2) concluded: "The party line, if there was one, was confused and poorly communicated. There was much individualization and autonomy, apparently, in the taking on and defining of party leadership roles." Mayntz (1961) concluded in her analysis of a CDU district organization: "Task-related expectations, for most party officials, were generally rather loose, lacking in specificity, and occasionally involved contradictions" (p. 169). The poor communication of role expectations is probably the result of a combination of factors, including the lack of clarity of formal role definitions and expectations, the often poorly developed party communications channels, and the volunteer character and high turnover rate of party activists. The latter two factors apply particularly to American parties.

3. Higher party officials generally lack effective sanctions for enforcing task performance of lower echelon leaders. We have noted that the hierarchical model is inappropriate to most, if not all, democratic political parties. There is thus little in the way of superior-subordinate status in political parties. In this regard, Eldersveld (Selection 1.3) states: "In fact, the basis for the authority of party organizations is one of the most puzzling to understand. It does not seem to be a function of expertise, or of role, or even of normative expectations. Rather, the party structure appears to be characterized as a 'rapport system.' " This "downward deference," whereby party leaders must leave it up to lower echelon officials to do their

job, Eldersveld contends, "stems from the absence of effective sanctions," among other things. Mayntz (1961) found that Berlin CDU officials likewise were in possession of few really effective sanctions. To be sure, the party statutes did provide for official sanctions such as expulsion from the party in extreme cases; furthermore, since party officials were elected by the members or their elected party representatives, support could be withdrawn at the next internal party election. But Mayntz points out that these were not practical courses of action: "While formal and informal sanctions can prevent or punish extreme departure from rules or norms, they can hardly insure optimal fulfillment of tasks. There is a connection between this lack of specific sanctions and the often vague definition of organizational tasks. Nonperformance of something that is not generally expected can hardly be punished as an extreme departure from norms" (p. 175).

4. As a result of the above factors — unclarity of formal role definitions and expectations, poor communication of expectations, and lack of effective sanctions — considerable leeway is left party officials to define their roles for themselves. The less clearly and comprehensively that roles are formally defined, the greater the leeway for private and idiosyncratic conceptions. In this situation, Mayntz (1961) contends, "Incumbents in such loosely defined roles behaved according to personality needs and private role conceptions to a greater extent than would have been possible were their roles more clearly defined in the minds of others" (p. 169).

5. It is not surprising, therefore, that a few party officials cannot articulate any role conception, while some can do so only in a rudimentary fashion. Still others define their roles exclusively in routine organizational maintenance terms. Probably only a minority hold and can articulate more sophisticated role conceptions. The degree of clarity of role definitions is in itself a significant datum, little use of which has been made in research on political parties. Mayntz (1961) states that the clarity and specificity of role definitions "may be regarded as an index of organizational formalization" (p. 165). Eldersveld (Selection 4.2) relates clarity of role perception or definition to organizational effectiveness; he hypothesizes that "an organization such as a political party loses effectiveness if roles are misperceived or improperly evaluated." This involves a clear conception of one's own role *and* the roles of others in the party structure. By these standards, political parties do not rank among the highly effective organizations.

6. The implication of the earlier discussion of the scope of task performance is that local party officials tend to define their roles

narrowly, partly as a result of their being volunteer activists devoting part of their leisure time to party activity and partly as a result of the aspects of party role structure cited above.

7. Most of the limited research on party roles involves the content of role definitions — i.e., role types or role-orientations. The role dimension most often used in studies of American parties is the distinction between internal or organizational and external or campaigning tasks. This is the only distinction made by Patterson (Selection 4.1) and Patterson and Althoff (1966), who classified county party officials as either campaign-oriented or organization-oriented, depending on whether they placed greater emphasis on winning elections or building the party organization. A third orientation is important conceptually and essential for purposes of comparative analysis of political parties. This type is the ideological mentor, who is most concerned with the discussion of issues and the formulation of policy. The two party models have the following implications for party role definitions. First, one expects to find and hypothesizes a high incidence of the campaign-oriented vote mobilizer and a low incidence of the ideological orientation in parties based on the Rational-Efficient model, and the reverse situation with a high incidence of ideological and a lower incidence of vote mobilizer orientations existing in parties based on the Party Democracy model. Second, organizational tasks serve different purposes in the two party models. In the Rational-Efficient party, organizational efforts are geared more or less directly to the party's electoral function; in the Party Democracy type, organizational activities relate more to the party's ideological function.

The findings of studies of American parties are generally consistent with these hypotheses. The vote mobilizer orientation is usually the most prevalent role type, and organizational activities tend to be geared to vote mobilization activities. One qualification must be made. These studies have found some diversity in role conceptions; local party officials are not single-mindedly preoccupied with "getting out the vote." Of the studies examined, only Bowman and Boynton classified a majority (60 per cent) of local party officials as primarily campaign-oriented. A minority of Oklahoma county chairmen and even fewer of the co-chairmen were labeled clearly as campaign-oriented by Patterson. Eldersveld (Selection 4.2) found that only 45 per cent of Wayne County precinct leaders "accepted the doctrine that their *primary* task was vote production" (original emphasis). Ippolito (1969) found that only 31 per cent of Nassau County Democratic and 38 per cent of Republican executive committeemen conceived their roles primarily in terms of campaign-related activities.

Generally, the second most prevalent role type in American studies is the "organizer." (Only Eldersveld does not use this category.) Beyond this point, there is less agreement on conceptualization of role types in American parties. In most cases, other orientations constitute "minor" or infrequent role types. Eldersveld did label one-quarter of Wayne County precinct leaders as "ideological mentors," but other studies have found less emphasis of this kind. Ippolito (1969) classified only 8 per cent of Nassau County Republican officials and 15 per cent of the Democrats as ideological mentors, and Bowman and Boynton determined that even fewer — between 3 and 9 per cent — of the local party officials in their study had this orientation. There are only a scattering of other role-orientations in studies of American parties — these include stress on service activities or candidate recruitment.

Comparable data on parties based on the Party Democracy model are even more limited, but some are available (Mayntz, 1961; Wright, 1970). As hypothesized, there is a lower incidence of vote mobilizer and a greater incidence of ideological orientations. In discussing the role of the CDU branch chairman, Mayntz states that he was *not* "expected to extend his activities beyond his unit's members to the population in his district," apart from participating in quadrennial election campaigns. "Aside from this, contact with the general population was not consciously sought; it was in fact exceedingly slight" (p. 170). Wright (1970) found that only 18 per cent of Berlin SPD and CDU branch chairmen were primarily campaign-oriented; the ideological mentor was the most prevalent role type with 49 per cent of the branch chairmen falling into this category. The remaining one-third were "organizers," with their organizational tasks related largely to the party's ideological or political education function (i.e., the planning and conduct of branch membership meetings). This latter point is consistent with Mayntz's findings.

Role Correlates. The final point in this discussion of party roles concerns attempts to account for variation in role-orientations. In a few studies, some attempt was made to relate role conceptions to other leadership and community characteristics; the question posed is whether certain kinds of party officials acquire particular role conceptions. No consistent general patterns have been found yet. Not only has very little research been done, but also party organizational and political environmental characteristics vary so greatly — especially in the United States — as to make generalizations difficult (Ippolito, 1969, p. 814). This point is illustrated by tests of the single general hypothesis concerning role correlates that has been tested in several studies. This may be termed the "party dominance" hypothesis, first eplicitly formulated and tested by Patterson (Selection 4.1). As stated most succinctly by Patterson and Althoff (1966), the hypothesis holds that "majority party leaders would incline to organization-oriented roles, while minority party leaders would be more campaign-oriented. The majority party has less electoral insecurity, and presumably wants to build and maintain their organization; the minority party needs to win elections and must emphasize campaign-waging" (p. 46). (This hypothesis applies to less than perfectly competitive situations.)

Patterson found that his data on Oklahoma county chairmen supported this hypothesis, as did data on party officials in a rural Ohio county (Patterson and Althoff, 1966). However, other studies which have tested the party dominance hypothesis have found a variety of patterns. In his study of Nassau County executive committeemen, Ippolito (1969) found the reverse relationship; the minority Democrats were more organization-oriented and the majority Republicans, more campaign-oriented. Bowman and Boynton tested this hypothesis on North Carolina and Massachusetts ward and precinct leaders and found no consistent patterns. The direction of the relationship was reversed for the two states studies, and little variation was found when community characteristics were examined. Eldersveld found yet another pattern: precinct leaders of both parties were most campaign-oriented in the "sure Republican" precincts.

Only a few studies have made a more extensive search for role correlates. Different independent and dependent variables were examined in these studies and no consistent and cumulative patterns have emerged. Bowman and Boynton (1966a) examined social background characteristics (occupational status, occupational role, and social mobility), parental political activity, and recruitment patterns for possible relationships with role conceptions. However, they found weak or no relationships with role definitions. Eldersveld made the most extensive search for role correlates. He analyzed social background and demographic characteristics, perceptions of party goals, political career patterns, and environmental characteristics such as party competition. It is difficult to briefly summarize his findings. Eldersveld concluded: "The proliferation of role perceptions, explicable by these variables—organizational status, political milieu, personal characteristics—and so closely linked to one's view of the party's goal as well as to one's own career aspirations suggests that it is indeed a diffuse organizational and personal context by which roles are assumed."

A focus on party structure and organizational processes necessitates concern with activities and role definitions of organizational leaders. In studying political parties, we have just begun to scratch the surface in this regard. The role concept has not been extensively used thus far. The main analytic utility of this approach is its broad applicability. More research is needed to link party organizational roles at all levels with those of elected public officials, party members or activists, and other party-related roles (e.g., interest group representatives). (See Olson, forthcoming, for an example.) There are conceptual and methodological problems which deserve more attention — particularly the need for standardized task classifications, role typologies, questionnaire items, and coding criteria — for the purposes of the comparative analysis of political parties.

REFERENCES

Barber, James David. *The Lawmakers.* New Haven: Yale University Press, 1965.

Barnes, Samuel H. *Party Democracy: Politics in an Italian Socialist Federation.* New Haven: Yale University Press, 1967.

Bowman, Lewis, and Boynton, G.R. "Recruitment Patterns among Local Party Officials: A Model and Some Preliminary Findings." *American Political Science Review,* 60 (September, 1966), 667-76.

_______ "Activities and Role Definitions of Grass Roots Party Officials." *Journal of Politics,* 28 (February, 1966), 121-43.

Crotty, William J. "The Party Organization and Its Activities," in *Approaches to the Study of Party Organization,* edited by William J. Crotty, pp. 247-306. Boston: Allyn and Bacon, 1968.

Cutright, Phillips. "Activities of Precinct Committeemen in Partisan and Nonpartisan Communities." *Western Political Quarterly,* 17 (March, 1964), 93-108.

Eldersveld, Samuel J. *Political Parties: A Behavioral Analysis,* Chapters 10 and 13. Chicago: Rand McNally, 1964.

Eulau, Heinz. *The Behavioral Persuasion in Politics*. New York: Random House, 1963.

Frost, Richard T. "Stability and Change in Local Party Politics." *Public Opinion Quarterly,* 25 (Summer, 1961), 221-35.

Greenstein, Fred I. *The American System and the American People.* Englewood Cliffs. N.J.: Prentice-Hall, 1963.

Hirschfield, Robert S.; Swanson, Bert E.; and Blank, Blanche D. "A Profile of Political Activists in Manhattan." *Western Political Quarterly,* 15 (September, 1962), 489-506.

Ippolito, Dennis. "Political Perspectives of Suburban Party Leaders," *Social Science Quarterly,* 49 (March, 1969), 800-15.

Ippolito, Dennis, and Bowman, Lewis. "Goals and Activities of Party Officials in a Suburban Community." *Western Political Quarterly,* 22 (September, 1969), 572-80.

Katz, Daniel, and Eldersveld, Samuel J. "The Impact of Local Party Activity Upon the Electorate." *Public Opinion Quarterly,* 25 (1961), 1-24.

Kornberg, Allan. *Canadian Legislative Behavior*. New York: Holt, Rinehart and Winston, 1967.

Leiserson, Avery. *Parties and Politics: An Institutional and Behavioral Approach.* New York: Alfred A. Knopf, 1958.

Mayntz, Renate. "Oligarchic Problems in a German Party District," in *Political Decision-Makers,* edited by Dwaine Marvick, pp. 138-92. New York: The Free Press of Glencoe, 1961.

Merton, Robert K. *Social Theory and Social Structure,* 1957 ed. rev. Glencoe, Ill.: The Free Press, pp. 72-82.

Neumann, Sigmund. "Toward a Comparative Study of Political Parties," in *Modern Political Parties,* edited by Sigmund Neumann, pp. 395-421. Chicago: The University of Chicago Press, 1956.

Niemi, Richard G., and Jennings, M. Kent. "Intraparty Communications and the Selection of Delegates to a National Convention." *Western Political Quarterly,* 22 (March, 1969), 29-46.

Olson, David M. *The Congressman and His Party,* forthcoming.

Patterson, Samuel C. "Characteristics of Party Leaders." *Western Political Quarterly,* 16 (June, 1963), 332-52.

Patterson, Samuel C., and Althoff, Phillip. "Political Activism in a Rural County." *Midwest Journal of Political Science,* 10 (February, 1966), 39-51.

Rossi, Peter, and Cutright, Phillips. "The Impact of Party Organization in An Industrial Setting," in *Community Political Systems,* edited by Morris Janowitz, pp. 81-116. New York: The Free Press of Glencoe, 1961.

Sorauf, Frank J. *Party and Representation: Legislative Politics in Pennsylvania.* New York: Atherton Press, 1963.

Thomas, Edwin J., and Biddle, Bruce J. "Basic Concepts for Classifying the Phenomena of Role," in *Role Theory: Concepts and Research,* edited by Bruce J. Biddle and Edwin J. Thomas, pp. 22-45. New York: John Wiley & Sons, 1966.

Valen, Henry, and Katz, Daniel. *Political Parties in Norway: A Community Study,* Chapter 4. Oslo: Universitetsforlaget, 1964.

Wahlke, John C., *et al. The Legislative System.* New York, John Wiley & Sons, 1962.

Wright, William E. "Role Definitions and Activities of Berlin Local Party Officials." Unpublished manuscript, 1970.

Characteristics of Party Leaders

Samuel C. Patterson

Organized partisanship is one of the fundamental functional requisites for a democratic polity. The effective presentation of some kind of alternative to the electorate, even if it be only alternative personalities, requires organization. In the United States the organization of partisanship can be described loosely as a congeries of party activists and their followers at local, state, and national levels who are combined under the respective rubrics of the Republican and the Democratic parties. These combinations customarily compete for political offices and their emoluments, nominating candidates and campaigning for their election. These are the commonplaces that depict the party battle in this country, and that lead to some of the central queries made about the political process: How are parties organized? What kinds of individuals are recruited into politics? Who are the party activists? How does party organization affect the political process, and what impact do parties and party leaders have on public policy?

NOTE: I should like to acknowledge gratefully the assistance of the Social Science Research Council and its Committee on Political Behavior for making this study possible. I am also grateful for the help of the Research Foundation of Oklahoma State University. I owe especial thanks to Eloise Dreessen, Billie Black, and Ida Linsenmeyer for their efficient and effective handling of the mailed questionnaires used as the basis for the study. I am, finally, indebted to Leon Epstein, University of Wisconsin, and Donald Johnson, University of Iowa, for their helpful comments and suggestions.

Reprinted from the *Western Political Quarterly,* XVI (June, 1963), 332-52, by permission of the University of Utah.

Some of these questions have been fathomed, and for them our body of knowledge is extensive. We know a great deal about the formal, and some about the informal organization of political parties. We have voluminous lore and data related to party operations in the processes of nominations, campaigns, and elections, and a considerable store of reliable knowledge on the nature and importance of party in the formulation of public policy.[1] What is more, in the last decade we have substantially improved our understanding of the kinds of individuals who get elected to public office, although our data are highly selective.[2] Perhaps the most neglected area of research on political parties has been that of party leadership. V. O. Key, in his provocative account of state politics, has pointed out that "while a great deal of information has been assembled about the composition of the electoral followings of the parties, the character and structure of the leadership corps are matters about which reliable data are scant."[3]

The data are scant, but not nonexistent. The vogue of the study of "machine" politics in cities in the 1930's produced analyses of precinct committeemen; Bone has suggested ways in which these data need to be updated in his study of Republican committeemen in Kings County, Washington.[4] Sawyer has presented findings on

---

[1]See Avery Lieserson, *Parties and Politics: An Institutional and Behavioral Approach* (New York: Knopf, 1958).

[2]See Donald R. Matthews, *The Social Background of Political Decision-Makers* (Garden City: Doubleday, 1954).

[3]V. O. Key, Jr., *American State Politics: An Introduction* (New York: Knopf, 1956), p. 255.

[4]Hugh A. Bone, *Grass Roots Party Leadership* (Seattle: Bureau of Governmental Research and Services, University of Washington, 1952). The principal older studies of precinct committeemen are: Harold F. Gosnell, *Machine Politics: Chicago Model* (Chicago: University of Chicago Press, 1937); Sonya Forthal, *Cogwheels of Democracy: A Study of the Precinct Captain* (New York: William-Frederick Press, 1946); William E. Mosher, "Party and Government Control at the Grass Roots," *National Municipal Review,* 24 (January, 1935), 15-18, 38; Leon Weaver, "Some Soundings in the Party System: Rural Precinct Committeemen," *American Political Science Review,* 34 (February, 1940), 76-84. See also Wallace S. Sayre, "Personnel of Republican and Democratic Committees," *American Political Science Review,* 26 (April, 1932), 360-62, and Austin Ranney and Willmore Kendall, *Democracy and the American Party System* (New York: Harcourt, Brace, 1956), pp. 239-41. Three recent studies have added significantly to our knowledge of the importance of local party leaders in elections. I refer to: Phillips Cutright and Peter H. Rossi, "Party Organization in Primary Elections," *American Journal of Sociology,* 64 (November, 1958), 262-69; Phillips Cutright and Peter H. Rossi, "Grass Roots Politicians and the Vote," *American Sociological Review,* 23 (April, 1958), 171-79; and Daniel Katz and Samuel J. Eldersveld, "The Impact of Local Party Activity upon the Electorate," *Public Opinion Quarterly,* 25 (Spring, 1961), 1-24.

Michigan Democratic State Central Committee, and Frost has examined informal county party leadership in New Jersey.[5] More studies of these kinds are badly needed, especially those that present or permit interparty, intraparty, and interstate comparisons.

Curiously, the level of party leadership that has been given least attention has been that of the county.[6] We have in the standard treatments of political parties countless admonitions as to the significance of the county committee and its chairman.[7] Yet we know very little about county party leaders. It is this deficit that the data presented in this paper seek to improve.

We know substantially more about sixty-odd million individuals who go to the polls to vote in presidential elections than we do about the three thousand county party chairmen in the several states who may occupy crucial positions in the party machinery. Thus our images of county party leaders are impressionistic and obscure. The county chairman may be pictured as the pliable hack of a state machine, the omnipotent dictator of a quaint and backward bailiwick, the bumbling conspirator in the courthouse gang, or the ineffective and inactive politico whose only motivation for party leadership is personal or political self-enrichment through graft and patronage. Again, the county chairman may be pictured as a dedicated party activist, like Johnny Welsh,

> a wiry, well-preserved, gray-haired, sharp-tongued politician whose iron will and personal integrity had kept the local Democratic party functioning for more than a quarter of a century. When others of us were working abroad, he and his six sons were at home doing the dirty work of running a complex party organization. When the Democrats were in such low esteem locally that not even candidates could be found, Johnny Welsh ran for office. He made his living selling real estate, but his real occupation was politics, and he

---

[5]See Richard T. Frost, "Stability and Change in Local Party Politics," *Public Opinion Quarterly*, 25 (Summer, 1961), 221-35; and Robert L. Sawyer, Jr., *The Democratic State Central Committee in Michigan* (Ann Arbor: Institute of Public Administration, University of Michigan, 1960).

[6]Both Leon Epstein and Eugene Lee have given some attention to the county chairman, for different purposes. See Leon D. Epstein, *Politics in Wisconsin* (Madison: University of Wisconsin Press, 1958), pp. 77-97; and Eugene C. Lee, *The Politics of Nonpartisanship* (Berkeley and Los Angeles; University of California Press, 1960), pp. 97-118.

[7]For example, see V. O. Key, Jr., *Politics, Parties, and Pressure Groups* (4th ed.; New York: Thomas Y. Crowell Company, 1958), pp. 359-60; and William Goodman, *The Two-Party System in the United States* (Princeton: Van Nostrand, 1960), pp. 76-77.

knew more about the workings of my county than any other man alive.[8]

None of these images is either completely true or false. Yet they do not help us very much in generalization about county party leaders.

The data to be presented here, while they do not shed light directly on the personalities of party leaders, contribute to our understanding of the characteristics of party leaders at the county level. Systematic empirical data were sought from county party leaders in one state to answer these questions: What kinds of party activists are recruited to the county party leadership role? How does the composition of this stratum of the party leadership corps compare with county leaders in other states? What kinds of previous political experience, in terms of office-holding, characterize county party leaders? Is the county-leader position a linkage for its occupants to other political positions, or not? Does the county leader conceive himself as playing an important part in the process of nominating candidates? How does the county leader conceptualize his job? The answers are much more modest than the questions, and yet they are suggestive of the nature and functions of party leadership at the county level.

Research Site and Procedure

The data for this analysis were gathered from Democratic and Republican county chairmen, Democratic co-chairmen, and Republican vice-chairmen in Oklahoma. In many ways Oklahoma is a valuable site for political research.[9] The state was not extensively settled by whites until the territory was first opened in 1889. When the area was settled, migration into the territory came from two distinct parts of the country, and settlers brought with them differ-

[8]James A. Michener, *Report of the County Chairman* (New York: Random House, 1961), pp. 67-68. The title of Michener's book is somewhat misleading, since he was not county *party* chairman during the 1960 presidential campaign. He was chairman of an *ad hoc* Kennedy-for-President committee in Bucks County, Pennsylvania.

[9]Oklahoma has a fascinating political history, and an extremely interesting contemporary politics which cannot be elaborated here. An adequate general description is not available, but short vignettes can be found in Angie Debo, *Oklahoma: Foot-Loose and Fancy-Free* (Norman: University of Oklahoma Press, 1949), pp. 39-53; and John Gunther, *Inside U. S. A.* (New York: Harper, 1951), pp. 970-74.

ent political traditions. The northwestern and north-central counties of Oklahoma were settled predominantly by people from the Midwest, while the southern and northeastern counties were settled mainly by Southerners. Those who moved across the border from Kansas brought with them their Republican political habits, while the Southerners brought to the southern part of the state (the southeastern counties are now identified as "Little Dixie") the Democratic political tradition. This intrastate sectional difference in the political tradition of Oklahoma voters still remains clearly identifiable in state politics. Republican political success, such as it is, is largely confined to the northern counties; and in the southern counties the Democratic party is dominant. These distinct political traditions are supported by cultural and economic differences between the two regions.[10]

Oklahoma, in a real sense, spans the hazy line of demarcation between North and South. In gubernatorial and other state elections Oklahoma has been predominantly Democratic. Compared to other states it is proper to classify Oklahoma as a "one-party" Democratic state.[11] On the other hand, Oklahoma is not properly written off as another one-party state like those of the Old South.[12] The Republican party has had electoral success in Oklahoma, however infrequently and tenuously. Once since Oklahoma entered the Union in 1907 the Republicans won a majority of the state House of Representatives, and nearly did so on another occasion. Three Republican United States Senators have been elected from Oklahoma, the last in 1942. Republican presidential electors have won in five presidential elections in the state. Eisenhower captured the Oklahoma electoral vote in both 1952 and 1956, and Nixon received a larger percentage of the two-party vote in Oklahoma than in any other state except Kansas and Nebraska. Even in gubernatorial and senatorial elections which have been won by Democrats, the Republican party in Oklahoma frequently has made a respectable

---

[10]See James D. Tarver, "The Regional Background of Oklahoma's People," *Proceedings of the Oklahoma Academy of Science,* 37 (1956), 95-99; and Key, *American State Politics . . .*, pp. 220-22. Key makes reference to the economic differences which lend support to the sectional basis of the Democratic-Republican cleavage in Oklahoma. Tarver's analysis demonstrates the difference between the Republican and Democratic sections and their differential religious inheritance, employing as his criterion the migration into the state of members of the northern and southern branches of the Methodist Church.

[11]Joseph A. Schlesinger, "A Two-Dimensional Scheme for Classifying the States According to Degree of Inter-Party Competition," *American Political Science Review*, 49 (December, 1955), 1120-28.

[12]Described by Key in *Southern Politics in State and Nation* (New York: Knopf, 1950)

showing. For instance, in two senatorial elections in the 1950's the Republican candidate polled nearly 45 per cent of the vote, and in three pre-1962 contests for the governorship Republican candidates received more than 40 per cent of the vote. In 1950 a Republican, Jo Ferguson, got nearly 49 per cent of the vote, and in 1962 Republican Henry Bellmon won the governorship, becoming the state's first Republican chief executive. The principal explanation for the presidential success of the Republican party in Oklahoma and its difficulty in electing a governor may lie in the fact that gubernatorial elections are held in off-presidential years.[13] Furthermore, the Republican party has a persistent base of strength in Tulsa and the remainder of the First Congressional District, where a Republican is regularly elected to the Congress.

The success of the Republican party in the three recent presidential elections, and the winning of the 1962 gubernatorial election, convinced many Oklahoma Republican leaders that a viable two-party system could be built in the state. The state Republican organization had been considerably revitalized and invigorated between 1959-62, most recently under the direction of state chairman (now governor) Henry Bellmon, a northern Oklahoma rancher.[14] For the first time in Oklahoma history, the Republicans now had county officers in nearly all of the state's seventy-seven counties, and efforts were devoted to precinct organizations in areas where no such activity had previously occurred. On the Democratic side, much the same process took place. Torpid, and under the direct control of the governor for many years, the Oklahoma Democratic party finally (though perhaps temporarily) became a political force independent of gubernatorial domination. This occurred, much to

---

[13]Key, *American State Politics* . . . , pp. 42-43.

[14]The Republican vitalization drive was labeled "GOP Countdown" in party literature, and it aimed at improved electoral activity in the 1962 elections. In addition to enhancing the regular Republican organization, Bellmon organized a "Republican Task Force" to raise funds, stimulate Democrats to re-register Republican, develop a public relations program, develop candidates, and improve campaigning. Republican registrations increased from 179,645 in 1959 to 215,344 in 1960. In May, 1961, the Republican state convention adopted a comprehensive party platform, probably the first in party history. As of this writing the Republicans had not as yet adopted a party constitution. The Democratic party has, of course, had a nominal organization for a long time, and its needs are not as great. Fund-raising and campaigning problems are not as acute for them. On the other hand, both organizations have only recently established permanent party headquarters in Oklahoma City. The Democratic party has a party constitution, badly out of date and now being revised. So far the Democrats have not prepared a formal state party platform. From the point of view of *organizational* development the two Oklahoma parties are not too different.

the consternation of some liberal Democrats, at the expense of reform Governor Howard Edmondson, and was widely interpreted as a victory for the Old Guard wing of the party.[15] In fact, it went deeper than this; it reflected to a significant degree the efforts of organization Democrats (like state Chairman Gene McGill, also a rancher) to build a real party organization. Perhaps stimulated by the potential Republican challenge, the Democratic party showed more life in Oklahoma than it had for many years.

Thus our data stem from a state characterized by Democratic one-party control, but where there is a traditional basis of Republican strength. What is more, both party organizations were meaningful in the sense that the Democratic party was not languid and the Republican party was not defunct. While the Democrats could still count on winning most elections for state offices, their leaders now believed party organization was necessary to assure it. While the Republicans could not hope for sweeping electoral successes, the probabilities had markedly improved.

The instrument employed for the purpose of gathering data for this study was the mailed questionnaire.[16] The two principal county party officers in every county where they existed were mailed a brief questionnaire in the summer, 1961, followed by a second mailing.[17] About three-fourths (74.8 per cent) of the questionnaires were re-

---

[15]Factionalism characterizes Democratic politics in Oklahoma to some extent, but not nearly to the extent that characterizes neighboring Texas politics. See Key, *Southern Politics . . .*, pp. 254-76.

[16]The standard handbook reference for the use of the mailed questionnaire technique is Mildred B. Parten, *Surveys, Polls, and Samples: Practical Procedures* (New York: Harper, 1950), pp. 383-402. See also: Donald S. Longworth, "Use of a Mail Questionnaire," *American Sociological Review*, 18 (June, 1953), 310-13; Sol Levine and Gerald Gordon, "Maximizing Returns on Mail Questionnaires," *Public Opinion Quarterly*, 22 (Winter, 1958-59), 568-75; and Marjorie N. Donald, "Implications of Nonresponse for the Interpretation of Mail Questionnaire Data," *Public Opinion Quarterly*, 24 (Spring, 1960). 99-114.

[17]At the time the data were accumulated, in the summer of 1961, there were 76 Democratic chairmen, 76 Republican chairmen, 76 Democratic co-chairmen, and 66 Republican vice-chairmen in the state. I am indebted to Democratic state chairman Gene McGill and Republican state chairmen Henry Bellmon for making lists of party officials available to me. It is quite correct that "if one sets out to interview 'county chairmen' only, much of the true leadership may be overlooked." See Frost, *loc. cit.*, pp. 224-25. Frost did find that 11 of the 16 county chairmen he studied in New Jersey were in the "leadership group." I do not maintain that there are no other important leaders, or that all chairmen and co-chairmen are "real" leaders. The data here are inherently limited by the fact that only those in official county leadership positions could be considered.

turned. Democratic county leaders returned questionnaires in a somewhat higher proportion than Republicans (Democrats, 76.9 per cent; Republicans, 72.5 per cent). A higher proportion of county chairmen returned questionnaires than did co- or vice-chairmen (Democratic chairmen, 77.6 per cent; Republican chairmen, 78.9 per cent; Democratic co-chairmen, 76.3 per cent; Republican vice-chairmen, 65.2 per cent). Obviously the small difference between parties in returning questionnaires stems mainly from the relatively lower proportion of returns among Republican vice-chairmen. There are no data available for all county party leaders on the basis of which to compare our large sample with the total population. A comparison of counties from whose county leaders questionnaires were returned with those whose leaders did not respond does not raise doubt about the validity of the sample.[18] Based on the minimal comparisons which can be made, if there be any noticeable category of non-returners it is among party leaders in the most overwhelmingly Democratic counties where, presumably, the Democratic leadership is inactive and the Republican, wasting.

The questionnaire, of necessity a rather limited one, included questions relating to the respondents' social backgrounds, political experiences and aspirations, roles in state legislative nominations, perceived contacts with state legislators, and conceptions of their jobs as county party leaders. Clearly the mailed questionnaire device limits the scope and depth of data gathered. On the other hand, it has many advantages and the data gathered, if not definite, are highly suggestive and of considerable value.

Profile of County Party Leaders

Social background data for Oklahoma county party leaders are available for occupation, educational attainment, income and age. The first three of these variables are useful in the determination of the socio-economic status of leaders, and are presented in Table 1. The general proposition that is obvious from this table is that Oklahoma county party leaders tend to occupy high socio-economic status. They tend to be employed in business or professional occupations, have high educational attainment, and command relatively high incomes. In marked contrast to the party committeemen in Chicago (in the 1930's), the Oklahoma county leader is a "man of

[18]The variables were rural-urban categorization, party competitiveness, and party dominance.

parts" in his community.[19] But the outstanding contrasts revealed by Table 1 are the differences between leaders of the two parties. Insofar as county leaders reflect the characteristics of the mass of party supporters, it certainly could not be maintained that the Republican party in Oklahoma is the party of business, managerial, and professional groups and the Democratic party the vehicle of the common man.

TABLE 1

OCCUPATIONAL, EDUCATIONAL, AND INCOME CHARACTERISTICS OF OKLAHOMA COUNTY PARTY LEADERS

	Democratic				Republican			
Characteristic	Chairmen		Co-Chairmen		Chairmen		Vice-Chairmen	
Occupation	Number	Per Cent	Number	Per Cent	Number	Per Cent	Number	Per Cent
Farmer-Rancher	11	18.6	3	5.2	15	25.0	1	2.3
Businessman	13	22.0	9	15.5	12	20.0	4	9.3
Sales-Clerical	6	10.2	4	6.9	8	13.3	4	9.3
Attorney	14	23.7	0		7	11.7	0	
Other professional	9	15.3	8	13.8	11	18.3	4	9.3
Public official	1	1.7	7	12.1	0		0	
Laborer	1	1.7	0		3	5.0	1	2.3
Housewife	1	1.7	26	44.8	0		29	67.4
Retired	2	3.4	1	1.7	2	3.3	0	
Other	1	1.7	0		1	1.7	0	
No response	0		0		1	1.7	0	
Total	59	99.9	58	100.0	60	100.0	43	99.9
Educational Attainment								
Grade school	1	1.7	4	6.9	1	1.7	2	4.7
Some high school	4	6.8	6	10.3	6	10.0	4	9.3
High school diploma	6	10.2	11	19.0	15	25.0	10	23.3
Some college	17	28.8	21	36.2	12	20.0	20	46.5
College degree	9	15.3	14	24.1	14	23.3	4	9.3
Graduate degree	21	35.6	2	3.4	12	20.0	2	4.7
No response	1	1.7	0		0		1	2.3
Total	59	100.1	58	99.9	60	100.0	43	100.1
Income								
Less than $4,000	1	1.7	15	25.9	8	13.3	8	18.6
$4,000 to $6,000	7	11.9	6	10.3	8	13.3	7	16.3
$6,000 to $8,000	5	8.5	10	17.3	10	16.7	4	9.3
$8,000 to $10,000	10	16.9	8	13.8	10	16.7	7	16.3
More than $10,000	34	57.6	15	25.9	23	38.3	14	32.6
No response	2	3.4	4	6.9	1	1.7	3	7.0
Total	59	100.0	58	100.1	60	100.0	43	100.1

[19]Gosnell, *op. cit.*, pp. 51-68. Bone found King County, Washington, Republican leaders better educated than were upstate New York Republican committeemen in 1932. See Bone, *op. cit.*, pp. 16-17.

Our assumptions about the social background differences between party leaders in northern two-party states have been that (1) Republicans are employed in higher status occupations than Democrats; (2) Republicans have higher educational attainment than Democrats; (3) Republicans tend more than Democrats to be recruited from high-income categories; and (4) Republicans tend to be older than Democrats. Table 1 clearly indicates that for the first three of these hypotheses the reverse is true for Oklahoma county chairmen. In the case of age, the data are not presented because of a very high no response rate; but the fragmentary data bear out the same relationship with respect to age. In general, Oklahoma Democratic chairmen tend more than Republicans to come from high-status occupations, to have more education, to have higher incomes, and to be older.

This reversal of our usual expectations about interparty differences in the social background characteristics of party leaders is made more explicit in the interstate comparisons supplied in Tables 2, 3, and 4.[20] Table 2 shows interparty breakdowns for county chairmen in Oklahoma, Kansas, and Wisconsin. Both Kansas and Wisconsin have been categorized as "one-party predominant" Re-

TABLE 2
INTERSTATE VARIATIONS IN THE OCCUPATIONAL BACKGROUNDS OF COUNTY PARTY CHAIRMEN
(In Percentages)

	OKLAHOMA		KANSAS		WISCONSIN	
OCCUPATION	DEMOCRATIC	REPUBLICAN	DEMOCRATIC	REPUBLICAN	DEMOCRATIC	REPUBLICAN
Farmer-Rancher	18.6	25.0	28.8	14.5	15.6	3.1
Businessman	22.0	20.0	19.2	32.5	17.2	45.3
Sales–Clerical	10.2	13.3	15.1	6.0	7.8	4.7
Attorney	23.7	11.7	13.7	27.7	18.8	29.7
Other professional	15.3	18.3	8.2	9.6	6.3	12.5
Laborer	1.7	5.0	1.4	3.6	23.4	0.0
Public official	1.7	0.0	1.4	1.2	1.6	0.0
Housewife	1.7	0.0	6.8	1.2	4.7	0.0
Retired	3.4	3.3	5.5	0.0	3.1	3.1
Other	1.7	1.7	0.0	0.0	0.0	0.0
No response	0.0	1.7	0.0	3.6	1.6	1.6
Total	99.9	100.0	100.1	99.9	100.0	100.0
N's	59	60	73	83	64	64

[20]Data for Wisconsin county chairmen are from Epstein, *op. cit.*, p. 186. Data for Kansas have been gleaned from the unpublished findings produced by a Citizenship Clearing House-sponsored project directed at the University of Kansas by James W. Drury. I am indebted to John G. Grumm for making the Kansas tabulations available to me in the absence of Dr. Drury.

publican states, although the classification for Wisconsin may be in need of revision.[21] In any event, here are three states with different kinds of political structures: Oklahoma is one-party Democratic; Kansas, one-party Republican; and Wisconsin, in between — traditionally Republican, but moving in the two-party direction. The differences in the occupational characteristics of county chairmen in these three states are striking. Though not inscrutable, these data raise interesting questions about the impact of party dominance

TABLE 3

INTERSTATE VARIATIONS IN THE EDUCATIONAL ATTAINMENT OF COUNTY PARTY LEADERS
(*In Percentages*)

	Oklahoma				Kansas			
	Democratic		Republican		Democratic		Republican	
Education	Chairman	Co-Chairman	Chairman	Vice-Chairman	Chairman	Vice-Chairman	Chairman	Vice-Chairman
Grade school	1.7	6.9	1.7	4.7	12.3	3.7	7.2	8.1
Some high school	6.8	10.3	10.0	9.3	5.5	13.0	2.4	3.2
High school diploma	10.2	19.0	25.0	23.3	24.7	35.2	7.2	29.0
Some college	28.8	36.2	20.0	46.5	26.0	25.9	28.9	38.7
College degree	15.3	24.1	23.3	9.3	13.7	11.1	18.1	16.1
Graduate degree	35.6	3.4	20.0	4.7	13.7	11.1	32.5	3.2
No response	1.7	0.0	0.0	2.3	4.1	0.0	3.6	1.6
Total	100.1	99.9	100.0	100.1	100.0	100.0	99.9	99.9
N's	59	58	60	43	73	54	83	62

on the recruitment of party leaders. Oklahoma is deviant from Kansas and Wisconsin with respect to the occupational categories of farmer/rancher, businessman, sales/clerical, and attorney. In each case the occupational composition of the Oklahoma leadership corps is the reverse of those in the other two states. Kansas and Oklahoma do not differ substantially in terms of professional occupations other than that of attorney. Similarly, in the manual-worker category Oklahoma and Kansas are parallel. Both differ markedly from Wisconsin in these categories in that a much higher proportion of Wisconsin Republican chairmen are in the "other professional" category than are Wisconsin Democratic chairmen. Also, while in Oklahoma and Kansas a higher percentage of Republican chairmen is in the laborer category than Democratic chairmen, in Wisconsin this condition is dramatically the reverse.

[21]Schlesinger, *loc. cit.*, p. 1125.

The explanation for some of these interstate differences is quite obvious. For instance, the more extensive industrial and manufacturing development of Wisconsin clearly explains the larger proportion of laborers and the smaller proportion of farmers among Wisconsin county chairmen in contrast to county leaders in Oklahoma and Kansas. That the interparty tendencies in Kansas and Wisconsin are largely similar, and generally dissimilar from Oklahoma, provides the interesting feature of Table 2. Tables 3 and 4 show education and income comparisons for both parties' chair-

TABLE 4

INTERSTATE VARIATIONS IN THE INCOME OF COUNTY PARTY LEADERS
(*In Percentages*)

	Oklahoma					Kansas			
	Democratic		Republican			Democratic		Republican	
Income Range	Chairmen	Co-Chairmen	Chairmen	Vice-Chairmen	Income Range	Chairmen	Vice-Chairmen	Chairmen	Vice-Chairmen
Less than $4,000	1.7	25.9	13.3	18.6	Less than $3,000	19.2	27.8	6.0	24.2
$4,000 to $6,000	11.9	10.3	13.3	16.3	$3,000 to $5,000	17.8	29.6	9.6	19.4
$6,000 to $8,000	8.5	17.3	16.7	9.3	$5,000 to $8,000	20.5	11.1	19.3	9.7
$8,000 to $10,000	16.9	13.8	16.7	16.3		17.8	7.4	13.3	4.8
More than $10,000	57.6	25.9	38.3	32.6		19.2	9.3	42.2	14.5
No response	3.4	6.9	1.7	7.0		5.5	14.8	9.6	27.4
Total	100.0	100.1	100.0	100.1		100.0	100.0	100.0	100.0
N's	59	58	60	43		73	54	83	62

men and co-chairmen in Oklahoma and Kansas. Here comparable data are not available for Wisconsin. However, they show that the generalizations which can be made for Oklahoma county leaders are the reverse of those which can be made for Kansas county leaders.

It seems likely that these interstate variations in the composition of Democratic and Republican county leadership are broadly related to the total political structures in the respective states, as well as to the differential compositions of the parties' supporters in these states. If we hypothesize that party leaders will tend to reflect in important ways the social characteristics of their supporters, then we can infer that interstate variations in party leadership reflect interstate differences in the electorates of the two parties. Unfortunately, we have no data describing the respective party supporters in these states. Whatever support we have for this hypothesis is based primarily on the national electorate and national political leaders, or on state legislators in predominantly urban two-party states. It seems doubtful that the Kansas and Oklahoma electorates as a whole differ very substantially, with the important exception that Kansas voters tend to vote Republican and Oklahoma voters tend to vote Democratic. Thus it is pertinent to suggest the significance of party dominance in the recruitment of party leadership.[22]

The channels of political success in Oklahoma have traditionally been through the machinery of the Democratic party; access to political power in Kansas has, except sporadically, been through identification with the Republican party. The active, ambitious, politically interested businessman, lawyer, or other professional man who is well-educated and well-paid could, in Oklahoma, best exploit his ambition or his talents in the Democratic party.[23] In fact, his esteem in the community might have been seriously damaged if he became identified as a Republican. When political parties are long in power, and their support is widely diffused in the political system, the composition of their leadership corps is increasingly likely to reflect heavy infiltration of individuals in the higher socioeconomic categories. The "better people" in the community will tend to gravitate toward political power, whether the Republican

---

[22]When an analysis of Oklahoma Democratic and Republican county chairmen by occupation and party dominance of counties is attempted the quantities in several cells of the table are very small even when occupational categories are combined, so that refined analysis may not be useful. This occurs because the number of Republican-dominant counties (defined as those in which Republican candidates won 75 per cent of the elections to the state House of Representatives between 1952-58) is so small. Such as it is, a breakdown by party dominance indicates that Democratic chairmen in Democratic-dominant counties conform in composition to the breakdown in Table 2, although the professional category (including lawyers) is somewhat higher. In Republican-dominant counties the proportion of Democratic chairmen in the farmer/rancher and businessman categories is somewhat higher than in Democratic-dominant counties, and the proportion of professionals is substantially lower. Also, a much larger proportion of Republican chairmen from Republican-dominant counties are farmer/ranchers and professionals than from Democratic-dominant districts, although the percentage of Republican chairmen from Democratic-dominant counties who are businessmen is higher than in Republican-dominant counties. On the whole, the analysis is not very conclusive, both because of the small number of Republican-dominant counties, and very likely because of the importance of the statewide pattern of politics, since the county chairman is not just a local party leader but an important linkage in the statewide organization.

[23]See Key, *Southern Politics* . . . , p. 432; and Seymour M. Lipset, *Political Man* (Garden City: Doubleday, 1960), p. 303.

or the Democratic party is dominant.[24] And, added to these considerations, state Republican leaders have often had difficulty in finding a business or professional man in a given county who was available to serve as county chairman for the very simple reason that such a large proportion of them count themselves as Democrats.

Political Experiences of County Party Leaders

Factors other than the socio-economic characteristics of party activists clearly affect the recruitment process for the selection of county leaders. The legitimacy of acquiring and holding a political position is affected by the degree to which individuals can claim to be of the community and by the incumbency of office. County party leaders tend to have been long-term residents of the counties in which they hold office: but also there tend to be important differences between the two parties' leadership corps insofar as length of residence and experience in office are concerned (see Table 5). Democratic county party leadership in Oklahoma tends to be more "home grown" than Republican leadership. While a sizable proportion of Republican leaders, like most Democratic chairmen and co-chairmen, have lived in their counties twenty years or more, a number of the newly appointed Republican county leaders are newcomers, some of whom got their initiation into politics in other parts of the country. One finds in the ranks of Republican chairmen, for instance, a young geophysicist recently resident in the state whose previous political experience was as a precinct chairman in Whittier, California; a former attorney for the federal government who retired to his boyhood home and took up politics; a lawyer, an engineer, a

[24]Of course, it is well known that individuals in business and professional occupations are over-represented in the occupancy of political positions. In connection with his study of Wisconsin party activists Epstein comments that "it may . . . be more important to note that many Democratic officers are business and professional men, rather than to emphasize how few they are relative to the number among Republican officers." See *op. cit.*, p. 89. Sawyer notes in his study of the Michigan Democratic state central committee, "the substantial increase in the number of people in the professional and managerial classes as one moves from the State Central Committee leadership group to the top leadership group," and the concomitant decline in the numbers of farmers and workers. See *op. cit.*, pp. 50-51. Sayre found both Democratic and Republican national committees dominated by businessmen. See Sayre, *loc. cit.*, p. 361. Weaver found that, with respect to precinct committeemen in ten downstate Illinois counties, "the committees of the two major parties in these counties recruit their membership from the various occupational strata in about the same way." See Weaver, *loc. cit.*, p. 80.

TABLE 5
Length of Residence in County and Years in Office of Oklahoma County Party Leaders

Characteristic	Democratic				Republican			
	Chairmen		Co-Chairmen		Chairmen		Vice-Chairmen	
	Number	Per Cent	Number	Per Cent	Number	Per Cent	Number	Per Cent
Years in County								
Entire life	27	45.8	27	46.6	23	38.3	15	34.9
At least 20 years	23	38.9	21	36.2	14	23.3	14	32.6
At least 15 years	2	3.4	3	5.2	5	8.3	1	2.3
At least 10 years	4	6.8	6	10.3	8	13.3	5	11.6
At least 5 years	3	5.1	1	1.7	10	16.7	7	16.3
Less than 5 years	0		0		0		1	2.3
Total	59	100.0	58	100.0	60	99.9	43	100.0
Years in Office								
Less than 1 year	6	10.2	1	1.7	29	48.3	20	46.5
1-2 years	22	37.3	26	44.8	20	33.3	10	23.3
3-5 years	13	22.0	20	34.5	4	6.7	9	20.9
6-10 years	13	20.0	10	17.3	6	10.0	3	7.0
More than 10 years	5	8.5	1	1.7	1	1.7	1	2.3
Total	59	100.0	58	100.0	60	100.0	43	100.0

sales manager, an office manager, and a chemist new to the state and to politics. It is also manifest from Table 5 that more than a half of the Democratic county leaders have served in office three years or more, while more than half of the Republican leaders have served less than three years. The very large proportion of Republican leaders who have served less than a year results in part from the fact that the Republican party has only recently filled county leadership posts in many counties and reflects the organizational development of Oklahoma Republicanism.[25]

An important feature of the political recruitment process is the operation of the principle of "availability." Leiserson points to the importance of this factor in observing how few elective politicians "come from a subordinate position in party organizations."[26] Availability as a selective factor in the recruitment process operates in such a way, Leiserson suggests, as to limit the extent to which party leaders run for elective public office because "they recognize, and the leaders of constituency organizations know, that competent party work alone does not constitute a qualification for a place on a winning ticket."[27]

> Local party workers tend to restrict their sights to the city council or county board, or to other executive boards or offices which con-

[25]Compare findings on Wisconsin in Epstein, *op. cit.*, p. 87.
[26]Leiserson, *op. cit.*, pp. 200-201.
[27]*Ibid.*, p. 201.

> stitute an advancement in their local position, rather than to aspire to a role in state or national politics. Perhaps the highest level which the locally oriented party workers normally reach is the state legislature, where they can promote projects of concern to their districts and protect the interests of the local party and community.[28]

One approach to the examination of this hypothesis is by analysis of the party-organization experience of public office-holders. It may be equally useful to examine it from the point of view of the party leaders themselves. To what extent, for instance, have county party leaders held elective or appointive public office, or, incidentally, prior party office? And, to what extent do county leaders aspire to run for public office?

TABLE 6
POLITICAL EXPERIENCE OF OKLAHOMA COUNTY LEADERS

TYPE OF POLITICAL EXPERIENCE	DEMOCRATIC				REPUBLICAN			
	CHAIRMEN		CO-CHAIRMEN		CHAIRMEN		VICE-CHAIRMEN	
	Number	Per Cent	Number	Per Cent	Number	Per Cent	Number	Per Cent
Held other party office	8	13.6	18	31.0	13	21.7	15	34.9
Held public office	23	38.9	6	10.3	14	23.3	3	7.0
Held both other party office and public office	3	5.1	3	5.2	3	5.0	0	
Never held other party office or public office	25	42.4	31	53.4	30	50.0	25	58.1
Total	59	100.0	58	99.9	60	100.0	43	100.0

The Oklahoma data suggest, first of all, that previous position in party officialdom or the holding of public office may reduce the individual's availability for county party leadership. It is clear from Table 6 that more than half of the county leaders in Oklahoma have never served in a previous political office, party or public. A higher proportion of Democratic chairmen has held public office for obvious reasons. Where county leaders have been elected to public office, or have served in other party offices, their experience has been predominantly at local levels. A tabulation of previous party and public offices held by county leaders, presented in Table 7, indicates that (1) those who have held party office tend to have held it at the precinct level — successful precinct leaders are to some degree promoted up; (2) most county leaders who have held elective public office (and some hold such offices coterminous with party leadership) have done so at the municipal and county levels; and (3) those who have held appointive public office have done so at the county and state levels.

[28]*Ibid.*

Of course, indications of offices held by county leaders, or evidence showing that a majority of party leaders had no previous office-holding experience, cannot themselves demonstrate that county leaders have not attempted to win office, or do not aspire to do so in the future. Losing an election is not as common for Democrats, and running for office is not as common for Republicans in Oklahoma as would be the case in more competitive states. Oklahoma leaders were asked, "Have you ever been a losing candidate for elective public office?" Tabulation of positive responses shows the following percentages:

Democratic chairmen	16.9
Democratic co-chairmen	8.6
Republican chairmen	20.0
Republican vice-chairmen	9.3

TABLE 7

PARTY AND PUBLIC OFFICES HELD BY OKLAHOMA COUNTY PARTY LEADERS
(*In Numbers*)

OFFICE	DEMOCRATIC LEADERS*	REPUBLICAN LEADERS*
Party Office		
Precinct	24	16
County	3	9
District	5	5
State	1	9
YDems/YGOP/Women's clubs	7	6
Total	40	45
Elective Public Office		
Municipal	16	10
County	15	6
State	3	1
National	0	0
Total	34	17
Appointive Public Offices		
Municipal	2	0
County	11	3
State	7	0
National	2	1
Total	20	4

*Each county leader was counted for each party or public office he held, which means, of course, that the total N's for this table are much higher than the total sample size. Though as Table 6 indicates, few county leaders held both public and party office, a sizable number held more than one party office, or more than one public office.

Furthermore, nearly half of those who had been defeated for elective public office had also been elected, so a marked increase in candidacy is not indicated.[29]

In addition, the degree of political aspiration among Oklahoma county leaders does not appear to be especially high. Here the data for Oklahoma county chairmen are illustrative, and the comparison with Epstein's Wisconsin data is particularly interesting.[30]

TABLE 8

POLITICAL ASPIRATION OF COUNTY CHAIRMEN
(*In Percentages*)

	OKLAHOMA COUNTY CHAIRMEN		WISCONSIN COUNTY CHAIRMEN	
POLITICAL ASPIRATION	DEMOCRATS	REPUBLICANS	DEMOCRATS	REPUBLICANS
Intend to run for elective public office	13.6	20.0	34.4	15.6
Desire to run for elective public office	23.7	40.0	48.4	23.4
N's	59	60	64	64

County leaders were asked about their political aspirations simply in terms of their intentions and their desires, and the percentage of positive responses is shown in Table 8. In addition to the generally somewhat lower degree of political aspiration among Oklahoma county chairmen, the table further suggests the function of party dominance for the political aspiration of party leaders.[31] Minority party chairmen in both states register a higher degree of aspiration than majority chairmen. Candidacy should be a more important factor for minority party members; majority party activists aspiring to unseat party incumbents are not likely to be chosen, or to remain county chairmen.

[29]It is interesting to note that Epstein (*op. cit.*, p. 187) found a substantially higher proportion of county chairmen had been defeated in elections in Wisconsin than were found in Oklahoma. He found that 54.7 per cent of the Democratic chairmen and 39.1 per cent of the Republican chairmen had campaigned unsuccessfully for public office.

[30]*Ibid.*

[31]In general, the degree of political aspiration among Democratic co-chairmen and Republican vice-chairmen is lower than for chairmen, but there is a distinct party difference. Democratic chairmen and co-chairmen do not differ much in their intention or desire to run for public office, but Republican vice-chairmen have a noticeably lower degree of aspiration than do Republican chairmen. Of all, the least aspiring category is that of Republican vice-chairmen, most of whom are housewives.

More than 40 per cent of the county chairmen in Oklahoma have not run for public office, do not intend to run, and do not desire to run; and in this Democratic and Republican chairmen do not differ significantly.[32] Indeed, the county party leader seems "more likely to seek his fortune through his party connections, and to carve his niche in life in his local community," than to seek or aspire to candidacy for public office.[33]

But the limited political aspirations and the local orientation of county party leaders ought not to obscure the important linkage the county leader provides between the local and the state and national party organizations. Epstein refers to the extent of county party-leader participation in state and national party conventions as an elementary index of the degree to which county leaders play roles in state and national party organizations. This kind of activity among county chairmen in Oklahoma exists at a lower frequency than in Wisconsin, and to about the same extent as in Kansas. Although somewhat higher proportions of both Democratic and Republican chairmen have been delegates to a state convention in Oklahoma (Democratic chairmen, 89.8 per cent; Republican chairmen, 86.7 per cent), nearly the same proportions as in Kansas have been delegates or alternates to their party's national convention (Democratic chairmen, 23.7 per cent; Republican chairmen, 8.3 per cent). In Wisconsin substantially higher proportions of county chairmen have attended state conventions as delegates, and much higher proportions of Republican chairmen have been delegates to their national convention than in either Kansas or Oklahoma.[34] In part the higher proportion of Democratic chairmen who have officially attended their national convention results from the larger membership of the Democratic convention. However, it does appear that, even so, grass-roots Democratic leaders tend to have a larger role in the deliberations of their national organization than Republicans.

---

[32]Compare Epstein, *op. cit.*, p. 91.

[33]Leiserson, *op. cit.*, p. 196.

[34]The comparable data for Kansas and Wisconsin are:

	Wisconsin County Chairmen	Kansas County Chairmen
Delegate to state convention:		
Democrats	95.3	71.2
Republicans	100.0	84.3
Delegates to national convention:		
Democrats	20.3	21.9
Republicans	21.9	8.4

Data for Wisconsin are from Epstein, *op. cit.*, p. 185. The Kansas data come from the unpublished CCH-sponsored study by Drury referred to in footnote 20.

The Role of the County Party Leader

We have suggested up to this point that among county party leaders high-status occupations are most predominant, and that county leaders seem both to have had limited office-holding experience and only temperate aspiration for public office. We have inferred that the county leader, while to some extent supplying an important linkage between the local party organization and the state and national party machinery, tends to be tied primarily to his party's cause in his own locality. It is appropriate to ask what role the county leader plays in his locality. Some have examined the activities of party leaders in campaigns, and others have attempted to assess the role of party leaders in candidate selection.[35] The latter course has been followed in this research.

County leaders were asked the question, "In your county, which of the following best describes what party leaders like yourself usually do with respect to the selection of party candidates for the Oklahoma state House of Representatives or state Senate?"[36] The results are reported in Table 9. In general, county leaders seem to regard candidate selection activity as at least of some importance in the performance of their role, although for about half of the Oklahoma county leaders such activity was confined to encouragement and persuasion.[37] Republican leaders, especially county chairmen, were involved to a greater degree than Democratic leaders.[38]

---

[35]For instance, see Frost, *loc. cit.*, pp. 221-35; and Epstein, *op. cit.*, pp. 92-93.

[36]The wording of the question is that of Epstein (*op. cit.*, p. 208).

[37]Epstein found that 86 per cent of the party officers for whom he had data in Wisconsin took some part in legislative candidate selection (*ibid.*, p. 93). Lee found that 53 per cent of the 58 California county chairmen for whom he had data "looked to the ranks of city, county, or school office-holders to seek candidates for state or national office," either "often" or "sometimes." He found no difference between Democratic and Republican chairmen. See Lee, *op. cit.*, p. 106.

[38]Drury found that a substantial proportion of Kansas county leaders had to search out candidates, and that Democratic leaders did so to a higher degree than Republican leaders. He asked, "Do you have to search out candidates, or do they file on their own accord?" The results in percentages, were:

	Republican Chairmen	Republican Vice-Chairmen	Democratic Chairmen	Democratic Vice-Chairmen
have to search	45.8	32.3	87.7	66.7
do not have to search	49.4	62.9	8.2	25.9
No answer	4.8	4.8	4.1	7.4

In addition, county party leaders appear to be interested in legislative business. Both Epstein and Drury found considerable professed contact with state legislators on the part of county party leaders, and the findings are the same for Oklahoma. Obviously, Oklahoma Democratic county leaders have more contact with legislators than do Republicans, and in Kansas the reverse is true although the party difference is not as great. For reference to the Kansas data see footnote 20.

Republicans in Oklahoma frequently find difficulty in convincing competent individuals to become their candidates, and much of their comment on questionnaires alluded to this difficulty. In one heavily Democratic county the Republican chairman said, "The Republican party has not had a candidate for the legislature for many years in [this] county . . . although individuals have been requested to run."

The county party leader's conception of his role in connection with candidate selection is clearly affected by the degree of political competitiveness in his county. The distribution arrayed in Table 10 needs to be interpreted in the light of the fact that all predominantly Republican counties are competitive, and all one-party counties are Democratic. The degree to which county leaders actively seek candidates for legislative elections clearly is reduced in one-party districts, where Democratic leaders may tend to remain neutral and Republican leaders may tend to feel helpless in the face of overwhelming odds.[39] In fact, there is impressionistic evidence from the questionnaires of the boredom of some Democratic leaders and the feeling of futility on the part of some Republican leaders. Furthermore, there is a relation between county leaders who take no part at all in candidate selection and political competitiveness. In one-party districts considerable proportions of both Democratic and Republican leaders rely on encouragement of candidates to run.

Above and beyond the county leader's conception of his proper role in the process of candidate selection, and probably partly independent of it, is the party leader's conception of his basic function. The party leader in a democratic competitive system plays a very difficult role; and it may be more difficult when the process in which he is involved does not conform to his normative standards. Both parties' county leaders, but especially the Republican's, frequently seem upset by the absence of two-party competitive standards. Many Republican leaders indicated that they went into politics in part to help build a two-party system in Oklahoma. But beyond this, conflicting demands on the party leader frequently lead him to orient his role in a particular direction. What are these conflicting demands? The political leader must constantly balance two very important demands on his ingenuity: he must maintain a viable

---

[39]This finding tends to support that of Seligman, who studied political recruitment in four legislative districts in Oregon. He found that "in areas safe for the majority party . . . party officials were least active in instigating or supporting candidates." See Lester G. Seligman, "Political Recruitment and Party Structure: A Case Study," *American Political Science Review,* 55 (March 1961), 77-86.

political organization, and he must wage campaigns. Part of his function is introversive — he must create and maintain working party machinery; and part of his function is extraversive — he must successfully move the party machinery into operation in campaigns against the other party. These two role demands are sufficiently separate in theory as to make it reasonable to presume that some party leaders will be oriented primarily toward their own party organizations, and that some will be oriented mainly in the direction of waging campaigns.[40]

In an effort to examine the differential role orientations of Oklahoma county party leaders, we asked each one to explain the most important things a county leader should do in order to be most effective in his job. Accordingly, insofar as possible county leaders were classified as either *organization-oriented* or *campaign-oriented.*

TABLE 9

PARTICIPATION OF OKLAHOMA COUNTY PARTY LEADERS IN LEGISLATIVE NOMINATIONS

Nature of Participation	Democratic				Republican			
	Chairmen		Co-Chairmen		Chairmen		Vice-Chairmen	
	Number	Per Cent	Number	Per Cent	Number	Per Cent	Number	Per Cent
Actively seek well-qualified candidates	17	22.1	16	16.8	29	34.5	19	28.8
Persuade well-qualified individuals to run	11	14.3	16	16.8	12	14.3	9	13.6
Encourage well-qualified individuals to run	31	40.3	34	35.8	31	36.9	19	28.8
Try to persuade individuals not to enter the primary against a well-qualified candidate already in the race	7	9.0	15	15.8	5	6.0	4	6.1
No part at all; individual candidates just come forward on their own to run in the primary	10	13.0	13	13.7	3	3.6	11	16.7
No response	1	1.3	1	1.1	4	4.8	4	6.1
Total responses*	77	100.0	95	100.0	84	100.1	66	100.1

*The total number of responses equals more than the sample size for each column because some individuals selected more than one type of participation, even though the questionnaire specified that the respondent select the *most important* type of participation.

[40]See Robert E. Lane, *Political Life* (Glencoe: Free Press, 1959), p. 307.

TABLE 10
PARTICIPATION IN CANDIDATE SELECTION AND POLITICAL COMPETITIVENESS OF COUNTIES
(In Percentages)

	Democratic Leaders			Republican Leaders		
	Highly Competitive	Semi-Competitive	One-Party	Highly Competitive	Semi-Competitive	One-Party
Actively seek well-qualified candidates	23.5	18.9	16.3	30.6	37.2	22.2
Persuade well-qualified individuals to run	20.6	15.8	11.6	22.2	12.8	8.3
Encourage well-qualified individuals to run	35.3	35.8	44.2	36.1	30.8	36.1
Try to persuade individuals not to run	11.8	14.7	9.3	2.8	7.7	5.6
No part at all	5.9	14.7	16.3	5.6	6.4	19.4
No response	2.9	0.0	2.3	2.8	5.1	8.3
Total	100.0	99.9	100.0	100.1	100.0	99.9
N's	34	95	43	36	78	36

The organization-oriented county leader is one who sees his most important function as that of building and developing the party organization itself. He believes that he should maintain contact with and the loyalty of precinct chairmen, keep harmony in the county organization, coordinate with the district and state party leaders, encourage party members to be more active in party affairs, be fair and impartial with respect to primary candidates, and equitably and judiciously dispense the party patronage.[41]

The campaign-oriented party leader is oriented principally in the direction of fighting the interparty battle. He thinks of his job primarily in terms of raising campaign funds, recruiting candidates to run in elections, preparing voter lists, urging citizens to register and vote, arranging party and public meetings for candidates and managing the party's campaign in his county.

That these broad role differentiations exist operationally is indicated by the data presented in Table 11. The considerable propor-

[41]Although the method of classification is different and probably more rigorous, the findings of Harned suggest the possibility that the organization-oriented role may in part be played by individuals characterized by distinctive personality syndromes. She found that ward committeemen in New Haven, Connecticut, who scored high on an "organizational emphasis scale" and low on an "ideological partisanship scale" tended to be more authoritarian. See Louise Harned, "Authoritarian Attitudes and Party Activity," *Public Opinion Quarterly*, 25 (Fall 1961), 393-99.

tion of Republican chairmen who defined their role in other ways is a consequence in part of the large percentage of new Republican chairmen who could not succintly define their job, or who did so in highly diffuse and universalistic terms. In the case both of Republican and Democratic co- and vice-chairmen, many were not able to define their job at all, and some frankly admitted it on their questionnaires. Inadequate role definition on the part of county leaders in all probability reflects the generally low level of political competition, the incipiency of party organization in the state, and the incomplete performance on the part of state leaders in replacing incompetent leaders or in clearly defining their role for them. In general, Democratic leaders have a clearer conception of their role than Republican leaders. To some degree Democratic leaders are more campaign-oriented than Republicans. The slightly greater organizational emphasis given by Republican leaders may be the result of temporary organizational demands in a party just beginning to build party machinery. In addition, it seems likely that the most effective county leader will be both organization- and campaign-oriented, that is, will effectively attempt to resolve his conflicting role demands; and if that be true the Republican leaders compare favorably with the Democratic leaders.

It was suggested earlier that these basic role conceptions may be partially independent of the activity of party leaders in candidate selection. When organization-oriented and campaign-oriented county leaders are compared on the basis of the nature of their participation in legislative nominations, the differences between them

TABLE 11

Role Orientations of Oklahoma County Party Leaders

Role Orientation	Democratic				Republican			
	Chairmen		Co-Chairmen		Chairmen		Vice-Chairmen	
	Number	Per Cent	Number	Per Cent	Number	Per Cent	Number	Per Cent
Organization-oriented	21	35.6	25	43.1	23	38.3	11	25.6
Campaign-oriented	15	25.4	13	22.4	9	15.0	5	11.6
Both organization- and campaign-oriented	12	20.3	8	14.0	13	21.7	9	20.9
Other	2	3.4	6	10.3	13	21.7	6	13.9
No response	9	15.3	6	10.3	2	3.3	12	27.9
Total	59	100.0	58	100.1	60	100.0	43	99.9

are not significant, although a somewhat higher proportion of campaign-oriented leaders *encourage* individuals to run, while a somewhat higher proportion of organization-oriented leaders plays no part at all in candidate selection.

It might be expected on a common-sense basis that party leaders in counties where their party is dominant should be more organization-oriented than in counties where the other party is dominant; that party leaders in urban areas should be more campaign-oriented than in rural areas; and that party leaders should be more campaign-oriented in competitive counties than in one-party counties. The Oklahoma data indicate that only the first of these propositions is wholly correct. A greater proportion of Democratic leaders in Democratic-dominant counties is organization-oriented than campaign-oriented, as is a greater proportion of Republican leaders in Republican-dominant counties (see Table 12). Party dominance

TABLE 12
ROLE ORIENTATIONS OF OKLAHOMA COUNTY PARTY LEADERS AND PARTY DOMINANCE OF COUNTIES
(In Percentages)

	DEMOCRATIC LEADERS		REPUBLICAN LEADERS	
ROLE ORIENTATION	DEMOCRATIC-DOMINANT COUNTIES	REPUBLICAN-DOMINANT COUNTIES	DEMOCRATIC-DOMINANT COUNTIES	REPUBLICAN-DOMINANT COUNTIES
Organization-oriented	65.1	50.0	68.4	75.0
Campaign-oriented	34.9	50.0	31.6	25.0
Total	100.0	100.0	100.0	100.0
N's	63	10	38	8

is operationally defined as those counties in which the dominant party won at least 75 per cent of the elections to the state House of Representatives between 1952 and 1958.

In the case of differences between urban and rural counties, urban party leaders appear on the whole to be somewhat more organization-oriented in Oklahoma.[42] In the Republican case, however, the difference between urban and rural leaders is slight, while urban Democratic leaders tend to be substantially more organization-

[42]Urban counties were defined as all counties in Standard Metropolitan Areas, and all counties with urban aggregates of 2,500 or more and a ratio of urban population of more than 55 per cent. Counties with urban aggregates of 2,500 or more but with a ratio of urban population of less than 55 per cent, and all counties without an urban aggregate of 2,500 or more were defined as rural.

oriented than rural Democratic leaders. The urban-rural difference among Democratic leaders may not be too difficult to account for: in some rural areas in Oklahoma there has been, and still is, very little Democratic party organization at all, and in urban areas the patronage functions and the exploitation of party perquisites hav sometimes supplanted campaign activity on the part of party leaders.

Similarily, party leaders from counties characterized by differential political competitiveness do not differ in line with expectations.[43] A very large proportion of Republican leaders in highly competitive counties (and this includes all the predominantly Republican counties) is organization-oriented. This may again be a ramification of the emphasis on party organization taking place in the Oklahoma Republican party. Again, more than half of the Republican leaders from Democratic one-party areas are campaign-oriented; and here it may be that Republican leaders have taken the campaigner role because of the impossibility of viable Republican organization, especially where campaigning alone seems to pay off in presidential elections. On the other hand, a higher proportion of Democratic leaders is campaign-oriented in highly competitive counties than in others.

Conclusion

Channels of access to political power are provided by party organizations. When the majority party is dominant in a political subsystem, high socio-economic status elements of the population are

[43]For this analysis counties were classified as "highly competitive," "semi-competitive," and "one-party." Highly competitive counties were those in which both parties won at least one election to the House of Representatives between 1952 and 1958, and those where each party won at least 40 per cent of the vote in 50 per cent of the elections during that period. Semi-competitive counties were those in which the minor party did not receive at least 40 per cent of the vote in any one of the elections for the legislature, but where the minor party contested at least 25 per cent of the elections between 1952 and 1958. One-party districts were those in which there were no general election contests for House seats in those years. In classifying counties I have benefited from the work of Heinz Eulau. See his "The Ecological Basis of Party Systems: The Case of Ohio," *Midwest Journal of Political Science*, 1 (August, 1957), 125-35. My colleagues, David Gold and John Schmidhauser, have correctly pointed out some of the weaknesses involved in classifying districts in terms of political competitiveness solely on the basis of state legislative elections (see Gold and Schmidhauser, "Urbanization and Party Competition: The Case of Iowa," *Midwest Journal of Political Science*, 4 (February, 1960), 62-75. A more refined classification of Oklahoma counties would have been desirable, but for this purpose the present scheme seems adequate.

likely to be inordinately represented among party leaders of the dominant party whether it be labeled Democratic or Republican. But county party leadership is not essentially a part of the recruitment pipeline for public office in the sense that few county leaders have held public office, and aspiration for elective public office is not particularly high among county leaders although minority party leaders have a higher aspiration for office. Finally, party leaders at the county level are differently oriented in their conceptions of their political leadership role, proportionately tending to be more organization-oriented where their party is dominant and more campaign-oriented where the other party is dominant.

Leadership Role Perceptions

Samuel J. Eldersveld

It is one thing for a party leader to have a clear conception of the primary goal of the group; it is quite another, although related, matter for him to have a clear perception of his personal task or role as the holder of a position in the hierarchy. His own interpretation of his job is involved, as well as a recognition of the expectations others have about his job. Further, for an organization to be ideally effective, there should be clarity in the comprehension and evaluation of tasks associated with the positions held by others at all levels of the party structure. Although no one perspective can be considered more vital to group success than another, one would certainly hypothesize that an organization such as a political party loses effectiveness if roles are misperceived or improperly evaluated. A party with precinct activists, for example, who differ in their own role perception from that assumed by the top elite, may find itself with no effective cadre of workers implementing command strategy in the field, or with a set of precinct leaders operating independently and accountable to no central command.

We approached the study of roles empirically by asking leaders at each level to define and evaluate their own tasks as well as those

---

Reprinted from *Political Parties: A Behavioral Analysis* (Chicago: Rand McNally and Company, 1964), pp. 245-46, 253-71, by permission of the publisher.

of persons holding other positions in the party structure. We could philosophize at great length on party leaders' role perceptions, drawing upon a rich body of social-psychological and political literature. We were, of course, interested in the degree of bureaucratization within the party, the number of leaders who believed they possessed specialized skills (organizational, financial, communicative, etc.), how much feeling existed for personal responsibility in party decision-making, how much professionalism and amateurism was found, and many other role-behavioral problems. At the outset, however, prior to such analyses, we wished to look at the statements made by party leaders in attempting to explain their roles. In probing, we usually asked some variant of this basic question put to precinct leaders: "Aside from your routine duties, what do you consider to be your most important job or task?" . . .

One would expect the precinct leader, in his role perception, to exemplify the "power-productive" character of the party structure. We have seen that the district chairman operated in all three role contexts — winning power, running the organization, and interacting with the community, especially as an ideological leader. The executive board, however, saw itself primarily as an organizational-integrating force. Since "the votes are in the precincts," we might assume that the vote-mobilization task would be impressed on the minds of the precinct leaders. As Avery Leiserson has put it: "the central function of the precinct organization is to carry the precinct for the party"; and, "the display of reliability and efficiency (by the precinct leader), rather than of original ideas and personal prominence before the electorate, is statistically the approved way to start up the ladder within the organization."[1]

Yet, an examination of empirical facts indicates precinct leaders' roles cannot be defined so simply. When asked what they considered their major task, a majority did not respond immediately that it was delivering votes. The actual distribution for the two parties, using our previous categories, is given in Table 1. From this distribution one can see that precinct leaders had by no means accepted the doctrine that their *primary* task was vote production. They actually saw themselves in an important "adaptive leadership" role in the community, much like the district chairmen — a role perception executive board members generally did not share. Thus at the apex and at the base of the hierarchy the parties contained leadership conscious of its interactive potential with the public. Less than one-fifth saw this interaction as exclusively part of the old New Deal

[1]Avery Leiserson, *Parties and Polities* (New York: Knopf, 1958), pp. 188, 192.

TABLE 1

Distribution of Role Perceptions for Precinct Leaders

Roles	Democrats	Republicans	Total
Vote mobilizer	45%	45%	45%
Ideological mentor	24	23	24
Social-economic welfare promoter	22	14	18
Have no role at all	9	12	10
Not ascertained	0	6	3

era stereotype of getting jobs for people, attending funerals, fixing traffic tickets, and providing for the needy. Though some still insisted on the priority of the service role, one-fourth thought of themselves in the "ideological mentor" role. That is, they felt their job was to define and explain public issue alternatives to the voters, to educate and inform the public about government generally, to instigate neighborhood action, and to fight for particular social legislation. This does not mean that they had no sense of responsibility for vote mobilization — after all, they were aware, theoretically, of the pressure from above to keep voter records up to date, engage in campaign activities, and conduct house-to-house canvasses. But at least 40 per cent of the precinct leaders either considered such voting efforts secondary, or they took a broad-gauged view of how the party was to maximize its voting appeals. This view of their own role was held also by the two state chairmen, Mr. Staebler and Mr. Feikens, though not as clearly articulated by either. From our interviews with district chairmen it was obvious that only two of three of them had this conception of the precinct leader's task. With few exceptions, district chairmen said that precinct leaders were important in the organization, and as influential, or more so, as executive board members. Their frame of reference, however, was different. District chairmen referred to the collective voting power of precinct leaders (in the party convention), to the importance of precinct organizations in rounding up the vote, and only rarely, and then ambiguously, to the fact that precinct leaders were "closest to the people" and "in touch with public opinion." Only two district chairment indicated that personal attention was given to training precinct leaders for the assumption of a community leadership or social welfare promotion role.

An interesting question arises about the efficient structuring of a party organization when only 45 per cent of those at the grass roots say their primary job is vote mobilization. On the surface this might seem dsyfunctional to the success-maximization goal of the party. Yet, this must remain an open question until further analyses are made. It may very well be that the ideological mentor and social-welfare promoter is just as efficient in winning or holding the precinct for the party as the overt vote mobilizer. A further question which must also be held in abeyance pending further analysis and interpretation is whether a party system with this type of role structure from top to bottom is not in essence a better balanced set of groups functioning more meaningfully in the society and the polity than a party system in which the political groups are exclusively role-conscious in a power-winning sense. Certainly, despite allegations about party politics in the United States to the contrary, it is significant that at the lowest echelons a sizeable percentage of activists had resisted the doctrine of the decline of ideology and saw as most salient their job as ideological surrogates for the community.

A revealing by-product of investigation was the set of views of party leaders concerning the importance of their leadership in influencing the political behavior of the public. We asked respondents to rank the opinions of "leaders of a political party" (as well as the opinions of "close friends," "family members," "religious leaders," "union leaders," "employers and business leaders," "nationality or racial group leaders") as "very important," "somewhat important," or "not very important" in "helping people decide how to vote." The relative self-esteem of party leaders can be seen in Table 2.

Party leaders tended to have a higher esteem of their own opinion influence than did the public. This perception correlated well with the insistence of a large number of precinct leaders on their role of community leadership and interaction.

TABLE 2

Ranking of Importance of Leaders' Opinions by Party (Precinct) Leaders and the Public

	Precinct Leaders	Public Cross-Section*
Party leaders' opinions:		
Very important	45%	19%
Somewhat important	34	32
Not very important	20	49
Which opinions most important?		
Party leaders	24	21
Union leaders	26	7
Family members	17	25
Nationality or racial leaders	12	2
Close friends	10	9
Religious leaders	6	14
Employers and business leaders	2	7

* Percentage of those whose opinion could be ascertained.

The image of the public differed substantially from that of the party leadership. At least 25 per cent of the public was unsure of the opinion influence role of various sectors of community leadership. But those who did commit themselves felt that union and nationality, or racial, leaders were less important than did precinct leaders, and placed somewhat more importance on the role of religious and business leaders. This differential image of political reality raises interesting questions about the perspectives of party leadership in activating the vote. This matter of the "realism" of party leadership will be examined with more care and detail in an ensuing section. Here it is important to note two tendencies. One is that the majority of grass roots party leadership sensed the importance of its own influence role. The other observation is that, despite this tendency, one-fifth of the local leadership felt they were not influential at all, corresponding to the finding that 13 per cent of precinct leaders were unable to explicate their primary role in the party structure. The implications of these tendencies will be analyzed in Part IV in our discussion of the "functional" competence or relevance of the party machine in the social and political system.

Role expectations or assumptions apparently varied greatly among party leaders, particularly precinct leaders. A central question to be posed, therefore, is why this variation, and under what political and social conditions does one or another type of role-perception motif develop? What types of precinct leaders in what organizational and/or social context are inclined to see themselves as "ideological mentors," "welfare promoters," and "vote mobilizers"?

Congressional district organizations differed greatly in the emphasis used by precinct leaders in defining their roles. Among Democrats, for example, three-fifths of those in the 15th District but only one-third in the 1st District defined their role primarily as vote mobilizing. On the other hand, over 50 per cent in the 1st District considered themselves ideological mentors, while less than 10 per cent in the 16th District assumed this role. Similarly, among Republicans, the highest percentage of vote mobilizers (75 per cent of precinct leaders) were found in the relatively competitive 14th District, while only one-fourth were in the 16th District. The ideological mentor role did not vary as greatly among Republicans, though the 16th was high (34 per cent) and the 13th was low (11 per cent). Thus, in both parties, in districts where the smallest percentage of precinct leaders declared their job was vote mobilization, the highest percentage claimed to be ideological leaders. There was also a tendency in both parties for precinct leaders in those districts which were least sure Democratic to be vote mobilizers.[2]

Significant, too, for both parties, were those districts in which the chairman was apparently most conscious about precinct delegates, asserted they were very important, claimed he saw them regularly, *and* had articulated a district organizational apparatus through which precinct leaders, he said, were consulted on party policy, trained for party work, and informed on party affairs. In these districts, two Democratic and two Republican, practically no precinct leaders replied "nothing" when asked to define their primary tasks or duties. There is a strong suggestion here, then, that these variations in role perception were linked to the competitive status of the district and the organizational plan for precinct leader communication and indoctrination.

An examination of precinct leaders' roles by the competitive status of the precinct itself (Table 3) adds to this analysis, and to some extent questions it, by indicating more precisely that both parties had the highest concentrations of vote mobilizing in sure Republican precincts. Although marginal precincts had a high proportion of Democratic vote mobilizers, they were not the highest.

The "get out the vote" doctrine had been communicated to the precinct leaders for the same types of districts, but with different strategy goals in mind — the Republicans seeking to hold their bastions of precinct voting power, the Democrats seeking to attack where they were weakest. Of course, role perception is not the same as "role activation," and it remains to be seen by later analysis to what extent precinct leaders' activities coincide with role evaluations. Nevertheless, it was not the doubtful precincts which revealed the heaviest concentration of overt vote mobilizers, but the definitely Republican precincts, indicating that the Democrats were competing with a vote-conscious set of percinct leaders in their weakest areas of strength. These data suggest also that the sure Republican precincts were the locale in which there may have been the most straightforward "struggle for votes," while in other precincts other types of leadership activity may have been more important. Finally, the Republican leaders were least conscious of their

[2]The one important exception was the Democratic 17th, which was somewhat marginal but had a fairly even distribution of precinct leaders in all three role categories. This may have been due to the personal battle between the congresswoman in this district and the district chairman, with the former developing her own campaign organization, she maintained. It also must be remembered that such a balancing of roles may not in any sense be assumed as dysfunctional to party success in a district.

TABLE 3

PRECINCT LEADERS' ROLE PERCEPTIONS BY PRECINCT COMPETITIVE STATUS
(PROPORTIONS OF LEADERS IN EACH PRECINCT TYPE)

	DEMOCRATS				REPUBLICANS			
Precinct type	*Vote mobilizers*	*Ideological mentors*	*Welfare promoters*	*No role*	*Vote mobilizers*	*Ideological mentors*	*Welfare promoters*	*No role*
Sure Democratic	37%	30%	28%	5%	41%	22%	10%	19%
Sure Republican	66	10	7	14	60	11	9	9
Doubtful	47	20	20	13	36	36	26	3

role in the sure Democratic precincts: almost one-fifth had no role perception at all.

When we join our data on the party career status of precinct leaders with role perceptions we find two career classes (those who had been party regulars and those who had achieved some upper mobility status) were least conscious of a vote-mobilization role (Table 4). It appeared that those precinct leaders who had served a long time in the organization without moving upward continued to work at the precinct level but perceiving themselves primarily as more broad-gauged community leaders. Vote mobilization became secondary to a great majority, about 70 per cent, of them. Similarly, from two-thirds to three-fourths of the top careerist elite among the precinct leaders, who had achieved higher positions while continuing as precinct leaders, also had a broad-gauged role perception. Vote mobilization was secondary to them, also. On the other hand, noncareerists were still relatively vote-mobilization-conscious, and thus of real value to the party machine despite their sporadic activity. But they included the largest percentage — about 30 per cent — of those who perceived themselves as having no role at all. It was the "informed influential" and "potential careerist" groups who were the vote mobilizers — those who were hoping for some eventual formal position in the hierarchy, who saw getting out the vote as the role most likely to result in political advancement. Above all, these data reveal again the great variety of personal role interpretations which prevail in a party, and suggest that the leader's own image of his present and future relationship to the hierarchy conditions his definition of his primary role. Perhaps vote mobilization is still the accepted avenue for recognition for the aspiring newcomer. But long-time precinct leaders who had begun to ascend in the hierarchy were more likely to define their job in less narrow terms. Perhaps this was because they visualized the party's place in the community in broader terms than winning elections, or they had a clearer view of how parties win elections.

In pursuing this last possibility, we correlated our data on party goal perspectives with role perceptions, with striking results (Table 5). It is clear that a close correspondence obtained between the two sets of perspectives. Those who did not articulate party goals in terms of winning power did not define their own role in vote-mobilization terms. And those with no party goal perspective tended to be unable to explain the expectations concerning their own role. Almost 10 per cent of precinct leaders fitted into both categories and demonstrated complete unawareness of party or their own job requirements — a significant finding in itself. On the other hand,

TABLE 4

CAREER STATUS AND ROLE PERCEPTIONS OF PRECINCT LEADERS
(PROPORTIONS OF LEADERS IN EACH CAREER STATUS)

	DEMOCRATS				REPUBLICANS			
Career status	*Vote mobilizers*	*Ideological mentors*	*Welfare promoters*	*No role*	*Vote mobilizers*	*Ideological mentors*	*Welfare promoters*	*No role*
Top organization mobiles	22%	17%	61%	0%	38%	54%	4%	0%
Informal influentials	60	8	22	11	68	0	21	5
Nonmobile regulars	29	43	29	0	32	14	32	7
Potential careerists	57	38	6	0	43	28	8	20
Noncareerists	44	20	0	32	63	0	6	31

those who were very conscious of the party goal of winning power did not necessarily see their own role as primarily vote mobilization. Fully 50 per cent saw themselves as ideological mentor or social and economic welfare promoter. This finding seriously questions the assumption that the power-oriented party leader is single-minded in his devotion to vote maximization.

There seemed, in fact, to be two distinct types of grass roots party leaders from the standpoint of role perspectives, perhaps also two types of doctrine on the meaning of a party leadership role. While there was considerable evidence that the party did communicate the concept of vote mobilization, especially in the recent joiners and upward aspiring, and in certain competitive areas and specialized organizational contexts, yet this doctrine was by no means uniform. It appeared that for many party regulars and those with some achieved status, though they were aware that the *party* goal was power, they might or might not take the view that their own role was an expanded one involving much more than merely producing votes.

There was undoubtedly also a tendency for leaders from certain social strata and backgrounds to assume particular role interpretations (Table 6). But for three variables (race, sex, and religion) these differences seemed to be party-conditioned. Negro Democrats were not as frequently vote mobilizers as are white Democrats, though the same distinction was not as true among Republicans. It is interesting that practically one-half of the Negro Democrats saw themselves in an ideological role, while little more than one-tenth of the Republican Negroes did. Sex functioned in contradictory ways also in the two party hierarchies, Democratic women leaders infrequently defining their role as vote mobilizing (19 per cent) compared to 64 per cent of Republican women. The Democratic women tended to be ideological leaders in role perceptions. Catholics again defined their roles differently in both parties — a majority were vote mobilizers in the Democratic party but many fewer in the Republican party.

For three factors (education, nationality, and family economic status) the differences seemed to be basic and uniform for both parties. Thus, it is significant that one found those leaders with only an elementary-school background most likely unable to articulate any personal role. Similarly, leaders with a northwestern European background were more inclined to think of themselves as vote mobilizers in both parties than those from a central, southern, or eastern European heritage. Middle-income leaders were somewhat more inclined to be vote mobilizers, although a party difference was also

TABLE 5

Party Goal Perspectives and Role Perceptions of Precinct Leaders (Proportions of Leaders in Each Goal Category)

	Democrats				Republicans			
Party goal perspectives	*Vote mobilizers*	*Ideological mentors*	*Welfare promoters*	*No role*	*Vote mobilizers*	*Ideological mentors*	*Welfare promoters*	*No role*
Power salients	44%	24%	27%	5%	64%	12%	7%	5%
Idealists	0	53	41	0	0	54	34	8
Unoriented	0	33	0	67	0	6	0	94

TABLE 6

PERSONAL CHARACTERISTICS AND ROLE PERCEPTIONS OF PRECINCT LEADERS (PROPORTIONS OF LEADERS IN EACH DEMOGRAPHIC CATEGORY)

	DEMOCRATS				REPUBLICANS			
	Vote mobilizers	*Ideological mentors*	*Welfare promoters*	*No role*	*Vote mobilizers*	*Ideological mentors*	*Welfare promoters*	*No role*
Race								
White	51%	17%	20%	11%	45%	25%	11%	11%
Negro	25	47	28	0	40	14	30	17
Sex								
Male	49	19	20	10	39	26	17	10
Female	19	52	29	0	64	11	4	18
Education								
Elementary	45	5	30	20	44	0	0	25
High school	46	22	22	10	32	30	25	11
College	43	38	16	0	53	23	9	9
Religion								
Catholic	52	17	17	12	24	35	12	18
Protestant	40	29	31	0	46	21	16	11
Nationality								
Northwestern European	56	5	29	9	47	20	7	16
Central, southern and eastern European	43	30	12	16	35	25	20	12
Family income								
Under $6,000	45	32	23	0	40	12	10	26
$6-10,000	53	9	31	7	47	28	25	0
Over $10,000	30	39	3	24	40	32	12	8
Union membership								
Belongs	43	22	19	16	43	12	12	24
Officer	48	22	30	0	*	*	*	*
Not a member	47	29	21	0	44	25	15	7

*Too few cases for analysis.

noticeable here — the wealthy Democrats were those who saw no personal role, while the poor Republicans had the same role perception. It may be that these were the deviants in role perception in both parties, their role interpretations reflecting an awareness that they did not fit into the party's socio-economic profile.

Union members were an unusual group within both parties — representing almost 70 per cent of the Democratic precinct leaders and 30 per cent of the Republicans. Union officers had clear role perceptions, but it is strange that relatively high percentages of nonofficer union members in both parties had difficulty (or skepticism) in defining their roles as leaders of a political party. This may have been due to ambivalence about party work, or the fact that they had been recruited for party work, or agreed to undertake party work with considerable reluctance or without adequate understanding of party tasks. They may also, of course, have had grave doubts about the efficacy of party precinct activity.

Returning to our "subcoalitional" and "deviant" analysis of the party structures, we found no exclusive preoccupation by subgroup representatives with winning votes. There was a good deal of overt commitment so far as own role is concerned with promotion of individual welfare as well as with ideological objectives (Table 7). Negroes, Poles, and Irish in the Democratic structure articulated roles highly suggestive of subgroup consciousness. Only the business and professional Democrats were not group-welfare-conscious. There was much less awareness of own role as well as much less concern for promoting social and economic welfare in the Republican subcoalitional structures.

The white labor element in the Republican party was a peculiar group. They were split — 43 per cent seeing no role for themselves, 46 per cent saying they were vote mobilizers. The English as a Republican subgroup were almost as divided. On the Democratic side the business and professionals were also split, but they were conscious of a role for themselves — 50 per cent vote mobilizers, 43 per cent ideologues. The Irish Democrats divided a different way — 50 per cent vote mobilizers, 44 per cent interested in social and economic welfare promotion.

The "deviants" in both parties, except for the German Democrats (who seemed to be ideologues) were as vote-mobilization-conscious as other subgroups. The English Democrats were particularly vote-conscious. Recruitment of deviants, thus, did not seem to mean that activists from these deviant groups would be less susceptible to indoctrination by the party in the success-maximization principle.

Democratic liberals were much less vote-conscious in role inter-

TABLE 7

ROLE PERCEPTIONS OF SUBCOALITIONAL AND DEVIANT GROUPS
(PRECINCT LEADERS)
(PROPOSITIONS OF LEADERS IN EACH SUBCOALITION)

Democratic Subgroups	Vote Mobilizers	Ideological Mentors	Welfare Promoters	No Role
Negroes	25%	47%	28%	0%
Poles	38	6	32	25
Irish	50	0	44	6
Other labor				
Officers	27	33	40	0
Nonofficers	65	15	0	20
Business and professional whites	50	43	7	0
All union members	43	22	19	16
All Germans	0	91	9	0
All English, Welsh, and Scottish	64	0	18	18

Republican Subgroups	Vote Mobilizers	Ideological Mentors	Welfare Promoters	No Role
Business-managerial whites	50%	30%	11%	9%
Other white collar (whites, northwestern European)	35	18	18	29
Labor whites	46	11	0	43
Negroes	40	14	30	17
All Germans	65	4	4	27
All English, Welsh and Scottish	43	7	11	39
Irish and Poles	39	33	28	0

pretations than were Republican conservatives. We arrived at this conclusion after an analysis of the role perceptions of the consistent liberals and conservatives in each party, contrasted to those who were inconsistent or took middle-of-the-road positions on current issues (Table 8). The two issues used here were foreign aid and medical assistance through governmental action. The data revealed that one-third of the Democratic liberals viewed themselves as vote mobilizers, in contrast to 63 per cent of the consistent Republican conservatives. In role definition, therefore, the conservatives seemed more alert to their vote-production task as party leaders. Perhaps more surprising is the fact that such a small percentage — no more than one-fifth or one-sixth of the consistent "ideologues" — actually assumed an *ideological* leadership role. This attests again to the low level of ideological saliency for many leaders. The Democrats were more inclined to be welfare promoters, the Republicans to be interested in votes. With 12 per cent of the Democratic liberals inarticulate on role, the consistent liberals seemed somewhat more confused than did the consistent conservatives. It was the ideological "fence-straddler" who was more vote-conscious and aware of his role in the Democratic party, while the Republican "fence-straddler" seemed less aware of his role and less inclined to be alert to his job of rounding up the votes in the precinct.

The power apex of each party was in charge of personnel with fairly clear role perceptions. They were aware of their jobs in a "power-productive," "community leadership," and managerial-organizational sense. Perhaps the Democrats in the Detroit area were more alert to their community adaptation responsibilities than were the Republicans. The internal management problems which beset a district chairman, however, were such in both parties that the top elite needed to concentrate the great proportion of its time on coordination, communication, and harmonizing the elements of dissension and factionalism in a local party structure. The secondary cadre of board members were strictly communicative links and representative agents of the precincts, performing organizational tasks of oversight and liaison.

It was at the base of the structure that one found a wide and unexpected role proliferation. The precincts in both parties were led by men and women with great variation in role interpretation. A majority did not see their *primary* task as vote maximization. Many felt they were ideological leaders or educators in the community, or charged first of all with the task of attending to social and economic demands of the party's constituent clientele groups. This may have been the result of the subcoalitional character of party structures.

TABLE 8

Ideology and Role Perceptions of Precinct Leaders (Proportions of Leaders in Each Ideology Category)

	Democrats				Republicans			
	Vote mobilizers	*Ideological mentors*	*Welfare promoters*	*No role*	*Vote mobilizers*	*Ideological mentors*	*Welfare promoters*	*No role*
Consistent liberals	37%	16%	35%	12%	*	*	*	*
Consistent conservatives	*	*	*	*	63%	22%	13%	0%
Inconsistent or middle of the road	50	43	7	0	29	29	20	16
Don't know, and not ascertainable	63	19	15	0	58	18	3	6

*Too few cases for analysis.

Over 10 per cent saw themselves as having no role at all. This means that the command posts in the field were populated with leaders who saw their tasks differently, however well they might perform as leaders. Why they differed in role definition is not absolutely clear, but the data suggest that the type of district party elite to which they were subordinate, and by which they were indoctrinated, may be of some relevance. Further, that the type of precinct, competitively, in which they found themselves may also be relevant. Then, too, the length of tenure in party work and the extent of their upward mobility in the hierarchy seems important — interestingly enough those who were newcomers were more likely to call themselves "vote mobilizers," while the others might define their role less narrowly. Finally, the leader's social and personal background and subgroup connections may also be related. The proliferation of role perceptions, explicable by these variables — organizational status, political milieu, personal characteristics — and so closely linked to one's view of the party's goal as well as to one's own career aspirations suggests that it is indeed a diffuse organizational and personal context by which roles are assumed.

Three observations seem overriding in this analysis. A minority of precinct leaders parroted the classical doctrine of students of party politics that precinct leaders had as their major task "getting out the vote." Second, parties did not communicate one particular role conception to rank-and-file leaders. The party line, if there was one, was confused and poorly communicated. There was much individualization and autonomy, apparently, in the taking on and defining of party leadership roles. Finally, a rather interesting balance of role interpretations emerges from our analysis — 45 per cent vote mobilizers, 24 per cent ideological leaders, 18 per cent socioeconomic welfare promoters. This raises significant questions. Is this balance conducive to effective party teamwork and immediate goal implementation? Does it mean that parties are effective functional groups at the grass roots in the community and the neighborhood?

Activities and Role Definitions of Grass Roots Party Officials

Lewis Bowman
G. R. Boynton

I. Introduction

Local party leaders are considered by many persons to be the base upon which the political party structure rests. It is often assumed that the precinct captains, the ward leaders, or the party elective committeemen (or whatever the grass roots party cadre is labeled in specific locales) are the leavening which provide the necessary ferment for effective party work. The tasks assigned the local party worker, generally on an *a priori* basis, are awesome. They are expected to mobilize voters, to espouse the party's ideology, to help recruit the party's leaders and workers, to dispense the party's favors, and to maintain a viable party organization all the while. But, if the demands of time, energy, and other resources which these "assigned" tasks place on the shoulders of local party cadre are considered, common sense alone is likely to dictate caution in accepting such a picture without adequate empirical evidence. All of us know of party situations, such as that described by Frank J. Sorauf when he wrote:

Reprinted from *The Journal of Politics,* XXVIII (February, 1966), 121-43, by permission of the journal and the authors.

> . . . some American parties may contain a series of groups differentiated by their activity and degree of involvement, others do not. It is a significant fact for countless local party organizations that their 'active cadre' consists of no more than a county chairman and a few spiritless hangers-on. The lines of authority and the degrees of activity also may shift in time.[1]

Hence, we are not surprised when informed that precinct workers do not operate very efficiently, even in highly politicized Wayne County, Michigan.[2]

Even though the range of activities is probably less than usually ascribed, American political parties do serve as one of the aggregates which helps structure societal conflict. Perhaps they play this role in the main at levels removed from the local scene; but we are uncertain about the accuracy of this because of the wide variations in the organizational levels. We must investigate the activities of local party officials, rather than writing them off as unimportant or so varied as to defy comparison. After all, structuring societal conflict is a latent function developing as the parties reciprocally interact with the larger political system within which they exist. As political parties perform their manifest functions (electioneering, making nominations, and supporting issues) with varying degrees of efficiency from locale to locale, they help structure societal conflict for the entire American political system.[3] Through nominations and electioneering they provide opposing sets of candidates for the public choice; through the development of issues in campaigns they give this public choice a policy content; and through communicating opinions and demands to public officials they serve as one channel of communication from the electorate to the office-holder as he established his policy position. In many local areas of the United States, these activities are not performed. Where they are performed, however, the party organization is likely to play a crucial role in local politics.

For the party organization adequately to perform these activities, it must be an effective grass roots organization. Except for Eldersveld's[4] recent comprehensive work, selected parts of the work by

---

[1]See his book, *Political Parties in the American System* (Boston: Little, Brown and Co., 1964), p. 6.

[2]These findings are reported by Samuel J. Eldersveld in his book, *Political Parties: A Behavioral Analysis* (Chicago: Rand McNally and Co., 1964), pp. 347-55.

[3]This interpretation follows that of Sorauf in important respects. See *op. cit.*, pp. 8-12.

[4]*Op. cit.*

Hirschfield and associates,[5] and the work of Rossi and Cutright,[6] little systematic empirical evidence exists regarding the adequacy of local party organizations to meet the demands imposed by these functions. The earlier works, such as those of Gosnell,[7] Forthal,[8] Mosher,[9] andKurtzman[10] are dated; most of them describe political organization in machine situations of the 1920's and 1930's. Also, much of the earlier and recent work emphasizes social backgrounds and/or the performance of selected activities (i.e., campaign techniques and their impact on voting) rather than getting the local officials to define their roles. Patterson[11] has tried the latter technique on county party chairmen in Oklahoma and developed some interesting hypotheses.

Our study was designed to allow us to investigate the activities, as well as the recruitment patterns and motivations to party work of local party officials in five locales. In this article we are reporting the findings relating to the range of activities and role definitions of these party officials.

---

[5]R. S. Hirschfield, B. E. Swanson, and B. D. Blank, "A Profile of Political Activists in Manhattan," *Western Political Quarterly*, 15 (1962), pp. 489-506.

[6]Peter H. Rossi and Phillips Cutright, "The Impact of Party Organization in an Industrial Setting," in *Community Political Systems*, ed. by Morris Janowitz (Glencoe, Illinois: The Free Press of Glencoe, 1961), pp. 81-116.

Also see, Phillips Cutright and Peter H. Rossi, "Grass Root Politicians and the Vote," *American Sociological Review*, 23 (1958), pp. 171-79.

[7]Harold F. Gosnell, *Machine Politics: Chicago Model* (Chicago: University of Chicago Press, 1937).

[8]Sonya Forthal, *Cogwheels of Democracy: A Study of the Precinct Captain* (New York: The Williams-Frederick Press, 1946).

[9]W. E. Mosher, "Party and Government at the Grass Roots," *National Municipal Review*, 24 (1935), pp. 15-18.

[10]D. H. Kurtzman, *Methods of Controlling Votes in Philadelphia* (Philadelphia: University of Pennsylvania Press, 1935).

[11]Samuel C. Patterson, "Characteristics of Party Leaders," *Western Political Quarterly*, 16 (June, 1963), pp. 332-52.

The following also provide helpful insights about party officials and/or leaders at other levels than that reported in this study. For more about the activities of county chairmen, see: Leon D. Epstein, *Politics in Wisconsin* (Madison: University of Wisconsin Press, 1958), especially, pp. 77-97; C. Eugene Lee, *The Politics of Nonpartisanship* (Berkeley: University of California Press, 1960), especially pp. 97-118. For information about volunteer party workers, see: Dwaine Marvick and Charles R. Nixon, "Recruitment Contrasts in Rival Campaign Groups," in *Political Decision-Makers: Recruitment and Performance*, ed. by Dwaine Marvick (New York: The Free Press of Glencoe, 1961), pp. 138-92.

Also of interest is the research of Lester G. Seligman into the part played by local parties in nominations to the state legislatures in four legislative districts in Oregon. See his article, "Political Recruitment and Party Structure: A Case Study," *American Political Science Review*, 55 (1961), pp. 77-86.

II. Methodology and Settings

Local party officials were interviewed in the Massachusetts communities of Holyoke, Northampton, and Medfield as well as in two North Carolina communities — Durham and Greensboro — during the fall of 1963.[12] No plea is made that these communities are representative of Massachusetts or North Carolina communities, and no such inference is intended. We selected the communities because of convenience (proximity) and because they offer some partisan balance in view of the two states' political systems.[13]

We designated the ranking official of each party's precinct organization in the two North Carolina communities, and the two ranking officials in each party's ward organization in the three Massachusetts communities as our universe.[14] We administered a structured interview lasting one-half to one hour to 138 officials. The response rate was 80.2 per cent.

A low response rate, while never desirable, apparently must be faced as a usual problem when interviewing "grass roots" politicans. Hirschfield and his associates were able to interview only 51.9 per cent of the sample which they drew from the universe (3,749) of Manhattan precinct committeemen.[15] In Wayne County, Michigan, Eldersveld found "a viable Democratic organization in less than half the precincts, and a working Republican organization in about one-

[12]The authors wish to acknowledge the assistance of Edward Lyle, Theodore Nelson, Thomas Albani, and Gordon Jones of Amherst College, and of Eleanor Main, Larry Flood, and Bob Craig, graduate students at the University of North Carolina. These students helped collect and analyze the data for this study.

[13]Both of the party systems in the two North Carolina communities can be characterized historically as modified one-party, although the Republicans recently made sizeable inroads on the traditional Democratic strength in one of the communities. In the two-party politics of Massachusetts, one of the community's party systems is strongly Democratic, one is strongly Republican and the third is a two-party situation.

[14]The organizational arrangement is such in the Massachusetts communities that two officials in each ward had to be designated in order to inflate the universe to a practical size. This means that for the purpose of this study "local party official" has been defined as the Republican and Democratic precinct chairmen in the North Carolina communities and as the two highest ranking Republican and Democratic ward officials in the Massachusetts communities. In some cases these are not exactly comparable because of wide variations in the formal (legal) arrangements of the party systems of the states; nevertheless, these are the "grass roots" party officials in both systems and are comparable in that important respect. They represent roughly comparable functional and organizational levels.

[15]See *op. cit.*, p. 490. Apparently much of the problem was caused by the highly resistant and well-placed (in socio-economic terms) Republicans who lived in rather inaccessible apartment surroundings. They completed interviews with only 36.5% of the Republicans in their sample.

third of the precincts."[16] Under these conditions, he found no Democratic precinct leaders in eleven per cent of the sample precincts, and no Republican leaders in five per cent.[17] We found several persons who were listed officially as precinct or ward chairmen who vehemently denied any such affiliation. Evidently their names had been used without their permission to complete an organizational chart. For these reasons, we do not question Duane Lockard's earlier judgment that the organizational state of the Massachusetts parties is poor.[18] The North Carolina organization seemed stronger, but left much to be desired organizationally. In one of the North Carolina communities we could find no trace of several persons who were listed officially as chairmen; the names seemed to be fictitious.

III. Self-Definition of Their Roles

Examining the local party officials' self-definition of their jobs could give at least two important insights. First, it might suggest activities which the party officials perceive as part of their party tasks, but which scholars have not ordinarily ascribed to them. (Conversely, there may be activities which are ordinarily ascribed to them, but which the party officials actually do not incorporate in the job.) Second, it would indicate how the activities of party officials in the Massachusetts and North Carolina locales differ from those performed by grass roots party workers elsewhere.

The party officials in the five communities were asked to describe the job of being a local party official. Also, they were asked to designate their most important activity.[19] It was possible to code the responses to these inquiries in four general categories: activities relating to campaigning and gaining votes for the party; party organizational work; activities calculated to encourage adherence to ideological orientation; and participation in the nominating process. As Table 1 shows, the bulk of the activities are concentrated in the campaign and in the organizational categories. This corresponds

---

[16] *Op. cit.*, p. 104.

[17] *Ibid.*, p. 103.

[18] *New England State Politics* (Princeton, New Jersey: Princeton University Press, 1959), p. 125.

[19] They were asked this open-ended question: "How would you describe the job of being *(current party office)* — what are the most important things you do?" Then, as a probe, the respondent was asked, "Which one of these activities do you consider the most important?"

closely to the general findings of Patterson[20] in his study of county party chairmen in Oklahoma. In Wayne County,Michigan, however, Samuel J. Eldersveld[21] found that party leaders at the precinct level were not nearly as task-oriented toward mobilizing the voters in their precincts as party theorists had assumed. Only forty-five per cent of the party leaders in the Wayne County study replied in terms

TABLE 1

ACTIVITIES MENTIONED BY THE PARTY OFFICIALS

ORIENTATION OF ACTIVITY	DESCRIPTION OF JOB	MOST IMPORTANT*
Campaign Related	(58.3%)	(67.8%)
Contacting voters	26.5%	43.5%
Raising money	12.5	6.9
Getting people to register	10.6	6.9
Campaigning	3.4	6.1
Public relations	3.4	1.7
Contacting new voters	1.9	1.7
Party Organizational	(27.6%)	(19.9%)
Participating in party meetings and business	11.7%	10.4%
Recruiting and organizing workers	9.8	5.2
County party organizational work	6.1	4.3
Ideological	(8.3%)	(9.6%)
Increasing political information	7.2%	9.6%
Policy formulation	1.1	0.0
Nomination	(5.7%)	(3.5%)
Getting candidates for local office	3.4%	2.6%
General activities	2.3	0.9

*According to the ratings assigned by the individual local party officials themselves.

of mobilizing the vote; Eldersveld found them much more concerned about tasks relating to ideological and social leadership at the precinct level than anticipated.[22] On the contrary, almost sixty per cent

[20]Patterson, *op. cit.*

And, as Patterson aptly pointed out, this corresponds to the general orientations of party leaders as reported in earlier studies. For a summary, see Robert Lane, *Political Life* (Glencoe, Illinois: The Free Press of Glencoe, 1959), pp. 303-307.

[21]*Op. cit.*, pp. 253-54.

[22]*Ibid.*

of the party officials in our sample (in answer to open-ended questions) described their jobs in voter mobilization terminology, and almost seventy per cent said a campaign-related activity was their most important task (when that question was put to them specifically). In fact, the single activity mentioned as "the most important task" of the party officials was "contacting voters." And, overall, eighty per cent of the local party officials mentioned campaign related activities at least once in their total response to the question asking them to describe their jobs.

The second most frequently mentioned type of activity was party organizational work. Although party organizational work sometimes is discussed as one of the two major task areas dividing the attention and energies of party workers, it often is passed over lightly. However, as Georgopoulos and Tannenbaum[23] have pointed out, organizations cannot invest all of their resources (time, energy, money, etc.) in goal-directed activity. It is necessary for organizations to place part of their resources in organizational maintenance activity. This is clearly shown in the local party officials' description of their job. Almost thirty per cent of the activities mentioned were of the organizational maintenance type, and forty-six per cent of the party officials mentioned organizational work as part of their tasks at least once. However, the percentage of the party officials who rate these organizational activities as most important is quite a bit smaller than is the percentage of those who mention them when describing their job. Thus, while the organizational activities are perceived as necessary, they are viewed as necessary for the performance of the major task of campaigning.

Neither activities related to the ideological tasks of the party, nor those related to the nominating process, are mentioned very often. Taken together they constitute less than fifteen per cent of the total activities named by the party officials.

Table 2 illustrates the variations in the role perceptions of the party officials when one takes into account the differing party and state political systems represented in the sample. Patterson[24] found that the Oklahoma county party chairmen tended to be more organizational-oriented if they were members of the dominant party, and more campaign-oriented if they were members of the minority party. Eldersveld[25] found little variation in role perception by party among the precinct leaders in Wayne County.

---

[23]B. S. Georgopoulos and A. S. Tannebaum, "A Study of Organizational Effectiveness," *American Sociological Review,* 22 (1957), pp. 334-40.

[24]*Op. cit.,* p. 352.

[25]See, *op. cit.,* p. 254, Table 10.1.

Our findings in the North Carolina and Massachusetts communities follow neither of the findings of Patterson or Eldersveld. Rather, eighty per cent of the North Carolina Democrats — long in a dominant situation — perceived their role as being campaign related. In the same state political system, the North Carolina Republicans were the most strongly organizationally-oriented of the four groups. How can these distinctive findings be explained? The most plausible hypothesis is that the majority-minority relationship in the local community, and shifts (plus "perceived" shifts and threats) in the

TABLE 2

GENERALIZED ROLE PERCEPTIONS HELD BY THE PARTY OFFICIALS*

INITIAL RESPONSE WAS DIRECTED TOWARD:	N.C. REPS.	N.C. DEMS.	MASS. REPS.	MASS. DEMS.	TOTAL
Campaign related activities	50%	80%	58%	39%	60%
Party organizational work	47	12	22	39	28
Ideological activities	3	3	8	9	5
Participation in nominations	0	3	8	9	5
DK/NA	0	2	4	4	2
	100%	100%	100%	100%	100%
N=	(34)	(41)	(40)	(23)	(138)

*Based on the first response of each party official in answer to the question: "How would you describe the job of being (current party office)—what are the most important things you do?"

relationship, causes a shift in role orientation among local party workers of the two parties. In analyzing our data on a community-by-community basis, this interpretation is supported. Respondents reported that a flurry of organizational activities had occurred among the Republicans in one of the North Carolina communities in the month just prior to the interviewing period. Twelve of the Republican party workers interviewed there mentioned an organizational activity first when asked to describe their job. Undoubtedly this helps explain the emphasis on this role by the North Carolina Republican aggregate. Whether, in turn, this may have inspired unusual emphasis on campaign related activities by the Democrats cannot be documented. More plausible, perhaps, is the fact that most elections are decided in the Democratic primaries in the two North Carolina communities; hence the Democrats are more concerned about campaigns which may actually work to divide the party, rather than unite it organizationally.

No explanation is available for the low Massachusetts Democratic identification with the campaign role. Analysis of the communities making up the aggregates shows low campaign role identification in all three areas. This may be related to the tendency in Massachusetts for candidates to run a rather personal campaign rather than to work through the party. Of course, this happens in both major parties in the state.

IV. The Performance of Campaign Activities

Anticipating that local party officials were likely to perceive their role as primarily that of campaign agents, we asked them if they had performed six standard campaign activities: personally talking to voters, door-to-door canvassing, transporting voters to polls, collecting money, distributing campaign literature, and organizing telephone campaigns.[26] In addition, we asked them if these activities were regularly carried out in their election districts, and, if so, by whom? By asking these questions we hoped to be able to differentiate levels and types of activities among the local party officials. Table 3 indicates the level of campaign activity (with regard to these six types of activities) in the four groups.

TABLE 3

NUMBER OF CAMPAIGN ACTIVITIES PERFORMED BY LOCAL PARTY OFFICIALS

# OF ACTIVITIES	MASS. REP.	MASS. DEM.	N.C. REP.	N.C. DEM.	TOTAL
6	72%	52%	47%	29%	50%
5	20	35	18	32	25
4	5	4	20	34	17
3	3	9	12	3	6
2 or less	0	0	3	2	2
	100%	100%	100%	100%	100%
N=	(40)	(23)	(34)	(41)	(138)
Mean score of activities	5.63	5.30	4.88	4.83	5.15

All six activities were performed in the election districts of fifty per cent of the local party officials and five of the activities were performed in the election districts of an additional twenty-five per cent. Overall, the level of activity proved to be quite high; however, there are substantial variations from group to group. The Massa-

[26]This checklist has been used in several other studies. For example, see the way it was used in: Daniel Katz and Samuel J. Eldersveld, "The Impact of Local Party Upon the Electorate," *Public Opinion Quarterly*, 25 (1961), p. 5.

chusetts local party officials performed a larger percentage of the six activities than their North Carolina counterparts. Seventy-two per cent of the Massachusetts Republicans performed all six of the activities and another twenty per cent said they performed five of the activities. Thus, over ninety per cent of the Massachusetts Republicans performed five or more of the activities. Eighty-seven per cent of the Massachusetts Democrats had five or more of the activities performed in their election districts. By comparison, only sixty-five per cent of the North Carolina Republicans and only sixty-one per cent of the North Carolina Democrats perform five or more of the activities. Thus, in terms of level of the activity, the state's political system seemed more important than did the party variation. There has been less political competition in North Carolina; consequently the local party cadre have performed specific campaign activities at a lower rate.

Personally talking to voters about elections is almost unanimously practiced in the election districts of the party workers (See Table 4). Distributing campaign literature and organizing telephone campaigns are also quite frequently practiced. Door-to-door canvassing and transporting voters to the polls are practiced less frequently. Raising money is the least practiced of the campaign activities.

Although each of the activities was performed in a majority of the districts represented, the extent of its performance and the emphasis given each varied widely by party and area. For example, the Massachusetts Democrats all transport voters to the polls, while only seventy-five per cent of the North Carolina workers practice this method of getting out the vote. Another point of interest concerns collecting money for campaign expenses; this is the activity least practiced by the other three groups, but *all* of the Massachusetts Republican workers collect money.

The local party officials interviewed were at the lowest level of officialdom in their party structure. In order to see if officials at this level are themselves organizers of campaign workers who do not hold official positions in the party structure, or if they are primarily the ones who do the work of campaigning, the party officials were asked whether they ordinarily had volunteers working with them during campaigns. Ninety-two per cent responded that they usually had volunteers working with them. This indicates the extent to which these local officials are themselves the organizers of campaign activity rather than just the "feet" of the party organization. A second way of getting at this question was by asking whether the six campaign activities were performed by the party officials themselves, by

TABLE 4

The Performance of Selected Campaign Activities by the Local Party Officials and Their Helpers

	Not done in the district	Done by the party official only	Done by someone else only	Done by the party official *and* someone else
	%	%	%	%
Personally talking to voters				
N. C. Republicans	6	12	6	76
N. C. Democrats	2	15	10	73
Mass. Republicans	8	40	12	35
Mass. Democrats	4	22	9	65
Distributing campaign literature				
N. C. Republicans	6	12	26	56
N. C. Democrats	15	5	29	51
Mass. Republicans	3	22	35	40
Mass. Democrats	9	4	30	52
Organizing telephone campaigns				
N. C. Republicans	20	12	18	50
N. C. Democrats	12	10	24	54
Mass. Republicans	5	28	32	35
Mass. Democrats	9	13	30	48
Door-to-door canvassing				
N. C. Republicans	12	12	24	53
N. C. Democrats	22	5	12	61
Mass. Republicans	10	35	28	28
Mass. Democrats	22	13	39	26
Transporting voters to polls				
N. C. Republicans	24	6	32	38
N. C. Democrats	24	5	17	51
Mass. Republicans	10	22	38	30
Mass Democrats	0	17	35	48
Collecting money				
N. C. Republicans	44	15	18	24
N. C. Democrats	39	17	7	36
Mass. Republicans	0	32	20	48
Mass. Democrats	26	9	30	35

others, or by both themselves *and* by others. While most active, the Massachusetts Republican party officials work alone more often than the other groups in performing each of the campaign activities, and, with one exception, are the group with the smallest number of party officials who worked with other volunteers in their election district. The exception is in raising money; in that activity the Massachusetts Republicans ranked highest in using volunteers to help them perform the activity.

How does one evaluate the performance of campaign activities by the local party officials? Eldersveld has said:

> Experience with party campaign work suggests *three* critical types of activities superseding the others in importance — registration drives, personalized canvassing (either house-to-house or by telephone), and the election-day roundup of votes. Admittedly, the importance of these may vary by party and by precinct, but generally one can consider them more important than literature distribution, rallies, etc.[27]

By these criteria of campaign task performance, he found that the precinct leaders in Wayne County rated much lower than one might expect. Only one-fourth performed all three critical tasks.

Although our data do not allow exact replication of Eldersveld's measure of campaign task performance, four of our six campaign items do involve these tasks, or somewhat the same level of commitment to campaign work in the precinct or ward. These include: organizing door-to-door canvassing, organizing telephone campaigns, transporting voters to and from the polls, and personally talking to voters about the campaign. An "index of campaign efficiency" was constructed and each party official was assigned a score from 0 to 4, corresponding to the number of campaign activities he performed. Only twenty-six per cent of the party officials in our sample performed all four the the critical tasks; just over

TABLE 5

PERFORMANCE OF CRITICAL CAMPAIGN ACTIVITIES BY THE LOCAL PARTY OFFICIALS

# OF ACTIVITIES PERFORMED	N.C. DEMS.	N.C. REPS.	MASS. DEMS.	MASS. REPS.	TOTAL
4	27%	30%	30%	20%	26%
3	39	23	13	38	30
2	20	35	35	22	27
1	10	6	22	12	12
0	4	6	0	8	5
	100%	100%	100%	100%	100%
N=	(41)	(34)	(23)	(40)	(138)
Mean score	2.73	2.65	2.52	2.50	2.61

*Includes these campaign activities: organizing door-to-door canvassing, organizing telephone campaigns, transporting workers to and from the polls, and personally talking to voters about the campaign.

[27] *Op cit.*, p. 349.
Other measures of organizational strength and vitality in campaigning are available. As pointed out in one study: "These elements of experience, of time devoted to party work, and of the particular pattern of campaign tasks are basic in determining an organization's strength and stability." See the work of Dwaine Marvick and Charles Nixon, *op. cit.*, p. 199.

TABLE 6

THE RELATION OF THE CAMPAIGN ACTIVITY PERFORMANCE LEVELS OF THE LOCAL PARTY OFFICIALS TO THEIR ROLE PERSPECTIVES

LEVEL OF CAMPAIGN ACTIVITY PERFORMANCE	ROLE PERSPECTIVE OF PARTY OFFICIAL		
	CAMPAIGN-ORIENTED	OTHER-ORIENTED*	TOTAL
High (3-4)	61%	52%	57%
Low (0-2)	39	48	43
	100%	100%	100%
N=	(82)	(52)	(134)
Mean score	2.71	2.50	2.63

*Includes those local party officials who were categorized in these role orientations: "party organizational," "ideological," and "participation in nominations."

one-half performed at least three (see Table 5). Hence, our findings approximate those of Eldersveld — for all their reputation as "vote-getters," local party officials do not efficiently utilize the techniques at hand to maximize the vote in their district nearly to the extent that one is often led to believe.

At this juncture a question arises: even though the party officials as a group are not as active in voter-mobilization as one might expect, are not those officials who articulate campaign-oriented roles likely to be exceedingly active when compared to the officials who perceived their roles as being oriented toward maintaining the organization, toward espousing an ideology, or toward gaining influence in the nomination process? In other words, are the campaign-oriented party officials "voter-mobilization specialists" who expend an unusual amount of time and energy in campaign activities? Apparently not. As Table 6 demonstrates, the campaign-oriented party officials do perform a higher number of campaign activities than do the remainder of the sample but their performance level is not sufficiently differentiated from that of the total sample to warrant accolades for them as "voter-mobilizers." In fact, the campaign-oriented officials' median score is 2.71, which is not even as high as the 2.73 median activity score of the North Carolina Democrats. Therefore, not even those party leaders professing a first interest in campaign activities performed anywhere near maximal strength on these four critical campaign activities.

The local party officials also were asked how actively they worked during the national, state, and local campaigns. The differences were not nearly as great as had been expected, but did run in the anticipated direction. Sixty-seven per cent of the local officials said they work "very actively" in national campaigns, sixty-three per cent say they worked "very actively" in state campaigns, and only sixty per cent said they worked "very actively" in local campaigns. Thus differences in the "noise" level of national, state, and local campaigns may be due more to the communication media and the interest of the electorate at large than to the activity of political party personnel.

V. Involvement in the Nomination Process

Schattschneider's now-classic proposition, "A party must make nominations if it is to be regarded as party at all,"[28] is an assumption widely held by political scientists. At the same time, it is quite obvious that the local party officials interviewed in this study do not consider participation in nominations a basic part of their role. Not six per cent of the activities mentioned were oriented toward activities related to nominations, and less than four per cent of the party officials thought that their activity in the nominating process was the most important part of their job.[29] What then of Schattschneider's oft-quoted dictum? Is it meaningless? One of the difficulties with his statement is that the meaning of "make nominations" is rarely spelled out. In one sense, of course, parties control or "make nominations" for most of the offices in the country; at the national and state level it is very difficult, though not impossible in most states, for a candidate to get his name on the ballot unless his name is placed there by a political party. And, a significant portion of the elective officials for local office are chosen in nonpartisan elections. Even in local partisan elections, if the candidate to be endorsed is chosen in a primary election in which the party organization either is only slightly involved or is not involved at all, this is "making the nominations" only in a very weak sense. These considerations mean that the political parties often have minimal control over which candidates will be placed on the ballot under their label.

Little systematic evidence is available about the extent to which parties are involved in the pre-primary selection of candidates and much of it is contradictory. Sorauf[30] has indicated that local political parties in Pennsylvania take a very active part at the pre-primary selection stage. Epstein found "limited organizational influence at this level"[31] in the open primary system of Wisconsin. Patterson[32] found that involvement in the nomination process by

---

[28]E. E. Schattschneider, *Party Government* (New York: Farrar and Rinehart, 1942), p. 100.

[29]See *supra,* Table 4, p. 47.

[30]Frank J. Sorauf, *Party and Representation* (New York: Atherton Press, 1963), pp. 54-56.

[31]Epstein, *op. cit.*, pp. 92-93.

[32]See Patterson, *op. cit.,* p. 347.

Oklahoma party chairmen varied according to majority or minority party membership. The minority party officials tended to be more involved in nominations than did the majority party chairmen. In the five communities of this study, it is our impression that pre-primary selection by the party organizations is sporadic at best. This is in agreement with Seligman's[33] findings in four districts in Oregon where he investigated the extent of party involvement in the nominations process. His findings also support Patterson's in finding greater involvement by the party officials of the minority party.

Overall, the evidence indicates that little involvement by either party organization occurs at levels lesser than the county, or comparable district. But, while the party organization as such may not be systematically involved in pre-primary recruitment, the local party officials may be active as individuals.[34] This may happen in two ways. In the first, and weaker, sense candidates may turn to local party officials seeking support before they decide whether to run and/or before they announce their decision to run. In a second, and stronger, sense the official may seek out potential candidates and ask them to run. We investigated both of these two methods of involvement in pre-primary selection of candidates. Almost eighty per cent of the North Carolina Democratic party officials say that they have been consulted by candidates before the candidates announced for office (see Table 7). In the two Massachusetts

TABLE 7

NUMBER OF CANDIDATES WHO HAVE CONSULTED LOCAL PARTY OFFICIALS

# OF CANDIDATES	N.C. REP.	N.C. DEM.	MASS. REP.	MASS. DEM.
0	41%	22%	30%	30%
1	41	39	18	9
2	12	20	25	30
3	3	7	20	13
4	3	10	5	13
5 or more	0	2	2	5
	100%	100%	100%	100%
N=	(34)	(41)	(40)	(23)
Average # of consultations	1.4	1.8	2.4	2.9

[33]Seligman, *op. cit.*, pp. 77-86 (*passim*).

[34]Peter H. Rossi and Phillips Cutright reported, in their study of party work in "Stockton," that, "At lower organizational levels . . . candidates attempt to gain the support of precinct workers. . . ." See their article, "The Impact of Party Organization in an Industrial Setting," in *Community Political Systems*, ed. by Morris Janowitz (Glencoe, Illinois: The Free Press of Glencoe, 1961), p. 98.

groups, seventy per cent of the local officials say that they have been consulted by candidates. Less than sixty per cent of the North Carolina Republicans report being consulted by candidates.

While the North Carolina Democrats have the largest percentage saying they have been consulted, they are not the aggregate who has been consulted by the most candidates. Over sixty per cent of the North Carolina Democrats say they have been consulted once, or not at all, and only thirty-nine per cent say they have been consulted twice or more. Fifty-two per cent of the Massachusetts Republicans, and sixty-one per cent of the Massachusetts Democrats say that they have been consulted twice or more. The minority party among the North Carolina aggregates has been consulted least; only eighteen per cent of the North Carolina Republicans have been consulted at least twice. A more striking way of demonstrating this is to take the average number of candidates who have consulted those local officials at least once (see Table 7). For the North Carolina Democrats the average number of candidates who have consulted them is 1.8; for the Massachusetts Republicans the average number is 2.4; and for the Massachusetts Democrats the average number is 2.9. Thus, the North Carolina Democrats, although having the largest group who say they have been consulted, are not the most active. They are somewhat less active than the Massachusetts Republicans and substantially less active than the Massachusetts Democrats.

The party officials were asked to name the offices of the candidates who had consulted them. These offices were divided into three categories: 1) those elected on a wider base than the local county; 2) those elected at the local level but who participated in state government (state senators, representatives, etc.); and 3) those elected at the local level to serve in local government (see Table 8). In all cases, a majority of the candidates who had contacted the

TABLE 8

OFFICE LEVEL OF CANDIDATES WHO HAVE CONSULTED LOCAL PARTY OFFICIALS ABOUT SEEKING OFFICE

OFFICE LEVEL	N.C. REP.	N.C. DEM.	MASS. REP.	MASS. DEM.
Governor, U. S. Congress	43%	20%	7%	10%
State legislature	24	26	23	28
Local office (mayor, city council, etc.	33	54	70	62
	100%	100%	100%	100%
N=	(21)	(50)	(60)	(39)

local party officials were elective at the local level (that is, they were state legislative or local office aspirants). However, there is a very striking difference between the North Carolina Republicans and the other three groups in this regard. Forty-three per cent of the contacts made with the North Carolina Republicans were by candidates running for an office with the widest areal constituency. This is true for only twenty per cent of the contacts with the North Carolina Democrats, seven per cent of the Massachusetts Republicans, and ten per cent of the contacts with the Massachusetts Democrats. The high number of contacts with candidates having the widest electoral base by North Carolina Republicans is probably a function of the peculiar development of the Republican party in the South. The Republican party in North Carolina was running candidates for state-wide and national offices long before it systematically ran candidates in local races. Also, because the party organization was much smaller in absolute terms (that is, in terms of the number of counties which had an ongoing organization), it probably was easier for the candidates to talk to a high percentage of the local party officials.

There is little variation in the four aggregates in terms of contacts with state legislators; and the variations in contact with local public officials is an inverse relation to the percentage of their contacts with officials with a wide electoral base.

One variation which is not shown in Table 8 concerns the local school board; the members are elective in all five communities in this study. In the North Carolina communities, no party officials mentioned being contacted by a candidate for the school board; but, in the three Massachusetts communities, seventeen per cent of the local contacts with Republicans and twenty-one per cent of the local contacts with Democrats were by candidates for the school board. Obviously a difference exists between the locales in the degree of politicization of the office, or in the involvement of local party officials in selecting nominees for the office.

The pattern for party workers who initiated the contact with a potential candidate — in an effort to get him to run — is essentially the same as that found above in the candidate-initiated contacts. However, slightly fewer of the local party officials had initiated such contacts. Seventy-one per cent of the party workers had been contacted by candidates, but only sixty-five per cent had initiated contact with potential candidates. The number of such contacts was also lower. Whereas the average number of contacts was 2.0 for those who had been contacted by a candidate, the average number of contacts for party workers who initiated contact with potential contacts was 1.7. However, there was little variation in the pattern among the party groups found in Table 8. The pattern of offices for which candidates were contacted is also quite similar to that of Table 8.

Opposite relationships have been reported between the probability of the party winning the election and the degree of pre-primary selection of candidates by the parties. In Pennsylvania, Sorauf[35] found that the party most likely to win is the party most likely to intervene at the pre-primary stage. In Oregon, Seligman[36] found just the opposite to be the case. In our study, the North Carolina Democratic candidates are most likely to win, and the North Carolina local party officials have a larger percentage of their group saying that they have been contacted. But those who have been contacted have been contacted less than those in the Massachusetts communities where the outcome is more in doubt. On the other hand, the North Carolina Republicans have the smallest percentage of precinct chairmen who have been contacted by candidates. This fits Sorauf's findings very neatly since there is very little likelihood of the North Carolina Republicans' candidates winning on a consistent basis. Thus, our findings do not completely follow those of Seligman, or Sorauf, but fall somewhere in between. Only when a considerable number of studies of local party organizations have been completed will we know which is the more consistent proposition and what the other determining variables are.

VI. Communicating Policy Preferences to Public Officials

The presumption often has been that one of the reasons people become active in politics is to ensure the implementation of policies which they feel are advantageous to themselves, their "group," or to the country. However, we have found that the party officials did not think of communication of policy beliefs as one of their more important activities. Despite this, they are involved in such communication to a much greater extent than the electorate at large.

The local party officials were asked if they had ever written to their congressman or senator. This question enabled us to compare the party workers and a national sample who were asked the same

---

[35]Sorauf, *Party and Representation,* pp. 54-58.
[36]Seligman, *op. cit.,* p. 85.

question.[37] Only fourteen per cent of the nationwide sample said that they had ever written to their congressman or senator. Sixty-nine per cent of the local party officials said that they had written their congressman or senator. This is a much greater percentage than found in social groups who were most active in writing. Thirty-two per cent of the business and professional people and thirty-five per cent of the college educated said that they had written to their congressmen.[38] Thus, the local party workers were twice as active as the most active groups in the electorate.[39]

Eighty-eight per cent of the North Carolina Democrats and seventy-one per cent of the North Carolina Republicans said that they had written their congressman or senator. This is substantially higher than the fifty-eight per cent of the Massachusetts Republicans and the fifty-two per cent of the Massachusetts Democrats who said that they had written their congressman or senator.

TABLE 9

FREQUENCY OF TALKING TO PUBLIC OFFICIALS

	N.C. REP.	N.C. DEM.	MASS. REP.	MASS. DEM.
Quite often	9%	34%	22%	22%
Often	15	22	30	22
Not very often	38	29	18	26
Never	38	15	30	30
	100%	100%	100%	100%
N=	(34)	(41)	(40)	(23)

In order to get a more complete picture of the policy communication activity of local party officials, they were asked how often they talked to public officials about public problems (see Table 9). Only fourteen and one-half per cent of the North Carolina Democrats say that they have never talked to public officials as compared with

[37]Robert E. Lane, *Political Life* (Glencoe, Illinois: Free Press of Glencoe, 1959), pp. 67-69.

[38]*Ibid.*

[39]As Fred I. Greenstein has pointed out in his recent work, *The American Party System and the American People* (Englewood Cliffs, New Jersey: Prentice Hall, Inc., 1963), pp. 10-11, evidence indicates that little change has occurred in the rate of letter writing to congressmen by the public. He reports that only thirteen per cent of an early national sample reported having written or talked to a congressman or other public official in the past year (according to data gathered by Elmo Roper and Associates in the late 1940's). Recently, only nine per cent said they had written their congressmen during the past year when asked by Gallup interviewers (see the American Institute of Public Opinion Release, October 20, 1961).

thirty per cent of the Massachusetts Republicans and Democrats and thirty-eight per cent of the North Carolina Republicans. Also, the North Carolina Democrats had the largest percentage saying they talked to public officials quite often. Both Massachusetts' aggregates again fell in the middle range. The North Carolina Republicans had only a very small percentage (9%) of their group who said that they talked to public officials quite often. Apparently, this is another illustration of the extreme importance of being in the majority party in a one-party situation, if access is desired. For example, North Carolina Democrats have not only written to their congressman or senator more often than the other three groups of local party officials, they have also engaged in personal contact with public officials much more regularly than have the other groups. The party workers also were asked to tell whether they talked to state, national, or local officials about public problems (see Table 10). The North Carolina Democrats, and the Massachusetts Democrats, mentioned the most contact—an average of 2.27 contacts and 2.04 contacts per party official, respectively. The North Carolina Republicans averaged less than one contact per respondent, and the Massachusetts Republicans averaged only one and one-half contact per local official. However, the variations in level of contacts are not great. The North Carolina Democrats mentioned about seven per

TABLE 10

PUBLIC OFFICIALS TO WHOM LOCAL PARTY OFFICIALS TALKED ABOUT PUBLIC PROBLEMS

	N.C. REP.	MASS. REP.	MASS. DEM.	N.C. DEM.
National officials	18%	20%	19%	26%
State officials	33	37	45	31
Local officials	49	43	36	43
	100%	100%	100%	100%
Total number of contacts mentioned	(33)	(60)	(47)	(93)
Average # of contacts	0.97	1.50	2.04	2.27
Total respondents	(34)	(40)	(23)	(41)

cent more contacts with national officials (congressmen or senators) than the other three groups. With the exception of the Massachusetts Democrats, who mentioned talking to more state officials than local officials, a substantial plurality of the contacts were with local officials.

All of the groups were quite active in talking to public officials about public problems. The North Carolina Democrats, however, are quite a bit more active than the other three groups. The major focus of this communication is at the local level where personal communication is easiest and where they have controlled most public offices for many years.

VII. Conclusion

When this research was initiated, it was assumed that political parties help structure societal conflict through their unique roles in campaigning, in the nomination process, and as an avenue for the expression of attitudes about policy to elected officials. The objective of the study was to contribute to an understanding of the degree to which local party workers are involved in these activities thereby gaining some indication of the extent of their role in structuring political conflict in their communities.

When asked about their job, local party workers in the five communities described their work primarily in terms of campaign related activities. Involvement in nominations was mentioned by only a few, and communicating policy preferences to elected officials was not mentioned at all. However, this is not an adequate measure of what they do. To a much greater extent than is true of most of the population they are involved in the recruitment of elected officials and they are involved in policy discussions with elected officials. It is possible to measure the extent to which local party workers are involved in the three activities and thus contribute to structuring political conflict. In the five communities investigated in this study the local workers were much more active than were members of the electorate at large.

The data delineate several variations between the two different parties and the workers from each of the two states. Some of these variations coincide with similar findings by other political scientists, but a number run counter to previous findings and quite obviously require further research. Two lines of further investigation might be fruitful. The first would be to study higher levels in the party hierarchy to examine shifts of emphasis in the performance of the three types of activity and possible shifts of emphasis in defining their job. The second would be a more systematic investigation of the effect of characteristics of the local political system on the way the three activities are performed by local party workers.

Type and Extent of Leadership Functions Undertaken by Party Leaders

Henry Valen
Daniel Katz

Organization leadership calls for many of the same qualities of behavior as does personal leadership, but in addition it requires an understanding of organizational structures and an ability to use them. Four basic functions of political leadership at the lower levels in the party hierarchy can be distinguished: (1) internal, or group organization, function — the ability to recruit, mobilize and motivate helpers to carry out the work of the unit; (2) the representative function, the maintenance of contact and communication with the upper levels in the party hierarchy; (3) the external, or foreign relations, role, establishing and maintaining good relations with the people in the district and the community; and (4) the administrative, or institutional, function of following the standard operating practices of the organization. Each of these functions is essential for an effective local organization. If a ward leader builds and maintains an energetic group of workers around him, he may still not contribute heavily to total organizational effectiveness if he neglects his representative role of communicating with those above him in the party structure. He will be less likely to follow party strategy and tactics and he will not be able to secure the recognition of his

---

Reprinted from *Political Parties in Norway: A Community Study* (Oslo, Norway: Universitetsforlaget, 1964), pp. 102-19 by permission of the publisher and Henry Valen.

followers by the party. On the other hand, if he devotes all his available time to attending party meetings and conferring with party leaders he will slight his function of securing support from the electorate. In other words, the effective local leader must relate well to three different groups of people, his own workers, his superiors in the party structure, and the voters in the community. Finally, the experiences of the organization in handling the many tasks of the campaign have been crystallized in standard procedures, and the strong leader must know and follow these practices. In some organizations some of these functions may be allocated to different roles and role incumbents, but almost every organizational leader has the two functions of relating effectively down the line and up the line. In the political party the local leader is in a key position in that in spite of his lowly status he must assume all four of these roles.

The function of establishing and maintaining relations with the electorate can be carried out in two ways: (a) through personal contact with the voters involving face-to-face communication; (b) through impersonal communication, for example, the use of mass media. Local party organization has been developed in part to emphasize the first method of personal communication. The objective is to have local leaders who know many of the people in their immediate area, who can extend their personal acquaintance to many more, and who can enlist other party members in their area as helpers in all types of primary group activity such as personal calls, coffee hours, and arranging appearances of candidates in the neighborhood. Studies in the United States have demonstrated the effectiveness of this personal type of influence in supplementing the impersonal approach of a mass media campaign. D. Cartwright, for example, has analyzed the effects of personal contact in the war bond campaigns during World War II (D. Cartwright, 1949). The extensive campaigns in the mass media did sell war bonds but when these campaigns were supplemented by community organization involving personal solicitation the results were spectacularly greater. American political parties believe in the doctrine of grass roots organization and they attempt to implement it through the precinct leader responsible for a limited geographical area. Since such local organization is on a voluntary basis and since patronage at the local level is no longer of much significance in American politics, precinct organization in the United States, though not ineffectual, is nonetheless not very strong.

Sometimes these two methods are combined as in the distribution of literature by party workers who leave their materials with the voters and talk to them about the materials. In the same way meetings or rallies can have features of both the personal and impersonal forms of communication.

This analysis of the functions and methods of political leadership furnished the guide lines for the questions put to party leaders in the Stavanger area about their practices, their activities, and their policies of operation as well as for the questions put to voters about party activities in their own neighborhoods.

Leaders' Perceptions of their Tasks

Local leaders tend to see their job as one of distributing election materials and of planning public meetings. The most salient task for leaders of all types of political persuasion is the distribution of campaign materials with 31 per cent of the leaders mentioning this aspect of their work (Table 1). Canvassing is much less salient with only 16 per cent emphasizing this task. Some interesting party differences do appear in that the Conservative leaders place relatively heavy emphasis upon the planning of public meetings and the Labor

TABLE 1
LEADERS' PERCEPTION OF THEIR TASKS

Q.: Would you have any objection to telling me what your job is during the campaign?

	LABOR	LIBERAL	CHRIS-TIAN	AGRARIAN	CONSERV-ATIVE	TOTAL
	%	%	%	%	%	%
Planning of public meetings	14	19	15	11	31	19
Organization of distribution of election materials	30	31	31	32	31	31
Planning of canvassing for subunits	19	12	4	5	14	12
Other planning and coordination of campaign activities	19	23	12	5	17	16
Mentions no coordination or planning	30	27	54	58	31	38
No basis for coding	12	12	8		9	9
N*	43	26	26	19	35	149

* Percentages add to more than 100 because the question called for multiple answers.

leaders are more likely than other leaders to mention personal canvassing. Though leadership of necessity involves some planning and coordination, over half of the leaders in the Agrarian party and the Christian People's party failed to talk in these terms. It should be mentioned in passing, though, that the planning of public meetings was the second most frequently mentioned task by all leaders, regardless of party.

Efforts Made to Come into Contact with the Voters

To the open question of 'What do you do to come into close contact with the voters in this district?' there was less agreement among the parties than to the previous question. In spite of the importance of this aspect of the local leader's role a third of the Agrarian party leaders frankly replied that they did nothing and 27 per cent of the Liberal leaders responded similarly (Table 2). Open member meetings were mentioned most frequently as a method of all the leaders, irrespective of party. The differences reported in the above para-

TABLE 2

EFFORTS MADE TO COME IN CONTACT WITH THE VOTER (FOR COMMUNE AND WARD LEADERS ONLY)

Q.: What do you do to come into closer contact with the voters in this district?

	LABOR	LIBERAL	CHRISTIAN	AGRARIAN	CONSERVATIVE	TOTAL
	%	%	%	%	%	%
Nothing is done in this respect	9	27	23	32	17	19
Open member meetings	12	31	38	5	54	29
Talks to people either when distributing literature or encouraging them to join, but casual not systematic	28	4	8	21	9	15
Systematic or strong emphasis on personal calls and canvassing	28	8	4	21	3	13
Not applicable	23	30	27	21	17	24
TOTAL	100%	100%	100%	100%	100%	100%
N	43	26	26	19	35	149

graph between the Conservative and Labor party methods are outlined here in even bolder relief. 54 per cent of the Conservative leaders compared with 12 per cent of the Labor leaders rely upon open party meetings. We may anticipate the results, . . . which show that the proportion of people attending such meetings is negligible. Some 28 per cent of the Labor leaders place heavy emphasis upon systematic personal calls and canvassing, and an equal number favor this method, though they are less systematic about it. Over half of the Labor leaders are thus enlisted on the side of personal communication in contrast to 12 per cent of the Conservative leaders. Agrarian leaders are closest to the Labor leaders in their emphasis upon personal contact. Again, however, our results indicate that the impact of personal communication upon the electorate is weak.

Relative Emphasis upon Internal, Representative, and External Functions

The responses of leaders to a series of questions about their activities reveals the limited conception many of them have of their leadership functions. Seventy per cent make no reference to their role of relationship with groups and people in the community, 61 per cent neglect to mention communication within the party structure and 56 per cent report no activity in mobilizing their own group of workers (Table 3). In some cases the failure to talk about relevant activities could mean that these were done so habitually that they were taken for granted or that a smooth functioning party organization had already taken care of the problem. In other cases, however, leaders were faithfully reflecting their own inadequacies in living up to the ideal requirements of a local political leader. This latter interpretation is certainly supported by the electorate's perception of the activities of the local party organization. . . . Coders' judgments of the concept the leader has of his position indicate that 38 per cent of the local leaders had a truly comprehensive notion of their role and 26 per cent had a very limited notion. Another 26 per cent fell between these extremes (Table 4).

Party differences in organization and practice are again in evidence (Table 3). The Liberal and Christian People's parties are at the head of the list in mentioning the mobilization of their own local groups. This conceivably could mean that this function had been so neglected between campaigns that it assumed special salience during the campaign for these parties. No differences appear among the parties concerning their relationships with the upper levels within their organizations with the exception of the Liberal party. Liberal leaders are much more likely than other leaders to report contact with those above them in the party structure. We do not know whether this again is a matter of salience for an otherwise neglected function or whether the Liberals do invest more energy in all types of discussion within the party structure. The Agrarian and Labor parties apparently invest more effort in coming into contact with individuals and groups in their communities. This is consistent with the fact that they are better integrated into the group structure of their communities than are the other parties.

A further indication of the closer tie-in of the Labor and Agrarian parties to the groupings in the community is found in the leaders'

TABLE 3

RELATIVE EMPHASIS UPON INTERNAL, REPRESENTATIVE, AND EXTERNAL FUNCTION

INTERNAL:	LABOR	LIBERAL	CHRISTIAN	AGRARIAN	CONSERVATIVE	TOTAL
	%	%	%	%	%	%
Involves others in campaign work	32	48	48	37	35	39
Mentions helping morale of workers	5	4	4	5	6	5
No mention of involvement of other workers	63	48	48	58	59	56
REPRESENTATIVE:						
Mentions relationship with own leaders and organization	34	56	32	37	38	39
No mention of relationship with own leaders and organization	66	44	68	63	62	61
EXTERNAL:						
Mentions external function of relationship with groups, leaders or people in community	37	28	12	47	26	30
No mention of external function	63	72	88	53	74	70
N*	41	25	25	19	34	144

*A few leaders are excluded because they were not asked the appropriate questions.

TABLE 4
Conception of Leadership Role

	Labor	Liberal	Chris-tian	Agrarian	Conserv-ative	Total
	%	%	%	%	%	%
Limited notion of task	16	23	48	32	21	26
Fairly comprehensive notion of task	16	35	32	32	23	26
Comprehensive notion of task	51	35	20	32	35	38
No basis for coding	17	7		4	21	10
TOTAL	100%	100%	100%	100%	100%	100%
N	43	26	26	19	35	149

answers to questions about particular groups or kinds of voters it was important for their parties to reach with their point of view (Table 5). Two-thirds or more of the Liberal leaders and the Christian leaders could think of no special groups, 40 per cent of the Conservative leaders were in the same category, whereas very few Agrarian or Labor leaders thought of their public in such blanket terms. The Labor leaders saw the need for reaching both occupational groupings, the different age groupings, including first-time voters, and the nonvoters. They were most concerned with the young first-time voter and with the white collar workers and governmental employees. More than any other party, Labor wanted to reach the nonvoters or stay-at-homes. The Agrarian leaders concentrate on two groups: farm families and first-time voters. Among Conservative leaders the first-time voters receive the most attention. A few of the Conservative leaders are also eager to reach white collar workers and farm families. The few Liberal leaders who feel they should reach special groups mention the first-time voters, nonvoters and working class people. For most Christian leaders the target is the general public, though a few do break apart the religious people as a special group. For all parties, the most frequently mentioned special group which should be reached by their message is the first-time voter. This mirrors the stability of Norwegian political behavior. Basically the older voters can be depended upon to stay with the party of their choice.

When the leaders were asked to mention the social groups from which their respective parties draw their main support at the polls, they answered with greater precision. . . . It is, therefore, surprising that many leaders are reluctant to see their party as appealing to specific target groups. The explanation lies in the growing ideology that a party should be a 'people's party,' a party representative of the whole nation and not any specific group. The Agrarian party is the only party, except the Communists, which does not claim to be a 'people's party.' The party may rather be labeled a 'single interest' party, or the political face of the farmers' interests. . . . Therefore, it is not surprising that Agrarian leaders are inclined to give differentiated picture of the party's target groups in the farm community.

Labor leaders also tend to hold a differentiated view of their party's group appeal. The Labor party certainly considers itself a 'people's party.' In this case, however, the basis of its support among the working class, among white collar workers, among intellectuals, and among small farmers and fishermen adds up to broad national support. . . . Labor leaders, however, have long thought in terms of

TABLE 5

Perceived Group Appeal of Parties

Q.: During a campaign the parties naturally appeal to all the voters with their basic policies and programs. But are there any particular groups or kinds of voters in this commune which the party considers it to be important to reach with its point of view? If yes: which groups or kinds of voters do you especially appeal to?

	Labor	Liberal	Christian	Agrarian	Conservative	Total
	%	%	%	%	%	%
Trade unionists	16	—	—	—	—	5
White collar, civil servants employees	37	—	—	—	11	13
Workers, people in working class areas	21	7	4	5	5	10
Farmers, farm families	—	—	—	63	11	11
Women	9	—	4	—	6	5
Youth, including first-time voters	42	15	4	32	34	28
Old people	12	—	—	—	6	5
The stay-at-homes	12	7	—	5	—	5
Religious people	—	—	15	—	—	3
Other groups	7	—	4	—	11	5
No special group	14	77	68	16	40	40
Don't know	—	—	—	—	9	2
N*	43	26	26	19	35	149

*Percentages add to more than 100 because the question called for multiple answers.

the interest of major interest groups and so are more specific about the targets to aim at in a campaign. It is also true that perceptual differences among leaders may be partly accounted for in terms of differences in organizational structure. The fact that Labor has established more suborganizations and more auxiliary agencies than other parties indicates that the party has a more articulated structure, and that it pays more attention to the social groups upon which the party is based, and that it applies a greater division of labor in handling organizational matters.

The Administrative or Organizational Function

Another way of looking at the effectiveness of local party organization is to examine the extent to which leaders follow the standard institutional practices of mobilizing the vote at the local level. The first question bearing specifically upon this function had to do with the keeping of records of voters in the leader's own election district (Table 6). Ideally from an organizational viewpoint the local leader should have a file of all voters in his area with information about their party preference, their voting behavior, and their possible availability for helping on some party tasks. As newcomers move into the area and as youngsters come of voting age they are added

TABLE 6

REGISTER KEEPING REPORTED BY PARTY LEADERS (COMMUNE AND WARD LEADERS ONLY)

Q.: Do you keep records of how people in this district voted and who turn out to vote in elections?

	LABOR	LIBERAL	CHRISTIAN	AGRARIAN	CONSERVATIVE	TOTAL
	%	%	%	%	%	%
Nothing done in this respect	26	50	54	26	51	41
Register kept in head	16	12	—	21	3	10
Register kept, no indication that it is used effectively	9	8	8	11	6	8
Register kept and effectively used	21	—	12	21	11	14
Don't know	2	—	8	—	6	3
Not applicable	26	30	18	21	23	24
TOTAL	100%	100%	100%	100%	100%	100%
N	43	26	26	19	35	149

to the file. This record thus can be used in a variety of ways; for example, to insure that one's own supporters get to the polls on election day. It is interesting to find that for the Liberal, Christian People's, and Conservative parties over half the local leaders do nothing about keeping records of voters. On this criterion the Labor and Agrarian parties again seem to have the stronger ward organizations in those districts where they have any ward organization at all. Even for these two more organizationally-minded parties, only one in five leaders made effective use of records. There was some tendency for local leaders to keep records in their heads rather than on paper. And among the twenty-six Liberal leaders not a single one gave evidence that he made any effective use of records of voters.

A majority of the leaders in each party, however, claimed that in his ward transportation was provided on election day for the voters who needed it (Table 7). On the other hand, for all parties, save the Labor party, only a minority of the leaders had organized their plans for transportation services in efficient fashion. The percentage of Labor leaders who indicated that they had arranged adequate transportation on election day was almost twice as great as in any of the other parties.

With the exception of the Conservative Party all the leaders interviewed at the ward level claimed that they had gotten election materials to the people in their election district (Table 8). The Liberals and Conservatives are more likely than other leaders to

TABLE 7

TRANSPORTATION PROVIDED BY PARTIES ON ELECTION DAY (FOR COMMUNE AND WARD LEADERS ONLY)

Q.: What do you do to provide transportation on election day?

	LABOR	LIBERAL	CHRISTIAN	AGRARIAN	CONSERVATIVE	TOTAL
	%	%	%	%	%	%
Transportation not provided	5	4	19	5	9	8
Transportation provided, no indication that it is well-organized	26	42	31	42	40	35
Well-organized transportation	44	23	23	26	20	29
Don't know	—	—	4	—	—	1
Not applicable	25	31	23	27	31	27
TOTAL	100%	100%	100%	100%	100%	100%
N	43	26	26	19	35	149

rely upon mail distribution. The strongest practitioners with respect to personal distribution are the Christian People's party's leaders with 65 percent of this group relying on personal distribution. This probably accords with their usual practices of achieving personal contact in their distribution of religious materials. The Agrarians are next in emphasizing personal distribution and the Labor leaders are third. Apparently, though, personal communication is more heavily valued by the Labor leaders than by the Christian leaders in all areas of politics; especially in canvassing, the Christian leaders will utilize the face-to-face technique in getting their literature to the people.

Evaluation of Campaign Methods by Party Leaders

Party leaders were asked to name the three most effective methods for reaching the voters in their commune or province with the message or point of view of their own party. The method which heads the list is the open party meeting with its discussion of the issues (Table 9). This accords with the question reported earlier about their conception of their task as local leaders. The leaders in their evaluation may be reflecting the past rather than the present because voters in the 1957 election just did not attend open meetings

TABLE 8

Distribution of Election Material
(Commune and Ward Leaders only)

Q.: What do you do to get election or campaign material to people in this district?

	Labor	Liberal	Christian	Agrarian	Conservative	Total
	%	%	%	%	%	%
Nothing done	—	—	—	—	9	2
Mail distribution	2	15	—	—	17	7
Some mail, some personal distribution	21	23	4	5	6	13
Personal distribution	35	19	65	47	31	38
Form of distribution not specified	19	12	15	26	14	17
Don't know	—	—	4	—	3	1
Not applicable	23	31	12	22	20	22
TOTAL	100%	100%	100%	100%	100%	100%
N	43	26	26	19	35	149

in sufficient numbers to have affected the election outcome in the slightest. But it is more likely that the leaders confused their answers to this question with the question of the general value to the party of such meetings. The open political meeting in which issues are discussed may give the party members ammunition to use on other occasions; it may help the morale of the local group by giving them a chance to express their views, and it may give social reinforcement to party workers. All of these benefits should not be underestimated, but it is still a widely held fiction among party leaders that they are reaching voters directly in this fashion. It is of interest in this connection that the party most concerned with old issues of individual rights is the party in which 25 out of the 26

TABLE 9

EVALUATION OF PARTY LEADERS OF THREE MOST EFFECTIVE CAMPAIGN METHODS

Q.: I have here a list of various campaign methods used by the parties. Which three of these methods do you think are the strongest and most effective for a party to reach the voters with its viewpoints in this commune (province)?

	LABOR	LIBERAL	CHRISTIAN	AGRARIAN	CONSERVATIVE	TOTAL
	%	%	%	%	%	%
Open meetings with speeches	5	12	19	21	29	16
Open meetings, discussions	79	96	62	74	71	77
Election movies	7	1	8	—	9	5
Posters	2	4	4	—	6	3
Distribution of slates, pamphlets, etc.	19	8	27	42	14	20
Election reviews	26	4	—	5	11	11
Political radio programs	67	88	81	47	54	68
Calling on people in their homes	33	12	35	47	20	28
The newspapers	26	62	27	53	40	39
Small meetings for special groups	23	8	19	5	20	17
Personal letters to the voters	—	4	4	—	14	5
No choice made	2	—	—	—	3	1
N*	43	26	26	19	35	149

*Percentages add to more than 100 because the question called for multiple answers.

leaders felt that open discussion meetings are the best method for reaching the people (the Liberal party). Apparently it is possible for party activists to talk to party activists and have the illusion that the public is somehow involved and listening.

The second most valued method is that of the radio debates, and this has a sound basis in reality, for people in fact do listen to the radio discussions by political leaders. The Conservative and Agrarian leaders are the most doubtful about this use of the mass media. The newspapers are regarded as the third most effective means, and again there is a reality basis for this belief. The newspaper which is often a party organ, not only reaches its regular subscribers, but is often sent free of charge during a campaign to a selected group of nonsubscribers. The Liberals are the strongest advocate of this method and they do have the newspaper with the widest circulation in Rogaland. The Labor leaders are the most doubtful about the efficacy of the newspaper. Calling on people in their homes, though not widely practiced in Norwegian politics, was named by 28 per cent of the leaders as one of the three most effective ways of reaching the people. It receives its heaviest support from the three parties who practice it the most, the Agrarian party, the Christian People's party, and the Labor party. The distribution of literature other than newspapers is favored by only 20 per cent of the leaders as a very effective device in spite of the common use of the method. The Liberals are the most skeptical on this score and the Agrarians are the most favorable. A number of Conservative leaders did emphasize a method almost exclusive to them, namely sending personal letters to voters.

In summary, then, *apart from open meetings* the ideal campaign for the Liberals would concentrate on the radio and the press, for the Conservatives the same pattern would be followed, the Labor party would use both radio programs and personal communication, the Agrarians would include both forms of the mass media as well as personal communication, and the Christian People's party would follow the pattern of Labor.

Leaders' Opinions of the Propriety of Certain Campaign Methods

Leaders were asked whether they considered any of the campaign methods to be morally objectionable. Eighteen per cent answered in the affirmative and a similar proportion said that some methods, while not immoral, were in poor taste (Table 10). The objections come primarily from the Conservatives, Liberals, and Christian

People's party's representatives and not from the Labor party or the Agrarian party. The objections are strongly focused on two methods: canvassing and election reviews (entertainment with political content). Canvassing is of particular interest in this connection. A substantial number of leaders regard it as an effective method, but apart from Labor party practice it is used relatively little. Apparently the leaders believe that voters dislike it as an invasion of their privacy and the leaders themselves regard it as improper. Most of the personal communication that takes place with voters occurs through informal communication with acquaintances, friends, or fellow workers, the great majority of whom are already party members or party supporters. The formalization of personal contact through systematic canvassing is not an accepted practice of most Norwegian political parties. Canvassing by telephone is completely unknown in a political campaign.

Time Devoted to Party Work by Local Leaders

Finally, as a measure of involvement leaders were asked to estimate the amount of time they spend a week on work connected with the campaign. Both Labor party leaders and Liberal party leaders tend to report more time devoted to party activities than do the leaders of other parties with Agrarian and Christian leaders giving the least time (Table 11). The greater activity of the Labor leaders is consistent with their responses to other questions but the estimate of the Liberals seems high and that of the Agrarians seems low.

TABLE 10

MORAL EVALUATION BY LEADERS OF CAMPAIGN METHODS

Q.: Do you personally find some of these methods mentioned on the card morally objectionable?

	LABOR	LIBERAL	CHRISTIAN	AGRARIAN	CONSERVATIVE	TOTAL
	%	%	%	%	%	%
Yes	3	23	29	11	29	18
No	75	65	50	78	48	63
Not immoral, but distasteful	22	12	21	11	24	19
TOTAL	100%	100%	100%	100%	100%	100%
N	43	26	26	19	35	149

TABLE 11

TIME SPENT ON CAMPAIGN WORK BY PARTY LEADERS

Q.: About how many hours do you spend every week on work connected with the campaign?

	LABOR	LIBERAL	CHRISTIAN	AGRARIAN	CONSERVATIVE	TOTAL
	%	%	%	%	%	%
Less than three hours	12	12	27	21	14	16
Three to five hours	9	15	8	32	11	13
Six to eleven hours	33	31	8	16	23	23
Twelve hours or more	30	27	31	21	29	28
Don't know	2	8	23	5	6	8
Not ascertained	14	7	3	5	17	12
TOTAL	100%	100%	100%	100%	100%	100%
N	43	26	26	19	35	149

Summary of Findings

1. The local leader tends to have a limited notion of his task in the campaign.
2. His major activities have to do with the distribution of election materials and the holding of open party meetings. Only a minority of the leaders attempt to come into contact with their electorate in any other fashion.
3. Party differences are fairly pronounced in the emphasis given to various activities. The Labor and Agrarian leaders invest much more energy in personal communication to the voters than do the other parties. And the leaders of these two parties have a much more differentiated picture of the groupings in the electorate which they must reach.
4. The Conservative and Liberal leaders rely heavily upon open party meetings as a method of campaigning — a method which may help internal party morale but which fails to reach the electorate.

Interpretative Summary

The nature of the local organizational structure and of the activities of the local leaders can be interpreted in part as a reflection of the philosophic orientation of the parties toward the political process. At the one extreme the philosophy of the Liberal party views the political process as occurring primarily among duly elected decision-makers whose election should be determined by people acting not as wage workers or business people but as citizens. In their citizen role people should strip themselves of their vested interests and concern themselves only with national interests. The Liberal Party thus views itself not as a class party or as a combination of the many interest groups making up the nation but as the expression of the common interests of all people. Society is not seen in pluralistic terms. The norm for political behavior, then, is not one of giving representation to specific interest groups or of seeking support through techniques of winning friends and influencing people. The less political the political process can be made the happier the Liberals are.

In contrast the Labor party has a down-to-earth orientation which sees the political process as a means of satisfying the interests of various groups in the society. It is moving toward becoming a people's party in the sense of including other sectors of the people besides the blue collar workers. But the conception of society is pluralistic and the norm is to bring as many groups into the party as possible and to handle their differences through participant decision-making within the party. This means involvement of members at the local as well as the higher levels in the party structure. The Labor party philosophy of politics is more pragmatic and sees the political process as one of the just allocation of resources to the different groups within the nation. The trade unionist need not completely divest himself of his role as a trade unionist to be a good citizen as in the philosophy of the Liberal Party.

These two orientations have many implications for party activity at the local level. The Labor party sees nothing shameful in engaging in politics by campaigning to reach different interest groups, whereas the Liberal party rebels against politics as the art of compromise and finds the technique of appealing to people in terms of their interests distasteful.

The Christian People's party reflects the same general orientation as the Liberal party. The Agrarian party is very much like the Labor party in its approach to politics. It is frankly partisan in appealing to one segment of society and makes no bones about going after support from this segment. Like the Labor party it is pragmatic and realistic about the political process. The Conservative party is somewhere in the middle between these two positions. It attempts to be a people's party but on the one hand lacks the pure idealistic appeal of the Liberals to the common citizen role of all people and on the other lacks the direct approach of the Labor Party to the interest groups with population concentration. It is consistent with Conservative tradition to stand above the political game. Practical American techniques for marketing products are unpalatable to many Conservative leaders.

Pragmatic and realistic approaches to politics are more congenial to underprivileged groups on their way up in the power struggle. The entrenched groups in a privileged position like to rationalize the status quo and to view the political process not as a vehicle for change but as a means of stability. Hence they deprecate class conflict and partisan struggle and they stigmatize as politicians those who play the game of the opposition. Since political demagoguery does occur they can point to some factual basis for their position. They are trapped, however, by their own ideology in that they often fail to play their own political roles to the full.

This account of the philosophical orientation of Norwegian political parties is of course but one interpretation. Our data do not permit a definitive test of it, but they do fit this pattern of interpretation.

SECTION FIVE

Party Processes: Leaders and Followers

Party Processes: Leaders and Followers

Any discussion of internal party processes, involving the distribution of power within the party, the nature of the policy-making process, and the relationship between leaders and followers brings the two basic party models into sharpest contrast. Concern for such matters is central to the Party Democracy model, but for several reasons is of only tangential interest in the Rational-Efficient model. First, the role of party in the determination of public policy is stressed in the Party Democracy model, but is less emphasized in the Rational-Efficient model. When the party is supposed to be influential in the policy-making process, the way policy is made within the party becomes a vital concern. Second, the two party models yield different answers to a basic question posed by Schlesinger (1965): Who "owns" the party? Who are the party's "prime beneficiaries?" The answer provided by the Rational-Efficient model is the voters, to whom party leaders as elected public officials in their representative capacity owe their prime allegiance, rather than to the party activists who are often considered to be ideologues who are unrepresentative of the broad mass of voters. (Actually, the logical implication of the attributes of the Rational-Efficient model point points to the elected public officials as the party's prime beneficiaries.) The prime beneficiaries in the Party Democracy model are the party members, who have a vital concern in what is done in the name of the party.

The two party models thus differ in their assessment of the policy role of the party in the political system and in their concern with the policy-making process within the party. A third difference concerns the nature of the internal party policy-making process. Questions raised about who makes party policy and the extent to which this process is democratic are central to the Party Democracy model, but of little concern in the Rational-Efficient model. In the latter model, emphasis is on the external democratization of political parties by such means as statutory regulation and the nomination of candidates for public office by direct primary rather than on democratization from within, as is the case with the Party Democracy model. Different answers to a basic question of democratic theory—whether in a democratic political system all subsystems such as political parties must be democratic — are given in the two party models. The Party Democracy model yields a strong affirmative answer to this question. The party is viewed as a miniature political system and is expected to serve as an exemplary model of democratic values and practices for the larger political system. Proponents of the Rational-Efficient model, usually operating with a conception of pluralistic democracy, tend to take the view that all subsystems of the political system need not be democratic. (On the latter point, see the discussion by Barnes, Selection 1.4.).

Although the concept of intraparty democracy has not been broadly applied to American parties, such concern is an important point made by reformist critics of American parties and it is a norm held by some party activists — particularly in the "club movement" type of American party organization (see Wilson, 1962; Sorauf, 1964). Questions of party democracy were given more public exposure during the 1968 Democratic National Convention. Contests over the seating of several delegations and criticisms of "undemocratic" convention procedures resulted in changes in the party rules calling for more democratic delegate selection procedures and demands for open and meaningful participation and broad representation within the party. Just how serious these concerns are and what organizational and policy consequences, if any, will follow are still open questions (McGovern, 1969).

What is involved in the concept of intraparty democracy which is so central to the Party Democracy model? How is the policy-making process viewed? The basic notion involved is that the rank-and-file membership is accorded a voice in the formulation of party policy and a substantial degree of control over the leadership — a norm held by both leaders and followers. The party organization is structured so as to make this possible, the most important structural requirement being the existence and effective operation of two-way channels of communication linking the party membership with the leadership. In order for the policy process to be considered democratic, the upward flow of communications — policy views of the members — should outweigh the downward flow of accomplished decisions and directives from the leaders to the members. (The obvious applicability of a communications model, suggested by Barnes, Selection 1.4, to this aspect of party is clearly indicated.) In order for the members to exert effective influence upon their leaders, leadership selection procedures within the party must be democratic. Moreover, since the members are considered to be the prime beneficiaries of the party, it follows that the membership organization is supposed to be able to influence the policy views and decisions of the party's elected public officials who constitute the governmental party. The view of policy formulation as an integrated process — both within the membership organization and the governmental party and between the two — is found in the Party Democracy model. The membership organization's claim of influence over the policies of the governmental party is the most controversial aspect of intraparty democracy.

The first two selections in this section deal with intraparty democracy generally, while the latter three selections examine aspects of the relationship between the external party organization and the governmental party.

Involved in the discussion of intarparty democracy are both normative and empirical questions: Is party democracy desirable? Is it possible? To what extent does it exist in the real world of party organizations? The classic formulation of the problem of organizational democracy — the contrast between the norm of internal democracy and organizational practice — remains that of Robert Michels (1949; first published in German in 1911). Michels was concerned with working-class organizations generally and the German Social Democratic Party (SPD) in particular—organizations which stressed the norm of internal democracy but which, according to Michels, did not practice it. The seeming inability of even these organizations to implement internal democracy in practice led Michels to question its attainability in complex organizations. Michels's most concise formulation of his famous "Iron Law of Oligarchy" reads "Whoever says organization says oligarchy." Complex organization, Michels argued, inevitably entails specialization or division of labor and requisite organizational skills, leading to the professionalization of a corps of leaders who become indispensible due to their monopoly of organizational skills, and resulting in a widening gulf between the leaders who constitute a minority and the majority followers. The leaders thus come to control the organization and, having attained power, seek to retain it—either directly through control of offices or indirectly by such means as coopting their successors as officials.

A crucial element in Michels's argument is his contention that in this process of differentiation the leaders become unrepresentative of the followers, in terms of values, attitudes, and policy views. In working-class organizations with which Michels was dealing, the leaders of working-class origins came to adopt a middle-class life style. One important reason for such leaders' efforts to retain power is that the acquisition of union, party, or public office as a career is often an important means of upward social mobility for them.

It is beyond the scope of this essay to consider the psychological as well as organizational factors which Michels discussed or to present a critique of his thesis. (For contrasting interpretations of Michels, see Cassinelli, 1953; and May, 1965; for an analysis of problems of organizational democracy, see Lipset, Coleman, and Trow, 1962; and Barnes, 1967, Chapter 1.) Certainly there remain serious problems of conceptualization and operationalization. Michels is never entirely clear just what he means by oligarchy, and is not concerned with empirically measuring this phenomenon. If Michels is merely saying that in all organizations, even in theoretically democratic ones, there is an active minority and a passive majority, this is a generally accurate but trivial statement (see Barnes, 1968, p. 135). Implied in the concept of oligarchic control are several factors which are capable of being tested empirically: (1) multiple office-holding as a means of control; (2) power drive of the leaders and their tenacity in clinging to office (e.g., a low rate of leadership turn-over); (3) control of the selection of their successors by co-optation and other means; (4) control of the channels of communication in the organization; (5) the "unrepresentativeness" of the leaders' values and attitudes; and (6) the leaders' control of policy-making, especially, as Dahl (1958) contends, in the case of controversial decisions. In any case, Michels did much to set the framework and tone of debate on this question and his influence is still felt in the study of political parties and voluntary associations. For example, Duverger's (1954) comparative analysis of political parties owes much to Michels's earlier work.

Renate Mayntz (Selection 5.1) tested the validity of Michels's thesis in her study of a West Berlin district organization of the Christian Democratic Union (CDU). Her analysis is based on extensive participant-observation, interviews with party officials, analysis of party records, and a mail questionnaire sent to rank-and-file members. Although Mayntz found a fairly low rate of member participation, evidence of pre-planning of internal party elections, and a high degree of independence of the district party leadership, she concluded that the conditions of oligarchic control were not met because of the *absence* of "overbureaucratization" of the leadership and their tenacity in clinging to office, monopoly of communications channels by the leaders, scarcity of political and organizational skills, or serious manipulation of internal party elections by the leaders.

Barnes (Selection 5.2) analyzed the interrelationships among the variables of education, political competence, and party participation for a sample of members of a federation of the Italian Socialist Party (PSI). He found these three variables to be positively intercorrelated. His main finding concerns the apparently crucial role of education: the better-educated PSI members were more knowledgeable about Italian politics, more ideologically sensitive, more efficacious, and participated more in party affairs. Compared with members with less education, the better-educated had several advantages with "vast implications for internal democracy in the PSI." Participation offered the poorly educated a "means to political competence," but did not overcome the advantages of a superior education.

In his larger study, Barnes (1967) extended the scope of his investigation of party democracy in the PSI. He found the extent of rank-and-file participation in party affairs to be positively associated with socio-economic status in occupation and, more especially, education; political competence or political knowledge, sense of political efficacy, and ideological sensitivity; extent of associational memberships; exposure to political communications both inside and outside the party; support of party democracy norms; and conception of democracy as process rather than an end-state to be attained. Most of these variables are correlates of political participation generally (Lane, 1959; Milbrath, 1965).

With these characteristics of the party activists in mind, the conditions favorable to internal party democracy are, according to Barnes, the following: (1) commitment by leaders and followers to norms of internal democracy in process terms — a necessary but not sufficient condition; (2) toleration of opposing viewpoints (pluralism, acceptance of factionalism); (3) structural provisions for multiple autonomous channels of communication (the crucial feature in Barnes's general conception of democracy); (4) open leadership recruitment; and (5) a sizeable core though not necessarily a majority of politically competent, knowledgeable, efficacious, and ideologically sensitive party activists (see also Barnes, 1968, pp. 137-38).

Empirical studies of leader-follower relations in political parties generally agree on several points. First, the extent of member participation in party affairs is generally low: only a small minority, generally not exceeding one-quarter of the membership, are highly active participants. Second, even active rank-and-file participants and lower-echelon leaders do not substantially determine higher-level party policy: party policy-making tends to proceed from the top down, rather than from the bottom up. Third, in most cases, party policy is determined by the party's elected public officials (the governmental party) rather than the extra-parliamentary membership organization, regardless of how much party norms support claims of the membership organization to influence or control over party policy-making.

The study of policy resolutions submitted by local party organizations to the annual conferences of the British Labour and Conservative parties already cited in the discussion of ideology (Rose, Selection 3.4) has as its analytical focus "the part played by party activists in policy formulation." Rose refers to the continuing debate among British party scholars and participants over the policy role of party activists and he concludes that ". . . there is consensus among students of British politics that party activists cannot and should not make party policy, or even influence it greatly." As a result of his own research, Rose concludes that constituency parties are neither as concerned with policy generally nor as ideologically extreme as often supposed. Policy disagreements thus divide the parties vertically in pitting some MPs, party organizational leaders, and party activists against others, rather than dividing them horizontally in a "conflict between a monolithic bloc of activists and a monolithic leadership." Considerable flexibility is apparently granted the party leadership and the leaders can count on a great deal of membership support; policy opposition tends to come from only a fraction of the party activists.

It should be noted that a great deal more policy debate takes place within subunits of mass membership parties than takes the form of formal conference resolutions; the views of the members may have some influence by being transmitted upward to the leaders. Moreover, policy debate is only one means by which party activists seek to influence the party leadership. Another channel of potential influence by party activists involves the selection of the party's candidates for public office, especially where the party organization controls the candidate selection process. (This aspect of leader-follower relations in political parties receives further comment below.)

As far as the relative influence of the membership organization and the governmental party in the party policy-making process is concerned, three general patterns are possible (see Duverger, 1954, p. 190): first, in accordance with an extreme interpretation of party democracy norms, the membership organization exerts dominant influence; second, the party policy-making process is the result of mutual influence between the membership organization and the governmental party; third, party policy is the exclusive jurisdiction of the governmental party. No example of a democratic political party which firmly fits the first pattern comes to mind, leaving two empirical types. According to Valen and Katz (1964, Chapter 3), Norwegian political parties, especially the Labour Party, may be taken as examples of the second pattern: in their discussion of party decision-making, Valen and Katz conclude that "party decisions are definitely the result of a mutual process of influence between the two subsystems" — the governmental party and the membership organization (p. 88). Although "the formal structure of the party gives the decisive weight to the membership organization in Norwegian parties" (p. 89), in practice the governmental party enjoys several advantages — among them greater information and greater access to communications channels, especially in the area of foreign policy; the norm of party unity and continuation of power due to an unwillingness to jeopardize party success; and inactivity of many party subunits. Although the party leaders — especially parliamentary leaders — are "very influential in all major decisions," the total picture, however, is not one which would confirm the iron law of oligarchy. The wishes of the membership, the processes of discussion at all levels within the party, the decentralized nomination procedure, and the democratic election system result in a complex interaction between leaders and followers characteristic of all large democratic organizations" (p. 96).

The third pattern, policy dominance by the governmental party, is most clearly illustrated by American parties, with little in the way of an organized membership and with the party organization serving elected officials in a service role. Robert McKenzie (1955) also places British political parties in this category — including the Labour Party, whose membership organization claims policy influence. The fact that the relationship between the membership organization and the parliamentary party in the policy-making process raises a "constitutional" issue within the Labour party, given the acceptance of the norm of internal party democracy, does not prevent policy dominance by the latter group. The operative features of British government, with its conventions of cabinet government and the role of the party leaders as Prime Minister or potential Prime Minister, are such, McKenzie argues, that the parliamentary party cannot allow its policy decisions to be dictated by the membership organization or any extra-parliamentary group, even if it were of a mind to do so.

The above comments, especially relating to the British and Norwegian Labour parties, illustrate a basic dilemma of political parties based on the Party Democracy model: the seemingly inevitable tensions between the norms of intraparty democracy and party unity. This is a conflict which tends to pit the governmental party, stressing the importance of party unity and cohesion in order to present a united front to opposing parties and the public in the interest of electoral and governmental success against the membership organization, emphasizing the norm and practice of full and free discussion of policy differences within the party. No successful democratic party can afford to opt exclusively for one or the other of these alternatives; how the continuing tension between the norms of intraparty democracy and party unity are handled in political parties is a theoretically significant problem that deserves more attention.

One aspect of the relationship between the governmental party and the party membership organization — relationships between national legislators and their constituency party organizations — is the subject of the last two studies in this section which deal with the United States and Canada. David Olson (Selection 5.3) investigates the relationship of congressmen to their congressional district party organizations; he is dealing here with congressmen's perceptions of their district parties. (Olson notes that the term "district party" in American politics is largely artificial, since it seldom constitutes a single entity but consists instead of several county parties or, in the case of metropolitan areas, part of a county party, the basic unit of American party organization.) His sample of 36 Democratic and Republican congressmen was selected to include a wide range of variation in party organizational characteristics and relationships. Olson found that party organizational realities varied "very extensively from all-powerful to almost nonexistent," a range not well predicted by the competitive status of the parties in the district. His first task was the development of a party organizational typology, based on the congressmen's reliance on their district parties, which was contingent upon the extent that the district parties could help them get re-elected. Olson found that only a minority of the district parties were characterized by "high reliance" because "only in some areas does party provide the electoral support usually ascribed to party as one of its 'functions.' "

Having classified district parties, Olson then analyzed both the involvement of district party officials with their congressman as perceived by the congressman and the role of the congressman in his district party organization. He found that "most congressmen feel that the local party leaderships are more interested in other offices and public arenas than in Congress, and that in relation to Congress, they are more interested in projects and patronage than in policy. The extent to which local party leaders are concerned with policy is seen as a product of their pragmatic concern with possible electoral consequences, not policy itself, of the congressman's position." (It should be noted that this statement is a classic depiction of the Rational-Efficient model.) Olson does point out that the perceived lack of policy concern by party organizational leaders must be viewed against a backdrop of "generalized policy agreement" with their congressmen. The role of the congressman in his district party also varied widely — from "avoidance" to "helpful" to "active": "The party of high reliance or of factional reliance he cannot ignore. If he and it cannot coexist in a mutually helpful relationship, he must actively fight it." Congressmen have greater latitude vis-à-vis the poorly organized district party: "He is free to mold his own role toward it," including the option of ignoring it.

Allan Kornberg (Selection 5.4) presents similar data on Canadian MPs' perceptions of their constituency party organizations, part of a more extensive study of Canadian legislative behavior (Kornberg, 1967). In the present context Kornberg comes up with three main findings. First, although the specific questions differed from those used by Olson, it would appear that Canadian MPs place greater reliance for electoral purposes on their constituency party organizations than do U.S. Congressmen: 85 per cent of the left-wing (Liberal and New Democrat) and 78 per cent of the right-wing (Conservative and Social Credit) MPs "described their local organizations' contributions as very important." Second, Canadian MPs perceived their constituency parties as "important reference groups"; MPs rated local party leaders and workers as the most important and accurate sources of information on constituency opinions on policy issues. Right-wing legislators indicated somewhat greater reliance on their constituency parties. A third finding concerns MPs' attitudes towards the influence that local party officials should have and actually do exercise on MPs. Two-thirds of left-wing and more than four-fifths (82 per cent) of right-wing MPs felt that legislators should be influenced by their local parties and even more (72 per cent and 85 per cent, respectively) thought that local parties did influence MPs.

Unlike these two studies, Epstein (1960) intentionally deals with exceptional rather than typical relations between British MPs — mainly Conservative — and their constituency parties. Epstein investigated the fate of 30 Conservative MPs who deviated from party and government policy during the Conservative Government's handling of the Suez crisis in 1956-57: ten anti-Suez Conservatives (eight of whom abstained on votes supporting the Eden government's intervention) and 20 pro-Suez Extremists, who abstained from supporting subsequent efforts by the Macmillan government to extricate itself from the disaster. The fate of the two groups of dissident Conservative MPs was strikingly different. All of the ten prominent anti-Suez Conservatives suffered varying degrees of criticism and pressure from their constituency parties. Six survived, five of whom were renominated by their local parties. (The sixth survivor had announced his intention not to seek re-election prior to Suez.) Three withdrew, declared they would not run again, or resigned; Nigel Nicholson (1958), the most prominent case, was rejected by his constituency association and a new candidate was selected for the next election. In contrast, not one of the 20 pro-Suez Extremists lost his seat because of abstention, nor did any suffer the criticism from their local parties that the ten anti-Suez Conservatives did.

Epstein offers several tentative generalizations concerning relations between British MPs and their constituency parties. His general conclusion is that the Suez experience affirms the basic model, whereby the power of constituency associations to select parliamentary candidates — as Ranney (1965) demonstrates, a very real power — entails the power to criticize and even reject "their" MPs. British Members of Parliament need the support and goodwill of their constituency parties. As a general rule, the safer the seat, the more vulnerable to local party pressure is the MP — i.e., where selection as a parliamentary candidate is tantamount to election, the MP owes more to his constituency party. Epstein considers the general pattern exhibited in these cases significant: Only those MPs who deviated from party policy in the direction of the opposition were criticized and disciplined, but not those MPs whose stands were more orthodox (i.e., more conservative in the Conservative Party) than the policy views of the parliamentary party leadership. Ranney (1968) concurs and finds the same principle to be operative in the Labour Party: "Thus in both parties not all breaches of party discipline have been frowned on — only those which support the opposition's position" (p. 152). Both Epstein (1967) and Ranney (1968) note that the potentially great power of constituency parties does not hinder cohesion of the national party, since the party activists have a national partisan orientation.

These comments provide no more than a bare introduction to a discussion of intraparty democracy and party processes, a discussion too often characterized by polemics and cast in extreme formulations. The question is not whether party activists are to be the final arbiters of party policy or whether party leaders make policy without regard for the views of party activists. Rather, the empirical question is the degree of constraint that norms of intraparty democracy place on party leaders. The norm itself can have some effect to the extent that party leaders in formulating policy engage in consensus-building policy discussion within the party — i.e., make policy with the expressed and perceived views of the members in mind, and seek actively to generate support for their policies within the party as well as within the electorate. Oligarchy and party democracy are a matter of degree.

REFERENCES

Barnes, Samuel H. "Participation, Education, and Political Competence." *American Political Science Review*, 60 (June, 1966), 348-53.

________. "Party Democracy and the Logic of Collective Action," in *Approaches to the Study of Party Organization*, edited by William J. Crotty, pp. 105-38. Boston: Allyn and Bacon, 1968.

________. *Party Democracy: Politics in an Italian Socialist Federation.* New Haven: Yale University Press, 1967.

Cassinelli, C.W. "The Iron Law of Oligarchy." *American Political Science Review*, 47 (1953), 773-84.

Dahl, Robert A. "A Critique of the Ruling Elite Model." *American Political Science Review*, 52 (1958), 463-69.

Duverger, Maurice. *Political Parties.* New York: John Wiley and Sons, 1954.

Epstein, Leon D. "British Members of Parliament and their Local Parties: The Suez Case." *American Political Science Review*, 54 (June, 1960), 374-90.

________. *Political Parties in Western Democracies.* New York: Frederick A. Praeger, 1967.

Gunlicks, Arthur B. "Intraparty Democracy in Western Germany." *Comparative Politics*, 2 (January, 1970), 229-50.

Janosik, Edward G. *Constituency Labour Parties in Britain.* New York: Frederick A. Praeger, 1968.

Kornberg, Allan. *Canadian Legislative Behavior.* New York: Holt, Rinehart and Winston, 1967.

Lane, Robert E. *Political Life.* Glencoe, Ill.: Free Press, 1959.

Lipset, Seymour Martin; Coleman, James; and Trow, Martin. *Union Democracy.* Garden City, N.Y.: Doubleday, 1962.

Lohmar, Ulrich. *Innerparteiliche Demokratie.* Stuttgart: Ferdinand Enke Verlag, 1963.

May, John D. "Democracy, Organization, Michels." *American Political Science Review,* 59 (June, 1965), pp. 417-29.

———. "Democracy, Party 'Evolution,' Duverger." *Comparative Political Studies,* 2 (July, 1969), 216-48.

Mayntz, Renate. "Oligarchic Problems in a German Party District," in *Political Decision-Makers,* edited by Dwaine Marvick, pp. 138-92, New York: The Free Press of Glencoe, 1961.

McGovern, George. "Commission on Party Structure and Delegate Selection Report." Adopted by the Democratic National Committee, November 19-20, 1969.

McKenzie, Robert T. *British Political Parties.* New York: St. Martin's Press, 1955.

McKitterick, T.E.M. "The Membership of the Party." *The Political Quarterly,* 31 (July-September, 1960), 312-23.

Michels, Robert. *Political Parties.* Glencoe, Ill.: Free Press, 1949.

Milbrath, Lester W. *Political Participation.* Chicago: Rand McNally, 1965.

Nicholson, Nigel. *People and Parliament.* London: Weidenfeld and Nicholson, 1958.

Olson, David M. *The Congressman and His Party.* Forthcoming.

Ranney, Austin. *Pathways to Parliament.* Madison: The University of Wisconsin Press, 1965.

———. "Candidate Selection and Party Cohesion in Britain and the United States," in *Approaches to the Study of Party Organization,* edited by William J. Crotty, pp. 139-58. Boston: Allyn and Bacon, 1968.

Rasmussen, Jorgen S. *The Relations of the Profumo Rebels with Their Local Parties.* Tucson: The University of Arizona Press, 1966.

Rose, Richard. "Parties, Factions, and Tendencies in Britain." *Political Studies,* 12 (1964), 33-46.

———. "The Political Ideas of English Party Activists." *American Political Science Review,* 56 (June, 1962), 360-71.

Schlesinger, Joseph A. "Political Party Organization," in *Handbook of Organizations*, edited by James G. March, pp. 764-801. Chicago: Rand McNally, 1965.

Sorauf, Frank J. *Political Parties in the American System.* Boston: Little, Brown, 1964.

Valen, Henry, and Daniel Katz. *Political Parties in Norway: A Community Study*, Chapter 3. Oslo: Universitetsforlaget, 1964.

Wilson, James Q. *The Amateur Democrat.* Chicago: University of Chicago Press, 1962.

Oligarchic Problems in a German Party District

Renate Mayntz

How Members are Attracted to the Party Organization

Since joining is voluntary, the party — like any other such organization — must offer some inducements to prospective members. It would be unrealistic to assume that more than a small minority deliberately joined as a means to reach a desired power position. Joining the party also provided limited opportunities for social and business contacts that could be of personal advantage. Beyond such inducements, the fund of more explicit "payments" was limited by the relatively scarce opportunities for patronage.

A further inducement may be a sense of moral satisfaction in taking part in public life. However, party membership is not commonly considered to be an essential element in an adult's social role — whether that of citizen, community member, or member of any occupational class. Only a comparatively small part of the Federal Republic's electorate are members of any political party (3.6 per cent), and, judging from the results of a 1954 public-opinion survey, only an added 6 per cent were willing (even conditionally) to join a party.

Reprinted from *Political Decision-Makers: Recruitment and Performance*, edited by Dwaine Marvick (New York: The Free Press, 1961), pp. 149-64, 187-89, by permission of The Macmillan Company. Footnotes omitted by permission.

The fact that being a party member is not a typical adult role, coupled with the negative attitude in Germany toward joining political parties, helps to explain why recruitment is sporadic. Thus, the motives of those who do join have greater significance. An organization, like an institution or profession (e.g., the police force or the priesthood), may unintentionally attract a particular type of person; subsequently, this type of person in turn may leave a distinctive mark upon the organization. Should this psychological selectivity in joining a political party tend to attract, say, corruptible persons bent upon achieving and wielding power for its own sake, the harm that could be done to the body politic served by that party would be great indeed.

During the interviews with District office-holders, they were asked their reasons for joining the CDU. From various observed and incidental documentary evidence, the motives of rank-and-file members may also be inferred. Although the data of this study are not sufficient to make quantitative statements about the proportions of different membership types or the relative importance of various motives for joining, a number of types of party members were found in the District. Stable patterns in their behavior served to differentiate them, and these in turn were readily related to particular reasons for joining party groups.

Three types of members were found to be characterized by different "instrumental motives," to use Parsons's terminology. First, is the opportunist and seeker of petty advantages. In fact, the party cannot give much help to those who are seeking jobs, housing accommodations, contracts, or free vacations for their children, and so forth. However, in the District, what little the party was believed to offer did attract some members. The opportunist's motive rarely led to very active participation, particularly not in any party office demanding much time or effort. This cost was apparently too great to be worthwhile, in light of the relatively small material gratifications offered or hoped for in party work.

A second type was motivated by a drive for power; political ambition led some members to participate actively and to strive for influential office. A third type seemed motivated by personal ambition; politics was a means of making a living, either directly by getting a paid party office or elective office on a higher level, or indirectly by furthering a career in the Berlin administration. Political and personal ambitions converge, but there are important distinctions: the personally ambitious often seems quite professionally oriented, little interested in wielding influence for its own sake, not attracted by political machinations, and often less ideological in his partisanship than the "politician."

A fourth observed type was normatively committed, motivated by genuine political interests and ideological identification with the party program. Frequently, one specific program was of greater importance than others to such ideologues. Most members of this type were willing to assume office, many quite desirous of doing so. Often, they had joined the CDU very soon after its foundation or their own return from captivity. The older usually had records of political activity dating back to the Weimer Republic. Among the younger, anticommunism and anti-Marxism were strong motivating factors Moreover, the normative commitment easily went hand in hand with a desire to link one's professional career with party activity. This subtype might be called the most valuable one found among CDU office-holders.

Normative or ideological commitment does not necessarily lead to active participation. This was shown by a fifth, quite frequent type: the person who joined the CDU to prove his faith in the *Weltanschauung*, or ideological basis of the CDU. Members like this were usually very partisan in their views, loyal in voting and continuing their membership, and regular in paying their dues. Otherwise, they were often inactive to the point of not even attending the monthly meetings of their locals.

A pure embodiment of any one of these types was, of course, rarely if ever found. This is even more true for the sixth and last type to be mentioned, the "joiner," who is apparently motivated by gregariousness and a desire to belong. He must have at least one other motive to make him join a political party instead of some social club or voluntary association, which might satisfy purely social needs even better. In the District, the joining motive in itself was not conducive to seeking higher office or the responsibility of leadership. But it did bring the member to his local unit's monthly meetings.

Nonparticipating members, participating rank-and-file, and office holders may be expected to reveal characteristically different motivational patterns. At this point, let us consider a few data about participation. The holders of the highest District offices — the chairmen of committees, District board members, and borough assemblymen — comprise only 4 per cent of the total membership; if lesser functionaries are included — such as local board members, regularly attending committee members, or delegates — office-holders account for roughly one-fifth of the total membership. Analysis of attendance at meetings of the District's largest local for a period of eighteen months revealed that about half the members came to only one-tenth of all meetings, i.e., came barely once a year. These we shall call "inactive members." Only a quarter of this local's membership attended an average of eight out of ten meetings; this included most office-holders. The meeting of a typical local at the time of the study and during the preceding years usually found from one-quarter to one-half of the members present. The average was about one-third. Even local chairmen who urged attendance strongly, by letter or in person, could not raise it above half the paper membership.

Selecting Leaders

The routine recruitment methods observed in the District in no way assured that party members were qualitatively select citizens. Perhaps it is generally the more active and politically responsible citizen who lets himself be inducted into a party. But our brief consideration of motives for joining suggests that this hope is only partly justified. It is, then, of crucial importance whether intraparty processes of leadership-selection tended to promote the best-qualified members.

The CDU party constitution provides for a selection process that moves in steps from the lowest to higher levels of office. Only offices at the local level are to be filled directly by the vote of the whole membership; at higher levels, delegates do the voting.

The election rules laid down in the constitution were, in general, closely adhered to in the District. Rare cases of slight deviation were observed. These were due mostly to negligence plus a desire for simplification, or to idiosyncratic interpretations of unclear rules; seldom were deviations the results of deliberate attempts at manipulation. Observing constitutional rules was a norm of primary importance; practically every member was strongly committed to do it. Indeed, on many occasions the constitution was quoted to decide controversies on procedural issues. Those whose views were not supported in the rules gave immediate, if disappointed, acquiescence.

Even full adherence to the letter of democratic rules does not guarantee, however, that their spirit will animate the selection process. Thus, formal constitutional provisions stipulate who elects the party officials at various organizational levels. These provisions had the probably quite unintended effect of producing markedly different interest in the elections for different offices. Local members were most interested in elections where they could vote directly. At the District level, delegates voted according to their own opinions, instead of expressing the wishes of those to whom they owed their mandates. Similarly, the practice of preplanning, observed in local elections, while it violated no formal rule, clearly ran counter to the meaning of intraparty democracy.

Selection processes were observably different for various offices. The number and quality of aspirants for a given office proved important factors. Certain kinds of positions, because of the opportunities they gave, attracted members with particular motives. Committee chairmanships or elective administrative offices thus tended to attract members with professional interest in the subject matter. The latter kind of office also attracted persons interested in political careers. Again, the offices in the upper party hierarchy that carried organizational authority, that gave the incumbent greater access to the public, and that enhanced his prestige, were the goals of those ambitious for deference and those striving for the inherent satisfactions of power.

Later, we will discuss the observed measure of correspondence between the type of office and the motivation and characteristics of office-holders. There was, for members highly motivated to assume office in the first place, an attraction toward higher party levels. This produced a dearth of better-qualified aspirants for lower-level offices; furthermore, the lower-level the office, the fewer its aspirants. These statements and their consequences for the selection process will be borne out as we turn now to the elections for various bodies.

1. Local Elections. Once a year, the members of a local elect their board (of eight to fifteen members), including its chairman and some delegates to the District Delegate Assembly. The interest of members in these elections proved to be very slight — evidenced by particularly low attendance on such occasions — unless a speaker or some other attraction had been scheduled for the same evening. Among those with no intention of seeking office, and with weak organizational identification (as distinguished from ideological orientation), the problems of city or federal politics generally evoked more interest.

Another important feature of local elections has been the shortage of aspirants, especially evident in the smaller locals. Aside from the chairmanship, local offices were not very attractive: the costs, in terms of time and effort, were relatively high; and the rewards, in terms of prestige, power, participation in policy-making, and material or job advantages, were rather low. For some, just beginning their political careers, service on a local board has been a stepping stone and precondition to higher offices. Once ther goal has been achieved, they often withdraw their services from the local. Others, with support from higher party officers or with noteworthy qualifications as an expert of some kind, can forego this step. No other party offices were filled as often as those on the local board by members who did not desire to hold office, but who consented to be elected out of a sense of party obligation.

The shortage of candidates necessarily lowered the qualitative selection standards. Only where several contestants aspired to an office could their respective abilities be compared before casting one's vote. Members who had to be urged to take office were probably less motivated to perform well in office than those who competed for a post. Many shortcomings in the locals were the result of these conditions.

Because of the shortage of candidates, the common practice of partially preplanning local-election choices seemed to contribute directly and effectively to the selection of a new board. This preplanning was usually done by the chairman and his board members, who got together before the election, discussed possible candidates, and agreed among themselves who would best fill at least the major offices of the board. Sometimes the preplanning group included only a part of the old board, or a clique within it. Preplanning was seldom applied to the party-assembly delegates, but it was more or less customary for newly elected board members to be named also to these delegate posts.

The agreed-upon nominations of such preplanning groups were subsequently made at the election meeting. Although the practice was not exactly constitutional, members did not ordinarily object if they saw that they themselves could not make better nominations. In fact, many were probably not aware of the planned origin of the nominations. Of course, the members at the meeting could advance counternominations. However, when they came to an election meeting, most of them had no specific plans in mind except for the office of chairman. They were quite satisfied if someone else made the nominations on which they were to vote.

Preplanning, as observed, was a local process into which the higher party officials hardly ever intruded. Of course, the opinion of a local member who held office on a higher party level would be considered, even if he had no official position in his local. A member of the District board or its chairman also occasionally was interested in who would be the next chairman of a local other than their own, particularly if there was reason to fear that a person considered unsuitable or even harmful to the party would be elected. But the most that could be, or was, done even in such a case was to give advice to an influential and personally known member of the local in question.

Constitutionally, locals possess considerable autonomy; this structural characteristic of the CDU is anchored in its ideology. The locals guard their autonomy firmly. Any visible attempt to exert pressure from outside would meet with fierce resistance and might well boomerang unpleasantly upon its initiators. This is substantiated by reports about incidents involving interference in previous years.

The dangers inherent in preplanning are easily noted: a tendency to perpetuate those already in office and to hold down new aspirants, particularly if their views are not congenial to the preplanning group. These dangers, however, only become real if there are more candidates than offices to be filled, which is practically never the case in local elections.

If nominations were made spontaneously by the rank-and-file members attending the election meeting, they would still focus largely around previous office-holders, because of their greater visibility and familiarity. The rank-and-file of a local, even that minority which regularly attended the monthly meetings, could hardly develop in the course of a single year adequate or extensive personal knowledge as a basis for an accurate judgment of potential candidates. Perhaps the situation would be different if the members of a local had frequent contact with each other outside of the party meetings, but in the District this was not often the case. The territorial boundaries of a local did not correspond to anything like a neighborhood in the sociological sense. Besides, sometimes up to half of a local's members lived outside of its territorial boundaries, in spite of the fact that this was deemed undesirable by constitutional provision. As a result, the chairman and his board members regularly had the most extensive personal knowledge of potential candidates and could judge best the abilities and possible willingness to serve of individual members.

Aside from incumbents, spontaneous nomination might be made of easily visible members, such as someone who stood out in the discussions at monthly meetings, or a person of high social status. In any case, only those present at an election meeting would thus be considered. Nonattendance was often an easy way out for members who were able but unwilling to assume the responsibilities of party office. Those in the preplanning groups, on the other hand, contacted the members they thought capable before the election and persuaded them to stand for an office. It was much more difficult to refuse such a direct request than merely to withdraw after being nominated spontaneously. Thus, the practice of preplanning actually activated members to serve the party. It was also observed that, rather than leave even a single willing party member without office, the chairman would often suggest, and the members vote to create, a new post on the board. Even in the 1957 election of the largest and particularly active local where some offices had several contestants, nobody nominated was left without an office, even if not the office originally desired. The reservoir of willing candidates was completely used up.

The local elections were thus largely rank-and-file acclamations of decisions made beforehand, at least as far as the more important party posts were concerned. Under such conditions, the election itself assumed the character of a ceremonial ritual which had the form but not the content of on-the-spot decision-making. The rank-and-file members seemed to delegate a good part of their elective functions to an active minority. Yet they did retain full opportunity for control, and figuratively stood ready to resume control should they become dissatisfied with the active minority's preplanning, or as soon as they had definite alternative preferences of their own. The preplanning minority was fully aware of this potential control, which kept them from openly acting contrary to the wishes and opinions of the rank-and-file members.

What appeared to be a mere ceremony at times suddenly sprang to life and became a process of decisive importance when conflict arose within a local and opposing candidates or factions fought for power. Such cases were very rare. In most years the elections in all thirteen District locals followed the pattern outlined above.

If conflict did arise, it was more often caused by individual ambition and personal animosity than by ideological issues. The rivals did, however, activate latent differences within the membership in their effort to secure a sizeable following, so that in the end the younger and older, Catholic and Protestant, left-wing and right-wing factions seemed to rally around opposing spokesmen. The fact that such divisions formed rarely, disappeared quickly, and hardly ever involved the whole membership of a local, is due to the relatively easy access to board offices which ambitious individuals have and to a general lack of pronounced tensions among the rank-and-file, whose limited interest and rather low organizational identifications made for considerable tolerance.

2. Election of the District Board. In marked contrast to the informal co-optation patterns that characterized local elections, the annual process by which the District board and its chairman were elected was both more competitive and more formalized.

First, there has been no scarcity of aspirants for District board offices. These posts carry more prestige, greater authority, constitute important stepping-stones for a political career, and permit participation in more important decision-making than occurs at the local level. At the some time, most of them require less time and effort than is called for from a local chairman or treasurer.

The election of District board members is performed by the District assembly. All local chairmen are *ex officio* members of the assembly; in addition, each local sends one elected delegate for every twenty-five members. In 1957, 80 per cent of these elected delegates were members of their local boards, and the rest were either past or present holders of other local offices.

Although the delegates who had the right to vote for District board members were typically interested and in full attendance at such elections, they did not feel accountable in any meaningful degree to the locals from which they came. Their votes were cast according to their own opinions and previous deliberations, although the local chairman has a particularly strong if not often decisive influence over others from his local. The members of their locals were not even asked for their opinions before District elections. Nor did the rank-and-file show much spontaneous interest. They lacked, even more than in local elections, the personal knowledge and insight necessary to form judgments concerning the suitability of alternative candidates, particularly candidates from other locals.

The members of a local had only sporadic opportunities to observe even incumbent District board members in action. Thus, they have little basis for evaluating their performance in considering their reelection. Of the rarely attending half of the membership of the largest local, 50 per cent reported in 1957 that they did not know the District chairman even by sight, although he had been in office several years. Fully 83 per cent reported they did not know any District board member except possibly the chairman. On the other hand, for the most regularly attending quarter of the same local's membership, which includes most of its office-holders, the corresponding figures were 7 per cent and 41 per cent.

Locals compete with each other for District board positions; this competition inhibits preplanning like that found in local elections. It is conceivable that a large clique within a District board could make an election plan. But this could only be successful if a full slate were agreed upon, and if the election strategy of the various locals could also be decisively influenced. Informants told of situations in other districts where clique control existed, but it definitely did not in the District studied, where no such unity existed in the board or in any large clique on it. Board members were more effective in influencing their locals to vote *against* certain incumbents seeking reelection or the favorites of rivals already on the Board. In 1957, the participant observer could watch as many local delegations made independent plans, some in opposition to each other, some forming coalitions and making agreements of mutual aid for election night.

Each year, prior to the District board election, a special committee with one representative from each of the thirteen locals met to draw up a nominations list. Usually such a list named only one candidate — the candidate getting the most committee votes — for each office. Since the delgates came with rather firm intentions, however, the committee's recommendation often did not affect their preconsidered course, taken either as a delegation or coalition. If necessary, they nominated their own candidate during the assembly meeting and voted for him.

The stimulus of committee nomination brings votes to a nominee only in a situation of pronounced fluidity of opinion and indecision among the voters. The main function of the nominations committee seemed to be that, while it met, each local (through its representative) gained an impression of how strong the backing for different candidates was likely to be. Sometimes a particular local was induced to change its plans. When strong and even open conflict existed, a local sometimes had its representative vote in the nominating committee so as to conceal its real plan. In 1957, the committee changed procedure and presented several nominations for each office. In this case, of course, the nomination list provided even less guidance.

These remarks do not mean that delegates never decided how to vote during the assembly elections after they got there. Delegations from particular locals did not always make plans for every office. The discussion of individual candidates at the assembly meeting itself sometimes drew attention to facts that changed some delegates' opinions; occasionally a favored candidate was unexpectedly rejected. The "counter measures" launched by his supporters called for a change in plans. Again, a new candidate might suddenly be thought of, nominated, and elected without much previous deliberation. In the 1957 District elections, examples of each of these possibilities were observed.

In general, each local delegation voted unanimously for or against particular candidates. There were some cases, however, where the voting alignment cut directly across delegations. Voting in 1957 was practically always by secret ballot, a procedure that a single assembly member may demand. Only when unanimity prevailed was voting done by raising of hands.

While attending numerous discussions where delegates tried to decide whether to vote for or against a particular candidate, this observer noted the use of a number of selection criteria. First, in deliberating about a candidate, his probable performance in office played a large part. A second factor was representativeness, considered in a variety of senses — political, geographic, and social. These rational criteria were sometimes applied in an emotional sense, when they became mere loyalty or attraction for a person possessing certain characteristics.

There is, prior to the discussion of a candidate's qualifications, a basic prerequisite of success which he must generally meet: he must be known to a majority of delegates. This could be achieved in a number of ways. Previous office-holders of district-wide renown had a distinct advantage. High professional prestige or being known as a former high official in a nearby district were among the other ways by which this basic requirement was met.

Although the constitution did not forbid it, it was practically unheard of for anyone not at least a delegate and thus present in the assembly at election time to be nominated to the District board. This effectively limited the number of possible candidates in yet another unwritten way.

Given some familiarity with a candidate, delegates were often preoccupied with his credentials and the quality of performance to be expected from him. A candidate was expected to have a record of active participation and familiarity with District and party politics. Beyond this, different qualifications were stressed depending on the office in question. There was, however, little agreement concerning what were a given office's most important requirements. In 1957, for instance, delegates debated whether, for the treasurer, occupational experience with bookkeeping was more important than personal connections with potential contributors. On that same occasion, there were delegates who felt that a District chairman should have a conciliatory and diplomatic attitude, while other delegates felt that a District chairman should be a man primarily known for the firmness of his views and the strength of his fighting spirit. On still another office, the problem was posed whether a person with an impressive record of party work and commitment to the District was to be preferred to a person with high party prestige as a member of the West Berlin government.

One explanation for the lack of agreement concerning desirable qualities is the lack of conciseness in defining many official roles. Moreover, those tasks which the constitution and the unwritten party tradition do assign to particular roles are diverse; sometimes they call for rather opposite kinds of skills, character traits, and social assets. Agreement among the delegates about the selective standards — which of course need not lead to unanimous voting for particular candidates — presupposes not only a clear image of an office's requirements but also agreement upon the relative weight given to different and not necessarily complimentary qualities. In the absence of both, fitting a candidate to an office is difficult. Lack of clarity concerning what should be expected from an office-holder also makes it difficult, after a person has achieved office, to judge his performance and thus his merits for re-election.

Another major selection criterion is related to the representativeness of a District board candidate. Whether representativeness referred to political subunits or to social and geographic groupings, applying it as a criterion could of course present serious conflicts with the application of probable performance standards. However, often the District board itself was seen as a coordinating and integrating center of party activity; in this sense, the representativeness of its composition was directly and functionally relevant.

Apart from constitutional provisions governing the District board's composition, the delegates openly or covertly consider the appropriate representation of major occupational and religious groupings. In 1957, propaganda for particular candidates as being labor representatives, self-employed artisans, or spokesmen for independent businessmen was made openly during assembly debate. On the other hand, a candidate's religion, while definitely of importance in the private deliberations, was never mentioned openly in discussing his merits. The CDU is strongly motivated to play down religious differences in its ranks and to prevent religious factions from developing. This is widely feared as a potential source of party disunity. As soon as strong rivalries develop on any other count, however, the campaign tends to activate any latent religious factionalism by bringing religion into the private deliberations.

Even among delegates who did consider the candidate's religion, there existed no agreement about the "right" board ratio of Protestants to Catholics. When the members of one religion felt that a proportionate representation norm would restrict the number of offices they could otherwise occupy, they denounced such quotas as unjust. When they saw such norms, on the other hand, as desirable barriers to the overproportionate success of the rival religious faction, they advocated them as reasonable.

In 1957, some Protestant delegates argued for a District chairman who was a Protestant, on the grounds that he represented the party's religious majority. Some Catholic delegates argued that this was not valid; they favored a rival candidate, a Catholic, on grounds of his ability and past level of activity.

In general, although religion was a criterion, it was only one among many aspects of "representativeness." The support for a candidate showed no obvious correspondence to his religion. A criterion of greater strength was the locality from which he came. Every local party unit preferred a candidate from its own ranks. This preference was sometimes observed to override considerations of probable poor performance. Although this kind of local partisanship may sometimes lead to a mediocrity's election, it does stir strong interest among a local's rank-and-file.

Geographically proportionate representation was clearly expected by most delegates. Thus, one relatively large local party unit covertly criticized a smaller one which had succeeded in filling more District board offices than it had. Every year since the foundation of the Districts, between seven and ten of the thirteen locals have had at least one member on the District board; only the smallest local has never had a representative.

Clearly, geographic representation operates as a criterion, but other kinds of representativeness and questions of the probable quality of performance have, in many cases, overridden the fact that a particular local already has its quota. Members of outstanding quality or ambition could reasonably hope to be elected.

One test of the probable performance from a candidate was his past performance. Those officers who had fulfilled their tasks adequately or had at least not shown serious deficiencies had rational arguments in their favor and also could claim a certain loyalty. For an incumbent seeking re-election to be supplanted by a newcomer was regarded as a personal rebuke and a vote of distrust. An incumbent is known, and in this minimum sense he has a good chance of being reelected. His experience can be looked upon as a relatively safe indicator of his future performance. Indeed, this may be so, where the job's requirements are little known, or varied and complex. In contrast, there is inevitably a risk involved in electing a new person, whose qualifications have had no empirical test.

This particular set of rational and emotional appeals prevents more incisive consideration of the qualifications needed for insuring high job performance. The very effectiveness of the "incumbency argument" strengthens a tendency toward oligarchy, the perpetuation of the current leading group in office. Thus, the argument is dysfunctional to selection of board members on grounds that relate to their qualifications and merit, and, at the same time, it is dysfunctional to rank-and-file control through intraorganizational democratic processes. Against these points, one must balance the fact that the effectiveness of the "incumbency argument" helps to preserve continuity in the party's leadership group and to inhibit the disruptive rivalries which develop when many people develop personal ambitions for more power.

A candidate's election to the District board is the result of a complicated process, involving both rational deliberation over his merits for the office and his "group representativeness" in a variety of appropriate senses, and also involving more emotional appeals to loyalty — to a member of one's own religion, to a member of one's own local party unit, and to an incumbent if there is one. In a later section, we will consider the effects of this selection process on the District board's composition.

3. Selection of Committee Chairmen. At the District level, the party apparatus involves a rather elaborate committee structure. The constitution establishes seven committees whose official functions may roughly be termed advisory; in addition, three "work-group" committees have constitutional status. Each annually elects its own chairman and other appropriate officers. Two of the three "work groups" (*Arbeitsgemeinschaften*) — those for women and work-place groups — in composition and actual functioning are very similar to the advisory committees.

The seven advisory committees are concerned with specific subject matters, as for instance, "economic policy" or "cultural and school affairs." In 1957, these committees averaged about thirty-five members, most of whom were representatives from local party units while the rest were *ex officio* members. Actually, these committees did not give advice to other party groups at the District level and they participated only very occasionally in policy formation on higher levels. Mainly they served to inform their own members about a policy field and to get them to understand and agree to CDU policy in a specific area. Moreover, they provided safety valves for the expression of doubt, opinion, or criticism, and thus provided a measure of organizational hygiene.

For the nine District-level committees thus in question, the processes by which leaders were selected showed a number of common characteristics. First, the interest of committee members in the annual election was rather low. The commitees had little group cohesion, due to infrequent meetings, annual changes in membership, and low attendance. Partly because committee work was informative but gave little real opportunity to participate in policy-formation, members were only limitedly involved. Second, there was little competition for committee offices and a strong tendency, reinforced by the members' inertia, to reelect incumbents. Here, loyalty and the other elements of the "incumbency argument" operated strongly. Demands for geographic representation were largely irrelevant in these elections, as is true also for notions that certain categories of members should be represented by quota. Except in very rare cases of dissent and rivalry, elections of committee officers were not preplanned, though their outcome was predictable in most cases. Finally, the most important selection criteria proved to be expertise. This criterion was, understandably, most specific in committees with a clearly defined and narrowly circumscribed area of interest, as for instance, cultural and school affairs. It became progressively more difficult to apply when the subject matter of a committee could only be characerized as "women's interests and problems" or "questions of general politics" *(allgemeine Politik)*.

4. Nomination of Candidates for General Elections. Every four years, when city-wide elections approach, the District assembly nominates candidates for the borough assembly. Their number is determined by how many seats the party expects to win (15 to 20 in past years), plus a sufficient number of substitutes. At the same time, the District assembly nominates for each precinct within its territory a candidate for the Berlin House of Representatives. (Until 1957, precinct and local boundaries did not coincide.) From the retrospective information available, the selection processes in determining these candidates were very similar to those involved in electing District board members, except for the relative importance of some selection criteria.

Thus, rivalry among the locals, especially concerning borough assembly nominations, appears to have been at least as great as in District board elections. Pronounced interest in these nominations existed even at the level of the local boards, although not among the majority of the rank-and-file members. Prior to the decisive assembly meeting, each local board decided upon the list of candidates it would like to see nominated. Typically, without seeking the views of the local party members, this list went to the District office. There, a master list of nominations was compiled and used as a guide during assembly voting.

Local patriotism was justified as a valid selection basis by the argument that borough assembly nominations should be based on territorial representation, i.e., that each local should have at least one member in the borough self-governing body. In 1954, only one very small local in the District had not achieved this aim.

Another criterion which weighs more heavily in borough assembly nominations than in filling District board positions is group representation. There were always more aspirants than nominations to be made. In making up the list of nominees, care was consciously taken to represent young members, women, major occupational categories, and special groupings such as refugees. Catholics and Protestants were deliberately nominated in the ratio corresponding to membership composition. Use of these criteria was justified by the argument that all important categories of the electorate deserved to have someone with whom they could identify or whom they would see as their representative or spokesman.

Whenever a means-end relationship was clearly perceived between a specific selection criterion and the shared goal of achieving election success, the District assembly showed remarkable agreement about its acceptance and the priority to be given to such a criterion. The desire to appeal to the electorate effectively thus lay at the base of efforts to nominate persons of high public prestige; this gave an advantage to ex-members of the borough administrative council. The related desire to avoid reinforcing unfavorable CDU stereotypes helps explain why the party conscientiously refrained from nominating religious figures.

Standards that have to do with the probable quality of a nominee's performance were difficult to apply in making nominations for the borough assembly. Performance standards and the credentials sought in nominees could not be very high, since the majority of the aspirants had little expert knowledge or experience in borough administration.

The position of borough assembly member per se was not very attractive: it involved much time and effort without substantial remuneration or significant increase in prestige for anyone beyond the lower social strata. Those who viewed borough assembly services as a stepping-stone in a political or administrative career normally refused renomination once they had achieved their higher goal. A significant number of qualified aspirants was probably eliminated by the rule that no one employed in the borough administration could be a borough assembly member, although the rule did not apply to someone employed by the city-wide administration.

For these reasons, although qualifications for office were considered important, they were neither very strictly defined nor very rigorously applied. District officials frequently commented that while there was no lack of candidates for borough assembly seats, there was a serious shortage of well-qualified aspirants. The majority of those elected to this office for the first time were, in fact, ill-equipped to fulfill their duties. After several years of incumbency, considerable improvement in skills and knowledge occurred. Functionally, renomination of incumbents was thus definitely advantageous.

In the past, the Land level of the party took little interest in the candidates nominated for borough assemblies in West Berlin. In accordance with the party constitution, this was every district's own affair. The situation was different when nominations were being considered for the Berlin House of Representatives. In this case, the constitution provides the Land board with a certain measure of influence over district nominations, and the actual influence was probably greater than the constitution visualized. Not only were the district nominations discussed beforehand with the Land board, but the higher body also used its rights to propose one candidate of its own for each district. In 1954, the District agreed to nominate a second candidate whom the Land board wanted. In this instance, both candidates backed by the Land board belonged to districts other than that which officially nominated them.

Berlin parliamentary candidates, in short, were thought of as drawn from city-wide rather than district bases, although the districts displayed considerable interest in having their own members nominated. Local patriotism was, however, largely irrelevant in view of the small number of such nominations made by each district — less than ten in the District investigated — and in view of the type of office involved. Criteria concerning the qualifications for performance were high and could be more freely and fully applied in these cases than for borough assembly nominations.

District level officials, including delegates also active on the Land and city levels of party work, showed especially strong interest in, and influence over, these nominations to the Berlin legislature. Among other reasons, this was because district-level officials had more insight into, were more familiar with, and were more involved in higher-level party politics and in city-wide politics generally.

According to the constitution, each district also selects city councilors who are to represent the CDU in the borough's administrative council. Nominations are formally made by the borough assembly *Fraktion*, and the whole borough assembly votes on such nominations. In selecting these candidates in previous elections, District officials had to take into account special considerations. First, they were sometimes hampered by coalition agreements made on a city-wide basis between the major political parties. For example, a coalition agreement once specified which political party was to have the position of borough mayor for each borough. Second, the opinion of the other political parties in the borough had to be taken into account, since a minimum level of good will and mutual acceptance of each other's councilors was considered necessary to secure continuing co-operation in borough administration. While the Land board has interfered only occasionally — and extraconstitutionally — in the selection of city councillors, the District has taken care not to nominate any one in disgrace with the Land board. The District chairman, as an *ex officio* member of the higher body, is usually the liaison figure in the informal consultations.

Candidates for city-councilor posts are also drawn from a city-wide rather than a district base. Two of the District's three city councilors, at the time of the study, had come from other districts when first nominated; one still retained his membership and even an office in another district. An extensive knowledge of persons is required for any district official who wants a decisive voice in these nominating deliberations.

The District also has a role in the annual election of a Land executive board. This board is elected by the Land assembly. In 1957, shortly before the election, its candidates were discussed in the District board. For this occasion, those delegates who were not *co ipso* District board members had been invited. The discussions were guided by candidate listings provided by a Land nominating committee. It was evident that board members without party offices taking them outside the District lacked the insight and knowledge necessary to form an independent judgment or to offer alternative candidates for these higher offices. Accordingly, they relied largely on the opinions of those who did have such credentials. Local boards and the District assembly were not asked for their own views and did not participate in the deliberations on the Land executive board selections.

Depending on its stake in a Land board election, a district delegation (present in the Land assembly for the voting) may vote according to a predetermined strategy. However, delegates in the Land assembly tend sometimes to be identified strongly with a special party grouping within the CDU, which cross-cuts district boundaries (such as the youth union), and accordingly cast their votes independently of, and even contrary to, the advice of their own district board.

It is not surprising to find a sharp increase in competition where these high party offices are involved. At the same time, however, the more exacting standards exclude aspirants with insufficient qualifications from being seriously considered as candidates. The field of possible candidates is further limited because no district delegation can afford to offer as its contender anyone who is unknown to other delegations. These conditions tend to strengthen oligarchic tendencies, which depend also on the widespread disinterest among the CDU rank-and-file membership.

Comparison of these different leadership-selection processes permits some summary statements. First, the amount of competition for a given type of office and the extent of interest displayed by those eligible to vote are positively correlated. Both interest and competition were higher for District board offices and for legislative nominations than for local board offices and committee chairs. The amount of competition itself, which depends largely on the attractiveness of an office, seems to stimulate interest among the voters. In addition, it is probable that District board offices and seats in the borough and city legislature are considered to be of greater consequence by the electors; therefore, the question of who will win them arouses more interest.

In local elections, where the reservoir of willing party-workers is in general fully utilized, the demands made of candidates in terms of skill are the lowest. The decisive factor is willingness to assume office, so that, in spite of the practice of preplanning, hopeful candidates easily find a post. Qualitative considerations begin to be made where voters can choose from among several candidates. But since qualitative standards are rather vague, and competing selection criteria enter the picture, there is no guarantee that the candidate most suited to an office is the one selected.

Role definitions and performance expectations play only a small part in party-leader selections. When the electorate is not guided by a clear qualitative frame of reference, other selection criteria gain more influence. Accordingly, a certain disjunction develops between selection and performance: performance comes to be determined largely by factors that operate after the winner assumes office. Analysis of leader performance bears this out fully, as will be seen; formal norms, informal expectations, subjective role perceptions, and elements inherent in an office's organizational situation are key factors that largely determine performance.

Finally, the leaders in higher offices were elected without any significant participation by lower party levels. In electing the District board, the assembly delegates (who were mostly local board officers) deliberated among themselves, without considering the opinions of local members. Correspondingly, Land assembly delegates (most of them District board officers) elected the Land executive board without deference to the opinions of other District officers (District delegates, for instance), or to the rank-and-file party membership. A potential danger exists in the degree of insulation against control from lower levels which this situation affords to higher party officers. Of course, the lower levels are by no means forcibly excluded from the deliberations; they do not rise up and demand to be heard. Moreover, the practice seems quite reasonable in view of the lack of insight and familiarity with potential candidates — the prerequisites for sensible judgment — among members not immediately involved in an election. In this situation of restricted democratic control in selecting leaders, democratic control via processes of opinion-formation and participation in policy-formation assumes increased importance as a possible alternative....

Summary and Outlook

Measured against realistic expectations, the picture presented by the District as of 1957 is favorable. From the viewpoint of an observer committed to the ideal of an efficiently functioning political democracy, however, there exist a number of more or less serious shortcomings and points of potential danger. Without repeating the arguments in detail, these points may now be summarized briefly.

There is a high degree of self-containment, not to say insulation, in the District. The lowest-level units of CDU do not constitute a region of high mutual permeability and interaction between the organization and the public. Furthermore, organized interest groups hardly interacted with the party at this level, although they surely did so at higher levels. Analysis of the activity of the borough assembly *Fraktion* and the party's city councilors in the District, not reported here, revealed some instances of such interaction; but, even there, much less was found than expected and less than would seem healthy in a pluralist power system where the parties play integrative roles. Finally, selection of party officers and candidates for general election was purely a party affair in the District, intra-organizational in scope. The participation of the electorate, organized or unorganized, was limited to deciding, every four years, how many of the party's nominees were to achieve office.

A second point of criticism is that through neither a deliberate recruitment of potential leaders, nor a corresponding orientation in intraparty elections, nor systematic training did the party purposefully insure having leaders and candidates of the highest possible ability or personal and political quality. If the present District leadership nevertheless displays positive characteristics, the credit goes only in part to the District's elective bodies. Some of the present qualified leaders at the local and District level received their positions with the help and upon the suggeston of other qualified leaders, i.e., through their urging, informal advice upon candidacies, personal campaigning, and so forth. The effects of the preplanning practice in local elections should be recalled.

The observed facts might be interpreted in part as evidence of a District leadership markedly oligarchical in character. Closer inspection, however, shows that this criticism hardly applied. Some factors ordinarily assumed to strengthen oligarchical tendencies were little in evidence at this organizational level. While there is much emphasis on organizational maintenance and its problems, there is no overbureaucratization that would strengthen the position of the "apparatus." Again, the District leaders, best informed and most frequently interacting among themselves, have no monopoly on communication media. Indeed, in 1957, no such media were relied upon in the District. Thirdly, most offices were not sufficiently attractive to motivate their incumbents to hold to them tenaciously merely to preserve status or material gratifications. Finally, the skills required, at least in the local and in several District-level offices, were not so rare that many ordinary members, far more than actually did so, could not reasonably aspire to these positions. At least at this lower party level, willingness to assume office was a more crucial factor than possession of special abilities.

A low turnover rate among office holders is another feature usually indicative of oligarchical leadership. In the District, however, this was in large part the result of tendencies among members and delegates to reelect incumbents. Elections in the District, except for local elections, were not manipulated in an oligarchic fashion, i.e., from above or by incumbents, and preplanning in the locals hardly deprived office to any interested persons. That delegates decided among themselves how to vote, rather than executing wishes of their parent bodies, did not violate the constitution—which gives no rules on this matter — and in fact corresponded to the actual level of limited interest and insight prevailing in the units from which the delegates came. Nor were the limited interest, low participation, and low involvement of large portions of the rank-and-file due to an entrenched leadership group deliberately usurping all responsibility and important functions, thus causing the remaining members to fall into apathy. Rather, this state of affairs was the consequence of the recruitment and admission standards, which permitted persons to join who never intended to participate actively. Nor should one evaluate this only negatively; even passive members may serve important functions in the larger context of a political system.

The District leadership was not oligarchic in the usual sense, yet it did display a high degree of independence as the result of several conditions, none of which these leaders had purposefully created. (1) Higher officeholders were insulated from lower-level control by the step-wise structuring of the election process. (2) The elected higher leaders were only limitedly visible to the lower levels, making assessment of their performance difficult by anyone outside of the small interaction group. Given the hierarchical structure of the organization, these two conditions may be unavoidable. The same was not true for two remaining conditions. (3) A large margin existed for self-definition of leadership tasks, because the norms and sanctions guiding leader behavior applied only to limited areas of their performance. (4) There was an absence of institutionalized participation by lower levels in matters of policy-formation dealing with programmatic value decisions (rather than the implementation of policy goals). The function of higher and intermediate ranks of party officials was presumably in part to translate general expectations relating to upward processes of policy-formation — and other negected functions such as the interaction with the public — into specific tasks allocated to specific office-holders, and to institute, for instance, procedures by which certain kinds of higher-level decisions could be presented to lower-level bodies with requests for their opinion. While it was not true that the divorce between higher decision-making bodies and lower party levels had been created by a deliberate usurpation of functions, the lower levels could have been activated more than they were.

The danger implied in the prevailing situation is potential more than actual; it lies less in the conditions of the District itself than in the fact that the decision-making bodies at the Land level were apparently as independent of District officials as the latter were of the local rank-and-file. If the lower party level is habitually only a resonating body for the decisions of leaders, it will presumably lack the disposition and the organizational instruments to assert its control, if, at some future time, these higher leaders should act against the latent wishes of the membership or in a way detrimental to the democratic political system. The danger, then, refers to a certain structured weakness in the substance of the democratic process. As such, it applies first of all to the German scene, but the same problem is posed in principle for all democracies.

The above problem may be rephrased, for the sake of added clarity. We have noted that the District membership at large accepted wholeheartedly the goal of political power of the CDU, as manifested in electoral success, and that any activity seen as directly related to electoral success was performed with particular willingness. However, instead of consciously perceiving power as a means for implementing a specific program, the membership received it as an end in itself. This left the elected leaders and representatives free to decide which policies should be pursued. Naturally, the leaders could not go directly against the general attitudes of the party membership, by pushing, for instance, the nationalization of industries. But the extent of the margin for independent decision-making at the highest level was seen, for example, in the event of the CDU's espousal of atomic armament in the famous parliamentary debate early in 1958. This issue had not been previously debated, at least at the District level in Berlin. It is by no means certain that the party rank-and-file, if consulted before any higher-level decisions had prejudged their opinion, would have supported the action. As it was, the District membership was simply presented with the decision, and many then felt called upon to defend it, as an action of their party, against outside criticism and particularly against that of the rival SPD.

This observation leads to a final point. Participant observation made it clear that the membership opinions voiced in discussions in local, committee, and assembly meetings in the District aimed primarily at creating consensus and support for the party's actions and legislative policy. While this may be important for maintaining organizational cohesion, it inhibits the development of independent political opinions among members. If the discussion of future policy were carried down to the lowest party level, intraorganizational conflict would be sharpened. A certain measure of such conflict seems essential for a vital democracy. . . .

Participation, Education, and Political Competence: Evidence from a Sample of Italian Socialists*

Samuel H. Barnes

Participation is one of the crises of political modernization. Along with the political awakening of masses of people has come the necessity of absorbing them meaningfully into the political system. The almost universally low levels of formal education and political competence contribute to the difficulties of mobilization. The most advanced polities are still seeking ways of making democratic participation effective; modernizing polities find the task even more formidable. This article examines the relationships among participation, education, and political competence in a sample of members of the Italian Socialist Party (PSI).

Although Italy is an advanced polity, in average education and industrialization it lags behind the world leaders in Europe and North America; and in some respects patterns of participation likewise reflect a transitional stage. The PSI is probably the only democratic Socialist party of the classic Marxian type left in Western Europe. It is devoted to the democratic mobilization of the indus-

*This research was accomplished while I was a Fulbright lecturer at the University of Florence in 1962-63. I wish to thank the Italian Fulbright Commission authorities, the Horace H. Rackham Graduate School of The University of Michigan, and the Olivetti Foundation for their assistance as well as the several professors, students, and party officials in Italy who made this research possible.

Reprinted from the *American Political Science Review*, LX (June, 1966), 348-52, by permission of the American Political Science Association and the author.

trial and agricultural masses. But it also contains a substantial middle-class element, and thus provides an opportunity to study the relationship between participation and political competence for persons of different levels of formal education.

There can be little doubt that differences in formal education have political consequences. The evidence is compelling that persons of high education participate more, are more knowledgeable, feel more efficacious, and exhibit greater sensitivity to the ideological dimensions of politics. Evidence from a sample of members of the PSI reinforces and refines these findings. Going beyond the simple associations between participation, education, and political competence, it is further evident that participation is more crucial as a means to political competence for the poorly educated than for the better educated. Formal education and participation in politics are both ways of achieving competence. There are undoubtedly many others, but participation is especially important for people of low education. The association between participation and political competence is not as strong for those of high education, as formal schooling and socialization in a sophisticated environment serve to develop competence independently of participation.

Three dimensions of political competence were investigated—factual knowledge about politics, sense of political efficacy, and ideological sensitivity. Measurements are discussed below. Although the data revealed the expected higher association between participation and political competence for those of low education, they also suggested some limitations on participation as a means to competence. At a given level of participation, the better educated always ranked higher on knowledge and efficacy. And high levels of ideological sensitivity were found *only* among members who ranked high on both education and participation. Finally, the relationship between participation and knowledge is stronger than that between participation and efficacy. Before discussing the implications of these findings I will examine some dimensions of the problem and present the data on which my conclusions are based.[1]

---

[1]These data are drawn from a research project on the internal politics of a PSI federation. While the larger study also includes interviews with all the formal leaders of the party in the province, plus extensive documentary research in party archives, the data analyzed here derive from 301 interviews with a dense sample of every third member of the party in the chief commune of the province. (The number of valid responses varies somewhat from table to table.) The interviews were administered in the spring of 1963 by students of the University of Florence. The response rate was 81% after at least two callbacks.

The larger study, which treats organizational democracy and oligarchy as problems in communications, is *Party Democracy: The Internal Politics of an Italian Socialist Federation* (forthcoming).

I. Participation, Education, and Voluntary Associations

One of the best documented conclusions about participation in voluntary associations in the United States is that high education and high participation are closely related. Studies further demonstrate that participation in voluntary associations is associated with increased political competence even if the associations are themselves nonpolitical. And the evidence is overwhelming that political competence and association membership correlated highly in the United States.[2] There is considerable evidence that these findings apply elsewhere. In their five-nation study, Gabriel Almond and Sidney Verba found that participation in voluntary associations is highly associated with political competence.[3] Similar conclusions are reported from a Finnish study cited by S. M. Lipset.[4]

Formal education is another method of acquiring both the substantive knowledge and the feeling of personal efficacy that are essential to political participation. That the better educated have higher rates of participation, regardless of how participation is measured, is demonstrated by a number of studies.[5] It is equally obvious that some individuals of meager formal education are active in politics and that some well-educated people are not: other variables clearly intervene between education and participation. In the PSI, for example, members are induced to join the party regardless of their levels of politicization and commitment. This seems to be a general phenomenon in voluntary associations. James March and Herbert Simon concluded, "There is evidence indicating that most union members become participants either more or less involuntarily or for limited special reasons . . ."[6] And, more nearly analogous to the PSI situation, Almond found that recruits were attached to the Communist Party by a wide variety of influences, but that

---

[2]See Howard E. Freeman, Edwin Novak, and Leo G. Reeder, "Correlates of Membership in Voluntary Associations," *American Sociological Review*, 22 (October 1957), 228-33; Herbert Maccoby "The Differential Political Activity of Participants in a Voluntary Association," *ibid*, 23 (October 1958), 524-32; Charles R. Wright and Herbert H. Hyman, "Voluntary Association Memberships of American Adults: Evidence from National Sample Surveys," *ibid*, 23 (June 1958), 284-94.

[3]*The Civic Culture* (Princeton: Princeton University Press, 1963), p. 320. Their measure of competence differs from that used in the present study.

[4]*Political Man*, (Garden City, New York: Doubleday, 1960), p. 202.

[5]For example, Almond and Verba, *op. cit.*, p. 304; Angus Campbell, Phillip E. Converse, Warren E. Miller, and Donald E. Stokes, *The American Voter* (New York: Wiley, 1960), pp. 475-81; the evidence cited in Lipset, *op. cit.*, pp. 187-89; and Lester W. Milbrath, *Political Participation* (Chicago: Rand McNally and Co., 1965), pp. 122-24.

[6]*Organizations* (New York: Wiley, 1958), pp. 72-73.

those who stayed in the party became more knowledgeable and committed.[7]

Members join the PSI for many different reasons. Class distinctions are sharply drawn in Italy. The extremes of rich and poor, the social stigma attaching to most nonwhite collar occupations, and the unequal sharing in economic prosperity give to parties a distinct social significance. In such an environment differences among parties are widely, if vaguely, perceived within the electorate. Social and traditional impulses motivate the voter to favor and join one party rather than another. It is easy to join a party without being highly politicized, without any real knowledge of politics, and without any excessive sense of efficacy. For many, formal party membership represents no level of politicization and commitment higher than that of a sympathizer or supporter. The difference may lie in having a husband, brother, father, close friend, or work colleague who was a member and who recruited those closest to him. The motivations for joining the PSI are thus varied. It is evident that it is not only the highly politicized and competent who are induced to join: yet, it is equally manifest that many poorly educated party members rank high on political competence.[8]

I have thus indicated that I do not believe that self-selection is the principal reason for the increased political competence of the high participants. There is plausible evidence that people join the PSI without prior development of political competence, and that competence results from participation and not the reverse. But cause and effect in social relations are difficult to establish with certitude. My argument is therefore not that participation results in increased political competence but rather that (1) they are closely associated; and (2) on some dimensions the association is stronger for members with low formal education than for those with high. More than this I do not claim.

II. The Measurements Employed

The model respondent had completed elementary school and hence had five years of formal education. However, more than one-third of the sample had less than five years, and only one in six had more. Consequently, the three categories of formal education are less than

---

[7]*The Appeals of Communism* (Princeton: Princeton University Press, 1955, esp., pp. 62-126.

[8]This phenomenon was noted by Almond and Verba, through its implications for working-class politics were not developed. *Op. Cit.*, pp. 300-22.

five years of school (low), five years (average), and more than five years (high).

TABLE 1

FORMAL EDUCATION OF SAMPLE

	N	%
Less than five years (Low Education)	116	39
Five years (Average Education)	135	45
More than five years (High Education)	48	16
	Total N=299	100%

Answers to two batteries of questions were utilized to construct indices of knowledge and efficacy. Respondents were asked whether each of eight statements about Italian politics was true or false.[9] To reduce guessing, respondents were asked whether they knew the answer to each question before replying true or false.[10] The distribution of the responses to the knowledge questions is shown in Table 2.

TABLE 2

NUMBER OF CORRECT ANSWERS GIVEN TO KNOWLEDGE QUESTIONS

CORRECT ANSWERS	%
0	32
1	12
2	15
3	9
4	10
5	7
6	6
7	5
8	4
	100%
	Total N=299

[9]The eight statements were: a) Calabria has a special regional status. b) Twenty-five is the minimum age for being elected a deputy. c) There are seven countries in the European Common Market. d) The PSI abstained on the vote of confidence for the center-left government (Fanfani, 1962). e) AGIP is a private industry. f) In the past the PCI has taken part in the government. g) The Constitutional Court has yet to be established. h) Everyone who has reached the age of 21 can vote for the Chamber and the Senate.

[10]The items were machined tested for scalability using the Multiple Scalogram Analysis developed by James C. Lingoes, "Multiple Scalogram Aanlysis: A Set-Theoretic Model for Analyzing Dichotomous Items," *Educational and Psychological Measurement*, 23 (Autumn, 1963). 501-24. They were also tested for scalability by conventional counter-sorter procedures. As the items did not form an acceptable and useful Guttman-type scale, the number of correct answers given by each respondent provided his position on an index of political knowledge.

The four statements concerning political efficacy were treated in a similar fashion.[11] Table 3 gives the pattern of responses.

TABLE 3

NUMBER OF RESPONSES INDICATIVE OF A SENSE OF EFFICACY

EFFICACIOUS ANSWERS	%
0	26
1	31
2	27
3	11
4	5
	100%
	Total N=295

Ideological sensitivity refers to the capacity to interpret political events in terms of some analytical scheme. Respondents were asked, "In your opinion what are the most important problems of Italian public life today?" And, "If you had to explain Italian political parties to someone who had spent all of his life in another country, in a few words, what would you say about the Italian Communist Party? About the Christian Democratic Party? About the PSI? About the Social Democratic Party?" Answers to these questions were divided into several categories.[12] Eight respondents who used ideological terms seriously and meaningfully were coded high on ideological sensitivity. An additional thirty-four respondents whose answers included references to democracy, totalitarianism, a planned economy, and similar concepts with ideological implications were coded as exhibiting some ideological sensitivity.

The remainder of the respondents were divided into four categories. Those who saw parties in terms of general group or class benefits, such as favoring the working class or capitalists, were separated from those who gave more limited or programmatic answers, referring, for example, to the interests of farmers or industrial workers. Many respondents held a simple good-bad view of the parties,

[11]The statements were: a) The average member has no influence at all on what the party decides. b) Sometimes politics seems so complicated that it is difficult to understand it. c) I don't think that public officials care very much about what people like me think. d) Voting is the only way for the rank-and-file member of the party to influence the policies of the party. The questions were taken from SRC American electoral studies. Although none of the items were reversed, there is no internal evidence of distortion due to response set.

[12]This measure of ideological sensitivity is adapted from Campbell, *et al*, *op. cit.*, Chapter 10.

saying merely that "The PCI is evil," or "I don't like Saragat." They were placed in a single category of respondents who viewed politics in terms of personalities or simple likes and dislikes. Finally, many respondents were simply unable or unwilling (and the former seems to be the case more often) to articulate anything about the parties that could be meaningfully coded. This latter category is excluded from the subsequent analysis, as it includes some who could not answer, others who refused, and a few who, for various reasons, were not asked these questions. The pattern of responses is given in Table 4.

TABLE 4

LEVELS OF IDEOLOGICAL SENSITIVITY

	%
No Meaningful content	17
Personalities or simple likes and dislikes	33
Limited benefits or programmatic	21
General group or class benefits	15
Some ideological sensitivity	12
High ideological sensitivity	2
	100%
	Total N=301

The respondents were divided into four levels of participation. The interview schedule contained questions concerning attendance at party-related meetings, activities performed for the party, and formal positions held in the party. To be classified as a *militant* a respondent must have carried out activities or held formal positions as well as attended meetings. A *participant* differed from a militant in the quality and quantity of his activities. A *marginal* member was one who exhibited at least some interest in the party as evidenced by having attended a meeting, or by having performed some activity on behalf of the party. The *nominal* member was a member in name only: he had done nothing more than take out a party card. The respondents divide as indicated in Table 5.

These categories combine ease of measurement with conventional usage. The militants, for example, are militants in the party's understanding of the term, and the participants are likewise a familiar party category. In evaluating the data that follow, it should be recalled that I am dealing with a sample of the rank-and-file. Everyone who held a post at the federation level or served as a secretary of section was excluded from the membership sample.

TABLE 5
LEVEL OF PARTICIPATION

	%
Unable to Participate	1
Nominal Members	14
Marginal Members	34
Participant Members	26
Militant Members	25
	100%
	Total N=301

III. Participation, Knowledge, and Efficacy

Previous findings of close association between education and knowledge are strikingly confirmed. A somewhat weaker association exists between education and efficacy, and between participation, on the one hand, and knowledge and sense of efficacy, on the other.

However, when these relationships are broken down by educational levels, important distinctions emerge. I hypothesized that the association between participation and competence would be stronger for those members in the low education category than for those in the two higher groups. The better educated generally have better educated parents; apart from their formal education, they are likely to acquire some political competence at home and from their peers. The poorly educated often are caught up in a cycle of ignorance and political incompetence. With poorly educated parents and associates and a long tradition of alienation and cynicism, they

TABLE 6
INTERCORRELATION MATRIX: PARTICIPATION, EDUCATION, KNOWLEDGE, AND EFFICACY ENTIRE SAMPLE[13]

	EDUCATION	KNOWLEDGE	EFFICACY
Participation	.22	.44	.33
Education	—	.61	.42
Knowledge		—	.42

[13]All measures of association herein are gamma rank order coefficients. Gamma was chosen because it does not require N×N tables in order to reach the values of ±1.0. For a discussion of gamma, see William L. Hays, *Statistics for Psychologists* (New York: Holt, Rinehart, Winston, 1963), pp. 655-56.

can escape only through great personal effort or good fortune. Participation in politics is one way for the poorly educated to acquire knowledge and a sense of efficacy; indeed, it may be the only avenue available. It is not nearly as important for the better educated.

Level of participation, for example, is related to the knowledge and efficacy of all groups. However, the regularity and magnitude of the increase are more impressive for the less well-educated, and the difference is greater for knowledge than for efficacy.

TABLE 7

PARTICIPATION AND KNOWLEDGE, BY EDUCATION

PARTICIPATION	EDUCATION		
	LOW	AVERAGE	HIGH
Nominal Members	.2*	2.0	**
Marginal Members	.8	1.8	4.6
Participant Members	1.4	3.0	5.0
Militant Members	2.1	4.4	6.1
N	116	133	47
Gamma	.52	.40	.35
		Total N=296	

*Figure is mean knowledge (0-8 possible).
**Less than five cases.

The association between participation and knowledge is stronger for the lowly educated (gamma .52) than for the average (.40) or highly educated (.35). Nominal members with low education have a *mean* of .2 on the index of knowledge (i.e., only one out of five in this category could answer even one of the eight questions correctly); the mean of the militants in the same category was 2.1. The importance of education is shown by the fact that the mean for nominal members with average education is 2.0, rising to 4.4 for militants with the same education. Those with high education scored much higher, from 4.6 for the marginal members to 6.1 for the militants. Marginal members of high education scored higher than militants of the lower two categories. The progression among the militants from 2.1 for the lowest educational category to 6.1 for the highest likewise demonstrates the importance of education for political knowledge even among the most active members. Further, while the association between participation and knowledge is stronger in the low education group, the absolute differences between the mean levels of knowledge in the low and high educational categories are relatively constant within each level of participation. Thus, among marginal members it is 3.8, participants 3.6, and militants 4.0.

TABLE 8

PARTICIPATION AND EFFICACY, BY EDUCATION

PARTICIPATION	EDUCATION		
	LOW	AVERAGE	HIGH
Nominal Members	.4*	1.0	**
Marginal Members	.8	1.6	1.9
Participant Members	1.0	1.6	1.5
Militant Members	1.3	1.9	2.6
N	112	133	47
Gamma	.38	.24	.33
		Total N=292	

*Figure is mean efficacy (0-4 possible).
**Less than five cases.

The association between participation and sense of efficacy is roughly similar for all groups. The increase in sense of efficacy by level of participation is monotonic for the lowest educational category; while there is an overall increase for the two other categories, it is irregular. Table 8 shows the mean sense of efficacy for each category, after the fashion of the above discussion of knowledge. It seems from these findings that knowledge about politics is very much a function of exposure to politics, as knowledge consistently increases with participation and education. A sense of efficacy, on the other hand, may have several origins; although in general it exhibits the same patterns as political knowledge, there are irregularities that elude simple interpretation.

IV. Ideological Sensitivity, Education, and Participation

There is an expected overall association between education, participation, and ideological sensitivity. For the entire sample, gamma correlations are as follows: participation and education, .22; participation and ideological sensitivity, .22; and education and ideological sensitivity, .47. These general patterns ars as anticipated. Few people of low education achieved the levels of ideologue or near-ideologue, however; and when the association between participation and ideological sensitivity is examined for each of the educational groups, significant differences emerge. Participation in the party is associated with a dramatic increase in the sensitivity of the best educated members, while the ideological sensitivity of the most poorly educated group hardly changes (see Table 9).

TABLE 9

PARTICIPATION AND IDEOLOGICAL SENSITIVITY

PARTICIPATION	EDUCATION		
	LOW	AVERAGE	HIGH
Nominal Members	1.6*	2.4	**
Marginal Members	1.6	1.9	3.0
Participant Members	1.8	2.2	2.0
Militant Members	1.7	2.5	4.1
N	89	116	37
Gamma	.09	.17	.43
			Total N=242

*Figure is mean level of sensitivity (5=Ideologue; 1=Good or Bad).
**Less than five cases.

Party ideologues generally are militants who also have considerable education. Among members of low education, participation is not associated with ideological levels of political understanding. Some ramifications of all these differences can now be examined.

V. Participation and Political Competence

I began with a review of other findings concerning participation and political competence. The data presented here confirm the generalization that high rates of participation are associated with high levels of political competence. It is now possible to suggest some refinements in the interpretation of this association. Participation is associated more strongly with knowledge, and to a lesser extent efficacy, among those of low than high education. This strongly suggests that participation in politics is a significant way for the poorly educated to break out of the circle of political ignorance and low sense of efficacy.

But the advantages of the better educated are strikingly confirmed also. For they rate high on political competence even when they are relatively uninvolved, and high participation is associated with even higher levels of competence. Low participants with high education excel other low participants in knowledge, sense of efficacy, and ideological sensitivity, and the absolute advantages of the better educated are maintained among the high participants. In other words, the poorly educated do not catch up through participation; they start behind and they stay behind.

This advantage of the better educated has vast ramifications for internal democracy in the PSI. Even through intensive participation in party life the poorly educated majority does not acquire as high a level of political competence as the small portion with more than average education. As differences in competence among the educational levels remain even among militants, the existence of formal opportunities to develop competence and leadership potentialities does not reduce the gap. Although a few persons may largely surmount their poor education, most do not.

This is especially apparent on the ideological dimension of competence. Participation is associated with increased ideological sensitivity only for the best educated; the poorly educated do not become ideologues. Political competence rises with participation and hence meaningful political action is possible for the poorly educated. But insofar as the goals of political action are conditioned by a sensitivity to ideological considerations, individuals with low educational achievement are dependent on others for the analysis and casuistry involved in applying ideological concepts to specific problems.

As many members affiliate and participate for nonideological reasons, the ideologically sophisticated possess an important weapon in internal party politics. They are in a position to interpret events, choose the alternatives presented to the membership, deal in dialectical niceties, and defend their actions in ideological terms. While often competent in practical politics, in fact sometimes more so than the ideologues, the poorly educated member is severely handicapped in dealing with abstractions and problems of general orientation. Ideological sensitivity is almost a monopoly of the educated members. Although participation in politics is undoubtedly a path to increased political competence, it nevertheless has severe limitations as a means to overcome the disadvantages of a poor education.

The Congressman and the Congressional District Party[1]

David M. Olson

If a political party reflects the horizontal divisions between the governmental party and the extragovernmental party, and the vertical divisions between local, state and national governmental levels, the American congressman is implicated in both. As an elected national public official, he belongs to one of the two congressional parties, which exists in an uncertain relationship to the extragovernmental units of that party, best typified by the national committees. Congressmen and the party national committees safely can, and usually do, pay scant attention to each other.

But congressmen can not so easily escape the tensions within party produced by geography and governmental levels. They are elected within a *local* congressional district to serve as an officer of the *national* government. Presidents can claim a national electorate, and, most U.S. Senators are elected by a heterogenous state-wide

[1]Revised version of a paper presented at the annual meeting of the Southern Political Science Association, New Orleans, Louisiana, November 2, 1967. This article was made possible in part by funds granted by the Carnegie Corporation of New York to the American Political Science Association for the Study of Congress, and in part by a grant from the University of Texas Research Institute. The statements made and views expressed are solely the responsibility of the author.

Written especially for this volume. An expanded and revised version can be found in the author's *The Congressman and His Party*, forthcoming.

electorate. Congressmen are elected from smaller and less diverse districts, composed of several counties, while some districts are themselves smaller than a whole county. While state assemblymen and senators exist in the same relationship to their local districts as do congressmen to theirs, they are probably subject to much less strain and conflict than are the members of the U.S. House of Representatives. State legislators escape the legal restraints of federalism, function within a common context of state-defined party and factional alignments, and usually represent a less diverse socio-economic complex than do national congressmen. Members of the U.S. House experience, more acutely than any other set of American public officials, the strain and stress of conflict bteween a national government and a local electoral district. Correspondingly, they are subject to potential conflicts in the relationship of the national with the county and district units of their political party.

This paper examines the relationship of U.S. Representatives with their congressional district party and is part of a larger undertaking to explore the reciprocal relationships and images of congressmen with their district party leaderships. This paper views that relationship from the perspective of thirty-six congressmen, interviewed in 1965-66.

The 36 congressmen and their district parties constitute more a selection than a sample. The purpose was to locate a number of congressmen whose district parties ranged along a continuum of party types, from the most strong and capable to the least capable and nonexistent. The criteria for judging party types is not well developed in the literature;[2] the criteria emerged from interviews with congressmen themselves, their staffs, and political practitioners and journalists in Washington, D.C. An effort was made to concentrate congressmen within state groupings both to hold the number of variables to a manageable number and to obtain built-in reality checks among congressmen and local respondents from the state. The expectation that the state was a meaningful context of political organization and interaction proved thoroughly justified. It also facilitated travel to and among the districts. The congressional districts in this study are located in the seven states of Con-

---

[2]Attempts to develop a classification of party types may be found in: Frank Sorauf, *Party and Representation* (New York: Atherton Press, 1963), Ch. 3; V. O. Key, *Southern Politics* (New York: Alfred A. Knopf, 1949), Ch. 14; Joseph A. Schlesinger, "Political Party Organization," in James March (ed.), *Handbook of Organizations* (Chicago: Rand McNally, 1965), pp. 754-801; and David M. Olson, "Toward a Typology of County Party Organizations," *Southwestern Social Science Quarterly*, 48: 558-572 (March, 1968).

necticut, New York, Pennsylvania, Maryland, California, Virginia, and Texas. While the 43 other states would undoubtedly provide an additional array of personalities, alignments, and practices, we simply do not know if they would yield different types of district parties or different relationships between the district parties and congressmen than has been generated by the included states. There are no handy indicators by which to judge. The analytic requirements of this study are met by including a diversity of district party types. The test of that diversity is presented in Table 2.

The balance of Democrats and Republicans among the congressmen is not even. The unevenness is in part a function of Democratic dominance of the South and in part is a function of the 1964 Democratic landslide which produced a large number of freshmen Democratic congressmen. An effort was made to include some of those freshmen elected under distinctive national political circumstances from long-term Republican districts.

Four topics were examined relating to the congressman's perception of and behavior toward the congressional district party:

1. The viability of the district itself as a locale of party.
2. The dependence and reliance by the congressman upon the local party in nominations and elections.
3. The extent to which the party leaderships involve themselves in the congressman's functions, i.e., projects, patronage, and issues.
4. The activity of the congressman in his district party.

I. The Congressional District as a Party Unit

Within a congressional district the party is seldom organized as a single unit. Rather it is a compound of county level parties. In multi-county districts, each county party functions autonomously, and usually their only point of contact is the congressional seat itself, though a few counties within the district may share a legislative or judicial seat. The unanimous sentiment of multi-county congressmen is summarized by the one who commented, "I have four counties in my district; hence I have four parties to deal with." The fact they shared the same partisan label seemed accidental if not irrelevant.

In the reverse situation, in which one county contains two or more congressional districts, the politics of each are derivative of county-wide politics. In those urban areas with strong township or ward party organizations, the congressional district may or may not be coterminous with a collection of township or ward boundaries. Either way, the congressional district is an artificial party jurisdiction, suspended between the more vital party units of town or ward, and county. Only in the single-county congressional district are the district boundaries coterminous with those of a viable party unit (Table 1).

TABLE 1
GEOGRAPHIC RELATIONSHIP OF CONGRESSIONAL DISTRICTS AND COUNTIES

	PARTY OF CONGRESSMEN		TOTAL	
	DEM	REP	No.	%
District and County				
Multi-county district	12	6	18	50
Coterminous	3	3	6	17
Multi-district Single county	10	2	12	33
Total	25	11	36	100

II. Reliance on District Party

Congressmen were asked for both general and primary elections, "To what extent can you rely upon your party?" Their answer was a compound of its organizational characteristics and of its competitive status. A party's organizational type can be defined independently of its competitive status,[3] although that status was one crucial determinant of the congressman's answer. As candidates in elections, congressmen do evaluate the ability of their party to command voter allegiance. If the party cannot command voter allegiance, it cannot be relied upon by the congressman. The degree of reliance the congressman places in the party organization indicates its operational utility and importance to him. This estimate of reliance is the basis for a typology of parties.

The types of party organization, characterized by the extent to which congressmen rely upon it in both general elections and in the nomination process, are listed in Table 2. The parties of high reliance in both general elections and in nominations are listed as Type A. Most of these parties have a comprehensive precinct struc-

[3]Sorauf, *op. cit.*, pp. 44-45.

TABLE 2
Types of District Party Organizations by Degrees of Reliance

Degrees of Reliance	Party Of Congressmen: Dem	Rep	Total
A. High reliance in both nominations and general elections	6	4	10 (28%)
B. High reliance on factional organization	4	0	4
C. Self reliance in nominations; High party reliance in general elections	3	5	8 (22%)
D. Party reliance in nominations; Self reliance in general elections	2	1	3
E. Self reliance in both nominations and general elections	10	1	11 (31%)
Total	25	11	36 (100%)

ture and all have a leadership corps which is able to recruit candidates, endorse and win in their nomination process, and to carry the general election. In the case of a few Democrats, high reliance was placed upon factional organizations rather than upon the regular and legal party (Type B). Types C and D are intermediate categories, in which congressmen rely upon the party in either general elections or nominations, but not in both. The party of low reliance, or rather of candidate self-reliance (Type E), is as frequent as the opposite party type of high reliance.

The relationship between party type and party's competitive status is complex if not confused. A few uniformities appear in Table 3. The parties and factions of high reliance, Types A and B, are found mostly in safe districts, and none in minority districts. The other three types, the partial and low reliance parties, are distributed among all competitive statuses.

The placement of minority parties mostly in the party types of low reliance (D and E) by congressmen is partly a consequence of its minority status. Five of the nine congressmen appearing in these party types and in the competitive and minority columns come from states and districts in which the party organization as such resembles those of Types A and B. The chairmen recruit candidates, executive committees successfully endorse in their own primaries, and precinct workers perform at least some election day tasks. Their minority status, however, prevents them from appealing to most voters, thus making them relatively useless to minority party congressmen in general elections.

TABLE 3
Types of District Party Organization by Competitive Status of District Party

Party Type	Competitive Status of Party			Total
	Safe	Competitive	Minority	
A	9	1	0	10
B	4	0	0	4
C	5	2	1	8
D	0	1	2	3
E	5	4	2	11
Total	23	8	5	36

Parties in the safe districts, however, were placed by congressmen in all categories except Type D. The safe district parties tend to the extremes, being evaluated as worthy of high reliance or as almost worthless. A congressman who relied almost completely upon his party organization in both nominations and general elections drew this portrait of his urban Republican cohesive and dominant party:

> The county committee of the party consists of elected precinct committeemen who elect a county chairman. But what really happens is that there is a leader, who is State Senator ———. He was the long-time party leader in the senate, the long-term state party chairman, and of course, the long-term leader of this county. The source of his power is patronage from lower levels of government (city and county) and his ability to win elections. He has survived state Democratic administrations and also an unfriendly Republican administration — remarkable!

This congressman has had little opposition in the primaries, for the reason, he thinks, that "no one could beat me." At the same time, however, he is endorsed by the regular organization, and few insurgents ever run for or win any office. He campaigns in the primary for and with the entire endorsed slate "because the organization supports me." He relies equally heavily upon the party organization in general elections.

Even in the strongly organized districts, congressmen usually indicate they do some independent campaigning. A congressman from such a party stated that the typical role of the party organization is to staff the election polls and bring in the voters. His own personal organization raises funds, arranges his schedule of appearances, and does some election day work. His personal campaign workers constitute a small number of persons who themselves are active in the regular party organizations of their communities. Hence, there is more a division of labor *within* the party organization than a separate and personal campaign structure outside the party.

This congressman's dependence upon the party is increased by joint campaigning by the party's candidates and by the practice of advertising party-wide tickets.

> We always have the governor or the president at the top of the ticket. The only time we are isolated is during a special election. Thus I run as part of the party and its ticket.

He also feels that he himself adds strength to the party ticket, for he can attract votes through his continual case work services.

If one-party areas spawn strong and cohesive party organizations, one-partyism is also associated with the absence of organization. One party dominance can mean merely the dominance of a party label — not an organization.

An inactive, if not nonexistent, party structure was described by a Southern Democrat from a dominantly Democratic and rural multi-county district:

> There is no party precinct organization, and I don't have one either. The way I get reelected is my 'sweetheart list.' These are people who have written me. I contact them and hope they will support me in an election. This is my only basis for an election organization.

There are, however, key people in each county:

> The county chairman, the county commissioners' chairman, and the sheriff — these are the leading party figures. Of course, it varies among the counties and it varies also with the personalities of each.

The personal manner in which the congressman relates to these potentially key position-occupants may be illustrated by his approach to his new counties acquired through redistricting:

> I visit the county chairmen of the new counties. I just say 'hello' and say I hope they can support me. Of course, I know most of the chairmen and other county officials already.

Another southern Democrat — urban — observed that the party is of no help to him. Democratic party officials in the county and precincts are inactive in general elections — or else support Republicans. They are likewise inactive in the primaries. In addition, he derives no support from other Democratic nominees. He leads the ticket in votes and usually wins easily even when his district has voted Republican for president or governor. "We have a system of purely *personal* organizations." At another point in the interview he observed, "The party doesn't help me. I always run ahead of the Democratic candidates."

He might have added that the system of personal organizations also characterizes the primaries in safe districts lacking strong party organization.

The necessity to adopt party labels for purposes of national politics has spread those labels throughout all 50 states, but these interviews indicate that the organizational realities of those party labels vary extensively from all-powerful to almost nonexistent.

The organizational attributes of party are not well-predicted by the competitive status of the party, indicating that definitions of party system, based upon the definition of competitive status from election statistics, cannot also serve as definitions of the internal characteristics of a political party considered as an organizational entity. The election statistics of Chicago and Texas are similar; their parties are not.

Once the congressman is elected to office, he and the party enter the inter-election portion of their work cycle. The immanence of the next election in two years presses in upon the congressman and local party even before the memories of the last election recede, but in between the periodic elections, he turns his attention to his congressional activities, and the local party may turn its attention to its internal affairs. The involvement of the congressman and the local party in each other's activities are explored in the next two sections.

III. District Party Role in Congressman's Job

Congressmen were asked, "How much interest does your district party show in what you do as congressman?"

This question was answered in terms both of the whole county committee (or executive committee) and individual party officials. Congressmen almost never receive communications from the whole party committee. Also, few congressmen speak of receiving communications from individual precinct chairmen. Rather, they communicate with the county chairman, or with ward or town chairmen within the county.

In operational terms, "the district party" for congressmen consists of "leaders." As one said, "For my purposes, it is sufficient to deal through the county chairmen when I want to deal with my district party." In more diffusely organized or factional parties, congressmen correspondingly relate to the leaders of those factions. The precinct captain, the election day workers, and the campaign volunteers disappear into the general population. These occupants of lower levels in a party organization become important in the congressman's consideration of party only as the local leadership is able to mobilize them into an active and effective body of campaign workers. If the leadership can perform that task, the congressman knows he does in fact have a leadership to deal with.

Most congressmen feel that local party leaders, regardless of type of party organization, are basically uninterested in and unaware of events in Congress. The local party is more interested in county and state government and particularly in electing its candidates to those offices. A Republican congressman from a particularly well organized rural party commented:

> Local party leaders don't care a fig about what I do. They don't give a continental about the congressman. The county chairman has never called me on a single vote. They view the congressman as a necessary evil. The job is a vacuum, so they have to fill it. They want someone who won't cause trouble — they don't want someone who is always causing trouble and agitating (in the county party). What they want is patronage, and this comes from the state capitol.

Patronage is an obvious source of party leadership interest in a public office, but the same phenomenon — of greater interest in state and county offices than in congressional — is reported by congressmen from nonpatronage states as well. These levels of government are viewed as being "closer" to the public and of being more in continuing contact with the electorate than is the congressional. In a few districts, congressmen felt the local party personnel were more interested in presidential elections than in the congressional. Whether they pointed to county-state or to presidential offices, most congressmen were of the opinion that their particular office was the stepchild — or orphan — of the district party units.

Congressmen do report a variety of contacts with individual party leaders. Table 4 presents such communications by topic, party, and faction. At times the distinction between party and faction is crucial.

Contacts with the chairmen of the formal and legal party, at either county or town level, are mostly confined to local projects and to patronage.

TABLE 4
NUMBER OF CONGRESSMEN REPORTING DISTRICT PARTY INVOLVEMENT IN ASPECTS OF THE CONGRESSMAN'S TASKS

CONGRESSMAN'S TASKS	DISTRICT PARTY ELEMENTS			
	REGULAR		FACTION	
	DEM	REP	DEM	REP
Patronage	9	3	3	0
Projects/cases	4	6	4	0
Legislation	4	2	9	1
None	6	2	0	0
	N= 34			

Projects and cases relate to obtaining federal funds for a municipal program or facility and to obtaining favorable agency action on social security and V.A. hospital care. Increasingly, the Viet Nam war brought a large increase in draft deferments and military service as topics of local party concern. The patronage available to congressmen are only the positions in their own office, postmasters and rural route carriers, military academies, and federal judgeships. In most cases, the congressman does consult with local party leaders (and probably other elites as well) about post master and judicial appointments, but most frequently makes his own appointments for his office staff.

Some congressmen report no communication of any sort with the chairmen of legal party organizations in their district. These are congressmen who are factional opponents of the leadership group of the formal party. One such congressman resentfully noted that the formal party leadership, who had opposed his nomination, had given "no acknowledgement of any kind that I even exist. I have not received a single word from them, not even a postcard. Nothing." Neither did they support one another in the general election. Another congressman stated the only contact he has had with the chairman of his local party has been the chairman's criticism of him as reported in the newspaper. When asked if he would clear patronage through the party committee and its chairman, the congressman replied, "No. Never. I wouldn't think of it!" Still another congressman observed that the party was badly split into many transient factions, that he and the county chairman opposed one another, but that he would "like to have a party committee I could talk to. There is no party, and that is the problem." Resentment is increased in those cases in which the county chairman himself challenges the incumbent congressman for the party's nomination.

A large proportion of congressmen in both parties reported specifically that the party leadership takes no part in policy and shows no interest in how they vote on legislation. One suburban congressman said, "Party leaders are interested in patronage, period," and added that he had never received any communication on legislation from his chairman. Another, a rural congressman, noted that his party leaders were interested only in "concrete and patronage."

Only six congressmen reported that party leaders of the legal and regular party organization took any role in policy determination (Table 5). Their role is viewed as helpful to the congressman. Local

TABLE 5
NUMBER OF CONGRESSMEN REPORTING DISTRICT PARTY INVOLVEMENT IN LEGISLATION

	District Party Elements			
	Regular		Faction	
	Dem	Rep	Dem	Rep
Some role in legislation	4	2	9	1
No role in legislation	19 (83%)	9 (82%)	0	0
Total	23	11		
N = 34				

leaders are interested in bills of "high local importance," as one congressman said, or in the local relevance of broader legislation, such as a housing bill.

Chairmen also advise on the local political impact of a congressman's vote on a controversial bill. A suburban Democratic congressman stated he consults with the chairman on "what the political effect would be of a given vote," and that he calls his chairman to

> inform him of what I'm going to do. Because he's going to hear about it and party leaders here (Washington D.C.) will call him to get that maverick congressman in line.

Local party leaderships inform their congressmen of what they hear in the district about their legislative voting and sometimes request information with which to defend that record. This thought was expressed by a legislative assistant to a suburban Republican congressman:

> Very seldom will the local party leadership call in on a vote. They do so apologetically because they have been called by a contributor. So they call us to inform the congressman of the first call they get — that's all.

Some congressmen noted their district party leaders were interested in legislation only in a derivative sense from their major concern with the election of party candidates. A rural Republican observed:

> My floor voting is important to the county party only as it affects my chances for reelection. Issues are not important to the party per se. The party is interested in getting its candidates elected; thus the party is concerned with how voters react to how I vote.

An urban Democrat noted that the local party was never concerned with specific bills or votes because "most voters don't know how I vote." But he felt that the party might become concerned if he jeopardized his own reelection — and hence his party's success — by "voting wrong on a whole succession of major items such as civil rights and unions." He was not likely to vote consistently against dominant district sentiment, however, and he did not anticipate any such reaction among the local party leaderships. He had certainly never experienced nor tempted it.

Here we come to the crux of the issue — and the probable explanation for the low concern of local party officials with their congressman's policy activity: they are in general agreement in advance of any specific vote. Hence, there is no need for contact.

A rural Republican, in discussing his House committee and the county chairman's reaction, noted:

> I am on a very good committee. My county chairman is very proud of this assignment. It is important to business in my state. But the county chairman does not suggest ideas for bills or try to tell me what to do, for the reason that we agree anyway.

An urban Democrat indicated similar policy agreement and the reason for such agreement:

> There is no need for contact on legislation. We all agree on general policy — liberal. We all came up together. No one has to persuade me to be for civil rights or fair employment!

One congressman, however, did report a voting consequence of his chairmen's concern with a bill. A dove on Viet Nam, the Democrat found that his several county chairmen

> tried to help me avoid being hurt politically in the district. Their view was that the less I say about it the better.
>
> Q. Have they talked with you about your voting on this issue?

A. Yes. They urged me to vote on a Viet Nam appropriations bill. That did carry some weight with me.

Only one congressman regarded his district party as a source of policy guidance. He consulted with the local organization's executive committee, both in person and in writing. He stated that in response, he had received only one statement. One member of the executive committee had urged him to vote against repeal of Section 14 (b) of the Taft-Hartley Act, a position which the congressman, a Republican, already held.

Factional contacts are far more important, especially for Democrats, on legislation than are contacts with the legal and formal party. They are mentioned more frequently and with greater fervor. In part, factional contacts replace formal party contacts for those congressmen reporting no contacts whatsoever with their party chairmen. They are factional opponents of the chairmen. One such congressman, when asked about his relationship with leaders of his faction, replied

> Oh, that's very different. Their interest is very high. On everything: legislation, community activities, attendance at political functions. I campaign with them, I raise money. My staff, too, has been active (in the faction) before coming with me in this office.

For congressmen engaging in frequent and friendly contacts with leaders of or associates in a faction, legislation is one of the topics of discussion. But it is rated as a subject of infrequent communication, even for those factions and congressmen who are highly ideological. One such congressman noted that

> There is not much contact on legislation. Civil rights is the biggest item. A few times the (factional) clubs have resolved on bills and issues. There has also been some talk of setting up a club committee to work with me on legislation, but I have discouraged it.

He felt that the factional members were sufficiently aware of issues, however, so that "I do have to be a liberal in order to keep their favor" and to retain their support. The fact that he was of that persuasion was the reason why the faction gave him its support in the first place.

In a factionalized party, congressmen may and do receive policy communications from hostile factions. These communications are rejected with hostility and characterized as pressure. One urban Democrat said he had been criticized by "the unwashed left" for his support of the President on Viet Nam, but that he "didn't pay a damn bit of attention to it." Another urban Democrat, who was opposed by the New Left in a primary, reported that the first intimation he had of this factional opposition to him came through their communication with him on Viet Nam. He replied rather sharply and negatively. The result for him was a difficult primary which he characterized as "a miserable, grueling campaign."

Most congressmen feel that the local party leaderships are more interested in other offices and public arenas than in Congress and that, in relation to Congress, they are more interested in projects and patronage than in policy. The extent to which local party leaders are concerned with policy is seen as a product of their pragmatic concern with possible electoral consequences, not policy itself, of the congressman's position. But these low-intensity relationships are also viewed as proceding within a generalized policy agreement. Those few congressmen lacking such agreement have experienced the eruption of policy conflicts in traumatic nomination contests.

IV. Congressmen in the District Party

All public officials, including congressmen, are potential actors within the parties of their districts. In broad terms, they may take 1) an active, 2) a helpful, or 3) an avoidance role toward the district party.

The helpful congressman inherits and accepts a given situation within his district party, accepts whatever later changes are initiated by others, and tries to be helpful to and cooperative with the existing leadership. The active role congressman attempts to initiate change or actively defend the status quo. The active congressman is a leader; the helpful congressman is more a follower. The avoidance role congressman, by contrast, "drops out"; he rejects participation in the district party.

The largest number of congressmen are helpful toward their local party, and the least assume the avoidance role, with roughly the same proportion of Republicans and Democrats exhibiting each (Table 6).

The situation in the party, as it affects the congressman, may change through time. Likewise, his own views of his proper role may change. Hence, the same man may play different roles within the same party at different times.

The competitive status of the party has limited relationship to these role categories; the helpful role is the largest single role in each competitive status. Nevertheless, the avoidance role is concentrated in the competitive districts, while the more engaged roles are concentrated in the safe districts (Table 7).

A more substantial relationship exists between party roles and types of party (Table 8). Congressmen with parties of high reliance appear only in the helpful role. No congressman, in this selection, is a major leader of his district party if it is a strong, cohesive, and,

TABLE 6
ROLES OF CONGRESSMEN IN THE DISTRICT PARTY

ROLES	PARTY OF CONGRESSMEN				TOTAL	
	DEM		REP			
	No.	%	No.	%	No.	%
Active	9	33	4	30	13	32
Helpful	14	52	8	61	22	55
Avoidance	4	15	1	9	5	12
Subtotal	27	100	13	100	40	99
Dual Roles	− 2		− 2		− 4	
Total	25		11		36	

TABLE 7
CONGRESSMEN IN THE DISTRICT PARTY:
BY ROLE AND PARTY'S COMPETITIVE STATUS

	PARTY'S COMPETETIVE STATUS			TOTAL
ROLES	SAFE	COMPETETIVE	MINORITY	
Active	7	4	2	13
Helpful	15	4	3	22
Avoidance	1	3	1	5
Subtotal	23	11	6	40
Dual Roles	0	− 3	− 1	− 4
Total	23	8	5	36

TABLE 8
CONGRESSMEN IN THE DISTRICT PARTY:
BY ROLE AND PARTY TYPE

DISTRICT PARTY TYPE	ACTIVE	HELPFUL	AVOIDANCE	SUB TOTAL	DUAL ROLES	TOTAL
A	0	10	0	10	0	10
B	4	0	0	4	0	4
C	4	3	1	8	0	8
D	1	3	0	4	−1	3
E	4	6	4	14	−3	11
Total	13	22	5	40	4	36

dominant organization (Green, Jr., of Philadelphia and Buckley of the Bronx were exceptions). Likewise, no congressman from this type of party is able to avoid participation, either. Type B congressmen, with strongly organized high reliance factions, are all active leaders of their respective factions.

The range of variation of roles in the district party is much wider for congressmen coming from parties of low reliance. These congressmen are found in all role categories. The several congressmen who have changed role categories since their entrance into Congress are also found only in the parties of low reliance, Types D and E. The lack of strong party structures grants congressmen considerable freedom to adopt varying roles.

Of the three roles toward the district party, the avoidance role is largely confined to the party of low reliance, Type E. These congressmen come from one minority party, two competitive parties, and one safe district. Their parties are either nonexistent or badly splintered. The safe district congressman acknowledged, about his legal party structure, that "I think I have their support but it doesn't mean much." The unofficial group in his district is badly split and "as a result, I leave it alone."

Most congressmen in the helpful category, however, like to cooperate with the party organization — regardless of type — and with the existing leadership. Congressmen from minority parties cannot rely on their party in general elections, but nevertheless would like to see their party prosper, and do cooperate with their party chairmen on patronage, in some joint campaigning with others on the ticket, and in quietly helping in reorganizing the party. By and large, congressmen from competitive and dominant parties attempt to be helpful in the same ways, even though their own fate in general elections is usually secure. The helpful role congressmen are basically in harmony with the outlook and personnel of the party organization, and have successfully coexisted with them over the years. They feel no need for any other type of relationship.

The active congressmen see themselves in a completely different situation. They either feel deeply dissatisfied with their district party *or* feel themselves under severe attack. Either way, they are highly active in the internal affairs of their district party. Their activism, and their sense of dissatisfaction or persecution, reflects a pervasive and serious factionalism within their district party. Factionalism may confront congressmen of all three roles. The strategy of the avoidance role congressman is to withdraw. The strategy of the helpful role congressmen is to adopt benign neutrality. The strategy of the active role congressman is to participate extensively if not abrasively. In some cases, the congressman is a leader of a faction initiating change; in other cases, his stance is more defensive.

Congressmen initiating change are usually part of an aspiring and generally young leadership group which attempts to "revitalize" or "reform" the party. Their more immediate objective is to capture control. This objective may be achieved by an election campaign directed specifically at the congressional nomination, but more commonly, the contest for Congress is part of a wider attack upon other offices, both public and party.

A particularly dramatic illustration of a coordinated attack upon an existing party group is provided by the Reform vs. Regular Organization struggle within the Democratic Party of New York City and especially within Bronx County.[4] They have launched an ideological (liberal) and organizational (reform) attack upon the old-line Flynn-Buckley Democratic organization. The culmination of their initial efforts was achieved in 1964, when Reform candidates were nominated for Congress in hotly contested primaries. The focal point for Reform-Regular factional conflict has been the congressional offices for the two accidental reasons that the leader, Buckley, was in Congress at that time, and that the Reformers' most substantial success has been in winning two of the three Democratic congressional seats in the Bronx. This intraparty conflict has been waged in contests for all offices, not just congressional. The purpose has been nothing short of capture of the entire party.

Congressmen tend to give active leadership for change at the time of their initial nomination. By contrast, most congressmen actively engaged in a defense of the status quo have held office for at least several terms. In such instances, the congressional nomination was one if not *the* focal point of a factional onslaught upon the entire party structure and upon a wide range of public offices within the district. In some instances, the local factional groups were associated with state-wide factions as well.

As example of the active congressman defending the party status-quo leadership and also defending his own seat under attack in the party's primary occurred in a southern urban district, in which a conservative Democratic incumbent was challenged in the primary by a liberal. His congressional district is one of several within an urban county; his contest was part of a long-term bifactional struggle for control of the party structure and for most public offices.

---

[4]For an account of the Regular-Reform struggle among New York City Democrats, see James Q. Wilson, *The Amateur Democrat* (Chicago: University of Chicago Press, 1962).

This county-level factionalism is closely associated with state-level factions, and, in fact, the Governor privately urged support of the conservative incumbent congressman in the party's primary, along with support for conservative candidates to other offices. The liberal challenger in the primary for Congress was the county party chairman.

The incumbent was understandably bitter about the role of the county chairman of his own party, and reacted to this experience by attempting to develop support for himself among conservative precinct chairmen and within the county party committee. This attempt, he anticipated, would involve him closely in intraparty fights and in the selection of party personnel.

His prior role in the party had been one of avoidance. Yet the pervasive factional struggle in his county, which had previously not seriously affected congressional elections, in this instance spilled over from the other offices into his own. The congressman found himself caught in a situation, not of his making, of a broad and enduring intraparty struggle. He thereupon adopted a leadership role in his own defense, although he had not originally thrust himself into that role.

The preceding examples have all been of hotly contested elections. One congressman, however, has been very active in his party even though he has had little opposition in either primary or general elections. This congressman's leadership in his district party is exerted on behalf of party harmony and unity.

He comes from a southern urban district, located in a state with deep factional divisions within the Democratic party revolving around the three foci of liberal-conservative ideologies, presidential Republicanism, and enduring personal bitterness. This congressman is contemptuous of Democrats, especially in the formal party structure, who openly campaign for Republicans. His personal response has been to replace Republican supporters with loyalists in the formal party:

> We began to try to build a party organization a few years ago. . . . We tried to qualify candidates for county and precinct posts who would at least vote for Democrats, even if they would not campaign for them.

This statement, however, also involved the congressman in attempting to mediate the factional disputes within the party:

> We tried to find someone acceptable to both sides. . . . I have and employ personal friendships with political antagonists. I talk to

> them, and tell them that each is not as evil as the other thinks. The trouble is that political rivalries have developed into personal bitterness and fear. I try to get them to meet together, to have lunch together. They discover that the other doesn't wear horns or that they pick up contagious diseases from the encounter.

In addition, he has worked to obtain conservative support for Democratic presidential nominees, and he himself campaigns for Democratic nominees to other offices even though he might be in strong policy disagreement with them. Further, he has attempted to encourage some joint campaigning within his county among candidates on the Democratic ticket.

The basic requirement a public official has of his local party is negative — that it not actively oppose him. Active hostility is the one condition the elected official cannot permit, unless the local party is impotent. If it is, he is likely to avoid it. But where the local party has at least a potential impact upon either primaries or general elections, the elected official cannot tolerate active and persistent hostility toward him. This condition forces him into activity, either to win office or to retain it. But if the local party's attitude toward him ranges anywhere from neutrality to complete support, the elected official is free to adopt either a helpful or an active role toward it. This choice is in part a function of his own goals and desires. It is also in part a function of the type of party in the district, with the parties of lower reliance permitting a wider range of choices than the parties of high reliance.

Conclusions and Discussion

Several conclusions emerge from this study.

1. The organizational realities of party in counties and congressional districts vary extensively. Only in some areas does party provide the electoral support usually ascribed to party as one of its "functions." And in most areas, in spite of primary election laws, party leaders either do, or would like to, actively work to gain the nomination of their favored candidates. But their capacity to do so reflects a combination of competitive status with internal leadership control, and that capacity becomes an important element in the congressman's evaluations of the adequacy of the party for his electoral purposes.

2. The congressman reports a general lack of either knowledge or concern by local party leaderships about his activities, unless those actions have some direct local impact. The directness of im-

pact is most easily seen in projects and patronage. Local party leaderships generally become concerned about policy only as a reflection of interest expressed by other segments of the district. These trends typify all types of district parties.

3. The type of district party is more directly related to the congressman's involvement within it than to its role in his activities. The party of high reliance or of factional reliance he cannot ignore. If he and it cannot coexist in a mutually helpful relationship, he must actively fight it. Although some local party leaders have served in Congress, none of the congressmen in this study were active leaders of parties of high reliance. The party of low reliance gives the congressman much more latitude, unless it actively opposes him. If there is no party threat to his nomination, he is free to mold his own role toward it.

This study of the relationship of one type of public officeholder—the American congressman—to the local extragovernmental party, raises similar questions about officeholders at different levels of government and in other countries. The American state legislator and county and city officials are probably more closely involved with their local extragovernmental parties than is the congressman. For reasons of both patronage and policy, congressmen and local party respondents alike agree that congressmen and the local party have little contact in comparison with the other levels of public officials. On the other hand, the U.S. Senator and the county party seem less involved with each other. While systematic interviews were not conducted concerning senators, few county and district party leaders reported contact with their senator; perhaps senatorial contacts exist primarily at the state level of party.

How national parliamentary members of other countries would compare with the U.S. congressman in their relationships to the constituency party is only a matter of conjecture. The literature on British parties[5] suggests that the parliamentary constituency is a, or perhaps *the*, viable unit of party organization. If local governmental units of the British party are subsidiary and derivative from the constituency organization, that circumstance is the exact reverse of the American party. Countries characterized by a strong and autonomous role of local elements in national government might be though to produce parties more similar to those of the United States. Germany, for example, has a federal constitution, and in Sweden, the members of the upper chamber of the national

---

[5]See for example, Austin Ranney, *Pathways to Parliament* (Madison: University of Wisconsin Press, 1965).

parliament are elected by provincial and city councils. In both of these countries, however, the parties appear to more resemble the British than the American in the extent to which they dominate the nomination and electoral process as well as the degree to which the local units of party are coordinated by national leaderships. These attributes, in turn, seem linked with the parliamentary system and also with policy consensus and organizational cohesion within the parliamentary party. Nevertheless, there would still seem to be room for variation in the ways in which European national legislators—and perhaps provincial and city legislators as well—relate to their constituency party. The range and content of such variation itself may result from, and be an indicator of, attributes of national party systems.

One of the dominant attributes of the American party is its decentralization. This study helps to document the extent and functioning of that decentralization. From the perspective, at least, of congressmen, the political party within the congressional district is viewed as a party unit isolated from any national unit of party. The county parties (within the district) seem to lack any form of either institutional or other connection to the national party.[6] The congressman himself would appear the only point of contact bridging the gap between the local and the national congressional party; even that bridge is lacking in each district for the party of the losing candidate for Congress.

[6]The "structural and functional autonomy" of the congressional district party is also noted in Avery Leiserson, "National Party Organization and Congressional Districts," *Western Political Quarterly*, 16: 633-49 (September, 1963), p. 649.

Party Organization in the Electorate

Allan Kornberg

Bowman and Boynton[1] have pointed out that local party organizations frequently have rather staggering tasks assigned to them a priori by party theorists. These include the mobilization of voters, the espousal of the party's ideology, the recruitment of workers and leaders, the dispensing of patronage, and so forth.

Although in the past few years there have been an increasing number of empirical studies of parties as organizations,[2] to the best of our knowledge there have been few, if any, that have studied party organizations from the viewpoint of their most immediate beneficiaries — the ones they elected to public offices.

---

[1]Lewis Bowman and George R. Boynton, "Activities and Role Definitions of Grassroots Party Officials," *Journal of Politics*, 28 (1966), 121-43.

[2]To date, the most ambitious has been Samuel J. Eldersveld's study of party organization in Wayne County. See Samuel J. Eldersveld, *Political Parties: A Behavioral Analysis* (Chicago, Ill.: Rand McNally & Company, 1964). See also Peter H. Rossi and Phillips Cutright, "The Impact of Party Organization in an Industrial Setting," in Morris Janowitz (ed.), *Community Political Systems* (New York: The Free Press, 1961), pp. 81-116; Lester Seligman, "Political Recruitment and Party Structure," *American Political Science Review*, 55 (1961), 77-86; and Samuel C. Patterson, "Characteristics of Party Leaders," *Western Political Quarterly*, 16 (1963), 332-52.

Reprinted from *Canadian Legislative Behavior: A Study of the 25th Parliament* (New York: Holt, Rinehart and Winston, Inc., 1967), Chapter 7, pp. 126-29, 138-39; by permission of the publisher.

Responses to the question, "How important was your party organization in determining the outcome of the election?" indicated that the majority of Canadian MPs, regardless of party affiliation, felt that their parties played a crucial role in electing them. Fully 85 percent of the left-wing and 78 percent of the right-wing party members described their local organizations' contributions as very important. When asked what tasks the party actually performed,[3] it was clear that, like the party organizations in the two states studied by Bowman and Boynton,[4] the direct canvassing of voters was the most important task performed by local party organizations. Local parties were also active doing committee-room work (making up and mailing party and candidate literature from party headquarters), providing opportunities for candidates to meet their constituents, performing election day chores, and raising campaign funds (see Table 1). Although relatively similar proportions of right-wingers and left-wingers reported committee work and fund raising[5] as important activities, it was evident that the left-wing party organizations were considerably more active in directly contacting voters or

TABLE 1
MOST IMPORTANT TASK PERFORMED BY LOCAL PARTY ORGANIZATIONS (PERCENTAGE)

	PARTY AFFILIATION	
TASK PERFORMED	LEFT-WING	RIGHT-WING
Canvass voters	38	28
Committee work[a]	20	21
Help candidates meet voters[b]	18	10
Election-day work[c]	8	22
Raise and provide funds	9	8
Nothing or practically nothing (no other reply)	7	11
	(N=76)	(N=89)

[a] Prepare and mail out literature.
[b] Arrange formal meetings, coffee, and cocktail parties.
[c] Baby-sit, provide transportation, check polls for irregularities.

[3]They were asked: "What were the chief things the party organization did to help you get elected?" Only their first responses have been analyzed.

[4]Unlike Bowman and Boynton, we have coded their first responses *only* on the assumption that they were the most important contributions of the organizations.

[5]Assuming that their responses were not overly influenced by the traditional reluctance of candidates for elected office to discuss campaign finances, it would appear that individual campaigns largely are financed (singly or in combination) by the central offices of the national or provincial party organizations, local donors outside the formal party, or by the candidates themselves.

enabling the candidates to have face-to-face contacts with voters. On the other hand, right-wing local party organizations were more active in performing what might be termed administrative tasks (committee work, election day work, and fund raising). If we label the former "direct contact work" and the latter "indirect contact work" we find a correlation of 0.34 between type of local party activity and left-right party affiliation.

After a lead-in question concerning their awareness of constituency opinions on policy issues the interviewees were asked, "How do you make sure about the accuracy of the information you get?" The responses revealed that local right-wing party organizations seem to be more important reference groups for their legislative representatives than do left-wing constituency organizations. In addition to local party organizations, the MPs also cited local newspapers, returns from mailed questionnaires,[6] and their own interaction with constituents as sources of information. Approximately 14 percent of the respondents said that it was difficult or impossible to ascertain opinions with any degree of accuracy. Another 10 percent said that they knew *intuitively* what constituents' opinions were. However, they refused to elaborate when probed for the bases of their insight (see Table 2). If nonparty sources are combined and compared with party sources we find a correlation of −0.42 between a left-right party affiliation and the employment of local party organizations (as opposed to other sources) as reference groups. In view of this, it was somewhat surprising that when the respondents were asked to rank their sources,[7] *there was little difference* (Gamma = 0.09) in the proportions of left-wingers and right-wingers who cited local party

TABLE 2

SOURCES FOR DETERMINING THE ACCURACY OF INFORMATION CONCERNING LEGISLATIVE DISTRICTS (PERCENTAGE)

	PARTY AFFILIATION	
SOURCES FOR DETERMINING ACCURACY OF INFORMATION	LEFT-WING	RIGHT-WING
Contacts with local party leaders and workers	46	69
Local newspapers	14	7
Polls (mailed questionnaires)	7	4
Intuition	15	7
Very difficult	16	12
Not ascertained	2	1
	(N=76)	(N=89)

[6]Compared with American Congressmen, Canadian MPs apparently make limited use of questionnaires and surveys to determine constituency attitudes.

[7]The question was: "From whom do you think you get the most accurate information about the feelings of your constituents?"

people as the source that provided the most accurate information concerning constituency feelings (see Table 3).

Taken together, the data contained in Tables 2 and 3 suggest that local party organizations constitute important reference groups for legislative incumbents. Because party activists are likely to view the world of the constituency through partisan blinkers, Canadian MPs, particularly members of the two right-wing parties, probably get a somewhat biased sampling of constituency opinions. That the right-wingers recognized this possibility is suggested by the substantially smaller proportion who perceived their local organizations as the best source of information. The fact that approximately similar proportions of left-wing and right-wing MPs cited personal friends and neighbors, also suggests that they look to the latter as possible correctives for what they have heard from party stalwarts. Finally, in view of the importance ascribed to them as "opinion leaders" in Canada,[8] it was not surprising that, as reference groups, business leaders ranked only behind the constituency parties.

In keeping with their somewhat greater reliance upon local party organizations, right-wing legislators were more inclined to accept the efficacy of those organizations exerting influence upon MPs. Thus a larger proportion of Conservatives and Social Creditors said local organizations *do* and *ought* to influence[9] their representatives in Parliament (see Table 4).

TABLE 3

MOST ACCURATE SOURCES OF INFORMATION BY PARTY (PERCENTAGE)

	PARTY AFFILIATION	
MOST ACCURATE SOURCES OF INFORMATION	LEFT-WING	RIGHT-WING
Local party leaders and workers	46	41
Business leaders	10	21
Local union officials	4	1
Local religious officials	4	7
Local ethnic leaders	6	2
Personal friends and neighbors	14	10
Depends on the issue[a]	16	18
	(N=76)	(N=89)

[a] The legislators in this category claimed it was impossible to ascribe to any single group or individual the accolade of "best" informant, as the knowledge and competence of most groups and individuals almost always is limited to a particular area.

[8] See, for example, Peter Regenstrief, *The Diefenbaker Interlude: Parties and Voting in Canada* (Toronto: Longmans, 1965).

[9] The two questions were: "Do you think the local party organization leaders have influence over the MPs?" and "Do you think they *should* have influence?"

TABLE 4
Local Party Influence on MPs by Party (Percentage)

Attitudes Toward Local Party Influence	Party Affiliation		
	Left-Wing		Right-Wing
Do They Influence?			
No	25		13
Depends	3		2
Yes	72		85
		Gamma = 0.29	
Should They Influence?			
No	32		13
Depends	1		5
Yes	67		82
		Gamma = 0.40	
	$(N=76)$		$(N=89)$

In summary, the members of the legislative parties differed somewhat in their perceptions of the functions carried out by their local organizations. Right-wing party members tended to see their local parties as being particularly busy on the day of an election, while members of the two left-wing parties tended to see their organizations as performing pre-election day activities. Apparently, the local organizations of the right-wing parties serve as reference groups for their MPs more frequently than do the local parties of the left. Relatedly, perhaps, a larger proportion of the right-wing respondents said that constituency parties do influence MPs. . . .

SECTION SIX

Environmental Change and Party Effectiveness

Environmental Change and Party Effectiveness

The discussion of larger questions concerning the role and effectiveness of contemporary political parties suffers both from inadequate guidance by theory and lack of relevant data. Even though political parties are ubiquitous elements of modern democratic political systems (Macridis, 1967, p. 10), there is substantial disagreement among political scientists as to the importance of parties and their effectiveness. Katz and Eldersveld (Selection 6.2) note the conflicting viewpoints: "On the one hand there are those who see the party as a major social structure mediating directly between the individual citizen and national, state, or local government. . . . On the other hand, others see parties today as obsolete, ineffective, atrophied, and incompetent. . . ." A discussion of the effectiveness of party organization returns us inevitably to our starting point — basic conceptions of party. Different criteria for judging party effectiveness follow from the two basic party models. The sole test employed in the Rational-Efficient model is efficient vote mobilization and electoral success. Since this objective is situationally determined, a variety of party attributes are consistent with it. In contrast, effective vote mobilization and electoral success, although important, yield the highest ranking as evaluative criteria in the Party Democracy model to effectiveness of policy-clarification and intraparty democracy.

If conclusions regarding the role and effectiveness of party are not to be determined by initial assumptions and value premises, two significant questions deserve attention: the impact of environmental change on political parties and the conceptualization and measurement of party effectiveness. The debate over the role of party and of its importance is set against a backdrop of technological and socio-political change, in terms of which questions about the contemporary relevance of traditional forms, functions, and activities of political parties are raised. Such modern communications and research techniques as technological developments in the mass media (particularly television), advertising and public relations, survey research techniques and computers, and their use by staffs of skilled specialists are increasingly viewed as rendering traditional organizational forms and practices of American and non-American parties outmoded.

An excellent illustration of how the impact of technological and other environmental change is viewed in terms of the Party Democracy model is Ulrich Lohmar's (1963) analysis of contemporary German parties. Lohmar's thesis is that German political parties are strongly influenced and even manipulated by (a) the mass media — especially television; (b) the increasing use of polls and modern public relations techniques by parties themselves; and (c) interest groups. The mass media and modern campaign techniques such as the use of polls, the centralization of campaigns, increasing emphasis on "personality" of the candidates and concern with the party "image," and the reduction of political issues to "slogans" are, in his view, depriving German party organization at the grass-roots level of some of its most important traditional functions. The important internal function of political education of the membership, designed to enable them to participate actively in the party opinion-formation and policy-making processes, is increasing jeopardized by the mass media, and member participation in party affairs is declining. The grass roots organization's traditionally important external function of developing and maintaining contact with the local electorate — a function broadly viewed as the extension of the party's political education and opinion-formation process to the general public — is also threatened by the increasing replacement of efforts of party activists by more sophisticated communications and research techniques. Lohmar considers the results of these changes to be a threatened loss of role of the lower levels of German party organization and a further de-politicization of the voters, turning them into "consumers" and "reducing the number of citizens who are prepared to be politically active" (p. 109). Hartenstein and Liepelt (1962) also discuss the decline in membership of German parties and Torgersen (1962) does the same for Norwegian parties. Torgersen "is concerned with what he regards as the ill effects of decreased citizen participation in party organizations, since he believes that such participation is essential to a vital political system" (Epstein, 1967, p. 253).

Epstein (1967, Chapter 9) discusses the impact of technological change in the mass media and research techniques and large-scale financing involved in the use of such techniques on political parties in industrialized Western politicial systems. While he generally agrees that the effects of modern communications techniques are weakening grass-roots party organization, operating as he does from the Rational-Efficient model, his evaluations differ sharply from those of Lohmar. Since these techniques tend to facilitate the electoral function of parties, "an organizational apparatus intervening between candidates and voters may be less necessary, or at any rate less efficient, as a vote-getting device" (p. 233). Thus the displacement of "certain membership functions" and the "trend toward less membership participation" are not deplored by Epstein: "Parties, it can be argued, successfully win votes, perhaps more votes, with fewer organizational members. The new campaign techniques may at least facilitate the electoral task" (p. 253). Epstein counters Duverger's (1954) argument that American parties, lacking a mass membership base, are archaic in structure with the viewpoint that American parties can be considered *more modern*, on the basis of their extensive use of sophisticated campaign techniques, because they are less encumbered than European parties by a high degree of organization: "By being organizationally backward, or even retrogressive compared to an earlier day, [American parties] were well suited to be especially advanced in campaign techniques" (p. 257). (For a concise propositionalized statement of Epstein's thesis, see May, 1969, p. 217.)

Modern communications techniques have made possible a sophisticated new style of politics that may be termed the "managerial" style, as represented by the 1968 Nixon campaign. This contrasts with the old style, the epitome of which is the patronage-fed, city machine typified today by Mayor Daley. But trends shaped by environmental factors are not that simple; 1968 also witnessed a different new style of politics that conflicts sharply with both the old style and the new managerial style — namely, the participatory style represented by the McCarthy forces. Demands for participatory democracy are not confined to the New Left but were expressed by a sizable number of somewhat older and more sedate delegates to the 1968 Democratic Convention. The coming trend in American party organization, Sorauf (1964) contends, may be the "club-movement" party composed largely of urban-suburban, well-educated, middle to upper-middle class members who tend to be ideologically-oriented, and who stress member participation in party affairs and intraparty democracy. (See also Wilson, 1962.) Epstein disagrees with Sorauf's assessment.

Increasing urbanization and, especially, education are key factors in this development. Rising educational levels offer a potential, though by no means certain check on the burgeoning technological potential for the manipulation of voters; greater education *may* lead to increased citizen participation in politics. In any case, American politics today is a diverse mixture of the old and the new, with the outcome uncertain. The same can be said of European politics. Although theories of convergence should be approached cautiously, European parties' increasing electoral orientation and use of modern communications techniques, their de-emphasis on ideology and declining policy differences among the major parties, and an increasing social heterogeneity in electoral support are factors leading them to more closely resemble their American counterparts. This is at a time when American politics may be moving in the opposite direction, if predictions of more class-based politics, increasing emphasis on ideology, and more activist participation in party affairs prove to be correct.

It is clear that we need more adequate conceptualization of the implications of environmental change for political parties. The potential utility of conceptualizing parties as organizational systems interacting with their environment should be noted. A related problem is that of conceptualizing and measuring party effectiveness — a problem to which little attention has been paid. The almost exclusive reliance on electoral success as a criterion follows from the Rational-Efficient model: "And, if the parties are simply electoral organizations, it is only a short step to the conclusion that the only relevant measure of the party's effectiveness and strength is its ability to win elections. The ability to win elections has become virtually the only measure of party functioning" (Sorauf, 1963, p. 44). Sorauf notes that involved here are also methodological considerations — the ready availability of hard data on this — and only this — aspect of party functioning: "Regardless of degree of influence, it seems undeniable that, in the study of parties, the availability of data has determined both research priorities and the shaping of concepts to best accommodate the handy data" (p. 46). Sorauf criticizes reliance on electoral success as the sole criterion for evaluating party effectiveness on three grounds: "In the first place, contesting elections involves more than drawing voters to the polls. Second, the evaluation of party as a winner or loser ignores it as a political organization. . . . Third, the criterion of victory is at best a partial test of the party's total electoral function. . . ." (pp. 44-45). In his study of local party organization in Pennsylvania, Sorauf (1963) concludes that the development and operation of party organization is not a simple matter; rather, it is the complex result of the interaction of several factors: constituency characteristics, political culture, party competition, party organizational characteristics, and "political style." He argues that party effectiveness is a more complex matter than "the easy assumption so common in the conventional wisdom of American politics that certain organizational types and patterns of activity accompany party because, as wisdom's logic would have it, they are essential ingredients of that victory" (p. 62).

Eldersveld (1964) takes a broad approach in using data from interviews with Detroit party officials and a cross-section sample of voters, as well as aggregate census and election data to measure the impact of local party activity upon the electorate and to assess organizational viability. He concluded that "ineffective and inadequate as much of its leadership and organization is," party efforts are functional for the political system in at least two respects: first, the stimulation of political knowledge, interest, participation, efficacy, and system support for those voters exposed to party activities; and second, the "maintenance of party loyalty and its implementation in voting regularity" (p. 471). Eldersveld also concluded that although parties today face increasing competition from interest groups and the mass media, they have not been supplanted by these competing institutions; rather, he views this competition as a "functional convergence of social forces."

The complexity of measuring party effectiveness is illustrated by the analyses of Sorauf and Eldersveld. The three studies included in this section are attempts to measure aspects of the impact of local party activity upon the electorate. These studies utilize census and election data on a ward or precinct basis, as well as interview or questionnaire data on local party activities and employ such statistical techniques as correlation and regression analysis. From multiple regression equations, the precinct voting results are predicted by various independent ecological and party organization variables. The difference between the actual and predicted results (the residuals) is attributed to party organizational efforts, the "breakage" or majority effect or the influence on the vote exerted by "the dominant political climate" of the precinct, and unexplained variance. One cannot simply attribute the residual difference to party organizational activities; rather, the latter must be measured and brought into the analysis at some point, either as an independent variable in the regression equation or in an examination of the residuals.

In a series of articles (Cutright and Rossi, 1958a, 1958b; Rossi and Cutright, 1961; Cutright, Selection 6.1) the impact of party organization is analyzed for contested local primary and general elections and the 1956 presidential election in Stackton, a Midwestern industrial city in which the Democratic Party is dominant and highly organized, and where patronage continues to play an important role in local politics. In their analysis of the presidential vote, Cutright and Rossi (1961) found precinct ecological characteristics such as ethnicity and socio-economic status to be better predictors of the vote than party activity indices; the later variable did have some effect (about five per cent) on the vote when the breakage effect was removed. They found that party activity played a more significant role in primary elections, where the party organization supplied effective cues to the voters (Cutright and Rossi, 1958b). Cutright (Selection 6.1) reanalyzed the Stackton (Partisan City) data and compared them to Nonpartisan City in an analysis of the 1956 presidential vote: he concluded that both the majority (or breakage) effect and local party activity "act to guide the voter to his final party choice" and that it is essential to correct for the majority effect in order to estimate accurately the impact of organizational activities.

Katz and Eldersveld (Selection 6.2) also found precinct ecological characteristics to be better predictors of the presidential vote in Detroit than party organizational measures. When they examined the partial correlations, the Democratic organizational leadership factor was found to be negligible, whereas "local Republican leadership did contribute significantly to the presidential vote." Katz and Eldersveld controlled for party competition and found a maximum difference in the presidential vote in those precincts where one party was organizationally strong and the other weak: In the Strong Democratic-Weak Republican precincts, Stevenson's actual vote was 5 per cent greater than expected; in Strong-Republican-Weak Democratic precincts, it was 5.5 per cent less. Unlike Rossi and Cutright, Katz and Eldersveld did not remove the majority or breakage effect before analysis of the data. They did find a majority effect, but not of such magnitude as to wipe out the effect of party organizational efforts. (They did not estimate the magnitude.) Both studies are in agreement that local party activity does make a modest difference in the presidential vote, especially for the minority party, which does not benefit from the dominant political climate of the area.

Raymond Wolfinger (Selection 6.3) studied the impact of precinct work on voting behavior in a different kind of election — the vote on a controversial city charter revision in New Haven, a city with strong local party organization (especially for the Democrats). As in Stackton, "all of the classic requirements for machine politics" were fulfilled in New Haven: strong ethnic groups, ample local patronage, and strong ward-based party organization. Passage of the charter revision which entailed strengthening the mayor's position was officially supported by the Democratic organization and opposed by the Republicans. To varying degrees, however, many Democratic ward leaders opposed passage since they feared that increasing the mayor's power would diminish the influence of the Democratic organization. Wolfinger interviewed a sample of Democratic ward chairmen to determine their position on the charter revision issue and their activities in this regard and analyzed absentee ballots turned in by the ward organization (a practice permitted by Connecticut statutes) as an index of party activity. He also utilized ward census and election data, as well as relevant data from a cross-section voter survey.

Wolfinger's findings point to a strong influence of precinct work on voting behavior with "virtually no influence" of "demographic variables such as education, income, and ethnicity" — variables which the other studies found to be most influential in presidential voting. In a situation in which (a) the issue was not salient for most voters; (b) party identification furnished less clear-cut cues than in presidential elections; (c) the local party organization's interests were threatened; and (d) turnout was low, the impact of party organizational efforts was greatest.

In their study of political parties in a Norwegian community, Valen and Katz (1964, Chapter 5) applied the techniques used by Cutright and Rossi; in addition, they sought evidence of the impact of local party activity on voting behavior in their voter survey data. Unlike the above-mentioned studies, Valen and Katz found virtually no relationship between local party activity and voting behavior. They advance several possible explanations for this, including methodological and situational (the character of the 1957 national election campaign) factors. They opt for the interpretation that "the other determinants [such as socio-economic status] are of such overriding importance in Norway that party organization is of no significance in mobilizing the vote through personal contacts with the voters, though it may be of significance in reaching people through mass media" (p. 128). Valen and Katz found that Norwegian local party leaders made little effort to come into personal contact with voters, apart from routine formal activities such as holding open party meetings and distributing campaign literature. Moreover, they found a very low rate of voter exposure to party efforts. The voters they interviewed were characterized by low scores on the following measures of exposure to party activities: knowledge of candidates and party leaders, attendance at election meetings and rallies, personal contact by party workers, receipt of party campaign literature, and exposure to and recall of content of radio debates which were a major campaign technique.

Valen and Katz did not develop an overall measure of voter exposure to party activities. Eldersveld (1964, Chapter 17) did construct a Party Exposure Index (exposure over time to any party efforts) and classified Wayne County voters as follows: highly exposed (17 per cent), moderately exposed (39 per cent), and not exposed (44 per cent) (p. 442). On those specific measures of voter exposure in these two studies that are comparable (e.g., knowledge of whether the parties had workers in the precinct, personal contact by party workers, receipt of campaign literature), Detroit voters tended to show a higher rate of exposure to party efforts than did the Norwegian voters interviewed by Valen and Katz. In both studies a factor to be taken into account in evaluating party impact is the relatively low rate of party effort. Thus Katz and Eldersveld note that "in general, organizational activity at the precinct level has an even greater potential for influencing the electorate in Wayne County, in that few of their precinct leaders carried out consistently all the necessary tasks for mobilizing the vote" (p. 24).

The paucity of empirical research in this area was noted by several of the authors. Wolfinger concluded: "The present research task in this area is to explore the effectiveness of vigorous party activity in conditions of varying public knowledge and interest, in different types of elections, and with different kinds of voters." The measurement of party effectiveness on a broader scale is an even greater task.

REFERENCES

Cutright, Phillips. "Measuring the Impact of Local Party Activity on the General Election Vote." *Public Opinion Quarterly,* 27 (Fall, 1963), 372-86.

Cutright, Phillips, and Rossi, Peter H. "Grass Roots Politicians and the Vote." *American Sociological Review,* 23 (1958), 171-79.

———. "Party Organization in Primary Elections." *American Journal of Sociology,* 64 (1958), 262-69.

Duverger, Maurice. *Political Parties.* New York: John Wiley and Sons, 1954.

Eldersveld, Samuel J. *Political Parties: A Behavioral Analysis,* Part IV. Chicago: Rand McNally, 1964.

Epstein, Leon D. *Political Parties in Western Democracies*, Chapter 9. New York, Frederick A. Praeger, 1967.

Hartenstein, Wolfgang, and Liepelt, Klaus. "Party Members and Party Voters in West Germany." *Acta Sociologica*, 6 (1962), 43-52.

Holt, Robert T. and Turner, John E. *Political Parties in Action: The Battle of Barons Court*, Chapter 5. New York: The Free Press, 1968.

Katz, Daniel, and Eldersveld, Samuel J. "The Impact of Local Party Activity Upon the Electorate." *Public Opinion Quarterly*, 25 (1961), 1-24.

Lohmar, Ulrich. *Innerparteiliche Demokratie*. Stuttgart: Ferdinand Enke Verlag, 1963.

Macridis, Roy C., ed. *Political Parties: Contemporary Trends and Ideas*. New York: Harper and Row, 1967.

May, John D. "Democracy, Party 'Evolution,' Duverger." *Comparative Political Studies*, 2 (July, 1969), 216-48.

Rossi, Peter, and Cutright, Phillips. "The Impact of Party Organization in an Industrial Setting," in *Community Political Systems*, edited by Morris Janowitz, pp. 81-116. New York: The Free Press of Glencoe, 1961.

Sorauf, Frank J. *Party and Representation: Legislative Politics in Pennsylvania*. New York: Atherton Press, 1963.

———. *Political Parties in the American System*. Boston: Little, Brown, 1964.

Torgersen, Ulf. "The Trend Towards Political Consensus: The Case of Norway," in *Approaches to the Study of Political Participation*, edited by Stein Rokkan. Bergen, Norway: Chr. Michelsens Institut, 1962.

Valen, Henry, and Katz, Daniel. *Political Parties in Norway: A Community Study*, Chapter 5. Oslo: Universitetsforlaget, 1964.

Wilson, James Q. *The Amateur Democrat*. Chicago: The University of Chicago Press, 1962.

Wolfinger, Raymond. "The Influence of Precinct Work on Voting Behavior." *Public Opinion Quarterly*, 27 (Fall, 1963), 387-98.

Measuring the Impact of Local Party Activity on the General Election Vote*

Phillips Cutright

Studies relating grass-roots political activities to voting behavior usually note the sharp differences in the vitality of political organizations from one state to another and the extreme differences in the long-run party loyalties of voters in different parts of the nation. Typically, however, an investigator focuses his attention on either the impact of party activities on the vote or the social-psychological effect of the varying levels of party loyalties of the electorate on the voters' decision-making processes preceding each election. Although investigators often comment on the interacting effects of existing party loyalties in an area on the level of party activity there, the political scientist follows his interest while the social psychologist follows his.[1]

[1]For examples of party-oriented research, see V. O. Key, Jr., *American State Politics*, New York: Knopf, 1956; and V. O. Key, Jr., *Southern Politics*, New York: Knopf, 1950. See also Daniel Katz and Samuel J. Eldersveld, "The Impact of Local Party Activity upon the Electorate," *Public Opinion Quarterly*, vol. 25, 1961, 1-24. Representative of the social-psychological interest is Bernard Berelson, *et al., Voting*, Chicago: University of Chicago Press, 1954; and Angus Campbell, *et al., The American Voter*, New York: Wiley, 1960.

*My thanks to Nelson W. Polsby and Robert A. Dentler for a helpful critical review of an earlier draft. It is a pleasure to acknowledge the support of the Department of Sociology of Washington State University, and the Social Science Research Council. The views expressed in the paper in no way reflect the opinion of the Social Security Administration.

The distinctive orientation of these two approaches has led to alternative explanations of the same phenomenon, e.g. the long-term stability of voter loyalties to a single party. The student with a concern for party-worker activities explains stable single-party loyalties in terms of the strength of the majority party's grass-roots activities and the comparative inactivity of the minority party. The scholar attentive to social-psychological effects speaks of a "majority effect" that acts to hold many voters to the majority party in spite of their ideological or other predispositions that may be counter to the existing majority party.[2] According to this second view, the majority-party activities need not be stronger than that of the minority party — the majority effect will hold dissident voters in line, given minimal support from the majority party. The meaning of "party activity" and the "majority effect" should be clear before we go further.

Our measures of party activity pertain to the activity of precinct workers and their interaction with voters in their precincts. Although much of the work in party organization has properly focused on the state political system, it is within the precinct or neighborhood that the party worker meets or fails to meet the voter. While the systematic analysis of the effects of these contacts are few, a method for assessing the impact of party workers on voting in general elections has been developed and applied to two cities.

Voters in a given area may or may not be evenly divided in their loyalties to political parties. The "majority effect" is the effect on an individual's party choice that is the result of living in a relatively homogeneous political environment. A person is in a majority situation when opinion on party choice strongly favors one party. Several studies have discovered a majority effect that delivers bonus votes to the dominant party in a one-party area. For example, a secondary analysis of the Survey Research Center's nationwide study of the 1952 presidential election, which classified voters according to their party voting predispositions, discovered that many voters in one-party counties were consistently voting against their party predispositions, while voters in "competitive" counties voted in line with their predispositions.[3] Cutright and Rossi found that voters in pre-

[2]See Berelson *et al.*, *op. cit.*, pp. 98-101. He observed that "The surrounding majority gets the benefit of the operation of cross pressures. One might call this the 'breakage' effect . . ." (*ibid.*, p. 100). We use the term "majority effect" in place of "breakage effect." See also S. M. Lipset *et al.*, *Union Democracy*, Glencoe, Ill., Free Press, 1956, for numerous examples of the effect of the majority "climate of opinion" on the voting behavior of printers.

[3]Warren E. Miller, "One Party Politics and the Voter," *American Political Science Review*, Vol. 50, 1956, 707-25.

cincts in which one party received more than 45 per cent of the vote tended to receive an additional 2.5 per cent of the vote over their expected level.[4] It seems clear that a party in its own majority area receives "bonus" votes. The issue is whether the Democratic Party, for example, is getting bonus votes in an area where it commands the loyalties of a strong majority of the voters because its party activities overwhelm Republican efforts or because of social-psychological effects resulting from the heavy concentration of Democratic voters in the area. The working hypothesis of this study is that both party activities and the balance of voting strength in an area work to determine the decisions of voters.

Using ecological data, it is possible to link the voting records of precincts with their social characteristics and, on the basis of a regression equation, calculate the vote that any precinct would be expected to give to each party on the basis of its own social composition. In previous research, the difference between the actual vote and the expected, or predicted, vote (this difference is called a "residual" in this paper) has been viewed as an outcome of differences between the activities of party workers in the precincts.[5] Using the same technique, however, we can also measure the majority effect: one simply examines the patterns of the residual differences (the differences between the actual and the predicted vote) in precincts with varying levels of party loyalties. By grouping precincts into strong Democratic, competitive, and strong Republican, one can see if the parties are receiving a systematic bonus vote in areas of varying partisanship.[6] By combining information about precinct-worker activities with residual values (measuring the extent of the "bonus vote") in different partisanship areas of the city, we can apply a rough test to the two competing explanations of the majority effect on voter decisions. We present data from two cities on the distribution of the activities of precinct committeemen in different political areas of the cities. We then examine the pattern of residual differences in Partisan and Nonpartisan City and assess the majority effect and the effect of party workers on the general election vote in the two cities.

---

[4]Phillips Cutright and Peter H. Rossi, "Grass Roots Politicians and the Vote," *American Sociological Review*, Vol. 23, 1958, 174.

[5]See *ibid.* for details of this method. See also Katz and Eldersveld, *op. cit.*, for a second application of this technique.

[6]The term "partisanship" in this paper refers to the percentage of the total vote a party gets in an area. It does not refer to the intensity of the feeling voters have toward the parties.

Data Collected in Partisan and Nonpartisan City

Data are presented from Democratic and Republican precinct committeemen in two cities, Nonpartisan City and Partisan City. (Partisan City is the same city referred to in earlier reports as "Stackton.") Both cities have some 160,000 inhabitants, but Nonpartisan City is located in the Pacific Northwest and Partisan City in the Middle West. We eliminate the nonwhite precincts in each city. Some of the differences in the characteristics of the local party workers that are consequences of the partisan and nonpartisan difference in the local electoral systems are reflected in the following tables, but the reader who is interested in a detailed analysis of these data and an interpretation of differences between the cities is referred elsewhere.[7] In this report we are primarily interested in studying local party activity and the majority effect in the two cities.

It should be noted that the responses from committeemen in the two cities are comparable, since the identical questions were used to study Nonpartisan City as were used in Partisan City. Every effort was made to have the research procedures make direct comparison between the two cities as reliable as possible.[8]

Party Activity and Contact with Voters in Different Areas of the City

The following two tables explore the contention that strong differences in party activity exist in different partisanship areas of the city. (For the evidence that a majority effect exists in these two cities, see Tables 4 and 5.) It is important to compare low and high Democratic partisan areas with each other, but it is also important to look at *all* the cases and include in the analysis the areas of "split" or nearly balanced party loyalty. Further, the behavior of both parties must be taken into account, because it is possible for the Democrats to be strong in heavy Democratic areas compared to their performance in Republican areas, but, at the same time, the Republicans may also be strong in Democratic areas compared to their performance in Republican areas. In the following two tables,

---

[7]Phillips Cutright, "Activities of Precinct Committeemen in Partisan and Nonpartisan Communities," *Western Political Quarterly*.

[8]When activity levels are low, as in Nonpartisan City, it is tempting to change the "cutting points" between "high" and "low" activity to satisfy statistical niceties. We will avoid artificial "high" activity splits by maintaining identical cutting points for both cities.

then, it is important not only to look for differences in Democratic and then Republican party contact with voters and political activities in different partisanship areas, but *to take account of the relative balance of party-worker activity a party has in a given partisan area.* This is done by controlling for the type of area and comparing the two parties within the same area. If the Republicans had a very strong advantage over the Democrats in Republican areas, the parties were about even in competitive areas, and the Democrats had a powerful advantage over Republicans in Democratic areas, we would have evidence that the party-activity explanation of the majority effect is plausible.

In Table 1 we present data pertaining to four committeeman attributes that affect their ability to influence voters.[9] The reader may observe the differences between the parties in the two cities, but our interest here is primarily on the net advantage a party has in different partisanship areas and how such differences are related to the patterns of residual differences we use to measure the majority effect. Again, if activity patterns are closely related to the pattern of residual party gains, then the majority effect can be thought of as a product of differential party strength in areas of varying party loyalties. If no systematic relationship is found, we will be obliged to reject the party-activity hypothesis as an adequate single explanation of the majority effect.

Looking first at Partisan City, we see that both Democratic and Republican daily contacts with their constituents increase as Democratic partisanship increases but no net party differences between "split" areas and heavy Democratic areas exists. The Democratic advantage is less, however, in Republican areas. This variable was, for Partisan City, the single best predictor of a committeeman's ability to influence voters in the 1956 presidential election. If the residuals are related to party activity, then the residuals of "split" areas and heavy Democratic areas should be about equally favorable to the Democrats, but this is not the case (see Table 5). The second type of contact measures the dependency of the voters in an area on local party organization, and this indicator changes dramatically with increasing Democratic voting strength. This change results in a pattern showing relatively stronger Democratic

[9] A detailed analysis of the relation of each indicator to voting behavior in Partisan City may be found in Peter H. Rossi and Phillips Cutright, "The Impact of Party Organization in an Industrial Setting," in Morris Janowitz, editor, *Community Political Systems*, Glencoe, Ill., Free Press, 1961, pp. 81-116. Party activity in both primary and general elections and the effect of this activity on voting behavior are examined in that article.

activity in heavy Democratic precincts. However, the third attribute, which measures the reaction of the committeemen to these requests for aid, shows that the greatest difference favors the Democrats in "split" areas. Finally, as revealed in the last entry for

TABLE 1

CONTACTS WITH VOTERS BY COMMITTEEMEN IN PRECINCTS OF DIFFERENT PARTISANSHIP, TWO CITIES

	PARTISAN CITY PRECINCTS, PER CENT DEMOCRATIC, 1956			NONPARTISAN CITY PRECINCTS, PER CENT DEMOCRATIC, 1958		
TYPE OF CONTACT	28-44	45-56	57-82	6-43	44-55	56-78
Median number of daily contacts in the precinct						
Democrats	12.8	12.0	15.2	2.9	3.8	4.5
Republicans	8.6	6.4	9.6	3.1	3.2	4.2
Democratic gain	4.2	5.6	5.6	−0.3	0.6	0.3
Per cent with 2 or more requests for aid in past 30 days						
Democrats	46	60	72	18	20	24
Republicans	10	8	10	3	6	6
Democratic gain	36	52	62	15	14	18
Per cent very responsive to voter requests for aid						
Democrats	21	38	33	0	3	8
Republicans	10	0	15	0	2	0
Democratic gain	11	38	18	0	1	8
Per cent of Committeemen holding patronage jobs, state and local						
Democrats	27	46	35	5	5	9
Republicans	13	15	15	3	0	0
Democratic gain	14	31	20	2	5	9
(N Democratic committeemen)*	(29-33)	(20-28)	(36-48)	(21-22)	(39-40)	(40-41)
(N Republican committeemen)*	(32-32)	(26-27)	(30-39)	(33-36)	(50-52)	(45-47)

*The smaller number applies to the first item, and the larger number to the remaining items.

NOTE: In Partisan City cutting points are based on the percentage of the total vote cast that was cast as a "straight" Democratic vote in each precinct. The mean for the 74 precincts was 53.3 per cent Democratic, S.D. = 12.18. Mean of the Democratic vote for President was 50.9. In Nonpartisan City cutting points are based on the percentage of the two-party vote cast in the precinct for the Democratic candidate for Congress, 1958 general election. The mean for the 107 precincts was 49.8 per cent Democratic, S.D. = 14.69.

Partisan City, there is little difference between Republican and Democratic areas in the proportion of committeemen holding patronage jobs.

Nonpartisan City reveals the same pattern of increasing contact between committeemen and voters as the areas become more Democratic, but this again holds for both parties' committeemen, and the net advantage of either party in any type of area is negligible. The last three indicators also reflect the strong differences between the parties' committeemen in Partisan and Nonpartisan City. Very few voters request the aid of committeemen in Nonpartisan City (the difference favors the Democrats, who were in power in the state and had the majority of county offices), but the net difference does not favor either party in any of the three partisanship areas. The third measure, of what committeemen do for their voters, and the fourth measure, of patronage job holding, reveal no pattern that we could assume would affect the relative strength of either party's activities in any area of the city.

In sum, Table 1 does not reveal a pattern of systematic differences between the net organizational strength of Democrats or Republicans in either of the two cities that would support the idea that the net party differences in day-to-day contact between the committeeman and his constituents or the relations of the party worker to the voter are notably different in different partisanship areas of either city. When the pattern of differences shown in Table 1 is compared to the pattern of residual differences in Table 5, it is clear that the patterns do not fit.

Table 2 presents measures of four types of political behavior and the distribution of these activities in the two cities. The first indicator discriminates between levels of activity of committeemen during primary elections. It is the best single indicator we have of attempts by committeemen to influence directly the choice voters make in primaries, and in Partisan City our interview data indicated that committeemen who were not active in the primary were not active in the general election.[10] In Nonpartisan City we asked about activity in both primary and general elections and found 29 committeemen doing door-to-door campaigning in the primary and 33 of the 236 respondents very active in the general election. This confirms our impression of stable activity levels gleaned from our Partisan City interviews; we present the primary election-activity data here to maintain comparability with Partisan City, and because the

---

[10] *Ibid.*

same pattern would be revealed in Nonpartisan City if the general election data were used. In Partisan City the greatest net advantage Democrats have over Republicans is in "split" areas, and there seems to be little difference between split and heavy Democratic areas on this indicator.

An interesting pattern in the time at which the precinct is polled (to register voters) is revealed in the next two indicators of activity. In Partisan City, Democrats poll during the primary and Republicans poll during the general election, but of interest here is the pattern of difference — there appears again to be no pattern similar

TABLE 2

POLITICAL ACTIVITIES OF VETERAN COMMITTEEMEN IN PRECINCTS OF DIFFERENT PARTISANSHIP, TWO CITIES

Type of Activity	Partisan City, Per Cent Democratic, 1956			Nonpartisan City, Per Cent Democratic, 1958		
	28-44	45-56	57-28	6-43	44-55	56-76
Per cent very active in last primary						
Democrats	50	65	70	0	19	20
Republicans	29	14	31	7	12	14
Democratic gain	21	51	39	−7	7	6
Per cent taking poll in primary						
Democrats	79	94	88	31	42	58
Republicans	42	33	26	48	30	29
Democratic gain	37	61	62	−17	12	29
Per cent taking poll in general election						
Democrats	46	53	48	28	52	62
Republicans	71	71	79	47	35	26
Democratic gain	−25	−18	−31	−19	17	36
Per cent with helpers in primary polling						
Democrats	42	38	64	17	33	45
Republicans	17	19	12	58	29	33
Democratic gain	25	19	52	−41	4	12
(N Democratic committeemen)	(24)	(17)	(25)	(19)	(33)	(36)
(N Republican committeemen)	(24)	(21)	(34)	(31)	(33)	(38)

to that shown by the residuals in Table 5. On the final indicator of helpers in primary polling (directly related, of course, to whether one polls in the primary or not), the pattern shows a sharp gain in heavy Democratic areas over the other two types of areas, but the Democratic gain in Republican areas where Democrats lose votes is larger than it is in split areas (where the Democrats come out even).

On the Nonpartisan City side of the table we see no significant difference among areas on the first indicator. However, the differences on the next three polling indicators reveals, for the first time, a pattern that would tend to give some support to the notion of sharply different types of organization in different partisanship areas. We see in the general election polling case that in Republican areas 28 per cent of Democrats polled while 47 per cent of the Republicans did, giving the Republicans a net gain of 19 per cent. However, the Democrats had a 17 per cent edge in split areas and a 36 per cent advantage in heavy Democratic areas.

Table 2 reveals, for Partisan City, differences among the areas, but these differences are not systematically related to the pattern of residuals shown in Table 5, while in Nonpartisan City our indicator of direct persuasion attempts did not correspond significantly to the concept of sharply different levels of precinct worker activity in different partisanship areas. We did find some evidence indicating a higher probability that a Republican or Democrat would poll his precinct in both primary and general elections if it was his party's precinct. It is clear that both party organizations in both cities make an effort in most precincts to poll during either the primary or the general election. This activity should be distinguished from attempts at persuasion, since it involves registration of voters, but it is also an opportunity for the committeemen to meet their voters (apparently for the first time in Nonpartisan City — see median number of daily contacts, Table 1) in a situation that is defined as a "public service" but that gives the committeeman an opportunity to sound out the voter and possibly use this contact to advantage on election day.

Our analysis of the distribution of organizational strength is not perfectly clear-cut, but it is clear enough to rule out the assumption that levels of party-worker activity in different partisanship areas vary systematically for most important activity indicators. While we should not misconstrue this to mean that party activities are equally distributed, we have shown for two very different types of cities that a number of precinct committeeman characteristics are not systematically related to precinct partisanship.

The Majority Effect and the Impact of Party Activity

A set of expected Democratic percentage values for each precinct in Nonpartisan City was constructed using the matrix of product moment correlations given in Table 3. It is from the prediction equation derived from this table that the residual values in Tables 4 and 5 were taken. In Nonpartisan City the economic level[11] of the precinct was far and away the best predictor of the vote and yields a correlation that is nearly as strong as the multiple correlation of .71. Although nearly identical measures of the demographic characteristics of the precincts were used in the two cities, a comparison of

TABLE 3
INTERCORRELATIONS AMONG PRECINCT CHARACTERISTICS AND PRECINCT VOTING RECORDS, 107 PRECINCTS, NONPARTISAN CITY

	PROPORTION HOMEOWNERS (2)	PROPORTION "NEW IMMIGRANTS" AND NONWHITES (3)	PROPORTION DEMOCRATIC 1958 CONGRESS (4)
(1) Economic level	.736	−.373	−.686
(2) Proportion homeowners		−.284	−.420
(3) Proportion "new immigrants" and nonwhites			.350

Regression equation and multiple correlation of precinct characteristics on the Democratic vote:

$$R_{4.123} = .71$$

$$Y = 85.9 - (-1.165)X_1 - .281X_2 - .163X_3$$

Regression equation and multiple correlation for Partisan City are:

$$R_{4.123} = -.908$$

$$Y = -108.2 - .422X_1 - .724X_2 - .112X_3$$

where X_1 = proportion "old immigrant"
X_2 = economic level
X_3 = proportion home ownership in precinct

An "old immigrant" is defined as a person of Anglo-Saxon, German, or Scandinavian descent. A "new immigrant" is any other white. In Nonpartisan City we combined the nonwhites with the "new immigrants" because they constituted only 1 per cent of the population and tend to vote Democratic.

The dependent variable was the proportion Democratic in the 1956 Democratic presidential election.

The matrix of intercorrelations can be found in Peter H. Rossi and Phillips Cutright, "The Impact of Party Organization in an Industrial Setting," in Morris Janowitz, editor, *Community Political Systems,* Glencoe, Ill., Free Press, 1961, p. 109.

[11]The economic level of the precincts in both cities was obtained by taking the regression of home valuation and average monthly rental for the precincts and estimating for each precinct an expected value based on the over-all regression. This expected value is an indicator of the economic level of the precinct. Economic, racial and home-ownership data were taken for the U.S. Census of Housing block book for each city, and a sample of names of registered voters in white precincts was "name-rated" for old or new immigrant ethnicity. See footnote, Table 3, for the definition of old and new immigrants.

the multiple R and prediction equation shows that the same variables did a more adequate job of accounting for variation in precinct voting patterns in Partisan City than in Nonpartisan City.[12] We have more unexplained variation in Nonpartisan City than in Partisan City, and therefore we will find larger residuals, but there is no reason to expect them to be patterned in any particular way. Table 4 is intended to make the actual pattern of the errors of prediction unmistakably clear. In Table 4 we take the ten precincts with the highest proportion of Democratic vote and the ten strongest Republican precincts in Nonpartisan City and show the actual, the predicted, and the residual "unexplained" vote. In 9 of the top 10 Democratic areas we find positive residuals, indicating a larger than predicted Democratic vote, while in 10 of the 10 strongest Repub-

TABLE 4

ACTUAL AND PREDICTED PROPORTION DEMOCRATIC IN STRONG DEMOCRATIC AND REPUBLICAN AREAS, NONPARTISAN CITY

ACTUAL PER CENT DEMOCRATIC	PREDICTED PER CENT DEMOCRATIC	RESIDUAL
Strong Democratic precincts:		
76	50.1	25.9
73	65.2	7.8
71	63.4	7.6
70	53.5	16.5
69	50.1	18.9
68	62.8	5.2
68	70.2	−2.2
68	67.6	0.4
68	59.6	8.4
67	51.2	15.8
Strong Republican precints:		
6	31.6	−25.6
19	29.1	−10.1
20	34.2	−14.2
22	35.2	−13.2
22	28.5	−6.5
22	37.7	−15.7
23	38.0	−15.5
24	39.5	−15.5
25	32.3	−7.3
25	30.7	−5.7

[12]The zero-order correlation between economic level, home ownership, and the proportion of the vote that was Democratic is virtually the same in the two cities, but the intercorrelation of these two predictors is very different, .73 in Nonpartisan City and only .15 in Partisan City. A second important difference is the absence of a strong zero-order correlation of the "ethnic" variable with voting in Non-partisan City (the zero-order correlation in Partisan City of the proportion "old immigrant" and proportion Democratic, 1956 presidential election, was −.76).

lican areas we find a larger than predicted Republican vote.[13] This table makes clear that, given the data presented in Tables 1 and 2, such a pattern of residual errors *could not arise solely from differences in party activity*. They are better explained as the result of the majority effect.

Table 5 summarizes the residual errors for Partisan and Nonpartisan City. The tables are constructed from the regression equations (see Table 3) utilizing the 74 white precincts of Partisan City and the 107 precincts of Nonpartisan City. Having a superior multiple correlation results in smaller errors of prediction, but it is important to note that this is not an adequate explanation for Table 5. Each cell in the table represents the *net mean residual*; if the residual errors were uncorrelated with the type of area, it would not make any difference how large the errors of prediction were because they would cancel out and the net mean residual in each cell would be near zero. This is not the case.

The available evidence indicates that the pattern taken by the residual errors of prediction is the same in the two cities—the errors are strongly related to the political-party partisanship of the precincts. What effect does this relationship have on our attempt to use these errors of prediction in assessing the impact of party activity on the precinct vote?

To handle this problem Cutright and Rossi subtracted out the majority effect from strongly partisan precincts before analyzing their data. Katz and Eldersveld did not. We can use Nonpartisan

TABLE 5

AVERAGE PERCENTAGE GAIN FOR DEMOCRATIC CANDIDATE IN PRECINCTS OF DIFFERENT DEMOCRATIC PARTISANSHIP, TWO CITIES*

	Partisan City Precincts, Per Cent Democratic, 1956			Nonpartisan City Precincts, Per Cent Democratic, 1958		
	28-44	45-56	57-82	6-43	44-55	56-76
Percentage gain for Democratic candidate	−2.4	−0.9	+3.0	−8.2	−2.1	+8.2
(N precincts)	(24)	(21)	(29)	(34)	(30)	(43)

*See Table 1 for details on cutting points and the campaigns studied.

[13]Statistically this means that the relationship between voting and the indipendent variables was curvilinear, but that does not explain the forces acting to distort the linear relationship. Also note that an area's net mean residuals need not be near zero simply because it is a "split" area — the distribution of the marginals in the heavy partisan areas is critical, as we can see by careful study of Table 5.

City as an independent test of the effects on our measurement of the impact of party-worker activities on the vote when we leave the majority effect in and when we remove it.

Table 6 compares the analysis of residuals before and after an adjustment for the majority effect. In the first row the majority effect is not removed. Precincts where the Democratic committeemen have more favorable characteristics relative to the Republican committeemen show a Democratic candidate gains between 5.6 and 3.6 percentage points, while in areas where the Republicans have the advantage they gain as much as 11 per cent of the vote in the extreme cases. If we average the last two categories on the right, we have 12 precincts with an average Republican gain of 4.4 per cent. The range in our extreme cells compares favorably with that demonstrated by Katz and Eldersveld (10.5 per cent) but hardly seems in keeping with the portrait we have seen (Tables 1 and 2) of the actual activities (or inactivity) of the precinct workers in Nonpartisan City. The second row of Table 6 removes the majority effect and recomputes the net gain for the Democratic candidate in precincts in which party activity varies. The effect is to reduce drastically the importance we gave to the impact of party activity on the vote. A combination of the last two cells on either side of the

TABLE 6

PERCENTAGE GAIN BY DEMOCRATIC CANDIDATE AND NET ACTIVITY BALANCE OF DEMOCRATIC OVER REPUBLICAN COMMITTEEMEN, NONPARTISAN CITY

	NET ADVANTAGE OF DEMOCRATIC OVER REPUBLICAN COMMITTEEMEN				
	3 OR 4 POINTS	1 OR 2 POINTS	0 POINTS	MINUS 1 OR 2 POINTS	MINUS 3 OR 5 POINTS
Percentage gain by Democratic candidate:					
Majority effect included	+5.6	+3.6	+1.3	−1.1	−11.0
Majority effect removed	+0.2	+2.4	−1.8	−1.1	−2.8
(N precincts)	(6)	(13)	(13)	(8)	(4)

NOTE: Forty-four precincts with interviews from both the Democratic and the Republican committeemen in the same precinct are used. Only veteran committeemen (incumbents before the most recent election) were used, because novice committeemen could not be questioned on political activity on behalf of candidates other than themselves.

Each committeeman could receive a score of 0 through 5. A score of 1 was given to the "high" response on these items: number of persons talked to daily (3 or more was "high"); being very active in the recent primary; polling the precinct during the general election; polling the precinct during the primary election; reporting additional party workers helping him during primary campaign.

table would yield an average gain in the 19 Democratic dominant precincts of +1.7, a loss of −1.8 per cent in the precincts where they were equal, and a loss to the Republicans of −1.7 per cent in the 12 precincts with superior Republican activities. The range is thus reduced to approximately 3 per cent when the majority effect is removed. How does this compare with the Partisan City case?

In Table 7 data from Partisan City reveal a range of about 4 per cent *after* the majority effect was removed for 51 precincts. This corresponds closely with the data analyzed earlier by Cutright and Rossi using 37 precincts.[14] The effect of party activity on voting in Partisan City seems to be about 4 to 5 per cent after we control for the majority effect.

A comparison of Tables 6 and 7 may lead to the false conclusion that party activity has only mild effects in most campaigns in most American cities. However, general elections for President or even Congress are not the only type of election that are important, and the same organizations in Partisan City that apparently can sway only 4 per cent of the voters in a presidential election have decisive and virtual command over voter decisions in primary elections. For this reason and because in many areas of the nation the primary election is *the* election, we should not be hasty in disparaging the vital role played by parties in determining the outcomes of elections in American cities, but neither should we fail to recognize the statistical pitfalls in the analysis of residual errors as a means of as-

TABLE 7

PERCENTAGE GAIN BY DEMOCRATIC CANDIDATE AND NET ACTIVITY BALANCE OF DEMOCRATIC OVER REPUBLICAN COMMITTEEMEN, PARTISAN CITY, MAJORITY EFFECT REMOVED

	NET ADVANTAGE OF DEMOCRATIC OVER REPUBLICAN COMMITTEEMEN			
	4 OR MORE POINTS	3 POINTS	1 OR 2 POINTS	0 OR NEGATIVE
Percentage gain by Democratic candidate	+2.06	+1.09	−0.08	−2.13
(N precincts)	(16)	(8)	(16)	(11)

NOTE: Fifty-one precincts with interviews from both the Democratic and Republican committeemen in the same precinct are used. Only veteran committeemen are used.

The activity index is based on two items: the number of persons talked to daily in the precinct (scored from 1 to 6 points), and the level of the committeeman's activity in the primary (scored from 1 to 4 points). We assume that our measure of primary activity carries over to general election activity.

[14]Cutright and Rossi, *op.cit.*, Table 10.

sessing the impact of precinct committeemen activity on voting behavior.[15]

Discussion

The hypothesis that the majority effect in voting behavior exists as the consequence of a differential distribution of political party activities in strong Democratic and Republican precincts was rejected. Neither Partisan City, with its powerfully organized political parties, nor Nonpartisan City, with its lower levels of party activities, revealed a pattern that would give to either party a sustained party-worker advantage in strong Republican, "split," or strong Democratic areas of the city.

A countermotion that local party workers lack effectiveness was not supported: both the majority effect and the party worker act to guide the voter to his final party choice. When we removed the majority effect, we found that the party worker was still "delivering the vote" but to a lesser extent than we would have believed had we not made the correction.

The size of the majority effect indicates that future investigators may be rewarded by further study of this phenomenon. Its systematic study in voting research is possible because we have at our command a simple technique, easily applicable to a sample of different types of political systems and any type of election we choose to study. Finally, a systematic study of the factors affecting the operation of the majority effect in voting behavior may suggest new questions and methods of assessing a wide variety of attitude and choice data.

---

[15]The method of residual analysis yields nearly equal numbers of positive and negative residuals, so in practice we could have 50 per cent of the precincts showing Republican gains even if there were no Republican organization whatsoever. Close attention to the volume and intensity of party work is necessary.

The Impact of Local Party Activity upon the Electorate*

Daniel Katz
Samuel J. Eldersveld

Interest in the role of political parties in the functioning of American democracy has increased in recent years as we have shifted from a description of political opinion to an analysis of its determinants. But authorities differ in the interpretations they draw from the scant evidence available. And these differing viewpoints emerge particularly in the discussion of local party organization and leadership.

On the one hand there are those who see the party as a major social structure mediating directly between the individual citizen and national, state, or local government. They see public policy as influenced by the party and its platform, interest groups aggregated through the party, social conflict resolved, public support mobilized, and public opinion represented. They maintain that the role of the party does not stop with elections. The party in power, as well as

---

*The writers are indebted to John Gilmore, Jose Armilla, and Wallace Wells for their contributions to the plan of the research and for their assistance in the analysis of data. They would also like to acknowledge the wise counsel of Donald E. Stokes in the programming of the correlational analysis. The analysis of the data was made possible by a faculty research grant from the Rackham School of Graduate Studies of the University of Michigan.

Reprinted from *The Public Opinion Quarterly* XXV (Spring, 1961), 1-15, by permission of *The Public Opinion Quarterly* and Samuel J. Eldersveld.

the party in opposition, together constitute a viable system through which citizens influence governmental action.

On the other hand, others see parties today as obsolete, ineffective, atrophied, and incompetent. They point out that the looseness of the party structure, the tenuousness of membership, the fluidity of affiliation mean that parties seem to be organizations in name only. Legislators and executives often appeal directly to their constituents or deal with pressure groups, circumventing the party mechanism. Party unity, responsibility, and discipline, it is pointed out, are much weaker in the United States than in Europe. In many areas parties will not take an official position regarding primary nominees; yet, paradoxically, informal party endorsements of primary nominees are often repudiated by the electorate in the primary. In this day of mass media and Madison Avenue, the local parties, it is claimed, have lost their competitive and integrative functional roles.

Since no great body of evidence can be marshaled on either side of this controversy, we clearly need more exact study of the relationships between our parties and American society, and of the effectiveness of our parties in influencing political behavior. The point of departure of this study was a concern with the functioning of parties at the local level. Our interest was at the point of personal contact of the individual citizen with the party organization. Specifically, we were interested in the types of activity conducted by local party leaders and their impact upon the electorate; our measures of impact were the perceptions, attitudes, and behavior of the electorate.

The dearth of previous research in this area is in strange contrast to the increase in both the quantity and quality of studies of the national electorate.[1] And it is all the more curious when one considers certain characteristic features of American politics. The major emphasis in party work is on mobilizing the vote through all the known organizational techniques. We stress especially the value of personal canvassing of all types in our mass campaigns, feeling that the efficacy of this approach has been amply demonstrated. Further, we consider that allegiance to political party is one of the most potent factors in determining choice of candidates on election day.[2] In this context of decentralized, grass-roots organizational party effort, one might have expected greater research concern over

---

[1]Angus Campbell, Philip E. Converse, Warren E. Miller, and Donald E. Stokes, *The American Voter*, New York, Wiley, 1960.

[2]Herbert H. Hyman, *Political Socialization*, Glencoe, Ill., Free Press, 1959.

the impact of party activity. Yet, the lone piece of research in the past three decades which is relevant to this problem is the work of Cutright and Rossi, who compared election statistics with the results of a mailed questionnaire from precinct leaders.[3]

In the present study intensive interviews were conducted both with a rank-and-file sample of the electorate and with precinct leaders from both parties. The interviews dealt at length with perceptions of party activities by the electorate and descriptions of such activities by the leaders. They also covered questions on voting behavior, attitudes on issues, knowledge of political matters, and strength of party identification. Election statistics for the precincts studied were also employed to measure party effectiveness.

Sample Design and Data-Gathering Procedures

The sample design was a modified version of the multistage area-probability sample in which the precinct was the primary sampling unit and the universe was Wayne County, Michigan. The four congressional districts in Wayne County were stratified according to ethnic homogeneity and political type, i.e. whether traditionally Democratic, or Republican, or mixed.[4] The preliminary selection of 500 precincts gave the following results:

Ethnic Composition	Political Preference		
	Republican	Mixed	Democratic
Heterogeneous	1/7	1/7	4/7
Homogeneous	0	0	1/7

Since no precincts were found which were ethnically homogeneous and Republican or ethnically homogeneous and mixed in political preference, these categories were dropped from the sample. The sampling ratios for the other types of precincts were determined by this preliminary study, and for the final study 87 precincts were selected: 18 ethnically heterogeneous Republican, 24 ethnically heterogeneous mixed, 24 heterogeneous Democratic, and 21 ethnically

[3]Phillips Cutright and Peter H. Rossi, "Grass Roots Politicians and the Vote," *American Sociological Review*, vol. 23, 1958, 171-79; and Phillips Cutright and Peter H. Rossi, "Party Organization in Primary Elections," *American Journal of Sociology*, vol. 64, 1958, 262-69.

[4]Paul Mott, "The Method of Selection of a Sample of Dwelling Units for the Detroit Area Study 1956-1957," Ann Arbor, Mich., University of Michigan, Survey Research Center, 1956, mimeographed.

homogeneous Democratic. Within the precincts a probability sample of households was employed; the objective was to obtain some seven or eight interviews from each precinct. In all, 596 interviews were taken and were weighted for analysis purposes to make the sample representative of Wayne County. The weighted sample gave an inflated N of 860.

In addition to this rank-and-file sample, personal interviews were planned with both the Republican and Democratic leader in each precinct. The names of the leaders were obtained from the two party organizations at the county and congressional district levels. The state party chairmen sent letters to these precinct leaders informing them of the nature of the study and asking them to cooperate with the University of Michigan interviewers. One hundred and forty-two interviews were obtained with 74 Republican and 68 Democratic precinct leaders.[5]

To obtain additional information on the characteristics of the precincts included in the sample, a census type of survey was conducted. In this survey some 2,400 households were enumerated to permit characterization of the precincts in terms of education, occupation, race, and religion.[6]

The interview schedules for both leaders and electorate were developed and pre-tested during the fall of 1956 by graduate students in the Detroit Area Study under the supervision of the authors and Dr. Harry Sharp, Director of the Detroit Area Study.[7] The interviewing of the rank and file was conducted during January and February of 1957 by this same group and by professional interviewers of the Survey Research Center. The interviewing staff was supplemented by political scientists from the staff of the University of Michigan for the questioning of the political leaders.

The Activities of Precinct Leaders as a Measure of Organizational Strength

Leadership is a complex phenomenon, and at least five dimensions can be identified as significant for local organizational purposes: (1)

---

[5]In addition, interviews were conducted with leaders at the ward level, the congressional district level, and the county level, but they are not included in the analysis reported in this article.

[6]This survey was the result of the resourcefulness of John Gilmore, who was its field director, its sampling expert, and its principal interviewer.

[7]The Detroit Area Study is a research facility associated with the Department of Sociology and the Survey Research Center of the University of Michigan.

the leader as the organizer of his own precinct workers, *the internal function*; (2) the leader as the communication center between the party organization above him and his precinct organization, *the representative function*; (3) the leader as the influential contact with the outside community, *the external function*; (4) the leader as the administrator of standard organizational practices, *the administrative or institutional function*; and, finally, (5) the leader's *strength of motivation* to carry on these various activities.

Indices were constructed for each of these five factors on the basis of answers to a series of specific questions about the leaders' activities. These five indices were also combined into a single over-all index of leadership strength. The types of questions on which these measures were based are indicated below:

1. *Internal leadership.* Was the precinct captain able to organize a local group of activists? For example, how many helpers did he mobilize and activate to work with him, did they hold regular meetings, did they help throughout the campaign, etc.?
2. *Representative leadership.* How much communication did the precinct leader have within the party? For example, how much contact did he have with the ward leader, the congressional district leader, the county committee, etc.?
3. *External leadership.* How well did the precinct leader relate to groups and people in his electorate? What were his contacts and group memberships outside the party?
4. *Administrative and institutional leadership.* How well did the precinct leader follow the role prescriptions for mobilizing the vote? Did he carry through the standard operating procedures of maintaining records and files of voters? Did he keep them up to date? How did he use them on election day in checking on voters? Were his files checked against official registration records? What was the nature of his registration activities, etc.?
5. *Strength of motivation.* Did the precinct leader plan to stay on with the party in his job, did he aspire to a more responsible position within the party, what things would he miss if he were able to leave his position of precinct leader?

Before summarizing the results for the two parties on these dimensions of leadership, it may be of interest to report that the findings on specific items show the characteristic uneven nature and weakness of voluntary organizations. Though a majority claimed they had done something in their precincts to get voters registered, on the more specific details of conducting an efficient operation the reports were less encouraging. Only 1 in 8 used his records to check on voting on election day. Below are the answers to some of the specific questions (in per cent):

Has done something to get voters registered	71
Kept some kind of record of voters in precinct	47
Has fairly complete records of own supporters and independents	20
Knows whether voters in precinct are registered or not	37
Uses records to check voters at polls on election day	12
Has helpers for precinct work	67
Had meetings of these precinct workers during campaign	32
Participated in fund raising in precinct	9
Contacted people in precinct by phone	16
Conducted door-to-door canvassing	29
Distributed literature in precinct	46
Has had contact with Wayne County leaders	40
Has had contact with congressional district leaders	67

The precinct worker is often glorified by the political party as the key person for maintaining contact between the party and people at the personal, grass-roots level. The facts are that in the Detroit area precinct organization functions fairly inefficiently and the precinct leader who carries out all his tasks is the exception rather than the rule. Party organization will often by-pass the precinct leader, as in fund-raising activities, membership drives, and even registration efforts. Such by-passing is both an effect and a cause of weak precinct organization. Since the precinct leaders, with their partial involvement and marginal time, are not the most reliable sources of help, special campaigns and activities will be sponsored and carried out by higher levels in the organization. But, in turn, this by-passing of the local leader lowers his morale and involvement in party activities.

The Democratic precinct leaders score higher on three of the five dimensions of leadership, as well as on the combined indices (Table 1). This may be due to the greater social reinforcement for Democratic workers in a community which is dominantly Democratic in party identification. The distributions of the two sets of leaders on the various indices of leadership are, however, fairly similar, and the edge the Democrats show is not great. On the combined index the findings are that some 9 per cent of the Republican as compared to 1 per cent of the Democratic leaders are leaders in name only and do nothing to help their respective parties. Only 14 per cent of the Republican group can be characterized as strong leaders compared to 30 per cent of the Democrats. The medians for the various indices show no difference between the two parties on motivational strength and on administrative or institutional leadership. The Democrats, however, seem to be more active in their contacts within the community and within their own party and also do a better job of mobilizing their own local groups for action. Apparently, there is the same willingness to work for the party and the same familiarity with organizational procedures in both parties, but the Democratic character of the area makes possible more social support for the Democratic local leaders.

The Effect of Precinct Leadership on Voting Behavior

The major problem in assessing the effectiveness of local party organization is to rule out the effect of other factors. In general, precincts which have strong local Democratic leadership are likely to be made up of people who would vote Democratic anyway, and the same observation holds true for precincts with strong local Republican leadership. Democratic strength is greater among people in the low income groups, of lower educational status, and of more recent American origin. The method which Cutright and Rossi employed to hold constant these demographic factors was to set up an anticipated vote for each precinct on the basis of its demographic composition and then see whether precincts that exceeded this expectation were precincts with effective local leaders and precincts that fell short of expectation were characterized by weak local leadership.[8] To determine the anticipated vote for the precinct Cutright and Rossi first computed a multiple correlation for the city as a whole, using three factors to predict the Democratic vote for President, namely, proportion old immigrant, estimated rental, and home ownership. For the aggregate data for precincts the multiple R was −.908. The regression equation thus provided weights for computing an expected vote for a given precinct on the basis of the distribution of these three factors within it. These investigators do not report, however, whether their multiple R would have been improved by adding local leadership as a determinant.

We have followed the general procedure of Cutright and Rossi but have used the following four factors in our multiple regression equation: religion, occupation, race, and education. In addition, we have included our index of strength of local leadership to see how much

---

[8]Cutright and Rossi, "Grass Roots Politicians and the Vote."

TABLE 1

Strength and Character of Precinct Leadership in Democratic and Republican Parties (in per cent)

Index	Negligible	Weak	Moderate	Fairly Strong	Strong	Total (N)	Median Score
Mobilization of own group:							
Republicans	18	24	27	23	8	100 (74)	4.0
Democrats	10	9	34	38	9	100 (68)	7.6
Contact within the party:							
Republicans	9	23	34	27	7	100 (74)	7.0
Democrats	9	7	32	34	18	100 (68)	9.2
Contact in community:							
Republicans	31	23	33	9	4	100 (74)	1.82
Democrats	19	16	31	12	22	100 (68)	2.67
Administrative leadership:							
Republicans	16	19	26	26	13	100 (74)	11.5
Democrats	7	15	43	25	10	100 (68)	11.5
Motivational strength:							
Republicans	14	18	32	28	8	100 (74)	8.6
Democrats	4	28	31	24	13	100 (68)	8.3
Combined index for:							
Republicans	9	18	31	28	14	100 (74)	31.0
Democrats	1	16	28	25	30	100 (68)	39.0

this contributes to the multiple R and have also computed the partial R's for all factors related to voting behavior.

For the sixty precincts where measures of local Democratic leadership were obtained, the multiple correlation between occupation, education, race, religion, strength of local Democratic leadership, and the Stevenson vote was .85 (Table 2). Occupation, education, and race (Negro-white) were all highly correlated with the Democratic vote for President. Democratic party leadership showed a positive but low correlation of .21 with the Stevenson vote, and Catholicism was negatively correlated with the Stevenson vote, —.29.

For the seventy-one precincts where measures of local Republican leadership were obtained, the same results are found, with a multiple R of .87 (Table 3). The index of strength of local Republican leadership shows a negative correlation (—.25) with the vote for

TABLE 2

CORRELATIONS BETWEEN DEMOGRAPHIC FACTORS, STRENGTH OF DEMOGRAPHIC LEADERSHIP, AND STEVENSON VOTE FOR SIXTY PRECINCTS WHERE DEMOCRATIC LEADERSHIP WAS MEASURED

	BLUE COLLAR	NEGRO	EIGHTH GRADE	DEMOCRATIC LEADERSHIP	STEVENSON VOTE*
Catholic	—.26	—.68	—.31	—.16	—.29
Blue collar		.62	.65	.19	.75
Negro			.70	.24	.71
Eighth grade				.14	.77
Democratic leadership					.21

Multiple correlation = .85
*From election statistics.

TABLE 3

CORRELATIONS BETWEEN DEMOGRAPHIC FACTORS, STRENGTH OF REPUBLICAN LEADERSHIP, AND STEVENSON VOTE FOR SEVENTY-ONE PRECINCTS WHERE REPUBLICAN LEADERSHIP WAS MEASURED

	BLUE COLLAR	NEGRO	EIGHTH GRADE	REPUBLICAN LEADERSHIP	STEVENSON VOTE*
Catholic	—.12	—.65	—.20	.01	—.19
Blue collar		.59	.69	—.13	.80
Negro			.65	—.10	.68
Eighth grade				—.10	.73
Republican leadership					—.25

Multiple correlation=.85
*From election statistics.

the Democratic presidential candidate. It should be noted, moreover, that Republican leadership is not correlated with the demographic character of the precinct.

Party organization, as measured by strength of local leadership, is thus correlated with voting behavior for the party in question, but demographic characteristics are more predictive of the vote. Hence it is necessary to look at the partial correlations to see how much of the variance is contributed by each factor when the others are held constant. In Table 4 the partial correlations indicate that in the precincts where Democratic leadership was measured the major factors predicting the Stevenson vote were occupation and education. The strength of local Democratic leadership was negligible — its partial correlation with the Stevenson vote was only .06. For the precincts where measures of Republican leadership were obtained, occupation again was a major determinant, with race being more important than education. (Table 5). Here, however, local Republican leadership did contribute significantly to the presidential vote. Strength of Republican leadership was significantly negatively correlated with the Stevenson vote (—.27) with the other factors held constant.

Apparently, then, the strength of party leadership at the local level cannot be discounted as a significant variable even in a national election. It is of interest that in Detroit, a Democratic stronghold with a tradition of voting Democratic and with strong union support for the party ticket, the degree of party activity at the local level seemed to make little difference in the vote for Adlai Stevenson but the strength of the local Republican leadership did make a difference. One explanation is that, where strong forces have been mobilized over time for one party, additional activity at the precinct level does not help it as much as local activity by the rival party

TABLE 4

PARTIAL CORRELATION BETWEEN THE STEVENSON VOTE AND FIVE VARIABLES FOR SIXTY PRECINCTS WHERE DEMOCRATIC LEADERSHIP WAS MEASURED

VARIABLE	CORRELATION	
Catholic	$r_{1y.2345} = .18$	
Blue collar	$r_{2y.1345} = .44$	$p < .01$
Negro	$r_{3y.1245} = .29$	$p < .05$
Eighth grade	$r_{4y.1235} = .39$	$p < .01$
Democratic leadership	$r_{5y.1234} = .06$	

NOTE: Degrees of freedom = .54.

may hurt it. Forces may be equipotential in getting the citizen with a leaning toward a given party to the polls. In an area where he is in the majority, his fellow workers, his neighbors, his union, or a local leader outside the party may play this role. Where he is in the minority, he lacks such support and the active local party leader may have a greater opportunity to activate him, since there are few competing positive forces. This is borne out by the experience of political parties invading areas where they have had little strength in the past. They find a local leader and encourage him to help set up

TABLE 5

PARTIAL CORRELATIONS BETWEEN THE STEVENSON VOTE AND FIVE VARIABLES FOR SEVENTY-ONE PRECINCTS WHERE REPUBLICAN LEADERSHIP WAS MEASURED

VARIABLE	CORRELATION	
Catholic	$r_{1y.2345} = .21$	
Blue collar	$r_{2y.1345} = .52$	$p < .001$
Negro	$r_{3y.1245} = .38$	$p < .001$
Eighth grade	$r_{4y.1235} = .23$	
Republican leadership	$r_{5y.1234} = -.27$	$p < .05$

NOTE: Degrees of freedom = 65.

a slate of candidates for local office and thus provide visible social support and encouragement for the otherwise discouraged political minority. One state chairman who followed this practice maintained that the activation of such local units made a difference of 10 per cent in the vote for the party ticket and an even higher difference in the vote for the local ticket.

Our correlational analysis, moreover, has not taken account of the relative strength of the Democratic leadership compared to the Republican leadership. Hence, precincts were divided into five groups on the basis of the combined index of leadership strength for each of the two parties: (1) much stronger Republican than Democratic leadership, (2) somewhat stronger Republican than Democratic leadership, (3) leadership about equal, (4) somewhat stronger Democratic than Republican leadership, and (5) much stronger Democratic than Republican leadership.

This more detailed analysis suggests that it does make some difference if one party has a strong local leader and the other party has a weak local leader. As Table 6 indicates, the eleven precincts which had strong Democratic and weak Republican organizations cast 5 per cent more votes for Stevenson than would have been expected in terms of the composition of the precinct. Eight of these eleven precincts were over the anticipated vote and only three were under. Similarly, in the twelve precincts with a strong local Republican leader and a weak Democratic leader, the vote for Stevenson fell 5.5 per cent under expectations. And of these twelve precincts

TABLE 6
Strength of Party Organization and the Stevenson Vote in Fifty-four Precincts*

Leadership	Number of Precincts	Actual Percentage of Stevenson Vote Minus Expected Percentage
Republicans definitely stronger	12	−5.5
Republicans somewhat stronger	5	−1.8
About equal in strength	15	+0.6
Democrats somewhat stronger	11	+4.5
Democrats definitely stronger	11	+5.0

*Two precincts omitted because of their high proporton of Jews, a faith not taken into account in predicting the vote.

nine were lower in Democratic vote than they should have been according to their demographic characteristics, and three were higher. For these two groups of extreme precincts, then, we find a total of 10.5 difference in voting behavior that can be attributed to the functioning of local party organization.

In addition to the comparison of precincts in which local leadership of one party is clearly stronger than the other, let us examine precincts in which the margin of superiority is not as great. Where there is some superiority of Democratic to Republican organization a 4.5 per cent gain for the Stevenson vote is found over that which the demographic characteristics of the precincts predicts. In the slightly stronger Republican precincts the gain for the Republicans is in the expected direction but is not great (1.8 per cent). For precincts in which organization of the two parties is about equal, the over-all vote for Stevenson is predicted by the demographic characteristics within 1 per cent.

The 10.5 percentage difference in votes which can be attributed to party activity between the extreme groups of precincts is double that reported by Cutright and Rossi for the city of Gary in the 1956 election.[9]

There were also percentage differences in the votes mobilized for the gubernatorial candidate, with the strongly led Republican precincts showing 31 per cent of their electorate favoring the Republican candidate and the strongly led Democratic precincts showing only 18 per cent favoring the Republican nominee. These figures are based on our cross-section sample and not on election statistics.

In spite, then, of the relative weakness of precinct organization, it cannot be discounted as a factor making some contribution to the total variance in voting behavior. The significant partial correlation between Republican leadership and voting behavior for the entire sample and the consistent trends where one party is stronger in local leadership than the other are evidence in point.

The Clustering Effect

It is possible, however, that the greater Democratic vote in precincts characterized by strong local Democratic leaders and the corresponding weak Democratic vote in areas characterized by strong Republican leadership can be due to the clustering of particular types of people in a given precinct.

In his analysis of Swedish election statistics of the 1920's, H. Tingsten demonstrated that members of the working class tended to vote proportionately more heavily for the socialist parties where they were more concentrated in an area than where they were less numerous.[10] Thus, where they comprised 34.5 per cent of the election district, the vote for the socialist parties was only 22.5 per cent, but where they made up some 83.8 per cent of the district, the vote for the socialist parties was 90.5 per cent. Tingsten attributed this clustering effect to three factors: (1) the different character of the wage workers in the more well-to-do districts compared to those in the poorer areas, (2) the influence of the social environment on the electors, and (3) the more active propaganda carried out by the party in the area of greater potential support. Valen and Katz found the same phenomenon in the 1957 Norwegian election. The percentage of working class voting for the Labor Party was greater in areas where workers were concentrated.[11] Berelson has used the term

[9] *Ibid.*

[10] Herbert Tingsten, *Political Behavior: Studies in Election Statistics*, London, King, 1937, pp. 177-80.

[11] H. Valen and D. Katz, "The Effect of Local Party Organization upon the Electorate in a Norwegian Province," in preparation.

"breakage effect" to take account of the tendency of the social forces of the community to pull voters in the direction of the general community, i.e. the dominant political climate of an area will exert some influence over people beyond that of the usual group determinants.[12] Thus the clustering effect may be a special case of the bandwagon effect, save that its reference is to the immediate social environment.

Controlling for occupation, then, does not rule out the possibility of the effects of concentrations of a given type of population in given precincts. Therefore, the three groups of precincts representing varying relative strengths of local party organization were divided into four subgroups on the basis of their white-collar and blue-collar concentrations and compared on percentage of vote cast for Stevenson. This control was run on the cross-section sample, since the aggregate data in the above analysis did not permit the identification of the individual voters. In Table 7 it is clear that both the clustering effect of concentrations of occupations and the strength of party organization influence voting behavior. The marginals show that in precincts where blue-collar workers constitute 85 per cent or more of the population some 72 per cent of them voted for Stevenson; where they constituted between 65 and 84 per cent of the population some 64 per cent voted for Stevenson; and where they were less than 65 per cent of the population only 36 per cent voted for Stevenson. In spite of the small numbers, this is convincing evidence of a clustering, or concentration, effect.

But the clustering effect does not account for all the superiority of certain precincts in proportion of Stevenson voters. There is a 21 per cent difference in the blue-collar vote for Stevenson in precincts with strong Democratic leadership as against precincts with strong Republican leadership. And this superiority is not wiped out when the concentration of blue-collar workers is held constant. For precincts with a heavy concentration of blue-collar workers (65 per cent or higher, combining the top two categories in Table 7), only 53 per cent voted for Stevenson in the strongly led Republican precincts, whereas 76 per cent voted for Stevenson in the strongly led Democratic precincts.

Though the numbers are small the trend clearly indicates that the effectiveness of local precinct leadership is not largely due to the concentration of blue-collar workers in a given area. There may, of course, be other types of clustering based upon ethnic and religious factors which would further affect our findings, but it should be re-

---

12Bernard R. Berelson, Paul F. Lazarsfeld, and William N. McPhee, *Voting*, Chicago, University of Chicago Press, 1954.

TABLE 7

Proportion Voting for Stevenson in Precincts Varying in Leadership, by Concentration of Occupational Groups

Concentration of Occupational Groups	Strong Republican, Weak Democrat		Strong Democrat, Weak Republican		Other Groups		Total	
	Blue Collar	White Collar	Blue Collar	White Collar	Blue Collar	White Collar	Blue Collar	White Collar
85 per cent blue collar	8/14 57%	1/1 100%	6/7 86%	3/3 100%	28/37 76%	3/8 38%	42/58 72%	7/12 58%
65-84 per cent blue collar	10/20 50%	2/6 33%	29/39 74%	2/8 25%	28/45 62%	11/22 50%	67/104 64%	15/36 42%
40-64 per cent blue collar	4/9 44%	2/11 18%	5/12 42%	1/7 14%	10/26 38%	6/24 25%	19/47 40%	9/42 21%
Less than 40 per cent blue collar	1/6 17%	8/25 32%	0 0%	2/2 100%	1/4 25%	2/17 12%	2/11 18%	12/44 27%
Total	23/49 47%	13/43 30%	40/59 68%	8/20 40%	67/112 60%	22/71 31%	130/216 60%	43/134 32%

membered that occupation is the most important correlate of voting behavior in this sample and that race is correlated with it. Hence our control on clustering by occupational groups is the most significant and relevant control that can be used for our data. The conclusion seems warranted, therefore, that when a political party neglects its organizational activities in an area in which the other party has a strong local leader, it will suffer in consequences at the polls.

It is possible, of course, that the increased vote for a party which we have attributed to local leadership activity is not the effect but the cause of strong leadership. Such an explanation, however, would not account for the results here reported. How can the discrepancy between anticipated voting behavior and actual vote be accounted for? We have already ruled out the factors which account for the major source of variance in terms of race, occupation, religion, and education and have further controlled on the clustering effect. There may, of course, be some idiosyncratic factor such as a local nonparty leader who exerts political influence and increases the support for one party, thus making it possible for the local party leader to operate with more workers and do more things. Against this very speculative interpretation is the fact that political parties, by increasing their local activity in areas where they have not been active before, do increase the turnout for their party. In one Michigan township not covered in this survey, Party X, the minority party in the township, set up a very active local organization and increased its support for the state ticket from 23 to 40 per cent of the total vote, while the increase in the state for Party X was only 2 or 3 per cent...

The Influence of Precinct Work on Voting Behavior*

Raymond E. Wolfinger

Most politicians believe that precinct work wins votes. This would seem also to be the verdict of common sense. But since direct evidence on the impact of party activity is hard to find, until recently social scientists have reserved judgment on its efficacy. In the past several years research has confirmed the politicians' faith in precinct work, although in the particular elections studied its influence was for the most part rather slight. In the study reported here precinct work was found to have a considerable impact on voting. It is likely that the difference between this finding and that of previous research is due in part to differences in the electoral decisions involved in the various instances. This paper thus confirms recent findings on the impact of party activity and also suggests some conditions under which that impact will vary.

---

*I am grateful to Robert P. Abelson, Theodore R. Anderson, and Morris Zelditch, Jr., for advice on statistical matters. Richard A. Brody, William Flanigan, Fred I. Greenstein, and my wife, Barbara Kaye Wolfinger, made many helpful comments on an earlier draft of this paper. I am greatly indebted to Morton Halperin, Sally McCally, Peter Savage, and Alan Shick for giving me much of the raw data on which this paper is based.

Reprinted from *The Public Opinion Quarterly*, XXVII (Fall 1963), 387-98, by permission of *The Public Opinion Quarterly* and the author.

Previous Research

Precinct work — including door-to-door canvassing, check-off registration lists, transportation to the polls, babysitting services, and various other interpersonal electioneering techniques — has two goals: getting the maximum number of favorably inclined people registered and then to the polls, and convincing voters to support the right ticket. The dearth of hard data on the effect of such activities has been due mainly to the difficulty of isolating it from the effect of other variables, chiefly demographic factors.[1] The famous panel studies of voting behavior shed no light on this issue. The subject is not discussed in the Erie County study,[2] while the researchers studying Elmira collected data on this subject only through late October and thus present no information on the period when the campaign reached its peak.[3] By late October only about 8 per cent of the Elmira respondents had been contacted by a party worker.[4] These respondents amounted to about seventy cases, too few for detailed analysis. The authors report that such contact increased turnout by about 10 per cent but had no effect in changing attitudes.[5]

---

[1]Circumstantial evidence for the effectiveness of party activity may be found in accounts of drastic changes in voting behavior from one election to the next that are consistent with known changes in the allegiance of a political machine. See, e.g., V. O. Key, Jr., *Southern Politics*, New York, Vintage Books, 1949, pp. 62-64.

[2]Paul F. Lazarsfeld, Bernard R. Berelson, and Hazel Gaudet, *The People's Choice*, New York, Columbia University Press, 2d ed., 1948.

[3]Bernard R. Berelson, Paul F. Lazarsfeld, and William N. McPhee, *Voting*, Chicago, University of Chicago Press, 1954, pp. 168-75.

[4]In at least those settled big-city neighborhoods that are the most hospitable environment for political organization, the extent of the machine's contact with the voters is not limited to explicit political solicitations during campaigns, but is a year-round matter. As one Chicago precinct captain described his activities, "I try to establish a relationship of personal obligation with my people. . . . I spend two or three evenings a week all year round visiting people, playing cards, talking, and helping them with their problems." Quoted in Fay Calkins, *The CIO and the Democratic Party*, Chicago, University of Chicago Press, 1952, p. 67. Despite this qualification, the most satisfactory available comparative index of party activity is the percentage of individuals who have been contacted by a precinct worker. In the 1952 presidential election about 12 per cent of a national sample were contacted; in 1956 this figure dropped to 10 per cent. (Sources: for 1952, Angus Campbell, Gerald Gurin, and Warren E. Miller, *The Voter Decides*, Evanston, Ill., Row, Peterson, 1954, p. 33; for 1956, Angus Campbell, Philip E. Converse, Warren E. Miller, and Donald E. Stokes, *The American Voter*, New York, Wiley, 1960, p. 427.)

[5]It would seem that this reported increase in turnout might indicate a higher vote for one party or the other, since the Elmira Republicans, at least, had a highly accurate canvass of the city and therefore probably did not ring doorbells at random. Unfortunately, the authors of *Voting* do not tell us whether one party was more successful in inducing higher turnout through precinct work, and hence there is no way of knowing whether such activities influenced the outcome in Elmira.

The Survey Research Center's well-known nationwide studies of the 1952 and 1956 presidential elections have also left this issue unilluminated.[6]

In the past few years several researchers have dealt with this topic. Rossi and Cutright measured the level of party activity in Gary, Indiana, by precinct committeemen's responses to a questionnaire on their campaign behavior.[7] In a Democratic primary, where demographic variables appeared to be unimportant, they found that the outcome was highly correlated with various indices of precinct work. Rossi and Cutright also found that in those precincts where Democratic committeemen were most active in the 1956 presidential campaign their ticket's average vote was 2.3 per cent higher than a predicted vote established by demographic analysis of previous election returns, while it was 1.6 per cent lower where the committeemen were least active. Differences of similar magnitude were found for the Republicans.

Katz and Eldersveld studied the 1956 presidential election in Wayne County, Michigan (Detroit), using questionnaires to measure the level of precinct leaders' electioneering.[8] Their research was handicapped by the rather low level of party activity in Detroit. Both parties had sketchy campaign organizations, and only 8 per cent of a sample of the electorate reported contact with a party worker. Although the Democrats seemed to have a somewhat less moribund organization, there was no correlation between their campaigning and the vote for Stevenson when demographic variables were controlled. The partial correlation coefficient between Republican Party activity and the Stevenson vote was — .27; this was significant at the 5 per cent level of confidence. In precincts where the Republican organization was definitely stronger than the Democratic one, Stevenson's vote was 5.5 per cent below the predicted vote. The same difference was found in the opposite direction where the Democrats had the stronger organizations.

This paper deals with the influence of precinct work in circumstances very different from the Wayne County study: the locality

---

[6]Respectively, *The Voter Decides* and *The American Voter*.

[7]Peter H. Rossi and Phillips Cutright, "The Impact of Party Organization in an Industrial Setting," in Morris Janowitz, editor, *Community Political Systems*, New York, Free Press of Glencoe, 1961, pp. 81-116. Earlier reports of this research appear in Cutright and Rossi, "Grass Roots Politicians and the Vote," *American Sociological Review*, vol. 23, 1958, 171-79; and "Party Organization in Primary Elections," *American Journal of Sociology*, vol. 64, 1958, 262-69.

[8]Daniel Katz and Samuel J. Eldersveld, "The Impact of Local Party Activity upon the Electorate," *Public Opinion Quarterly*, vol. 25, 1961, 1-24.

had flourishing political organizations and the issue was a local one about which most voters were ignorant and apathetic. The data were gathered in the course of an intensive study of the politics of New Haven, Connecticut.[9]

The Political Culture of New Haven

New Haven fulfills all the classic requirements for machine politics. The original settlers were affronted, outnumbered, and finally displaced by the immigrants who came to dig their ditches and work in their factories. Such anti-plebeian devices as the city manager plan had not been invented when the Yankees lost control of the city government, and so they withdrew, first from the political scene, and later, with the growth of suburbs, from the city as well. In 1959, 56 per cent of the city's registered voters were Catholics (largely of Italian and Irish descent), 9 per cent were Negroes, and 15 per cent were Jewish.[10] Since the war the Yankees fleeing to the suburbs have been joined by the more affluent and assimilated Catholics and Jews. Since the city's newcomers tend to be poor Negroes and Puerto Ricans, the population remains at low income and educational levels, and thus a constituency for machine politics is maintained.

New Haven is an extreme example of the proletarianization that has occurred in most American cities in the past generation. In 1949 the median income there was a little over $2,700, compared with the national median of over $4,000.[11] In 1950 the median number of school years completed by adults was 9.1, compared to 10.2 in all American urban areas. In 1959 2 out of 5 registered voters had not completed one year of high school.

The city's governmental structure perfectly complements its social composition in providing fertile soil for the maintenance of political machines. In this city of 152,000, aldermen are elected from

---

[9]This study was conducted primarily by Robert A. Dahl, Nelson W. Polsby, and Raymond E. Wolfinger. Various aspects of this project are reported in Dahl, *Who Governs?* New Haven, Yale University Press, 1961; Polsby, *Community Power and Political Theory*, New Haven, Yale University Press, in press, Chap. 4; and Wolfinger, *The Politics of Progress*, New Haven, Yale University Press, forthcoming.

[10]Source: A survey of 525 randomly selected registered voters conducted under the direction of William Flanigan in the summer of 1959.

[11]Data on education and on income in New Haven are from the U.S. *Census of Population, 1950*, Bureau of the Census, Part 7, *Connecticut*, Vol. II, *Characteristics of the Population*, 1952; data on income in the United States are from *U.S. Income and Output*, Department of Commerce, 1958, p. 41.

each of thirty-three wards, an arrangement which facilitates ethnic appeals to small, homogeneous constituencies. A long ballot for municipal offices gives further opportunities for slate making. The city charter prescribes a "weak mayor" form of government, with a number of appointive boards. These boards provide more opportunities for appointments that bestow "recognition." Largely because residents of Italian descent, who comprise one-third of the city's population, have voted Republican, New Haven has had vigorous two-party competition in municipal elections, which are conducted on a partisan basis.

The law permits and custom provides for a variety of very tangible rewards for political activity. Any mayor taking over City Hall can make about 600 patronage appointments almost immediately. Service to the party and influential connections are prime criteria for promotions in hundreds of other municipal positions. Such jobholders are assessed a percentage of their salaries for campaign contributions. Most government contracts are given on a political basis. The right connections are highly useful in numerous judicial and administrative interactions.[12] Three thousand people are employed by the city. In addition, there are more than 150 members of municipal boards and commissions, many of whom receive annual stipends of up to $500. For many of these people political activity is

TABLE 1

POLITICAL PARTICIPATION BY REGISTERED VOTERS IN THE UNITED STATES AND IN NEW HAVEN*

(*in per cent*)

QUESTION	UNITED STATES 1956	NEW HAVEN 1959
Did you give any money or buy tickets or anything to help the campaign for one of the parties or candidates?	11	26
Did you go to any political meetings, rallies, dinners or things like that?	8	23
Did you do any other work for one of the parties or candidates?	4	8

*The data for New Haven are from the 1959 survey. The data for the United States are from the University of Michigan Survey Research Center's 1956 national election study, computed by the author from IBM cards supplied by the Inter-University Consortium for Political Research. The questions in the table are those in the latter source. The same questions were used in the New Haven survey, except that they were phrased in the present tense, e.g., "Do you give any money . . .?"

[12]A considerable amount of patronage and other spoils was also available in local state government offices, the Probate Court, and county offices. These other sources of patronage have helped to maintain two-party competition in New Haven by sustaining the party that did not control City Hall.

motivated not so much by enlightened sentiments of citizen duty as by economic self-interest.[13] With these powerful inducements, perhaps it is not so surprising that the rate of political participation is about twice as high in New Haven as in the country as a whole, despite the city's rather depressed socio-economic status (see Table 1).

A Democratic mayor, Richard C. Lee, entered City Hall in 1954 and in 1955 and 1957 led his party to victories over the Republicans with 2 to 1 majorities. Also out of power at the state level, the Republicans were generally supposed to have fallen on hard times. Yet by some standards they were not in such bad shape. A disconsolate Republican leader complained that even in a strong ward his party could count on only fourteen or fifteen "really good, active workers." In 1957 the Democrats officially reported that they had spent $18,000 for campaign expenses on election day alone, while the Republicans could find only $10,700 for this purpose. This kind of campaigning reaches a majority of the electorate: fully 60 per cent said that they were contacted by one party or the other during campaigns. New Haven is, as Elmira and Detroit were not, an excellent locale for the study of precinct work.

The Election Issue

This research is concerned with the impact of precinct work on the outcome of an election on a proposed city charter revision. The charter revision was conceived by Mayor Lee, who overrode the objections of the Democratic Board of Aldermen to put the proposal on the ballot in the November 1958 general election, in which candidates were running for state and national offices.

One major provision of the proposed charter would have lengthened the mayor's term of office from two to four years. This, together with proposed increases in the mayor's formal powers, incurred the wholehearted and unambiguous opposition of the city's Republican leaders.[14] The two local newspapers waged a vociferously hostile

---

[13]In the country as a whole, campaign participation increases markedly with education. In New Haven this is much less true, and at the highest level of campaign activity the percentage of better-educated participants drops off appreciably. (Sources: for New Haven, Dahl, *op. cit.*, pp. 285-87; for the United States, *The American Voter*, p. 476.)

[14]An important Republican politician, on the outs with the party regulars for years, was the chairman of the charter commission. This service to the Lee Administration, the culmination of several years of friendly relations, further estranged this man from his party and reduced his influence there. The following year the Democratic Governor, Abraham Ribicoff, appointed him to a highly prized judgeship.

campaign against the proposed charter, culminating in a series of eight editorials prior to election day. The well-heeled pro-charter forces saturated the city with brochures, full-page newspaper ads, television programs, and spot announcements on radio and television.

Some of the charter's provisions would have diminished the Democratic organization's considerable influence in some types of governmental decisions. Although the Mayor induced the reluctant Democratic Town Committee to issue a formal endorsement of his proposal, it was clear that the new charter's threat to ancient prerogatives aroused the opposition of many members of the Democratic organization. The disaffection was so widespread that Mayor Lee had no means, short of a thoroughgoing purge, to compel his party's ward organizations to campaign for his charter. Some ward leaders, however, out of loyalty, obligation for past favors, or hope of future ones, supported the charter. Others, for fear of the Mayor, did nothing. Thus the thirty-three Democratic ward organizations varied from vigorous support of the charter to equally vigorous hostility.

On election day Democratic candidates for state and national offices rolled up enormous majorities in New Haven. Forty-five per cent of the voters made a choice on the charter issue, rejecting it by a 2 to 1 majority. The following analysis deals with the influence on charter voting of campaigning by the Democratic ward organizations.

Indices of Local Party Activity

Fourteen of the thirty-three Democratic ward chairmen were interviewed early in 1959.[15] Among other questions, each was asked his position on the charter and what he did on this issue during the campaign. On the basis of these interviews it was possible to classify the electioneering of these fourteen chairmen as vigorous support, passivity, or active opposition. The voting records of the wards in each of these categories will be examined in the following section.

Another, more important index of precinct work may be found in the absentee ballots turned into the registrar of voters by each party organization in each ward. Connecticut laws permit the blank ballots to be taken to voters by party workers; after the ballots are filled out, they may be taken from the voter to the registrar of

[15]These interviews were conducted by Morton Halperin, Sally McCally, Peter Savage, and Alan Shick.

voters by the same intermediaries. Most ballots are not from soldiers and traveling salesmen, but from the sick, aged, and incompetent. Given the ready availability of precinct workers in New Haven, it is not too surprising that the absentee ballots represent for each party a pool of sure votes, subject, as politicians freely concede, to the preferences of the various ward organizations.

In the 1958 election 2,576 absentee ballots were cast in New Haven. In eighteen of the city's thirty-three wards these ballots can be classified according to which party turned them in.[16] The vote in favor of the charter on the Democratic absentee ballots from these wards ranged from 5.3 to 78.6 per cent. These returns can be used as an index of the precinct work for the charter by the respective Democratic ward organizations, as the following discussion of the findings demonstrates. An organization that turned in a 78.6 per cent "yes" vote on its absentee ballots will be assumed to have worked for the charter in all its campaign work, while the organization that produced a 5.3 per cent absentee ballot "yes" vote will be taken as hostile to the charter in other activities as well.

Finally, some data relevant to this problem come from a survey conducted in January 1959 under the direction of William Flanigan. The respondents, randomly selected from the voting lists, were 192 persons who had voted in the 1958 election.

Findings

An analysis of the absentee ballot returns by party illustrates the failure of many Democratic ward organizations to give vigorous support to the charter. Whereas 83 per cent of the Republican absentee ballots had votes on the charter issue, only 65 per cent of the Democratic absentee ballots did. This silent treatment of the charter by the Democratic organizations extended to other forms of precinct work. While 24 per cent of the survey respondents were contacted by a party worker during the 1958 election campaign, more than half these people said that the charter was not mentioned. As one Democratic ward chairman remarked, "When a thing is so confusing that you can't even understand what it means, you aren't going to work too hard for it."

Many Democratic precinct workers did more than ignore the charter: they actively opposed it. Thirty per cent of the charter votes on the Democratic absentee ballots were cast against the

[16]These wards exhibit as much ethnic diversity and as great a range of education and income as the entire city.

party's official position, compared with less than 8 per cent anti-party votes on the Republican ballots. That is, 30 per cent of the Democratic ballots had anti-charter votes, while less than 8 per cent of the Republican ballots had pro-charter votes. When votes are computed on a base of all absentee ballots, less than half the Democratic absentee ballots were cast for the charter, while more than 75 per cent of the Republican absentee ballots carried opposed votes. These data are summarized in Table 2. In the succeeding analysis of these ballots, percentages are computed on a base of the total number of absentee ballots, i.e. on line 3 rather than line 2 of Table 2.

TABLE 2

ABSENTEE BALLOT VOTES ON THE CHARTER IN 18 WARDS, BY PARTY
(*in per cent*)

	DEMOCRATIC (*N* = *776*)	REPUBLICAN (*N* = *636*)
1. Percentage of ballots on which a vote for or against the charter was cast	65.2	83.2
2. Votes for the party's official position (D—for, R—against) as a percentage of votes on the issue	70.0	92.2
3. Votes for the party's official position as a percentage of all absentee ballots	45.6	76.7

Demographic variables such as education, income, and ethnicity had virtually no influence on charter voting.[17] Neither ward-by-ward correlations with any of these variables nor the survey data show any meaningful relationships. Presumably because the charter was so closely identified with a Democratic mayor and so vehemently denounced by Republican leaders, there was a strong association between Republican allegiance and a negative vote. Only three Republican survey respondents voted for the charter,[18] while Democrats and independents were more evenly divided pro and con. For

[17]Ethnicity was a variable only with respect to Negroes, who were concentrated largely in the three wards where the charter fared best. These wards are in Lee's home neighborhood, where he has friendly relations with the party leaders. Lee is very popular with Negroes because of various civil rights measures and his diligent courting of Negro leaders.

[18]For this reason the current controversy about the validity of ecological correlations is not relevant to this discussion. See W. S. Robinson, "Ecological Correlations and the Behavior of Individuals," *American Sociological Review*, vol. 15, 1950, 351-57; Leo Goodman, "Some Alternatives to Ecological Correlation," *American Journal of Sociology*, vol. 64, 1959, 610-25; and the works cited there.

thirty-two wards[19] the correlation coefficient between the Democratic vote[20] and votes for the charter was .72.

As Table 3 shows, in those wards where the Democratic chairmen reported that they worked hard for the charter, the proportion of "yes" votes was considerably greater than in those wards where the Democratic chairmen actively opposed the charter. Where little or no electioneering on this issue was reported by the chairmen, the percentage of affirmative votes fell between these two poles. In order to control for the effect of Democratic sentiment on these differences, the pro-charter vote in each group of wards is also presented as a percentage of the Democratic vote. The Democratic vote was virtually identical in the "active support" and "passive" wards, but the pro-charter vote was 10 per cent higher in the former group. Where the Democratic ward chairmen campaigned against the charter, the Democratic: charter ratio was 37.8; where they worked for it, it was 65.6.

For five wards both absentee ballot returns and interviews with Democratic ward chairmen are available. A comparison of these two types of data further validates the use of absentee ballots as an index of party activity. In one ward where the chairman reported that he was in active opposition to the charter, only 26.4 per cent of the absentee ballots favored it, while in two wards where the chairman claimed active support, 61.8 per cent of the absentee ballots favored it. (In the two wards where the chairman reported little or no action, 35.6 per cent of the absentee ballots were in favor.)

TABLE 3

CHARTER VOTING AND AVOWED CAMPAIGN ACTIVITY OF DEMOCRATIC WARD CHAIRMEN ON CHARTER*

(in per cent)

	Chairman's Avowed Campaign Activity on Charter		
	Active Support *(N = 5)*	No Action *(N = 6)*	Active Opposition *(N = 2)*
Vote in favor of charter	46.8	36.7	22.0
Democratic vote	71.3	69.2	58.2
Vote for charter as a percentage of Democratic vote	65.6	53.0	37.8

*Since the respondents were promised that they would not be identified, the voting returns for individual wards are not given.

[19]Official voting returns from one ward were erroneous.

[20]The "Democratic vote" is an average of the votes for the Democratic candidates for lieutenant governor and secretary of state.

For seventeen wards the correlation coefficient between the vote in favor of the charter on the ward's voting machines and pro-charter votes on the Democratic absentee ballots was .73. The relationship between these two values can be isolated by a partial correlation that holds constant the only other independent variable, the level of Democratic sentiment. The partial correlation coefficient of the absentee ballots with the pro-charter vote on the voting machines is .58. This explains about 34 per cent of the variance. That is, precinct work by the Democratic ward organizations was strongly associated with voting behavior and may be assumed to have had an important influence on the outcome of the charter election. These data are presented in Table 4.

TABLE 4

WARD-BY-WARD CORRELATIONS BETWEEN VOTE FOR THE CHARTER AND SELECTED VARIABLES, FOR 17 WARDS

	VARIABLE	CORRELATION COEFFICIENT
Vote in favor of the charter on the Democratic absentee ballots	.73	(r_{12})
Democratic vote	.72	(r_{13})
Median income	.04	
Partial correlation	.58	$(r_{12.3})$

Conclusion

The much greater importance of precinct work as a variable in the charter election, as compared with the 1956 presidential election in Detroit, may be explained not only by the vastly stronger party organizations in New Haven, but also by the different character of the two elections. For one thing, "regular" organizations usually are not strongly impelled to maximum exertion in presidential elections, where the outcome has so little to do with the distribution of their customary rewards: jobs, contracts, and favoritism.[21] All-out effort is usually reserved for elections for local offices, control of the party organization, and occasional referenda that threaten the organization's interests. These are often contests about which most voters

[21] People interested primarily in national politics — and particularly liberal Democrats — periodically complain that powerful local organizations have betrayed their party's presidential candidate. The likelihood of such "betrayal," which is really lack of interest, decreases with the candidate's estimated chances of winning. Such complaints were more common after Stevenson's campaigns than in 1960.

know little and care less. As the precinct captain quoted earlier remarked, "If they [the voters] have their own opinions on certain top offices, I just ask them to vote my way on lower offices where they usually have no preferences anyway."[22]

Second, party identification, the appeal of well-publicized and familiar candidates, and the influence of recurring issues provide guideposts for voting decisions in presidential elections. Most voters have made their decisions on the presidential election by the time the candidates are nominated. Many others decide as the campaign reminds them of past political habits and structures their perceptions of the current situation along familiar lines. Exposure to the campaign in the mass media hardens predispositions and reduces persuasibility.[23]

Popular interest in and knowledge of politics usually reach their peak in presidential election years. The authors of *The American Voter* present data on public familiarity with sixteen national issues in 1956.[24] On eight of these issues more than two-thirds of their sample both had an opinion and knew what the government was doing on the issue. This level of knowledge was reached by less than a majority on only one issue.

In New Haven, despite the vehemence and visibility of the major local newspaper's opposition to the charter, two-thirds of the voters did not know its position on the issue, nor that of the Republican party. Only 15 per cent of the sample could mention any good feature of the charter — usually "it's time for a change" — while twice this many could name a bad feature. This general apathy and ignorance were due to both the uncompelling nature of the topic (municipal administration is not a field that quickens many pulses) and the unfamiliarity of the issue, and hence the absence of habits and relevant criteria to guide voters' thoughts.

In the charter election, as in many primaries, nonpartisan elections, and referenda, the issues appeared before most voters more or less *de novo*. Customarily there is less interest and involvement in such elections. Exposure to campaign news persuades voters, rather than merely activating predispositions, as in presidential elections. In these circumstances voters will be most open to persuasion and, as is well established, interpersonal communication is more effective than the mass media.[25] It is in just this sort of low-salience election

---

[22]Quoted in Calkins, *op. cit.*, p. 68.

[23]Berelson, *op. cit.*, pp. 246-50.

[24]P. 174.

[25]A good deal of evidence on this point is summarized by Joseph T. Klapper, *The Effects of Mass Communication*, New York, Free Press of Glencoe, 1960, pp. 31-38.

that political machines are supposed to be most potent, both because their precinct workers encounter less sales resistance and because the lower turnout enhances the importance of their pool of sure votes. In the case of the charter, the low salience of the issue and the fact that less than half the people who went to the polls voted for or against the proposal suggest that here precinct work had its effect by persuasion rather than by mobilizing an already predisposed body of partisans.

While high-salience elections would seem to offer more limited scope for precinct work, they still present two areas of opportunity: (1) getting favorably inclined people to the polls, and (2) persuading, at least for the day, those voters whose political perspectives are so dim that other campaign stimuli never really make an impression.[26]

The bald proposition that precinct work can have an impact has been established. A comparison of the data in this paper with those presented by Katz and Eldersveld suggests that this impact will vary in inverse ratio to the salience of the election to the voters. The present research task in this area is to explore the effectiveness of vigorous party activity in conditions of varying public knowledge and interest, in different types of elections, and with different kinds of voters.

---

[26]Political machines classically have registered and herded to the polls such extreme examples of this group as derelicts and unacculturated members of minority groups. Beyond such marginal members of the electorate, however, there are a good many more socially integrated people with very feeble political perspectives. For a discussion of the size and characteristics of this rather large group, see *The American Voter*, Chap. 10.